Leadership

Seventh Edition

D0103248

Leadership

A Communication Perspective

Seventh Edition

Craig E. Johnson
George Fox University

Michael Z. Hackman
late of University of Colorado–Colorado Springs

WAVELAND
PRESS, INC.

Long Grove, Illinois

For information about this book, contact:
Waveland Press, Inc.
4180 IL Route 83, Suite 101
Long Grove, IL 60047-9580
(847) 634-0081
info@waveland.com
www.waveland.com

Mike, this one's for you.

About the Authors

Craig E. Johnson (PhD, University of Denver) is emeritus professor of leadership studies at George Fox University, Newberg, Oregon, where he taught a variety of courses in leadership, ethics, communication, and management at the undergraduate and doctoral level. During his time at the university he served as chair of the Department of Communication Arts and founding director of the George Fox Doctor of Management/Doctor of Business Administration program. Though retired from full-time teaching, Dr. Johnson continues to serve as an adjunct professor. He is author of *Organizational Ethics: A Practical Approach* (4th ed.) and *Meeting the Ethical Challenges of Leadership: Casting Light or Shadow* (6th ed.). His articles have appeared in such journals as *Communication Quarterly, The Journal of Leadership Studies, The Journal of Leadership and Organizational Studies, Academy of Management Learning and Education, The Journal of Leadership Education, Communication Education, Communication Reports,* and *International Listening Association Journal.* Johnson has served in leadership roles in several nonprofit organizations and has participated in educational and service trips to Kenya, Rwanda, Honduras, Brazil, China, and New Zealand. Professor Johnson is a past recipient of George Fox University's distinguished teaching award and 2016 recipient of the outstanding graduate faculty researcher award. When he is not writing or teaching, Dr. Johnson enjoys working out, fly fishing, camping, and reading.

Michael Z. Hackman (PhD, University of Denver) was a professor in the Department of Communication at the University of Colorado–Colorado Springs and an adjunct at the Center for Creative Leadership. He taught courses in communication, including Foundations of Leadership, Leadership Theory and Practice, Organizational Leadership, Leadership Communication in a Global Environment, and Leadership and Organizational Change. In 1995, he was awarded the university-wide Outstanding Teacher award. Dr. Hackman's research focused on a wide range of issues, including the impact of gender and culture on communication and leadership behavior, leadership succession, organizational trust, and creativity. His work appeared in such journals as *Communication Education, Communication Quarterly, The Journal of Leadership Studies, Leadership, The Leadership Review,* and the *Southern Speech Communication Journal.* He was the coauthor (with Craig Johnson) of *Creative Communication: Principles and Applications* and (with Pam Shockley-Zalabak and Sherwyn Morreale) of *Building the High-Trust Organization.* Dr. Hackman served as a visiting professor at the University of Waikato in Hamilton, New Zealand, on four separate occasions between 1991–2002. He also served as an adjunct professor at the University of Siena (Italy) and the University of Vienna (Austria), and lectured at the China Executive Leadership Academy Pudong in Shanghai and the SP Jain Center of Management in Dubai (UAE).

Acknowledgments

The inspiration for this text came while Michael Hackman and I were graduate students at the University of Denver. We agreed to write a book together but weren't sure what topic to write about. Mike called me a couple of years after we had both graduated to propose a leadership text from a communication vantage point. That collaboration, which produced the previous six editions, was truly a labor of love and served to shape our friendship and our careers.

In 2016 Mike died after battling cancer. The world lost an outstanding educator, scholar, international consultant, professional colleague, friend, and father. This edition is dedicated to him.

Thanks to all who adopted previous editions. Based on your positive response, I remain convinced that there is value in examining leadership from a communication vantage point. To those considering this text for the first time, I hope that it will prove to be a useful tool for both you and your students.

Over the years many students and colleagues provided their own leadership stories along with encouragement, advice, and support. In particular I want to recognize Alvin Goldberg, our mentor at the University of Denver, who was instrumental in igniting our interest in the topic of leadership.

Thanks to Carol Rowe at Waveland Press who has been a constant source of encouragement and inspiration over the years. Laurie Prossnitz prepared this edition for publication. A number of research assistants from the University of Colorado–Colorado Springs and George Fox University helped with the previous editions. Linda Crossland assisted in preparing materials for this version. I am grateful for all of your help. My greatest appreciation, however, is reserved for the Hackman and Johnson families, who lovingly supported our continuing journey to explore the latest developments in leadership.

—Craig E. Johnson

Contents

11 Ethical Leadership and Followership

12 Leader and Leadership Development

Preface

Readers of the previous editions of *Leadership: A Communication Perspective* will note a variety of changes. New material and research highlights have been added on a number of topics. For instance: transcendent followership, the leadership skills approach, alternative pathways to outstanding leadership, team coaching, escalation of commitment, strategy, invisible leadership, cultural intelligence, raising leadership development readiness, 360-degree feedback, trigger events, situational crisis communication theory, and resilience. You'll find revised coverage of a number of other topics, including, for example, identity and leadership, the traits approach, authentic leadership theory, Taoism, public relations, and persuasive campaigns.

Examples, sources, and cases have been updated throughout the book. All of the films and documentaries described in the Leadership on the Big Screen feature at the end of every chapter are new to this edition as are a majority of the Cultural Connections features. There are new case studies on The Container Store, Alibaba's Jack Ma, Zappos, Airbnb, Sheryl Sandberg, Uber, Colombian President Juan Manuel Santos, Waffle House, Chipotle, and leadership in Antarctica. New self-assessments measure readers' perceptions of emotional language, personal leadership style, motivation to lead, organization-public relationships, cultural intelligence, servant leadership, and personal leadership skills. *Leadership: A Communication Perspective* continues to integrate theory and practice. Each chapter blends discussion of research and theory with practical suggestions for improving leadership effectiveness. Chapter takeaways highlight important concepts and action steps. Application exercises provide the opportunity to further explore and practice chapter concepts.

Chapter 1 examines the relationship between leadership and communication with an in-depth look at the nature of leadership, both good and bad, and the leader/follower relationship. Chapter 2 surveys the research on leader and follower communication styles as well as the link between information processing, identity, and style selection. Chapters 3 and 4 summarize the development of leadership theory with an overview of the traits, situational, functional, relational, transformational, charismatic, CIP, and authentic approaches. Chapters 5 and 6 focus on two elements—power and influence—that are essential to the practice of leadership.

The next three chapters provide an overview of leadership in specific contexts. Chapter 7 introduces group and team leadership and describes the special challenges of leading project and virtual teams. Chapter 8 is a discussion of organizational leadership with particular focus on the creation of culture, developing strategy, sense making, and the communication of expectations. Chapter 9 examines the power of public leadership, highlighting public relations, public speaking, and persuasive campaigns.

The final four chapters look at important leadership issues. Chapter 10 describes the impact of cultural differences on leading and following, how to foster diversity, and how to narrow the gender leadership gap. Chapter 11 outlines the ethical challenges facing leaders and followers, components of ethical behavior, and ethical perspectives that can guide both leaders and followers. Chapter 12 identifies proactive leader development strategies as well as tools for managing leadership transitions. Chapter 13 examines the role of leadership in preventing and responding to crises and addresses leadership in extreme contexts.

As noted in the preface to previous editions, this text is designed as an introduction to leadership from a communication vantage point, not as the final word (as if there could be one) on the topic. Please consider *Leadership: A Communication Perspective* as our contribution to a continuing dialogue with you on the subjects of leading and following. Throughout the book we'll invite you to disagree with our conclusions, generate additional insights of your own, debate controversial issues, and explore topics in depth through research projects, reflection papers, and small group discussions. We hope you will discover additional topics that you think are essential to the study and practice of leadership and will investigate them on your own.

1

Leadership and Communication

Leadership is action, not position.

—*Donald McGannon*

OVERVIEW

Leadership: At the Core of Human Experience

Leadership attracts universal attention. Historians, philosophers, and social scientists have attempted to understand and to explain leadership for centuries. From Confucius to Plato to Machiavelli, many of the world's most renowned thinkers have theorized about how people lead one another.[1] One reason for the fascination with this subject lies in the very nature of human experience. Leadership is all around us. We get up in the morning, open up our tablets or smart phones, turn on our computer, radio, or television, and discover what actions leaders all over the world have taken. We attend classes, go to work, and interact in social groups—all with their own distinct patterns of leadership. Our daily experiences with leadership are not that different from the experiences of individuals in other cultures. Leadership is an integral part of human life in rural tribal cultures as well as in modern industrialized nations. Assessing your past leadership efforts can provide a good starting point for understanding why the success of leadership often varies so significantly. Identify your own best and worst leadership moments and what you learned from these experiences by completing the self-assessment exercise in box 1.1.

Followers prosper under effective leaders and suffer under ineffective leaders whatever the context: government, corporation, church, mosque or synagogue, school, athletic team, or class project group. The study of leadership, then, is more than academic. Understanding leadership has practical importance for all of us. (See the case study in box 1.2 for a dramatic example of how important leadership can be.) In this text we will examine leadership in a wide variety of situations. The perspective, however, remains the same—leadership is best understood from a communication standpoint. As Gail Fairhurst and Robert Sarr explain, effective leaders use language as their most tangible tool for achieving desired outcomes.[2] Let's begin our exploration of leadership by considering the special nature of human communication and the unique qualities of leadership.

Defining Leadership

As noted above, leadership is a fundamental element of the human condition. Wherever society exists, leadership exists. Any definition of leadership must account for its universal nature. Leadership seems to be linked to what it means to be human. As communication specialists, we believe that what makes us unique as humans is our ability to create and manipulate symbols.

I take leadership to signify the act of making a difference.
—Michael Useem

| **Box 1.1   Self-Assessment** | **Your Best and Worst Leadership Moment[3]** |

We all have had leadership success at some point. Whether in high school, college, in a music group, in sports, in a condominium association or religious group, or on the job, we have all accomplished goals through other people. We have all acted as leaders. Looking back over your experiences, what is the moment that you are *most* proud of as a leader? Describe the details of that moment below.

_____

_____

_____

Not only have we had leadership success, we've also endured leadership failure. Becoming a leader requires reflecting on and learning from past miscues so that you don't repeat errors. What was your *worst* experience as a leader? Record your thoughts in the space below.

_____

_____

_____

Given the best and worst leadership experiences you identified, consider the lessons you have learned about leadership in the past. In working through this assessment it can be very helpful to share your leadership stories with others so that you have a richer set of examples from which to compile a list of leadership lessons. The lessons learned from past leadership experiences might be things like: *It is difficult to succeed as a leader when followers are not motivated; leadership works best when you have a clear sense of direction;* or *a leader must be sure his or her message is understood to ensure followers stay involved.* Try to identify 10 leadership lessons your experiences (and, if possible, those of others) have provided.

Leadership Lessons

1.

2.

3.

4.

5.

6.

7.

8.

9.

10.

Box 1.2 Case Study	**Death and Heroism on the Savage Mountain**[4]

Mountaineers call K2 the Savage Mountain. The world's second tallest peak, K2 claims a greater percentage of climbers (1 in 3) than Mt. Everest, the world's tallest mountain (1 in 10). Fewer than 300 climbers have topped K2 as compared to over 3,000 on Mt. Everest. The Savage Mountain is not only steeper and harder to climb than Mt. Everest; its location further north makes it even more susceptible to bad weather. There are only a few days when high winds and snow abate, allowing climbers to attempt to reach the summit at over 27,000 feet.

In summer 2008, ten expeditions made up of members from Serbia, the United States, France, South Korea, the Netherlands, Italy, Nepal, and Pakistan huddled in their small tents at the highest camp on K2 waiting for the weather to break. Because so many people were on the mountain, team leaders knew they had to coordinate their efforts, particularly to navigate the Bottleneck. The Bottleneck is a narrow, sheer section of trail that requires climbers to go single file. At the Bottleneck, a slow climber can delay all those who follow. Team leaders agreed that on the day of the summit one group would go first and lay out ropes for the other teams to use as they ascended and descended the Bottleneck. Another group would put willow wands in the snow to mark the path back to camp.

On August 1 the weather cleared and 20 climbers launched their mass assault on the summit. Problems arose almost immediately. The lead team didn't have enough rope and started to lay rope too soon so that there wasn't enough to reach the top of the Bottleneck. The wands weren't planted. The only climber to have previously made it to the top took sick and couldn't summit. Some groups were slow to start and, as feared, a cluster of climbers got stuck below the Bottleneck, waiting to ascend. A Serbian fell to his death during the initial ascent and another climber died while trying to retrieve his body.

Descending in darkness is highly dangerous, as is bivouacking at 27,000 feet without shelter in intense cold. To avoid these dangers, climbers should have turned back by 2 PM. Instead, most pressed on to the top, not reaching their goal until much later. Eighteen reached the summit—a K2 record—with the last team arriving at 7 PM. As a result, some decided to stop for the night while others made their way back down the mountain. That's when disaster struck. A huge overhanging piece of ice broke off. Tumbling through the Bottleneck, it buried one climber and scoured away the ropes. Subsequent icefalls and avalanches, as well as the elements, disorientation, and deadly climbing conditions, would take additional lives. The total death toll was 11, making this one of the worst mountaineering disasters ever.

While nothing could have prevented the huge icefall, the loss of life was greater than it should have been. To begin, members of the various expeditions never bonded but instead remained strangers. They had difficulty communicating with each other because of language differences, and operated independently. Members of some teams were highly critical of the preparation and skills of those on other teams. This apparently contributed to a disregard for human life when the crisis struck. Far too many ignored those in need, failing to offer assistance to those likely to perish. According to a Dutch survivor, "Everybody was fighting for himself and I still do not understand why everybody were leaving each other."

Summit fever drove many to continue to climb when they should have turned back, putting them at high risk. So close to reaching their goal, they feared that they would never have another chance to reach their objective. Some had corporate sponsors and felt additional pressure to summit. The high-altitude porters had an incentive to support their efforts because they would earn a $1000 bonus if their clients succeeded. Those on the mountain also became too dependent on the ropes, even though the peak can be successfully climbed without them. In fact, the first climber to summit and successfully descend that day did so using only his personal alpine gear.

Sherpa are often overlooked in tales of mountaineering, which focus on the exploits of European and North American alpinists. However, Sherpa climbers earned international recognition as the heroes of the K2 disaster. Pemba Sherpa repeatedly left the safety of camp to assist stranded climbers. Pasang Lama gave his ice axe to another climber while above the Bottleneck. When his colleague Chhiring Dorje saw his plight, he climbed back up to help. Chhiring roped himself to Pasang and they descended step by step to safety. Two other Sherpa lost their lives in an avalanche after they ascended to assist three Korean climbers tangled in rope.

The disaster on the Savage Mountain illustrates the high cost of ineffective and unethical leadership and followership. However, these events also demonstrate how individuals can make a life-and-death difference when they put aside selfish concerns to help others.

Discussion Questions

1. Have you ever followed a leader in a high-risk situation? How did you determine that this person was worthy of your trust?

2. Have you ever been the leader in a high-risk activity? How did you approach this task?

3. Have you ever let pursuit of a goal override your common sense and put you in danger? How can you prevent this from happening again?

4. What steps, if any, could have been taken to prevent the disaster on K2 or to lessen the death toll?

5. Why do some people, like the Sherpa on K2, rise to the challenge of a crisis while others do not?

6. What leadership and followership lessons do you take from the disaster on K2?

The Symbolic Nature of Human Communication

Communication theorist Frank Dance defines symbols as abstract, arbitrary representations of reality agreed upon by human users.[5] For example, there is nothing in the physical nature of this book that mandates labeling it a "book." We have agreed to use this label, or symbol, to represent a bound collection of pages; this agreement is purely arbitrary. The meaning of a symbol, according to Leslie White, does not come from the intrinsic properties of the idea, concept, or object being represented. The value is "bestowed upon it by those who use it."[6] Words are not the only symbols we use; we attach arbitrary meanings to many nonverbal behaviors as well. Looking someone in the eye symbolizes honesty to many North Americans. However, making direct eye contact in some other cultures is considered an invasion of privacy. Meaning is generated through communication.

> *[Humans] differ from the apes, and indeed all other living creatures so far as we know, in that [they are] capable of symbolic behavior. With words, [humans] create a new world, a world of ideas and philosophies.*
>
> —Leslie White

Communication is based on the transfer of symbols, which allows individuals to create meaning. As you read this text, the words we have written are transferred to you. The meanings of these words are subject to your interpretation. It is our goal to write in a way that allows for clear understanding, but factors such as your cultural background, your previous experience, your level of interest, and our writing skills influence your perception of our message. The goal of communication is to create a shared reality between message sources and receivers.

The human ability to manipulate symbols allows for the creation of reality. Simply labeling someone as "motivated" or "lazy," for example, can lead to changes in behavior. Followers generally work hard to meet the high expectations implied in the "motivated" label; they may lower their performance to meet the low expectations of the "lazy" label. This phenomenon, discussed in detail in chapter 8, is known as the Pygmalion effect.

Symbols not only create reality but also enable us to communicate about the past, present, and future. We can evaluate our past performances, analyze current conditions, and set agendas for the future. In addition, symbolic communication is purposive and goal driven. We consciously use words, gestures, and other symbolic behaviors in order to achieve our goals. The purposeful nature of human communication differentiates it from animal communication.[7]

The communication patterns of animals are predetermined. For example, wolves normally travel in small groups known as packs. Dominance within the pack is based on such characteristics as size, physical strength, and aggressiveness. Humans, on the other hand, consciously select from an array of possibilities for achieving their goals. Human leadership is not predetermined as in the animal world; rather, it varies from situation to situation and from individual to individual.

Leadership shares all of the features of human communication just described. First, *leaders use symbols to create reality.* Leaders use language, stories, and rituals to create distinctive group cultures. Second, *leaders communicate about the past, present, and future.* They engage in evaluation, analysis, and goal setting. Effective leaders create a desirable vision outlining what the group should be like in the future. Third, *leaders make conscious use of symbols to reach their goals.* (See the case study in box 1.3 for examples of the effective and ineffective use of symbols by leaders.) We will have more to say about how leaders adapt their behaviors to reach their goals later in the chapter. In the meantime, let's take a closer look at the characteristics of human communication.

Words can destroy. What we call each other ultimately
becomes what we think of each other, and it matters.

—Jeane Kirkpatrick

Box 1.3 Case Study	The Importance of Symbols

Leadership is primarily a symbolic activity. The words and behaviors of leaders greatly influence the reactions of those who follow. Consider these examples:

Don Isley is the General Manager of Renco Manufacturing, a medium-sized manufacturing company producing precision components for the airline industry. The Renco plant is located in an office park near a commercial airport and parking is limited. Employee parking areas at the plant are divided into two lots. In one lot, managers and office staff park their vehicles near the main entrance to the Renco plant. On the other side of the building, those who work in the production area park near a side entrance to the plant. This parking arrangement is more informal than formal, but employees are consistent in their behavior and rarely park in the "wrong" lot. Isley parks in neither lot. He parks his vehicle, a new Corvette, directly in front of the building in a fire lane designated as a no parking area. Isley claims he needs to park in this location so that he can have easier access to his office. Some of the production workers who earn salaries just above minimum wage feel like Isley is "showing off." What do you think?

Peter Houghton is the CEO of a large privately owned utility company—Valley Electric. Houghton came to Valley Electric from a competitor where he was highly regarded for his successful management practices. Despite this reputation, employees at Valley Electric were nervous when Houghton was hired. He replaced a well-regarded CEO who had been at the helm during a period of rapid growth and profitability. Sensing this uneasiness, Houghton made the decision to spend his first month on the job meeting as many Valley Electric employees as he could. Houghton visited offices, power stations, and field sites. He introduced himself to employees, asked questions, and learned policies and procedures. At the end of his first month on the job, Houghton finally reported to his office. He felt ready to assume the challenge of leading Valley Electric. What do you think of this strategy?

Mark Ayala is the owner of a small T-shirt printing business. His company employs about 15 full-time staff members who are responsible for the production of a variety of custom-designed T-shirts. Most of the staff work for minimum wage, and turnover is high. The clothing produced ranges from special-order logo shirts for corporate clients to mass-produced shirts celebrating sports team championships. Ayala started the business in his garage five years ago and has built a loyal clientele by providing high-quality products that are delivered on time to his customers. Ayala and his staff must, at times, work around the clock to meet deadlines for special orders. Through his persistence and hard work, Ayala has developed a very successful business. Recently, Ayala noted that his total revenue for the year exceeded $1 million for the first time in company history. To mark this accomplishment and to thank his employees, Ayala came in late one night and printed T-shirts for his staff. The shirts featured a depiction of a $1 million dollar bill with Ayala's picture in the center. On the back each shirt read, "Thanks a Million." When Ayala announced the $1 million milestone to his employees and handed out the shirts, many of his employees were appreciative. Some, however, found the T-shirt giveaway insulting. What do you think?

Eric Littleton is the president of Bald College, a small, private, residential school in the South that is heavily dependent upon tuition revenue. Due to a drop in the number of incoming students, Bald had to reduce costs. Littleton called an all-employee meeting to announce that department budgets would be cut and that some employees would be laid off. He delivered this message to faculty and staff while wearing workout clothes—a T-shirt, Bald College sweatshirt, and running pants. At the end of the meeting he declined to take questions. Instead he told the crowd that he was headed over to the athletic complex to work out with the college's highly successful men's basketball team. A number of employees were upset with the way the president handled this important announcement. What do you think?

(continued)

Margaret Gates is the superintendent of schools in the Elmwood Hills school district. Elmwood Hills is an affluent community located in the suburbs of a large metropolitan area. The schools in the Elmwood Hills district have an excellent reputation, and many parents choose to live in the area so their children can attend the schools. Gates was hired as superintendent after her predecessor (who had been in the district for 37 years as a teacher and administrator) retired. Gates was a well-regarded candidate; she had years of experience leading high-performing programs in school districts in another state. Within two months of her arrival at Elmwood Hills, Gates assembled the more than 2,000 faculty and staff members within the district. Although few of these teachers or staff members had met Gates yet, most were eager to hear what their new leader had to say. In the meeting, Gates unveiled a new vision statement and a set of 12 initiatives, including mandatory nightly homework assignments, a greater emphasis on core academic subjects, and revamping many of the existing programs within the district. Although many of the initiatives Gates presented had merit, most of those attending the meeting left with a very negative impression of their new leader. What do you think went wrong?

Shirley Phillips is the CEO of Hilcrest Laboratories, a multinational pharmaceutical company. As CEO, Phillips has exhibited an antipathy toward corporate perks. Like all other Hilcrest executives and managers, Phillips has a cubicle, not a private office. When Phillips travels, she flies coach class and rents a subcompact car, as do all Hilcrest executives and managers. Employees jokingly refer to these small rental cars as "Hilcrest limousines." Phillips's efforts are viewed by some as merely an attempt to cut costs. Some senior managers feel they have earned the perks of first-class travel and full-size rental cars. Others contend that Hilcrest's profit-sharing plan is perk enough and that money shouldn't be wasted on costly airfares and rental cars. Phillips argues her actions communicate a belief that all at Hilcrest are equal in importance. What do you think?

After considering these six examples, think of some of the leaders with whom you have worked in the past. Identify examples of effective or ineffective symbolic behavior on the part of these leaders. Discuss your examples with others in class.

The Human Communication Process

Noted communication scholar Dean Barnlund identified five principles that reflect the basic components of human communication.[8]

Communication is not a thing, it is a process. Communication is not constant; it is dynamic and ever changing. Unlike a biologist looking at a cell through a microscope, communication scholars focus on a continuous, ongoing process without a clearly defined beginning or end. Take a typical conversation, for example. Does a conversation begin when two people enter a room? When they first see each other? When they begin talking? Barnlund, and others, would suggest that a conversation actually "begins" with the experiences, skills, feelings, and other characteristics that individuals bring to an interaction.

Communication is not linear, it is circular. Models depicting the process of communication have evolved from a linear explanation, first developed by ancient Greek rhetoricians over 2,000 years ago, to a circular explanation, offered by Barnlund. In the earliest description of the communication process, a source transmitted a message to a receiver in much the same way that an archer shoots an arrow into a target. Only the source had an active role in this model; the receiver merely accepted messages. This view, known as an action model, is diagrammed below.

Action Model of Communication

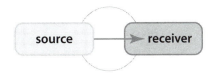

The action model provided an incomplete depiction of the communication process because the response of the receiver was ignored. Reactions to messages, known as feedback, were included in the next explanation of communication—the interaction model. The interaction model described communication as a process of sending messages back and forth from sources to receivers and receivers to sources. From this perspective, diagrammed below, communication resembles a game of tennis.

Interaction Model of Communication

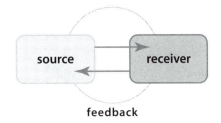

The evolution of the circular explanation of communication was completed with the development of Barnlund's transactional model. The transactional approach assumes that messages are sent and received simultaneously by source/receivers. The ongoing, continuous nature of the process of communication is implicit in this model.

In the transactional model, diagrammed at the top of p. 10, communicators simultaneously transmit and receive messages. Effective communicators pay close attention to the messages being sent to them as they talk with others. The typical classroom lecture demonstrates how we act as senders and receivers at the same time. Even though only one person (the instructor) delivers the lecture, students provide important information about how the lecture is being received. If the lecture is interesting, listeners respond with smiles, head nods, and questions. If the lecture is boring, class members may fidget, fall asleep, text their friends, or glance frequently at their phones. These responses are transmitted throughout the lecture. Thus, both the instructor and students simultaneously act as message source and receiver.

Transactional Model of Communication

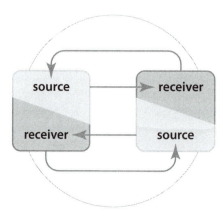

Communication is complex. Communication involves more than just one person sending a message to another. The process involves the negotiation of shared interpretations and understanding. Barnlund explains that when you have a conversation with another person there are, in a sense, six people involved in the conversation.

1. Who you think you are
2. Who you think the other person is
3. Who you think the other person thinks you are
4. Who the other person thinks he or she is
5. Who the other person thinks you are
6. Who the other person thinks you think he or she is

Communication is irreversible. Like a permanent ink stain, communication is indelible. If you have ever tried to "take back" something you have said to another person, you know that while you can apologize for saying something inappropriate, you cannot erase your message. Many times in the heat of an argument we say something that hurts someone. After the argument has cooled down, we generally say we are sorry for our insensitive remarks. Even though the apology is accepted and the remark is retracted, the words continue to shape the relationship. The other person may still wonder, "Did he/she really mean it?" We can never completely un-communicate.

Communication involves the total personality. A person's communication cannot be viewed separately from the person. Communication is more than a set of behaviors; it is the primary, defining characteristic of a human being. Our view of self and others is shaped, defined, and maintained through communication.

Now that you have a better understanding of the process of human communication, we will examine the special nature of leadership communication.

Leadership: A Special Form of Human Communication

One way to isolate the unique characteristics of leadership is to look at how others have defined the term. According to James MacGregor Burns, the scholar attributed with founding contemporary leadership studies, "Leadership is one of the most observed and least understood phenomena on Earth."[9] Indeed, Joseph Rost found there were 221 definitions of leadership published in books and articles between 1900 and 1990—a number that likely has gone up dramatically given interest in leadership since his review.[10] With so many definitions of leadership in print it is helpful to classify these conceptions into broader categories. Four primary definitional themes emerge.

Leadership is about who you are. This definitional theme focuses on leader traits and attributes and is one of the oldest ways of conceptualizing leadership. The emphasis is on identifying the characteristics that define "born leaders." Examples of such definitions of leadership published in the early part of the twentieth century are "personality in action . . . in such a way that the course of action of the many is changed by the one,"[11] and "[the] person who possesses the greatest number of desirable traits of personality and character."[12]

Leadership is about how you act. From this perspective, leadership is defined as the exercise of influence or power. To identify leaders, we need to determine who is influencing whom. For example, Paul Hersey defines leadership as "any attempt to influence the behavior of another individual or group."[13] Bernard Bass argues that "an effort to influence others is attempted leadership."[14] When others actually change, then leadership is successful. Swedish researcher Mats Alvesson focuses on the influence process from a communication perspective, arguing that leadership is a "culture-influencing activity" that involves the "management of meaning."[15]

Leadership is about what you do. This definitional thread focuses on the importance of followers. Leader influence attempts are neither random nor self-centered. Instead, leaders channel their influence and encourage change in order to meet the needs or to reach the goals of a group—task force, business organization, social movement, state legislature, military unit, nation. Note the group orientation in the following definitions:

- the behavior of an individual when he/she is involved in directing group activities;[16]
- the process (act) of influencing the activities of an organized group toward goal setting and goal achievement.[17]

Placing leadership in the context of group achievement helps to clarify the difference between leadership and persuasion. Persuasion involves changing attitudes and behavior through rational and emotional arguments. Since persuasive tactics can be used solely for personal gain, persuasion is not always a leadership activity. Persuasion, although critical to effective leadership, is only one of many influence tools available to a leader.

Leadership is about how you work with others. This definitional theme emphasizes collaboration. Leaders and followers establish mutual purposes and work together as partners to reach their goals. Success is the product of leaders' and followers' joint efforts. Joseph Rost highlights the interdependence of leaders/ followers this way: "Leadership is an influence relationship among leaders and their collaborators [followers] who intend real changes that reflect their mutual purposes."[18] Others, such as Peter Block and Robert Greenleaf, discuss concepts such as "stewardship" and "servant leadership" in defining leadership as a partnership with followers.[19]

> *Leadership is not something you do to people,*
> *but rather something you do with people.*
>
> —*Kip Tindell*

Combining our discussion of human communication with the definitional elements above, we offer the following communication-based definition of leadership: **Leadership is human (symbolic) communication that modifies the attitudes and behaviors of others in order to meet shared group goals and needs**. (For a sampling of how other textbooks have defined leadership, see box 1.4.)

Box 1.4	**Leadership Definitions: A Textbook Sampler**

"Leadership is a process whereby an individual influences a group of individuals to achieve a common goal."—Peter Northouse[20]

"Leadership is the process of influencing others to understand and agree about what needs to be done and how to do it, and the process of facilitating individual and collective efforts to accomplish shared objectives."—Gary Yukl[21]

"A leader [can be defined as] a person who influences individuals and groups within an organization, helps them in the establishment of goals, and guides them toward achievement of those goals, thereby allowing them to be effective."—Afsaneh Nahavandi[22]

"The process of influencing an organized group toward accomplishing its goals."—Richard Hughes, Robert Ginnett, and Gordon Curphy[23]

"Leadership is social influence. It means leaving a mark, it is initiating and guiding, and the result is change. The product is new character or direction that otherwise would never be."—George Manning and Kent Curtis[24]

"Leadership. . . . a dynamic (fluid), interactive, working relationship between a leader and one or more followers, operating within the framework of a group context for the accomplishment of some collective goal."—Jon Pierce and John Newstrom[25]

". . . We can define leadership as the ability to inspire confidence and support among the people who are needed to achieve organizational goals."—Andrew Dubrin[26]

Leaders vs. Managers

Management is often equated with leadership. However, leading differs significantly from managing. Managers may act as leaders, but often they do not. Similarly, employees can take a leadership role even though they do not have a managerial position. Leadership experts James Kouzes and Barry Posner suggest the following exercise to highlight the differences between leaders and managers. Take a sheet of paper and make two columns. In the first column, identify the activities, behaviors, and actions of leaders. In the second column, list the activities, behaviors, and actions of managers. Now compare the two lists. Kouzes and Posner predict that you will associate leaders with factors such as change, crisis, and innovation and that you will associate managers with organizational stability. According to these authors, "When we think of leaders, we recall times of turbulence, conflict, innovation, and change. When we think of managers, we recall times of stability, harmony, maintenance, and constancy."[27]

> *You manage things; you lead people.*
> —*Grace Murray Hopper*

John Kotter uses three central activities to highlight the differences between management and leadership: creating an agenda, developing a human network for achieving the agenda, and executing the agenda.[28] The management process for creating an agenda involves planning and budgeting. Managers at this stage tend to focus on time frames, specific details, analysis of potential risks, and resource allocation. By contrast, leaders create an agenda by establishing direction and communicating long-range views of the big picture. This process involves developing a desirable and attainable goal for the future, otherwise known as a vision. The actions of Herb Kelleher during his tenure as CEO of Southwest Airlines are examples of this type of leadership activity. In taking a fledgling airline to prominence in the U.S. airline industry, Kelleher had a clear vision of the strategy and leadership practices necessary to make Southwest Airlines a success. He made employees top priority by making work fun, communicating constantly with workers and empowering them to do whatever it takes to satisfy customers. As other airlines moved in and out of bankruptcy, Southwest was consistently profitable. The presence of a shared and meaningful vision, as we'll see in chapter 4, is a central component of effective leadership.

Once the agenda is established, people must be mobilized to achieve the plan. Managers mobilize others through organizing and staffing. The focus of this management activity involves getting individuals with the right training in the right job and then getting those individuals to carry out the agreed-upon plan. Leaders mobilize others by aligning people. Alignment focuses on integration, teamwork, and commitment. (The Leadership on the Big Screen feature at the end of the chapter describes a leader who was able to align both his superiors and his followers behind his vision.)

The execution of the agenda from a management perspective involves controlling and problem solving. This process usually focuses on containment, control, and predictability. Leaders execute their agenda by motivating and inspiring. This process focuses on empowerment, expansion, and creativity. One organization that does an excellent job of motivating and inspiring followers is Dutch Brothers Coffee. The drive-thru coffee chain headquartered on the West Coast operates under an Optimist's Creed that encourages enthusiasm and looking at the "sunny side of everything." The company was rated highest in customer satisfaction among specialty coffee retailers largely because of its fun-loving, high-energy baristas.[29]

According to Kotter, the outcomes of management and leadership differ significantly. Management produces orderly results. Leadership, on the other hand, often leads to useful change. Both these activities are important in the overall success of groups and organizations. To be successful, organizations must consistently meet their current commitments to customers, stockholders, employees, and others, and they must also identify and adapt to the changing needs of these key constituencies over time. To do so, they must not only plan, budget, organize, staff, control, and problem solve in a competent, systematic, and rational manner, they must also establish and reestablish, when necessary, an appropriate direction for the future, align people to it, and motivate employees to create change even when painful sacrifices are required.

The Question of "Bad" Leadership

Most of those who study and write about leadership have focused on the more positive connotations of the concept. Recently scholars have devoted increasing attention to the "bad" or "toxic" side of leadership.[30] Those interested in destructive leadership believe that researchers and practitioners must embrace a more honest and holistic view that acknowledges the dark side of human nature. These investigators argue for a broader conception of leadership that includes an exploration of those whose impact on others is damaging, noting that bad leadership is more common that we would like to think.[31] (For a closer look at bad followership, turn to box 1.5.)

Like many leadership scholars, we believe that leaders should be ethical and serve the common good. Yet, we recognize that far too many individuals fall short of this standard, driven by personalized or harmful motives that make them more power wielders than leaders who serve the needs of the group.[32] These bad leaders can teach us a great deal about good leadership, however. Studying examples of bad leaders can alert us to the ethical dangers of being in a leadership role (see the discussion of the ethical shadows of leadership in chapter 11); help us prevent ethical abuses in ourselves and others; and clearly demonstrate what we DON'T want to do when our time comes to lead.

There are a number of reasons why leaders engage in destructive behavior. Important causes or antecedents of bad leadership include:

Selfishness. Self-centeredness is a particular problem for leaders. That's because impulsive, selfish individuals are more likely to seek positions of power and, at the same time, they are more likely to be identified as leaders by others.

They are extroverts who are seen as energetic and charismatic.[33] Once in power, impulsive leaders are free to satisfy their own desires at the expense of others. For example, they consume more than their share of organizational resources and violate group norms (including rules about sexual behavior). They justify their actions by defining morality in terms of rights instead of responsibilities. They believe that resources should go to those who contribute the most (which favors them) instead of to the needy (which favors less powerful individuals) and generally ignore other points of view when making moral determinations. Organizations can reinforce these selfish tendencies. Those in power frequently silence the critiques of followers. Unchallenged, they exert even more control and, over time, low power individuals modify their emotions and attitudes to match their leaders.

Box 1.5   Research Highlight   **Bad Followership[34]**

There are bad followers just as there are bad leaders. In fact, bad followership makes bad leadership possible. For example, top executives at Volkswagen wouldn't have been able to install software that defeated emissions tests in 11 million diesel cars without the help of a host of followers. Engineers designed the "defeat device," managers authorized its installation, and engine and product development personnel incorporated it into the vehicles.

Pennsylvania State University professor Christian Thoroughgood and his colleagues believe that there are factors that make followers susceptible to the influence of destructive leaders. They divide susceptible followers into two categories—conformers and colluders. Conformers engage in bad behavior as they obey their leaders. (They wouldn't misbehave on their own.) Colluders, on the other hand, actively support and contribute to the leader's destructive mission. Conformers and colluders then break down into these categories:

Conformers: Lost Souls. Lost souls are highly needy. They are vulnerable to destructive leaders because (1) they have basic unmet needs (for love and recognition, for instance), (2) are experiencing high levels of stress (e.g., going through a divorce, flunking out of school), (3) lack a clear sense of identity, and (4) have low self-esteem. They comply because they admire and identify with the leader, who offers them direction and community, and seek the leader's approval.

Conformers: Authoritarians. Authoritarians have a strong belief in hierarchy. They reflect an unconditional respect for authority, reject uncertainty, and believe in a just world where people get what they deserve. They comply because they are convinced that leaders have a legitimate right to demand obedience because they occupy leadership roles.

Conformers: Bystanders. Bystanders appear to be the most common type of bad followers. Passive, they are motivated by fear. They comply because are convinced that they will be punished if they object or disobey the orders of their destructive leaders. Bystanders typically have negative self-evaluations that persuade them that they can't resist, must submit to whoever is in power, and are victims. Good at reading elements of the situation, they stay passive in order to avoid punishment. These individuals are often introverts who lack a courageous, prosocial orientation.

Colluders: Opportunists. Opportunists share the dark qualities of their destructive leaders. They carry out the unethical and illegal directives of leaders because they believe they will be rewarded for doing so. Opportunists are ambitious, greedy, exploitive, and lacking in self-control. Rewards—money, status, power—are the key to motivating their compliance.

Colluders: Acolytes. Acolytes are true believers who actively partner with their leaders. Self-motivated, they share the leader's vision and values. If they believe the leaders can achieve the organization's toxic goals, they are highly motivated to join in destructive behavior.

Many leaders are narcissistic.[35] The term *narcissism* is derived from Greek mythology. In the ancient Greek fable, Narcissus falls in love with his image that he sees reflected in a pond. Contemporary narcissists are just as self-absorbed as their namesake. Thinking highly of themselves, they are attracted to leadership roles that make them the center of attention. Narcissists often succeed in their bids for power because they are socially skilled and make a positive first impression. In a small group, for instance, they are likely to emerge as leaders when none are appointed because they are quick to speak up and come across as bold and competent.[36] They are effective at holding on to their authority once in power, convinced that they deserve to be where they are. Narcissistic leaders engage in a variety of bad leadership behaviors, including claiming special privileges, demanding obedience and admiration, dismissing negative feedback, abusing power for personal goals, ignoring the welfare of followers, and acting like dictators. They put their organizations at risk because they have unrealistic visions and expectations of what they and their groups can achieve.

Machiavellianism is another selfish trait that drives leaders to engage in destructive behavior.[37] Italian philosopher Niccolò Machiavelli argued in *The Prince* that political leaders should maintain a positive public image while using any means possible (ethical or unethical) to achieve their goals. According to modern psychologists and communication scholars, highly Machiavellian individuals (high Machs) follow this advice. They are skilled at manipulating others to achieve their ends, a fact that makes them more likely to end up in leadership positions. Compared to narcissists, Machiavellian leaders have a more accurate sense of their abilities and are more in touch with reality. However, they too engage in lots of self-promotion, tend to be emotionally cold, and are likely to be aggressive. High Machs frequently deceive others because they are out to generate positive impressions while getting their way. They may pretend to care about coworkers to secure their cooperation, for instance, or work overtime only to score points with the boss. (We'll have more to say about ethical impression management later in the chapter.)

Machiavellian leaders enjoy successful careers because they are so skilled at manipulation and hiding their true intentions. However, they put their groups and followers in danger. They may be less qualified to lead than those who don't make as good of an impression. High Machs are also tempted to engage in unethical behavior because they want to succeed no matter what the cost. When followers suspect their supervisors are manipulative, they are less trusting and cooperative, which lowers organizational productivity.[38]

Cognitive errors. Bad leadership is also the product of poor decision making.[39] Officials at NASA ignored the possible damage to the *Columbia* shuttle, for example. A piece of debris hit the capsule upon liftoff but mission leaders didn't think the problem was even worth mentioning to the shuttle crew. The spacecraft then disintegrated upon returning from space when superheated gas entered through a hole in its protective shield (caused by the debris strike), killing seven astronauts. Common leader errors occur when (1) gathering and organizing information (e.g., failing to contact an important client for feedback, putting off the most important tasks, using the wrong criteria to evaluate a training program); (2) deciding how to use information (e.g., ignoring safety reports, basing decisions on outdated data); (3) managing personnel resources (e.g., hiring the wrong employees, assigning workers to tasks they aren't prepared for); and (4) managing tasks and resources (e.g., purchasing unneeded office equipment and factory machinery, failing to repair equipment).

Environmental factors. Selfishness and decision-making errors are internal sources of bad leadership. However, outside forces can also encourage leaders to engage in destructive behaviors. Leaders are more likely to initiate and persist in unethical behaviors when they experience the following:[40]

- pressure to meet aggressive goals
- intense competition to maintain market share, profitability, etc.
- organizational instability and uncertainty caused by downsizing, mergers, recessions, rapid technological developments, shortage of resources
- perception of an outside threat
- pressure from followers to engage in unethical behavior
- organizational climates that encourage unethical behavior
- pressure to conform
- lack of checks and balances both inside (governing boards, performance appraisal systems) and outside the organization (the media, governing agencies) to check toxic behavior
- cultural values that encourage destructive leadership (tolerating large power differences, putting the needs of the group above those of outsiders)

According to Harvard University professor Barbara Kellerman, bad leadership falls into two categories—ineffective and unethical—and is exhibited through destructive behaviors and dysfunctional personality characteristics. Ineffective leaders are not successful in achieving desired outcomes. These "bad" leaders may be poorly skilled, may exhibit ineffective strategic or tactical planning, or may not have the requisite traits to succeed. Unethical leaders are unable to distinguish between right and wrong, often engaging in behaviors that maximize their rewards while harming others. Kellerman identifies seven types of "bad" leaders.[41]

Incompetent. These leaders do not have the desire or skill (or both) to sustain effective action. They may lack practical, academic, or social intelligence and can be careless, dense, distracted, lazy, or sloppy. Former Home Depot CEO Bob Nardelli illustrates incompetence in action. Recently named one of the worst CEOs of all time by *CNBC* television, Nardelli helped the company earn a reputation for poor customer service by laying off knowledgeable workers and slashing costs. During his tenure, Home Depot's stock price dropped and the company lost market share to competitor Lowe's. (He left with a $210 million severance package.) Later Nardelli was forced out as head of Chrysler.

Rigid. These leaders are unyielding. Although the rigid leader may be competent, he or she is unable or unwilling to adapt to new ideas, new information, or changing times. Russian President Vladimir Putin is one such leader. He jails his opponents and critics while refusing to yield to world opinion, sending troops into the Ukraine.

Intemperate. These leaders lack self-control and are aided and abetted by followers who are unwilling or unable to intervene. President Donald Trump is considered by many (including some of his fellow Republicans) to be an intemperate leader. He tweets out attacks on his opponents and former allies at all hours of the night. He claims that he won the popular vote in the 2016 election (he did not) and that there was widespread voter fraud in the election (there is no credible evidence to back up this assertion). Trump raised fears of nuclear war with his pledge to bring "fire and fury" down on North Korea in response to that nation's threat to fire a missile near Guam.

Callous. These leaders are uncaring or unkind. Martin Shkreli is a contemporary example of a callous leader. Shkreli, founder of Turing Pharmaceutical, raised the price of a drug largely used by HIV patients and minority and low-income women by 5,000%. When the US Senate investigated, he complained that the senators were "trying to make a tempest out of a teacup."

Corrupt. These leaders, and at least some of their followers, lie, cheat, or steal—putting self-interest ahead of the public interest. Former FIFA president Sepp Blatter was forced to resign after many of the leaders of the governing board of soccer were charged with corruption for taking bribes from broadcasters, athletic apparel companies, and countries hoping to host the World Cup. Investigations into corruption among FIFA officials continue.

Insular. These leaders, and at least some followers, minimize or disregard the welfare of others outside the group or organization for which they are directly responsible. Former Austrian Chancellor Werner Faymann is one example of an insular leader. After first welcoming Syrian refugees, he then changed course, severely limiting asylum applications, erecting a fence to keep immigrants out, and deploying armed forces to the border. As a consequence, many fleeing the civil war in Syria are stranded in overcrowded camps in Greece.

Evil. These leaders, and at least some followers, commit atrocities that inflict physical and/or psychological harm on others. Pol Pot, the Cambodian leader from 1975 to 1979, is a chilling example of evil leadership. His Khmer Rouge army was one of the most brutal in history. During his time as leader, violent deaths in his country were more common than deaths by natural causes. More than 1.7 million Cambodians—one-third of the population—were murdered in just four years.

While Kellerman developed her typology based on case studies of prominent leaders, other investigators focus on ordinary leaders. A group of Norwegian researchers, led by Ståle Einarsen, offers an alternative typology of destructive leadership behaviors derived from the organizational context.[42] They are careful to say that organizational leaders are typically not totally good or bad, toxic or nontoxic. Instead, leaders engage in a mix of constructive and destructive behaviors. The investigators discovered that constructive behaviors are far more common but the majority of the respondents they surveyed noted that their immediate supervisors engaged in at least one type of negative behavior. Destructive leadership is directed primarily at subordinates, the organization, or at both. Based on these dimensions, Einarsen's group outlines five types of leadership behaviors.

1. *Constructive leadership behavior* supports both the organization as well as subordinates. Constructive leaders motivate and inspire employees while using resources wisely to reach organizational goals.

2. *Tyrannical leadership behavior* serves organizational goals at the expense of followers. Tyrannical leaders may be highly competent (have technical and planning skills, for example) but they are abusive to subordinates, using intimidation, manipulation, and humiliation to try to improve organizational performance.

3. *Derailed leadership behavior* works against the interests of both the organization and subordinates. These leaders skip work, shirk their duties, commit fraud, and steal company equipment and supplies. At the same time, they attack and undermine subordinates using many of the tactics employed by tyrannical leaders.

4. *Supportive-disloyal leadership behavior* is pro-follower but anti-organization. These leaders care for their subordinates and build positive relationships with them. However, they allow employees to benefit at the expense of the organization by, for instance, allowing them to take too much time off, shirk their duties, steal, and so on. Supportive-disloyal leaders may also pursue goals that are different than those of the organization, encouraging employees to work hard but for the wrong objectives.

5. *Laissez-faire leadership behavior* is passive behavior that undermines the organization as well as subordinates. Laissez-faire leaders avoid interacting with followers when they can, delay decisions, provide little feedback, and make no effort to motivate employees to reach organizational goals. Doing nothing reduces employee satisfaction and commitment and hurts group performance.

The Leader/Follower Relationship

Clarifying the relationship between leading and following is the final step in defining leadership. Earlier we noted that leaders and followers function collaboratively. Recognizing that leaders and followers work together toward shared objectives should keep us from overemphasizing the importance of leaders or ignoring the contributions of followers. Unfortunately, we generally pay a lot more attention to leaders than to followers. Using "leadership" as a Google search term, for example, generated approximately 774 million results while "followership" only generated 546,000. (The Microsoft Word spell-check feature marks the word "followership" as a misspelling.) Leaders get the vast majority of credit when businesses like Facebook or Twitter are successful. However, these companies would not have succeeded without the hard work of software and hardware engineers, programmers, supervisors, customer service representatives, administrative assistants, and other followers. Scholars, too, have been slow to recognize the value of followers. An analysis of articles in *The Leadership Quarterly* from 1990 (the first year the journal was published) to 2008 revealed that only 14% included any form of the word "follower" in the title or abstract.[43]

Shifting some of the spotlight from leadership to followership is one way to assure that followers get the credit they deserve. This shift appears to be taking place. Not only are more followership books and articles being published, but there is also evidence that followers play an increasingly important role in the modern world. In America, the decades of the 1960s and 1970s saw the birth of the civil rights, antiwar, and gay rights movements, all of which were driven by followers. Americans of all political persuasions learned to distrust authority. As a result, constituents gained power at the expense of leaders, a trend that has continued to the present. Information and computer technology have empowered followers around the world. *Time* magazine recognized the power of followers by naming "the protester" as the 2011 Person of the Year.[44] Protesters brought down regimes in the Middle East, challenged corruption in India and Russia, and drew attention to economic inequality in Europe and North America.

Recognizing that leadership duties can be widely distributed is another way to ensure that followers are properly recognized. In *shared leadership*, group and organizational members share the responsibility for achieving collective goals.[45] Shared leadership can take several different forms. Two individuals might function as co-leaders by jointly occupying a leadership position, as in the case of William Hewlett and David Packard, cofounders of the technology giant HP. In another form of shared leadership, group members divide up leadership functions or take turns rotating in and out of leadership roles. For instance, members of a firm's executive team may each take responsibility for one component of a merger plan—finance, operations, products, personnel. Or different team members may take the lead depending on the plan's stage of development. The chief financial officer (CFO) might be in charge as the company determines if a proposed merger will be profitable. The human resource director will likely coordinate salary and benefits when the two groups of employees are brought together after the merger is approved. In yet another form of shared leadership, leadership duties are disbursed throughout the organization rather than concentrated in the hands of a few individuals at the top of the hierarchy. Frontline supervisors and their teams are empowered to make hiring and firing decisions (see chapter 5), for example, or to shut down the production line.

Describing leaders and followers as relational partners who play complementary roles is the best way to capture what followership means.[46] Leaders exert a greater degree of influence and take more responsibility for the overall direction of the group. Followers, on the other hand, are more involved in implementing plans and carrying out the work. Most people routinely shift between leader and follower functions during the course of the day. As a student you must follow in the classroom, but you may also lead a class project group or an intramural sports team. In recognition of this fact, we suggest that you make a mental note to think of yourself not as a leader or a follower, but as a *leader-follower*. Recognize, too, that you can learn to lead by following and learn to follow by leading. Leadership can prepare us for followership in the same way that following prepares us for leading. By observing our followers we can gain insights into what we should (and shouldn't) do when we serve in a follower role.

~

A good leader can't get too far ahead of his [her] followers.

—Franklin D. Roosevelt

As you can see, followers play an active, vital role in the success of any group, organization, or society. They are neither passive nor subservient. Throughout this text we will use alternative terms like "constituents," "stakeholders," or "collaborators" along with "followers" to help drive home this point. We also believe that effective leadership is based on service, not hierarchy. In the upcoming discussions of transformational leadership in chapter 4 and ethical leadership in chapter 11, we suggest that truly great leaders serve rather than rule because they recognize that those whom they lead entrust them with leadership responsibilities.

Followership expert Robert Kelley sums up the work of followers and leaders this way:

> *In reality followership and leadership are two separate concepts, two separate roles. . . . Neither role corners the market on brains, motivation, talent, or action. Either role can result in an award-winning performance or a flop. The greatest successes require that the people in both roles turn in top-rate performances. We must have great leaders and great followers.*[47]

Viewing Leadership from a Communication Perspective

From our perspective, leadership is first, and foremost, a communication-based activity. Leaders spend much of their time shaping messages that are then presented to a variety of follower, constituent, and stakeholder groups. It is also true that the more leadership responsibility one has, the more one's job focuses on communication. Certainly political leaders, executives, coaches, educators, and religious figures alike all share this common characteristic—the higher the level of leadership, the higher the demand for communication competence. Highly competent leaders are willing to engage in communication, use stories effectively, skillfully use and respond to emotions, and create the desired impressions.

Willingness to Communicate

Leadership effectiveness depends on our willingness to interact with others and on developing effective communication skills. Those who engage in skillful communication are more likely to influence others. Communication professors James McCroskey and Virginia Richmond developed the Willingness to Communicate (WTC) scale to measure the predisposition to talk in a variety of situations.[48] Take a few minutes to complete the WTC instrument in box 1.6, and then compute your total score as well as your scores for each of the subscales.

Box 1.6 Self-Assessment	Willingness to Communicate Scale (WTC)[49]

Directions: Below are 20 situations in which a person might choose to communicate or not to communicate. Presume you have completely free choice. Indicate in the space at the left what percentage of the time you would choose to communicate in each type of situation. You can choose any percentage ranging from 0% (never communicating) to 100% (always communicating).

_____ 1. Talk with a service station attendant.

_____ 2. Talk with a physician.

_____ 3. Present a talk to a group of strangers.

_____ 4. Talk with an acquaintance while standing in line.

_____ 5. Talk with a salesperson in a store.

_____ 6. Talk in a large meeting of friends.

_____ 7. Talk with a police officer.

_____ 8. Talk in a small group of strangers.

_____ 9. Talk with a friend while standing in line.

_____ 10. Talk with a waiter/waitress in a restaurant.

_____ 11. Talk in a large meeting of acquaintances.

_____ 12. Talk with a stranger while standing in line.

_____ 13. Talk with a secretary.

_____ 14. Present a talk to a group of friends.

_____ 15. Talk in a small group of acquaintances.

_____ 16. Talk with a garbage collector.

_____ 17. Talk in a large meeting of strangers.

_____ 18. Talk with a spouse (or girl/boy friend).

_____ 19. Talk in a small group of friends.

_____ 20. Present a talk to a group of acquaintances.

The WTC is designed to indicate how willing you are to communicate in a variety of contexts, with different types of receivers. The higher your WTC total score, the more willing you are to communicate in general. Similarly, the higher your given subscore for a type of context or audience, the more willing you are to communicate in that type of context or with that type of audience.

Scoring: The WTC permits computation of one total score and seven subscores. The subscores relate to willingness to communicate in each of four common communication contexts and with three types of audiences. To compute your scores, merely add your scores for each item and divide by the number indicated below.

Subscore Desired	Scoring Formula
Group discussion	Add scores for items 8, 15, and 19; then divide by 3.
Meetings	Add scores for items 6, 11, and 17; then divide by 3.
Interpersonal conversations	Add scores for items 4, 9, and 12; then divide by 3.
Public speaking	Add scores for items 3, 14, and 20; then divide by 3.
Stranger	Add scores for items 3, 8, 12, and 17; then divide by 4.
Acquaintance	Add scores for items 4, 11, 15, and 20; then divide by 4.
Friend	Add scores for items 6, 9, 14, and 19; then divide by 4.

To compute the total WTC scores, add the subscores for stranger, acquaintance, and friend. Then divide by 3.

Norms for WTC Scores

Group discussion	> 89 High WTC, < 57 Low WTC
Meetings	> 80 High WTC, < 39 Low WTC
Interpersonal conversations	> 94 High WTC, < 64 Low WTC
Public speaking	> 78 High WTC, < 33 Low WTC
Stranger	> 63 High WTC, < 18 Low WTC
Acquaintance	> 92 High WTC, < 57 Low WTC
Friend	> 99 High WTC, < 71 Low WTC
Total WTC	> 82 High Overall WTC, < 52 Low Overall WTC

McCroskey, Richmond, and their colleagues report that overall scores on the WTC scale are directly related to communication behavior. Individuals with high WTC scores communicate more frequently and for longer periods of time than people with low WTC scores. Increased communication activity, in turn, leads to a number of positive outcomes in the United States, a society that values individualism and assertiveness (see chapter 10). Speaking up is not viewed as favorably in other cultures, such as some Asian societies, that put more emphasis on the needs of the group as a whole.[50] In the United States:

- High WTCs are viewed as more credible and attractive and are more often identified as opinion leaders.
- People who speak frequently in small groups are more likely to hold leadership positions (see chapter 7).
- Talkative people are more likely to be hired and promoted. They also stay with organizations longer than their quiet colleagues.
- Willing communicators rate themselves higher as competent communicators and report that they are more skilled at using humor.[51]
- High WTCs are rated as more socially and sexually attractive by members of the opposite sex.
- Students who are more willing to communicate with people from different cultures have more friends from other countries and are more willing to interact with international students on campus.[52]
- Soldiers release stress by being willing to talk about problems in group settings.[53]
- Those who are more willing to communicate are also more open to change and enjoy tasks that require thought.[54]

There are a number of reasons why we may be reluctant to interact with others: we may have inherited a tendency to be shy, introverted, and anxious about communication; put a low value on talk; feel alienated from other people; suffer from low self-esteem; or experience fear or anxiety about specific communication situations. In some cases, we're reluctant to communicate because of a skill deficiency. We don't know how (or think we don't know how) to communicate effectively. This perceived deficiency becomes a vicious cycle. Thinking we can't communicate successfully, we avoid interaction. As a consequence, we don't get the practice we need and therefore can't communicate as well.

We can reverse the cycle by developing our skills. Skill development builds confidence and encourages us to talk. When we communicate, we practice our skills and increase our effectiveness. This results in greater self-assurance, making it even more likely that we'll participate in future interactions. In one study, for example, students enrolled in an introductory public speaking course significantly increased their willingness to give speeches during the semester. Those who were the least willing to give speeches at the beginning of the class saw the most rapid improvement.[55] (Box 1.7 describes another leadership skill we can improve through practice.)

Box 1.7 Research Highlight	**Leading with Questions[56]**

Asking effective questions is a critical skill for leaders. In his book, *Leading with Questions*, professor and consultant Michael Marquardt builds a case for exercising leadership through questioning. To discover how successful leaders use inquiries, Marquardt interviewed 22 leaders from around the world who are known for their questioning abilities. His sample included top-level executives at DuPont, Novartis, and ConocoPhillips Petroleum, as well as academic leaders and nonprofit officials drawn from Brazil, Finland, North America, Malaysia, Korea, Mauritius, and Switzerland.

Professor Marquardt found that asking questions instead of providing answers creates a "questioning culture." In a questioning culture, members challenge assumptions, encourage inquiries, and find creative ways to solve problems. Both groups and individuals benefit as a result. Questions promote organizational learning; improve collective problem solving and decision making; produce greater adaptability; energize followers; encourage teamwork; and foster innovation. Individuals working in a questioning climate experience greater self-awareness, self-confidence, openness, and personal flexibility. They become better listeners; are more comfortable expressing and managing conflict; develop keener insight into organizational dynamics and relationships; and demonstrate stronger commitment to learning and personal development.

Unfortunately, leaders are often quick to provide answers instead of asking questions, based in part on their belief that followers are looking to them for solutions. When leaders do ask questions, they may put others on the defensive. Examples of judgmental questions include: "Why are you behind schedule?" and "What's the problem with this project?" According to Marquardt, leaders must admit when they don't have the answers and ask questions that encourage followers to come up with their own solutions. For example: "How do you feel about the project thus far?"; "What have you accomplished so far that you are most pleased with?"; "What key things need to happen to achieve your objective?"

Moving from judgmental questions to productive ones takes a shift in mind-set as well as behavior. Leaders need to begin with a commitment to learn rather than to judge. They should frame questions in a nonthreatening manner to express curiosity and to open dialogue. They can set the stage for inquiries by spelling out what they desire from the conversation ("I hope to get a better idea of why costs are up," "I want to understand your feelings about the reorganization plan"). The questioning leader should allow the other person enough time to reflect and to respond and show genuine interest in the reply. Finally, it is critical to follow up on information and concerns. As one nonprofit executive in Marquardt's sample noted: "The power of questions can only be realized through learning, follow up, and change. The leader who asks questions and doesn't pay attention to the answers quickly loses credibility."

Storytelling as Leadership

One of the primary ways in which leaders shape reality is through storytelling. As Washington College professor Michael Harvey explains, "Leaders frame stories and events to help [followers] understand the world, themselves, and other groups, as well as to identify or solve problems."[57] Stephen Denning suggests that leadership is an "interactive" endeavor largely shaped by narrative.[58] This is not to suggest that abstract reasoning and analysis are not important to leadership, but rather that storytelling is a valuable supplement to these generally recognized aspects of leadership. Leaders tell their stories in a variety of informal and formal contexts, from conversations over a cup of coffee to formal presentations. Through stories leaders can connect themselves with others, building strong relationships and a sense of affiliation. Stories carry multiple messages. Among other functions, they reflect important values, inspire, and describe appropriate behavior. Further, when leaders tell compelling stories they influence others to pick up the same story line, thus extending the narrative. This process of retelling stories (often in a revised form by those who follow) is part of the cocreation of meaning that is central to storytelling. Royal Dutch Shell Group offers a good example. The group's managing directors first developed their own story lines about needed change and the future and then engaged the next layers of management in crafting their versions. Tales were told for years of profitable growth and technical leadership. These stories were then retold throughout the company across sites in more than 100 countries. As a result, all those concerned understood the case for change and told each other what they would have to do to bring the "new reality" into being.[59]

The right anecdote can be worth a thousand theories.

—Warren Bennis

Denning proposes that there are eight general categories of stories that leaders can use to assist in achieving their goals.[60]

Sparking action. These stories describe how a successful change was implemented in the past, allowing listeners to imagine how such a change might work in their situation. These "springboard" stories enable listeners to visualize the large-scale transformation required. For example, as program director of knowledge management for the World Bank in the mid-1990s, Denning struggled to get his colleagues to see the importance of the need for a central repository for the information scattered throughout the organization. The message was falling on deaf ears until Denning found a "springboard" story. He framed the need for collecting and sharing information at the World Bank by describing how technology was changing the landscape of our planet. The story he told involved a health worker in 1995 in a remote village in Zambia who logged on to the website of the Centers for Disease Control and Prevention in Atlanta, Georgia, and got an answer to a question on how to treat malaria. When this story was added to the presentation, audience members were able to visualize how the information collected in their organization might be used.

Communicating who you are. These stories reveal your identity to an audience, building trust and creating a connection. Political leaders such as Elizabeth Warren and Sarah Palin, for example, write books, maintain websites, and give speeches designed to present a desired image of themselves to the electorate.

> *Leadership is personal. Do the people you lead know who you are,*
> *what you care about, and why they ought to be following you?*
>
> —*Ron Sugar*

Communicating the brand. These organizational stories are designed to communicate brand image to customers. Cosmetic retailer The Body Shop created a global brand without using conventional advertising. Brand identity was communicated through the stories of the company founder, the late Anita Roddick, and through commitment to a model of commerce-with-a-conscience.

Transmitting values. These stories reflect and reinforce organizational values by telling audience members "how things are done around here." Leaders at Costco are particularly skilled at telling stories as a means for transmitting organizational values. Costco is an $89 billion business. Jim Sinegal, the founder and retired CEO of the company, loved to tell visitors the "salmon story" to highlight Costco's focus on raising quality while lowering prices. A team of employees was able to improve the quality of salmon filets by removing excess parts while, at the same time, lowering the cost from $5.99 to $4.99 a pound. The story is told in a wall display in the lobby of corporate headquarters and the firm created the Salmon Award. This annual award recognizes outstanding employee performance. New salmon stories are generated every time it is given out.[61]

Fostering collaboration. These stories encourage people to work together by generating a narrative to illustrate common concerns and goals. (Turn to the Cultural Connections feature at the end of the chapter to see how one cultural group uses storytelling to foster connection.) As noted earlier, Southwest Airlines is an organization with a clear set of common concerns and goals. Stories are frequently used to reinforce this collaborative culture. One such story is that of a Southwest Airlines pilot who quickly exited his flight after arrival only to return a short time later for preflight checks for his return trip. Where had he been? Getting a quick cup of coffee? No, he had climbed in the front bin of the aircraft on a cold and windy day to unload all of the mail and freight—with no gloves, knee pads, or coat—while the other agents off-loaded the bags in the back.[62]

Taming the grapevine. These stories highlight the incongruity between rumors and reality. For example, one might deal with a false rumor of imminent corporate-wide reorganization by jokingly recounting how difficult it is to work out the seating chart at the executive committee meetings. It is important to be careful with these types of stories as mean-spirited humor can generate a well-deserved backlash and the denial of a rumor that turns out to be true can have a devastating impact on credibility.

Sharing knowledge. These stories focus on problems and show, in detail, how corrections were made and why the solution worked. Many organizations use an after-action review (AAR) in this manner. AARs are assessments conducted after a project or major activity that allow employees and leaders to explore what happened and why. They may be thought of as a professional discussion of an event that enables employees to understand why things happened during the progression of the process and to learn from that experience. AARs can be useful in a variety of situations, including: following the introduction of a new product line or computer system upgrade, after a busy holiday season in a retail store, or after a major training activity or a change in procedures. The discussion during the AAR allows leaders to use sharing knowledge stories to improve subsequent organizational responses to similar situations. (We'll take a further look at debriefing in chapter 7.)

Leading people into the future. These stories evoke images of a desired future. Often such stories provide limited detail while encouraging listeners to imagine what the future might be. There are many fine historical examples of such stories, but none, perhaps, had more impact on twentieth century life in the United States than Martin Luther King, Jr.'s "I Have a Dream" speech. King had a vision of whites and blacks living in racial harmony; where his children "would be judged, not by the color of their skin, but by the content of their character."

Emotional Communication Competencies

The rational dimension of leadership is critical. In the chapters to come, we'll outline ways that leaders use thinking and reasoning skills to solve problems, set goals, negotiate, argue, shape public opinion, adapt to cultural differences, and organize and deliver effective presentations. Forgetting the emotional side of leadership, however, would be a mistake. Effective leaders are also skilled at sharing and responding to emotions. For example, they know how to communicate affection, liking, and excitement to followers. In addition, they know how to channel their emotions in order to achieve their objectives and to maintain friendly group relations.

Neal Ashkanasy and Peter Jordan argue that successful leaders effectively utilize emotions at five different levels of the organization.[63] In their Multilevel Model of Emotion in Organizations (MMEO), *Level 1* is *within the person*. At this level the focus is on how leaders experience and respond to emotions. During the course of a day, leaders must cope with a variety of events beyond their control (rising and falling stock prices, customer feedback, news stories) that generate positive and negative responses. Effective emotional leaders communicate confidence and stability in the face of these emotional ups and downs. *Level 2* is *between persons*. Leaders differ in emotional intelligence (EI), which is the ability to perceive, respond to, and express emotions.[64] Evidence suggests that outstanding (transformational) leaders have high levels of EI.[65] They use emotions to encourage, inspire, stimulate, and motivate followers, resulting in significantly higher performance.

(We'll take an in-depth look at transformational leadership in chapter 4.) High emotional intelligence also helps leaders make better decisions, as we'll see in the discussion of emotional competencies that follows.

Level 3 is the *interpersonal* level, which is concerned with interaction within dyads in the organization. Effective leaders use emotional displays to accomplish tasks. For instance, an instructor may make supportive comments to students when they feel overwhelmed by assignments but later express disappointment about the results of a test to motivate class members to study harder for the next exam. In addition to employing emotional expressions to achieve goals, successful leaders use positive, supportive displays to manage relationships and to build trust.

Level 4 describes the *group level*. Work teams as a whole develop an "affective tone." Informal leaders influence moods indirectly through emotional contagion. Through their example, they help spread emotions like happiness or sadness throughout the group. Formal leaders exert direct influence on moods. For example, groups accomplish more when their appointed leaders are in a positive frame of mind. The affective tone of the group as a whole improves when formal leaders develop positive emotional relationships with individual group members.

Level 5 is the *organizational level*. Effective leaders at this level help create an emotional tone for the entire organization. Virgin's Richard Branson, for instance, is out to create a "fun" organization. Successful leaders don't suppress emotions but recognize their importance. They realize that there may be times when negative feelings should be expressed. For instance, employees under particularly high levels of stress may need to voice their frustrations.

Unfortunately, some proponents of emotional leadership appear to overstate its importance. They go so far as to argue that nearly all of the competencies that account for executive success are emotional rather than cognitive in nature.[66] They also label as "emotional" some competencies that seem to have more to do with thinking than feeling. For instance, some researchers identify conflict management and influence as emotional skills, but we consider them to be largely rational leadership communication abilities.

Striking a balance between logic and emotion is safer than making one more important than the other. When it comes to leadership, **both** are essential.[67] Crisis decision making provides one example of the importance of both cognitive and emotional competencies (see chapter 13). To avoid making a hasty decision in a crisis, leaders must exercise a variety of cognitive skills, such as rejecting their faulty beliefs and assumptions, gathering facts, identifying stakeholders, soliciting a broad range of opinions, keeping records, and perspective taking. At the same time, they must employ such emotional skills as managing stress, overcoming mental and physical fatigue, expressing compassion, and resisting group pressures.

The following set of emotional competencies demonstrates that the success of followers and leaders depends on how well are they able to integrate emotion and cognition. Skillfully blending feeling and thinking requires the following five skills.[68]

1. *Perception, appraisal, and expression of emotion.* Emotional intelligence begins with the ability to identify, evaluate, and then express emotional

states. These skills may seem rudimentary, but some people are "emotionally illiterate." For example, people can be oblivious to the fact that they are irritating everyone else in the group. While most of us are not this insensitive, we frequently suffer from emotional blind spots. There are times when we feel uneasy but can't identify our emotions or when we don't know exactly how to express our affection for friends or loved ones.

2. *Attending to the emotions of others.* Those in a leadership role must understand the feelings of followers in order to connect with them. Consider the case of a CEO who doesn't understand that his employees are feeling overworked and discouraged. If he fails to acknowledge their frustration and tries to inspire them to work harder, they aren't likely to put forth additional effort. Instead, he will appear out of touch.

3. *Emotional facilitation of thinking.* Emotional states impact decision-making styles. Good moods facilitate creative thinking while sad moods slow the decision-making process and encourage more attention to detail. Both emotional states have a role to play in problem solving. Some problems require intuitive, broad thinking; others demand a more linear, logical approach. Emotionally intelligent leaders know how to match the mood with the problem. Further, they recognize the dangers of ignoring risks when in an optimistic frame of mind, or of being too critical when feeling pessimistic. Using emotions to facilitate thinking also means channeling feelings in order to reach goals. For instance, moderate fear of failure can spur us to prepare before making a presentation. Remembering past successes can reduce our anxiety before we deliver the speech.

4. *Understanding and analyzing emotional information and employing emotional knowledge.* This cluster of competencies links symbols to emotions. Leaders must be able to label what they feel and recognize the relationship between that label and other related terms. For example, "anger" belongs to a family of words that includes "irritation," "rage," "hostility," and "annoyance." (To determine your ability to identify emotional labels, complete the self-assessment in box 1.8.) The internal states identified by these labels are connected in specific ways. Irritation and annoyance lead to anger and rage, not the other way around. Understanding this fact can empower leaders. A supervisor may decide to postpone a meeting with a disagreeable employee, for instance, when she senses that her irritation with this individual could escalate into unwanted anger. Recognizing how emotions blend together is also important. Surprise is one example of an emotion that rarely stands alone. When we feel surprised, we generally experience some other emotion—perhaps happiness, disappointment, or anger—at the same time.

5. *Regulation of emotion.* The last component of emotional intelligence puts knowledge into action. This set of competencies enables leaders to create the feelings they desire in themselves and in others. They recognize the power of *emotional contagion,* the fact that emotions of one person quickly spread to

others.[69] Emotionally skilled leaders know how to maintain positive moods and how to repair negative ones. To do so, they employ such tactics as avoiding unpleasant situations, engaging in rewarding tasks, and creating a comfortable work environment. In addition, they can step back and evaluate their feelings to determine if their responses in a situation were appropriate. Such evaluation can encourage them to remain calm instead of getting upset and to be more supportive instead of only focusing on the task. Effective leaders also help others maintain and improve their moods. They use these skills to create cohesive groups and to inspire and motivate followers.

Humans are not, in any practical sense, predominantly rational beings, nor are they predominantly emotional beings. They are both.

—*Peter Salovey*

. . . leadership is an emotion-laden process, both from a leader and a follower perspective.

—*Jennifer M. George*

Box 1.8   Self-Assessment   **Emotional Word Matrix[70]**

Instructions: You have ten minutes to fill in the boxes below with high-intensity, moderate intensity, and low-intensity descriptors for each of the primary emotions. For example, descriptors for "happy" can range from ecstatic (high) to delighted (medium) to glad (low). When time is up, respond to the following questions: Did you find it difficult to complete the matrix? If so, why? How can you improve your emotional vocabulary?

	Intensity		
Category	**High**	**Moderate**	**Low**
Happy			
Sad			
Scared			
Angry			
Confused			
Strong			
Weak			

Playing to a Packed House: Leaders as Impression Managers

From a communication standpoint, leaders are made, not born. We increase our leadership competence as we increase our communication skills. We can compare the leadership role to a part played on stage to illustrate how effective communication skills translate into effective leadership.

Sociologist Erving Goffman and others have adapted Shakespeare's adage that life is a stage to develop what is called the *dramaturgical approach* to human interaction. Proponents of this perspective argue that, like actors in a drama, people create meaning and influence others through their performances.[71] Let's look at a typical date, for example. The date is a performance that may take place on any number of stages: the dance floor, the coffee house, the movie theater, the football game. The actors (the couple) prepare in their dressing rooms at home before the performance and may return to the same locations for a critique session after the date ends. Particularly on the first date, the interactants may work very hard to create desired impressions—they engage in "impression management." Each dating partner tries to manage the perceptions of the other person by using appropriate behaviors, which might include dressing in the latest fashions, acting in a courteous manner, engaging in polite conversation, and paying for meals and other activities.

To see how impression management works, change one aspect of your usual communication and watch how others respond. If friends have told you that you seem unfriendly because you are quiet when meeting new people, try being more assertive the next time you meet strangers at a party. If you make a conscious effort to greet others, introduce yourself, and learn more about the others at the gathering, you may shake your aloof, unfriendly image.

Leaders also engage in impression management to achieve their goals. Remember that as a leader you'll play to a packed house. People in organizations carefully watch the behavior of the CEO for information about the executive officer's character and for clues as to organizational priorities, values, and future directions. They seek answers to such questions as: "Can I trust him/her?" "What kind of behavior gets rewarded around here?" "Is she or he really interested in my welfare?" "Is dishonesty tolerated?" "Are we going to survive the next five years?" "Is this an enjoyable, exciting place to work?" (See box 1.9 for a closer look at impression management in a public setting.)

Important clues to how we can shape the impressions others have of us can be gleaned from the examples of outstanding leaders. Charismatic or transformational leaders are skilled actors who create the impression that they are trustworthy, effective, morally worthy, innovative, and skilled.[72] To see how they create these and other favorable images, turn to chapter 4. Those who study *aesthetic leadership* also focus on the performance dimension of leadership. Aesthetic scholars look at how individuals embody leadership through their actions.[73] Effective leaders put on beautiful (aesthetically pleasing) performances. To lead beautifully, they demonstrate mastery, coherence, and purpose. *Mastery* means knowing a particular subject matter (such as the topic of a speech), knowing a communication skill (like public speaking), and knowing how to use that skill (how long to speak, for instance). *Coherence* refers to matching the form of the message with the message and objective. Coherent messages authentically reflect the leader's self. (Breaking up with a long-term romantic partner via a text message would be considered inauthentic, for example.) *Purpose* refers to the goal of leadership. Beautiful performances are ethical—they serve the common good and moral purposes. Robert Kennedy put on such a performance in 1968. Scheduled to give a presidential campaign speech in Indianapolis right after the assassination of Martin Luther King Jr., Kennedy faced a largely black audience primed for violence and revenge. Kennedy stood on the back of a flatbed truck and for the first time spoke in public about the assassination of his brother, President John Kennedy. He ended by urging blacks and whites to put aside their hatred to work together to create a better society. The crowd peacefully dispersed and the city remained calm.[74]

Box 1.9 Research Highlight	Performing on the Debate Stage[75]

Presidential debates highlight the importance of impression management. Williams College professor George Goethals analyzed presidential debates from 1960–1992 and found that nonverbal behaviors have a significant impact on the perception of candidates, complementing or undermining their words. Goethals came to his conclusions after viewing recordings of the debates, reading the comments of contemporary observers, and showing edited clips to Williams College students to determine their responses.

Radio audiences gave Richard Nixon higher ratings in his 1960 debate with John F. Kennedy while television audiences were more favorable to Kennedy. Kennedy appeared confident and relaxed on screen, while Nixon fidgeted and moved his arms awkwardly. When assuming his position at the podium, Kennedy walked confidently while Nixon appeared unsure of himself. Kennedy's behavior undercut Nixon's campaign slogan, "experience counts," and made Kennedy appear more like the "ideal president."

During the 1976 campaign (the next time debates were held), Gerald Ford, a former football player, appeared to dominate the much smaller Jimmy Carter, making Ford appear more commanding. That same year, during the vice-presidential debates between Bob Dole and Walter Mondale, Bob Dole stumbled when he referred to the wars of the twentieth century as "democrat wars" while leaning against the podium "much like a gunslinger in a saloon in an old west cowboy movie."

Ronald Reagan's calm, slow manner of speaking reassured debate viewers that he could be trusted in his campaign against Jimmy Carter in 1980. In 1984, his one-liners about him not holding opponent Walter Mondale's youth and inexperience against him played a major role in his success. In fact, when these jokes and audience reactions were edited out, Mondale came out the winner among student viewers. Mondale, for his part, failed to communicate warmth in his facial expressions.

In 1988, George H. W. Bush had a large height advantage over Michael Dukakis (which was apparent the moment they shook hands at the start of the debate). Bush alluded to Dukakis as the "iceman who never makes a mistake," turning a liability into an advantage by implying that Dukakis might be smarter and more articulate but that he (Bush) was "imperfect but warm." Later in the debate Dukakis showed little emotion when asked if he would seek the death penalty should someone rape and murder his wife. In 1992, Bill Clinton's sympathetic voice and direct physical approach to citizens in a town hall debate format made him appear caring and engaged. On the other hand Bush, who looked at his watch, appeared aloof and distant.

Many people are uncomfortable with the idea of impression management. They equate playing a role with being insincere, since true feelings and beliefs might be hidden. They note that far too often fellow students and coworkers get ahead by acting like chameleons, changing their behaviors to conform to the wishes of whatever group in which they find themselves. As we saw in our earlier discussion of narcissistic and Machiavellian leaders, these are very real dangers. Self-promotion and ingratiation can trump competence and hard work. However, research suggests that individuals typically use impression management to project a public image that is congruent with their self-concepts.[76] Followers continually watch for inconsistencies and often "see through" insincere performances of leaders. Further, impression management is part of every human interaction. Others form impressions of us, whether or not we are intentional about our behaviors. Frequently, we have no choice but to play many roles. We are forced into performances as job applicants, students, dating partners, and leaders each day. The real problem is that we often mismanage the impressions we make. Our behaviors may make us appear dull or untrustworthy when we really are interesting and honest.

Some fear that leaders can manipulate impressions to mislead the group. This is a legitimate concern (we'll discuss the ethical dimension of leadership in greater detail in chapter 11). Yet, impression management is essential for achieving worthy objectives. The state human services director who inspires her employees to meet the needs of more clients through her use of impression management is helping the disadvantaged, making better use of state funds, and boosting the morale of her organization.

Because impression management can be used to further group goals or to subvert them, it should be judged by its end products. Ethical impression management meets group wants and needs and, in the ideal, spurs the group to reach higher goals. Organizational impression experts Paul Rosenfeld, Robert Giacalone, and Catherine Riordan offer the following guidelines for determining if impression management is beneficial or detrimental to an organization.[77] Beneficial impression management helps the organization achieve its objectives by: (1) promoting positive interpersonal relationships and increasing cooperation with both those inside and outside the organization; (2) accurately portraying positive persons, events, or products to insiders and outsiders; and (3) facilitating decision making, helping management and consumers make the right choices. Detrimental or dysfunctional impression management damages the organization by (1) blocking or undermining relationships with those who work with or do business with the organization; (2) incorrectly casting people, events, or products in a negative light to insiders and outsiders; and (3) distorting information that results in managers and consumers reaching the wrong conclusions and/or decisions.

In this theater of man's [woman's] life it is reserved
only for God and the angels to be lookers on.

—*Francis Bacon*

∽ CHAPTER TAKEAWAYS

- Leadership attracts universal attention. Historians, philosophers, and social scientists have attempted to understand and to explain leadership for centuries.

- Leadership is a fundamental element of the human condition. Wherever society exists, leadership exists. Any definition of leadership must account for its universal nature. Leadership seems to be linked to what it means to be human. What makes us unique as humans is our ability to create and manipulate symbols—abstract, arbitrary representations of reality.

- One way to isolate the unique characteristics of leadership is to look at how others have defined the term. Four primary definitional themes have emerged in the leadership literature: (1) leadership is about who you are; (2) leadership is about how you act; (3) leadership is about what you do; and (4) leadership is about how you work with others. We offer the following communication-based definition of leadership: Leadership is human (symbolic) communication that modifies the attitudes and behaviors of others in order to meet shared group goals and needs.

- Management is often equated with leadership. However, leading differs significantly from managing when it comes to creating an agenda, developing a human network for achieving the agenda, and executing the agenda. While the manager is more absorbed in the status quo, the leader is more concerned with the ultimate direction of the group.

- Most of those who study and write about leadership have focused on the more positive connotations of the concept. Recently researchers have devoted attention to the bad or "toxic" side of leadership. Bad leadership is the product of selfishness, cognitive errors, and external forces. Destructive leaders can be classified as incompetent, rigid, intemperate, callous, corrupt, insular, or evil. In the organizational context, destructive leadership behaviors are directed at followers, the organization, or at both.

- Leaders and followers are relational partners who play complementary roles. Leaders exert a greater degree of influence and followers have more responsibility for carrying out the work. Followers are playing an increasingly important role in modern society.

- In shared leadership, responsibility for achieving shared goals is distributed throughout the group.

- Leaders spend much of their time shaping messages that are then presented to a variety of follower, constituent, and stakeholder groups. It is also true that the more leadership responsibility you have, the more your job will focus on communication.

- Viewing leadership from a communication perspective recognizes that your leadership effectiveness depends on your willingness to interact with others (the willingness to communicate) and on making skillful use of storytelling, emotional communication competencies, and impression management.

• Leadership is an interactive endeavor largely shaped by narrative. Storytelling is a valuable supplement to abstract reasoning and analysis. Important types of stories include those that: (1) spark action, (2) communicate who you are, (3) communicate the brand image to customers, (4) transmit organizational values, (5) foster collaboration, (6) tame the grapevine by pointing out the disconnect between rumors and reality, (7) share knowledge about problem solving, and (8) lead people into the future.

• Effective leaders know how to utilize emotions at all organizational levels— within the person, between persons, interpersonal, group, and organization wide. They demonstrate five emotional competencies: (1) perception, appraisal, and expression of emotion; (2) attending to the emotions of others; (3) emotional facilitation of thinking; (4) understanding and analyzing emotional information and employing that information; and (5) regulation of emotion.

• To achieve your goals as a leader, you'll need to manage the impressions others have of you. Strive for beautiful (ethical, effective) performances that demonstrate mastery, coherence, and a worthy purpose.

• Ethical leaders use impression management to reach group objectives rather than to satisfy selfish, personal goals. Beneficial impression management promotes positive interpersonal relationships and cooperation; accurately portrays people, events, or products; and facilitates effective decision making.

APPLICATION EXERCISES

1. Take a trip to a local bookstore and check to see how many books you can find on leadership. Did you find more or fewer titles than you expected? Report your findings in class. Or select a leadership topic and see how many books you can find on Amazon.com.

2. Conduct a debate regarding the relative importance of leaders and followers. Have one-half of your class argue that leaders are more important than ever and have the other half argue that followers are becoming more influential than leaders. As an alternative, debate the concept of "bad" leadership. Should we consider people like Hitler, Stalin, Pol Pot, and Osama bin Laden leaders or are they merely "power wielders"?

3. Develop your own definition of leadership. How does it compare to the ones given in the chapter?

4. Make a list of the characteristics of leaders and managers. Are your characteristics the same as those described by Kouzes, Posner, and Kotter? To clarify the differences between leaders and managers, describe someone who is an effective leader and then someone who is an effective manager. How do these two people differ? Share your descriptions with others in class.

5. Select one of your follower roles (student, employee, team member, etc.) and then select one of your leadership roles (team captain, project group leader,

coach). Consider the behaviors and qualities you appreciate or dislike in those who lead or follow you. What can you learn from those strengths and weaknesses that you can apply as a leader-follower? What conclusions can you draw about being an effective leader or follower? Write up your findings.

6. In a group, determine the advantages and disadvantages of sharing leadership responsibilities in a group or organization. Based on your discussion, what conclusions do you reach about shared leadership?

7. Pair off with someone and compare your overall Willingness to Communicate (WTC) scores as well as your seven subscores. What factors make you and your partner reluctant to communicate in all situations or in particular contexts? What can each of you do to increase your willingness to communicate? What communication skills do you need to sharpen? Or, as an alternative, find a partner and discuss your responses to the Emotional Word Matrix.

8. Consider the stories you have heard from leaders in the past. Discuss with others in class which stories you found to be most/least effective and why.

9. Identify individuals in leadership roles you believe have low or high emotional intelligence. Discuss what you feel the impact of these ratings is on leadership effectiveness.

10. Analyze the impression management strategies of a well-known leader. What image does this individual create? How effectively does he/she use the dramatic elements described in the chapter? Does she/he make ethical use of impression management? Write up your findings. Or analyze a specific performance of a leader. Does she or he put on a beautiful performance by demonstrating mastery, coherence, and purpose?

∿ CULTURAL CONNECTIONS: FOSTERING CIRCLES THROUGH STORIES[78]

Indigenous groups in Canada and the United States take a very different approach to leadership than their fellow citizens who draw from Western tradition. Believing that all things are related (people, nature, past, and present), First Nations leaders strive to meet the needs of the entire community. Instead of hierarchy, they emphasize equality. Driven by a sense of calling, they focus on long-term results—looking seven generations into the future—and turn to spiritual traditions for guidance. This approach to leadership is captured in the image of a circle. A circle is equalitarian and consensual. The circle or wheel functions only when everyone is united and working together. Some tribes incorporate four quadrants of life into the Medicine Wheel version of the circle: physical, mental, spiritual, and emotional. The responsibility of leaders is holistic, helping followers develop in all four areas of life.

Storytelling, which draws upon tribal oral tradition, plays a critical role in indigenous leadership. Aboriginal leaders use imagery to communicate messages and to reinforce connection. For example: "The idea is that you stay in your canoe and we'll stay in our canoe and we'll follow our culture and traditions and you'll follow yours." "We [the leaders] may be out at the pointy end of the spear, but the big weight of the spear, the broad part of the spear, is behind us and that's the people."

Aboriginal leadership has much to offer modern organizations that want to eliminate levels of hierarchy, foster connection and spirituality, strive for work-life balance, and develop sustainable business practices that protect future generations. Western-oriented leaders can learn from First Nations leaders who practice equalitarianism, service, spirituality, connection, consensus, meeting the needs of the total person, sustainability, and storytelling.

∿ LEADERSHIP ON THE BIG SCREEN: *THE BEST OF MEN*

Starring: Eddie Marsan, Rob Brydon, Niamh Cusack, George MacKay, Leigh Quinn, Richard McCabe

Rating: PG for language and mature themes

Synopsis: In 1944 neurosurgeon Ludwig Guttmann, a Jewish refugee from Nazi Germany, is appointed to run the spinal injury unit of Britain's Stoke Mandeville hospital. Conditions in the ward are appalling. Paralyzed soldiers arrive from the battlefield in coffins, are heavily sedated, and left to "rot" in their beds from bed-sores. Some 80% die within a year from their injuries, sores, and urinary tract infections. Those who survive face a lifetime in institutions. Guttmann (played by Marsan) addresses this hopelessness, convinced that his patients can become active members of society. He institutes a series of changes that include ending the use of shipping coffins and sedation, turning the young men once every two hours so they don't develop bed sores, moving patients to wheelchairs, and engaging the soldiers in upper body exercise. Progress is far from easy, however. Guttmann must battle fellow doctors and nurses (and patients) who oppose his initiatives, lobby for staff and resources, and deal with layers of bureaucracy. In 1948 he hosts the first competition for wheelchair athletes, which later becomes the International Paralympics drawing thousands of participants from around the world. (Guttmann was knighted for his work with spinal patients in 1966.)

Chapter Links: vision, leading change, emotional communication competencies, symbols, willingness to communicate, leader-follower relationships

2

Leadership and Followership Communication Styles

OVERVIEW

The Dimensions of Leadership Communication Style

Think of the leaders with whom you have worked in the past. Chances are you enjoyed interacting with some of these people more than others. The leaders you enjoyed working with were most likely those who created a productive and satisfying work climate. Under their guidance, you probably accomplished a great deal and had a pleasant and memorable experience.

One factor that contributes to variations in leader effectiveness is communication style. Leadership communication style is a relatively enduring set of communicative behaviors in which a leader engages when interacting with followers. The communication style a leader selects contributes to the success or failure of any attempt to exert influence.

Researchers have identified a number of leadership communication styles. These varying styles can be pared down to two primary models of communication: one model compares authoritarian, democratic, and laissez-faire styles of leadership communication; a second model contrasts task and interpersonal leadership communication. Let's look more closely at these two models of communication.

Authoritarian, Democratic, and Laissez-Faire Leadership

Kurt Lewin, Ronald Lippitt, and Ralph White undertook one of the earliest investigations of leadership communication style.[1] They studied the impact of authoritarian, democratic, and laissez-faire leadership communication styles on group outcomes.

Each of these styles of communication has unique features that affect how leaders interact with followers. The authoritarian leader maintains strict control over followers by directly regulating policy, procedures, and behavior. Authoritarian leaders create distance between themselves and their followers as a means of emphasizing role distinctions. Many authoritarian leaders believe that followers would not function effectively without direct supervision. The authoritarian leader generally feels that people left to complete work on their own will be unproductive. Examples of authoritarian communicative behavior include a police officer directing traffic, a teacher ordering a student to do his or her assignment, and a supervisor instructing a subordinate to clean a workstation. (See the Leadership on the Big Screen feature at the end of the chapter for another example of an authoritarian leader in action.)

Democratic leaders engage in supportive communication that facilitates interaction between leaders and followers. The leader adopting the democratic communication style encourages follower involvement and participation in the determination of goals and procedures. Democratic leaders assume that followers are capable of making informed decisions. The democratic leader does not feel intimidated by the suggestions provided by followers but believes that the contributions of others improve the overall quality of decision making. The adage that "two heads are better than one" is the motto of the democratic leader. A group leader soliciting ideas from group members, a teacher asking students to suggest the due date for an assignment, and a district manager asking a salesperson for recommendations regarding the display of a new product are examples of democratic communicative behavior.

> *I not only use all the brains that I have, but all that I can borrow.*
> —*Woodrow Wilson*

Laissez-faire, a French word roughly translated as "leave them alone," refers to a form of leader communication that has been called nonleadership by some.[2] An ineffective version of this leadership communication style involves abdication of responsibility on the part of the leader; leaders withdraw from followers and offer little guidance or support. As a result, productivity, cohesiveness, and satisfaction often suffer. A supervisor who is incompetent, nearing retirement, or in jeopardy of being laid off or fired may exhibit the abdicating form of the laissez-faire leadership communication style. A more positive form of the laissez-faire leadership communication style affords followers a high degree of autonomy and self-rule while, at the same time, offering guidance and support when asked. The laissez-faire leader providing guided freedom does not directly participate in decision making unless requested to do so by followers or if such intervention is deemed necessary to facilitate task completion.[3] Examples of guided-freedom communicative behavior include a leader quietly observing group deliberations (providing information and ideas only when asked), a teacher allowing students to create their own assignments, and a research and development manager allowing his or her subordinates to work on product designs without intervention.

How can you tell if a leader is using an authoritarian, democratic, or laissez-faire style? Pay close attention to the leader's communication. The communication patterns in table 2.1 will help you recognize the style of leadership.

Lewin and his colleagues taught these communication styles to adult leaders who supervised groups of 10-year-old children working on hobby projects at a YMCA. The authoritarian leader was instructed to establish and to maintain policy and procedures unilaterally, to supervise the completion of task assignments directly, and to dictate follower behavior in all situations. The democratic leader was told to encourage the participation of followers in the determination of policy and procedures related to task completion and follower behavior. The laissez-faire leader was instructed to avoid direct involvement in the establishment of policy and procedures by supplying ideas and information only when asked to do so by followers.[4]

The responses of the children in these experiments led to the formation of six generalizations regarding the impact of leadership communication style on group effectiveness.[5]

1. Laissez-faire and democratic leadership communication styles are not the same. Groups with laissez-faire leaders are not as productive and satisfying as groups with democratic leaders. The amount and quality of work done by chil-

Table 2.1   Styles of Leadership Communication

Democratic	Authoritarian	Laissez-Faire
Involves followers in setting goals	Sets goals individually	Allows followers free rein to set their own goals
Engages in two-way, open communication	Engages primarily in one-way, downward communication	Engages in noncommittal, superficial communication
Facilitates discussion with followers	Controls discussion with followers	Avoids discussion with followers
Solicits input regarding determination of policy and procedures	Sets policy and procedures unilaterally	Allows followers to set policy and procedures
Focuses interaction	Dominates interaction	Avoids interaction
Provides suggestions and alternatives for the completion of tasks	Personally directs the completion of tasks	Provides suggestions and alternatives for the completion of tasks only when asked to do so by followers
Provides frequent positive feedback	Provides infrequent positive feedback	Provides infrequent feedback of any kind
Rewards good work and uses punishment only as a last resort	Rewards obedience and punishes mistakes	Avoids offering rewards or punishments
Exhibits effective listening skills	Exhibits poor listening skills	May exhibit either poor or effective listening skills
Mediates conflict for group gain	Uses conflict for personal gain	Avoids conflict

dren in laissez-faire groups was less than that of democratic groups. Additionally, the majority of children in laissez-faire groups expressed dissatisfaction despite the fact that more than twice as much play occurred in these groups.

2. Although groups headed by authoritarian leaders are often most efficient, democratic leaders also achieve high efficiency. The greatest number of tasks were completed under authoritarian leadership. This productivity depended on the leader's direct supervision. When the authoritarian leader left the room, productivity dropped by nearly 40% in some groups. Democratic groups were only slightly less productive. Further, productivity in these groups remained steady with or without direct adult supervision.

3. Groups with authoritarian leadership experience more hostility and aggression than groups with democratic or laissez-faire leaders. Hostile and aggressive behavior in the form of arguing, property damage, and blaming occurred much more frequently in authoritarian groups than in other groups.

4. Authoritarian-led groups may experience discontent that is not evident on the surface. Even in authoritarian-led groups with high levels of productivity and little evidence of hostility and aggression, absenteeism and turnover were greater than in democratic and laissez-faire groups. Further, children

who switched from authoritarian groups to more permissive groups exhibited tension-release behavior in the form of energetic and aggressive play.

5. Followers exhibit more dependence and less individuality under authoritarian leaders. Children in authoritarian groups were more submissive than those in other groups. These children were less likely to initiate action without the approval of the leader and less likely to express their opinions and ideas than children in the democratic and laissez-faire groups.

6. Followers exhibit more commitment and cohesiveness under democratic leaders. Children in democratic groups demonstrated a higher degree of commitment to group outcomes. The climate in democratic groups was generally supportive and friendly.

A number of follow-up studies to the work of Lewin, Lippitt, and White have provided additional information about the effects of authoritarian, democratic, and laissez-faire leader communication. Box 2.1 summarizes these findings.

> *I love disagreements. I love the democratic process. If I'm in a room where everybody agrees, I start to nod off.*
>
> —*Gina McCarthy*

Box 2.1 Research Highlight	The Effects of Authoritarian, Democratic, and Laissez-Faire Leadership Communication Styles	
Authoritarian Leadership	**Democratic Leadership**	**Laissez-Faire Leadership**
Increases productivity when the leader is present[6]	Lowers turnover and absenteeism rates[7]	Decreases innovation when leaders abdicate, but increases innovation when leaders provide guidance as requested[8]
Produces more accurate solutions when leader is knowledgeable[9]	Increases follower satisfaction[10]	Decreases follower motivation and satisfaction when leaders abdicate[11]
Is more positively accepted in larger groups[12]	Increases follower participation[13]	Results in feelings of isolation and a decrease in participation when leaders abdicate[14]
Enhances performance on simple tasks and decreases performance on complex tasks[15]	Increases follower commitment to decisions[16]	Decreases quality and quantity of output when leaders abdicate[17]
Increases aggression levels among followers[18]	Increases innovation[19]	Increases productivity and satisfaction for highly motivated experts[20]
Increases turnover rates[21]	Increases a follower's perceived responsibility to a group or organization[22]	Increases stress and conflicts when leaders abdicate[23]

The findings related to leadership communication style suggest that leaders adopting authoritarian communication can expect: high productivity (particularly under optimal conditions: a simple task completed over a short period of time with direct supervision by the leader); increased hostility, aggression, and discontent; and decreased commitment, independence, and creativity among followers. This style of communication would seem best suited for tasks requiring specific compliance procedures and minimal commitment or initiative. Routinized, highly structured, or simple tasks are often effectively accomplished under authoritarian leadership. Authoritarian leadership is also recommended when a leader is much more knowledgeable than his or her followers, when groups of followers are extremely large, or when there is insufficient time to engage in democratic decision making. Certainly a military combat leader would not stop to discuss the possibilities of advancing or retreating while under enemy fire.

Democratic leadership communication contributes to relatively high productivity (whether or not the leader directly supervises followers) and to increased satisfaction, commitment, and cohesiveness. This style of communication is best suited for tasks that require participation and involvement, creativity, and commitment to a decision. The only significant drawbacks to democratic leadership are that democratic techniques are time consuming and can be cumbersome with larger groups. (See the case study in box 2.2 to see how democratic leadership has been used at one successful company.)

Box 2.2 Case Study	The Reluctant Executive: Sustainability, Surfing, and Leadership Style at Patagonia[24]

Yvon Chouinard was an accomplished mountain climber in the 1960s, successfully ascending peaks throughout the world. To support his climbing activities, he began selling mountaineering equipment out of the back of his car. This endeavor evolved into Chouinard Equipment, a full-service climbing gear manufacturing and sales operation located in Ventura, California. Chouinard increased sales volume by importing rugby shirts, gloves, hats, and other clothing from Europe and New Zealand. Soon, the focus turned to manufacturing clothing, and in 1973 the Patagonia clothing company was born. The business struggled at first, but by the mid-1980s sales began to increase, growing from $20 million to over $100 million by 1990. Today, sales volume at Patagonia is around $575 million per year. The company makes a wide range of products from outdoor clothing and travel gear to surfboards and fishing equipment.

Chouinard never aspired to be an executive, but he soon found himself facing business challenges as the founder and owner of an expanding company. Despite the growth, he held fast to the values of teamwork and camaraderie he had enjoyed as a mountaineer. Employees at Patagonia dress as they please (often in t-shirts and shorts, sitting barefoot at their desks); surf when the conditions at nearby beaches are good (the daily surf report is prominently displayed in the lobby of the corporate headquarters, and employees can take advantage of liberal flextime policies); and enjoy company-sponsored ski and climbing trips; a cafeteria serving high quality, healthy food (including a wide range of vegetarian options but no beef); a subsidized on-site day care center; and the option to take a leave of absence from work for up to two months at a nonprofit of their choice, while still receiving their full pay from Patagonia. These benefits make the company a very desirable place of employment—on average some 900 people apply for every open position.

The company is highly committed to environmental causes and a corporate philosophy to "do no harm." Chouinard and each of Patagonia's 2,000 employees try to make decisions based on the impact that will be felt 100 years from now. That approach requires asking tough questions about manufacturing processes and making the right choices, even if production costs increase. In the early 1990s, for example, an environmental audit revealed that the chemicals commonly used for growing and harvesting cotton made it one of the most damaging fibers used by Patagonia. Cotton farming, Chouinard discovered, consumes 25% of the world's pesticides on just 3% of the world's farmland. As a result, the company switched its entire product line to organic cotton, a decision that ultimately improved profitability. In 2011 Patagonia ran a full-page ad in The New York Times on Black Friday headlined "Don't Buy This Jacket." The rest of the ad described the environmental costs of buying the firm's top-selling garment, asking readers to think carefully before buying the fleece jacket or any other product. (Sales went up significantly after the ad appeared.) The company repairs garments purchased from Patagonia for free and has started selling used items. One percent of the firm's sales go toward environmental causes like creating a national park in Chile.

How does Chouinard lead the company and drive this environmental mission? Through a hands-on, directive approach? No, he uses what he calls his MBA theory—management by absence. Chouinard travels the globe developing and testing Patagonia products and serving as a crusader for environmental issues. To run his business, he hires employees who will question authority—challenging bad decisions and working with others to seek out the best solutions. As he explains, "The best democracy exists when decisions are made through consensus . . . decisions based on compromise often leave the problem not completely solved, with both sides feeling cheated or unimportant."[25] And the most effective leaders, Chouinard argues, are those who can communicate their ideas to others, not via e-mail, but by talking face-to-face to work out collaborative agreements. To support this democratic approach, there are no private offices at Patagonia—everyone works in open rooms with no doors or separations. When Chouinard is at the Patagonia headquarters, he does not have a reserved parking spot (such spots are reserved for those who drive fuel-efficient cars) or special perks or office space; he considers himself no more important than others in the organization. Such treatment would only damage the democratic spirit of the company. Chouinard believes: "Finding the right balance between the management problems that come with growth and maintaining our philosophy of hiring independent-minded people and trusting them with responsibility is the key to Patagonia's success."[26]

Discussion Questions

1. What is your opinion regarding the corporate policies at Patagonia? Would you like to work for a company like this?

2. Why do you think Patagonia sales increased after it urged consumers to buy less?

3. Do you believe that focusing on sustainability and environmental issues is important for leaders?

4. How effectively do you think Chouinard's MBA philosophy might work in other organizations?

5. Do you agree that consensus is critical in organizational decision making?

6. What advantages/disadvantages do you see in leading the way that Chouinard does?

The leader adopting the laissez-faire communication style may be accused of leadership avoidance. This communication style results in decreased productivity and less satisfaction for most followers and can increase their stress levels. A number of variables, including the personality, age, and job experience of followers, impact the effectiveness of laissez-faire leadership. A group led by a laissez-faire leader, particularly when the leader engages in abdication, may be less innovative than groups with leaders employing authoritarian or democratic communication styles.

However, laissez-faire leadership can be highly effective with groups of motivated and knowledgeable experts. These groups often do not require direct guidance and produce better results when left alone. A group of medical researchers, for example, might function very effectively when provided with the necessary information and materials without any direct guidance or intervention by a leader. (See box 2.3 for an example of what happens when highly motivated and knowledgeable followers are supervised too closely).

> *Treat people as if they were what they ought to be and you may help them to become what they are capable of being.*
>
> *—Johann Wolfgang von Goethe*

Researchers have concluded that the democratic style of leadership communication is often most effective. Generally, the benefits derived from democratic communication far outweigh any potential costs. Democratic leadership is associated with increased follower productivity, satisfaction, and involvement/commitment. A negative element is that democratic leadership can become mired in lengthy debate over policy, procedures, and strategies. In most cases, the increase in follower involvement and commitment more than make up for any such delays. Authoritarian leadership is effective in terms of output (particularly when the leader directly supervises behavior) but is generally ineffective in enhancing follower satisfaction and commitment. The abdication factor in laissez-faire leadership often damages productivity, satisfaction, and commitment. The laissez-faire style can be effective when it represents guided freedom or when it is used with highly knowledgeable and motivated experts. In many situations, the costs associated with the authoritarian and laissez-faire styles of leadership can seriously hamper a leader's effectiveness.

Task and Interpersonal Leadership

Closely related to the authoritarian, democratic, and laissez-faire model of leadership style is the task and interpersonal model. From the late 1940s until the early 1960s, several groups of researchers worked to identify and to label the dimensions of leadership communication. These researchers used different methodologies and measurement techniques but came to similar conclusions. Each of

Box 2.3 Case Study	The Importance of Leadership Communication Style: SuperNova Microcomputer

Jay Brooks is the project director of a product development team at SuperNova Microcomputer. His team of 30 employees has been charged with the task of developing a new "cutting edge" tablet computer for the consumer market. This group of 30 consists of the best technicians within the organization.

Unfortunately, Jay's team has been experiencing numerous difficulties and delays in the development of the new computer system. A number of team members have complained to the president of SuperNova, Sam Lowell, that Brooks is stifling creativity within the team and that Laura Martin, the project assistant, would be a much more effective leader. "We could get this project moving if Laura were in charge," claims one team member.

Brooks, who was hired from a major competitor six months ago, is a very directive leader. He holds a daily meeting from 8 to 10 am in which each unit of the entire team presents its latest innovations. All new ideas must be cleared through Brooks. Many team members have complained about these meetings, claiming that "Brooks might as well build this system by himself if he is going to approve every chip." In addition, all team members must complete a worksheet isolating the specific tasks they have undertaken each day. This worksheet, wryly called "form 1984" by members of the team, is a major source of dissatisfaction among team members.

Laura Martin has been with the company since its inception a decade ago. Laura was passed over for the job as project director because Sam Lowell felt that she was not as technically competent as she needed to be. Laura was disappointed, but she accepted the decision because, overall, she has been very happy at SuperNova. Indeed, Laura has been instrumental in promoting the open, democratic, employee-oriented management style that is characteristic of SuperNova. As project assistant she interacts frequently with all members of the team. She has discovered that many of the members feel unappreciated. One team member complains, "We are expected to create one of the most advanced home computer systems in existence, but we are treated like a bunch of rebellious third graders."

Sam Lowell is disturbed because the project is falling way behind schedule. After only six months, major delays have pushed back the target date for the project by a full year. The team members themselves don't seem to be aware that they are falling behind any projected schedule; they only realize that the project is bogging down.

Things have gotten to the point that a number of team members are threatening to quit. If they leave, the entire project will be jeopardized. Further, rumors are spreading through the team that upper management is disappointed with productivity and may replace several key members. All in all, members of the team seem very frustrated. "We just want to build the best product that we can," says one team member, adding, "I only wish they would let us."

Discussion Questions

1. What problems can you identify at SuperNova Microcomputer?

2. Which leadership style (s) would be most effective in working with the product development team? Why?

3. How would you suggest a leader might get the product development team back on schedule? What policy and/or personnel changes would you recommend?

4. What recommendations would you make concerning the overall operation at SuperNova Microcomputer?

5. How might the leaders at SuperNova Microcomputer assure their employees that problems like this can be avoided in the future?

the research teams suggested that leadership consists of two primary communication dimensions: task and interpersonal. Although each group of researchers applied its own unique label to the communication styles discovered, the groups were essentially talking about the same set of communicative behaviors.

Task-oriented communication has been referred to as: production oriented, initiating structure, Theory X management, concern for production. Interpersonal-oriented communication has been called: employee oriented, consideration, Theory Y management, concern for people.

The similarity in findings among these researchers is not surprising. Leadership boils down to two primary ingredients: work that needs to be done and the people who do the work. Without these ingredients there is no need for leadership!

The leader employing the task style is primarily concerned with the successful completion of task assignments. The task-oriented leader demonstrates a much greater concern for getting work done than for the people doing the work. The task leader is often highly authoritarian. In contrast, the interpersonal leader is concerned with relationships. This style, similar to the democratic style, emphasizes teamwork, cooperation, and supportive communication.

Ernest Stech describes the typical communication patterns of task- and interpersonal-oriented leaders in his book *Leadership Communication*.[27] He lists the distinctions between these two styles of leadership in table 2.2.

In the next sections, we will focus on four of the most significant attempts to identify the communication patterns of leaders: (1) the Michigan leadership studies, (2) the Ohio State leadership studies, (3) McGregor's Theory X and Theory Y, and (4) Blake and McCanse's Leadership Grid.* (Turn to the Cultural Connections feature at the end of the chapter for a closer look at leadership styles research conducted outside the United States.)

Table 2.2   Leadership Communication Distinctions

Task Orientation	Interpersonal Orientation
Disseminates information	Solicits opinions
Ignores the positions, ideas, and feelings of others	Recognizes the positions, ideas, and feelings of others
Engages in rigid, stylized communication	Engages in flexible, open communication
Interrupts others	Listens carefully to others
Makes demands	Makes requests
Focuses on facts, data, and information as they relate to tasks	Focuses on feelings, emotions, and attitudes as they relate to personal needs
Emphasizes productivity through the acquisition of technical skills	Emphasizes productivity through the acquisition of personal skills
Most often communicates in writing	Most often communicates orally
Maintains a "closed door" policy	Maintains an "open door" policy

The Michigan Leadership Studies

Shortly after World War II, a team of researchers at the University of Michigan set out to discover which leadership practices contributed to effective group performance. To determine the characteristics of effective leaders, the Michigan researchers looked at both high- and low-performing teams within two organizations. Twenty-four groups of clerical workers in a life insurance company and 72 groups of railroad workers were studied in an attempt to identify the factors contributing to satisfactory and unsatisfactory group leadership.[28]

From their observations of these work groups, the Michigan researchers noted a distinction between what they called "production-oriented" and "employee-oriented" styles of leadership communication. Production-oriented leaders focus on accomplishing tasks by emphasizing technical procedures, planning, and organization. The production-oriented leader is primarily concerned with getting work done. Employee-oriented leaders focus on relationships between people and are particularly interested in motivating and training followers. Employee-oriented leaders demonstrate a genuine interest in the well-being of followers both on and off the job.

The Michigan researchers believed that the production-oriented and employee-oriented styles were opposing sets of communicative behaviors. They suggested these leadership communication styles could be described along a continuum as illustrated in figure 2.1. A leader could choose either a production-oriented style, an employee-oriented style, or a neutral style of communication. According to the Michigan research, leaders who exhibited employee-oriented styles had more productive and satisfied work groups.

Figure 2.1   Continuum of Leadership Communication Style

This one-dimensional view of leadership communication style was short lived.[29] Follow-up studies performed by the University of Michigan researchers suggested that it was possible for leaders to adopt both production-oriented and employee-oriented styles. Further, leaders who demonstrated high concern for both production and people were found to be more effective than leaders who exhibited only employee-oriented or production-oriented communication.[30] Production-oriented and employee-oriented leadership styles were not polar opposites but rather two distinct dimensions of leadership communication style.

The Ohio State Leadership Studies

While the Michigan researchers were involved in their observations of work groups, an interdisciplinary team of researchers at The Ohio State University attempted to identify the factors associated with leadership communication.[31] The Ohio State researchers developed a questionnaire they called the Leader Behavior Description Questionnaire (LBDQ). The LBDQ was administered to groups of military personnel who were asked to rate their commanders.

Statistical analysis of the LBDQ indicated two primary dimensions of leadership. These dimensions were labeled consideration and initiating structure. Consideration consisted of interpersonal-oriented communication designed to express affection and liking for followers; the consideration of followers' feelings, opinions, and ideas; and the maintenance of an amiable working environment. Inconsiderate leaders criticized followers in front of others, made threats, and refused to accept followers' suggestions or explanations. Initiating structure referred to task-related behaviors involved in the initiation of action, the organization and assignment of tasks, and the determination of clear-cut standards of performance.

Consideration and initiating structure were believed to be two separate dimensions of leadership. As a result, a leader could rate high or low on either dimension. This representation of leader communication style allowed for the development of a two-dimensional view of leadership. As depicted in figure 2.2, the Ohio State researchers believed that it was possible for a leader to demonstrate varying amounts of task (initiating structure) or interpersonal (consideration) communication.

Conclusions drawn from the Ohio State research focusing on the use of task and interpersonal styles of leadership communication are complicated by variations in methodology and instrumentation. Over the years, several different versions of the LBDQ, such as the one found in the self-assessment in box 2.4, have been used to measure task (initiating structure) and interpersonal (consideration) related messages. As a result, the findings of the Ohio State team are inconsistent.

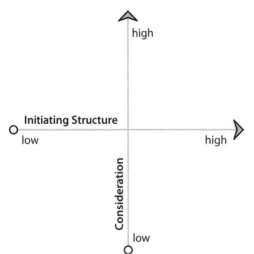

Figure 2.2   A Two-Dimensional View of Leadership

In general, both consideration and initiating structure are important to effective leadership. Considerate leadership communication seems to increase follower satisfaction while decreasing hostility and strife. Initiating structure appears important in guiding and organizing the completion of tasks.[32]

Box 2.4 Self-Assessment	Leadership Style Questionnaire[33]

Instructions: Read each item carefully and think about how often you engage in the described behavior. Indicate your response to each item by circling one of the five numbers to the right of each item.

Key: 1 = Never   2 = Seldom   3 = Occasionally   4 = Often   5 = Always

1. Tells group members what they are supposed to do.		1 2 3 4 5
2. Acts friendly with members of the group.		1 2 3 4 5
3. Sets standards of performance for group members.		1 2 3 4 5
4. Helps others in the group feel comfortable.		1 2 3 4 5
5. Makes suggestions about how to solve problems.		1 2 3 4 5
6. Responds favorably to suggestions made by others.		1 2 3 4 5
7. Makes his or her perspective clear to others.		1 2 3 4 5
8. Treats others fairly.		1 2 3 4 5
9. Develops a plan of action for the group.		1 2 3 4 5
10. Behaves in a predictable manner toward group members.		1 2 3 4 5
11. Defines role responsibilities for each group member.		1 2 3 4 5
12. Communicates actively with group members.		1 2 3 4 5
13. Clarifies his or her own role within the group.		1 2 3 4 5
14. Shows concern for the well-being of others.		1 2 3 4 5
15. Provides a plan for how the work is to be done.		1 2 3 4 5
16. Shows flexibility in making decisions.		1 2 3 4 5
17. Provides criteria for what is expected of the group.		1 2 3 4 5
18. Discloses thoughts and feelings to group members.		1 2 3 4 5
19. Encourages group members to do high-quality work.		1 2 3 4 5
20. Helps group members get along with each other.		1 2 3 4 5

Scoring: First, sum the responses on the odd-numbered items. This is your task score. Second, sum the responses on the even-numbered items. This is your relationship score.

Total scores: Task _____   Relationship _____

Interpretation

45–50	Very high range
40–44	High range
35–39	Moderately high range
30–34	Moderately low range
25–29	Low range
10–24	Very low range

In recent years scholars have isolated a third leadership style called change-centered leadership. Change-centered or development-oriented leadership encourages creativity, experimentation, risk taking, and the adoption of innovations. Swedish investigators first noted this style when reexamining the original Ohio State studies. They and other researchers subsequently found that change-oriented leadership improves work performance and employee job satisfaction while stimulating learning.[34] After reviewing 50 years of research, professors Gary Yukl, Angela Gordon, and Tom Taber conclude that change-centered behaviors should join task and relational behaviors as components of leadership styles. All three types of behaviors play a role in effective leadership, though not all behaviors are equally important in every context and every behavior is not significant in every leadership situation. Here are the specific behaviors that Yukl and his colleagues associate with each leadership style:[35]

Task Behaviors

- Short-term planning—"deciding what to do, how to do it, who will do it, and when it will be done." Includes writing plans and budgets, making schedules, and coordinating with others to determine a plan of action.
- Clarifying responsibilities—guiding and coordinating work activity. Involves setting objectives, looking for the best way to do the work, and evaluating performance against benchmarks.
- Monitoring operations and performance—gathering data about operations, work progress, the performance of individual followers, product and service quality, and project and program success. Takes the form of observation, reading reports, reviewing performance data, inspecting quality, and holding progress review meetings.

Relations Behaviors

- Supporting—demonstrating consideration, concern, and acceptance for the needs and feelings of others.
- Developing—coaching others. Examples: helping someone learn how to do a task or learn from a mistake, explaining how to solve a problem, providing opportunities for followers to develop their skills and confidence.
- Recognizing—expressing praise and appreciation for excellent performance, significant contributions, and noteworthy achievements. Often combined with tangible rewards.
- Consulting—involving followers in important decisions.
- Empowering—delegating to followers and giving them autonomy and discretion.

Change Behaviors

- External monitoring—scanning the environment to identify threats and opportunities from customers, clients, suppliers, government policies, market trends, and so on. Includes reading industry reports, attending professional meetings, talking to customers, studying competitors, and conducting market research. Monitoring also incorporates analyzing the information and interpreting events to lay the foundation for change.

- Envisioning change—creating an inspiring vision to encourage followers to commit to change; connecting with the values, goals, and ideals of followers.

- Encouraging innovative thinking—sparking innovative thinking in others and in oneself; proposing innovative ideas.

- Taking personal risks—stepping out to push for change in the face of opposition, which may result in loss of job, reputation, or career.

McGregor's Theory X and Theory Y

In the late 1950s, Douglas McGregor, a professor of management at the Massachusetts Institute of Technology, attempted to isolate the ways in which attitudes and behaviors influence organizational management. The result of this investigation was McGregor's classic work, *The Human Side of Enterprise*.[36] In his book, McGregor identifies two basic approaches to supervision—Theory X management and Theory Y management.

Theory X and Theory Y represent basic approaches for dealing with followers. Both approaches are based on a set of assumptions regarding human nature. Theory X managers believe that the average person has an inherent dislike for work and will avoid engaging in productive activities whenever possible. Managers must coerce, control, direct, and threaten workers in order to ensure performance. Indeed, Theory X management assumes that most people actually desire strict supervision as a means of insuring security. If workers are told what to do, they can have little doubt that they are performing as expected. This approach emphasizes task supervision with little or no concern for individual needs.

Theory Y managers work to integrate organizational and individual goals; Theory Y assumes that work is as natural as play or rest. Work is not viewed as inherently unpleasant but rather as a source of satisfaction. Therefore threats, punishment, and direct supervision are not necessary to ensure productivity. Personal commitment and pride are sufficient to ensure quality workmanship. Further, Theory Y argues that the average person seeks responsibility as an outlet for imagination and creativity. This approach emphasizes individual commitment by recognizing individual needs as well as organizational needs.

The leader employing a Theory X orientation adopts a task-oriented approach. This leader focuses on methods for getting work done. Little consideration is given to those doing the work. The Theory Y leader, on the other hand, focuses on the unique characteristics of the individuals performing the tasks. The tasks themselves are not ignored but are viewed in terms of the people involved.

The Theory X–Theory Y dichotomy has been criticized for being an overly simplistic attempt to identify polarized extremes of human nature. McGregor responded to his critics by explaining that Theory X and Theory Y are not polar opposites. Rather, they are independent options from which a leader can select, depending on the situation and the people involved.

Blake and McCanse's Leadership Grid®

One of the most commonly cited examples of the task and interpersonal approach to leadership communication styles is the Leadership Grid by Robert Blake and Anne Adams McCanse (formerly the Managerial Grid developed by Blake and Mouton).[37] Blake and McCanse identify communication styles based on the degree of concern for production (task orientation) and concern for people (interpersonal orientation) exhibited by a leader. These communication styles are plotted on a graph with axes ranging from one to nine (see figure 2.3).

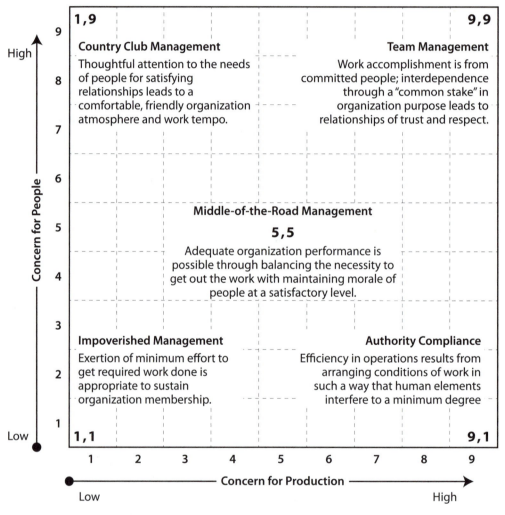

1,9

Country Club Management
Thoughtful attention to the needs of people for satisfying relationships leads to a comfortable, friendly organization atmosphere and work tempo.

9,9

Team Management
Work accomplishment is from committed people; interdependence through a "common stake" in organization purpose leads to relationships of trust and respect.

Middle-of-the-Road Management

5,5

Adequate organization performance is possible through balancing the necessity to get out the work with maintaining morale of people at a satisfactory level.

Impoverished Management
Exertion of minimum effort to get required work done is appropriate to sustain organization membership.

Authority Compliance
Efficiency in operations results from arranging conditions of work in such a way that human elements interfere to a minimum degree

1,1

9,1

Concern for People — High / Low

Concern for Production — Low / High

Figure 2.3   The Leadership Grid[38]

The five plotted leader communication styles are:

1,1 Impoverished Management. The impoverished leader demonstrates a low concern for tasks and a low concern for relationships. The leader with a 1,1 orientation does not actively attempt to influence others but rather assigns responsibilities and leaves followers to complete tasks on their own.

9,1 Authority Compliance. This leader is highly concerned with the completion of task assignments but demonstrates little concern for personal relationships ("produce or perish"). The primary function of the 9,1 oriented leader is to plan, direct, and control behavior. Followers are viewed as human resources who facilitate the completion of tasks. Input from followers is not encouraged; the 9,1 oriented leader attempts to dominate decision making.

5,5 Middle-of-the-Road Management. This middle-of-the-road leader is adequately concerned with both production and people. In an attempt to involve followers, the 5,5 leader engages in compromise. Middle-of-the-road leaders do not rock the boat—they push enough to achieve adequate productivity but yield if they believe increasing the workload will strain interpersonal relationships. As a result, the 5,5 leader often achieves mediocre results.

1,9 Country Club Management. The country club leader is more concerned with interpersonal relationships than with the completion of tasks. The 1,9 leader seeks to establish a supportive, friendly environment. Although country club leaders may want tasks to be completed effectively, they will emphasize factors that contribute to the personal satisfaction and happiness of followers. The 1,9 leader believes his or her primary responsibility is to provide a positive working environment.

9,9 Team Management. Team leadership involves a high concern for both production and people. The 9,9 leadership style is the ideal in which the successful execution of task assignments as well as individual support and caring are emphasized. The 9,9 leader nurtures followers so that they are able to achieve excellence in both personal and team goals. Under team leadership, both leaders and followers work together to achieve the highest level of productivity and personal accomplishment.

Leaders generally adopt one leadership communication style, which they use in most situations. This is called a dominant style. A second orientation from the model may be used as a backup style. For example, a leader might generally adopt a 5,5 leadership communication style but might shift to a 9,1 style when pressured to get orders out to an important customer.

The most effective leadership communication style, according to Blake and McCanse, is team management (9,9). Implementation of the 9,9 style in organizational contexts is associated with increased productivity and profitability, increased frequency of communication, and improved leader-follower relations.[39]

Follower Communication Styles

Followers, like leaders, need to understand their communication styles to carry out their roles successfully.[40] In this section we'll examine four systems for categorizing followers. Each typology provides insights into the characteristics of ineffective and effective followers; each offers guidelines for functioning more effectively in the followership role.

Engaged Followers

Political scientist Barbara Kellerman places followers along a continuum based on how willing they are to engage with their leaders and with their fellow followers.[41]

Isolates are the least engaged followers. In fact, they barely qualify as followers because they don't care about their leaders or communicate with them. The millions of Americans who don't vote are isolates as are the members of a club that never show up for meetings. Isolates, by refusing to become involved, empower leaders and other, more engaged, followers to make decisions for them.

Bystanders observe what is going on but do not actively participate. Many citizens in Nazi Germany acted as bystanders by refusing to oppose Hitler. They stood by as the nation's leadership plunged the world into war and slaughtered millions in concentration camps. Some employees at Penn State University apparently stood aside instead of intervening when they suspected that a long-time assistant football coach was sexually abusing children. By standing aside, followers allow the status quo to continue.

Participants are moderately engaged with their leaders and organizations, offering support or opposition. Employees at Merck were supportive participants when they developed and marketed the painkiller Vioxx despite concerns about its safety. Later the drug was withdrawn from the market because it dramatically increased the likelihood of heart attacks in patients. Faculty members who hold a vote of "no confidence" in the university president would be categorized as oppositional participants.

Activists are motivated by strong feelings about their leaders. They are energetic and highly engaged, working to serve or to undermine their leaders. Activist volunteers and small contributors helped Bernie Sanders mount a significant presidential bid in 2016, one that surprised political pundits. Loyal supporters were also key to the election of Donald Trump, which also took political experts by surprise. Activist Republican members of Congress ousted House Majority Leader John Boehner from his position in 2015.

Diehards are totally committed to or opposed to their leaders. They are willing to die in order to support them or to perish in an attempt to remove them from their positions of power. Diehards are at the heart of the civil war in Syria. Rebels are risking death to overthrow President Assad while his loyal supporters are risking death to keep him in power.

Kellerman argues that two criteria separate good followers from bad followers. First, better followers are engaged with their leaders. That's because silence signals that followers are ignorant, apathetic, or too frightened to speak up. When followers remain quiet, bad leaders are able to stay in power. Good followers, on the other hand, speak out the first time they note leader misbehavior, before it becomes ingrained. When confronting leaders, they are well prepared, arming themselves with the facts, seeking advice, and recruiting allies. Motivation is the second criterion separating good from bad followers. The best followers are motivated by the public interest, not self-interest. They seek to serve their organizations, communities, and countries.

Exemplary Followership

To identify the components that make up follower styles, Robert Kelley asked individuals and focus groups to describe the best, worst, and typical followers in their organizations.[42] He found that followers differ on two dimensions—independent/critical thinking and active engagement. The best followers are people who think for themselves and take initiative. The worst followers have to be told what to do and require constant supervision. Typical followers take direction and complete jobs on their own after being told what is expected of them.

Once he had isolated the key characteristics of followership, Kelley then developed the questionnaire found in box 2.5. Followers fall into one of five categories based on how they respond to the independent thinking and active engagement sections of this test. Alienated followers are highly independent thinkers who put most of their energies into fighting rather than serving their organizations because they've become disillusioned with their leaders or feel unappreciated. Alienated followers provide a dose of healthy skepticism for the group but generally come off as cynical. An example of an alienated follower would be the class critic who sits in the back of the room and continually challenges what the instructor has to say. In contrast, conformists are committed to organizational goals but express few thoughts of their own. These followers (often referred to as "yes men/women" in popular culture) may hold back their ideas out of fear or deference to authority. Pragmatists are moderately independent and engaged. Pragmatism is a way of coping with organizational uncertainty caused by frequent changes of leadership, layoffs, and restructuring. These organizational survivors hold on to their jobs but are not likely to be promoted. Passive followers demonstrate little original thought or commitment. They rely heavily on the leader's direction and meet only minimal expectations. Their passivity may stem from a lack of skills or be a response to serving under authoritarian leaders. Passive followers can be found at many fast-food restaurants where teenagers with limited job experience work under highly directive supervisors. Exemplary followers rate highly as both critical thinkers and active participants, contributing innovative ideas and going beyond what is required.

Kelley outlines three sets of skills and values that characterize exemplary followership. Utilizing these skills can help us shift from the alienated, conformist, pragmatist, and passive styles to the exemplary category. First, exemplary followers add value to the organization by helping it reach its objectives. They know what they want to achieve in life and commit themselves to organizations that share the same purposes. They understand what tasks are most important to achieving an organization's vision and develop the skills necessary to carry out these critical path activities. Second, outstanding followers "weave a web of relationships" through joining teams, building bridges to others throughout the organization, and working as partners with leaders. Third, exemplary followers cultivate a coura-

Box 2.5 Self-Assessment	Followership Style Questionnaire[43]

For each statement, think of a followership situation and how you acted. Choose a number from 0 to 6 to indicate the extent to which the statement describes you. 0 indicates rarely applies and 6 indicates almost always applies.

_____ 1. Does your work help you fulfill some societal goal or personal dream that is important to you?

_____ 2. Are your personal work goals aligned with the organization's priority goals?

_____ 3. Are you highly committed to and energized by your work and organization, giving them your best ideas and performance?

_____ 4. Does your enthusiasm also spread to and energize your coworkers?

_____ 5. Instead of waiting for or merely accepting what the leader tells you, do you personally identify which organizational activities are most critical for achieving the organization's priority goals?

_____ 6. Do you actively develop a distinctive competence in those critical activities so that you become more valuable to the leader and the organization?

_____ 7. When starting a new job or assignment, do you promptly build a record of successes in tasks that are important to the leader?

_____ 8. Can the leader give you a difficult assignment without the benefit of much supervision, knowing that you will meet your deadline with highest-quality work and that you will "fill in the cracks" if need be?

_____ 9. Do you take the initiative to seek out and successfully complete assignments that go above and beyond your job?

_____ 10. When you are not the leader of a group project, do you still contribute at a high level, often doing more than your share?

_____ 11. Do you independently think up and champion new ideas that will contribute significantly to the leader's or the organization's goals?

_____ 12. Do you try to solve the tough problems (technical or organizational), rather than look to the leader to do it for you?

_____ 13. Do you help out other coworkers, making them look good, even when you don't get any credit?

_____ 14. Do you help the leader or group see both the upside potential and downside risks of idea or plans, playing the devil's advocate if need be?

_____ 15. Do you understand the leader's needs, goals, and constraints, and work hard to help meet them?

_____ 16. Do you actively and honestly own up to your strengths and weaknesses rather than put off evaluation?

_____ 17. Do you make a habit of internally questioning the wisdom of the leader's decision rather than just doing what you are told?

_____ 18. When the leader asks you to do something that runs contrary to your professional or personal preferences, do you say "no" rather than "yes"?

_____ 19. Do you act on your own ethical standards rather than the leader's or the group's standards?

_____ 20. Do you assert your views on important issues, even though it might mean conflict with your group or reprisals from the leader?

Finding Your Followership Style
Use the scoring key below to score your answers to the questions.

Independent Thinking Items	**Active Engagement Items**
Question 1. _____	Question 2. _____
5. _____	3. _____
11. _____	4. _____
12. _____	6. _____
14. _____	7. _____
16. _____	8. _____
17. _____	9. _____
18. _____	10. _____
19. _____	13. _____
20. _____	15. _____
Total Score _____	Total Score _____

Add up your scores on the independent thinking items. Record the total on a vertical axis, as in the graph below. Repeat the procedure for the active engagement items and mark the total on a horizontal axis. Now plot your scores on the graph by drawing perpendicular lines connecting your two scores. The juxtaposition of these two dimensions forms the basis on which people classify followership styles.

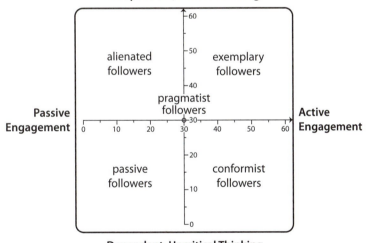

Followership Style	Independent Thinking Score	Active Engagement Score
EXEMPLARY	High	High
ALIENATED	High	Low
CONFORMIST	Low	High
PRAGMATIST	Middling	Middling
PASSIVE	Low	Low

geous conscience by making the right ethical judgments and then following through on those choices. They anticipate and eliminate ethical problems before they pose a significant threat and disobey leaders who issue directives that put the organization at risk. (For an example, see the case study in box 2.6; for an in-depth discussion of courageous followership, see chapter 11.)

Box 2.6 Case Study	**When Followers Dare**

National Insurance Company is a full-service insurance provider with corporate divisions in 15 locations in the United States. Each division is responsible for writing and servicing policies within its geographic area. For several years the general manager of the Western Division was Fred Jackson. Under Jackson's leadership, the Western Division became the most successful division in the company, achieving a goal of policy sales of $100 million a full 18 months ahead of projections. The success of the Western Division was directly attributable to Jackson's open, democratic leadership style. Jackson knew all of his 250 employees by their first names and was always willing to talk with an employee who had a question or concern. Jackson, who had worked his way up from an entry-level position in the company, was a tireless cheerleader for his staff and never failed to recognize his employees' achievements. When his division reached its goal of $100 million in policy sales, Jackson hired a local high school band to march through the parking lot and then invited all of his employees to join him for a catered lunch-hour barbecue. Senior management at National recognized Jackson's leadership prowess, and he was promoted to the corporate headquarters in New York.

Jackson's replacement in the Western Division was a recent Stanford MBA graduate named Jason Hirsch. Hirsch's leadership style was very different than his predecessor's. Where Jackson had been open and interactive, Hirsch was closed and private. He spent most of his time alone in his office and made only token appearances at company meetings and functions. Most of Hirsch's communication consisted of directives handed to the senior management team. Within a few months of Hirsch's arrival, the mood at the Western Division began to change. The energy and team spirit that had been so prevalent under Jackson's leadership was significantly diminished. Sales declined dramatically, and rumors surfaced suggesting the Western Division would be closed with its business moving to other National Insurance Company divisions.

These rumors were the catalyst for a plan among the senior management team in the Western Division. These managers felt that it was their responsibility to communicate their dissatisfaction to Hirsch to save jobs in the Western Division. One morning when Hirsch entered the building, he was greeted by his 12 senior managers dressed in military fatigues. Hirsch was informed that his managers had "taken over the office," and he was escorted to a meeting room. The managers explained to Hirsch that the military uniforms were a joke and that their "coup" was only an attempt to sit down with Hirsch and discuss how to improve the Western Division. Surprisingly (some of the managers fully expected they might be fired for their actions), Hirsch was very open to discussing the situation. As a newcomer to the Western Division, he had felt like an outsider. This bold move by his followers offered an opportunity for communication. Hirsch admitted that he was very nervous about taking charge of the division after the departure of the very popular and successful Fred Jackson. Once Hirsch and his managers began to communicate, they were able to identify strategies for improving the situation in the Western Division. Although it took time, the managers' coup helped to develop a much improved relationship between Hirsch and his staff. Within six months the Western Division was, once again, among the most successful divisions within National Insurance Company.

Discussion Questions

1. Do you think it was appropriate for the followers to approach Jason Hirsch the way they did? Why? Why not?

2. Do followers have a responsibility to take action when a leader's ineffectiveness may have negative consequences on others? How can followers determine when it is time to take action?

3. What can followers do to help a new leader succeed?

4. Robert Kelley suggests that two components make up follower communication styles: independent/critical thinking and active engagement. How would you rate the follower communication of the senior management team in the Western Division? In what category on the Kelley model would you place the followers who organized the "coup"?

5. What impact do you think each of the follower communication styles has on organizational effectiveness? What style of follower would you like to lead?

The 4-D Followership Model

Organizational consultant Roger Adair categorizes employees according to their degree of job satisfaction, their productivity, and turnover—their intention to leave their organization.[44] In his 4-D Followership model, Quadrant I Disciple Followers are focused on serving the needs of others. Disciples are totally committed and are willing to sacrifice for the company or organization. They are inclusive, friendly communicators, willing to share their ideas and to learn from others. They are not likely to leave the organization. Quadrant II Doer Followers focus on meeting their personal needs. These individuals are productive "go-getters." Though they may appear to be disciples at first, they are quick to move on when new opportunities present themselves. Doers are hard workers but can be competitive and are focused on furthering their careers. Quadrant III Disengaged Followers take a passive approach when under stress. These followers are detached and carefully limit their communication, appearing nonresponsive, closed minded, and guarded. Inertia keeps them in their current organizations. Quadrant IV Disgruntled Followers respond actively to stress. These constituents tend to be vocal, aggressive, and combative. They are unforgiving and closed to other points of view. Disgruntled followers are more than ready to leave their current organizations, believing that any new situation has got to be better than their current one.

Adair believes that most employees function as either disciples or doers. They are most productive and satisfied when they operate within the quadrant that naturally fits them best. Further, both types of followers are essential to organizational success. Stress can push disciples and doers into the disengaged or disgruntled quadrants, however. In order to shift back to their natural quadrant, followers need to change their attitudes and, at the same time, work with their leaders to make this change. For example, the disciple follower who wants to function independently may become passive if supervised closely. To return to the discipleship quadrant, this follower will need to give up some of her autonomy and the leader will need to relinquish a degree of control. A doer follower who is used to being a top performer is likely to become aggressive in the face of failure. To return to the doer quadrant, the disgruntled employee will have to change from within by accepting the fact that he may not always excel. His leader will need to set limits on how vocal the worker can be in expressing his displeasure about his current situation.

Transcendent Followership

Advocates for transcendent followership argue that the best followers demonstrate knowledge and skills that transcend or cross multiple levels or domains.[45] They show competence in managing themselves, working with others, and supporting and changing the organization as a whole. Followership at the domain of the self describes the ability to direct one's activities while remaining true to personal values and beliefs. Self-leadership rests on self-direction and self-motivation. (We'll have more to say about self-leadership in chapter 5.) Competent followers know their strengths and weaknesses and engage in self-criticism. They assume responsibility for developing their skills, which may mean stepping out beyond their comfort zones. For example, frontline employees at Toyota demonstrate self-leadership by acting as problem solvers and change agents who tie their work to that of their leaders. Followership at the domain of others is competence in relating to peers and leaders. Those skilled in this domain relate to others in a positive fashion by helping out coworkers, demonstrating kindness, and expressing gratitude. They build trusting relationships with leaders and function effectively in teams, building on the leader's strengths and minimizing her/his weaknesses. Followership at the organizational level is competence at supporting the group as a whole by, for example, scanning the environment for potential trouble spots and dealing with unexpected situations that might disrupt service to customers. Organizationally skilled followers are also supportive of the organization when speaking to outsiders. Effectiveness at this level requires that followers be proactive and persistent.

Proponents of the multi-domain approach argue that there are significant limitations to only demonstrating competence at a single level. Followers who are only skilled at self-leadership often focus on themselves and demonstrate limited concern for others and the organization as a whole. They don't like to share their knowledge and may damage working relationships. As the founder of Pixar noted, it is difficult "getting talented people to work effectively with one another." The self-oriented follower is most effective when he or she doesn't have to depend on others to complete a task. Followers skilled only at relationships are tempted to put the goals of the team above that of the organization. They are most effective when they are charged with executing a task or mission, not when called upon to generate creative ideas. Followers who are only competent at the organizational level often promote better collective performance in the short run but at a high cost to self and others. They may ignore their own needs or create an atmosphere of dependence. This type of follower can't be counted upon to engage in the independent thinking that the group needs over time.

Followers who demonstrate two out of the three levels of competence are more effective than single-level followers. However, constituents should strive to work effectively at all three domains. Transcendent followers help the organization adapt to rapidly changing conditions. At the same time, these followers believe they are contributing to something bigger than themselves; they are convinced that their work is important. Transcendent followers are emotionally connected to their coworkers and feel personal responsibility for their actions.

Communication Styles, Information Processing, and Identity

So far in this chapter we have focused on the observable behaviors of leaders and followers and explored the link between communication styles and performance. However, this approach leaves a number of important questions unanswered. For example: What process do leaders and followers use when choosing one style over another? How do constituents decide if someone is a leader? What factors make leaders and followers more receptive or resistant to influence from the other party? Information-processing scholars Douglas Brown, Robert Lord, and others argue that we must look inside the minds of leaders and followers to answer questions like these.[46] They focus on cognitive processes that determine behavior, "attempting to discern how individuals acquire, store, retrieve, and use information to better understand how those individuals (i.e., leaders and followers) function and adapt to the current context."[47]

Three concepts are crucial to understanding the information-processing perspective. First, the basic building blocks of knowledge are symbols and categories of symbols. These symbols (generally words) are stored in long-term memory and allow us to engage in conceptual thinking. We draw on language whenever we think, problem solve, plan, and remember.[48] Second, these symbolic bits of knowledge form interconnected networks called schemas or schemata, which assist us in interpreting and making sense of the world around us. Imagine, for instance, how confusing it would be to attend a wedding for the first time without any schema for figuring out what is going on. You would have no idea how to dress, where to sit, how to behave during the ceremony, the roles of the wedding party, and so forth. Leaders and followers, too, have schemata that guide their behaviors, helping them determine who is a "motivated" or "unmotivated" follower or a "successful" or "unsuccessful" leader, for example. Third, schemas must be activated in order to influence perceptions, attitudes, and behavior. The large volume of schemata in long-term memory and the limited capacity of working memory mean that only a small subset of schemas can be activated at a given time.

A leader's selection of a particular behavioral style depends in part on the schemata that she or he has stored in long-term memory. The leader who thinks of followers as generally incompetent, for instance, is much more likely to engage in authoritarian leadership that calls for strict supervision and direction on his or her part. (See the earlier discussion of Theory X.) If the leader's schema holds that followers perform better when they like their supervisors, she or he will adopt a relationally oriented style. Not surprisingly, leaders can't utilize an alternative style unless they have established a schema for the beliefs, attitudes, and behaviors of that style. In the case of our authoritarian leader, it would be difficult for this individual—perhaps someone raised by authoritative parents—to adopt a more democratic approach unless he or she understands what this style entails.

Researchers report that leaders with a broader variety of schemata are better able to adjust their behavior to the situation and to generate superior solutions more quickly. Experience plays an important role in developing expert knowledge that leads to improved performance. For instance, when compared to junior officers, senior military officers have schemata that are better organized and that are based on principles that can be applied to a variety of situations.[49] Experience isn't the only way to develop new schemata, however. New symbolic networks can be created through training programs, books, TED talks and YouTube videos as well.

Leaders also respond to the situation when choosing which communication style to use. In particular, they must "make sense" of their followers through categorization. How they categorize followers determines their style, which, in turn, has a direct impact on the performance of subordinates as well as the organization as a whole. As we'll see in our discussion of leader-member exchange theory in chapter 3, followers selected to be members of the leader's "in-group" have more flexibility when it comes to completing their tasks and exert more influence in decision-making. In contrast, leaders are more dominant in interactions with followers who make up the "out-group." In-group members are more productive and satisfied than their out-group counterparts as a result.

Categorization extends to attributions about the causes of the followers' behaviors. Superiors are more likely to punish poor performance (e.g., a delayed shipment) if they perceive it is the product of internal forces (lack of motivation) rather than external forces (unexpected delays caused by the weather). These attributions are often biased. Leaders will protect themselves by blaming failure on external forces, such as the shortcomings of followers, rather than on internal factors, such as the leaders' failure to provide adequate guidance and resources. Supervisors are generally more tolerant of the failings of subordinates they like.

Schemas guide followers as well as leaders. To begin, followers construct different definitions of what it means to be a follower.[50] Passive followers define their role as taking orders and following through on directions from leaders who have more expertise. To them, a successful follower never challenges authority and avoids taking risks. Active followers believe that it is important to express their opinions and give input when asked by their leaders. But, according to their schema, the good follower is loyal and supports the leader even when disagreeing with the leader's decision. Proactive followers take the initiative, offering feedback, advice, and dissent even when they haven't been asked to do so. They continue to resist even after the decision has been made. Researchers Melissa Carsten and Mary Uhl-Bien report that followers who view themselves as partners with their supervisors (as co-producers of leadership) are less likely to give into unethical requests from their leaders and are more likely to voice their opposition. In contrast, passive followers comply rather than resist.

The impact of a leader's style rests on how subordinates interpret his/her actions. Consider who gets selected for a leadership role, for example. Judgments of who is suitable to lead are largely based on implicit leadership theory—our beliefs about what distinguishes a leader from a nonleader.[51] The ideal small-group leader takes an active role in the discussion through setting goals, giving directions, managing conflict, and summarizing the group's deliberations (see chapter 7). The group member who engages in these prototypical behaviors is most likely to emerge as leader when one has not been appointed ahead of time. It should be noted that a leader candidate doesn't have to have all the prototypical characteristics to be selected for the role, and that the ideal leader will vary between situations. We have different expectations of a military leader than of a religious one or of a frontline supervisor and the CEO in the same organization. (Take a look at box 2.7 to see how the prototypical leader in the United States compares to those in other countries.)

Performance outcomes serve as indirect cues for evaluating those in leadership roles. Observers make judgments about a leader's effectiveness based on how well the group performs and on whether or not they believe the leader is responsible for

Box 2.7	National Differences in Leadership Prototypes[52]
Nation	**Prototype**
United States	*Free Agent Star*—a winner who gets short-term results; sees money as an indicator of worth
Latin America	*General*—strong man in charge, keeps order, promotes change, controls
France	*Genius*—smartest one, best exam score, member of intellectual elite, graduate of the best school
United Kingdom	*Diplomat*—big thinker, well-educated, well-traveled, good social skills
Germany	*Master*—most respected by peers, expert in field, has in-depth knowledge
Italy	*Godfather*—holds together conflicting factions, punishes and favors, paternalistic
Holland	*Marathon Winner*—outworks the rest, runs hard, trains well, endures, at head of pack
Poland	*Baron*—protects castle and fiefdom, exercises power for self and close associates
Japan	*Senior Statesman*—older, wiser; from the group; survivor, consensus builder
China	*Warlord*—local power; uses quanxi (favors) for loyal supporters; rich
Vietnam	*Communist Party Boss*—wears numerous hats; favors to family and friends; ideological
Israel	*Field Commander*—smart, energetic, creative, tactical, self-made
Africa	*Tribal Chief*—older, wiser, consultative; orchestrates various networks, builds factions

its successes or failures. We generally infer, for example, that the CEO of a highly profitable company is effective due to the success of the corporation and our belief that she or he plays a critical role in the organization's high performance.[53]

Social psychologists have increasingly focused on the role of identity in leadership and followership. Some identity theorists examine how leaders achieve their goals by influencing the ways that followers think of themselves, their self-identity.[54] The self-concept is made up of many different self-schemas, which are activated at different times. When you are sitting in class, your student script is active. If you call your mother on your cell phone after class, your son or daughter schema takes center stage. Levels of self-identity range from individual (defining the self as different from others), to the interpersonal or relational (defining the self in terms of relationships with others), to the collective (identifying with the group or larger organization).

To be effective, leaders must both tailor their communication styles to the self-identification level of their followers and, at the same time, help followers change how they view themselves. Those followers who think of themselves as individuals will be more open to personal performance feedback and rewards. Those operating at the interpersonal level will be looking to establish a positive emotional relationship with their leaders. Followers who define themselves at the collective level will be more motivated by messages that emphasize teamwork and organizational goals. Outstanding leaders encourage followers to shift their focus from personal concerns to the group as a whole, which increases individual commitment and collective performance. Often this shift begins with establishing good relationships with new followers. Over time, these followers develop schemas that highlight their group membership. They adopt the values and standards communicated by the leader and begin to regulate their own behavior according to these guidelines. Their personal goals—their images of what they would like to be in the future—become linked to the vision of the organization.

Other theorists believe that social identity, not individual identity, is the key to leadership effectiveness.[55] The more an individual identifies with the group (the more salient the group is to the person), the more important it is for the leader to uphold the group's identity. Followers like leaders who are "one of us," who (a) emphasize how the group is unique and distinctive ("we" are different from "them"), and (b) communicate that the group is superior ("we" are better than "them"). For example, the leader of an institutional technology department might reinforce the idea that IT staff members are more creative and committed than employees in other units. When social identity is strong, followers look to leaders to support the interests of the group and group members, even at the expense of other groups. The IT leader might argue for a larger department budget and lobby for raises for department employees. If she or he is successful, other departments may receive less money and their employees may not get raises. Setting the emotional tone is an important element of leadership in social identity theory. Leaders let followers know how they should feel and behave (see our discussion of emotional intelligence in chapter 1). Followers, for their part, express disapproval and anger towards leaders who threaten the group's identity by acting unfairly or in a self-serving manner. They also disapprove of leaders who demonstrate emotions that don't fit with the group's situation, such as a coach laughing and joking in the locker room right after a loss.

The information processing and identity approaches deepen our understanding of leader and follower styles by shifting the focus to intrapersonal communication—communication that occurs within the individual. The selection and effectiveness of leadership styles depend on the storage and activation of symbols and symbolic networks. Here are some implications of this approach for aspiring leaders and followers.

1. Develop your knowledge and experience base. The more you learn about leadership and get firsthand experience serving as a leader, the greater your ability to meet the demands of the situation and to generate good solutions.

2. Acknowledge the power of categorization. How you categorize others will determine how you respond to those individuals, how they respond to you, how well they perform, and how well the group as a whole performs. Beware of possible perceptual biases that unfairly categorize followers or protect you at the expense of others.

3. Be careful how you view yourself as a follower. If you define the follower role as passive, you will find it hard to resist unethical directives and to oppose poor decisions. Think of yourself as a partner with your leader.

4. Know your audience. Determine the leadership prototypes held by the group and act in a way that fulfills those expectations. What followers expect of you, as a leader, will depend on a variety of factors including organizational and national culture, group history, and elements of the situation. Not fulfilling leadership prototypes is a major cause of failure when leaders are placed in other cultures. Know, too, how your followers define themselves and direct messages to their level of identity—self, relational, or organization centered.

5. Performance counts. Recognize that performance counts or, rather, your connection with performance counts. To emerge as a leader and to be effective in a leadership role, you'll need to be perceived as contributing to the group's success. Increase your power or discretion to influence events through your knowledge and example (see chapter 5) while establishing coalitions with others in the organization.

6. Be flexible. Different audiences and situations will call for a variety of responses. A style that works in one setting may not work in another. Seek feedback about how followers are responding to your behavior and adjust accordingly.

7. Focus attention on the "we" not the "me." Emphasize the importance of the group or organization's shared mission and goals to encourage followers to activate their collective identities. Such shared focus can boost individual motivation and performance, which, in turn, helps the group become more productive. One simple way to start this process is through your choice of

words. Use more inclusive language like "us" and "we" instead of "I" and "you." Frequently communicate shared values and reward behavior that serves common goals.

8. Respect and maintain the group's social identity. Once collective identity is activated, it exercises strong influence over the thoughts and behavior of group members. Emphasize how your group is distinctive and look out for the interests of the team and team members. Be prepared to sacrifice on the group's behalf; follow fair procedures. Set the emotional tone for the group while expressing emotions appropriate to the situation.

~ CHAPTER TAKEAWAYS

- One factor that contributes to variations in leader effectiveness is communication style. Leadership communication style is a relatively enduring set of communicative behaviors that a leader engages in when interacting with followers.

- Authoritarian leaders maintain strict control over followers by directly regulating policy, procedures, and behavior. Authoritarian leaders create distance between themselves and their followers as a means of emphasizing role distinctions. Many authoritarian leaders believe that followers would not function effectively without direct supervision. The authoritarian leader generally feels that people left to complete work on their own will be unproductive. As a leader, recognize that an authoritarian style can boost output, but reduces follower satisfaction and commitment.

- Democratic leaders engage in supportive communication that facilitates interaction between leaders and followers. The leader adopting the democratic communication style encourages follower involvement and participation in the determination of goals and procedures. Democratic leaders assume that followers are capable of making informed decisions. The democratic style of leadership is often most effective, being associated with increased follower productivity, satisfaction, and involvement/commitment.

- Laissez-faire refers to a form of leader communication that has been called non-leadership by some. An ineffective version of this leadership communication style involves abdication of responsibility on the part of the leader; leaders withdraw from followers and offer little guidance or support. As a result, productivity, cohesiveness, and satisfaction often suffer. A more positive form of the laissez-faire leadership communication style affords followers a high degree of autonomy and self-rule while, at the same time, offering guidance and support when requested. The laissez-faire approach works best when used with highly knowledgeable and motivated experts.

- A number of researchers have concluded that leadership consists of two primary communication dimensions: task and interpersonal, which focus on work that needs to be done and the people who do the work. Recently change-oriented communication has emerged as a third dimension. Change- or development-oriented communication fosters innovation and change.

- Several models focusing on the task and interpersonal dimensions of leadership have been developed. Most notable are: (1) the Michigan leadership studies, (2) the Ohio State leadership studies, (3) McGregor's Theory X and Theory Y, and (4) Blake and McCanse's Leadership Grid.®

- As a follower, you also need to understand your communication style to carry out your role successfully. Engaged followership, exemplary followership, the 4-D followership model, and transcendent followership are four ways to categorize follower styles. The best followers are highly engaged and take initiative. They are also committed to other followers, their leaders, and to their organizations. They demonstrate competence across three levels or domains: self, others, and organization.

- Information-processing theory looks inside the minds of leaders and followers to determine how they select and respond to communication styles. A leader's selection of a particular style depends (1) on schemata (interconnected bits of symbolic knowledge) stored in memory, and (2) on the categorization of followers and other elements of the situation. For their part, followers construct passive, active, and proactive definitions of their roles, which determine how willing they are to disobey unethical orders and to resist their leaders.

- To be selected as a leader, you will generally need to resemble the image of the ideal or prototypical leader. Followers also make inferences about your effectiveness based on performance outcomes or cues.

- In order to achieve your goals, influence how followers think of themselves. Tailor your style to the self-concepts of followers, who may be individually, relationally, or organizationally focused; at the same time, encourage followers to identify with collective values and goals.

- The more salient the group identity is to members, the more important it is for you as a leader to uphold that social identity. Effective leaders emphasize what makes the group distinctive and superior. They also lobby on behalf of the team and team members. Team members express anger and disapproval towards leaders who are self-serving, unfair, and express inappropriate emotions.

- Important implications of the information-processing and identify approaches include: (1) develop your knowledge and experience base as a leader, (2) acknowledge the power of categorization, (3) be careful how you view your follower role, (4) know your audience, (5) don't underestimate social influence, (6) performance counts, (7) be flexible, (8) focus attention on the "we," not the "me," and respect and reflect the group's identity.

∼ APPLICATION EXERCISES

1. Make a list of the qualities that you believe are important for effective leadership. Compare your list with the communicative behaviors listed in table 2.1, p. 42. Do effective leaders seem to adopt one leadership communication style more than others?

2. In what types of situations do you believe each of the leadership communication styles identified in this chapter would be most effective? Least effective?

3. Try to think of historical examples of leaders who adopted one of the five grid positions identified by Blake and McCanse. Which of these leaders was most effective? Why?

4. In a group, develop a list of the characteristics of good and bad followers. Report your findings to the rest of the class.

5. Determine if you are a task or relationally oriented leader using the scale found in box 2.4. Then divide into task and relational groups. In your group, discuss the following: What are the advantages and disadvantages of your style? Of the other style? What frustrates you about the other style? What do you wish they knew about your style? Then meet with the other team and share your responses. Draw conclusions based on what each group shares.

6. Identify your follower communication style using the self-assessment questionnaire found in box 2.5. Why do you think you have adopted this style? What are your strengths and weaknesses as a follower? If you're not an exemplary follower, develop a strategy for becoming one. If you categorized yourself as exemplary, what can you do to become even more effective? Write up your findings.

7. In a group, discuss the relationship between leadership and followership styles. Based on your past experience, identify how leader communication styles have affected your performance as a follower. Try to pinpoint the leadership behaviors you think are most important in promoting exemplary and transcendent followership.

8. Reflect on your past experiences with leadership and try to identify how your view of the most/least desirable leadership communication styles has been affected. What have been the primary influences on your view (home, work, school, other)?

9. Describe your prototypical political leader, student body president, professor, and supervisor at work. How are these images similar? Different? Why? As an alternative, select a group that you might want to lead. Describe the prototypical leader for this group. What leadership communication style would you need to use to be selected for this role?

10. Keep a record of your leadership/followership activities over a period of one to two weeks. Evaluate your efforts in light of the information-processing and identity approaches.

⌒ CULTURAL CONNECTIONS:
THE PERFORMANCE-MAINTENANCE (PM) THEORY OF LEADERSHIP[56]

Shortly after World War II, American social psychologist Kurt Lewin urged a colleague in Japan to investigate whether the findings of leadership style researchers in the United States would generalize to Japanese culture. In response, Jyuji

Misumi and his colleagues carried out a 40-year research program that generated the Performance-Maintenance (PM) Theory, which is based on two dimensions of leadership—performance (P) and maintenance (M). Performance behavior involves pressure to follow regulations and to produce. Maintenance behavior is aimed at preserving the social stability of the group. A leader falls into one of four quadrants: performance oriented (P), maintenance oriented (M), not exhibiting either performance or maintenance behaviors (pm), or demonstrating both (PM). Studies with Japanese subjects found that the PM style is most effective, followed by the M style, P style, and pm-oriented style.

While Western task-relationship theory focuses on the behavior of leaders, PM theory examines the experiences of followers with their leaders. Thus, the same leader behavior may have a different meaning depending on the context. Pressure to complete a task is more acceptable when the leader and follower have a strong relationship, for example. Overall, performance and maintenance behaviors are similar to the task and relationship behaviors identified in the Michigan and Ohio State studies. Yet, the classification of behaviors as P or M differs between cultures. For instance, Japanese maintenance behaviors include teaching new job skills, talking about work problems, and sending written notes to subordinates. In the United States, supervisors are rated as higher in maintenance if they do NOT engage in these activities. Similarly, Japanese supervisor performance behaviors, like meeting socially after work hours or arranging help for a worker with personal problems, would be considered maintenance behaviors by many US followers. Discussing an employee's personal problems with others when he or she isn't around, which is seen as promoting group solidarity in Japan, would not be accepted in the West.

The Leadership Grid, developed in the US, emphasizes that leaders need to be high in both task and relationship behaviors. PM theory, on the other hand, asserts that moderation is best. The best leaders display "substantial" amounts of both behaviors and adjust their level of P or M communication depending on the situation. More P-type behavior is needed at the beginning of new project or with a temporary group assigned a simple task. M-type leadership is best with anxious, highly aroused followers. Further, the PM dimensions, rather than being seen as opposites or distinct, interact with each other. That explains why P-oriented leadership without maintenance behavior is largely ineffective.

∽ LEADERSHIP ON THE BIG SCREEN: *IN THE HEART OF THE SEA*

Starring: Chris Hemsworth, Benjamin Walker, Cillian Murphy, Tom Holland

Rating: PG-13 for intense action scenes and mature themes

Synopsis: Herman Melville based his novel *Moby Dick* on the story of the *Essex*, a real-life ship sunk by a whale in the Pacific in 1820. This film recounts the last voyage of the *Essex*, which is troubled from the start. Successful whaler Owen Chase (played by Hemsworth) expects to be named captain. Instead, George Pollard (Walker) is given command and Chase is appointed first mate. Pollard, though young and inexperienced, is named captain because he is a member of a prominent

Nantucket whaling family. The autocratic Pollard mocks Chase's humble origins and puts his crew in danger by sailing into a storm against the first mate's advice, nearly sinking the ship. Realizing that returning to port without any whale oil would ruin both of their reputations (and leave them broke), the two set aside their differences and sail thousands of miles to better hunting grounds off the coast of South America. There a white whale destroys the *Essex*, leaving the crew drifting for weeks in three small boats. Pollard and Chase develop a grudging respect for one another as the survivors fight to stay alive. After their rescue, Pollard and Chase appear at a public hearing and are urged by the ship's owners—hoping to protect the image of the whaling industry—to say the ship ran aground. Both the captain and first mate refuse to lie.

Chapter Links: authoritarian and democratic leadership styles, task-oriented leadership, Theory X, followership communication styles, leader and follower schemas

3

Traits, Situational, Functional, Skills, and Relational Leadership

Great leaders are never satisfied with current levels of performance.
They are restlessly driven by possibilities and potential achievements.

—*Donna Harrison*

OVERVIEW

Understanding and Explaining Leadership

Much of what was written about leadership prior to 1900 was based on observation, commentary, and moralization. The increasing use of "scientific" procedures and techniques to measure human behavior, which blossomed in the early twentieth century, changed the way scholars looked at leadership. Over the past 130 years, seven primary approaches for understanding and explaining leadership have evolved:

1. Traits approach
2. Situational approach
3. Functional approach
4. Skills approach
5. Relational approach
6. Transformational approach
7. Authentic approach

Early social scientists believed that leadership qualities were innate; an individual was either born with the traits needed to be a leader, or he or she lacked the physiological and psychological characteristics necessary for successful leadership. This approach to leadership, known as the traits approach, suggested that nature played a key role in determining leadership potential. The idea that inherent leadership traits could be identified served as the impetus for hundreds of research studies in the early part of the twentieth century. After being challenged in the late 1940s, the popularity of the traits approach waned. However, in recent decades there has been renewed interest in the significance of traits in shaping performance and the perceptions of leadership effectiveness.

The situational approach argues that the traits, skills, and behaviors necessary for effective leadership vary from situation to situation. Think of a successful leader you know; perhaps he or she leads a student club, social group, or religious congregation. Now imagine this leader as a union boss, school principal, football coach, lab supervisor, or military commander. Is it difficult to picture this person playing different leadership roles effectively? A leader is not always successful in every situation. A leader's effectiveness depends on his or her personality, the behavior of followers, the nature of the task, and many other contextual factors. The eighteenth president of the United States, Ulysses S. Grant, is an example of how a leader's effectiveness varies between situations. Grant was a highly effective military leader but was considered inept as president.

While many researchers have attempted to identify factors influencing leadership effectiveness in various contexts, others have studied the functions of leadership. The functional approach looks at the way leaders behave. The underlying assumption of the functional approach is that leaders perform certain functions that allow a group or organization to operate effectively. An individual is considered a leader if he or she performs these functions. The functional approach has been applied primarily to group leadership. The perspective is important to communication scholars because it attempts to identify specific communicative behaviors associated with leadership.

The skills approach identifies the abilities that individuals need to effectively carry out their leadership functions. Unlike traits, these skills can be learned and developed through training and experience; skill building is the focus of leadership education and training. A variety of leadership skills lists have been offered, including those based on organizational levels, leadership tasks, and problem solving.

The relational approach focuses on the links or relationships between leaders and followers. This approach to leadership explores the unique interactions a leader has with each of her or his followers. These interactions are critical in developing leader-follower relationships, which, in turn, impact effectiveness. Those who have positive relationships with their leaders are generally more satisfied and productive. Effective leaders try to establish high-quality relationships with as many followers as possible.

In this chapter we will explore the traits, situational, functional, skills, and relational approaches to leadership. The transformational and authentic approaches will be discussed in the next chapter. All seven approaches provide perspectives for understanding and explaining leadership—frameworks that guide leadership theory, research, and practice. Sometimes the approaches overlap; other times they contradict one another. No single approach provides a universal explanation of leadership behavior, but each provides useful insights. As you read, try to identify at least one concept from each approach that you can use to become a more effective leader (see Application Exercise 10 on p. 101).

A good theory is one that holds together
long enough to get you to a better theory.

—D. O. Hebb

The Traits Approach to Leadership

In the early part of the twentieth century, it was widely believed that leaders possessed unique physical and psychological characteristics that predisposed them to positions of influence. Researchers were not completely sure which characteristics were most important, but they assumed that an individual's physical and psychological features were the best indicators of leadership potential. Scores of leadership studies focused on factors such as height, weight, appearance, intelligence, and disposition. Other studies looked at status, social skill, mobility, popularity, and other social traits in order to determine which of these characteristics were most strongly associated with leadership. Researchers wanted to know, for example, were leaders: tall or short? bright or dull? outgoing or shy?

In 1948, Ralph Stogdill published a review of 124 studies that had appeared in print between 1904 and 1947 with a focus on traits and personal factors related to leadership.[1] Stogdill's review uncovered a number of inconsistent findings. Leaders were found to be both young and old, tall and short, heavy and thin, extroverted and introverted, and physically attractive as well as physically unattractive. Further, the strength of the relationship between a given trait and leadership prowess varied significantly from study to study. Stogdill concluded, "A person does not become a leader by virtue of the possession of some combination of traits, but the pattern of personal characteristics of the leader must bear some relevant relationship to the characteristics, activities, and goals of the followers."[2]

In 1974, Stogdill again published an exhaustive review of traits research. This time he analyzed 163 traits studies published between 1949 and 1970.[3] Fewer inconsistencies were uncovered in this research, but Stogdill remained convinced that personality traits *alone* did not adequately explain leadership. Once again, Stogdill concluded that *both* personal traits and situational factors influenced leadership.

> *Leaders are made, they are not born. They are made by hard effort, which is the price which all of us must pay to achieve any goal that is worthwhile.*
>
> —*Vince Lombardi*

Stogdill's work has sometimes been cited as evidence that personal traits have no bearing on leadership. Stogdill himself did not hold this view. In 1974, he wrote:

> [I] have been cited frequently as evidence in support of the view that leadership is entirely situational in origin and that no personal characteristics are predictive of leadership. This view seems to overemphasize the situational and underemphasize the personal nature of leadership. Strong evidence indicates that different leadership skills and traits are required in different situations. The behaviors and traits enabling a mobster to gain and maintain control over a criminal gang are not the same as those enabling a religious leader to gain and maintain a large following. Yet certain general qualities—such as courage, fortitude, and conviction—appear to characterize both.[4]

Later researchers used advanced statistical techniques to reanalyze previous reviews of trait research as well as to conduct additional reviews.[5] The updated analyses (as well as new analyses) revealed that personal characteristics do have an influence on leadership behavior and perceptions. Contemporary research has identified the following as important leader traits.[6]

Cognitive abilities. Investigators have discovered a link between intelligence and effective leadership. Those who score higher on mental ability tests are generally more likely to emerge as leaders and perform successfully. Creative or divergent thinking is also important, particularly in solving complex problems.

Locus of control. Individuals with an internal locus of control (internals) believe that the rewards they receive are largely under their control and rest upon their own efforts. Individuals with an external locus of control (externals) believe that their rewards are determined by outside forces like chance, powerful people, and fate.[7] Internals are more likely to emerge as leaders; to rely more on persuasion than on coercion; to pursue more innovative, risk-taking corporate strategies; and to engage in outstanding leader behaviors that promote higher organizational performance.[8]

Personality. Personality studies have largely centered on the relationship between leadership and the Big Five Model. The Big Five personality model organizes personality traits around five dimensions: neuroticism (emotional stability), extraversion (sociability), openness to experience (creative and curious), agreeableness (trusting and nurturing), and conscientiousness (organized and dependable).[9] Meta-analysis of 78 leadership and personality studies has linked the Big Five personality factors (often referred to by the acronym NEOAC) to leadership effectiveness. Extraversion was found to have the strongest positive relationship to leadership, followed by conscientiousness, and openness. Agreeableness was found to have only a weak association with leadership. Neuroticism had a negative relationship with leadership.[10]

In practical terms, those with higher or lower ranges within these personality dimensions can be expected to experience work differently. High extroverts like to be around people and enjoy interaction and social settings, while those scoring lower on this dimension are more energized by working alone. (Turn to box 3.1 for a closer look at introverted leaders.) Those with a higher openness to experience are intrigued by new ideas and activities, while workers scoring lower on this dimension prefer the familiar and tend to be more practical. Highly agreeable people have a tendency to accommodate the needs of others, while those scoring lower on this dimension are more inclined to focus on their own personal needs. Those with high conscientiousness scores tend to be more focused and organized, while those scoring lower on this dimension are more spontaneous and tend to be more comfortable with multitasking. Those who are higher on neuroticism tend to be more reactive and affected by stress, while those scoring lower on this dimension are generally calm and less impacted by stress.[11]

Motivation. Three motives have drawn the most attention from traits researchers: power, achievement, and affiliation.[12] Generally speaking, the most effective leaders are high in power motive, moderate to high in achievement motivation, and lower in the need to affiliate with others. Power motivation encourages individuals to seek and exert influence as leaders. However, power should be exercised on behalf of the group instead of personal gain.[13] Leaders also seek achievement but, as they take upper level positions, they must set aside the desire for personal achievement and focus on achieving through others. Those with a strong need to relate to others (affiliation) are typically not as successful because their need to please others interferes with their ability to make tough decisions like laying people off or denying promotions.

Investigators have also discovered that individuals differ in their motivation to lead (MTL).[14] MTL determines how much a person seeks out leadership roles as

---

Box 3.1   Research Highlight   **The Introverted Leader**[15]

It's easy to see why extroverts would be more likely to emerge as leaders. They fulfill the image of the prototypical leader by speaking up, asserting themselves, and making connections with others. As we saw in chapter 1, in the United States willingness to communicate is tied to leadership emergence and a number of other positive outcomes. Writer Brian Walsh sums up the nation's bias toward extroversion this way:

> Simply being an introvert can also feel taxing—especially in America, land of the loud and home of the talkative. From classrooms built around group learning to open-plan offices that encourage endless meetings, it sometimes seems that the quality of your work has less value than the volume of your voice.[16]

A number of scholars argue that all the focus on the extroverted leader overlooks the fact that introverted people can also be effective leaders. They point to Mohandas Gandhi, Moses, Warren Buffet, Bill Gates, Rosa Parks, and Albert Einstein as prominent examples of leader-introverts. In fact, introverts have significant advantages over extroverts. Introverts are better listeners, which enables them to gather the ideas of followers. They also are more aware of risk and are more innovative. Because they work well alone, introverts can concentrate on developing their skills.

An exchange between Bill Clinton (an extrovert) and Barack Obama (an introvert) illustrates the differences between the two leader types. After attending the funeral of Israel's Simon Perez, the departure of Air Force One was delayed because former president Clinton was still shaking hands on the tarmac. Finally, President Obama, who had already boarded, had to come out of the door of the plane to urge Clinton to get on the plane.

When it comes to leadership, introverts and extroverts can learn from each other. Introverts need to adopt extroverted behaviors when needed—engaging in small talk, leading meetings, approaching strangers, public speaking. For their part, extroverts need to adopt introverted behaviors—listening, seeking out solitude for thought, and resisting unnecessary risk taking.

---

well as the amount of effort he or she puts forth to succeed once in a leadership position. MTL is made up of three factors. Those with *affective-identity* leadership motivation are driven to express domination and power. They are generally outgoing and confident, value achievement, and have significant past leadership experience. Those with *social-normative* leadership motivation lead because they are driven by a sense of duty and obligation to the group. Those with *non-calculative* leadership motivation don't consider the cost of leading but, instead, lead because they want to preserve group harmony. People with high overall motivation to lead are more likely to be both informal and formal leaders, receive higher effectiveness ratings, and benefit more from leadership training. (To determine your motivation to lead, complete the self-assessment in box 3.2.)

Social appraisal (social intelligence). Social appraisal is the ability to recognize the feelings and behaviors of others in social situations and to respond effectively based on that knowledge. A number of researchers argue that this trait is essential to effective leadership. They report that individuals who are better at monitoring their thoughts and feelings are more likely to emerge as leaders. Once in leadership roles, those who are skilled at responding flexibly to a variety of contexts experience more success. Emotional intelligence is a subset of social intelli-

Box 3.2 Self-Assessment	Motivation to Lead Scale[17]

Instructions: Respond to each of the following items on a scale of 1–5; 1 = strongly disagree, 5 = strongly agree.

_____ 1. Most of the time, I prefer being a leader rather than a follower when working in a group.

_____ 2. I am the type of person who is not interested in leading others. (reverse)

_____ 3. I am definitely not a leader by nature. (reverse)

_____ 4. I am the type of person who likes to be in charge of others.

_____ 5. I believe I can contribute more to a group if I am a follower rather than a leader. (reverse)

_____ 6. I usually want to be the leader in the groups that I work in.

_____ 7. I am the type who would actively support a leader but prefers not to be appointed as leader. (reverse)

_____ 8. I have a tendency to take charge in most groups or teams that I work in.

_____ 9. I am seldom reluctant to be the leader of a group.

_____ 10. I am only interested in leading a group if there are clear advantages for me. (reverse)

_____ 11. I will never agree to lead if I cannot see any benefits from accepting that role. (reverse)

_____ 12. I would only agree to be a group leader if I know I can benefit from that role. (reverse)

_____ 13. I would agree to lead others even if there are no special rewards or benefits with that role.

_____ 14. I would want to know "what's in it for me" if I am going agree to lead a group. (reverse)

_____ 15. I never expect to get more privileges if I agree to lead a group.

_____ 16. If I agree to lead a group, I would never expect any advantages or special benefits.

_____ 17. I have more of my own problems to worry about than to be concerned about the rest of the group. (reverse)

_____ 18. Leading others is really more of a dirty job rather than an honorable one. (reverse)

_____ 19. I feel that I have a duty to lead others if I am asked.

_____ 20. I agree to lead whenever I am asked or nominated by the other members.

_____ 21. I was taught to believe in the value of leading others.

_____ 22. It is appropriate for people to accept leadership roles or positions when they are asked.

_____ 23. I have been taught that I should always volunteer to lead others if I can.

_____ 24. It is not right to decline leadership roles.

_____ 25. It is an honor and privilege to be asked to lead.

_____ 26. People should volunteer to lead rather than wait for others to ask or vote for them.

_____ 27. I would never agree to lead just because others voted for me. (reverse)

Scoring: Reverse scoring where indicated, and add up scores for each of the three dimensions. Range: 9–45 on each dimension; 27–135 for total score.

Affective-Identify MTL Items 1–9 _____

Noncalculative MTL Items 10–18 _____

Social-Normative MTL Items 19–27 _____

Total MTL Score _____

The higher your score on a set of items, the greater your motivation to lead based on that dimension. The total score reveals your overall motivation to lead.

gence. Leaders who can identify, use, understand, and manage emotions are generally more successful (see chapter 1).

Research findings establish that there are traits that are advantageous for leaders. These characteristics increase the likelihood that someone will emerge as a leader and perform successfully in that role. However, the trait approach leaves many unanswered questions: (1) What is a trait? Items on some lists—like integrity, knowledge, or social intelligence—appear to be learned or developed rather than innate. (2) What, if any, traits are universally needed? Ask a group of people to generate a list of essential leader traits and you are likely to find little agreement (see Application Exercise 3.2). (3) How do we account for successful leaders who seem to lack many of the personal characteristics deemed necessary for leadership? (See box 3.3.) (4) How much does success depend on meeting the demands of the situation in addition having important traits? A leader's cognitive abilities will equip her to problem solve in a particular setting, for instance. But general intelligence is not enough in and of itself to guarantee success in that situation. The effective leader must analyze the context, identify and solve problems, and apply relevant experience and knowledge.

Box 3.3 Case Study	**Eleanor Roosevelt: The Timid Child Who Became the World's First Lady**[18]

Eleanor Roosevelt was one of the most important leaders of the twentieth century. While her husband Franklin Delano Roosevelt was president, she devoted herself to promoting social issues like civil rights, better treatment for the poor, workers rights, and equality for women. She had a hand in creating the National Youth Administration (a work-training program for young people) and keeping other New Deal programs operating during World War II. Eleanor served as Franklin's "eyes and ears," traveling extensively as his representative to visit combat troops, coal miners, farmers, housewives, school children, and other groups. Franklin supported her efforts, even though he didn't always know what she was up to. In one case, she left early to visit a prison without saying goodbye to her husband. When he asked Eleanor's secretary where she was, the secretary replied, "She's in prison, Mr. President." "I'm not surprised," Franklin replied, "but what for?"[19]

Mrs. Roosevelt continued her activism after FDR died. President Truman asked her to be a delegate to the first session of the United Nations after World War II. There she chaired the UN committee that drafted the Universal Declaration of Human Rights. She made a number of international trips promoting understanding between cultures. At her death many considered her to be the "First Lady of the World."

Mrs. Roosevelt's emergence as a world figure is surprising given that she had few of the qualities typically associated with leaders. She began life as a shy and unattractive child who earned the family nickname "Granny" because she was so somber. In Eleanor's words, "I was a solemn child, without beauty and painfully shy and I seemed like a little old woman entirely lacking in the spontaneous joy and mirth of youth."[20] Her insecurity grew when she was orphaned (her mother died of diphtheria and her father of alcoholism). After her marriage to FDR, her timidity kept her out of the limelight as she gave birth to six children. Her fear made her a poor public speaker when she finally did start campaigning on behalf of her husband. Through diligent preparation, she overcame her fears and changed her speaking voice, eliminated her nervous giggle, and learned to make eye contact. She also had to learn to deal with the media. (In one bold step, Mrs.

Roosevelt began to hold press conferences for women reporters only.) Once she found her voice, she had to endure verbal assaults that would shake the confidence of even the most assured leader. She became the brunt of jokes and vicious attacks, particularly in the South, for her efforts to end lynching and for her friendship with black leaders. Eleanor summed up her evolution as a leader this way:

> [O]ne can, even without any particular gifts, overcome obstacles that seem insurmountable if one is willing to face the fact that they must be overcome; that, in spite of timidity and fear, in spite of a lack of special talents, one can find a way to live widely and fully.[21]

What enabled Mrs. Roosevelt to overcome personal and societal obstacles? To begin, it is clear that she did have some "special talents"—the ability to write, to empathize with the needs of others, to persevere. She also had a learning attitude, which enabled her to reflect on her childhood, grow from mistakes, accept help from mentors, listen to others, and respect people from other cultures. Eleanor didn't appear to have a strong achievement orientation but was motivated instead by her passion: to help others. To pursue her vision, she took risks, endured criticism, and created networks of friends and supporters.

Discussion Questions

1. What do you know about Eleanor Roosevelt from prior courses and study? How would you evaluate her as a leader?

2. What leadership traits did Eleanor Roosevelt appear to lack? What traits, if any, did she have?

3. Does Mrs. Roosevelt demonstrate that leaders are made rather than born? Why or why not?

4. Can you think of other leaders who succeeded even though they lacked important characteristics that we associate with effective leadership? What accounts for their success?

5. What principles do you see in the life of Eleanor Roosevelt that can help you become a better leader?

The Situational Approach to Leadership

As the traits approach became less accepted as an explanation of leadership behavior, many researchers began to pursue situational explanations for leadership. These approaches, often called contingency approaches, assume that leadership behavior is contingent on variations in the situation.[22] For example, the strategy for effectively leading a high-tech research and development team is much different from the strategy for effectively leading a military combat unit. The differences in leadership style might be attributed to task and relational structure, superior-subordinate interactions, the motivation of followers, or any one of a number of other situational factors. Two of the most commonly studied situational approaches are path-goal theory, and Hersey and Blanchard's situational leadership model.

Path-Goal Theory

Path-goal theory is based on a theory of organizational motivation called expectancy theory. Expectancy theory claims that followers are more motivated to be productive when they believe that successful task completion will provide a path to a valuable goal. According to Robert House and his associates, leaders play an important role in influencing follower perceptions of task paths and goal desirability.[23] It is a leader's responsibility to communicate clearly what is expected of followers and what rewards can be anticipated when tasks are successfully completed. He or she is also responsible for helping followers overcome obstacles to completing the task. Take, for example, a group of students assigned to give a classroom presentation. How might the leader of such a group apply expectancy theory? By providing specific expectations for individual task assignments and reinforcing the group goal (a quality product that will receive a good grade), the group leader can increase the motivation and satisfaction level of followers. She or he may also need to help the group deal with such barriers as limited practice time and computer software problems.

According to House and Terence Mitchell, the ability to motivate followers is influenced by a leader's communication style as well as by certain situational factors. Four communication styles are identified.

1. *Directive leadership*—procedure-related communication behavior that includes planning and organizing, task coordination, policy setting, and other forms of specific guidance.

2. *Supportive leadership*—interpersonal communication focusing on concern for the needs and well-being of followers and the facilitation of a desirable climate for interaction.

3. *Participative leadership*—communication designed to solicit opinions and ideas from followers for the purpose of involving followers in decision making.

4. *Achievement-oriented leadership*—communication focusing on goal attainment and accomplishment, emphasizing the achievement of excellence by demonstrating confidence in the ability of followers to achieve their goals.

In path-goal theory, two situational variables are most influential in the selection of an appropriate leadership communication style: the nature of followers and the nature of the task. Follower characteristics thought to be important include follower needs, abilities, values, and personality. Important task factors include task structure and clarity. These factors influence motivation and satisfaction levels among followers and determine the most effective leader communication style. Box 3.4 diagrams the use of particular leader communication styles depending on follower characteristics and abilities, and task structure.

Directive leader communication is most effective when followers are inexperienced or when the task is unstructured. In these situations, followers might have a low expectation of their ability to perform satisfactorily. This expectation can lead to decreased motivation and satisfaction. In general, when expected behavior and task assignments are ambiguous, such as in a new position or job function, followers need directive leadership. On the other hand, if behavioral expectations are clearly understood and followers are competent in performing tasks, directive leadership lowers motivation and satisfaction. Nobody likes to have someone looking over her or his shoulder when the task is clear and performance is not problematic.

Box 3.4				Path-Goal Theory Factors
Communication Style	Achievement-Oriented	Participative	Supportive	Directive
Nature of Followers	Followers possess necessary skills and have high need to succeed.	Followers are unsure (particularly if uncertainty prompts apprehension) and have an internal locus of control.	Followers are skilled and have a need for affiliation.	Followers are inexperienced or unsure, have an external locus of control and a strong belief in authority.
Nature of Task	Task is unstructured and under the control of followers.	Task is unstructured.	Task is structured (particularly if task is stressful).	Task is unstructured.

When followers confront structured tasks that are stressful, tedious, frustrating, difficult, or dissatisfying (such as working on an assembly line), a leader can make the situation more tolerable by engaging in supportive leader communication. In situations such as these, followers might have the necessary skills to complete tasks effectively, but they may lack confidence or commitment. This lack of confidence or commitment can produce a low self-expectation, resulting in poor performance. Supportive communication bolsters confidence and commitment and offers social rewards that can enhance motivation and satisfaction. Simply recognizing the difficulty of a task and expressing your appreciation for a follower's efforts can increase motivation and satisfaction levels. Supportive communication will contribute less to motivation and satisfaction when tasks are already stimulating and enjoyable.

*Good leadership consists of showing average people
how to do the work of superior people.*

—John D. Rockefeller

Situations in which tasks are unstructured and behavior expectations are ambiguous are good opportunities for participative leader communication. Participating in decision making allows followers to think critically about expected behavior and task performance. Becoming more intimately involved with an unclear task can increase understanding and motivation. A follower struggling to develop a program to simplify a new computerized accounting system might benefit from participative communication. When uncertainty is uncomfortable for followers, participative communication stimulates understanding and clarity and can increase satisfaction. In situations where the task is highly structured and followers are aware of behavior expectations, participative leadership will have a minimal effect on motivation and satisfaction, according to path-goal theory.

Achievement-oriented leader communication increases a follower's confidence in his or her ability to realize challenging goals. By emphasizing excellence and demonstrating confidence in a follower's abilities, a leader can create a positive performance expectation. We are more likely to produce excellent results when others have expressed confidence in our ability to excel. The expectations of his coach and teammates might offer a partial explanation for the incredible success of Michael Jordan when he played for the Chicago Bulls. When the coach was asked what his game plan was, he claimed, "We give the ball to Michael and get out of his way." Achievement-oriented communication is most effective in unstructured situations. Followers performing highly structured tasks will not be as effectively motivated by achievement-oriented messages.

Twenty-five years after first presenting the theory, House offered an updated version that addressed the motivation of work units (not just individuals) and introduced additional leader behaviors that are "theoretically acceptable, satisfying, facilitative, and motivational for subordinates."[24] These include: (1) clarifying behaviors that sharpen understanding of goals, means, standards, and rewards and punishments; (2) work facilitation behaviors that address planning, scheduling, and organization as well as coordinating and overseeing the work of subordinates; (3) interaction facilitation behaviors that resolve disputes, foster collaboration and teamwork, and encourage communication, resulting in member satisfaction; (4) group oriented decision processes that improve decision quality and acceptance, like involving all participants, drawing on the skills of expert members, identifying mutual interests, presenting alternatives, and breaking the problem into smaller parts; (5) representation and networking behaviors that secure resources for the unit from outside groups; and (6) values-based leader behaviors that motivate by appealing to the values of followers and tying follower identity to the group and organization.

Path-goal theory attempts to explain follower motivation and satisfaction in terms of leader behavior and task structure. Although the approach neglects many situational variables that might potentially be important (such as power, organizational climate, and group cohesiveness), path-goal theory provides a viable explanation of the relationship among leaders, followers, and tasks. Nevertheless, path theory development has been hampered by inconsistent research findings and problems with how to assess the styles and outcome variables. Path-goal theory initially generated a large number of projects (more than 100) but few path-goal studies have been conducted in the past few years.[25]

Hersey and Blanchard's Situational Leadership Approach

Paul Hersey and Kenneth Blanchard originated the situational leadership approach in the late 1960s while working on the first edition of their book, *Management of Organizational Behavior*, and later independently refined the model—Hersey as the Situational Leadership Model, and Blanchard as the Situational Leadership II Model. The situational leadership approach posits that different situations call for different styles of leadership. Hersey and Blanchard suggest that the readiness level of followers plays an important role in selecting appropriate leadership behavior.[26] As does path-goal theory, Hersey and Blanchard divide leader behavior into task and relationship dimensions. The appropriate degree of task and relationship behavior exhibited by a leader depends on the readiness of followers.

According to the situational leadership approach, follower readiness consists of two major components that can be plotted along a continuum: ability and willingness. In Blanchard's later version of the model, he uses the terms competence and commitment to refer to these components. Ability/competence refers to skills, knowledge, and experience. A medical intern making rounds for the first time has low ability. A budget officer preparing a yearly financial statement for the twentieth consecutive year has high ability. Willingness/commitment relates to feelings of confidence and motivation. A factory worker who is bored and unchallenged by a repetitive task has low willingness, while a teacher committed to excellence in the classroom has high willingness. Readiness levels can fluctuate as a follower moves from task to task or from one situation to another.

Four combinations of ability and willingness indicate follower readiness:

Readiness Level 1:   Low ability and low willingness (follower lacks skills and motivation)

Readiness Level 2:   Low ability and high willingness (follower lacks skills but is committed)

Readiness Level 3:   High ability and low willingness (follower is skilled but lacks motivation)

Readiness Level 4:   High ability and high willingness (follower is skilled and motivated)

According to Hersey and Blanchard, the readiness level of followers dictates effective leader behavior. By adapting the Blake and McCanse Leadership Grid* discussed in chapter 2, Hersey and Blanchard suggest appropriate task and relational orientations for each of the four levels of follower readiness. R1 followers require specific guidance. The most effective leader behavior with R1 followers is high task-directed communication and low relationship-directed communication (*directing*). Task-related messages direct and guide follower behavior. The use of supportive, relationship-directed communication should be avoided at this level, as such messages might be interpreted as a reward for poor performance.

R2 followers lack skills but are willing. Because they do not possess necessary task skills, they need direct guidance. Because they are putting forth effort, they need support. Thus, the most effective leader behavior with R2 followers is high task/high relationship (*coaching*). At this level, the leader is "selling" the belief that the necessary skills can be acquired. R3 followers are skilled but lack the willingness to perform. Leaders need to promote follower participation in decision-making. Task guidance is not necessary since performance has been demonstrated, but leaders must encourage R3 followers to discuss problems or fears hampering commitment or confidence (*supporting*). The most effective leader behavior facilitates involvement by using low task and high relationship behavior.

R4 followers are skilled and willing. Giving authority to these performers is the best strategy (*delegating*). Since task skills are well developed, task guidance is not necessary. Relationship behavior is not required because commitment and confidence are not a problem. This does not mean that relationship behavior should be completely ignored. Certainly a leader needs to offer support and recognition periodically to maintain the level of excellence of the R4 follower.

> *Things do not change, we change.*
>
> —*Henry David Thoreau*

By engaging in appropriate leadership behavior, Hersey and Blanchard suggest a leader can influence follower behavior. The manipulation of task and relationship behaviors in accordance with follower readiness can facilitate growth and development among followers. If leaders carefully diagnose the situation, communicate accordingly, and maintain flexibility as the situation changes, the situational leadership approach claims that they will be more effective in influencing followers. (Practice applying this approach by analyzing the case study in box 3.5.) However, investigators have been unable to consistently substantiate Hersey and Blanchard's claims.[27] Not only are there problems with the instrument used to measure the situational flexibility of leaders, but also the styles recommended for each of the readiness levels do not always produce the best results. For example, a high task/high relationship can be effective for R1 followers. As a consequence, some scholars suggest that situational leadership should be treated more as a teaching tool than a theory. It can be used to introduce the importance of the situation (particularly follower readiness) to leadership success.

The Functional Approach to Leadership

Traits and situational approaches focus primarily on the individual characteristics of leaders and followers. The functional approach looks at the communicative *behavior* of leaders. The functional approach suggests that it is the ability to communicate like a leader that determines leadership. Imagine that while driving you witness an accident. Several motorists, including you, stop to offer assistance. Who will become the leader in this emergency situation? Will the leader be the person with the most knowledge regarding first aid? Perhaps. Will the leader be the person with the right combination of motivation and willingness for the situation? Maybe. Most likely the leader will be the person who starts behaving like a leader. Leadership functions in this situation might include assigning tasks ("You call 911"), initiating action ("I'll put my jacket on him so he'll be warm"), giving support ("The ambulance will be here in just a few minutes"), and mediating conflict ("Let's not worry about whose fault it was until everyone is feeling better"). By performing the functions of leadership, an individual will be viewed as a leader by others.

Many ordinary people took on leadership functions during the horrific events of September 11, 2001. Office workers carried injured colleagues down the stairs of the World Trade Center, while firefighters rushed up to help victims. Those in

---

Box 3.5 Case Study	**Leadership at *The Campus News***

Maryanne Norton is the faculty advisor to *The Campus News*, the student newspaper at Algonquian University. She oversees production of the weekly publication and advises the newspaper's editor, Mark Lee, and his staff. Mark is a junior political science major with little experience in journalism. He is, however, enthusiastic and excited about his role as editor of *The Campus News*. Mark is typical of many of the staff in his lack of journalistic skills. In fact, many of *The Campus News* reporters have no background in news writing. As a faculty member in the Department of Communication, Maryanne teaches four courses per semester and is responsible for several other projects, including supervision of the internship program. Maryanne has a keen interest in student journalism and has long been an advocate of the rights of student reporters. Although Maryanne is very busy, she takes time to meet with the staff of *The Campus News* each week prior to publication and often hosts social gatherings for the students at her home. Although the staff of *The Campus News* is comprised of students, Maryanne believes the most effective approach to leading is to treat followers as peers and colleagues; she is most comfortable serving as a confidant and a friend to her advisees. She rarely criticizes a story and feels it is not her place to correct the work of the student reporters. She is quick to offer suggestions or guidance when asked for advice, but mainly she tries to make the experience of working for *The Campus News* enjoyable and rewarding for students.

Although there have been minor problems in the past during Maryanne's term as advisor, *The Campus News* has been heavily criticized recently. The inexperience of Mark and his staff has been evident in the last few issues of the student newspaper. In one headline, the name of the Dean of Engineering was misspelled, and details have been inaccurately reported in several stories. The most troubling error occurred in a story about Algonquian's attempt to settle a dispute with a faculty member who had been denied tenure. The story did not present the situation accurately and contained several quotes attributed to administrators at Algonquian that were later determined to have been taken out of context. One of the statements was so inflammatory that the administrator quoted was subpoenaed and asked to explain his comments in a deposition.

Shortly after that incident, Maryanne was called into the university president's office to discuss the situation at *The Campus News*.

Discussion Questions

1. What is the problem at *The Campus News*?

2. How would you rate Maryanne Norton as a leader? How would you rate Mark Lee as a follower?

3. Which leadership style discussed in the Hersey and Blanchard situational leadership approach does Maryanne exhibit? How would you rate the readiness level of the student followers at *The Campus News*?

4. What situational leadership style would be most effective with the students working for *The Campus News*? Why?

5. What would you advise Maryanne to tell the president of Algonquian University she will do to improve the situation at *The Campus News*?

buildings near Ground Zero pulled pedestrians off the street and out of harm's way. Staff at Starbucks and other businesses organized to provide food to relief workers. Employees at many firms in Manhattan refused to be cut off from their jobs, finding new ways to get to work by kayaking the East River, renting buses, and hiking.

One of the earliest contributions to the functional approach was Chester Barnard's 1938 classic, *The Functions of the Executive*.[28] Barnard's work isolated communication as the central function of organizational leadership. Since then, a number of researchers have attempted to identify the various behaviors associated with leadership in organizations and groups. Kenneth Benne and Paul Sheats were pioneers in the classification of functional roles in groups.[29] After analyzing group communication patterns, they identified three types of group roles: *task-related, group building and maintenance,* and *individual.*

Task-Related Roles

According to Benne and Sheats, these roles contribute to the organization and completion of group tasks. Six task-related roles are described below.

The initiator. This person defines the problem, establishes the agenda and procedures, and proposes innovative strategies and solutions. The initiator makes statements such as: "I see our problem as maintaining our market share," or "Let's begin by just throwing out some possible ways to approach this problem."

The information/opinion seeker. Someone in this role solicits ideas, asks questions about information provided by others, and asks for evaluations of information and procedure. The information/opinion seeker makes statements such as: "Why do you think our production costs will increase in the next quarter?" or "Do you think we are spending enough time discussing possible solutions?"

The information/opinion giver. In contrast to the above, this person presents and evaluates facts and information and evaluates procedure. The information/opinion giver makes statements such as: "I think we will serve our students better by offering more night courses next semester," or "I learned in my group communication course that we shouldn't offer solutions until we have thoroughly analyzed the problem."

The elaborator. The elaborator provides examples and background as a means for clarifying ideas and speculates how proposed solutions might work. A person in this role makes statements such as: "A raffle may be an effective way to raise money. Last year, the Ski Club made $1,000 from its raffle."

The orienter/coordinator. This group member summarizes interaction, looks for relationships among ideas and suggestions, and focuses group members on specific issues and tasks. The orienter/coordinator makes statements such as: "That suggestion seems to fit with Glenn's idea about training," or "Maybe if we all come to the next meeting with a few pages of notes we could put together an outline for our presentation."

The energizer. In groups, the energizer stimulates or arouses the group to achieve excellence and promotes activity and excitement. The energizer makes statements such as: "If we can get this product out on schedule, I think it will revolutionize the industry."

Group-Building and Maintenance Roles

People who fulfill these roles contribute to the development and maintenance of open, supportive, and healthy interpersonal relationships among group members. Four group-building and maintenance roles are described below.

The encourager. Someone in this role supports and praises the contributions of others, communicates a sense of belonging and solidarity among group members, and accepts and appreciates divergent viewpoints. The encourager makes statements such as: "I agree with Susan," or "I am confident that our group will do a great job next week," or "I can appreciate your concern about reaching a decision too quickly. We must be careful not to jump to premature conclusions."

The harmonizer/compromiser. This group member mediates conflict, reduces tension through joking, and attempts to bring group members with opposing points of view closer together. The harmonizer/compromiser makes statements such as: "What's the worst thing that could happen if we don't get this project done on time? Okay, what's the second worst thing that could happen?" or "Is there any way both you and Brett can get what you want from this decision?"

The gatekeeper. This person encourages the involvement of shy or uninvolved group members and proposes regulations of the flow of communication through means such as time and topic limitation. The gatekeeper makes statements such as: "I'd be interested to hear what Luisa has to say about this," or "Why don't we limit our discussion of the budget to twenty minutes."

The standard-setter. This person in this role expresses group values and standards and applies standards to the evaluation of the group process. The standard-setter makes statements such as: "Our goal has always been to develop user-friendly products," or "Let's try to be critical of ideas, not people. That has always been our policy in the past."

Individual Roles

When a group member's behavior is not supportive of task or group relationships, group effectiveness can be minimized. Although a certain degree of individuality is healthy, individual-centered behaviors do not contribute to task completion or relationship development and maintenance. Five possible disruptive individual roles are included here. Playing any of these roles can seriously disrupt a group and keep it from carrying out its task.

The aggressor. This person attacks the ideas, opinions, and values of others; uses aggressive humor; and makes personal judgments. The aggressor makes statements such as: "It is better to keep your mouth shut and appear stupid than to open it and remove all doubt," or "Pete's concern for equal workloads is the reason this group is so unproductive."

The blocker. This group member resists the ideas and opinions of others and brings up "dead" issues after the group has rejected them. The blocker makes statements such as: "I don't care if we already voted against it; I still think that we ought to go ahead with the project."

The recognition-seeker. Another individual who minimizes group effectiveness is the person who relates personal accomplishments to the group and claims to be more expert and knowledgeable than other group members on virtually every topic. The recognition-seeker makes statements such as: "I know I am not a nurse, but I might as well be, considering how much time I spent with my husband when he was ill."

The player. This group member maintains a noncaring or cynical attitude and makes jokes at inappropriate times. The player makes statements such as: "We can't get much accomplished in one hour. Let's knock off early and get a beer."

The dominator. Particularly disruptive, the dominator lacks respect for the views of others, disconfirms the ideas and opinions of others, and frequently interrupts. The dominator makes statements such as: "Rahid's idea doesn't seem worthwhile to me. The way to get this program to run is to do what I have suggested."

Roles associated with the successful completion of the task and the development and maintenance of group interaction help facilitate goal achievement and the satisfaction of group needs. These roles serve a leadership function. Roles associated with the satisfaction of individual needs do not contribute to the goals of the group as a whole and are usually not associated with leadership. By engaging in task-related and group-building/maintenance role behaviors (and avoiding individual role behavior), a group member can perform leadership functions and increase the likelihood that he or she will achieve leadership status within the group. (Turn to chapter 7 for an in-depth look at group leadership.)

In addition to the Benne and Sheats categories, several other communicative behaviors associated with leadership have been identified. Box 3.6 lists three sets of proposed leadership functions.

The functional approach provides guidelines for the behavior of leaders by suggesting the necessary functions that a leader should perform. Functional theorists offer this advice: "To be a leader you've got to act like a leader." In its present form, the functional approach does not provide a clear, well-developed prescription for leader behavior. Many of the identified leader behaviors are vague, and some are contradictory. How, for example, can a leader increase interdependence among group members? What specific leader behaviors facilitate work? How can a leader both set standards and compromise? Still, the functional approach does provide a useful framework for identifying communication behaviors that contribute to the exercise of leadership.

The Skills Approach to Leadership

The skills approach fills in some of the gaps of the functional approach by identifying the abilities leaders need to carry out their functions. Effectiveness is the key criteria for skills theorists and researchers. First they want to learn what makes leaders effective when carrying out their leadership roles. Then they want to use this information to help aspiring leaders increase their chances of success. This approach is based on the premise that, unlike traits, skills can be developed. Thus,

Box 3.6 Research Highlight	The Functions of Leadership

Krech and Crutchfield (1948)[30]

- executive
- planner
- policy maker
- expert
- external group representative
- facilitator of internal relationships
- supplier of rewards and punishments

- arbitrator
- role model
- group symbol
- surrogate for individual responsibility
- ideologist
- parental figure
- scapegoat

Bowers and Seashore (1966)[31]

- supporter of others
- interaction facilitator

- goal emphasizer
- work facilitator

Cartwright and Zander (1968)[32]

- goal achievement (including: initiating action, focusing on goals, clarifying issues, developing procedural plans, and evaluating outcomes)
- maintenance behavior (including: keeping interpersonal relationships pleasant, mediating disputes, providing encouragement, involving reticent followers, and increasing interdependence among members)

skill building is a major focus of most university leadership classes, corporate training programs, and leadership texts like this one. Theorists, consultants, instructors, and writers offer a great many skill typologies or classifications to guide developing leaders. Some are based on personal experience and observation while others have a stronger theoretical and research base. In this section we'll focus on three influential skill typologies: the three-skill model, task-based competencies, and problem-solving capabilities.

The Three-Skill Model

Robert Katz presented one of the earliest skill-based models in a 1955 *Harvard Business Review* article.[33] Katz developed his model based on field research and observations of executives. He identified three types of skills and argued that the importance of each skill varies, depending on the leader's level of responsibility. *Technical skill* refers to understanding and becoming proficient in a particular activity such as accounting, web design, carpentry, or sales. *Human skill* refers to working with people. This skill is demonstrated through communication that accurately reflects the intent of the manager while anticipating the reactions of others. Those with this skill work well with others and create an atmosphere of trust and security. *Conceptual skill* is "big picture" thinking that encompasses the entire organization. Conceptual thinkers understand how organizational systems interact and the relationship of the business to its industry, community, and the economy. They set the direction and tone for the organization. To put it another way, technical skill is concerned with *things*, human skill is concerned with *people*, and conceptual skill is concerned with *ideas*.

Katz argued that technical skill is most important at lower levels of the organization where employees are focused on completing tasks. Human skill is most important at the next level as forepersons and middle managers must foster collaboration. Conceptual skill becomes most important at the top level where executives make strategic decisions. Katz believed that top executives could be effective even if they had few technical skills. However, human skills remain essential to their success.

To see how the three skills might operate at different organizational levels, consider the case of a recent college graduate. She's been hired by a public relations firm to work on a team designing social media strategies for small corporate clients. Her ability to work with social media is the technical skill that got her the position and one that she will need to exercise to keep her job. If she ever wants to lead her team, however, she will need human skill to enable her to build trust, foster collaboration, convince others to accept her ideas, and so on. If later in her career she aspires to move into a vice-president role, she will have to demonstrate an in-depth understanding of both her public relations agency as well as the larger environment. She will likely be called upon to work with the CEO and other vice-presidents in crafting organizational strategy and shaping the agency's corporate culture.

Task-Based Competencies

Researchers and trainers at the Center for Creative Leadership (CCL) organize their skills typology around the three major tasks of leadership described in chapter 1: setting direction, gaining commitment, and creating alignment. To accomplish these tasks, individuals need to lead themselves, to lead others, and to lead the organization. Based on decades of leadership development in a variety of organizations, CCL scholars identify the following sets of leader competencies, which can be improved through training and experience.[34]

Leading Oneself

- *Self-awareness*: understanding personal strengths and weaknesses and how those strengths and weaknesses impact others; understanding cultural assumptions and biases.
- *Ability to balance conflicting demands*: balancing the demands of bosses, subordinates, clients, personal life, and work life.
- *Ability to learn*: recognizing when new behaviors, skills, and attitudes are needed; accepting responsibility for personal development; taking steps to acquire new knowledge and behaviors.
- *Leadership values*: demonstrating honesty and integrity, which engender trust from followers; developing personal initiative and drive and an optimistic attitude.

Leading Others

- *Ability to build and maintain relationships*: developing cooperative relationships with diverse individuals; demonstrating respect for people from all different backgrounds and perspectives.

- *Ability to build effective work groups*: helping group members develop positive relationships with one another; bridging differences between work groups.

- *Communication skills*: ability to communicate effectively through a variety of media and to understand and process what others are thinking and feeling.

- *Ability to develop others*: helping others determine their development needs; providing feedback and learning opportunities; coaching and mentoring followers; recognizing and rewarding improvements in behavior.

Leading the Organization

- *Management skills*: facilitating and coordinating daily work; setting goals and plans, putting systems in place; monitoring progress, solving problems, and making decisions.

- *Ability to think and act strategically*: supporting the long-term vision and mission of the group or organization though daily decisions; balancing global needs with local demands.

- *Ability to think creatively*: seeing new possibilities, making connections, developing new ideas; implementing innovative solutions.

- *Ability to initiate and implement change*: establishing the need for change; convincing followers to change; putting new systems and procedures into place.

Problem-Solving Capabilities

Professor Michael Mumford of the University of Oklahoma and his colleagues define leadership as an ongoing process of solving complex, ill-defined problems.[35] Unlike a math problem or a true/false quiz, ill-defined problems don't have one clear answer and a workable solution is often sought instead of an ideal solution. Examples of ill-defined problems faced by leaders include, for example, whether to sell a division of the company or to initiate a new compensation system. Ill-defined problems are challenging because, first of all, it can be hard to figure out just what the problem is. Product defects on a manufacturing line may be increasing but it might not be clear why, for instance. Moreover, it may be hard to get timely, accurate information and to determine which data is relevant to the issue at hand. Ill-defined problems are generally novel (they involve new situations), generate conflict, and must be solved within a limited time frame. Implementing the solution means involving a variety of stakeholders both inside and outside the organization. To be effective, leaders must possess the necessary knowledge and skills (capabilities).

Problem-solving theorists identify three sets of skills that are key to solving complex dilemmas: (1) problem-solving skills, (2) solution construction skills, and

(3) social judgment skills. *Problem-solving skills* include defining the problem, gathering information, identifying the key facts and concepts to apply to the dilemma, combining the concepts in new ways (creativity), and developing an answer. *Solution construction skills* describe the ability to develop solutions that work within the context of a specific organization. To do so, leaders must be objective, self-reflective, understand the system, work within organizational restrictions, anticipate the long-term impact of changes, and so forth. They also need insight into the needs, goals, and problems of different organizational groups. *Social judgment skills* are used to implement the solution. Leaders must build consensus as well as coordinate the activities of departments and individuals. Persuasion, negotiation, and other influence tactics (see chapter 6) are critical to rallying support for proposals. Knowledge is the key to effectively using all three of these skill sets. Effective leaders have developed complex schemas (see chapter 2). They recognize prototypical problems; identify relevant problem-solving strategies based on past experience; master concepts they then can combine in creative ways; understand their tasks, organizations, and colleagues; know how to exercise influence, and so forth.

To test their theory, Mumford and his colleagues conducted a research program with officers from the United States Army. They discovered that skill levels increased with rank. Mid-level leaders demonstrated more complex knowledge than junior level officers. Senior-level officers mastered new knowledge and skills most rapidly and scored highest on measures of problem solving, social construction, and social judgment. In order to progress, junior leaders need to develop their abilities to solve problems and their knowledge of relevant situations.

The skills approach underlies leadership development by emphasizing that leaders are *made* not born. No matter what our particular personality traits, we can learn to become better leaders by gaining further knowledge and developing our skills. Time spent in leadership classes and workshops is time well spent. Theorists not only identify capabilities that are critical to overall leadership effectiveness, they also highlight the fact that senior leaders often need different skills than lower-level leaders.

Despite its insights, the skills/capabilities approach suffers from significant limitations. There is no universally accepted list of skills just as there is no universal list of traits. Instead, writers offer a variety of skills lists, many of which are not supported by research. The conclusions of Mumford and his colleagues, who studied military officers, may not generalize to other settings.

The Relational Approach to Leadership

The relational approach to leadership shifts the focus from the characteristics of leaders and followers (traits and situational) and leadership behaviors (functional and skills) to the relationships among leaders and followers. The relational approach has progressed through an early phase focusing on vertical dyadic relationships to the notion of leader-member exchange.

Vertical Dyad Linkage Model

The most significant early relational approach to leadership was the vertical dyad linkage (VDL) model developed by George Graen and his associates.[36] Until the development of VDL theory, researchers believed that leaders used the same style, on average, with all the members of the group. Graen and his colleagues discovered that this was not the case. They found that leaders treat individual followers differently and that followers offered differing descriptions of the same leader. Some followers reported their relationship with a leader to be very positive. These followers indicated they felt high levels of trust and respect for the leader. In such relationships, followers felt a sense of duty and obligation to the leader and to the tasks of the group or organization. Other followers perceived their relationship with the leader to be strained. In these cases, the perception of the leader and the importance of the work being done were lower. These variations in linkage patterns resulted in two types of relationships: in-group and out-group. Members of the "in-group" play the role of assistant, lieutenant, or advisor to a leader. The remaining followers will be members of the "out-group." Leader-follower exchanges differ in each group. *High levels of trust, mutual influence, and support characterize in-group exchanges.* In-group exchanges allow for wider latitude in task development; followers are granted more responsibility and influence in decision making. *Low levels of trust and support characterize out-group exchanges.* Authoritarian and task-oriented leadership communication is often evident in out-group exchanges.

Leaders make choices regarding the inclusion of followers in both the in-group and the out-group. Such factors as compatibility, liking, similarity in values, and personality influence in-group/out-group determinations. Leaders and followers also negotiate their respective roles. The leader might offer a follower more responsibility. If the follower accepts these additional duties and performs well, he or she may become a member of the in-group. Conversely, a follower may volunteer to work extra hours and move from the out-group to the in-group. (Box 3.7 highlights how in-groups and out-groups develop in the classroom.)

To fulfill leader expectations, members of the out-group must meet formal role expectations, such as following company procedures, meeting deadlines, or submitting work containing few errors. In-group members are expected to work harder, be more committed, take on more administrative duties, and be more loyal to the leader than out-group members. The assistance of committed followers can be very useful to a leader. Nonetheless, the leader must be mindful of maintaining the in-group relationship by paying attention to the needs of in-group followers. An in-group relationship is reciprocal; both the leader and the follower must maintain it.

Leader-Member Exchange Theory

Vertical dyad linkage marked the first stage of what was to become leader-member exchange (LMX) theory. LMX theory focuses on the quality of the relationship between an individual leader and follower rather than on categorizing followers as either a member of the in-group or the out-group.[37] The quality of a

---

Box 3.7   Case Study   **In-Groups and Out-Groups in the Classroom**

Todd Higuera recently joined the faculty of Belmont University after earning his PhD. This is his first full-time teaching position. Belmont, a branch of the larger state university system, is known primarily as a teaching institution. Professor Higuera is expected to publish the occasional book or article, but most of his success will depend on his performance in the classroom. So far Todd is off to a good start. His evaluations are high, with students reporting that he is both enthusiastic and knowledgeable about his subject.

There is one consistent negative thread in the feedback that Todd receives that might cause him difficulty when he comes up for promotion and tenure. A number of students rate him low on the item on the instructor evaluation form that reads "Treats all students fairly." Written comments on the form include such remarks as: "The instructor plays favorites"; "I felt ignored in the class"; and "I am concerned that some students are given second chances while others are not." Todd finds these comments particularly troubling since he believes that it is unethical to treat people unfairly and, coming from a Hispanic background, he has experienced discrimination firsthand. Yet, as the primary instructor in a small major, he knows some students better than others since he has taught them in several classes. He can see how students he meets for the first time could think that they were at a disadvantage.

The beginning of the semester is approaching, and Todd wants to address the fairness issue before he creates his syllabi for the upcoming term. He is open to advice from both students and his fellow professors.

Discussion Questions

1. What instructor behaviors create in-groups and out-groups in the classroom? How do these behaviors influence student performance?

2. Which of the behaviors you identified might be occurring in this case?

3. What advice would you give to Dr. Higuera for building high-quality relationships with his students?

4. Should Dr. Higuera expect that he can establish in-group relationships with all of his students? A majority of them? Can he still be perceived as fair if he doesn't?

5. What responsibilities do students have for creating high-quality relationships with their instructors? What steps should they take to help this happen?

---

leader-follower relationship (which ranges from low LMX to high LMX) can be plotted along a continuum using the scale found in the self-assessment in box 3.8.

LMX researchers report that there is a link between relational quality and personal and organizational effectiveness. Followers who have high LMX relationships with their leaders are:[38]

- more productive (produce a higher quality and quantity of work)
- more satisfied with their jobs
- less likely to quit
- enjoy better psychological health
- more satisfied with their supervisors
- more committed to the organization

- more satisfied with the communication practices of the group and organization
- clearer about their roles in the organization
- more likely to go beyond their job duties to help other employees
- more successful in their careers
- likely to provide honest feedback
- highly motivated
- more influential in their organizations

Box 3.8 Self-Assessment	Recommended Measure of Leader-Member Exchange (LMX-7)[39]

Directions: Rate your relationship as a follower with a leader of your choice by circling the numbers preceding your responses to these seven items. You can also rate your relationship as a leader with a follower of your choice (leader items are in parentheses).

1. Do you know where you stand with your leader; that is, do you usually know how satisfied your leader is with what you do? (Does your member usually know?)

   (1) Rarely   (2) Occasionally   (3) Sometimes   (4) Fairly Often   (5) Very Often

2. How well does your leader understand your job problems and needs? (How well do you understand the problems and needs of your member?)

   (1) Not a Bit   (2) A Little   (3) A Fair Amount   (4) Quite a Bit   (5) A Great Deal

3. How well does your leader recognize your potential? (How well do you recognize member potential?)

   (1) Not at All   (2) A Little   (3) Moderately   (4) Mostly   (5) Fully

4. Regardless of how much formal authority he/she has built into his/her position, what are the chances that your leader would use his/her power to help you solve problems in your work? (What are the chances that you would use your power to help a member solve problems?)

   (1) None   (2) Small   (3) Moderate   (4) High   (5) Very High

5. Again, regardless of the amount of formal authority your leader has, what are the chances that he/she would "bail you out," at his/her expense? (What are the chances that you would use your power to cover a member's shortcomings?)

   (1) None   (2) Small   (3) Moderate   (4) High   (5) Very High

6. I have enough confidence in my leader that I would defend and justify his/her decision if he/she were not present to do so. (Your member would support your decisions.)

   (1) Strongly Disagree   (2) Disagree   (3) Neutral   (4) Agree   (5) Strongly Agree

7. How would you characterize your working relationship with your leader? (How would your member characterize your working relationship?)

   (1) Extremely Ineffective   (2) Worse Than Average   (3) Average   (4) Better Than Average
   (5) Extremely Effective

Scoring: Total the numbers preceding your responses. The higher the score, the better your perceived relationship with your leader. To determine if your view matches that of your relational partner, compare your rankings with those of your leader or follower.

While Graen and his colleagues initially believed that leaders could only maintain a few high-quality relationships with trusted assistants due to limited time and resources, they later became convinced that leaders should attempt to build high-quality partnerships with *all* their followers, not just a chosen few. This marked a shift to the third stage of LMX theory—leadership making. Leadership making focuses on how leaders can establish partnerships with followers. Not all relationships will become partnerships, but leaders have a duty to make the offer of partnership to all of their followers. Doing so will increase the number of high-quality relationships, bond the organizational unit (build social capital), and improve performance. Graen and Mary Uhl-Bien offer a three-phase model of the leadership-making process.[40] In the first phase—*stranger*—leaders and followers are essentially strangers who occupy their respective roles. The rules and the organizational hierarchy determine their interactions, which are largely formal in nature. The leader makes requests, and the follower complies based on self-interest. In the second phase—*acquaintanceship*—the parties begin to build more productive working relationships. They begin to share social as well as task information. This is a testing phase, though, and the relationship could return to phase one. The third and final phase—*partnership*—marks the highest level of relational maturity. Leaders and followers exert mutual influence on one another, sharing a wide range of task and social information. They enjoy a high level of mutual trust, respect, and sense of obligation. Each feels empowered to provide criticism and support to the other. Their relationship has expanded well beyond the formal work contract and work rules that define the stranger phase.

Interest in LMX theory has not waned, even though it was first developed decades ago, making it one of the "most durable theories for describing supervisory behavior and understanding its consequences."[41] In fact, over half of the articles published on LMX were published recently along with an Oxford University Press handbook devoted entirely to Leader-Member Exchange.[42] There are several possible reasons for the enduring popularity of the relational approach to leadership. First, it is confirmed by our personal experiences. We have all experienced in-group and out-group relationships. Teachers, coaches, and bosses, among others in leadership roles, often spend more time with and give more attention to those students, team members, and employees they prefer. We know firsthand the costs of being in low-LMX relationships and the benefits of high-LMX relationships. Second, there is a strong link between relational quality and important individual and organizational outcomes. Developing relational partnerships pays off for the individual and the group.

Third, LMX theory has matured, moving from descriptive to prescriptive while becoming more equitable. In its early stages, the model described differences in leader-follower relationships and appeared to promote inequality. Leaders could only develop quality exchanges with a few followers and the rest of the group suffered as a result. Now theorists offer prescriptive advice to leaders, urging them to develop high-LMX relationships with as many followers as possible. Following this advice fosters justice and fairness. When they share leadership duties with subordinates, leaders should encourage followers to develop high member-member exchange (MMX) relationships with one another. Fourth, the theory highlights the importance of communication. Communication patterns differ between in- and out-groups. Partnerships are built and maintained through communication.

While influential, LMX theory has not escaped criticism.[43] Critics point out that a variety of measures have been used to measure leader-member exchanges, generating confusion and making it hard to compare the results of different studies. Superiors and subordinates often don't see "eye to eye" when it comes to judging the quality of their relationships, with leaders giving higher ratings. Some observers complain that LMX theorists provide little practical advice to leaders who want to develop relational partnerships. Others believe that the LMX model, despite its evolution, still promotes inequality and injustice. These appear to be valid criticisms, but the relational approach will likely continue to guide leadership scholarship for decades to come. (Turn to the Cultural Connections feature at the end of the chapter for a description of another relationally based approach to leadership.)

∿ CHAPTER TAKEAWAYS

- Over the past 130 years, seven primary approaches for understanding and explaining leadership have evolved: the *traits approach*, the *situational approach*, the *functional approach*, the *skills approach*, the *relational approach*, the *transformational approach*, and the *authentic approach*.

- The traits approach asserts that nature plays a key role in determining leadership potential. Individuals are born with certain characteristics that equip them to become leaders and to function effectively. Key leader traits appear to be cognitive abilities, locus of control, personality, motivation, and social intelligence.

- The situational approach argues that the traits, skills, and behaviors necessary for effective leadership vary from situation to situation. Two commonly studied situational approaches are path-goal theory, and Hersey and Blanchard's situational leadership theory.

- According to path-goal theory, leaders influence followers' perceptions of the task and the goal. When choosing a communication style, consider two factors: the nature of the followers and the nature of the task. Directive leader communication is most effective when followers are inexperienced or when the task is unstructured. Supportive leadership is appropriate when the task is stressful and dissatisfying and followers lack confidence and commitment. Participative leader communication is best when tasks are unstructured and followers feel uncertain as a result. Achievement-oriented leadership boosts follower's confidence that they can reach challenging goals and is most effective when performing unstructured tasks.

- According to the situational leadership approach, you should focus on the job maturity and psychological maturity of followers. A telling style (high task/low relationship) succeeds with followers who are both unskilled at the tasks and unwilling to do the job. A selling style (high task/high relationship) should be used with followers who lack skills but are willing. A participating style (low task/high relationship) should be employed when dealing with skilled followers who are unwilling. A delegating style (low task/low relationship) generates the best results with followers who are both skilled and willing.

- The underlying assumption of the functional approach is that leaders perform certain functions that allow a group or organization to operate effectively. You will likely be considered a leader if you perform (1) task-related roles that contribute to the organization and completion of group tasks and/or (2) group-building and maintenance roles that develop and maintain supportive and healthy interpersonal relationships. However, you will undermine your group's effectiveness if you play selfish individual roles that are disruptive.

- The skills approach identifies the competencies (capabilities) leaders need to carry out their functions. Unlike traits, we can develop skills through training and experience. Three notable skills typologies are the three-skill model (technical, human, conceptual), task competencies (leading oneself, leading others, leading the organization), and problem-solving capabilities (problem solving, solution construction, social judgment).

- The relational approach to leadership shifts the focus from the characteristics of leaders and followers (traits and situational), leadership behaviors (functional) and leader capabilities (skills) to the relationships between leaders and followers. According to vertical dyad linkage (VDL) theory, some followers (in-group members) enjoy a closer relationship or linkage with their leaders than other followers (members of the out-group). In-group leader-follower exchanges are marked by higher levels of trust, mutual influence, and support than out-group exchanges.

- Leader-member exchange (LMX) theory focuses on the quality of the relationship between an individual leader and follower. Followers in high-quality (high-LMX) relationships are generally more productive and satisfied. You should try to establish partnerships with all of your followers, not just a few. The greater the number of high-quality relationships you build with followers, the higher the likely performance of your work group or organization.

∼ APPLICATION EXERCISES

1. Make a list of the five traits you think every leader must have. Then pair up with someone else and create a joint list consisting of ONLY the traits you both had on your individual lists. Then repeat the process, creating a joint list in groups of four, eight and so on until the entire class meets together. Put the surviving traits (those that appeared on everyone's lists) on the board. Were any left? What does this exercise say about the potential strengths or weaknesses of the trait approach?

2. Complete the Motivation to Lead Scale on p. 79. What motivates you to lead? How strong is your motivation to lead? What accounts for your score? How

has your motivation to lead (or lack of motivation) contributed to your performance as a leader?

3. Reflect on a time when you were part of a successful (or unsuccessful) group. Apply path-goal theory to account for the group's success or failure. What was the nature of the task and the makeup of group members? What obstacles did the group face and how did the leader help the group overcome these barriers? What leadership style did the leader use and was it effective? Why or why not?

4. Discuss the Hersey and Blanchard situational leadership approach (on pp. 84–86) with someone who is currently in a management position. Ask the person to evaluate this model's effectiveness given his/her past experiences. Share your findings with others in class.

5. Either alone or in a group, make a list of leadership functions. Try to engage in these behaviors the next time you participate in a group. See if others look to you for leadership because you are acting like a leader.

6. Next time you are in a problem-solving group, make a list of positive and negative leadership actions you observe from other group members. Compare your list with the Benne and Sheats typology on pp. 88–90. Compare the similarities and differences in the two lists.

7. Describe a time when you or someone you know became a leader by communicating like a leader. Identify the specific behaviors that led to you or the person you observed becoming the leader. What can you learn from the situation to apply to other leadership situations? Write up your analysis and conclusions.

8. Complete the LMX scale on p. 97. What factors contribute to your ratings on each of the items? What can you do to improve your relationship with this leader or follower?

9. Analyze your skills (capabilities) as a leader using one of the skills lists described in the chapter. What skills do you already possess? Which ones do you need to develop? How will you acquire these competencies? Outline a strategy for doing so.

10. Conduct interviews with several effective leaders. Try to identify which approach to leadership provides the best explanation for their success. Share your results with your classmates. As an alternative, identify the skills they need to succeed in their leadership positions.

11. Create a list of concepts from the chapter that can help you become a more effective leader. Gather with others and create a group list. Compare your group's list with those of other groups.

～ CULTURAL CONNECTIONS: PATERNALISTIC LEADERSHIP[44]

Nearly all the theories in the first section of this text were developed in the United States. Researchers then determine how well these ideas translate to Europe, Africa, Latin America, Asia, and other regions. In contrast, paternalism is an approach to leadership that has its origins outside the United States. Investigators then study how paternalistic leadership translates to U.S. society.

Paternalistic leaders act as father figures who treat subordinates like family members. They take a personal interest in the lives of employees both on and off the job. For example, bosses may attend the weddings, funerals, and baptisms of workers and their families. In addition to being concerned and supportive, paternalistic leaders act as authority figures who make decisions for followers. Followers willingly submit to their power in return for their care and protection. Paternalistic leadership shares elements in common with leader-member exchange theory. Like LMX, paternalism is a relationship-based approach to leadership. High-quality relationships encourage leaders to invest in their followers and followers to offer their trust and loyalty to their leaders. Both LMX and paternalistic leadership spotlight the importance of supportive communication and the exchange of resources.

Paternalism is a popular form of leadership in Asia, Latin America, and the Middle East. It is effective in traditional cultures that believe that fathers should be caring but demanding (India, for example), as well as in societies like China and Mexico that value the collective good and hierarchical relationships. Obligation and loyalty play an important role in these cultures and followers want their leaders to be involved in their personal lives. Researchers in Turkey, Malaysia, Japan, China, India, and Mexico report that paternalistic leadership practices increase organizational commitment levels and foster trust and harmony.

Paternalism is not as well accepted in cultures (Israel, Germany, Canada) that value individualism and equality. Constituents in these societies are likely to take offense when leaders get involved in their personal lives, seeing such interest as a violation of privacy. They have more difficulty accepting the idea that leaders should have significantly more power and status than they do. Some Western leadership scholars believe that paternalistic leaders are oppressive dictators who hide their true intentions in order to get what they want from followers. However, these critics may be confusing paternalism with authoritarianism. Genuine or benevolent paternalistic leaders are follower centered, not self-centered, which keeps them from abusing their authority. In addition, benevolent leaders demonstrate high character by setting a good example and using their power to serve others.

In one study, employees from both India and the United States were more committed to their organizations when their leaders acted in a paternalistic fashion. This suggests that elements of paternalistic leadership may have universal appeal. Followers from a variety of cultures apparently appreciate supportive leaders who express genuine interest in their welfare.

∼ LEADERSHIP ON THE BIG SCREEN: *CONCUSSION*

Starring: Will Smith, Alec Baldwin, Albert Brooks, Gugu Mbatha-Raw

Rating: PG-13 for mature subject matter and language

Synopsis: Allegheny County (Pittsburgh) forensic pathologist Bennet Omalu (played by Smith) conducts an autopsy on the body of Pittsburgh Steeler football hall of famer Mike Webster in 2002 to determine the cause of Webster's bizarre behavior. Depressed, confused, and frequently enraged, Webster ended up living in his truck and dying of heart failure at age 50. Omalu discovers that Webster's brain is riddled with tiny packets of tau protein, which destroy reasoning and emotional control. He names this brain pattern CTE: chronic traumatic encephalopathy. The brains of players Terry Long, Justin Strzeleczyk, and Andre Waters show the same damage. With the help of former Steeler team doctor Justin Bailes (Baldwin) and his boss, county coroner Cyril Wecht (Brooks), Omalu tries to convince the National Football League to acknowledge that players are in danger. League officials respond by denying that there is any link between repeated football collisions and brain trauma. Instead, they put pressure on Dr. Omalu to back off his claims. Wecht comes under federal indictment (charges were later dropped) and Omalu and his wife (Mbatha-Raw) are forced to relocate to California. Omalu is later vindicated when five thousand former players successfully sue the NFL for failing to acknowledge or treat brain injuries.

Chapter Links: cognitive abilities, internal locus of control, Big Five personality traits, motivation, leadership skills, problem solving, leader-member exchange

4

Transformational and Charismatic Leadership

The new leader is one who commits people to action, who converts followers into leaders, and who may convert leaders into agents of change.
—*Warren Bennis*

OVERVIEW

The Transformational Approach to Leadership

The Characteristics of Transformational Leadership
   Creative
   Interactive
   Visionary
   Empowering
   Passionate

Perspectives on Charisma
   The Sociological Approach
   The Behavioral/Attribution Approach
   The Communication Approach

Transformational and Charismatic Leadership: Interchangeable or Distinct?

Alternative Approaches to Outstanding Leadership
   Authentic Leadership
   The CIP Model

The Transformational Approach to Leadership

Beginning in the late 1970s, the transformational approach emerged as a new perspective for understanding and explaining leadership. The transformational approach was first outlined by James MacGregor Burns. He compared traditional leadership, which he labeled as *transactional*, with a more "complex" and "potent" type of leadership he called *transformational*.[1] The motivational appeals of the transactional leader are designed to satisfy basic human needs; the appeals of the transformational leader go beyond those basic needs to satisfy a follower's higher-level needs.

According to Abraham Maslow, five hierarchically arranged human needs exist: physiological, safety, belonging and love, self-esteem, and self-actualization.[2] (See figure 4.1.) The most basic human needs are physiological. Before we can concern ourselves with other needs, we must secure the basic necessities: oxygen, food, water, and sleep. If you study for several days without sleeping, the need for sleep takes precedence over any other concern. Once physiological needs are satisfied, we can turn our attention to the second level of the hierarchy, safety needs. Humans seek predictability and protection. We are generally most comfortable in environments that are familiar and free from danger. If you become lost in the desert in the heat of the day, one of your first priorities will be finding a safer, cooler environment. After environmental factors are satisfied, social belonging and love needs surface. Humans desire affiliation with others. Whether you are a member of

Figure 4.1   Maslow's Hierarchy of Needs

a group or an organization, involved in a friendship or an intimate relationship, all these situations involve seeking social connections with others.

Self-esteem needs become important after the first three levels have been reasonably well satisfied. Self-esteem needs relate to our desire to feel good about ourselves. Self-esteem consists of internal feelings of competence, respect, and self-worth as well as external feedback and recognition that support positive esteem. The feeling of satisfaction you get when you finish a difficult assignment, and the "A" your instructor gives you for your hard work, help to satisfy your self-esteem needs.

When all other needs are satisfied, we can turn our attention to self-actualization needs. Self-actualization is the process of applying your own unique set of interests and abilities to become the best person you can possibly become. If you are self-actualized, Maslow claims you will feel a sense of fulfillment and purpose. He also suggests those who achieve self-actualization have a strong urge to help others satisfy their self-actualization needs.

For Burns, the distinction between transactional and transformational leadership is dichotomous—leaders are either transactional or they are transformational. Subsequent research proposed that transformational leadership augments the effects of transactional leadership.[3] Similar to the hierarchy Maslow described, lower-level transactional leadership is the foundation for higher-level transformational leadership. As leadership expert Bernard Bass explains: "Many of the great transformational leaders, including Abraham Lincoln, Franklin Delano Roosevelt, and John F. Kennedy, did not shy away from being transactional. They were able to move the nation as well as play petty politics."[4]

The transactional leader is most concerned with the satisfaction of physiological, safety, and belonging needs. To meet these needs, a transactional leader exchanges rewards or privileges for desirable outcomes—much the way a Marine drill sergeant would trade a weekend pass for a clean barracks. Transformational leaders also attempt to satisfy the basic needs of followers, but they go beyond mere exchange by engaging the total person in an attempt to satisfy the higher-level needs of self-esteem and self-actualization. Transformational leadership is empowering and inspirational; it elevates leaders and followers to higher levels of motivation and morality. According to Burns, "The result of transforming leadership is a relationship of mutual stimulation and elevation that converts followers into leaders and may convert leaders into moral agents."[5]

*The function of leadership is to
produce more leaders, not more followers.*

—Ralph Nader

In a series of research studies involving groups of military leaders, university students, corporate managers, and educators, Bernard Bass and his associates looked at the factors of transactional and transformational leadership.[6] These researchers identified seven leadership factors: two dimensions of transactional leadership, four dimensions of transformational leadership, and one nonleadership dimension (see box 4.1).

| **Box 4.1** | **Dimensions of Transactional and Transformational Leadership[7]** |

Transactional Leadership Factors

Contingent reward: Provide rewards for effort; recognize good performance.

Management-by-exception: Maintain the status quo; intervene when subordinates do not meet acceptable performance levels; initiate corrective action to improve performance.

Transformational Leadership Factors

Charisma: Provide vision and a sense of mission; inspire; build trust and respect.

Individualized consideration: Exhibit considerate and supportive behavior directed toward each individual subordinate; coach and advise.

Inspiration: Communicate high expectations; use symbols to focus efforts and enhance understanding of goals.

Intellectual stimulation: Promote innovative ways of viewing situations; stimulate intelligent problem solving and decision making.

Nonleadership Factor

Laissez-faire (abdication): Abdicate leadership responsibility; avoid problem solving and decision making.

Transactional leadership is primarily passive. The behaviors most often associated with transactional leadership are establishing the criteria for rewarding followers and maintaining the status quo. Those leaders who went beyond transaction and engaged in transformational leadership demonstrated active behaviors that included providing a sense of mission, inspiration, emotional support, and intellectual stimulation. As Bass notes:

> Unlike the transactional leader who indicates how current needs of followers can be fulfilled, the transformational leader sharply arouses or alters the strength of needs that may have lain dormant. . . . It is leadership that is transformational that can bring about the big differences and big changes in groups, organizations, and societies.[8]

Whether or not a leader exhibits transformational behavior may be directly related to his or her communication skills. Ted Zorn discovered a relationship between the complexity of a leader's communication system and the tendency to exhibit transformational leadership behavior.[9] Zorn found those leaders with the most developed cognitive and communicative abilities were the most likely to be perceived as transformational by their followers.

Evidence from a large body of studies conducted in a variety of settings (military units, schools, religious congregations, *Fortune 500* companies) demonstrates that transformational leaders are highly effective. Their followers give them higher evaluations and are more committed, satisfied, and engaged. Their organizations, in turn, achieve outstanding results: more military victories, greater profits, higher quality, and improved service.[10] (Complete the self-assessment in box 4.2 to determine if you engage in transformational behaviors.)

Box 4.2 Self-Assessment	**Transformational Leadership Scale**[11]

Instructions: Think about a situation in which you either assumed or were given a leadership role. Think about your own behaviors within this context. To what extent does each of the following statement characterize your leadership orientation?

Very little			A moderate amount			Very much
1	2	3	4	5	6	7

_____ 1. Have a clear understanding of where we are going.

_____ 2. Paint an interesting picture of the future for my group.

_____ 3. Am always seeking new opportunities for the organization/group.

_____ 4. Inspire others with my plans for the future.

_____ 5. Am able to get others to be committed to my dreams.

_____ 6. Lead by "doing," rather than simply by "telling."

_____ 7. Provide a good model for others to follow.

_____ 8. Lead by example.

_____ 9. Foster collaboration among group members.

_____ 10. Encourage employees to be "team players."

_____ 11. Get the group to work together for the same goal.

_____ 12. Develop a team attitude and spirit among employees.

_____ 13. Show that I expect a lot from others

_____ 14. Insist on only the best performance.

_____ 15. Will not settle for second best.

_____ 16. Act without considering the feelings of others.

_____ 17. Show respect for the personal feelings of others.

_____ 18. Behave in a manner thoughtful of the personal needs of others.

_____ 19. Treat others without considering their personal feelings.

_____ 20. Challenge others to think about old problems in new ways.

_____ 21. Ask questions that prompt others to think.

_____ 22. Stimulate others to rethink the way they do things.

_____ 23. Have ideas that challenge others to reexamine some of their basic assumptions about work.

_____ 24. Always give positive feedback when others perform well.

_____ 25. Give special recognition when others' work is very good.

_____ 26. Commend others when they do a better-than-average job.

_____ 27. Personally compliment others when they do outstanding work.

_____ 28. Frequently does not acknowledge the good performance of others.

(continued)

Scoring: Reverse your scores on questions 16, 19, and 28. There are seven dimension scores to be computed. *Articulate vision*—Sum your responses to questions 1–5 and divide by 5. *Provide appropriate model*—Sum your responses to questions 6-8 and divide by 3. *Foster acceptance of goals*—Sum your responses to questions 9–12 and divide by 4. *High performance expectations*—Sum your responses to questions 13–15 and divide by 3. *Individual support*—Sum your responses to questions 16-19 and divide by 4. *Intellectual stimulation*—Sum your responses to questions 20–23 and divide by 4. *Transactional leader behaviors*—Sum your responses to questions 24–28 and divide by 5.

My scores are

Articulate vision _____

Role model _____

Foster goal acceptance _____

Performance expectations _____

Individual support _____

Intellectual stimulation _____

Transactional leader behavior _____

A high score of 6 and greater reflects a strong orientation to engage in each of these behaviors. A low score of 2 or less reflects that you are unlikely to engage in each of these behaviors.

The Characteristics of Transformational Leadership

Many researchers have attempted to describe the characteristics of transformational leaders. In one of the earliest projects, Tom Peters and Robert Waterman studied 62 successful American companies. They discovered that excellent companies were most often blessed with extraordinary leadership.[12] Warren Bennis and Burt Nanus studied 90 successful leaders from business, government, education, and sports in an attempt to identify the strategies used by transformational leaders.[13] James Kouzes and Barry Posner surveyed more than 1,300 managers in order to discover practices common to successful transformational leaders.[14] Bruce Avolio and Bernard Bass developed a series of leadership case studies suggesting the most successful leaders exhibit transformational leadership behaviors.[15]

The characteristics of transformational leaders identified by all of these researchers are strikingly similar. Five primary characteristics appear, in one form or another, in all of the classification systems dealing with extraordinary leaders. Transformational leaders are *creative, interactive, visionary, empowering*, and *passionate*. Further, since transformational leadership can convert followers into leaders themselves, these characteristics are often filtered throughout transformed groups and organizations.

Creative

Transformational leaders are innovative and foresighted. They constantly challenge the status quo by seeking out new ideas, products, and ways of performing tasks. Transformational leaders recognize that satisfaction with the status quo poses a serious threat to group or organization survival. Resting on past achievements can blind members to new opportunities and potential problems. As organizations such as AOL, Blockbuster, Circuit City, Bear Stearns, and Borders Books have discovered, the most successful organizations are often in the most danger. Transformational leaders ignore the adage, "If it ain't broke, don't fix it." Instead, the transformational leader adopts the attitude, "If it ain't broke, you're not looking hard enough."[16] As Toyota executive Iwao Isomura explains, "Success is the best reason to change."[17]

The Process of Creativity

To clarify the relationship between creativity and leadership, we first need to understand how the creative process works. Creativity, like leadership, is based on our capacity for creating and manipulating symbols. Not only does creative problem solving involve abstract thought (which is made possible by language), but creative ideas nearly always take a particular symbolic form—as chemical formulas, sentences, drawings, ad slogans, and so on.

Experts suggest that creativity involves making new combinations or associations with existing elements. Educator Sidney Parnes, for example, describes creating as "the fresh and relevant association of thoughts, facts, ideas, etc. in a new configuration."[18] Psychologist Sarnoff Mednick defines creativity as "the forming of associative elements into new combinations which either meet specified requirements or are in some way useful."[19]

Creative thinking is frequently referred to as divergent or lateral thinking because it requires looking at problems from a number of different perspectives, thinking in broad categories, and producing a variety of solutions. Once a creative idea is generated through lateral thinking, however, the concept is refined through analysis, evaluation, and other convergent (vertical) thinking strategies. For example, to develop his theory of relativity, Einstein used lateral thinking to visualize himself as a passenger holding a mirror as he rode on a ray of light. He determined that his image would never reach the mirror because both he and the glass would move at the speed of light. In contrast, a stationary observer could catch Einstein's reflection in a mirror as the scientist passed by. Einstein started work on his theory of relativity as a result of this visualization. In order to complete the task, he worked for a decade using such vertical thought processes as calculation and reasoning.

One widely used description of creative problem solving was developed by George Graham Wallas. Based on research done with problem solvers, Wallas claimed that there are four steps to the creative process.[20]

1. *Preparation.* Creativity often begins with a conscious attempt to define and solve a problem. The preparation stage involves days, months, and even years of reading, gathering information, and repeating experiments. Com-

posers, for example, may spend more than 10 years in study before their first important compositions are finished. The more extensive the preparation, the more likely the creative solution. As two-time Nobel Prize winner Linus Pauling once pointed out: "The best way to get a good idea is to get lots of ideas." In addition, valuable new insights often come from unrelated fields of study. Take the case of Steve Jobs (profiled in the Leadership on the Big Screen feature at the end of the chapter) who co-developed the Apple computer. Before starting Apple, Jobs designed video games at Atari. He attributes his success in developing the game Breakout to what he learned about movement and perception in a college dance class.[21]

2. *Incubation.* During the incubation period, the conscious mind shifts to other interests and the subconscious has an opportunity to make new associations, which lead to creative problem solving. To see how the incubation process works, build in an incubation period as you write your next major paper. Work as hard as you can for a few hours, and then turn your attention to other matters. When you return to write, you may find that ideas come more easily.

3. *Illumination.* Ideas may appear as sudden inspirations during the creative process. These flashes of insight come during the illumination stage, often when a person is alone and more sensitive to intuitive messages.

Carol Orsag Madigan and Ann Elwood compiled the stories of many such inspirational moments in a book called *Brainstorms and Thunderbolts.*[22] Here are a few examples of famous flashes of illumination:

- While in the bathtub, the ancient Greek scientist Archimedes discovered the principle that "a body immersed in liquid loses as much in weight as the weight of the fluid it displaces." Afterwards he celebrated his discovery by running naked through the streets, shouting "Eureka!" ("I have found it!")

- The formula for the structure of benzene came to German chemist Friedrich August Kekule (1847) in a dream. Dreams were also a source of story plots for Robert Louis Stevenson. Mary Shelley, on the other hand, got her inspiration for the novel *Frankenstein* during a sleepless night.

- William Booth, the founder of the Salvation Army, came home after a walk through the slums of London to announce to his wife, "Darling, I have found my destiny."

- Mary Baker Eddy used her recovery from a fall on the ice to launch a new faith—Christian Science.

4. *Verification.* In this last stage, the creator develops the ideas that have come through preparation, incubation, and illumination. Verification can include writing poetry and novels, testing mathematical theorems, or checking with suppliers and running cost data.

Becoming a Creative Leader

One common misconception about creativity is the belief that only a few people are blessed with creative ability. According to this view, some outstanding individuals like William Shakespeare, Marie Pasteur, Bill Gates, or artist Georgia O'Keefe have large amounts of creative talent while most people have little or none. Research suggests, however, that everyone can think creatively—not just a few creative superstars. Studies of creative people reveal that they do not fit a single profile. Creative individuals are both aggressive and passive, introverted and extroverted, unstable and adjusted. Creative people share only three characteristics: (1) they are hardworking and persevering, (2) they are independent and nonconformist in their thinking, and (3) they are comfortable with complexity and ambiguity.[23]

Becoming a creative leader means thinking more creatively yourself, while at the same time helping followers develop their creative abilities. To achieve these goals, leaders need to adopt a problem-finding perspective, learn to tolerate failure, and focus collective attention on innovation.

Identifying new problems is called the ***problem-finding orientation*** to creativity.[24] In order to develop a problem-finding orientation, keep in constant touch with sources both inside and outside the organization or group—employees, members of other task forces, customers, stockholders, government officials, media outlets, industry officials, and others. These linkages will reveal gaps between what the organization is and should be doing, shifts in the political or social climate, and so on. In addition, go looking for "trouble" by posing questions that challenge current products, practices, procedures, and beliefs. Psychologists Robert Kriegel and David Brandt call this process "hunting for sacred cows."[25] Sacred cows are outmoded, usually invisible ways of doing things that blind organizations to new opportunities. For example, many reports, proposals, and publications could be eliminated because nobody reads them. To round up sacred cows, leaders should listen to complaints, identify and analyze basic assumptions, and form cow-hunting groups. Pay particular attention to the way you spend your time. Keep a daily log for an average week and then eliminate the sacred cows by asking yourself: (1) Why am I doing this activity, and what would happen if it didn't exist? (2) Is someone else doing this task? (3) How and when did this practice come into being, and who started it? and (4) Can another person, department, or company do it faster, better, or more easily? (Application Exercise 4.4 provides practice with another problem-finding technique.)

A leader is someone who can take a group of people
to a place they don't think they can go.

—Bob Eaton

Because every creative idea carries with it the risk of failure, we need to tolerate mistakes if we hope to foster creativity in ourselves and those we lead. Creative leaders concentrate on the task rather than on what can go wrong. They recognize that failure is a significant learning tool; the only people who don't fail are those who don't try. The founder of the Johnson & Johnson company once declared: "If I wasn't making mistakes, I wasn't making decisions."[26] IBM's first president, Thomas Watson, took this philosophy to heart. After making a $10 million blunder, a young executive walked into his office and began the conversation by saying, "I guess you want my resignation." Watson replied: "You can't be serious. We've just spent $10 million educating you!"[27] Microsoft's Bill Gates likes to hire people who have made mistakes: "It shows they take risks. The way people deal with things that go wrong is an indicator of how they deal with change."[28] Tesla Motors founder Elon Musk says, "If things are not failing, you are not innovating enough."[29] One study of 90 successful public and private leaders found that they simply didn't concern themselves with failing, seeing failure as a learning tool. The researchers call this positive approach to failure the "Wallenda factor" after famed tightrope artist Karl Wallenda. In 1978 he fell to his death because he focused his energies on not falling rather than on walking across the wire.[30]

If you want to foster creativity, you need to help your group focus on generating new products, ideas, and procedures. In an organizational setting, invest your own time in project start-ups and other innovative activities. Encourage creativity by measuring and rewarding creative efforts. At 3M, for instance, innovative employees receive cash awards and are honored every year for their scientific achievements. The top 20 recipients receive a four-day holiday at the firm's corporate retreat. Under the company's dual track career system, creators don't have to move into management roles in order to earn more money or gain status.[31] Box 4.3 describes another company known for being highly innovative.

Interactive

Transformational leaders are masterful communicators able to articulate and define ideas and concepts that escape others. As suggested earlier, the process of leadership depends on the existence of symbols that facilitate coordinated action. Transformational leaders transmit their ideas through images, metaphors, and models that organize meanings for followers. Extraordinary leadership is first, and

---

Box 4.3 Case Study	**Innovation: The Soul of Google[32]**

Ask people to name the world's most innovative companies and chances are Google will appear near or at the top of the list. And for good reason. Google has revolutionized the way most of us gather information. The company's servers handle billions of searches every day. Even our language reflects the impact the company has had on our lives. We don't search for information anymore, we "Google" it.

Google was founded in 1998 when Stanford students Larry Page and Sergey Brin developed a mathematical formula to simplify online searches based on ranking websites. Prior to Google, searches were chaotic, with some companies unable to find themselves on the Web. Google's second important innovation, and the one that made the firm extremely profitable, was developing a way to make money off the service in 2001. (A number of dot.com firms went broke because they didn't generate a profit.) Advertisers, who bid on search terms, pay only for each person who clicks on an ad.

Given the firm's history, it's no wonder that innovation continues to be the "soul" of Google.[33] Company leaders realize that Google could fall victim to the next big technological advance. They hire talented, risk-taking engineers (many of them PhDs) who are more focused on problem solving rather than on generating profits. Researchers work with projects all the way to fruition instead of passing them off to other groups to perfect. According to the director of search quality, "We don't want to create different classes of engineers where the researchers get to do the really fun stuff and someone else gets to do the grunt work."[34] And creative ideas can come from anywhere in the company. A staff medical doctor successfully argued that Google had an ethical obligation to help those searching with the phrase "how to commit suicide." The top of the screen now shows the toll free number of the National Suicide Prevention Hotline. Call volume to the hotline went up nine percent soon after.

Instead of waiting to see if all the "bugs" have been worked out before launching products, engineers go "public," releasing programs and then modifying them based on input from users. They realize that not every idea will work and are on the lookout for "good failures." Good failures are those that (1) provide insights that can be applied to future projects and (2) fail rapidly, before they become too costly. Ideas are embraced based on the philosophy that if users come, then the company can figure out how to make money on the new services later. Engineers can spend 20% of their time on their own projects. In the past they could pursue any idea they wanted but executives now limit projects to those that are directly related to company strategy.

Page and Brin encourage employees to have fun. The atmosphere at company headquarters (the GooglePlex) is casual, featuring lava lamps, foosball, beanbag chairs, and massage chairs. The company founders also want information to "cross-pollinate." One way they encourage cross-pollination is by providing free meals to employees so they interact over lunch. In addition, the corporate culture is one that fosters public communication or "living out loud." According to a VP of engineering, "Everything that's done privately is done publicly here. We make decisions in public. We expect people to debate. You're supposed to engage. You're supposed to disagree."[35]

Fostering innovation has resulted in a host of new products including Gmail, Google News, Google Games, Google Scholar, Google Earth, Google+, Google Desktop, Google Spreadsheets, Instant (which displays search results while the user is still typing), and self-driving cars. Some services are more successful than others, of course. Google Video failed to unseat YouTube. (Google later bought YouTube.) Google Answers no longer takes new questions because users can go directly to websites that provide specific information. However, if the past is any indication, Google's passion for innovation will enable it to continue to play an important role in the lives of millions of users around the world.

Discussion Questions

1. Does a company need to have a history of innovation like Google in order to be highly creative? If not, how can an innovative climate be fostered?

2. What are the advantages and disadvantages of restricting what engineers can develop on their own? Do the advantages outweigh the disadvantages? Should Google leaders go back to the old system where engineers could pursue any idea they wanted?

3. Could Google's practice of going public with new ideas and then modifying them based on feedback be effective in other fields besides technology?

4. How would you define "good" failures?

5. Is there a danger in focusing first on attracting users to a new service without knowing how to make money from it?

6. Could any of the methods for fostering creativity employed at Google be used in an organization with which you are familiar?

foremost, a product of extraordinary communication. To communicate success-fully, a transformational leader must be aware of the needs and motivations of his or her followers. Only when a leader is involved with followers can he or she find ways to do things better. "Managing by wandering around" (MBWA) is one way to become involved with followers.[36] MBWA involves walking the floor, interacting with followers on a regular basis. The transformational leader engaging in MBWA does not play the role of a cop on patrol but acts as a coach whose primary activi-ties are listening, teaching, and helping followers with problems.

One organization that embodies the transformational philosophy is Johnson-ville Foods of Sheboygan, Wisconsin. At Johnsonville, traditional organizational structure was replaced in the early 1980s by self-directed work teams. Middle man-agers adopted the leadership roles of coordinators and coaches rather than the tra-ditional roles of supervisors and disciplinarians. Leaders were responsible for teaching team members how to lead themselves more effectively. In short, the pri-mary job responsibility of organizational leaders at Johnsonville Foods became one of interacting with team members.

Thomas Neff and James Citrin, senior executives at Spencer Stuart, one of the best regarded executive search firms in the world, surveyed more than 500 leaders in business and education to identify the 50 best public and private sector business lead-ers in the United States. One common trait among the 50 top-rated business leaders was the ability to communicate effectively. As Neff and Citrin explain, "Nowhere is it more critical to be a strong communicator than in leading people."[37] One of their most powerful examples is Mike Armstrong, the former CEO of AT&T. Every Monday, Armstrong brought together the company's top executives—eight to ten people—who met for the entire day to make sure the company was on track. Armstrong said the key was to "communicate, communicate, communicate. You cannot be a remote image. You've got to be touched, felt, heard, and believed."[38] This is particularly important in times of change. In the days following the September 11, 2001, terrorist attacks, Con-tinental Airlines CEO Gordon Bethune recorded a daily voice-mail message to keep all of his employees fully informed about the rapidly changing situation in their indus-try.[39] (Turn to chapter 13 for a closer look at the communication lessons to be drawn from the events of 9/11.) These examples illustrate the importance of communication to successful leadership. Indeed, the more leadership responsibility an individual has, the more likely that his or her job includes a significant communication component. Political and social leaders, CEOs, and senior executives all devote a great deal of energy to clearly communicating their message to followers.

By encouraging open communication, a leader allows followers to share their ideas and insights. The experience of the US Forest Service provides a good example of how simplifying the communication process can help foster employee participa-tion. The Eastern Region of the Forest Service had a system for suggestions that required employees to fill out a four-page form each time they had an idea. In a four-year period the region's 2,500 employees submitted 252 ideas for consideration, or about one idea per person every forty years. To see if they could improve participa-tion, Forest Service officials changed the process to make it easier for employees to communicate with their superiors. The new system allows anyone with an idea to submit a brief description by e-mail. Under the new system, employees sent in 6,000 new ideas in the first year, an average of more than two ideas per employee each year![40]

Openness to interaction and feedback extends beyond the leader/follower relationship. Transformational leaders also engage in frequent communication with suppliers, customers, and even with industry competitors. In 2002, executives from the aircraft manufacturer Boeing met with a group of global airline representatives. Leaders at Boeing scheduled the meeting to determine customer needs in the face of increasing competition from rival manufacturer Airbus. The feedback from the airline industry was clear—Boeing's customers were much more interested in fuel efficiency than the speed of an aircraft or the number of passengers that could be carried. Based on this information, Boeing scrapped its plans for a high-speed, high-cost jetliner and began work on a new fuel-efficient airplane, the 787 Dreamliner. Five years after that meeting, Boeing had orders for nearly 700 Dreamliners totaling some $114 billion in sales.[41] The manufacturing process for BMW automobiles built in Leipzig, Germany, has been streamlined by including suppliers onsite. The French auto-parts company Faurecia assembles cockpits and seats for the BMW in the plant, not at an off-site location as is the norm. As a result of the frequent interaction among employees from the two companies (workers from both companies even share the same cafeteria), custom vehicle orders can be filled in just 20 minutes, a process improvement that is central to BMW's goal of improving efficiency by 5% each year. One of the strategies for cutting costs is to solicit creative ideas from suppliers, like Faurecia. Over a three-year period some 10,000 suggestions have been offered—and about a third have been put into practice.[42]

Visionary

Communicating a vision to followers may well be the most important act of the transformational leader. A vision is a concise statement or description of the direction in which an individual, group, or organization is headed. Compelling visions provide people with a sense of purpose and encourage commitment. Followers achieve more and make more ethical decisions when they pursue a worthy goal. To be compelling, a vision must be both desirable and attainable. Uninspiring or unachievable visions are ineffective and may demoralize followers.

Warren Bennis and Burt Nanus found that transformational leaders spend a good deal of time talking with employees, clients, other leaders, and consultants before developing a vision for their organization.[43] They study the history of their organization to determine the reasons for past successes and failures; they study the present to determine current strengths, weaknesses, and resources; and they look to the future to identify possible long-term social, political, and environmental changes. The leaders then interpret the information and construct a realistic vision that fits the norms of the group and inspires followers to put forth more effort.

Burt Nanus lists four characteristics of effective visions.[44]

1. *An effective vision attracts commitment and energizes people.* People are willing, even eager, to commit to worthwhile projects. An effective vision

inspires people by transcending the bottom line. Whether it involves something that improves conditions for others (such as the development of new medical technology) or something that allows for growth and development on the part of the follower (such as increased autonomy), people are motivated to meet challenges that make life better.

2. *An effective vision creates meaning for followers.* People find meaning in their work lives. When groups and organizations share a vision, individuals see themselves not just as salesclerks or assembly workers or whatever their job description names, but as part of a team providing a valuable product or service.

3. *An effective vision establishes a standard of excellence.* Most people want to do a good job. A shared commitment to excellence provides a standard for measuring performance. Establishing a standard of excellence helps followers identify expectations and provides a model for the distinctive competence of a group or organization.

4. *An effective vision bridges the present and the future.* A vision is a mental model of a desirable and idealistic future. By bridging the present and the future, an effective vision transcends the status quo by linking what is happening now with what should happen in the future.

Extraordinary leaders at every level communicate compelling visions. Whether the vision is to have the best customer service in the industry or the fewest defects on an assembly line, a sense of direction and purpose is essential to inspired leadership. The behavior exhibited by a transformational leader provides the basis for reinforcing a vision. When the plant manager jumps into a delivery truck to rush an order to an important customer, people notice. This kind of dramatic behavior reinforces priorities and values and sets a standard for follower behavior. As James Collins and Jerry Porras explain in their book *Built to Last*, organizations with a well-articulated vision that permeates the company are most likely to prosper and have long-term success.[45] Visionary companies such as Boeing, General Electric, Nordstrom, Sony, and Walt Disney tend to be the premier market leaders in their industries. Collins and Porras found that visionary companies were more likely to prosper over long periods of time—even through multiple product cycles and changes in corporate leadership.

According to John Kotter, an effective vision is specific enough to provide real guidance to people, yet vague enough to encourage initiative and remain relevant under a variety of conditions.[46] If a vision is too specific, it may leave followers floundering once the goals it articulates are achieved. An example of an overly narrow vision statement was President John F. Kennedy's vision for NASA. In 1962, Kennedy defined NASA's vision as "landing a man on the moon and returning him safely to earth before this decade is out." When a vision this specific is achieved (as it was in 1969), followers may feel a sense of confusion regarding what to do next (as NASA did in the 1970s and 1980s).[47]

If you do not know where you are going, every road will get you nowhere.

—Henry Kissinger

More effective vision statements offer general guiding philosophies without detailing specific end results. The following vision statements are examples of well-conceived organizational visions:

Amazon.com	To be Earth's most customer-centered company, where customers can find and discover anything they might want to buy online.
American Medical Association (AMA)	To promote the art and science of medicine and the betterment of public health.
Bristol-Myers Squibb	To discover, develop and deliver innovative medicines that help patients prevail over serious diseases.
Facebook	To give people the power to share and make the world more open and connected.
Ford Motor	People working together as a lean, global enterprise for automotive leadership.
Google	To organize the world's information and make it universally accessible and useful.
McDonald's	To be our customers' favorite place and way to eat and drink.
Nike	To bring inspiration and innovation to every athlete in the world.
REI	At REI, we inspire, educate and outfit for a lifetime of outdoor adventure and stewardship.
Wendy's	To be the quality leader in everything we do.[48]

These vision statements provide a general philosophy that guides the actions of members of the organization while simultaneously reflecting key organizational values. Well-conceived vision statements evolve directly from the core values shared by members of a group or organization. (Try the self-assessment activity in box 4.4 to see how the process of developing a personal vision statement works.)

Experts have traditionally distinguished between vision and mission, arguing that the vision provides a sense of direction and an idea or image of a desirable future, while the mission is a description of the organization and how it is aligned to achieve its vision. Yet, in practice some vision statements describe the company's purpose and some mission statements are inspirational. To further confuse matters, the terms are often treated interchangeably. Whatever label is used, the research is consistent with regard to the importance of having a unifying vision. Well-articulated visions have the potential to inspire and guide organizational behavior; they are associated with higher levels of performance.[49]

| Box 4.4   Self-Assessment | Developing a Personal Vision Statement[50] |

Values are at the core of individual, group, and organizational identity. Values are relatively enduring conceptions or judgments about what we consider to be important. According to Milton Rokeach, there are two types of personal values.

1. **Terminal values.** Lifelong goals (e.g., freedom, inner harmony, salvation)

2. **Instrumental values.** Behaviors that help people achieve lifelong goals (e.g., independence, ambition, obedience)

Values guide and direct behavior. There is substantial research suggesting that a number of positive effects result from agreement between personal values and the values most prized in the organization at which we work. Agreement between personal and organizational values results in increased personal identification with the organization, higher levels of job satisfaction, greater team effectiveness, and lower turnover rates. Values play a key role in the development of vision. Try to identify your own personal vision by ranking the values on the lists below. These two lists represent key terminal and instrumental values as identified by Rokeach. There are 18 values on each list. Rank order each from 1 (most important) to 18 (least important). Remember to consider the values on each list separately. You are to create two rank-ordered lists. Many people find this to be a very difficult process. Remember, you are ranking values from most important to least important—not from important to unimportant. Because values are so central to our personality, there are few unimportant values.

Terminal Values

____ Freedom (independence, free choice)

____ Self-respect (self-esteem)

____ Mature love (sexual and spiritual intimacy)

____ An exciting life (activity)

____ A comfortable life (prosperity)

____ Family security (taking care of loved ones)

____ True friendship (close companionship)

____ Social recognition (respect, admiration)

____ Wisdom (an understanding of life)

____ Happiness (contentedness)

____ A world at peace (free of war and conflict)

____ A world of beauty (beauty of nature and art)

____ Pleasure (an enjoyable, leisurely life)

____ Equality (brotherhood, equal opportunity for all)

____ A sense of accomplishment (lasting contribution)

____ Inner harmony (freedom from inner conflict)

____ National security (protection from attack)

____ Salvation (saved, eternal life)

Instrumental Values

____ Loving (affection, tenderness)

____ Independent (self-reliant, self-sufficient)

____ Capable (competent, effective)

____ Broad minded (open minded)

____ Intellectual (intelligent, reflective)

____ Honest (sincere, truthful)

____ Responsible (dependable, reliable)

____ Ambitious (hardworking, aspiring)

____ Imaginative (daring, creative)

____ Helpful (working for the welfare of others)

____ Forgiving (willing to pardon others)

____ Logical (consistent, rational)

____ Cheerful (lighthearted, joyful)

____ Self-controlled (restrained, self-disciplined)

____ Courageous (standing up for your own beliefs)

____ Polite (courteous, well-mannered)

____ Obedient (dutiful, respectful)

____ Clean (neat, tidy)

When you complete your rankings, write down six of the top-rated values from each of your lists in the space below.

Terminal Values	Instrumental Values
1.	1.
2.	2.
3.	3.
4.	4.
5.	5.
6.	6.

Carefully examine the list of your top-rated terminal and instrumental values. Look for similarities, patterns, and themes. Using this as a starting point, try to create your own personal vision statement. Remember, this vision statement should emerge from the top-rated core values you identified. Your vision statement should be concise (usually a single sentence). Look back at the examples of well-conceived organizational vision statements on p. 119 if you need a reminder of what a vision statement looks like.

My Personal Vision Statement:

_____

_____

_____

_____

_____

Once you have developed your personal vision statement, try to shorten your statement into a slogan. A slogan is a shorter version of the vision statement you previously created. Slogans are most often associated with corporate advertising (e.g., Just Do it—Nike; One Team. One Plan. One Goal—Ford; Whole Foods, Whole People, Whole Planet—Whole Foods Market; Because I'm Worth It—L'Oreal). Write your slogan below and share it with others in your class.

My Personal Slogan:

_____

_____

_____

_____

Discussion Questions

1. How does your personal vision statement and slogan match that of your present or past employer? How do think your personal vision statement might impact your job satisfaction?

2. Based on the slogans presented, what values do you perceive to be most prized in your class?

3. How can learning what is important to us (as well as to others) help organizations operate more effectively?

4. What is the most significant thing you learned about yourself in this exercise?

> *The growth and development of people*
> *is the highest calling of leadership.*
>
> —*Harvey S. Firestone*

Empowering

Transformational leaders empower others. Even an extraordinary leader cannot accomplish a great deal without capable followers. Transformational leaders encourage participation and involvement. The exchange of ideas between leader and follower does not pose a threat to the transformational leader. Extraordinary leaders realize that individual achievement and success are the basis for team achievement and success. Transformational leaders know how to give power away and how to make others feel powerful. Transformational leaders give followers access to the funds, materials, authority, and information needed to complete tasks and to develop new ideas. (See chapter 5 for an in-depth discussion of empowerment.) These leaders allow others to make decisions rather than insisting on making all the decisions themselves. Implicit in the concept of empowerment is the fact that such autonomy encourages employees to take ownership of their work. The Ritz-Carlton hotel chain exemplifies this type of ownership. The company wants the first person receiving a guest's complaint to handle the problem. It empowers employees to own the problem by allowing them to spend up to $2,000 per guest to solve any customer complaint. As one of the company's corporate trainers put it, at Ritz-Carlton no one says "That's not my job."[51] Box 4.5 describes another company that empowers employees to serve customers.

> *Many hands, and hearts, and minds*
> *generally contribute to anyone's notable achievements.*
>
> —*Walt Disney*

Passionate

Transformational leaders are passionately committed to their work. They love their jobs and have a great deal of affection for the people with whom they work. This passion and personal enthusiasm motivates others to perform at their highest levels as well. Transformational leaders are able to encourage others because they, first and foremost, encourage themselves.

One organization that has received cult-like recognition for the passion exhibited by its employees is the Pike Place Fish Market in Seattle. Books and training videos have documented the popularity of the seafood store as a tourist attraction. Thousands flock each day to watch the employees perform their jobs.

Box 4.5 Case Study	**Working by the Rule Book at Nordstrom**

Nordstrom began as a small shoe store in Seattle in 1901 and has grown into a retail giant with 119 large department stores and 194 outlet clearance centers (Nordstrom Rack) in the United States, online customer apparel companies (Nordstrom.com and nordstromrack.com), a private sale website (HauteLook), and Trunk Club, a personalized clothing service. Together they generate over $14 billion per year in sales (up from $10 billion in 2010). Although other retailers may be larger, few engender so much enthusiasm and loyalty from both customers and employees.

From the beginning, Nordstrom incorporated the idea that outstanding customer service offers a competitive advantage. Stories abound concerning the almost mythic levels of assistance offered by Nordstrom staff. This (well-deserved) reputation has turned the opening of new Nordstrom stores into civic events. When the first Nordstrom was built in Denver in the 1990s, hundreds of shoppers camped overnight in the parking lot in anticipation of the store's grand opening.

The key to Nordstrom's success is a leadership philosophy based on empowering employees to do whatever it takes to satisfy customers. As in many companies, new hires at Nordstrom attend a day-long employee orientation before they begin work on the sales floor. Unlike other companies, however, the training focuses almost exclusively on customer service. They learn that Nordstrom sales people never point but walk customers to where items are located, for example, and walk around the counter to hand customers their bagged purchases. While the company does outline standards for employees, the heart of the handbook is captured in the following statement, which for many years was written on a card and given to new hires:

> WELCOME TO NORDSTROM
> We're glad to have you with our company.
> Our number one goal is to provide
> **outstanding customer service.**
> Set both your personal and professional goals high.
> We have great confidence in your ability to achieve them.
> We only have one rule:
> **Use your good judgment in all situations.**
> Please feel free to ask your department manager,
> store manager, or Human Resources office
> any questions at any time.[52]

This entrepreneurial spirit allows Nordstrom sales associates to perform at levels that often exceed customers' expectations. For example, a Nordstrom sales associate in suburban Washington DC received a letter from a Swedish business executive who had purchased $2,000 worth of shirts and ties from Nordstrom while in the United States. After returning to Sweden, he washed the shirts in hot water; they shrank. He wrote to Nordstrom to ask for advice on how he might deal with his problem. The Nordstrom sales associate immediately put through a call to Sweden and told the customer he would replace the shirts with new ones at no charge. He asked the customer to mail the damaged shirts to the store—at Nordstrom's expense—so he could send back the appropriate replacements. Such a move would likely require several levels of approval—if it would happen at all—at most stores, but as the Nordstrom sales associate explained, he "didn't have to ask for anyone's permission.... Nordstrom would rather leave it up to me to decide what's best."[53] In another example, a woman lost the diamond from her wedding ring while shopping at Nordstrom. She returned to the store and started crawling around the women's

(continued)

department looking for the diamond. The store's loss prevention agent got down on his hands and knees and began to help but without success. When the woman left, the loss prevention agent recruited two building service employees to look. After further search they decided to tear open the vacuum cleaner bags. There it was. The company then created a video clip on the incident to show other employees and encouraged them to develop their own version of the "diamond story."[54]

Nordstrom also has extremely liberal return and exchange policies. In one case it accepted a set of tires (the company had recently acquired local stores that carried this item). In another case a New York City shopper brought a pair of shoes purchased at Bloomingdale's into a New York area Nordstrom. The customer explained the shoes were too small. She had purchased them because she liked the style, but Bloomingdale's didn't have her size. After being fitted with the same shoe in the proper size (the average Nordstrom store carries over 150,000 pairs of shoes), the customer started to pay for the shoes. The salesperson suggested the customer simply exchange the too-small shoes and take the correctly fitting pair for free. When the customer reminded the sales associate she had purchased the shoes at Bloomingdale's, the Nordstrom salesperson explained, "If I take these shoes for you, you won't have any reason to return to Bloomingdale's."[55] These liberal return and exchange policies might invite abuse, but the company's unconditional money-back guarantee is designed for the 98% of customers that Nordstrom finds to be honestly seeking fair treatment.

Developing this level of customer service can be challenging. Nordstrom prefers to hire people without previous sales experience. As Jim Nordstrom, the late co-chairman of the company once explained, those with little sales experience "haven't learned to say 'no' to customers, because they haven't worked for anybody else."[56] Nordstrom expects its sales staff to exhibit high levels of professionalism and initiative and pays its sales associates the second-highest wages in retail fashion (an average of $11.89 an hour). (Most exceed their base pay rate by earning a higher commission-based pay of approximately 6.75% of their sales volume.) Some employees generate over a $1 million in annual sales. Thus Nordstrom staff members have the opportunity to earn exceptional salaries as their sales increase, benefiting both the employee and the bottom line at Nordstrom. Salespeople also receive full benefits, including retirement, and medical and dental insurance. They report that the company is a great place to work. As Nordstrom has learned, high performance comes when employees are empowered to offer the highest imaginable levels of customer service and attention.

Discussion Questions

1. What constitutes outstanding customer service? What are the best and worst customer service experiences you have had?

2. What is the relationship between empowerment and customer service?

3. What do you think of the one rule? Would you like to work for a company like this? Why? Why not?

4. Do you think the Nordstrom return and exchange policies might be abused by more than the estimated 2% of its customers?

5. If a company expects people to take on more responsibility at work, what, if anything, should an employer be expected to offer in return?

The onlookers are treated to a spectacle that includes constant banter with customers, fish flying through the air to the cashier, and countless other zany antics.[57] Another example is the FedEx advertising campaign that highlighted the passion of company employees around the globe. The focal point of the advertisement was a website, fedexstories.com, that chronicled the exploits of workers who went above and beyond for their customers. Examples included an Italian courier who drove 300 miles in his own vehicle to deliver a late package, an Australian FedEx Kinko's manager who came to work at 3:00 AM to assist his employees with a malfunctioning copier machine, and a delivery manager in Michigan who went to extraordinary lengths to deliver a mobility scooter to a customer with a ruptured tendon. The scooter arrived too late for delivery at the customer's home address in Michigan. When the delivery manager found out the customer was limping around on crutches in New York where he was visiting his children at summer camp, the manager mobilized a team of FedEx employees who assembled the vehicle, charged the battery, and shipped the fully constructed scooter at no additional charge to New York for the man to use on his trip.

Organizational consultant Richard Chang suggests that passion is the single most important competitive advantage an organization can have.[58] For example, when Gillette executives made the choice to build sophisticated and more expensive shaving systems rather than expand in the low-margin disposable market, they did so in large part because they had little enthusiasm for developing cheap disposable razors. For executives at Gillette, the technical design of shaving systems sparks the same type of excitement that might be expected from an aeronautical engineer working on the latest advancements in aviation. People who aren't passionate about Gillette are not welcome in the organization. One top business school graduate wasn't hired by the company because she simply didn't show enough passion for deodorant.

> *Nothing great in the world has ever been accomplished without passion.*
> —*Georg Friedrich Wilhelm Hegel*

By demonstrating the characteristics of transformational leaders, individuals can begin to transform themselves and their organizations. By encouraging creativity, fostering open communication, demonstrating forward thinking, sharing responsibility, and exhibiting commitment, leaders can help construct organizations that are prepared to meet the challenges of the future.

Perspectives on Charisma

Charismatic leaders are the "superstars" of leadership. We usually reserve the label "charismatic" for well-known political, social, and business leaders who have had significant impact on the lives of others. Notable historical figures such as Joan of Arc, Queen Elizabeth I, Henry Ford, John F. Kennedy, Martin Luther King, Jr., and Nelson Mandela likely come to mind when we think of charisma. More recent conceptions of charisma, however, suggest that charismatic leadership can be found at all levels—not just among those in senior positions. By discovering how charismatics communicate, we can increase our effectiveness as leaders. In this section of the chapter, we'll look at some of the most significant approaches to the study of charismatic leadership.

The Sociological Approach

German sociologist Max Weber, writing in the early twentieth century, was one of the first scholars to use the term *charisma* to describe secular leaders. The term, which Weber borrowed from theology, means "gift" in Greek. Early Christians believed that God gave special gifts or abilities to church leaders.[59] Weber expanded the definition of gifted leadership to include all leaders, both religious and nonreligious, who attracted devoted followers through their extraordinary powers. In summarizing the nature of the charismatic leader, Weber wrote:

> [H]e [she] is set apart from ordinary men [women] and treated as endowed with supernatural, superhuman, or at least specifically exceptional powers or qualities. These [powers] are such as are not accessible to the ordinary person, but are regarded as of divine origin or as exemplary and on the basis of them the individual concerned is treated as a leader.[60]

According to Weber, a leader retains charismatic status as long as he or she is seen as charismatic. A charismatic must periodically demonstrate his or her exceptional personal gifts in order to maintain power over followers. Harrison Trice and Janice Beyer found five key components in Weber's foundational conception of charisma.[61]

1. A leader with extraordinary, almost magical, talents
2. An unstable or crisis situation
3. A radical vision for providing a solution to the crisis
4. A group of followers attracted to the extraordinary leader because they believe they are linked through the leader to powers that exceed usual limits
5. A validation, through repeated success, of the extraordinary leader's talents and power

Great crises produce great deeds of courage.

—*John F. Kennedy*

A number of important details are missing from Weber's pioneering theory of charismatic leadership. Weber never describes the origin or exact nature of the charismatic leader's extraordinary powers, nor does he clarify how charismatic authority rests both on the traits of the leader and on the perceptions of followers.

Much debate is also generated by the claim that instability or crisis is a necessary condition for charismatic leadership. Many scholars argue that charisma can be demonstrated in the absence of crisis, noting that charismatic leaders with compelling visions often appear in the business world in times of stability and calm.[62]

The Behavioral/Attribution Approach

Behavioral scientists argue that organizational leaders, like Thomas Watson of IBM and George Johnson of Endicott-Johnson Shoes, can also be described as charismatic. Behavioralists try to quantify the differences between charismatic and noncharismatic leaders, hoping to clarify what charisma is and to predict the effects of charismatic leadership.

> *Do what you can, with what you have, where you are.*
> —*Theodore Roosevelt*

Jay Conger and Rabindra Kanungo claim certain leader behaviors motivate followers to regard individuals as charismatic. Five behaviors that encourage followers to attribute charismatic characteristics to leaders are:[63]

- *Possess a vision that is unique, yet attainable.* A charismatic leader's vision differs markedly from the status quo. It is unique, innovative, and energizing. At the same time, the charismatic leader's vision is not too radical. A vision that challenges conventional wisdom too greatly (for example, a CEO promising to triple the size of the company in one year) will promote distrust. Followers attribute powers of observation and insight to a leader who communicates a singular, achievable vision.

- *Act in an unconventional, counternormative manner.* By engaging in behaviors that are outside traditional normative bounds, a charismatic demonstrates he or she is different from other leaders. When such behaviors produce successful outcomes, a leader appears to transcend the existing societal, organizational, or group order. (Turn to box 4.6 to learn about one such unconventional charismatic leader.)

- *Demonstrate personal commitment and risk taking.* Trust is an important component of charisma, and followers have greater trust for a leader who is personally committed to his or her own vision. Most impressive is a leader who is willing to risk losing such things as power, status, or money.

- *Demonstrate confidence and expertise.* Leaders who appear confident and knowledgeable are far more likely to be viewed as charismatic than those who seem unsure and confused. A leader's confidence can be infectious. When a leader believes in his or her decision making, followers are likely to be more confident in their judgments as well. This shared confidence increases the likelihood of success for both leaders and followers and

Box 4.6   Case Study   **Jack Ma: China's Unlikely Billionaire[64]**

Jack Ma is a most unusual billionaire. He is the head of one of the world's largest technology companies (the Alibaba group) but knows little about technology. Short (around 5 feet tall), thin, with a prominent forehead and protruding ears, he doesn't resemble the typical corporate executive. Some journalists call him "Crazy Jack" based on his animated speaking style as well as his risky corporate strategies. He dresses in wild wigs and lipstick to serenade employees at annual meetings, belting out renditions of Elton John's "Can You Feel the Love Tonight" and other tunes. Ma remains humble though he is the richest man in China and one of the richest men in the world. He spends his free time practicing tai chi, and reading and writing Kung Fu novels.

The unusual billionaire followed an unlikely career path. His family faced the wrath of the Chinese communists because his grandfather fought against Mao. Ma's parents were performers who practiced Pingtan, a traditional folk art form combining storytelling and music, which Mao banned during the Cultural Revolution of the early 1970s, when Jack was a child. His family's low status, along with his physical appearance, meant that he was the target of bullying at school. But Ma fought back, getting in trouble for his frequent fights with classmates. (He told biographers: "I was never afraid of opponents who were bigger than I.")[65] Once he learned that tourists were returning to visit his scenic hometown of Hangzhou following the Cultural Revolution, he got up at 5 AM every morning to befriend visitors so he could learn English. Since they couldn't pronounce his Chinese name, the Western visitors nicknamed him "Jack." Through this experience Jack not only polished his English skills, he made friends he would visit later and learned that much of what he was being taught in school was not true.

When it came time to enter university, Jack flunked the entrance exam twice due to poor math skills. He was finally accepted into what he refers to as "the most terrible school" in town—the Hangzhou Teacher's Institute. After graduation he got turned down for jobs with the city police, a hotel, and the local KFC. (Ma claims he was the only one of 24 applicants not hired by the restaurant chain.) He then took a job teaching English for $20 a month. At the same time, he started his own translation service. Jack's introduction to the Internet came when he traveled to the US to collect a bill for a client (an effort that failed when the American pulled a gun on him). Staying with a friend in Seattle, he entered the words "China" and "beer" into a search engine and could find no entries. He received 5 visits within 24 hours of setting up his own website and was convinced that there was a future for e-commerce in China though, at the time, few Chinese knew about the Internet.

Ma quit his job as a teacher and started an online directory, which was soon taken over by China Telecom; he then worked briefly for the Chinese government. In 1999 Ma and 17 friends used $60,000 to start Alibaba, which means "open sesame." Alibaba puts foreign buyers in touch with Chinese suppliers. In 2003 he started Taobao ("searching for treasure"), an online auction site that put him in direct competition with eBay. eBay chair Meg Whitman mocked Ma's decision to offer his service for free, declaring, "Free is not a business model." Ma's gamble paid off—eBay left the Chinese market and Taobao began making money by charging fees. Other branches of Alibaba include Alipay, which, similar to PayPal, guarantees payment for online transactions; and Tmall.com, which operates much like Amazon.com, serving buyers and retailers. In 2011 Alibaba made the largest initial public offering (IPO) in the history of the New York Stock Exchange ($160 billion) and is the seventh largest company in the world, surpassing General Electric and Walmart. Currently Alibaba handles more Internet traffic than eBay and Amazon combined and accounts for 60–70% of all packages shipped in China. The conglomerate has recently diversified into financial services, travel booking, a football team, the film industry, and other businesses.

Ma started his company just as China was moving to a socialized market economy and discovering the Internet, which was key to his success. The arrogance and cultural insensitivity of foreign competitors also gave the company a chance to succeed. Executives at Yahoo!, eBay, and

Google not only showed disdain for Ma and his company, they failed to adapt to the Chinese market. Recognizing the importance of relationships in China, Alibaba officials held face-to-face gatherings around the country to recruit businesses to the Internet. While eBay keeps buyers and sellers from contacting the other party, Taobao provides chat software so they can talk directly with one another. Click on Taobao in China and moving icons and animations come up, a feature not found when visiting eBay or Amazon.com.

Despite Ma's good timing, Alibaba wouldn't have succeeded without Ma's charismatic leadership. As Porter Erisman, who served as an Alibaba VP explains, there were lots of other people who were more qualified to start an e-commerce business in China but Jack was the only one who seized the opportunity: "He was the right *person* in the right *place* at the right *time*."[66]

Ma is a skilled communicator. Since stepping down as CEO he has maintained the role of chairman and spends much of his time representing the company. While Western executives are fond of outlining leadership principles, Ma is fond of images and sayings. For example, when describing Alibaba's relationship with the Chinese government, he notes, "While we are in love with them we don't have to be married to them." He describes his early days at Alibaba and his lack of technical skill as a "blind man riding on a blind tiger." During the struggle with eBay he comforted employees through this image: "eBay is a shark in the ocean; we are a crocodile in the Yangtze River. If we fight in the ocean, we will lose, but if we fight in the river, we will win." As a reminder to entrepreneurs to stay focused on the central mission of their firms, he evokes another animal image: "If you are a wolf chasing rabbits focus on one rabbit. Change yourself to catch the rabbit, but don't change rabbits." He exhorts followers through such declarations as "Never give up. Today is hard, tomorrow will be worse, but the day after tomorrow will be sunshine."

Like his parents, Ma is a performer, which made him a popular teacher and helps him inspire the loyalty of his current employees. Annual meetings resemble pep rallies. (He also presides over the mass weddings of Alibaba employees.) The entrepreneur makes work enjoyable. When the company made its first profit, he handed out a can of Silly String to everyone to celebrate. Ma encouraged the team launching Taobao to do handstands during their breaks to keep their energy up.

Ma's vision is clear. He is passionate about fostering the growth of small businesses by enabling them to sell goods globally over the web. He is also clear about his priorities. "Putting shareholders first is capitalism's biggest mistake," he claims. "Shareholders do not have a long-term vision for the company."[67] Instead, Ma believes customers come first, employees (who serve customers) come second, and investors come third. He summed up his philosophy in a letter sent to Alibaba employees when the firm filed for its IPO:

> We know well we haven't survived because our strategies are farsighted and brilliant, or because our execution is perfect, but because for 15 years we have persevered in our mission of "making it easier to do business across the world," because we have insisted on a "customer first" value system, because we have persisted in believing in the future, and because we have insisted that normal people can do extraordinary things.[68]

Discussion Questions

1. How did Ma's childhood and early failures prepare him for later success?
2. What makes Ma such an effective communicator?
3. Can you think of other leaders who use images and sayings to motivate followers? What images do they use?
4. What elements of charismatic leadership do you see in Jack Ma?
5. When entering overseas markets, how can leaders avoid the mistakes made by US technology companies in China?
6. Would you like to work for Jack Ma?
7. What do you learn from Jack Ma that you can apply as a leader?

enhances the status of a leader among his or her followers. At the same time, when a leader demonstrates a high level of expertise, followers may believe the leader has privileged knowledge. The leader's successes will be attributed to expert decision making as opposed to chance.

• *Demonstrate personal power.* Followers are more likely to attribute charisma to leaders who use personal power to meet the objectives of their vision than to those who use authoritarian or democratic approaches. Leaders who use authoritarian means based on position power when implementing a vision are not likely to be perceived as charismatic. Likewise, leaders who delegate responsibility by asking followers to develop their own strategies for achieving a vision are unlikely to be seen as charismatic. Although these democratic leaders are generally well-liked, they usually are not considered extraordinary by followers. Those leaders who demonstrate their personal power through the use of compelling oratory or persuasive appeals, however, are likely to be viewed by followers as possessing charismatic characteristics.

The Communication Approach

Neither of the perspectives on charisma that we have discussed so far view the topic specifically from a communication vantage point. Nonetheless, sociologist Weber emphasized that charisma is perceived by followers who look to the leader to illustrate his or her charismatic standing through communication. Conger and Kanungo emphasize the importance of articulating a compelling vision, appearing confident, and demonstrating personal power through oratory.

Communication is more than an important element of charismatic leadership, however. We believe that ***charisma is the product of communication.*** We agree with Robert Richardson and Katherine Thayer who point out that "charisma isn't so much a gift as it is a specific form of communication."[69] Richardson and Thayer argue that we can exert charismatic influence by working to improve our communication skills.

Charismatic leaders excel in four core functions of communication:

Charismatics as Relationship Builders

Charismatic leaders are skilled at linking with others. Their relationships with followers are characterized by strong feelings. As we've seen, such terms as excitement, adventure, loyalty, and devotion are frequently used to describe charismatic leader/follower relations. In addition, charismatics convince followers that as leaders they have a significant impact on the course of events—that they are "at the center of things."[70]

Charismatics as Impression Managers

Charismatics excel at creating the desired impressions through skillful use of the following elements:[71]

Framing. Successful leaders help followers interpret the meaning of events. A CEO, for example, might explain that layoffs are only a temporary measure that will guarantee the long-term health of the company or that market trends point to a bright future for the firm's products. Notable leaders also frame the organization's purpose in a way that inspires followers by tying into audience values and stressing the vision's importance and feasibility. (We'll take a closer look at framing in chapter 8.)

Scripting. Scripts are directions or guidelines for behavior. While frames define the situation, scripts outline the roles of players, what they are to say, and how they are to act. Scripting begins with *casting*, the process of identifying and then defining the roles of the main performers, supporting players, audiences, and enemies. Charismatic and transformational leaders outline their role in the drama, convince followers that they have a significant part to play in achieving shared goals, and identify outside groups that need to be approached for support. They then script the *dialogue* or interaction with followers. Powerful dialogue techniques include storytelling, which was discussed in chapter 1, as well as creating metaphors, drawing analogies, and communicating overarching goals. Successful leaders provide *direction* to guide performances, with specific attention to nonverbal behaviors and emotional displays. When they want to be perceived as dynamic, for example, they exhibit more eye contact, vocal variety, relaxed posture, and animated facial expressions. When they want to be seen as considerate, they are less animated and expressive.

Staging. Charismatic leaders pay close attention to how performances are staged, making sure that their personal appearance, the setting, and props support the image they want to project. For instance, when addressing the nation in times of crisis, presidents dress formally in dark colors and speak from the Oval Office surrounded by such props as the American flag and the presidential seal.

Performing. Performing is carrying out the behaviors outlined in the script. Outstanding leaders make effective use of four types of impression management. The first type is *exemplification*, which refers to living out or role modeling desired values and behaviors. For example: engaging in self-sacrificing or risky behavior like working extra hours or investing in a new venture, helping others, or demonstrating personal integrity. The second type is *promotion*—the communication of favorable information. The leader can promote (1) him- or herself (skills and accomplishments), (2) the vision (selling its merits and the leader's ability to bring it to pass), and (3) the organization (highlighting the success of the collective, which reflects well on the leader). Charismatic leaders are careful not to overstate their accomplishments, the vision, or the group's success. Overpromoting the self can backfire, generating skepticism and resentment; overpromoting the vision and organization can be seen as overzealous and unrealistic.

The third type of impression management used by notable leaders consists of *facework*, communication designed to protect or repair damage done to personal or collective images. Charismatic leaders know how to account for their missteps in ways that reduce their negative impact. They may deny responsibility for what happened, excuse their behavior, or justify their actions based on the fact that they were right to act as they did. Ronald Reagan successfully used accounting tactics to protect his image during the Iran-Contra scandal, when his administration was accused of trading weapons for hostages. He took "full responsibility" but yet blamed others for acting without his knowledge.

The fourth type of impression management is *ingratiation*. Effective leaders make themselves appear more attractive and likeable to others through complements, praise, agreeing, and offering to do things for others. They create the impression that they are warm and friendly. They take care to avoid intimidating behaviors that make them appear dangerous and threatening.

Charismatics as Visionaries

Charismatic leaders can also be defined in terms of their ability to create symbolic visions. Above all, charismatics emphasize the transcendent. According to one scholar, "They provide in themselves and in their visions an opportunity for the follower to imagine himself and his society transformed into something entirely new."[72]

Although the visions of charismatic leaders are new images of the group's future, they are built on the foundation of previous myths and values. The power of the charismatic grows as larger and larger numbers of people accept his/her symbolic focus. Stressful events like unemployment, war, fear for the future, and racial strife discredit current definitions of reality. This creates a more receptive audience for the charismatic leader's new vision. For example, the civil rights movement of the 1960s made many white Americans aware of the extent of racial injustice. Martin Luther King, Jr.'s nonviolent message gained wide acceptance because people of all racial groups could accept King's vision of a world united by love.[73]

Charismatics as Influence Agents

Charismatics are masters at influence and inspiration. In some instances, their influence is so great that followers never question their decisions or directives. Charismatic leaders project an image of confidence, competence, and trustworthiness. They utilize the power of positive expectations to generate high productivity, and they make effective use of language and persuasion to achieve their goals. Such leaders rely heavily on referent power—their influence as role models—to encourage others to sacrifice on behalf of the group.

If the perception of charisma is the result of communication behaviors, then we all have the potential to act as charismatic leaders. We can generate charismatic effects as small group, organizational, and public leaders. Though we may never influence millions as did Mahatma Gandhi, Martin Luther King, Jr., or Steve Jobs, we can have a strong impact on the lives of others through shaping the symbolic focus of the group, generating perceptions of confidence and competence, communicating high expectations, and inspiring others.

Transformational and Charismatic Leadership: Interchangeable or Distinct?

Scholars disagree as to whether transformational and charismatic leadership should be treated as interchangeable or considered separately.[74] There is no doubt that these two approaches share much in common. Both transforming and charismatic leaders have a powerful effect on followers and organizations; both achieve extraordinary results; both inspire; both are skilled communicators. Both approaches even appear to share the same potential weaknesses. Critics complain that they are "leader-centric" because they seem to focus almost exclusively on leaders while ignoring followers.[75] It is the leader who crafts the vision, inspires, fosters creativity, motivates employees, empowers, and so on. Influence flows in one direction—top down. In some cases, like Steve Jobs's refusal to do market research, we admire leaders who ignore the wishes of followers. Followers, who are just as important to the success of the group, are overlooked. They are far too often treated as empty vessels waiting to be filled or directed by their leaders.

Initially, both the transformational and charismatic approaches were criticized for overlooking the bad or dark side of leadership. As we noted in chapter 1, leaders are frequently destructive. Selfish, exploitive leaders can use transformational strategies to achieve unworthy objectives; some of the most terrifying leaders in history were considered to be charismatic. To their credit, transformational and charismatic scholars now acknowledge that both approaches can be used for good or ill.

In order to distinguish between authentic and self-interested transforming leaders, Bernard Bass and others differentiate between transformational and pseudotransformational individuals.[76] (See box 4.7.) The behavior of authentic transformational leaders is aligned with those actions in the first column while pseudotransformationals exhibit the unethical behaviors in the second column. (We'll have more to say about authenticity in the final section of this chapter.)

Box 4.7	Products of Transformational and Pseudotransformational Leadership
Transformational Leaders[77]	**Pseudotransformational Leaders**
• Raise awareness of moral standards	• Promote special interests at the expense of the common good
• Highlight important priorities	• Encourage dependency of followers and may privately despise them
• Increase followers' need for achievement	
• Foster higher moral maturity in followers	• Foster competitiveness
• Create an ethical climate (shared values, high ethical standards)	• Pursue personal goals
	• Foment greed, envy, hate, and deception
• Encourage followers to look beyond self-interests to the common good	• Engage in conflict rather than cooperation
• Promote cooperation and harmony	• Use inconsistent, irresponsible means
• Use authentic, consistent means	• Use persuasive appeals based on emotion and false logic
• Use persuasive appeals based on reason	
• Provide individual coaching and mentoring	• Keep their distance from followers and expect blind obedience
• Appeal to the ideals of followers	• Seek to become idols for followers
• Allow followers freedom of choice	• Manipulate followers

For their part, charismatic theorists distinguish between personalized (unethical) and socialized (ethical) charismatics based on their motivation.[78] Personalized charismatics use power to reach their goals. Their followers passively submit to their authority. Socialized charismatics seek to exercise power on behalf of the group instead, serving follower needs. Followers become more autonomous as a result of their relationship with the leader. Personalized (unethical) charisma has a detrimental effect on the organization by fostering dependency and instability. Socialized (ethical) charisma brings about positive change and equips followers to function more effectively.

While transformational and charismatic leadership share common ground, there appear to be significant differences as well. To begin, charismatic leadership is more person centered. The success of the charismatic leader rests on her or his personal characteristics (or perceptions of those characteristics). He or she must demonstrate high energy, self-confidence, risk taking, courage, and superior impression-management skills. When the charismatic leader leaves, so does her or his charismatic authority; it can't be transferred to a successor. The transformational leader, on the other hand, is more group-centered, appealing to the values and needs of followers. He or she wants to elevate the aspirations and morality of followers and leaders alike. This dimension is missing in many discussions of charismatic leadership.

There appears to be a stronger emotional connection to charismatics than to transformational leaders. Crisis also seems to be a critical element for the emergence of charismatic leadership (in most cases) but not for transformational leadership. The behaviors of the two types of leaders differ as well. Empowerment is a key characteristic of transformational leadership but charismatic leaders are often more authoritative, giving direction instead of enlisting the help of subordinates. Because of these differences, we believe that it is useful to view transformational and charismatic leadership as overlapping yet distinct approaches. We think each offers important insights into the success of highly effective leaders. However, we leave it to you to determine if you think that transformational and charismatic leadership are different names for the same approach (see Application Exercise 9 on p. 141).

Alternative Approaches to Outstanding Leadership

Together, transformational and charismatic leadership are the dominant theories in the field of leadership studies. However, alternative ways to explain outstanding leadership are emerging. We'll close out the chapter by looking at two of these approaches—authentic leadership and the CIP model.

Authentic Leadership

In the previous section we saw that Bernard Bass and others differentiate between authentic and pseudotransformational (inauthentic) leadership. While they introduced the notion of authenticity, it was up to other scholars—starting with Fred Luthans, Bruce Avolio, and others associated with the Gallup Institute at the University of Nebraska—to describe authentic leadership more fully and to determine how this type of leadership impacts performance. Initial interest in authentic leadership came at a time (right after the turn of the century) when the nation was rocked by a series of corporate scandals at Waste Management, Enron, WorldComm, Arthur Anderson, Tyco, and other firms. Researchers and practitioners were looking for ways to promote ethical leadership. The positive scholarship movement in the social sciences also influenced them. Positive psychologists and organizational scholars argue there is more to gain by building on the strengths of individuals and organizations than on addressing their weaknesses. (We'll have more to say about positive psychology in chapter 11.). However, modern theorists aren't the first scholars to be interested in authenticity. Both ancient Greek and Roman philosophers put a high value on this quality. "Know thyself" appears in the writings of Cicero and Ovid and is inscribed on the frieze about the oracle of Delphi. Greek thinkers also urged listeners "to thine own self be true."[79]

Authentic leadership theorists believe that authenticity is the root construct or principle underlying positive leadership and leadership development. According to proponents, practicing authentic leadership leads to sustainable (long-term) and veritable (ethically sound) organizational performance. Authenticity has four components, all of which are grounded in intrapersonal and interpersonal communication.[80] *Self-awareness* means being aware of, and trusting in, personal motives, desires, feelings and self-concept. Self-aware people know their strengths and weaknesses, personal characteristics, and emotional responses and patterns. They use this knowledge when interacting with others and their environments. *Balanced processing* describes remaining objective when receiving information. Inauthentic processing involves denying, distorting, or ignoring feedback. Leaders may have to acknowledge the fact that they are reluctant to delegate or that they fall back on an authoritarian style when they feel stressed. *Internalized moral perspective* is regulating behavior according to internal standards and values, not according to outside pressures. Authentic leaders act in harmony with what they believe and don't change their behavior to please others or to earn rewards or avoid punishment. *Relational transparency* is the presentation of the authentic self to others, openly expressing honest thoughts and feelings appropriate to the situation. These four elements are summarized in the following definition of authentic leadership:

> A pattern of leader behavior that draws upon and promotes both positive psychological capacities and a positive ethical climate, to foster greater self-awareness, an internalized moral perspective, balanced processing of information, and relational transparency on the part of leaders working with followers, fostering positive self-development.[81]

Authentic leadership can have a profound effect on followers.[82] Leader authenticity fosters feelings of self-efficacy (competence), hope, optimism, and resilience in subordinates. These factors, which together make up *positive psychological capital*, increase job performance. Followers who believe in their own abilities are more likely to take initiative and achieve more, even when faced with difficult circumstances. Feelings of hope and optimism foster will power. Resiliency enables followers to more quickly recover from setbacks and failures.

Investigators report that followers of authentic leaders demonstrate higher commitment, satisfaction, and effort. They also demonstrate higher moral performance. Authentic followers are likely to emulate the example of authentic leaders who set a high moral standard. They feel empowered to make ethical choices on their own and are more likely to act courageously. (We'll take a closer look at follower courage in chapter 11.) They align themselves with the values of the organization and set a moral example themselves. Authentic followers provide honest feedback to their leader, which increases the leader's self-knowledge. They also give their leaders more freedom to make difficult, unpopular choices.

Authentic Leadership Theory (ALT) has moved into the next phase of development. At first, articles and chapters on authentic leadership offered observations and propositions that weren't supported by empirical research. But an ALT scale has now been developed which tests the four dimensions described above. Sample scale items include: "Seeks feedback to improve interactions with others" (self-awareness); "Says exactly what he or she means" (relational transparency); "Demonstrates beliefs that are consistent with actions" (internalized moral perspective); and "Solicits views that challenge his or her deeply held positions" (balanced processing).[83] In devising the scale, developers found that authentic leadership shares some features with transformational and servant leadership but is a distinct construct. Authentic leadership is now being examined in other cultural settings like Brazil, India, Iran, Australia, and China. To date, the positive effects of authentic leadership appear to generalize across a variety of cultures, reducing follower stress and insecurity while increasing trust, job satisfaction, safety, performance, and willingness to blow the whistle on organizational wrongdoing.

Authentic leadership theory is highly attractive. The theory has developed at a time when many people are disillusioned with the poor ethical performance of business, political, and nonprofit leaders. Then, too, there is a commonsense appeal to the theory: "After all, who would advocate for inauthentic leaders?"[84] Many of us can point to authentic leaders (teachers, coaches, supervisors) in our own lives or we can name prominent leaders who demonstrate authentic characteristics. Former president Jimmy Carter, for example, continued his commitment to service after his election defeat. He founded the humanitarian Carter Center, builds homes for Habitat for Humanity, and teaches at his church despite a brain cancer diagnosis. Former first lady Betty Ford encouraged others to seek help for addictions by openly seeking treatment for alcoholism. In addition, she revealed her struggles with breast cancer at a time when few women did so. ALT is also attractive because it highlights the fact that outstanding leaders are moral leaders. A growing body of evidence demonstrates that authentic leaders have a significant positive influence on followers and lay the foundation for long-term organizational success.

Despite its attraction, there are serious concerns with authentic leadership. The theory's underlying premise that authenticity is the source of all positive forms of leadership is controversial. There may be other sources as well. In addition, authenticity may be overrated. Stanford business professor Jeffrey Pfeffer points out that leaders frequently act in ways that contradict their feelings in order to carry out their roles.[85] They have to preside over annual meetings when they are ill, overcome insecurity to express confidence to attract investors and customers, and comfort others when they (the leaders) are still grieving.

> *Authenticity is the alignment of head, mouth and feet—*
> *thinking, saying, feeling and doing the same thing.*
>
> *—Lance Secretan*

The CIP (Charismatic/Ideological/Pragmatic) Leadership Model

Psychologist Michael Mumford points out that many noncharismatic leaders have also had a profound effect on society. Take Benjamin Franklin, for instance. Franklin doesn't appear on lists of charismatic leaders, but the nation and world would be much different without him. He helped draft the Declaration of Independence and led efforts to establish the US postal system. In addition, he is credited with inventing the lightning rod and bifocal lenses.

Mumford and his colleagues acknowledge the impact of charismatic leaders but identify two additional tracks or pathways to outstanding leadership.[86] Each track—charismatic, ideological, pragmatic (CIP)—is based on the mental model or schema leaders use to make sense of the world. *Charismatic leaders* believe that people can act on the environment to achieve their goals. They look to the future and present a vision that will lead to positive outcomes and address social needs. *Ideological leaders* believe that situational forces are keeping followers from reaching their goals and propose changes that will eliminate those blockages. They look to the past, believing it is much better than the present. Highly committed to personal beliefs and values, they present visions that stress values and adhering to standards. *Pragmatic leaders* focus on the causes—both people and situational influences—that pose threats and opportunities in the current context. They look to the present, using a variety of skills to deal with complex problems, rather than offering inspirational visions or images of the idealized past.

Mumford and his associates initially relied heavily on the historiometric method to test the CIP model. In the historiometric approach, investigators apply statistical methods to analyze historical figures. CIP researchers identified notable leaders for each category, selected speeches and other material from each individual, and then asked judges to rate the leaders' behaviors to determine how charismatic, ideological, and pragmatic leaders differ. Some of the historical figures in their sample included Jomo Kenyatta, Margaret Thatcher, Martin Luther King, Jr., and Eva Peron (charismatic); Jane Addams, Susan B. Anthony, Dietrich Bonhoeffer, and Fidel Castro (ideological); and Katharine Graham, Booker T. Washington, Rupert Murdoch,

Richard Nixon, and Martha Stewart (pragmatic). The theorists also used a similar approach to analyze successful college and professional football coaches.

CIP investigators found significant differences among charismatic, ideological, and pragmatic leaders in both the historical figure and football coach samples. These differences include:

1. *Problem solving*: Charismatic leaders generate more ideas, ideologues focus on evaluation, and pragmatics rely on detailed analysis and expertise.

2. *Relationships with followers*: Charismatic leaders give and receive support; ideological leaders share power and direction with key followers who hold the same values; pragmatic leaders are less likely to share direction.

3. *Communication strategies*: Charismatic leaders seek to motivate; ideologues appeal to follower needs; pragmatics offer logical, problem-oriented appeals.

4. *Political tactics*: Charismatic and ideological leaders rely heavily on such tactics as controlling decisions, coalition building, and intimidation. Pragmatic leaders rely more on rational influence (expertise) and allocating resources.

5. *Machiavellianism*: Pragmatic leaders are most likely to manipulate subordinates; followed by charismatic leaders. Ideological leaders are least likely to engage in Machiavellian behavior.

6. *Emotional displays*: Charismatic leaders express more positive emotions as they envision a desirable future; ideological leaders express more negative emotions, particularly if events don't align with their beliefs, and are also more volatile; pragmatic leaders use both positive and negative displays closely tied to the current situation.

The CIP model highlights the fact that outstanding leadership takes different forms. Leaders who (1) look to the past and appeal to shared values, or (2) focus on solving immediate problems can be as effective as their transformational/charismatic counterparts. The CIP approach also raises important questions about how we measure the influence of a leader. Charismatic leaders might have the most immediate impact but the influence of ideological and pragmatic leaders may be greater over time. There are significant limitations in using historical figures to support the model, however. Observers may disagree about how to classify leaders. Moreover, evaluators have to rely on biographical accounts, which reflect the biases of the historian. Coaching (where each game may pose a crisis and emotions run high) might differ from leadership in other contexts.

CIP researchers have begun to address these concerns by developing ways to identify the three styles in college students and then measuring their performance on games and problem-solving tasks. To date, most US students surveyed have a pragmatic orientation. The effectiveness of each style in simulations and in problem-solving exercises depends on such factors as the complexity and type of dilemma being solved.[87]

⌒ CHAPTER TAKEAWAYS

- Beginning in the late 1970s, the transformational approach emerged as a new perspective for understanding and explaining leadership.

- The transformational approach contrasts traditional leadership, labeled as *transactional*, with a more "complex" and "potent" type of leadership known as *transformational*.

- The motivational appeals of the transactional leader are designed to satisfy basic human needs; the appeals of the transformational leader go beyond those basic needs to satisfy a follower's higher-level needs.

- Transformational leaders are *creative, interactive, visionary, empowering*, and *passionate*. Further, since transformational leadership can convert followers into leaders in their own right, these five primary characteristics are often filtered throughout transformed groups and organizations. You can act as transformational leader by demonstrating these behaviors.

- Transformational leaders are innovative and foresighted. They constantly challenge the status quo by seeking out new ideas, products, and ways of performing tasks.

- Transformational leaders are masterful communicators able to articulate and define ideas and concepts that escape others.

- Communicating a vision to followers may well be the most important act you engage in as a transformational leader. A vision is a concise statement or description of the direction in which an individual, group, or organization is headed. Compelling visions provide people with a sense of purpose and encourage commitment.

- Transformational leaders empower others. These leaders encourage participation and involvement. The exchange of ideas between leader and follower does not pose a threat to the transformational leader. Extraordinary leaders realize that individual achievement and success is the basis for team achievement and success. Transformational leaders know how to give power away and how to make others feel powerful.

- Transformational leaders are passionately committed to their work. They love their jobs and have a great deal of affection for the people with whom they work. This passion and personal enthusiasm motivates others to perform to their highest levels as well. Transformational leaders are able to encourage others because they, first and foremost, encourage themselves.

- Charismatic leaders are the "superstars" of leadership. We usually reserve the label "charismatic" for well-known political, social, and business leaders who have had significant impact on the lives of others.

- Weber's sociological approach to charisma included five key components: a leader with extraordinary talents; an unstable or crisis situation; a radical vision for providing a solution to the crisis; a group of followers who believe the extraordinary leader links them to powers that exceed usual limits; and a validation of the extraordinary leader's talents and power through repeated success.

- By describing charisma as a set of behaviors, the behavioral approach attempts to clarify what charisma is and to predict the effects of charismatic leadership. Followers attribute charisma to leaders who: possess a vision that is unique, yet attainable; act in an unconventional, counternormative manner; demonstrate personal commitment and risk taking; demonstrate confidence and expertise; demonstrate personal power.

- The communication approach suggests that charisma is a specific form of communication. You can create perceptions of charisma by excelling in four core functions of communication: relationship building, impression management, visioning, and influencing.

- Transformational and charismatic leadership are overlapping yet distinct approaches. Both achieve outstanding results. However, charismatic leadership is more person centered and the charismatic leader is more likely to direct than to empower followers.

- Authentic leadership theory (ALT) is based on the premise that authenticity is the basis of positive leadership. Authentic leaders, in turn, often have profound effects on followers, raising their organizational and moral performance. Authentic leaders demonstrate self-awareness, balanced processing, an internalized moral perspective, and relational transparency.

- According to the CIP model, there are three pathways to highly successful leadership: charismatic, ideological, and pragmatic, each based on a different mental model. The charismatic looks to the future, the ideologue looks to the past, and the pragmatic leader looks to the present.

∼ APPLICATION EXERCISES

1. Select a particular leader discussed in one of the many books focusing on transformational leadership (*Leaders, The Leadership Challenge, Built to Last, Lessons From the Top, Leadership on the Edge, Developing Potential Across a Full Range of Leadership,* or *Good to Great,* for example). Analyze how effectively the leader applies transformational techniques. Does he/she meet the higher-level needs of followers? Is he/she an effective communicator? Does he/she have a clearly stated vision?

2. Develop a case study based on an organization that embodies one or more of the characteristics of transformational leadership.

3. Think of a time when you came up with a creative solution to a major problem. Analyze your problem-solving effort based on the four stages of the creative process identified by Wallas: preparation, incubation, illumination, and verification. Did you experience each stage? Which was most difficult for you? How can you overcome creative blocks and increase your flow of creative ideas in the future? Report your findings.

4. In a group, generate ideas about how to improve your school or business by asking "What if?" and then filling in the rest of the sentence. For example,

"What if students could get their undergraduate degrees in three years instead of four?" "What if the university required every student to spend at least one term in another country?" "What if our company only sold its products online?" Select the most promising ideas and present them to the rest of the class or to colleagues at work.

5. Collect vision statements from several sources. Share your examples with others in class. Identify the common characteristics of the vision statements you think are most effective.

6. Make a list of your passions. How could these passions be used to guide your career and future leadership experiences?

7. Form a small group and generate a composite list of 10 charismatic leaders. To make the group's list, all the members of the group must accept a leader as charismatic. Keep a record of those individuals who fail to receive unanimous support. Present your findings to the rest of the class. As part of your report, describe the criteria that the group used to compile its list. In addition, name those individuals who were rejected by the group. Explain why these leaders failed to make the master list.

8. Conduct a debate on whether or not charismatic and transformational leadership should be treated as different or interchangeable approaches. As an alternative, debate whether authenticity is the most important quality for leaders.

9. Determine if your supervisor at work is charismatic, ideological, or pragmatic. Offer evidence to support your conclusion.

10. Do an in-depth study of a public charismatic or an authentic leader. Describe how this person's use of communication resulted in his/her emergence as a charismatic or authentic figure. Write up your findings.

∼ CULTURAL CONNECTIONS: IS TRANSFORMATIONAL/CHARISMATIC LEADERSHIP A UNIVERSAL CONCEPT?[88]

As society becomes increasingly global in its focus, it is important to assess the universality of leadership research and theory. Bernard Bass argued that the concept of transformational leadership may be truly universal—transcending organizational and national boundaries. Evidence supporting the viability of the transformational approach has been gathered from all continents except Antarctica. The results suggest leadership, in general, and transformational leadership, in particular, are found in one form or another at all levels and in all cultures.

Bass and fellow researcher Bruce Avolio offered three assertions about transformational leadership, which have subsequently been supported across a variety of cultures.

1. *Transformational leaders are more effective than leaders adopting a more transactional approach.* This has been verified in research conducted in the United States, Canada, Austria, Belgium, Italy, Germany, Spain, India, Singapore, Japan, China, New Zealand, and several other countries. Based on

the perceptions of followers and organizational outcomes, including performance appraisals, career advancement, and performance of the work unit, transformational leaders consistently exceeded the performance of transactional leaders.

2. *Transformational leadership adds value to transactional leadership, but the inverse is not true.* Results supporting this assertion or corollary have been obtained in the United States, Canada, the Dominican Republic, India, Singapore, and other nations. While transformational leadership appears to augment transactional leadership, transactional leadership does not enhance transformational leadership.

3. *Whatever the country, when people think of leadership, their prototypes and ideals are transformational.* Participants in research conducted in the United States, Canada, South Africa, Spain, Austria, Sweden, Italy, Israel, Japan, Taiwan, Sri Lanka, New Zealand, and elsewhere consistently described the ideal leader as possessing the traits and characteristics of transformational leaders.

Researchers affiliated with the Global Leadership and Organizational Behavior Effectiveness (GLOBE) project surveyed more than 15,000 middle and senior managers in 1900 corporations from 69 different cultures. Their research, like that conducted by Bass and his colleagues, suggests that attributes of transformational leadership (what they call charismatic/values-based leadership) are universally endorsed and lead to higher employee and firm performance. These attributes include: (1) performance orientation, (2) visionary, (3) integrity, and (4) inspirational. According to the GLOBE researchers, "What this means is that leaders in all GLOBE countries studied are expected to develop a vision, inspire others, and create a successful performance-oriented team within their organizations while behaving with honesty and integrity—easier said than done."[89] However, though these behaviors appear to be universal, cultural influences still play a role. Societies have different expectations for charismatic behavior. Effective CEOs exceed the expectations of their particular cultures; ineffective CEOs fell short of societal expectations.

Bass acknowledged that there may be cultures in which transformational leadership is not found. In those cultures, trust between the leader and the led would be unimportant, and followers would have to demonstrate no concern for self-esteem, intrinsic motivation, consistency in the actions of leaders, or meaningfulness in their work and lives. Such cultures would be the exception rather than the rule.

⁓ LEADERSHIP ON THE BIG SCREEN: *THE MAN IN THE MACHINE*

Starring: Steve Jobs, Regis McKenna, Joe Nocera, Chrisann Brennan, Sherry Turkle, Bob Belleville

Rating: NR but probably PG for language

Synopsis: Documentary filmmaker Alex Gibney puzzled over the worldwide outpouring of grief at the death of Apple CEO Steve Jobs in 2011. After all, Jobs was not a civil rights leader or a great artist. Why, then, were so many people moved to mark his passing by placing flowers in front of their local Apple store and by posting condolences on social media? And what did this mean for our culture? To answer these questions, Gibney provides an in-depth look at the life of Jobs through archive footage and interviews. The portrait that emerges is of a troubled entrepreneurial genius. Jobs successfully battled IBM and revolutionized personalized technology through the Apple computer, iPad, iPhone, and other devices, forever changing the way that people interact with machines and with one another. Under his focused leadership, Apple became the most valuable as well as one of the most popular corporations in the world. While Jobs could inspire his followers to accomplish more than they ever dreamed possible, he could also treat them with contempt. Near the end of his life, Jobs and Apple engaged in a number of unethical and illegal activities, including mistreating foreign workers, using overseas shell companies to reduce corporate taxes, and back dating stock options for executives. Gibney concludes that Jobs and Apple may not be worthy of all the admiration they have received but acknowledges the impact of the man and the company on the world in which we live.

Chapter Links: charismatic leadership, creativity, vision, passion, impression management

5

Leadership and Power

Leadership begins and ends with the problem of power.

—Abraham Zaleznik

OVERVIEW

Power: Mixed Emotions

Power and Leadership
Interdependent But *Not* Interchangeable
Sources of Power

Deciding Which Types of Power to Use

Engaging in Constructive Organizational Politics

Powerful and Powerless Talk

Empowerment
Components of the Empowerment Process
Empowerment Models

Power: Mixed Emotions

Many of us have contradictory feelings about power. On the one hand, we are fascinated by the power and wealth we see on television and in movies. We admire those with clout, those who move quickly and decisively to get things done. We also loathe the corruption and greed that often comes with power. We're uneasy with exercising power—just discussing the topic can make us uncomfortable. According to power expert Julie Diamond, "Power, like sex and death, is a taboo topic."[1]

As a society, we pay a high price for our ambivalence toward power. Avoiding the subject makes us more vulnerable to the misuse of power by those in authority. A chilling example is cult leader Jim Jones, who presided over the mass suicide of 800 followers in Guyana. This tragedy might have been prevented if cult members and outsiders had recognized and challenged Jones's unhealthy use of power.[2] Conversely, our discomfort with the subject of power diminishes our capacity to be successful. Leaders can only bring about change if they skillfully use power to enlist the support of followers, overcome resistance, collect resources, create alliances, and so on. If we ignore the reality of power, we won't learn how to exercise power effectively on behalf of worthy goals.

Power is a given. Refusing to talk about it won't make it go away. Instead, we need to acknowledge the importance of power and determine how to use it appropriately. In the words of John Gardner:

> To say a leader is preoccupied with power is like saying that a tennis player is preoccupied with making shots his [her] opponent cannot return. Of course leaders are preoccupied with power! The significant questions are: What means do they use to gain it? How do they exercise it? To what ends do they exercise it?[3]

Power and Leadership

Sorting out the relationship between power and leadership can be confusing. Is using power the same as exerting leadership? Does having power automatically make you a leader? Power and leadership are obviously interdependent; however, they are not interchangeable. While power can exist without leadership, leadership cannot exist without power.

Interdependent but *Not* Interchangeable

We define power as *the ability to influence others.* Leadership is impossible without power since a leader must modify attitudes and behaviors. Yet influencing others does not automatically qualify as leadership; power must be used in pursuit of group goals to merit leadership classification.[4] Imagine a robber armed with a semiautomatic weapon bursting into a bank, ordering everyone to lie on the floor. The group obeys. The bank robber certainly exerted power—a very negative manifestation of power. We would not label him a "leader," however. His power was exercised only on behalf of his own interests. In other instances, powerful individuals do not use their power and thus fail to take a leadership role. The small-group member who knows the most about a topic would be a natural candidate for group leadership. However, this person may refuse to participate in the group's discussion.

Leadership experts Warren Bennis and Burt Nanus summarize the relationship between power and leadership this way: "Power is . . . the *capacity to translate intention into reality and sustain it.* Leadership is the wise use of this power. . . . Vision is the commodity of leaders, and power is their currency."[5]

> *Being powerful is like being a lady.*
> *If you have to tell people you are, you aren't.*
>
> —*Margaret Thatcher*

Sources of Power

If power is the "currency of leadership," then understanding the sources and uses of power is essential to effective leadership.[6] The ability to influence others can be based on a wide variety of factors. John French and Bertram Raven have isolated five primary sources of power.[7] Chances are you prefer to use one or two of these power bases more than the others (see the self-assessment exercise in box 5.1).

Coercive power is based on the ability to administer punishment or to give negative reinforcements. Examples of coercion range from reducing status, salary, and benefits to requiring others to do something they don't like. In the most extreme form, coercive power translates into brute physical force. Whistle-blowers—employees who have pointed out unethical practices like cost overruns and safety hazards—often experience coercion. They may be fired, assigned to distasteful jobs, or socially ostracized.

Coercion is most effective when those subject to this form of power are aware of expectations and are warned in advance about the penalties for failure to comply. Leaders using coercive power must consistently carry out threatened punishments. A parent who punishes without first establishing expectations and the consequences for failure will be less effective than a parent who clearly sets the ground rules. The effective parent says: "I expect you home by 10:00. If you're not home by then, you will be grounded for the rest of the weekend." The user of coercive power must then follow through with the announced consequence. Threatening over and over again to ground a teenager for being late without ever carrying out the punishment significantly diminishes coercive power. The same is true in organizational settings. A supervisor who threatens to take action against a subordinate must carry out the threat if coercive power is to remain a viable source of power.

Failure to execute threats can produce a cycle of negative behavior. Warnings to punish represent attention. Although humans certainly prefer positive reinforcement, they will select negative reinforcement over no reinforcement at all (apathy). Humans would rather be punished than ignored. If a child is unable to attract positive attention, he or she may begin to misbehave in an attempt to attract

| Box 5.1 Self-Assessment | | | | Personal Power Profile[8] |

Directions: Below is a list of statements describing possible behaviors of leaders in work organizations. Carefully read each statement, thinking about *how you prefer to influence others.* Mark the number that most closely represents how you feel.

I prefer to influence others by	Strongly Disagree	Disagree	Neither Agree nor Disagree	Agree	Strongly Agree
1. increasing their pay level	1	2	3	4	5
2. making them feel valued	1	2	3	4	5
3. giving undesirable job assignments	1	2	3	4	5
4. making them feel like I approve of them	1	2	3	4	5
5. making them feel that they have commitments to meet	1	2	3	4	5
6. making them feel personally accepted	1	2	3	4	5
7. making them feel important	1	2	3	4	5
8. giving them good technical suggestions	1	2	3	4	5
9. making the work difficult for them	1	2	3	4	5
10. sharing my experience and/or training	1	2	3	4	5
11. making things unpleasant here	1	2	3	4	5
12. making work distasteful	1	2	3	4	5
13. helping them get a pay increase	1	2	3	4	5
14. making them feel they should satisfy job requirements	1	2	3	4	5
15. providing them with sound job-related advice	1	2	3	4	5
16. providing them with special benefits	1	2	3	4	5
17. helping them get a promotion	1	2	3	4	5
18. giving them the feeling that they have responsibilities to fulfill	1	2	3	4	5
19. providing them with needed technical knowledge	1	2	3	4	5
20. making them recognize that they have tasks to accomplish	1	2	3	4	5

Scoring: Record your responses to the 20 questions in the corresponding numbered blanks below. Total each column, then divide the result by 4 for each of the five types of influence.

	Reward	Coercive	Legitimate	Referent	Expert
	1 _____	3 _____	5 _____	2 _____	8 _____
	13 _____	9 _____	14 _____	4 _____	10 _____
	16 _____	11 _____	18 _____	6 _____	15 _____
	17 _____	12 _____	20 _____	7 _____	19 _____
Total	_____	_____	_____	_____	_____
Divide by 4	_____	_____	_____	_____	_____

Interpretation: A score of 4 or 5 on any of the five dimensions of power indicates that you prefer to influence others by using that particular form of power. A score of 2 or less indicates that you prefer not to employ this particular type of power to influence others. Your power profile is not a simple addition of each of the five sources. Some combinations are more synergistic than the simple sum of their parts. For example, referent power magnifies the impact of other power sources because these other influence attempts come from a "respected" person. Reward power often increases the impact of referent power because people generally tend to like those who can give them things. Some power combinations tend to produce the opposite of synergistic effects. Coercive power, for example, often negates the effects of other types of influence.

negative attention. Employees in organizations are no different. "Problem" employees who receive warning after warning may simply need attention. Following the guidelines regarding the use of coercive power and offering positive reinforcement minimizes the negative behavior.

I praise loudly, I blame softly.

—*Catherine the Great*

Reward power rests on the ability to deliver something of value to others. The reward can be tangible (money, health benefits, or grades, for example) or something intangible like warmth and supportiveness. Many organizations use both tangible and intangible rewards to recognize superior performance. Pride, for instance, is a particularly powerful intangible incentive. The Marines, Southwest Airlines, Aetna Insurance, and other organizations foster institution-building pride that comes from doing something well in service to the group's mission. Members focus on the organization's performance—customer satisfaction, product quality, respect of peers—rather than on themselves.[9]

Any reward must be desirable and attractive to serve as a sufficient motivator. One student worked in a large organization that decided to change computing systems. The changeover took six months and required employees to work many hours of overtime. When the new system was finally in place, the corporation hosted a Friday afternoon party and rewarded those who had worked such long hours with T-shirts that said, "I Survived the Changeover." The student and her coworkers were insulted. More suitable rewards, like giving workers the day off after so many weeks of overtime, might have been more appreciated and more attractive to employees. This student's unhappy experience with rewards is all too common, prompting some experts to suggest that leaders should strictly limit their use of tangible rewards as a motivational strategy.

Legitimate power resides in the position rather than in the person. Persons with legitimate power have the right to prescribe our behavior within specified parameters (for example, judges, police officers, teachers, and parents). Although we may disagree with our supervisor at work, we go along with a decision because that person is the boss. The amount of legitimate power someone has depends on the importance of the position she or he occupies and the willingness to grant authority to the person in that position. Individuals grant legitimate power based on particular circumstances. An assistant will comply when the boss assigns a word-processing project or requires the phone to be answered because those are legitimate requests. The assistant may not be willing to assent to tasks that are not related to work.

Expert power is based on the person, not the position, in contrast to legitimate power. Experts are influential because they supply needed information and skills. In our culture, it is particularly important to be perceived as an expert. Those with credentials are more powerful than those without appropriate certification. When visiting a new physician, do you immediately check his/her diploma? Our culture mandates that certain credentials must be obtained before an individual can be considered a professional. Demonstrating practical knowledge and skills can also build expert power. For this reason, members of an organization often have little legitimate power but a great deal of expert power. Receptionists can be extremely influential because of what they learn through talking to employees, managers, customers, and others. School janitors are often powerful because they know how to fix bulletin boards, open locked doors, and so on.

Referent power is role model power. When people admire someone, they confer on the admired person the ability to influence their behavior. Referent power depends on feelings of affection, esteem, and respect for another individual. This loyalty generally develops over an extended period of time. Since referent power takes so long to nurture, it should be used carefully. A supervisor who asks a subordinate to work overtime as "a personal favor" will succeed if the employee likes and respects the supervisor. Referent power will probably be effective the first weekend and possibly the second, but after several weeks the employee will tire of doing "favors" for his/her supervisor. Once depleted, referent power must be replenished by engaging in behavior that will produce new feelings of affection, esteem, and support.

In recent years, scholars have identified two additional sources of power to French and Raven's original list.[10] These are information power and ecological power.

Information power is based on access to, and distribution of, data. Those in roles that span organizational boundaries—marketers, salespeople, public relations staff—have access to information about outside events. Managers have inside knowledge about personnel moves, possible mergers and acquisitions, new products, and other information vital to organizational members. They also have control of over how and when such data is released and to whom. Followers often have control over operating information that managers need to make effective decisions.

Ecological power arises out of control over the physical environment, technology, and how work is organized. Examples of exerting ecological power include designing the layout of a manufacturing assembly line, installing a new software program, and changing the duties assigned to organizational departments.

> *The measure of a [hu]man is what he [she] does with power.*
>
> *—Pittacus*

Deciding Which Types of Power to Use

A useful way of determining the relative advantages and disadvantages of each source of power is to view leadership as a reciprocal relationship. While leaders exert more influence than other group members, leaders are also influenced by followers. According to social exchange theory, leaders must maintain profitable relationships with followers.[11] They do this by providing rewards like approval, information, or salary in return for such commodities as labor, compliance, and commitment. When the relationship becomes unprofitable to either party (the costs outweigh the benefits), then the relationship is redefined or ended. There are potential costs and benefits associated with using each power type. For example, coercion can be used by followers as well as by leaders. Students may punish instructors who rely heavily on threats and other coercive tactics by giving them low course evaluations. Politicians who legislate unpopular tax measures are often removed from office.

A list of the benefits and costs of each type of power is given in table 5.1. The list—which incorporates the thoughts of the authors and a number of researchers—is not exhaustive.[12] In fact, we hope that you will add your own costs, benefits, and conclusions (see Application Exercise 2).

The cost/benefit ratios suggest that leaders should rely heavily on expert and referent power. These forms of power have a positive effect on the performance and satisfaction of those being influenced and are less costly to use. They are most likely to maintain a profitable relationship between leader and follower. Yet, effective leaders need access to all types of power. Taking charge may require discipline through coercion, the judicious use of rewards, and the power of position. In fact, a leader's impact is enhanced if, for example, she or he combines legitimate power with expert and referent power. A highly respected group member who is appointed the chair of a committee is in a very powerful position. Or, to put it another way, leaders need both hard power and soft power. *Hard power* uses

Table 5.1   Benefits and Costs of Power Types

BENEFITS	COSTS
Coercive Power	
Effective for gaining obedience	Drains physical and emotional energy from user
Appropriate for disciplinary actions	Lowers task satisfaction of followers
Achieves quick results	Destroys trust and commitment
	Becomes less effective over time
	Followers may respond in kind
	Most likely to be abused
Reward Power	
Culturally sanctioned	Lower task satisfaction than with expert and refer-
Focuses attention on group priorities	ent power
Effective for gaining obedience	Not consistently linked with high task performance
Boosts short-term performance	Escalating financial and material costs to provide
	ever-greater tangible rewards
	Some groups, like nonprofit agencies, have lim-
	ited tangible rewards to give
	Ineffective or destructive if rewards are not desir-
	able or attractive, or if the wrong individuals are
	rewarded
Legitimate Power	
Culturally sanctioned	Lowers follower task performance
Incorporates weight of the entire organization	Lowers follower task satisfaction
Effective for gaining obedience	May become less effective over time
Helps large organizations function efficiently	
Expert Power	
High follower task satisfaction	Takes a long time to develop
High follower task performance	Must possess the necessary knowledge and skills
Drains little, if any, emotional energy from the user	Not as effective in gaining obedience as coercion,
	reward, or legitimate power
	May not be effective if followers do not share the
	leader's goals
Referent Power	
High follower task satisfaction	Takes a long time to develop
High follower task performance	Can diminish if overused
	Must possess the necessary knowledge and inter-
	personal skills
	Not as effective for gaining obedience as coer-
	cion, reward, or legitimate power
Information Power	
Available to both leaders and followers	Distorting information
Information can be acquired through effort	Hoarding information
Ecological Power	
Can be used to empower followers	Only available to those with legitimate power
Can improve job satisfaction	Costly to implement
Can increase efficiency and productivity	Possibility of costly errors

inducements (bonuses, raises) and threats (firings, lawsuits) to get people to go along. *Soft power* is based on attracting others rather than forcing them or inducing them to comply. Leaders using soft power set a good example, outline a worthy vision, and build good relationships with subordinates. Effective leaders combine hard and soft power into *smart power* to achieve their goals. For example, a manager may try to persuade an employee to follow a new work procedure while also outlining the penalties the subordinate will face if she or he does not comply.[13]

To summarize, group members seem to prefer leaders who rely on power associated with the unique characteristics of the person (expert and referent) rather than leaders who rely on power related to their position (coercion, reward, legitimate). Since effectiveness is more directly tied to personal performance than to official position, we can manage our communication behaviors to increase our power—which, in turn, can increase our ability to lead. Later we'll take a closer look at one cluster of communication behaviors—powerful forms of talk—that seem particularly well-suited to building both expert and referent power. But first we'll examine how leaders can put their power to good use in the organizational context.

Engaging in Constructive Organizational Politics

In organizational politics, leaders accumulate and use informal power to achieve their own objectives and/or the objectives of the organization.[14] Political behavior is not officially sanctioned by the organization and operates outside the formal power structure. Examples of engaging in organizational politics include lobbying for a promotion, forming a coalition with other leaders to bring a new product to market, or loaning an employee to another department in hopes that the other department will return the favor in the future.

"Playing politics" is generally associated with backstabbing, hidden agendas, secret deals, selfishness, and deceit. Often those who are skilled at politics get what they want (raises, promotions) at the expense of more deserving, nonpolitical individuals. Employees who believe that they work in highly political environments are less satisfied with their jobs and less committed to their organizations. At the same time, they report that they are more stressed and more likely to quit.[15] (To determine your perceptions of the negative political climate in your organization, complete the self-assessment in box 5.2.)

Leaders can't afford to dismiss organizational politics due to its unsavory image. To begin, politics is an inescapable part of organizational life. Organizations are political institutions complete with competing interest groups, coalitions, power brokers, and power struggles. Successful leaders know how to navigate this political environment. They recognize that engaging in political activity is just as important as carrying out traditional management functions like negotiating and decision making.[16] Also, informal power is generally used for constructive purposes. Managers engage in positive politics on a daily basis to allocate people and equipment, manage product development, coordinate workflow, and so on. Sometimes going outside formal power channels is the only way to achieve important organizational objectives like removing an incompetent executive or getting corporate headquarters to deal with product quality issues.

Dwight Eisenhower is one example of a leader who used his political skill for constructive purposes.[17] From a young age, Eisenhower was good at settling disputes and getting others to focus on a shared goal. He was a careful observer of people and could sense what each individual needed. His strongest skill was his ability to build networks. Early in his career, he developed a web of friendships with George Marshall, Omar Bradley, and George Patton. Later these generals played a critical role in the invasion of Europe during World War II. Eisenhower used the relationships he developed during the war in his postwar career as commander of NATO and President of the United States.

Engaging in constructive organizational politics requires a shift in mind-set. Organizational behavior experts Ronnie Kurchner-Hawkins and Rina Miller argue that leaders and followers need to set aside their negative image of organizational

---

Box 5.2 Self-Assessment	**Perceptions of Organizational Politics Scale (POPS)[18]**

Directions: Rate your workplace on each of the following items:
(5 = strongly agree, 1 = strongly disagree)

_____ 1. Favoritism rather than merit determines who gets ahead around here.

_____ 2. There is no place for yes-men and women around here; good ideas are desired even when it means disagreeing with superiors.

_____ 3. Employees are encouraged to speak out frankly even when they are critical of well-established ideas.

_____ 4. There has always been an influential group in this department (organization) that no one ever crosses.

_____ 5. People here usually don't speak up for fear of retaliation by others.

_____ 6. Rewards come only to those who work hard in this organization.

_____ 7. Promotions in this department (organization) generally go to top performers.

_____ 8. People in this organization attempt to build themselves up by tearing others down.

_____ 9. I have seen changes made in policies here that only serve the purposes of a few individuals, not the work unit or the organization.

_____10. There is a group of people in my department who always get things their way because no one wants to challenge them.

_____11. I can't remember when a person received a pay increase or a promotion that was inconsistent with the published policies.

_____12. Since I have worked in this department, I have never seen the pay and promotion policies applied politically.

Scoring: Reverse your scores on items 2, 3, 6, 7, 11, and 12 and then add up the total score from all twelve items. The higher the score, the greater your perception that negative politics operates in your workplace. Range: 12–60.

politics and recognize instead that informal power can foster collaboration and help the organization achieve its objectives.[19] To drive home this point, they contrast the traditional view of organizational politics as manipulative and exploitive (the "dark" side of political behavior) with a more optimistic view (the "bright" side of political activity). Negative politics is self-serving and uses power to intimidate and control others. Destructive politicians are out to win at all costs without consideration for ethical standards. In contrast, positive politics serves the vision of the group and brings people together to achieve worthy goals. Constructive politicians act as stewards, serving the future of the organization and society. They focus on achieving goals through collaboration not competition, and carefully consider the ethical implications of their actions.

Kurchner-Hawkins and Miller note that developing a strategy can help leaders and others reach their goals through positive political means. A positive political strategy, whether to introduce a new software system or enter a new market, should keep the following elements in mind:

1. Identify the political behavior you want to engage in. (This makes it easier to understand and manage it.)

2. Articulate your purpose and what you want to achieve; keep the focus on the group's vision.

3. Consider important elements of the context, including history, culture, past interactions, ethics, and the motivations driving the behaviors of organizational members.

4. Name those involved who need to be influenced or who can exert influence.

5. Anticipate the possible reactions to your plan and political activities. Consider what's at stake.

6. Take responsibility for your role in the strategy. Determine how you are contributing and how your behavior may impact others and the organization as a whole both immediately and in the future.

7. Consider whether your actions will be consistent with your values and those of the organization; take into account how they reflect your ethical values and the needs of others.

8. Determine how to leverage change. Consider how you can employ your power, communication/information, relationships/alliances, and networks.

Carrying out a constructive political strategy takes four sets of capabilities.[20] First, politically skilled leaders demonstrate a conceptual understanding of the nature of power and how it can be used to achieve worthy goals. They identify which relationships are essential to getting things done and nurture those partnerships. In addition they know how to gather support (lobby), how decision-making processes work, how to operate quietly and effectively, how to build their credibility by meeting the requirements of their jobs, and how to create pockets of change. Second, constructive political leaders understand themselves. They set aside the desire for job security and promotion in order to pursue a worthy cause. They simultaneously challenge current practice while retaining respect for the values of the group. Third, effective politicians demonstrate a high level of awareness about their political situations, continually seeking out information about influential individuals, where and how decisions are made, and the agendas of other leaders. Further, they are aware of what is happening beyond the organization because they ask questions of insiders and outsiders and systematically gather data through market research, reading, seminars, forums, and other means. Fourth, skillful political leaders develop their interpersonal skills. They persuasively present their ideas through supplying information, acting collaboratively, maintaining flexibility, and demonstrating respect for the other person. They avoid direct challenges to decision makers but use questions and listening to get influential individuals to analyze their ideas and behavior. At the same time, constructive politicians identify the motives of other parties by observing their behavior and by comparing their words to their actions.

> *It is impossible to avoid organizational politics—as a natural form of human behavior it is a natural part of the institutional landscape.*
>
> *—Gerald Egan*

Powerful and Powerless Talk

Sociolinguists, anthropologists, communication specialists, and others have long been fascinated with the two-way relationship between language and power. Viewed from the perspective of society, language is a mirror reflecting power differences. Every culture has a "standard language" that is spoken by the highest socioeconomic group in that society. Nonstandard languages are dialects spoken by less advantaged people.[21] The use of language both reflects and creates power differentials.[22] Speakers are stereotyped as powerless or powerful based on their word choices.

The fact that speakers are perceived as powerless or powerful based on the way they talk means that language can be an important tool for building power bases. Conversely, inappropriate language can reduce perceived power and leadership potential. A number of language features have been identified as "powerful" or "powerless" by researchers.[23] Powerful talk makes speakers seem knowledgeable and confident; powerless talk is tentative and submissive. Most researchers have concentrated on identifying powerless speech forms, while powerful speech has been treated as speech without powerless speech features. Here are some forms of powerless talk.

- *Hesitations* ("uh," "ah," "well," "um," "you know") appear to be the most frequently used form of powerless talk and have been identified as the least powerful speech feature in some studies. The characteristic that is most likely to clutter our talk is apparently also the most likely to reduce our power.

- *Hedges* ("kinda," "I think," "I guess") may occasionally be appropriate (when we truly are not sure of our facts, for example), but they greatly reduce the impact of what we say. Compare "I think you should have that report in by Friday" to "Have that report in by Friday."
- *Tag questions* ("isn't it?"; "wouldn't it?") on the end of a sentence indicate uncertainty. These expressions make a declarative statement much less forceful. For example, "That presentation was unorganized, wasn't it?"
- *Disclaimers* ("Don't get me wrong, but"; "I know this sounds crazy, but") can be a useful conversational tool. Speakers use disclaimers when they are not sure if listeners will accept what they have to say. For instance: "I'm not trying to be critical, but your speech was way too long." They should be used with caution, however, since they can signal that we lack confidence in our statements.
- *Accounts* (excuses or justifications) deny responsibility for what happened. Speakers employ accounts after they say or do the wrong thing: "It was an accident," or "I wasn't ready for the test because I stayed up all night helping my roommate with a problem." A speaker who frequently excuses or justifies his/her behavior will be seen as inept or uncertain.
- *Side particles* ("like," "simply," "that is") detract from a powerful image. They can be irritating for listeners.

Researchers report that the use of powerless speech in experimental settings significantly lowers source credibility (we'll have more to say about believability—what communication experts call credibility—in the next chapter.) Listeners consistently rate the knowledge and ability (competence) of powerless speakers lower than that of powerful speakers when both deliver the same message. In addition, they find such sources less trustworthy, less dynamic, less attractive, and less sure of themselves. Audiences don't retain as much information from a speech or lecture if the message is delivered in a tentative style.[24] Powerless language also makes speakers less persuasive, serving as a distraction and weakening their arguments.[25]

Language choices clearly have a strong influence on the two bases of power most easily controlled by the communicator: expert and referent power. Powerless speakers often *appear* to be uninformed and unskilled even if they do, in fact, possess the necessary knowledge and abilities. On the other hand, powerful speakers are frequently seen as competent and attractive, and their messages have more persuasive and informational impact. Some evidence suggests that powerful talk can help overcome the disadvantages that come from having low legitimate power.[26] It should be noted, however, that other variables may moderate or override the influence of powerless speech. For example, students are less distracted by an instructor's use of powerless talk if they like that professor or if the information contained in the lecture is important to them.[27] Strong persuasive arguments are still more effective than weak arguments no matter what style a speaker uses.[28] Also, powerful speech is most effective when speakers are trying to be authoritative. There are times when a powerless style may be more appropriate, such as in a conversation between friends or when a superior is trying to establish common ground with a subordinate. The key is to adopt the appropriate style for the situation.

Fortunately, we can eliminate powerless language features if we choose to do so. Lawyers report that they can teach clients to avoid powerless language. Public speaking instructors help their students eliminate powerless talk by noting powerless speech features on speech evaluation forms. To become a more powerful speaker, start by monitoring your powerless speech habits. Record a conversation and count the number of powerless speech features you used, or ask a friend to give you feedback about your powerless speech patterns. Make a conscious effort to eliminate powerless language. Keep track of your progress using the recording and feedback methods described above. Another way to become a more powerful speaker is by monitoring public speakers (including instructors). Evaluating what others do can help to improve your own performance.[29]

Empowerment

Up to this point, we have emphasized how power is the essential currency of leadership. There is no leadership without power, and some forms of power are more effective for leaders than others. Further, leaders need to systematically use their power for constructive purposes. However, a leader will frequently want to distribute rather than to maintain power. Reducing power differentials often enhances group performance and may be the key to organizational survival. (Take a look at the case study in box 5.3 to see how empowerment can increase productivity.)

Paradoxically, leaders gain more power by empowering others. There are five major reasons why leaders choose to share power. In an organizational setting, distributing power *increases the job satisfaction and performance of employees.* People like their jobs more, generally experience less stress, and work harder when they feel that they have a significant voice in shaping decisions.[30] Withholding power has the opposite result. Those who feel powerless often respond by becoming cautious, defensive, and critical.[31] In extreme cases, they lash out at coworkers and damage the organization through such tactics as work slowdowns and equipment sabotage.

Box 5.3 Case Study	**Empowerment on the Load Line at Techstar Industries**

Techstar Industries is one of several companies responsible for assembling the circuit boards used in personal computers and tablet devices. Companies like Techstar compete with many other organizations doing the same type of work. The assembling of circuit boards is tedious and demanding; the work is often repetitive and dull. At the same time, there is tremendous pressure to assemble large numbers of boards with very few rejects. The only competitive advantage a company like Techstar can hope for is to produce a higher quality product at a lower price than its competitors.

Boards at Techstar are assembled on the load line. Parts are loaded by hand onto the board as it travels along a conveyer belt. The most recent Techstar board, the MT2000, has 27 parts that are loaded at six different stations by a team of operators. To be profitable, Techstar must manufacture 600 usable boards with fewer than 10 rejects during each eight-hour shift.

The load line team has averaged fewer than 500 usable boards with as many as 30 defective boards produced on each shift. The supervisor, Tom Friedman, decided that the only way to improve the situation was to turn the problem over to the operators. Tom called a meeting to announce his intentions. Despite his team's apprehension, he told the operators he wanted them to generate ideas for improving their productivity. To get the team started, Tom chaired the first few meetings. He told the team he would provide all the necessary support required to improve the situation. Further, Tom made it clear that he was willing to turn over control of the load line to the operators if they could meet the production goal for profitability and keep him apprised of their progress.

Over the next two months, the load line team met on a regular basis. They identified 20 ways to improve the process. Among the most important suggestions were: cross-train operators, develop a system for keeping the line stocked with parts, and reengineer the line to optimize efficiency. The team based these suggestions on several problems that they identified during their meetings. First, each operator was trained to work at only one of six stations. When an operator needed to leave the line for any reason, the entire assembly process came to a halt. Second, when an operator on the line ran out of parts, the line had to be stopped until the parts were replenished. Finally, with six stations operating at once, all members of the load line team were tied to the line. This became even more problematic when the team realized that the demands of each station were very different. Because workloads were unevenly distributed, some operators were rushing to get their parts loaded while those at other stations worked at a much slower pace.

The team presented its plan to Tom. They requested downtime to train each member of the team to work at each station. The team felt the process could be improved if there were only five stations rather than six. This would enable the team to balance the workload so that the demands of each station would be roughly equal. In addition, five workstations would allow one team member to circulate between stations. This team member would be responsible for filling in for other team members when they left the line, for stocking parts, and for troubleshooting before defective boards were produced.

Tom liked the team's ideas and, as he promised, offered his support. Within a few days the line was reconfigured and the load line team began assembling MT2000 boards on their new five-station line. With team members working together and rotating positions on the load line throughout their shift, the number of MT2000 boards produced began to climb. Within three months, the team not only met Tom's production goal, they exceeded it—producing more than 700 usable boards with an average of only three defective boards per eight-hour shift.

Discussion Questions

1. How do you think the assembly process would have been affected if Tom had decided to reconfigure the load line without consulting the team?

2. What are the major advantages/disadvantages of the type of empowerment strategy Tom used?

3. What advice would you offer Tom for dealing with the load line team members if their suggestions for improvement had not resulted in increased productivity?

4. Discuss a time when you have been empowered to make a decision. What were the results?

5. What kinds of tasks do you think should be among the first delegated to followers as part of a leader's empowerment effort? Why?

Sharing power *fosters greater cooperation among group members.* Cooperation, in turn, increases group accomplishment. The effectiveness of any group depends in large part on the cooperation of group members. For instance, a small group cannot get an "A" on a class project if members withhold information from each other or if a number of members refuse to participate at all. The same is true for a sales team or computer project group. The genius of organizing lies in combining individual efforts in order to achieve goals that would be beyond the capability of any one person. The group advantage is lost or diluted when participation is only halfhearted. James Kouzes and Barry Posner report that enabling others is a key to leadership; accomplishment results from the efforts of many people, not just the leader. According to Kouzes and Posner: "We developed a simple test to detect whether someone is on the road to becoming a leader. That test is the frequency of the word *we.*"[32]

> *There is no limit to what you can do if you don't care who gets the credit.*
>
> —*John Wooden*

Distributing power means *collective survival*; the group endures rather than fails. One of the best ways to stay competitive in a fast-paced, global environment is to develop a "flat" organizational structure. Flat structures are decentralized and grant a great deal of decision-making authority to lower-level leaders. For instance, branch managers in flat corporations control decisions affecting their operations. They do not have to check with headquarters constantly. In these companies, project groups blur traditional lines of authority in order to develop new ideas. Flat organizations offer two advantages: (1) they can move quickly to meet changing market conditions, and (2) they foster innovation—the development of new products and processes on which a business ultimately depends.

Effective leadership facilitates *personal growth and learning.* Group members become more mature and productive than they were before. Empowerment is one way to stimulate growth. Sharing power with followers can help them tackle new challenges, learn new skills, and find greater fulfillment.[33] In the end, both the group member and the group are transformed when power is shared. Not only does the individual grow, but the collective gains a more committed and skilled member.

Sharing power *prevents power abuses.* Concentrating power in the hands of a few individuals is dangerous. As Britain's Lord Acton observed, "Power corrupts, and absolute power corrupts absolutely." Individuals who do not share power are free to project their insecurities, fears, and hostility on others and to further their own interests at the expense of followers. Tyrannical bosses, for example, seek to maintain their positions by (1) tracking every move of employees, (2) sending conflicting messages about what they want, (3) engaging in angry outbursts, (4) demanding absolute obedience, (5) putting followers down in public, (6) acting arbitrarily, and (7) coercing subordinates into unethical behavior.[34] (Turn to Leadership on the Big Screen at the end of the chapter for a film that highlights the dark side of power.)

Powerful individuals often ignore the needs of others. Compared to the powerless, they typically devote less attention to finding out how other people think and feel. As a consequence, they are more likely to hold and to act on harmful stereotypes, particularly of minority group members. They are overconfident and take foolish risks. Leaders who distribute power, on the other hand, are less likely to abuse their positions, to take advantage of followers, to ignore the needs of others, to stereotype or to take unnecessary chances.[35]

> *Oh, it is excellent to have a giant's strength,*
> *but it is tyrannous to use it like a giant.*
>
> —*William Shakespeare*

Making a case for empowering followers is easier than making empowerment happen. Many organizations continue to operate under the traditional, hierarchical model where top executives often get treated like royalty, and middle- and lower-level managers are rewarded for keeping, not sharing, their authority. Giving power away is difficult in these hostile environments. (Turn to the research highlight in box 5.4 for some humorous examples of how organizations create feelings of powerlessness.) Other organizations fail to reward followers who take on added

Box 5.4 Research Highlight	Stories of the Dumbemployed[36]

Writers Phil Edwards and Matt Kraft operate the website dumbemployed.com. On their site they invite visitors to share their stories of the dumb, funny, and demeaning things that happen to them at work, what the webmasters/researchers call being "dumbemployed." They have collected 800 of these stories (all 300 characters or less) in a book of the same name.

Edwards and Kraft divide their book into the five factors that "make your job infuriatingly dumb." Each of these factors shares a common theme—the powerlessness employees frequently experience at work. Here is a sampling of the stories appearing under each of the five elements of dumbemployment.

Factor 1: Bosses

- A supervisor assigns a worker to clean out his pickup truck. Unfortunately, the boss is a hunter and the employee ends up smelling like a dead deer.
- When recommending a subordinate for a promotion, the boss says she "didn't believe any of the bad things people were saying" about the employee.

Factor 2: Customers

- On a trip to the zoo, a father gets angry with the tour guide for not letting his son touch a lion.
- A student believes his professor can help him with his knee pain because he is a doctor. The professor's doctorate is in Renaissance literature.

(continued)

Factor 3: Just Dumb

- A front desk clerk is asked to hold a package for a tenant. It turns out that the woman wants the clerk to hold her infant while she goes jogging.
- An enterprising worker steals business cards from another worker just in case he runs out of his own cards.

Factor 4: Overtime

- At one elementary school, the principal makes his commute easier by parking his car where the school buses drop off students.
- One employee asks for time off to attend her sister's wedding. She is told to ask if the sister "could have it on another day instead."

Factor 5: Weird Shift

- One employee receives a 20% off coupon from Office Depot given by management as a "reward for friendliness."
- A worker comes back to his desk to find a post-it note on his computer screen asking him to turn his radio down. After being angry about the note for five minutes, the employee realizes he doesn't have a radio.

responsibilities. Then, too, some employees resist empowerment, wanting only to follow orders.[37] Yet, empowerment efforts can and do succeed. Leaders have relinquished much of their legitimate, reward, expert, and coercive power bases at companies like Gore and Associates (makers of Gore-Tex fabric), Johnsonville Foods, Harley-Davidson, Morning Star (the world's largest tomato processor), McCormick Spice Company, and many other successful organizations. Self-directed work teams (SDWTs) have taken over many of the functions traditionally reserved for lower- and middle-level managers and are being rewarded for doing so.

Power sharing is most likely to occur when leaders understand the components of the empowerment process and are equipped with implementation strategies. With that in mind, we'll take the remainder of the chapter to outline the important elements of empowerment and to describe two models that take a systematic approach to giving power away.

Components of the Empowerment Process

Component 1: Modifying the Environment

Environment refers to the setting where work occurs. Important elements of the environment include reward systems, job tasks, organizational structure and workflow, rules, charts, and physical layout. The first step in the empowerment process is often the elimination of situational factors that create feelings of powerlessness, like inappropriate rewards, authoritarian supervision, and petty regulations (see box 5.5). Next, the environment is redesigned to shift decision-making authority to followers. Those assigned to do the work get a great deal of say in how the job gets done.

Box 5.5 **Research Highlight**	**Situational Factors Leading to a Potential State of Powerlessness**[38]

Organizational Factors
  Significant organizational changes/transitions
  Start-up ventures
  Excessive, competitive pressures
  Impersonal, bureaucratic climate
  Poor communications and limited network-forming systems
  Highly centralized organizational resources

Supervisory Style
  Authoritarian (high control)
  Negativism (emphasis on failures)
  Lack of reasons for actions/consequences

Reward Systems
  Noncontingency (arbitrary) reward allocations
  Low incentive value of rewards
  Lack of competence-based rewards
  Lack of innovation-based rewards

Job Design
  Lack of role clarity
  Lack of training and technical support
  Unrealistic goals
  Lack of appropriate authority/discretion
  Low task variety
  Limited participation in programs, meetings, and decisions that have a direct impact on job performance
  Lack of appropriate/necessary resources
  Lack of opportunities to form networks
  Highly established work routines
  Too many rules and guidelines
  Low advancement opportunities
  Lack of meaningful goals/tasks
  Limited contact with senior management

Component 2: Building Intrinsic Motivation

Empowered followers are energized to carry out tasks associated with their work roles. They take an active, not passive, approach toward their job responsibilities. Such intrinsic motivation is the product of the following four factors.[39]

Meaning. Meaning is the value placed on a task, goal, or purpose based on personal ideals or standards. Low levels of meaning produce apathy and detachment; higher levels focus energy and produce commitment and involvement. You can foster a sense of meaning by (1) hiring those who share the group's values, (2) promoting the organization's purpose and vision, (3) clarifying work roles, (4) matching individuals with jobs they find meaningful, and (5) explaining how individual tasks support the group's mission and goals.

Choice (self-determination). Choice reflects a sense of self-direction or control. Those who have choice about how to carry out their jobs (when to start, how fast to work, how to prioritize tasks) feel a greater sense of responsibility and are more flexible, creative, and resilient. Shifting decision-making authority to followers is one way to encourage a sense of self-determination. In addition, create a participative climate that values employees and takes their ideas seriously. Emphasize the importance of taking individual initiative and making a personal contribution. Make followers accountable for their choices and set boundaries on what they can and cannot do. Finally, support those who take risks. Years ago, a UPS employee ordered an extra plane to make sure that packages left behind during the Christmas rush were delivered on time. Rather than punish this individual for going above the budget, company leaders praised him. His story—still told at the company—sends the message that UPS leaders will stand behind those who take initiative.

Competence. Competence is based on the individual's assessment that he or she can do the job required. It is a subset of what psychologist Albert Bandura refers to as *self-efficacy* or personal power. Self-efficacy is the sense that we can deal with events, situations, and people at work and in other environments as well. Followers who have a sense of self-efficacy or personal power are more likely to take initiative, to set and achieve higher goals, and to persist in the face of difficult circumstances. Constituents who believe that they have limited self-efficacy and feel powerless dwell on their failures. They are less inclined to offer new ideas, to set and meet challenging standards, or to continue when they encounter obstacles.[40] Leaders can build followers' perceptions of their personal power by:[41]

- providing positive emotional support, particularly during times of stress and anxiety. Stress, fear, depression, and other negative factors reduce feelings of personal efficacy. The impact of these factors can be diminished if a leader clearly defines the task, offers assistance, engages in play to create a positive emotional climate, and uses films, speakers, seminars, and other devices to build excitement and confidence.

- expressing confidence. The most effective leaders spend time every day encouraging others and expressing confidence in their abilities at meetings, during speeches, in the lunchroom, in hallways, and in offices.

- modeling successful performance themselves or providing opportunities to observe others who are successful. Knowing that someone else can handle a task makes it easier for a worker to continue to learn the same task even after repeated failures.

- structuring tasks so that followers experience initial success. Initial victories build expectations for future triumphs. Effective leaders structure tasks so that they become increasingly complex. Completing one part of the job is followed by training and then greater responsibilities. The same strategy can be used to introduce large-scale change. A new marketing strategy or billing system can be started in one plant or region and then adopted by the organization as a whole. (See chapter 8 for additional information on demonstration projects.)

Impact. Impact describes the individual's belief that he or she can influence the environment of the organization. Followers with a high sense of impact are convinced that they can make a difference in the work group's plans, goals, and procedures. You can foster this perception by including workers in strategic planning and by involving them in setting collective rules and standards. Encourage their efforts to introduce innovations.

Component 3: Supplying Resources

Empowerment increases the demand for resources. No follower, no matter how motivated, can complete a task if she/he doesn't have adequate funds and supplies, enough time to devote to the job, and a place to work. Political support—the approval of important individuals—is essential for the completion of major projects. Leaders supply this resource when they publicly endorse the work of stakeholders and encourage other leaders to "buy in" to initiatives.[42]

Information is a particularly important resource for newly empowered followers. Consider the machine operator who has just joined a self-directed work team, for example. Under the old system, she had to know how to run a single piece of equipment. Now she's part of a group that makes decisions for an entire department: planning, scheduling, hiring, and quality control. In addition to operating her machine, she must learn how to work in a team, set objectives, measure results, read a profit-and-loss statement, conduct a hiring interview, and so forth. She can only succeed if she receives adequate training and if company management supplies the team with financial and performance data for planning and measurement.

Empowerment Models

Two widely used models—Superleadership/Self-Leadership and Leading the Journey—provide road maps for implementing the components of empowerment described above.

Superleadership/Self-Leadership

Management professors Henry Sims and Charles Manz argue that the ultimate goal of leadership is empowering followers to take charge of their thoughts and behaviors. Sims and Manz use the term "superleaders" to describe those who help followers learn to lead themselves. They use the label "self-leaders" to refer to followers who act on their own.[43]

Guiding followers from dependence to independence (see box 5.6) is a process that begins with the leader modeling the desired behaviors. Followers then work under the guidance of the leader who encourages and rewards initiative and provides the necessary resources and training. In the final stage, followers act on their own with minimal direction from the leader.

Box 5.6	Shifting Followers to Self-Leadership[44]
FROM (DEPENDENT)	**TO (INDEPENDENT)**
External observation	Self-observation
Assigned goals	Self-set goals
External reinforcement for task performance	Internal reinforcement plus external reinforcement for self-leadership behavior
Motivation mainly based on external compensation	Motivation also based on the "natural" rewards of the work
External criticism	Self-criticism
External problem solving	Self-problem solving
External planning	Self-planning
External task design	Self-design of tasks
Obstacle thinking	Opportunity thinking
Compliance with the organization's vision	Commitment to a vision that the follower helped to create

Superleaders use three strategies to create a climate that promotes independent thought and action.

1. *Changing organizational structures.* They reconfigure roles, functions, and responsibilities to reduce hierarchy and specialization; create self-managing teams; remove layers of organizational structure; and reduce job and pay classifications. (Box 5.7 describes a company that is reorganizing to promote self-leadership.)

2. *Changing organizational processes.* Superleaders redesign the way that communication and materials flow in the organization. They push decisions down to the lowest possible level, encourage teams to solve their own problems, and reengineer jobs so that followers have the responsibility for the whole project, not just part of it.

3. *Changing interpersonal communication patterns.* Effective leaders use verbal and nonverbal behaviors to build follower confidence. They listen more and command less, ask followers to solve their own problems, express confidence in employees, and compliment initiative.

According to researchers, self-leadership can pay significant dividends for followers and their organizations. Self-led employees are more self-confident, satisfied with their jobs, productive, and successful.[45] Followers can learn to lead themselves without the guidance of those in authority if they become self-disciplined, find rewards in the task, and adopt positive thought patterns. We will illustrate these self-leadership tactics by applying them to a common classroom assignment: the term paper.

The first set of self-leadership strategies involves self-behavior modification. Most of us complete jobs we enjoy, but we often miss deadlines when tackling diffi-

Box 5.7 Case Study	Self-Leadership at Zappos[46]

Online shoe retailer Zappos has always prided itself on being playful and unconventional. In fact, one of the firm's core values is "Create Fun and a Little Weirdness." For example, the firm sponsors "Bald and Blue" events where employees get their heads, legs, and eyebrows shorn for charity by a group of their colleagues known as the "Blue Man Group." Company meetings can include comedians, live music, circus performances, costumes, and appearances by CEO Tony Hsieh's favorite animal—a llama. The firm's mission is to "deliver happiness." To fulfill that mission it pays for shipping both ways (many customers order several different pairs of shoes, try them out and return the ones that they don't like or don't fit), provides free overnight shipping to loyal customers, and staffs 24-hour call centers. Customer service representatives are evaluated on how well they meet the needs of callers, not on how quickly they end the calls. They might provide free fashion advice, for instance, or talk with someone who is lonely. If Zappos is out of a specific style and size, the customer service representative will visit at least three other websites and then direct the customer to competitors. Hsieh credits the firm's success to its unique culture. Zappos reached $1 billion in sales in its first ten years and was purchased by Amazon.com for $1.2 billion in 2009. As part of the sales agreement, Amazon CEO Jeff Bezos agreed to let Zappos operate independently as long as it met its financial targets.

In 2013 Hsieh took a step that made Zappos even more unconventional. Worried that the firm was turning into a traditional bureaucracy, he introduced a new operational structure called holacracy designed to foster creativity and risk taking. (Holacracy describes a collection of holons, which are parts that function simultaneously as parts and wholes, much like the organs in the human body.) Instead of being organized around hierarchy and job titles, employees take on a variety of roles to get work done, roles that are constantly changing. A worker without a marketing background might take on a marketing role along with several other roles, for instance. When conflicts arise, employees air their issues at governance meetings that focus on accomplishing goals. Tactical meetings are held to coordinate team members to complete specific tasks. Each circle or team of employees must coordinate its work with other circles. Individuals called "lead links" assign roles to individuals in their circle and represent their circle as a whole. However, lead links have no control over individuals. Instead, power to hire and fire and approve expenditures is made by a committee. Employees must record their activities on the company's software program.

According to those spearheading the transition, self-leadership is at the heart of the new model.

> One of the core principles is people taking personal accountability for their work. It's not leaderless. There are certainly people who hold a bigger scope of purpose for the organization than others. What it does do is distribute leadership into each role. Everybody is expected to lead and be an entrepreneur in their own roles, and holacracy empowers them to do so.[47]

Hsieh first rolled out holacracy in the human resources department and by 2015 85% of employees had started the new process. Frustrated at what he viewed as a slow rate of adoption, Hsieh wrote the entire workforce that "having one foot in one world while having the other foot in the other world has slowed down our transformation towards self-management and self-organization." He then made an ultimatum: Get with the program or take a three-month severance package and leave. Fourteen percent of the staff took him up on the offer, helping send the company's one-year turnover rate to 30%, well over its average.

Both those who left and those who stayed report a number of problems with holacracy. To begin, there is widespread confusion about who does what. Employees complain that they spend endless time in meetings. They don't have bosses to turn to for advice and there is no longer any opportunity to move up in the company. Managers must give up their power, and skilled

(continued)

employees may no longer be able to use the expertise they spent years developing. Then, too, the lack of job titles has made it hard to set compensation levels. Employees don't know how to represent themselves outside the firm and those who leave don't know what to put on their resumes. The company dropped off the Best Places to Work list after holacracy was rolled out. (Employees gave management especially low scores on the question of whether leaders have a "clear view of where the organization is going and how to get there.")

Some workers have responded well to the new model. Said one employee who took on new job duties: "My worst day at Zappos is still better than my best day anywhere else. I can't imagine going back to traditional hierarchy anymore." More junior and nontraditional employees have been able to exert more influence. One introvert noted: "The structure of meetings forces each person to . . . say what they want. Before I might've thought something and wouldn't have jumped in."[48]

Outside observers are skeptical that Hsieh's self-leadership experiment will succeed. They note that while other companies have tested the model, they are much smaller than Zappos. Some of these businesses, like the content site Medium, have discontinued the experiment. (Estimates are that less than 1% of all companies in the world operate without traditional hierarchy.) Journalists point to the recent exodus of Zappos employees as a sign that the company has veered off course. Then, too, critics have taken issue with the way the program was implemented—from the top down. Stanford business professor Jeffrey Pfeffer points out, "It's deliciously ironic that self-management is being decreed from above."[49]

Hsieh appears more committed than ever to self-leadership. He is not concerned about those who have left the firm, believing they weren't a good fit for the company. While admitting that he was surprised by the level of resistance, "at how hard it is to let go of the psychological baggage," he wishes he had implemented the change faster. "In retrospect, I would have probably ripped off the Band-Aid sooner."[50] Hsieh expects the new system to make the company more successful: "I'm personally excited about the potential creativity and energy of our employees that are just waiting for the right environment and structure to be unlocked and unleashed."

Discussion Questions

1. Are some organizations too large to function without traditional hierarchies?
2. Are some types of employees a better fit for the holacracy model? What characteristics do they need to succeed in this system?
3. Did Hsieh move too fast or too slow in implementing the new system? What mistakes, if any, did he make?
4. Would you like to work at Zappos? Why or why not?
5. Does a change to self-leadership have to be imposed from the top?
6. Do you think that Zappos' transition from hierarchy to holacracy will succeed or fail?

cult or unpleasant tasks like research papers. To succeed we need self-discipline, which we can foster by altering our immediate physical environments. Use reminders and attention-focusing devices like computer calendar notifications and sticky notes as prompts to keep you focused on the term paper. Eliminate those cues that undermine performance. Remove the cell phone that would distract you from your project, for instance. Instead, determine those conditions that encourage peak performance and build those elements into the work setting. If you write best in a quiet location, take your laptop computer or tablet to the library or work when your roommates or family members are gone. Hang around those who model good study habits. Self-discipline can also be strengthened by deliberately taking actions that enhance our performance on challenging assignments. Goal setting is one such self-behavior modification strategy. Chances are you already engage in goal setting by keeping a to-do list on your phone or keeping a record of upcoming assignments for class. Effective goals, whether as simple as a daily list or as complicated as a five-year plan, put specific completion dates and benchmarks in writing. Goal setting for a term paper project would mean breaking the assignment into a series of smaller sections or tasks and making up a schedule of completion dates.

Mastering others is strength, mastering yourself is true power.
—Lao Tzu

Seeking out opportunities to observe and evaluate your actions is the best way to determine if you're reaching your goals. Don't wait for feedback from others; instead, watch your own behavior to determine what factors raise or lower your performance. Track how frequently you carry out a desired behavior, such as searching databases or completing sections of your paper. When self-observation indicates you're achieving your objectives, reward yourself (take a break, play a video game, fix your favorite meal). Avoid self-punishment because it focuses on past failures rather than on improvement. Use rehearsal strategies to prepare for particularly important communication performances like speeches, interviews, sales calls, or presenting your research paper to the rest of the class. Identify the key elements of the situation and rehearse by visualizing the setting and a successful performance. Practice out loud whenever possible.

The second set of self-leadership strategies focuses on the task itself. We achieve more when we are attracted to a project. The key is finding enjoyment or pleasure in the job itself. Naturally rewarding activities make us feel competent and in control and contribute to our sense of purpose. When it comes to term papers, you may enjoy mastering a difficult subject, setting your own work pace for a project, or learning material that will further your career and benefit others. Focus on the rewards, not the unpleasant aspects of the task—the investment of time and energy, the difficulty of writing. The setting also plays an important role in how we feel about a task. Whenever possible, pleasurable features should be built into the work environment. Put on your favorite music when writing, for instance, or settle in to read with your favorite drink or snack.

The final set of self-leadership strategies fosters self-confidence through positive thinking. Eliminate critical and destructive self-talk, and challenge unrealistic beliefs and assumptions. In the case of a term paper, damaging self-statements like "I can't complete this project" can be changed to "There's no reason I can't finish if I set my goals and follow my timeline." Irrational beliefs like "I must get an A on this paper or I'm a failure" can be reframed as "I'm going to give this paper my best effort, but I can't expect to excel in every situation." Use mental rehearsal as a preparation tool. Recognize that failure is often the precursor to success. Finally, think in terms of opportunities rather than limitations or obstacles.

Former president Ronald Reagan provided one of the best examples of opportunity thinking when he was wounded in an assassination attempt. He tried to relieve the tension of the nation rather than focusing on his own condition. Reagan told his wife: "Honey, I forgot to duck." He pleaded with his doctors: "Please say you're Republicans." To the medical staff, he quipped: "Send me to L.A. where I can see the air I'm breathing." (Another example of an opportunity thinker can be found in box 5.8.)

Our life is what our thoughts make it.

—Marcus Aurelius

Box 5.8 Opportunity Thinking in Action	**The One-Armed Explorer**[51]

In the years immediately following the Civil War, much of the American Southwest surrounding the Colorado River was marked "unexplored" on maps. There were rumors that the region contained towering waterfalls and that the Colorado River disappeared underground.

In 1869 amateur geologist and map maker Major John Wesley Powell set out with a team of nine other men to travel the Green and Colorado Rivers, to explore the "Great Unknown." He hoped to map the area and to observe its geologic features. Powell had taken previous surveying trips to the West but this was his first river journey. The Major was an unlikely leader. He was small even for his time—5 feet 6½ inches and 120 pounds. He lost most of his right arm in the Battle of Shiloh and suffered chronic pain. His father advised him to avoid exploration after the war. "Wes," he said, "you are a maimed man. Settle down at teaching. It is a noble profession. Get this nonsense of science and adventure out of your mind." Powell did take up teaching, but used his academic positions to launch scientific expeditions to the West with student recruits.

No one in Powell's river expedition had any experience navigating rapids so they had to learn how to run white water on the fly. They loaded themselves and their supplies into three heavy boats that were hard to maneuver in fast water. Powell had the only life jacket. (The rest of the group believed that wearing life jackets was not manly.) Science writer Edward Dolnick describes the dangers facing the group this way:

> Between their starting point and safety, though they could not have known it, stretched a thousand miles of river and nearly five hundred rapids. At spots beyond counting, a moment's inattention or the briefest of mistakes could prove fatal. Drowning was only the most obvious hazard. A capsizing that left the food stores soaked or sunk would mean death just as surely, though more slowly. A boat damaged beyond repair could be a calamity. A broken leg could be a death sentence. . . . The river could grab a boat and trap it in a "hole," a kind of whirlpool turned on its side . . .

Powell traveled in the first boat and scouted the river ahead. He would signal if the group would run the rapids or "line the boats," a back-breaking process of towing them along the edge of the rapids to calmer water. Disaster soon struck when one of the boats sank, destroying much of their food. Later they barely escaped from a burning campsite, and water spoiled most of their remaining supplies. If the desert heat wasn't burning them, downpours were drenching them.

Throughout the trip Powell remained optimistic despite the danger and discomfort. He marveled at the geology revealed by the canyons and realized that they were created by erosion over thousands and millions of years. At nearly every stop, as his men rested or repaired the boats, he would scale the canyon walls (a thousand feet or more), hoping to see the surrounding country while identifying the river's course. On one occasion he was "rim rocked," meaning he couldn't go up or down the cliff. His climbing companion took off his long underwear, lowered the garment down to Powell and then hauled him up to safety.

Ragged and starving, Powell and five of his men came out of the Great Unknown three months after they started. (One member of the expedition abandoned the journey early on, while three others hiked out near the conclusion of the trip—never to be seen again.) At the end of the journey even Powell was focused more on survival than science, as most of his instruments and notes were lost. The Major and his crew have been hailed as some of the greatest explorers in US history. Their feat is even more impressive given that other adventurers of their time who also tried to travel down the river either gave up or died in the attempt. By World War II (70 years later), only 250 people had successfully traveled the Colorado River through the Grand Canyon.

Major Powell's refusal to be limited by his disability continued the rest of his life. (Surgeries to end the pain in his arm were not successful.) He led other survey trips to the West as well as another trip down part of the Grand Canyon. He became an expert on Indian life and, as an employee of the federal government, he founded and directed the US Geological Society and the Bureau of Ethnology, which studied Native American culture. Despite never finishing college, Powell led a variety of scientific clubs and organizations, including the Anthropological Society, the National Academy of Sciences, and the Association for the Advancement of Science. He told politicians that the West was arid and could not sustain a large population. (His warning was ignored.) Powell was even able to make light of his physical limitation. He became friends with Mississippi Congressman C. E. Hooker, who lost his left arm fighting for the South. The two agreed that when they bought a new pair of gloves, they would send the other the glove they didn't need. The two friends shipped useless gloves to one another for 30 years.

Leading the Journey

Leaders who empower followers take on different tasks than they do under the traditional, hierarchical model. According to James Belasco and Ralph Stayer, an empowering leader acts more like a lead goose than a head buffalo.[52] As head buffalo, a leader takes charge while loyal followers look on, waiting for direction. In contrast, geese flying in a V formation on their annual migrations frequently shift leaders and roles in response to travel conditions.

Belasco and Stayer call their model for a systematic approach to empowerment "Leading the Journey." In this model, leaders (acting as lead geese) are responsible for determining vision and direction, removing obstacles, developing ownership, and stimulating self-directed action.

- *Determining focus and direction.* Leaders at all levels of an organization are responsible for setting vision and direction. Staying in touch with customers (those who use an organization's products and services) is the key to determining direction. The goal is to put on an outstanding performance for the end user, not just an adequate one.

- *Removing obstacles.* Eliminate obstacles that keep followers from providing outstanding performances. Help ensure that all systems (compensation, information, procedures) support this one objective. At Johnsonville Foods, product quality improved when customer complaint letters, which used to go to the marketing department, went directly to line workers instead. The people on the line responded to the complaints and then took responsibility for measuring product quality. Soon these measurements led to improvements in production processes. (Quality also improved when workers began sampling the sausages.)

- *Developing ownership.* Refuse to accept responsibility for problems that can be solved by followers. Use questions to coach followers instead of providing answers. Coaching questions include:

  — "In the best of all worlds, what is great performance for your customers?"

  — "What do you want to achieve in the next two or three years?"

  — "How will you measure your performance?"

  — "What things do you need to learn in order to reach your goals?"

  — "What work experience do you need to help you learn what is needed to achieve your goals?"

- *Stimulating self-directed actions.* Decide what you do best and give your other responsibilities away. Change systems and structures so that followers are rewarded for solving their own problems and not for bringing their problems to you. Hire the best performers and fire or transfer those who aren't contributing.

Belasco and Stayer argue that the only way to master the leadership tasks described above is to learn by doing. Test these behaviors and learn from your failures. Use mistakes, fear of failure, anger, terminations, and other obstacles and setbacks as teachers. In sum: "Leading requires learning. Learning requires doing. So get on with the doing. Then study how you did it."[53]

Buffalo are loyal to one leader; they stand around and wait for the leader to show them what to do. When the leader isn't around, they wait for him to show up. That's why the early settlers could decimate the buffalo herds so easily by killing the lead buffalo. The rest of the herd stood around, waiting for their leader to lead them, and were slaughtered.

—James Belasco & Ralph Stayer

CHAPTER TAKEAWAYS

- Power is defined as *the ability to influence others.* Leadership is impossible without power since a leader must modify attitudes and behaviors. Yet influencing others does not automatically qualify as leadership; power must be used in pursuit of group goals to merit leadership classification.

- *Coercive power* is based on the ability to administer punishment or to give negative reinforcements.
- *Reward power* rests on the ability to deliver something of value to others.
- *Legitimate power* resides in the position rather than in the person. People with legitimate power have the right to prescribe our behavior within specified parameters.
- *Expert power* is based on the person, not the position. Experts are influential because they supply needed information and skills.
- *Referent power* is role model power.
- *Information power* is based on access to, and distribution of, data.
- *Ecological power* arises out of control over the physical environment, technology, and how work is organized.
- Group members prefer leaders who rely on power associated with the unique characteristics of the person (expert and referent) rather than leaders who rely on power related to their position (coercion, reward, legitimate).
- To engage in constructive organizational politics, use your informal power to foster collaboration and to help the organization reach its objectives. Politically skilled leaders understand power and themselves, demonstrate awareness of the political environment, and develop their interpersonal skills to influence others.
- A number of language features have been identified as "powerful" or "powerless" by researchers. Powerful talk makes you seem knowledgeable and confident; powerless talk is tentative and submissive.
- You can gain more power by empowering others. There are five major reasons why leaders choose to share power: (1) distributing power increases the job satisfaction and performance of employees; (2) sharing power fosters greater cooperation among group members; (3) distributing power means collective survival—the group endures rather than fails; (4) effective leadership helps personal growth and learning; and (5) sharing power prevents power abuses.
- Components of the empowerment process include modifying the environment to eliminate situational factors that create feelings of powerlessness; building intrinsic motivation though meaning, choice, competence, and impact; and supplying information and other resources.
- "Superleaders" help followers learn to lead themselves, guiding them from dependence to independence. Become a "self-leader" by acting on your own through self-behavior modification, finding enjoyment in the task, and building self-confidence through positive thinking.
- In the "Leading the Journey" empowerment model, leaders determine vision and direction, remove obstacles, develop ownership, and stimulate self-directed action.

∽ APPLICATION EXERCISES

1. Is power a taboo subject? Discuss your answer to this statement in class or in a reflection paper.

2. Create your own cost/benefit ratios for each type of power. Do you agree that leaders should strive for expert and referent power?

3. Identify the sources of power you respond to most/least favorably. Analyze the differences.

4. Create a case study based on how a leader engaged in constructive organizational politics.

5. Develop a strategy for overcoming your powerless talk using the techniques discussed in the chapter. Report on your progress to another person in the class.

6. Brainstorm a list of strategies for eliminating environmental factors that cause powerlessness.

7. Evaluate your intrinsic task motivation as a student using the four factors described in the chapter. Share your analysis with others in the class.

8. Interview employees (leaders and followers) in an organization to determine how empowerment is/is not used effectively. Share your results with others.

9. Write a paper describing why an empowerment effort succeeded or failed based on the components and models of empowerment presented in the chapter.

10. Identify the job/situation/or context in which you have felt most/least empowered as a follower. Compare your effectiveness in these two situations.

11. Select a major task or project facing you this term (a major speech, a professional exam, getting in shape, training for a long race) and apply the self-leadership strategies described in this chapter to completing this task. Develop specific goals and determine how you will observe and evaluate your behavior, reward yourself, modify the physical environment, and rehearse. Consider the elements of the project that might be naturally rewarding and how you can think in terms of opportunities instead of limitations. Turn in your preliminary plan. At the end of the quarter or semester, after the project has been completed, reflect on your performance. Did using these tactics produce better results? How would you rate yourself as a self-leader? Record your conclusions and submit them to your instructor.

∿ CULTURAL CONNECTIONS: A DIFFERENT VIEW ON POWER— THE SOUTH AFRICAN CONCEPT OF UBUNTU[54]

As we have discussed in this chapter, using power effectively is critical to the success of leadership. Whether power is centralized or distributed, its use or misuse has much to do with overall leadership outcomes. This becomes more complex, however, when crossing cultural boundaries. Inhabitants of different countries have sometimes radically dissimilar viewpoints on power. In some countries, such as Israel, Denmark, and New Zealand, workers often expect that power will be shared. In countries like Malaysia, India, and the Philippines, followers are generally much more willing to be directed. One country with a very unique view on power is South Africa.

Since the collapse of the oppressive apartheid system, black empowerment has been a priority. Over three-fourths of the population in South Africa is black; yet many of these indigenous people live in poverty in rural settlements outside major cities. The South African government has been working to integrate traditional black African cultural values into mainstream society. One option for development that has gained popularity embraces the traditional African concept of ubuntu. In Zulu, *ubuntu* roughly translates as: "a person is a person through other persons." As such, ubuntu is based on caring for the well-being of others through a spirit of mutual support and the promotion of individual and societal well-being. Ubuntu basically views an enterprise as a community of relationships that reflect group solidarity. The ubuntu philosophy of democracy is not based simply on majority rule; rather it focuses on building consensus through shared power. The ubuntu philosophy helps to create a community built on interdependent and equal participation.

This can be seen in the nearly one million South African collectives known as *stokvels*. These joint undertakings—savings clubs, burial societies, and other cooperatives—offer community-based services to members and are led through a process of shared decision making based on the ubuntu philosophy. Power is distributed within South African society in ways that place the good of the collective above the needs of the individual. For the stokvels, making a profit is important, but never if it involves the exploitation of others. Although similar practices are found in many other cultures, this approach would seem quite different than the view of power held by many in Western industrialized society, which often focuses on maximizing profits whatever the costs.

～ LEADERSHIP ON THE BIG SCREEN: *STAR WARS EPISODE VII—THE FORCE AWAKENS*

Starring: Daisy Ridley, John Boyega, Harrison Ford, Carrie Fisher, Oscar Isaac, Adam Driver, Mark Hamill

Rating: PG-13 for violence and intense action scenes

Synopsis: Thirty years after the triumph of good in the earlier Star Wars film *Return of the Jedi*, the dark side of the powerful Force is active again. Only the last remaining Jedi knight, Luke Skywalker (Hamill), can restore order—and the search is on to find him. Both the Resistance and the evil First Order want the map that pinpoints Skywalker's location. The Resistance secures the map but must destroy the First Order's super weapon and vanquish its second in command, Ren (Driver), the son of Resistance leaders Han Solo (Ford) and Princess/General Leia (Fisher). This sequel introduces new characters to the Star Wars franchise, including young scavenger Rey (Ridley) who demonstrates Jedi powers, former First Order storm trooper Finn (Boyega) who supplies valuable intelligence about the enemy, and Resistance pilot Poe Dameron (Isaac). Han Solo makes his final appearance, dying at the hands of his son.

Chapter Links: use and abuse of power; coercive, legitimate, reward, expert, and referent power; powerlessness; self-leadership

6

Leadership and Influence

Leadership is serious meddling in other people's lives.

—*Max DePree*

OVERVIEW

Exercising influence is the essence of leadership. Leading means influencing since leaders must shape the attitudes and behavior of others to help groups reach their goals. In the last chapter, we examined the sources and uses of power. In this chapter, we continue our discussion of influence by taking a closer look at how leaders modify the behavior of others through symbolic communication. We will focus on four sets of influence tools particularly significant to leaders: (1) credibility-building behaviors, (2) compliance-gaining strategies, (3) argumentation competencies, and (4) negotiation tactics. We'll conclude by examining ways to resist unethical influence attempts.

Credibility: The Key to Successful Influence

Credibility is the foundation for successful influence because the success or failure of a particular influence strategy ultimately depends on the credibility of the influencer. The results of surveys of 100,000 global managers over a period of 30 years demonstrate how important credibility is to leaders. When the managers were asked what characteristics they admired most in their leaders, the answers were forward looking, honest, inspirational, and competent. Taken together, these elements comprise what researchers label as believability or credibility.

> People everywhere want to believe in their leaders. They want to have faith and confidence in them as people. People want to believe that their leaders' words can be trusted, that they have the knowledge and skill necessary to lead, and that they are personally excited and enthusiastic about the direction in which they are headed. *Credibility is the foundation of leadership.*[1]

Credibility has always been central to the study of communication and leadership. The ancient Greeks studied the public speaking techniques of leaders and used the term "ethos" for what we now call credibility. For Plato, Aristotle, and others, ethos consisted of high moral standards, intelligence, and other speaker character traits.[2] An orator swayed an audience through logic (logos), emotion (pathos), and, most importantly, personal characteristics (ethos). Interest in credibility among communication scholars remains high in the modern era.[3]

The strong tie between credibility and influence is the reason scholars have been interested in ethos through the ages. No matter what the setting, credible sources are more effective. Consider the following:

- Highly credible public speakers are more likely to convince audiences to accept their arguments. By citing credible sources, speakers build their own credibility and generate greater attitude change.[4]
- Successful counselors first earn the trust of their clients.[5]
- Salespeople are more productive if they sell themselves (build their credibility) before they sell their products.
- Editorials are more persuasive if they come from highly credible newspapers like *The New York Times* or the *Chicago Tribune*.[6]

- Trust in leadership significantly affects basketball team performance.[7]
- Juries are more swayed by credible witnesses.
- The higher the credibility of instructors, the more students learn.[8]

> *Leader credibility is the cornerstone of*
> *corporate performance and global competitiveness.*
>
> —*Tom Peters*

Dimensions and Challenges of Credibility

Modern investigators no longer treat credibility as a set of speaker traits. Instead, they isolate factors that audiences use to evaluate the believability of speakers. The most significant elements or dimensions of credibility are *competence*, *trustworthiness*, and *dynamism*.[9]

Competence can be defined as knowledge of the topic at hand, intelligence, expertise, skill, or good judgment. The term "value-added" best describes the kind of competence that leaders need to demonstrate.[10] A leader must provide the skills that the group needs at a particular time. For example, boards of directors often look for top executives who can take their organizations in new directions. In one case, they may be looking for someone with a strong marketing or fund-raising background to increase sales or donations. In another, they may want a chief executive who knows how to cut costs or streamline operations.

Trustworthiness (character) is another name for honesty and consistency.[11] This dimension of credibility is critical to effective leadership since the leader-follower relationship is built on trust. Managers rate honesty as the most important leader quality; the most influential public opinion leaders are also the most trustworthy. Unfortunately, trust is lost when CEOs get huge contracts when ordinary workers are suffering. In 2011, for example, as the nation was coming out of one of the biggest economic downturns in history, CEOs at Qualcomm, JC Penney, Tyco, and several other firms earned over $50 million even as many of their fellow citizens struggled to find work and stay in their homes.[12]

Dynamism refers to perceptions of a source's confidence, activity, and assertiveness. Dynamic leaders communicate confidence in their visions for the future. They inspire others to work harder and to make greater sacrifices. Dynamism appears to be an integral part of what many people call charismatic leadership, a topic we discussed in detail in chapter 4.

Leaders face some special challenges when it comes to establishing and maintaining their credibility.[13] First, followers pay more attention to leaders than leaders do to followers. As a result, they are quick to note when leaders fall short. Any failure (a supervisor violating a promise, for example) is seen as evidence of the leader's poor character rather than as the product of situational factors (the supervisor may have been forced to break the commitment by top management). One negative incident can undo the goodwill built with followers over a long period of time and makes receivers more sensitive to possible future violations. Heightened scrutiny also leads to charges of inconsistency when leaders present themselves in different ways to different audiences (stockholders, customers, employees).

Second, leaders must respond to the conflicting demands of multiple constituencies. Fulfilling the expectations of one group may mean violating the expectations of another. For instance, a pledge to increase the budget of the marketing department may mean a reduction in the amount previously committed to research and development. Third, leaders often feel the pressure to treat organizational "stars" better than their peers, creating perceptions of injustice. Fourth, leaders may seek to improve performance by communicating high expectations that turn out later to be unrealistic. Fifth, following the latest management fads can lead to a gap between words and deeds because leaders start using new terminology ("employee engagement," "total quality") that doesn't match reality. Finally, leaders hired solely for their technical competencies may overlook the importance of interpersonal skills like acting consistently, treating others justly, and following through on promises.

While the challenges of building leadership credibility are great, so are the rewards for doing so. Followers who believe that their leaders are trustworthy, for instance, are more satisfied with their jobs as well as more committed to their organizations. These followers are more willing to help out coworkers and to treat others with respect. They are also more supportive of organizational decisions and receive higher performance evaluations.[14] (We'll take a closer look at the importance of building a trusting organizational culture in chapter 8.)

A single lie destroys a whole reputation for integrity.

—*Baltasar Gracian*

Building Your Credibility

Discovering how others assess your competence, trustworthiness, and dynamism is an excellent way to start building your credibility as a leader. Rate yourself on the credibility scales found in Application Exercise 1 at the end of this chapter. Then ask someone else to rate you and compare the responses. You will probably rank higher on one dimension of credibility than on others. In addition, your self-ratings might be either above or below the ratings you receive from your partner. Once you've targeted the dimension(s) of credibility most in need of improvement, you can start to change your behaviors in order to generate more favorable impressions. In chapter 1, we called this process impression management. The following sets of behaviors are particularly effective in managing perceptions of credibility. These tactics boost your credibility by increasing your perceived similarity with observers and linking you to groups that have reputations for competence and integrity.[15]

Self-presentation behaviors. Use statements that reveal that you are "human" with similar emotions, limitations, and experiences as your audience. Distance yourself from untrustworthy groups by pointing out how dissimilar you are to them. For example: you are *not* a manager who follows the latest management fads or you are *not* like other salespeople who will lie to sell their products. Introduce your qualifications—job title, experience, research—to address the issue at hand. Identify your credentials at or near the beginning of messages to have the greatest impact.[16] However, your message can change attitudes and behavior even if you don't have impressive qualifications. According to the "sleeper effect," the source is forgotten as time passes, but the message is remembered and judged on its own merits. If the ideas you introduce are well-crafted and supported (see the discussion of argumentation to follow), they may be adopted later.[17]

Language. Avoid technical, jargon-laced language that will distance you from your audience and may give the impression that you are hiding behind the terminology because you don't really understand the topic. Use common, clear, and understandable terms.

Physical appearance and other nonverbal behaviors. Dress appropriately for your profession; choose a style similar to that of your audience; reject clothing or accessories that might match negative stereotypes. For instance, avoid darkly tinted glasses or sunglasses. The stereotype holds that untrustworthy people wear dark eyeglasses. In addition:[18]

- Make sustained eye contact when communicating with others. Avoid shifting your eyes, looking away, keeping your eyes downcast, or excessive blinking.

- Use gestures to add emphasis to the points that you make. Try to appear spontaneous and unrehearsed; let your gestures convey the depth or intensity of your emotions. Hand wringing, finger tapping, tugging at clothing, and tentative movements undermine credibility.

- Maintain a relaxed, open posture when talking with others. Lean forward and smile when answering a question in order to establish rapport. Change your posture frequently and forcefully to communicate responsiveness. Try to avoid those behaviors that make you look timid or nonassertive—holding your body rigid, keeping arms and hands crossed and close to the body, and so on.

- Pay attention to your voice. Strive to sound confident by using a conversational speaking style and vary your rate, pitch, and volume. Sounding nasal, tense, or flat can make you appear significantly less credible. In addition, frequent pauses, speaking too rapidly, repeating words, and stuttering have a negative impact on credibility.

Modifying behaviors to make the desired impression on others is the first step to building your credibility. However, our credibility as leaders also depends on the quality of the relationships we maintain with followers. Ellen Whitener and her colleagues identify five sets of behaviors that foster perceptions of trustworthiness in manager-employee relationships.[19] These include: (1) *Behavioral consistency;* acting consistently over time and in a variety of situations makes it easier for followers to predict your behavior and to take risks. (2) *Behavioral integrity;* match what you say and do, particularly by telling the truth and keeping promises. (3) *Sharing and delegation of control;* inviting participation in decision making enables employees to protect their interests, reduces the likelihood that you will take advantage of the situation, and signals trust and respect for their worth and standing in the organization. (4) *Communication;* provide accurate information, supply explanations for decisions, and reveal your openness through sharing your thoughts and feelings. (5) *Demonstration of concern;* reflect your concern for followers by focusing on their needs and interests, protecting their rights, and refusing to take advantage of them (i.e., keep confidences, give credit to others).

James Kouzes and Barry Posner emphasize that perceptions of all three dimensions of credibility build over time. They outline the following credibility-building practices that are effective in the long term.[20]

Discover yourself. Know yourself in order to lay the foundation for consistent behavior. Start by identifying your credo, which is the set of values and beliefs you consider to be important. Values serve as principles or standards by which we evaluate our actions and the actions of others. To clarify what you believe, imagine that you'll be going on a six-month sabbatical to a location where you cannot be reached by phone, letter, fax, or e-mail. Write a short memo before you go in which you identify the values and beliefs you think should guide the decision making and actions of colleagues when you're gone. (Turn to Application Exercise 2 for a complete description of this project.) Next, develop the necessary skills or competencies to put your beliefs into action along with the confidence to do so. Skill and confidence levels can be built through mastering current tasks, following effective role models, seeking support from others, and recognizing that experiencing stress does not signal lack of ability.

Appreciate constituents. Credible leaders have a deep understanding of the values, needs, and desires of constituents. In particular, they appreciate the perspectives of an increasingly diverse workplace (see chapter 10 for a discussion of leading diversity). To cultivate an in-depth understanding of followers, listen (visit the sales force, hold feedback sessions, monitor social media, call customers), be willing to learn from others, solicit feedback from superiors and subordinates, encourage dissent or controversy about ideas, and put your trust in others at the same time you live up to the trust they put in you.

Affirm shared values. Kouzes and Posner refer to shared values as the "internal compasses that enable people to act independently and interdependently." Shared values provide a reference point for decisions and actions, creating a common language for collaboration that boosts productivity. We've already seen how important it is for a leader to have a clear set of personal values. However, you must not unilaterally impose your values on others. Instead, work together with followers through discussion groups and other forums to develop shared values statements.

Additional ways to encourage shared beliefs and actions include advocating cooperation and resource sharing, as well as developing recruiting and hiring procedures, orientation programs, training and development efforts, recognition and promotion, and other organizational structures that highlight organizational values. You may also have to help groups with competing values discuss their differences and come to agreement.

Develop capacity. Like leaders, followers need to develop skills and self-confidence to put their beliefs into action. You can help constituents increase their capacity by (1) providing educational opportunities, (2) giving followers the latitude and authority to make significant decisions, (3) helping followers believe in their own abilities (for a discussion of empowerment strategies, turn to chapter 5), (4) giving followers the opportunity to make mistakes (fostering confidence), (5) sharing information and feedback, and (6) ensuring that everyone accepts responsibility for her or his own actions.

Serve a purpose. Serving a purpose refers to creating a sense of direction for the group. Leaders can communicate direction by:

- *going first*. Demonstrate commitment by taking the initial step, like being the first to volunteer to work overtime to get a product out on schedule, and by how you spend your time and respond to challenges.
- *staying in touch*. Maintain regular contact with constituents; listen and be approachable.
- *making meaning on a daily basis*. Send consistent messages about attitudes, values and commitments through how you respond to routine events like interruptions, stress, meetings, and complaints; set a consistent example.
- *storytelling*. Teach others through narratives that involve your own experience and that of your audience.
- *regaining lost credibility*. Every leader, no matter how conscientious or successful, will fail on occasion. The effects of such failures do not have to be permanent, however. Restoring your credibility involves the six "As" of leadership accountability: accept responsibility, admit mistakes, apologize, take immediate remedial action, make amends or reparation (you should share in any penalty for the mistake), and pay close attention to the reactions of followers. (More information on repairing trust can be found in chapter 8.)

Example is not the main thing in influencing others. It is the only thing.
—*Albert Schweitzer*

Sustain hope. Leaders play a critical role in boosting the spirits of followers in a world marked by stress and failure. Hopeful followers, in turn, achieve high levels of performance. If you want to keep hope alive, you must first believe that you can take charge of your life and persist in the face of obstacles. You and your constituents need to combine hope with work, recognizing reality but acting to change things for the better. Create positive images of the future that, in turn, generate positive thoughts and images in the minds of followers. Be passionate about your organization or cause; suffer together with constituents. (Freeze your salary and benefits along with those of your employees, for example.) As a supportive leader, show genuine concern for others by listening to their problems, offering words of encouragement, fostering friendships between coworkers, and nurturing a sense of community.

Compliance-Gaining Strategies

Compliance-gaining strategies are the verbal tactics that leaders and others use to get their way in face-to-face encounters. These strategies are based on the types of power we described in chapter 5. Attempts to get others to do what we want are a frequent occurrence in everyday life. Requesting notes from a classmate, convincing a friend to take Uber or Lyft rather than driving home drunk from a party, enlisting volunteers for a fund drive, and persuading a neighbor to keep her dog chained up are all examples of interpersonal compliance-gaining situations.

Managerial Influence Tactics

Organizational compliance seekers face a number of constraints not present in the interpersonal context. First, they have less freedom to decide whether or not to engage in persuasion. Middle managers and supervisors must influence others if they are to perform their roles. Second, the statuses of both the compliance seeker and the target of the request in an organization are clearly defined. Third, organizational influence agents aren't free to pursue their personal goals only; they must direct most of their efforts at achieving organizational objectives like increasing productivity, reducing tardiness, and improving service. Fourth, the rules and culture of the organization may favor some influence methods while discouraging others.

Gary Yukl of the State University of New York at Albany and his associates identify the following common managerial influence tactics.[21]

- *Rational persuasion.* Use of logical arguments and factual evidence to demonstrate that a request or proposal will attain organizational objectives.

    Examples: "Getting the additional funds will help our department reach its goals."
    "Research shows there is a market for a new online MBA program."

- *Apprising.* Explaining how compliance will benefit the target and his or her career.

    Examples: "Learning the new accounting software will make you a more valuable employee."
    "Taking this overseas assignment will help you qualify for a division manager position."

- *Inspirational appeals.* Generating enthusiasm by appealing to values and ideals; arousing emotions.

    Examples: "Hiring more service representatives will help us provide world-class customer care."

    "Joining our project team will put you on the cutting edge of emerging technology."

- *Consultation.* Seeking suggestions for improvement; asking for input for planning an activity, strategy, or change.

    Examples: "How do you think we can reduce the time it takes to bring a new product to market?"

    "Take a look at this proposal and let me know what you think before we implement it."

- *Collaboration.* Providing resources and assistance if the target complies with the request.

    Examples: "We could both come in on Saturday morning to make sure the product gets shipped."

    "If you can help, I'll provide you with the equipment and personnel you need."

- *Ingratiation.* Use of flattery and praise before or during a request; expressing confidence in the target's ability to fulfill a difficult request.

    Examples: "Since your handwriting is better than mine, you should record the group's findings on the board."

    "You're the only person in the department who can make this sale."

- *Personal appeals.* Appealing to feelings of loyalty and friendship when asking for something.

    Examples: "As a friend, do me a favor, and cover my shift."

    "We've been colleagues for a long time, so please back me up when I approach the boss."

- *Exchange.* Trading favors; promising to reciprocate later or to share the benefits when the task is completed.

    Examples: "If you support my legislation, I'll support yours."

    "If you put in additional hours now, you can have additional time off when the project is done."

- *Coalition tactics.* Soliciting the aid of others or using the support of coworkers to convince the target to go along with the request.

    Examples: "The CEO really likes this proposal."

    "Your friend Jim is behind this idea."

- *Legitimating tactics.* Claiming the right or authority to make a request; aligning the request with organizational policies, rules, traditions, and so forth.

Examples: "The policy manual states that I am entitled to two weeks of vacation."

"Your firm signed an agreement to buy a shipment of our product."

- *Pressure.* Demanding, threatening, checking up; persistent reminders.

Examples: "If you don't honor the contract, we will take you to court."

"You had better finish creating that contract by Friday afternoon."

In evaluating the effectiveness of individual managerial influence tactics, Yukl concludes that any given strategy is more likely to be successful if:

1. the target perceives the influence attempt as socially acceptable;

2. the influencer has the position and personal power to use the tactic;

3. the strategy makes the request seem more desirable to the target;

4. the tactic is used skillfully; and

5. the request is legitimate and doesn't violate the needs and values of the recipient.[22]

Rational persuasion, consultation, collaboration, and inspirational appeals are most likely to generate commitment to the task, whether the target is a superior, peer, or subordinate. Ingratiation, exchange, and apprising are moderately effective with subordinates and peers but not with superiors. Personal appeals secure compliance in friendly relationships. A coalition can encourage support for a major organizational change but may be seen as ganging up on a target when used to convince someone to carry out an assignment or to improve her or his performance. Pressure and legitimating tactics gain compliance at the expense of long-term commitment. You can practice these strategies by applying them to your organization in Application Exercise 4.

Combinations of tactics also vary in effectiveness. Tactics based on the soft power described in chapter 5—rational persuasion, apprising, consultation, ingratiation, inspirational appeals—work better when combined than when used alone. Combining a soft tactic with supporting evidence generally increases the chances of success. However, some tactics are incompatible. Mixing hard and soft power strategies (i.e., pressuring someone while asking him or her to do a favor based on loyalty or friendship) can derail a request.

Yukl reminds us that we can't take effective influence for granted. Subjects in his studies report many examples of when they originated or received "inept influence attempts."[23] Managers may combine incompatible tactics, make clumsy attempts at being helpful or friendly, fail to recruit allies, try to gain compliance for an improper or unethical request, and so forth. One common mistake is using hard tactics when softer ones would have been more successful.

In chapter 5 we developed a cost/benefit ratio for each of the types of power. The same approach can be used to determine the best compliance-gaining strategy. John Hunter and Franklin Boster suggest that persuaders should balance the cost of using a tactic against the objective they seek by considering the *emotional threshold*.[24] Compliance-gaining attempts produce emotional responses in targets. Pro-social tactics, such as rational persuasion, inspirational appeals, collaboration and consultation, are widely accepted and are more likely to produce positive feelings in recipients. Antisocial strategies like pressure and legitimation raise threat levels and thus are more likely to generate negative emotions. Hunter and Boster believe that leaders must decide just how much negative emotion they are willing to generate to get their way. In some situations, the emotional threshold is high; for example, when asking a colleague to do a personal favor like covering a shift at work. In other cases, the threshold is low; for example, when safety is threatened or when addressing destructive behaviors like stealing and sexual harassment. In these cases of dangerous, unethical activities, antisocial tactics are in order, even if they provoke anger and resentment in targets.

Upward Dissent

Expressing disagreement or dissent upward to management and supervisors is a particularly challenging form of compliance gaining. Followers who take issue with decisions, policies, and procedures lack the power to make the changes themselves so they have to express their opposition to those who can take action. Upward dissent is risky because there is always the threat of retaliation. However, those who express their frustrations to management do their organizations a valuable service because dissent can alert the group to problems and help it operate more efficiently and ethically.

According to University of Arizona West communication professor Jeffrey Kassing, satisfied workers who identify with their organizations are more likely to express upward dissent. Followers are also more likely to speak up if they (1) have higher status, (2) believe that they can exert significant influence, and (3) have high-quality relationships with their supervisors. Kassing offers the following typology of upward dissent strategies.[25] Complete the self-assessment in box 6.1 to determine the tactics you are most likely to use when expressing disagreement to your leaders.

- *Direct-factual appeal*: supporting the complaint with facts drawn from physical evidence, knowledge of the organization, and personal work experience. For example: producing examples of shoddy work, telling stories of unhappy customers.

- *Repetition*: repeatedly drawing attention to a topic over a period of time. For example: reminding the boss several times about unsafe working conditions during the course of several weeks.

- *Solution presentation*: offering a solution along with drawing attention to the problem. For example: writing an e-mail that includes new procedures; meeting with the supervisor to outline a different manufacturing process.

- *Circumvention*: dissenting to someone above the immediate supervisor. For example: talking to the boss's boss when the immediate supervisor is not receptive to dissent or when the dissent issue involves the direct supervisor.

- *Threatening resignation*: threatening to resign in order to get the supervisor and management to act. For example: promising to quit unless managers end illegal accounting practices.

Box 6.1 Self-Assessment	The Upward Dissent Scale[26]

Instructions: On a scale of 1 to 5, indicate how likely you are to use each of the following behaviors when expressing disagreement to supervisors and higher level managers. 1 = strongly disagree, 5 = strongly agree.

_____ 1. I talk to someone higher up in the organization than my direct supervisor.

_____ 2. I gather evidence to support my concern.

_____ 3. I bring up my concern numerous times.

_____ 4. I say I'll quit if the organization doesn't do something about the problem.

_____ 5. I focus on the facts surrounding the issue.

_____ 6. I raise the issue repeatedly.

_____ 7. I suggest that I'm considering quitting if the organization doesn't do something.

_____ 8. I talk to an organizational officer higher in the chain of command.

_____ 9. I threaten to resign if my concerns aren't addressed.

_____ 10. I present solutions not just problems.

_____ 11. I talk to my boss's boss.

_____ 12. I make several attempts to draw attention to the concern.

_____ 13. I use facts to support my claim.

_____ 14. I claim that the problem is serious enough to make me quit.

_____ 15. I go above my direct supervisor's head to voice my concern.

_____ 16. I continue to mention my concern until it gets addressed.

_____ 17. I go over my boss's head.

_____ 18. I repeat my concern as often as possible.

_____ 19. I threaten to quit.

_____ 20. I present a well-thought-out solution to the problem.

Scoring: Scores for each tactic range from 5 to 25. The higher the score, the more likely you are to use that strategy. Items 2, 5, 10, 13, and 20 = Prosocial; items 4, 7, 9, 14, and 19 = Threatening Resignation; items 1, 8, 11, 15, and 17 = Circumvention; and items 3, 6, 12, 16, and 18 = Repetition.

Employees clearly identify some upward dissent strategies as more effective than others. Strategies that threaten the "face" or image of the receiver are rated least competent; strategies that protect the face of the supervisor are judged most effective. Threat of resignation is the least competent tactic because it promotes the face of the subordinate at the expense of the supervisor, doing the most relational damage. Circumvention and repetition are more effective than vowing to resign but are still considered less competent because they continue to pose a threat to the supervisor's image. Direct-factual appeal and solution presentation (prosocial strategies) are the most successful because they reduce threat through clear and direct communication. These two influence tactics are also the ones most frequently used by workers.

Because upward dissent is so beneficial to organizational health and increases employee satisfaction, Kassing suggests that leaders take steps to encourage this type of communication. They should develop high-quality partnerships with followers, be trained to be receptive to disagreement and criticism (and resist the temptation to retaliate), and develop systems—hotlines, ethics offices—to encourage employees to raise concerns about safety and ethical issues. Finally, leaders need to learn how to effectively express dissent to their managers. Doing so not only alerts the organization to issues but also encourages followers to express their concerns as well.

> *The humblest individual exerts some influence,*
> *either for good or evil, upon others.*
>
> —*Henry Ward Beecher*

Developing Argumentative Competence

When two or more people take different sides on a controversial issue like immigration policy or how to fund local schools, they generally try to establish the superiority of their positions through argument. To be successful, arguers must build a strong case for their positions while simultaneously refuting the arguments of those who take other positions. The introduction of controversy and dialogue sets argumentation apart from compliance-gaining strategies that also rely on reason and evidence. Compliance gainers may provide evidence even when there is no significant disagreement, and compliance-gaining messages often take only a few seconds to deliver. Argumentation always involves controversy and extended discussion.

Argumentation is important to leaders at every level. In small groups, argumentative individuals are more likely to emerge as leaders, and groups that argue about ideas generate higher quality solutions.[27] In organizations, supervisors must defend their own ideas and argue on behalf of subordinates.[28] In the public arena, political leaders, public relations specialists, and social activists engage in argument to support new government regulations, promote industry interests, or defend the rights of disadvantaged groups. (Complete the argumentativeness scale in box 6.2 to determine how likely you are to engage in arguments.)

While argumentation is an essential leadership activity, many of us view arguments with suspicion. Although you have probably had enjoyable arguments that stimulated your thinking, chances are you've also been in unpleasant arguments that resulted in hurt feelings and broken relationships. The key to understanding the mix of good and bad experiences we've had while arguing lies in distinguishing between argumentativeness and verbal aggression.[29] Argumentativeness involves presenting and defending positions on issues. Verbal aggressiveness is hostile communication aimed at attacking the self-concepts of others instead of (or in addition to) their positions on the issues.

Box 6.2   Self-Assessment   **Argumentativeness Scale**[30]

Directions: This questionnaire contains statements about arguing controversial issues. Indicate how often each statement is true for you personally by placing the appropriate number in the blank to the left of the statement. If the statement is almost never true for you, place a "1" in the blank. If the statement is rarely true for you, place a "2" in the blank. If the statement is occasionally true for you, place a "3" in the blank. If the statement is often true for you, place a "4" in the blank. If the statement is almost always true for you, place a "5" in the blank.

_____ 1. While in an argument, I worry that the person with whom I am arguing will form a negative impression of me.

_____ 2. Arguing over controversial issues improves my intelligence.

_____ 3. I enjoy avoiding arguments.

_____ 4. I am energetic and enthusiastic when I argue.

_____ 5. Once I finish an argument I promise myself that I will not get into another.

_____ 6. Arguing with a person creates more problems for me than it solves.

_____ 7. I have a pleasant, good feeling when I win a point in an argument.

_____ 8. When I finish arguing with someone I feel nervous and upset.

_____ 9. I enjoy a good argument over a controversial issue.

_____ 10. I get an unpleasant feeling when I realize I am about to get into an argument.

_____ 11. I enjoy defending my point of view on an issue.

_____ 12. I am happy when I keep an argument from happening.

_____ 13. I do not like to miss the opportunity to argue a controversial issue.

_____ 14. I prefer being with people who rarely disagree with me.

_____ 15. I consider an argument an exciting intellectual challenge.

_____ 16. I find myself unable to think of effective points during an argument.

_____ 17. I feel refreshed and satisfied after an argument on a controversial issue.

_____ 18. I have the ability to do well in an argument.

_____ 19. I try to avoid getting into arguments.

_____ 20. I feel excitement when I expect that a conversation I am in is leading to an argument.

Argumentativeness Scoring

1. Add your scores on items: 2, 4, 7, 9, 11, 13, 15, 17, 18, 20.
2. Add 60 to the sum obtained in step 1.
3. Add your scores on items: 1, 3, 5, 6, 8, 10, 12, 14, 16, 19.
4. To compute your argumentativeness score, subtract the total obtained in step 3 from the total obtained in step 2.

Interpretation

73–100 = High in Argumentativeness

56–72 = Moderate in Argumentativeness

20–55 = Low in Argumentativeness

Aggressive tactics include:

- Character attacks
- Background attacks
- Insults
- Teasing
- Ridicule
- Profanity

- Threats
- Competence attacks
- Physical appearance attacks
- Nonverbal indicators that express hostility (looks of disgust, clenched fists, rolling eyes, demeaning tone of voice)

If our arguments have been unpleasant, it is probably because one or both parties engaged in verbal aggression. Verbally aggressive communication is destructive. Such behavior has been linked to spousal abuse and family violence, for example, and reduces student learning and instructor credibility. In contrast, argumentativeness produces a variety of positive outcomes. Organizational followers prefer to work for supervisors who are argumentative but not aggressive, and such leaders have higher salaries and career satisfaction. Organizational leaders favor followers who have similar traits, giving argumentative (but not aggressive) subordinates higher performance reviews.[31]

Recognizing the difference between argument and aggression is the first step to building our argumentative competence.[32] We may need to jettison our negative images of the term argument and recognize its positive features. We must avoid the aggressive behaviors listed earlier and sharpen our argumentation skills instead. Dominic Infante outlines five skills that, collectively, constitute argumentative competence: stating the controversy in propositional form; inventing arguments; presenting and defending your position; attacking other positions; and managing interpersonal relations.[33]

Stating the controversy in propositional form. Productive arguments begin with a clear understanding of the argumentative situation. Stating the problem in the form of a proposition or proposal is the best way to clarify what the conflict is about. Propositions of fact deal with what happened in the past ("the college grew after 2010 largely due to its president's leadership"), the present ("enrollment is down due to higher tuition"), or future ("unless the college cuts its rate of tuition increase, it will be in financial trouble within five years"). Propositions of value deal with issues of right or wrong ("it's unethical to lay off employees when profits are rising" or "everyone ought to do their part on the group project"). Propositions of policy are concerned with what course of action should be taken, such as how to reduce the number of homeless people in a city or how to market a new financial service. By framing an argument in the form of a proposal, we identify the sides that people are likely to take on the issue, clarify where we stand, and determine who has the burden of proof. Those who favor a proposition must demonstrate that the status quo ought to be changed.

Inventing arguments. Careful examination of the proposition is the key to developing a case either for or against the proposal. The set of questions in box 6.3 can help us analyze controversies systematically. To illustrate how this system

Box 6.3	Inventional System[34]

Major Issues and Sub-Issues

1. Problem
   a. What are the signs of a problem?
   b. What is the specific harm?
   c. How widespread is the harm?

2. Blame
   a. What causes the problem?
   b. Is the present system at fault?
   c. Should the present system be changed?

3. Solution
   a. What are the possible solutions?
   b. Which solution best solves the problem?

4. Consequences
   a. What good outcomes will result from the solution?
   b. What bad outcomes will result from the solution?

works, we'll use the example of a student government faced with the following proposition: "Student activity fees should be increased to help pay for a new fitness center on campus." Proponents of this idea might argue that long waiting lists for racquetball courts, weight rooms, gyms, and physical education classes are signs that current facilities are too small. Overcrowding means that students can't exercise when they want and can't get the classes they need for graduation (specific harm). The problem appears widespread because of the large number of students who express frustration with the current situation.

In answering questions related to blame and possible solutions, proponents might conclude that the problem of overcrowding stems from the fact that student enrollment has outgrown current facilities. A change is in order because current facilities are inadequate (sub-issues b and c). More efficient scheduling and sharing community facilities might help relieve some of the pressure, but the best solution appears to be to build a new, larger building on campus. Since the college does not currently have enough money to build the center, student activity fees must be raised to pay for the project.

Possible positive outcomes or consequences of using fees for the building include more health and human performance classes, an expanded intramural program, additional recreational opportunities, and a higher level of fitness on campus. These positive benefits, advocates might suggest, should outweigh the negative consequence—having to pay higher fees.

Those who oppose the idea of using student fees to pay for a new fitness center could use the same set of questions to generate arguments for opposing the project—the problem does not affect that many students, other solutions can be found, the hardship caused by the additional fees would outweigh any benefits, and so on.

Presenting and defending your position. Most arguments involve four parts—claim, evidence, reasons, and summary. Begin by stating what you want others to accept—the conclusion or claim of your argument. Provide evidence in the form of statistics, examples, or testimonials from others and supply reasons or logic for taking your position. Common patterns of logic include:

1. inductive (generalizing from one or a few cases to many),

2. deductive (moving from a larger category to a smaller one),

3. causal (one event causes another), and

4. analogical (argument based on similarities).

All four types of reasoning could be used in the fitness center argument. If you supported this idea, you could argue that the frustration experienced by some students is typical of the student body at large (inductive), that most colleges have developed new fitness facilities in the past 10 years (deductive), that building a new fitness center will improve student retention (causal), or that billing students for a new fitness center worked well for a similar college in the next town (analogical). End your presentation with a summary that shows what you've established. Be prepared to supplement your position with further evidence and reason once it comes under attack.

Attacking other positions. This argumentative skill is based on identifying weaknesses in the evidence and reasoning of the other party. Questions to ask when attacking evidence include: Is the evidence recent enough? Was enough evidence presented, and was it from reliable sources? Is the evidence consistent with known facts? Can it be interpreted in other ways, and is it relevant to the claim of the argument? Look for these common fallacies or errors when evaluating reasoning.[35]

- *False analogy.* The differences in the two items being compared outweigh their similarities.

- *Hasty generalization.* Drawing conclusions based on a sample that is (a) too small or (b) isn't typical of the group as a whole.

- *False cause.* Assuming that one event caused another just because it happened first, or using only one cause to explain a complex problem like illegal immigration or international terrorism.

- *Slippery slope.* Assuming that an event (outlawing the use of torture on suspected terrorists) is the first in a series of steps that will inevitably lead to a bad outcome (more terrorist attacks). No proof is offered for the claim that the subsequent events will actually take place.

- *Begging the question (circular reasoning).* Using the premise of the argument to support the claim instead of bringing in outside evidence. (For example: "Jennifer Lawrence is popular because she is a movie star.")

- *Non-sequitur ("it does not follow").* The evidence doesn't support the arguer's claim.

- *Misdirection.* Diverting attention from the central argument to an irrelevant argument. This includes attacking the opponent instead of his/her position, appealing to popular opinion or tradition, and destroying a weak or false version of an opponent's case (a "straw" or "strawperson" argument).

- *Equivocation.* Exploiting the fact that a word has more than one meaning to generate a false conclusion. Television ads for indoor air filters, steak knives, and juicers often promise to include an extra "free" item if we call now. "Free" for the consumer means without cost. However, in this case, the cost of the additional item is already built into the original price and the buyer ends up paying for both products.

- *Amphiboly.* Using grammatical structure to mislead or confuse. For example: "Our product is new and improved." There is no basis of comparison offered in this claim. Is the current product better than previous versions or better than other brands?

- *Emotive language.* Selecting words that generate positive ("innovative," "captivating," "luxurious") or negative ("outdated," "dull," "cheap") emotional images and associations that undermine the ability to judge proof and reasoning.

Managing interpersonal relations*.* There are a number of tactics that can be used to keep an argument from deteriorating into verbal aggression. Reaffirm the sense of competence of other participants through appropriate complements ("Though I don't agree, I can see that you've studied this issue thoroughly"). Emphasize what you have in common and show that you're interested in their views. Let your opponents finish what they're saying instead of interrupting, and deliver your messages in a calm voice at a deliberate pace. If opponents become verbally aggressive, you can point out the differences between argument and verbal aggression, ask them to focus on the point of controversy, or appeal to them to act in a rational manner. You may need to leave if these tactics fail. As a general rule of thumb, never respond to verbal aggression with aggressive tactics of your own.

The Leader as Negotiator

Like argumentation, negotiation comes into play when leaders must influence those who actively disagree with them. However, while the goal of argumentation is to establish the relative superiority of one position over another, the goal of negotiation is to reach a conclusion that is satisfying to both sides. Negotiation consists of back-and-forth communication aimed at reaching a joint decision when people are in disagreement. A mix of compatible and incompatible interests marks all negotiation situations. Negotiators must have some common goal or they wouldn't negotiate. On the other hand, at least one issue must divide them or they wouldn't need to negotiate to reach an agreement. Consider the relationship between members of the production and marketing departments. Although both share a common interest in seeing company sales increase, marketing wants fast product turnaround to capture a new market; production wants to minimize costs while maintaining quality. These departments must resolve their differences through negotiation in order to be successful. Similar disagreements can be found in small groups. Everyone working in your class project group probably wants a high grade. However, some group members may prefer to spend their time relaxing or studying for other classes instead of meeting with the group or gathering research. The amount of work each member does for the group then becomes a matter for negotiation.

> *The very essence of all power to influence*
> *lies in getting the other person to participate.*
>
> —*Harry A. Overstreet*

All types of leaders engage in negotiation. Union and company representatives come to agreements on salary and benefits packages. The United States House and Senate must settle differences in the bills passed by each body. Realtors try to strike the best deals for homebuyers and sellers while sports agents try to do the same for their clients. Lawyers negotiate the terms of plea deals and financial settlements. Small business owners bargain with commercial property companies over lease agreements. CEOs and their boards negotiate the price they will pay when acquiring other companies.

Creating a Cooperative Climate

Our discussion of compliance gaining and argumentation emphasized the activities of the persuader. The outcome of the negotiation process depends on the *joint* efforts of the parties involved. As we indicated earlier, negotiators have compatible and incompatible goals. Since they have both similar and different interests, the two parties simultaneously possess the incentive to cooperate and to compete. Participants must foster cooperation and reduce competition if they are to reach a mutually satisfying solution. According to conflict expert Morton Deutsch, there are sharp differences between cooperative and competitive negotiation climates, as noted in table 6.1.[36]

Table 6.1   Differences in Negotiation Climates[37]

Cooperation	Competition
Open and honest communication	Very little communication; messages often negative and misleading
An emphasis on similarities	An emphasis on differences
Trusting, friendly attitudes	Suspicion, hostility
Mutual problem solving	One party wins over the other
Reduction of conflicting interests	Escalation of conflict and negative emotions

Those who want others to cooperate act in a cooperative manner. Conversely, those who compete meet resistance. Both cooperation and competition get "locked in" to a negotiation relationship at an early stage and persist throughout the negotiation process.[38] One way to foster cooperation is by using the Tit for Tat strategy. The three rules of Tit for Tat are (1) be nice, (2) respond to provocation, and (3) be forgiving. Begin the negotiation by offering to cooperate. If the other negotiator tries to take advantage of you, respond in kind. When he or she switches to a cooperative approach, begin to cooperate again.[39] Promises and concessions are two ways to signal that you are willing to cooperate. Offer to share important information, for example, or back away from one of your initial demands. If the other party responds in kind, make further concessions. However, if the other party does not match your concession, he or she may be looking to compete rather than to cooperate. In this case, follow the rules of the Tit for Tat strategy and make no further concessions until the other negotiator becomes more conciliatory.

To prevent being taken advantage of, it helps to know some of the common destructive tactics used by competitive negotiators. Some common deceptive tactics that promote competition rather than collaboration include:[40]

- *Good cop/bad cop.* This is a variation of interrogation techniques portrayed on *Blue Bloods, Law & Order Special Victims Unit,* and other police shows. The good cop is friendly and cooperative, while the other is tough and demanding. The temptation is to offer more information and concessions than you should to the "good" negotiator. A variation of this approach is the good cop asking for concessions that he or she can offer to his or her unreasonable partner.

- *Bad-faith negotiation.* The other party states that he or she is willing to collaborate but is really just stalling for time or looking for more information to use against you later. The negotiator may also try to reopen discussion on earlier points of agreement in hopes of getting greater concessions. You may yield based on the belief that you have come too far to back out now.

- *Lack of authority.* Your counterpart claims that a third party who doesn't participate in the discussion must approve agreements. This technique is common at auto dealerships where salespeople turn to the sales manager for approval. The third party often overrules or changes the agreement, bringing pressure to bear to complete the negotiation.

- *Inaccurate data.* Information supplied by the other negotiator may be inaccurate, deceptive, or incomplete, putting you at a serious disadvantage.

- *Many for one.* This tactic rests on the norm of reciprocity (to be discussed in more detail later in the chapter). The other party makes small concessions early in the negotiations only to ask for large, important concessions from you near the end of the talks.

- *Information overload.* The other negotiator tries to overload you by providing a flood of data. This mass of information may be intimidating (there is too much to read and understand); can be used to stall talks or manipulate them; and may hide errors and distortions.

To cope with these strategies, be firm but reasonable. Identify the tactic being used and warn the other party that such deceptive strategies may undermine any hope of reaching an agreement. State that you'll keep talking as long as he or she appears to be genuinely interested in reaching a mutually satisfying solution.

Perspective-Taking Skills

Understanding the other negotiator's perspective is a valuable leadership skill. A negotiator with high perspective-taking ability anticipates the goals and expectations of the other party. He or she can encourage concessions that lead to agreement. Perspective taking reduces the defensiveness of the other negotiator and makes him/her more conciliatory. The result is faster, more effective negotiations.[41] However, trying to see the other person's point of view in a negotiation is difficult for these reasons:

- strong emotions, such as anger, may be aroused;
- both parties may be highly committed to their positions;
- negotiators may have significantly different values, beliefs, and experiences; and
- interactants may be unequal in power, which increases uncertainty about how the other person will respond.

Perspective taking begins before any actual negotiation. Start by gathering information about the issues and individuals involved in the future negotiation. For example, if you want to negotiate for more funding for your organization from the student government, find out the amount of money available, past grants to your group and other campus organizations, the interests of those serving on the funding committee, and other relevant facts.

Once you've gathered as much information as you can, role play the negotiation by taking the part of the other negotiator. This should give you a greater understanding of that person's vantage point. For instance, if you are a manager preparing for labor negotiations, act out the role of the union negotiator. Do symbolic role playing if you can't physically role play. Imagine how the other party thinks and feels in the situation. As a manager in contract negotiations, consider the relationship between the union negotiator and the union membership. This person may have to make unreasonable demands at first in order to satisfy union members.

Active listening skills are critical once the negotiation begins. Ask for clarification when needed and paraphrase the speaker's comments. By making an effort to listen actively to the other negotiator, you demonstrate that you want to understand his or her point of view. This makes conciliation more likely. (A comprehensive list of productive negotiation behaviors is found in the research highlight in box 6.4.)

Box 6.4 Research Highlight	**Effective Negotiation Skills[42]**

Researchers in a variety of fields, including communication, management, economics, law, psychology, sociology, political science, and psychology, study negotiation. Those who want to become better negotiators must draw on insights from many different disciplines. Michael Roloff, Linda Putnam, and Lefki Anastasiou analyzed the results of studies from across academic fields to develop a comprehensive list of negotiation skills. They examined projects that focused on (a) professional negotiators or (b) successful negotiation outcomes.

(continued)

Planning emerged as a critical negotiation skill based on Roloff, Putnam, and Anastasiou's analysis of the behavior of experts. Professionals who negotiate as part of their jobs are well informed on the issues and are therefore better able to question the position of the other party and to stay away from personal attacks. They are more flexible because they have considered a larger range of options. Once discussions begin, professionals exercise self-control, actively seek additional information, and keep the process from being competitive.

The researchers found that, when it comes to generating successful outcomes, the most effective negotiation behaviors vary depending on whether parties take a win-lose (distributive) or problem-solving (integrative) orientation toward negotiation. Successful distributive negotiators who seek to maximize their personal outcomes are tough bargainers who may mislead their opponents. However, the distributive approach has many limitations, including unethical behavior, increased resistance, and potential deadlock. Those who want to avoid the pitfalls of hard bargaining should engage in the following behaviors instead. Roloff, Putnam, and Anastasiou report that these skills consistently produce high-quality solutions that benefit both parties:

1. **Set specific and reasonably high goals.** Failure to specify objectives encourages participants to take shortcuts (split the difference) instead of working toward a creative solution. Negotiators who set challenging goals are motivated to analyze the situation in more detail and to come up with a win-win outcome. However, setting unrealistically high goals makes it harder to reach integrative solutions. Discouraged participants may give up.

2. **Lower goals reluctantly.** Successful negotiators resist the temptation to back off their objectives once talks begin. They recognize that giving in leads to a compromise instead of a mutually beneficial outcome. They practice flexible rigidity, holding on to their goals but identifying many ways these objectives can be reached.

3. **Share information about priorities and make trade-offs among issues of differing importance.** Effective negotiators build momentum by logrolling. In this technique (visualize a log rolling down a hill, gathering speed as it travels), participants build momentum by trading concessions on low priority items to get agreement on more significant issues. Successful logrolling depends on acquiring accurate information about the priorities of the other party.

4. **Be aware of and control cognitive biases.** Thinking errors can undermine negotiation. The first important bias is the mistaken assumption that the priorities of negotiators are identical. This false assumption prevents logrolling. The second error is the faulty belief that all of the positions and priorities of the negotiators are incompatible when they are not. This fallacy encourages the parties to compromise instead of reaching integrative agreements.

5. **Be selectively contentious.** Integrative negotiators function as problem solvers, analyzing the issues and engaging in cooperative behaviors. However, being contentious signals that negotiators are committed to their goals and may lead to a better understanding of the positions of the other parties. The best negotiators take care to reduce the potential damage that can come from contention. They are specific about their concerns and use threats sparingly—to keep the negotiations moving and to avoid repeating issues. Their challenges are focused on solutions, not on the personality of the other party or on that individual's interests and goals. They also try not to take unsupportive comments from others personally, recognizing that these remarks may be mistakes or may be the product of poor preparation.

6. **Signal concern about the opponent's needs and interests.** Effective negotiators signal flexibility by communicating concern about the other party. They express commitment to generating joint benefits, use "we" instead of "I" language, and create rapport through accommodating nonverbal communication (mirroring the other person's posture, matching gestures, using appropriate facial expressions).

Negotiation as Joint Problem Solving

As we've seen, effective negotiators create a cooperative atmosphere and take the perspective of others. The most productive approaches to negotiation incorporate these two elements by viewing negotiation as a problem-solving process rather than as a competitive tug of war. In contrast to the win-lose approach, problem-solving negotiation fosters cooperation and focuses on generating solutions that will meet the interests of both sides. Perhaps the best-known example of the problem-solving style of negotiation is the principled negotiation model developed by Roger Fisher, William Ury, and associates of the Harvard Negotiation Project.[43] Following the four steps of principled negotiation will help you reach a solution that is satisfactory to both you and the other party. After you've read the description of the four steps, apply them to the case study in box 6.5.

1: Separate the People from the Problem

Avoid defining the situation as a test of wills. Focus instead on working side by side on a common goal—resolving the issues at hand. Build trust to defuse strong emotions and to keep conflict from escalating. Colonial activist John Woolman is an excellent example of a negotiator who was able to tackle tough issues without attacking the people with whom he disagreed.[44] Woolman, a prominent Quaker cloth merchant in Philadelphia, spent 30 years negotiating the end of slavery in Pennsylvania. Woolman assumed that there was good in everyone, including slave owners. He believed that slaveholders, rather than being evil, were "entangled" in a corrupt system. They had been socialized to believe that blacks were lazy and didn't want to oppose the practice of slavery for fear of alienating their parents and the rest of the community. Woolman was friendly and cheerful when he confronted slave owners and encouraged consensus building and experimental learning. As a group, Woolman and local farmers designed an experiment that freed a few slaves to sharecrop. The productivity of the sharecroppers was higher than that of the slaves, proving that blacks could be just as industrious as whites. Woolman's "friendly disentangling" strategy paid off. By 1770 Quakers were forbidden to own slaves, and by 1800 Pennsylvania became the only state south of New England to make slavery illegal.

2: Focus on Interests, not Positions

A negotiating position is the negotiator's public stance (i.e., "I want $70,000 a year in salary from the company."). An interest, on the other hand, is the reason why the negotiator takes that position ("I need to earn $70,000 so that I can save for a down payment on a house."). Focusing on positions can blind you and the other negotiator to the fact that there may be more than one way to meet the underlying need or interest. The company in the example above might pay less in salary and yet meet the employee's need for housing by offering a low-cost home loan. The Camp David peace treaty between Egypt and Israel demonstrates how making a distinction between interests and positions can generate productive settlements. When the two nations first sat down to negotiate with the help of President Jimmy Carter in 1978, they argued over the return of the Sinai Peninsula, which had been seized by Israel from Egypt during the Six-Day War in 1967. Egypt took the position that all occupied lands should be returned, while Israel took the position that only some of the Sinai should be returned to Egyptian control. As a result, the talks stalled. However, once the negotiators realized that Israel's real interest was national security and Egypt's interest lay in regaining sovereignty over her land, an agreement was reached. Israel gave back the occupied territory in return for pledges that Egypt would not use the Sinai for military purposes.[45] Despite recent unrest in the region, the two nations remain at peace.

3: Invent Options for Mutual Gain

Spend time brainstorming solutions that can meet the needs of both negotiators. Obviously, this is impossible unless you first separate the people from the problem and focus on interests rather than on negotiating positions. Fisher and Ury offer the following example of a creative solution, which met the interests of both parties.

> Consider the story of two men quarreling in a library. One wants the window open and the other wants it closed. They bicker back and forth about how much to leave it open: a crack, halfway, three quarters of the way. No solution satisfies them both. Enter the librarian. She asks one why he wants the window open: "To get some fresh air." She asks the other why he wants it closed: "To avoid the draft." After thinking a minute, she opens wide a window in the next room, bringing in fresh air without a draft.[46]

4. Insist on Objective Criteria

Find a set of criteria on which you both can agree when determining the terms of the settlement. This reduces the possibility that one party will force the other into accepting an unsatisfactory solution. In most cases, negotiators will be comfortable with an agreement that corresponds to widely accepted norms. Such standards can range from used car price books to legal precedents for insurance settlements to industry standards for wages. Use fair procedures (taking turns, turning to outside experts) as well. Your parents may have used one such fair procedure—the forced choice technique—to divide up cakes and pies between you and your siblings. In this strategy one child cuts the pie and the other gets first choice of what slice to take. This approach was used to divide deep-seabed mining sites in the Law of the Sea negotiations. Half of the sites were to be mined by private companies from wealthier nations and the other half by the United Nations on behalf of poorer countries. The poorer nations worried that the more knowledgeable private mining companies would keep the best sites to themselves. To break the stalemate, the negotiators determined that the private firm would present the UN group with two sites and the UN would select one. The private company then had an incentive to present two promising locations since it didn't know which site it would get.

Box 6.5 **Case Study**	**Negotiating Homes for Students**

Higgins College is a private, residential four-year liberal arts school located in a small rural community in the Northeast. Over the past three years it has experienced a surge in enrollment, growing from 1,400 to 1,900 students. Unable to build student housing fast enough to meet demand, the college has purchased houses in the adjoining neighborhood as a temporary solution to its housing crisis. Unfortunately, resentment toward the college grows with each additional house it buys. Neighbors complain that student tenants are noisy and that the college lets the condition of its properties deteriorate. Some individuals who sold their homes to the school believe that they were paid less than full market value.

Imagine that you are the special assistant to the president at Higgins, newly hired with special responsibility for property acquisition. You must negotiate the purchase of two additional homes to help house this fall's incoming freshman class, the largest in the college's history. Higgins' president, a forceful personality largely credited with the college's rapid growth, has made it clear that this is to be your top priority. You've also received several e-mail messages from the student housing director, who says she needs to know if you can complete the deal in three weeks so she can finish housing assignments. The two most desirable properties are located next to each other right across the street from the college's science building. Other options are located much farther away from campus in a more expensive area. Fearful of being "ripped off," the owners of the homes near the science building have hired a real estate agent to represent them in this transaction. When you call the realtor to set up a meeting, you learn that members of the neighborhood association have urged the homeowners to sell to private individuals, not to the college. You have three days to get ready for the first negotiation session.

Discussion Questions

1. What steps will you take to build a cooperative climate?
2. Describe the perspectives of all the parties, including yourself.
3. What are the interests of both sides and how can they be met?
4. What solutions could meet the needs of both parties?
5. What objective criteria could be used to determine the terms of the settlement?
6. What alternatives does each side have to reaching a settlement? How will this influence the likely outcome of the negotiation?

Resisting Influence: Defending against the Power of Mental Shortcuts

Up to this point in the chapter we've focused on how leaders exercise influence to carry out their roles. Yet, leaders must resist influence as well as exert it. Succumbing to dishonest or poorly reasoned persuasive appeals can be costly to leaders and to their groups and organizations. Among the possible negative consequences are supporting bad proposals, hiring the wrong employees, paying too much for goods and services, giving to unworthy causes, and engaging in illegal (and even deadly) activities.

Arizona State University social psychologist Robert Cialdini believes that mental shortcuts leave leaders and others vulnerable to unethical influence.[47] In the modern age it is impossible to carefully evaluate every piece of information that comes our way through cable and streaming television, cell phones, websites, social media, and other channels. Faced with a flood of data, we often make decisions based on a single piece of information that we believe accurately represents the total situation—we use shortcuts to save time.[48] Automatic responses produce poor choices if advertisers and others manipulate information to their advantage. Cialdini believes in the adage "forewarned is forearmed." If you are aware of the following tactics, you are more likely to analyze persuasive attempts critically, bolster your existing position, and develop counterarguments, all of which will help you avoid the negative consequences that come from falling victim to manipulative influence attempts.[49] However, keep in mind that, when it comes to persuasion, most of us have "illusions of invulnerability."[50] We believe that advertising has an impact on others but not on us, for example. If we are to successfully resist, we need to first acknowledge that we can fall victim to the tactics described below.

Reciprocation (Give and Take)

The rule of reciprocity (that people are obligated to return favors) appears to be a universal guideline, which encourages individuals of every culture to cooperate with one another. People can offer assistance to others with the confidence that they will be repaid in the future, thus creating mutually advantageous relationships where none existed before. Solicitors and advertisers take advantage of this basic standard of human behavior. The March of Dimes, the Audubon Society, and other charities send out free address labels and calendars in hopes that recipients will return the favor by making donations. Other examples of this strategy (known as "foot-in-the-door") are the product representatives who line supermarket aisles on weekends handing out samples of cheese, sausage, pizza, and other foods. Shoppers often respond by buying the items, partly out of a sense of obligation. The reciprocal concessions strategy (referred to as the "door-in-the-face" or "rejection and retreat" technique) is an interesting variation on the theme of give and take. In this strategy, persuaders make an extreme request and then back off, asking for less. Making a smaller request is viewed as a concession and, as a result, targets are more likely to comply with the second attempt. Also, the follow-up request appears more reasonable in contrast to the original one. Cialdini and his colleagues first tested this procedure by asking strangers to make a two-year commitment as youth volunteers. The researchers then followed up their initial request by asking these same individuals to take children to the zoo for two hours. To create a comparison group, they approached a separate group of strangers with only the second request. Those who had first been asked to make the long-term commitment were more likely to agree to go to the zoo.[51]

The reciprocity rule can result in unwanted debts and trigger unequal exchanges. Concerns about the dangers of reciprocity are behind attempts to restrict gifts from lobbyists. Accepting meals, golf outings, and overseas junkets can put legislators in debt to special interest groups.

Cialdini outlines three strategies for resisting the power of reciprocity. One, turn down initial favors. Some political candidates refuse large contributions, for instance, and universities return gifts from controversial donors. Two, do not feel obligated to return favors that are tricks, not genuine favors. Three, turn the tables on unethical influencers by exploiting the exploiters. Take the free gift—a cracker, a free weekend visit at a time-share resort, a road atlas—and walk away without giving anything in return.

> *Nothing is more costly than something given free of charge.*
> —*Japanese saying*

Commitment and Consistency

This shortcut is based on the desire to appear consistent with previous choices and actions. Consistency prevents feelings of dissonance while reducing the need to think carefully about an issue after making a choice. Commitment goes hand in hand with the drive for consistency. Once we've made a commitment, no matter how small, we want to remain consistent with that decision or action. Using small commitments to leverage bigger ones is called the "foot-in-the door" strategy.

One sobering example of the effectiveness of the foot-in-the-door technique came during the Korean War. People were shocked by the fact that many captured U.S. soldiers readily informed on one another and offered other help to the enemy. This collaboration was not forced through torture or harsh treatment; it was the product of a series of small commitments. First, the captors convinced their prisoners to agree to such statements as "the United States is not perfect." Interrogators then asked these same men to make a list of problems in the United States and to sign their names. These lists were shown to other prisoners, and the prisoners wrote essays expanding on the nation's weaknesses. Later the names and essays were broadcast to other POW camps and U.S. soldiers still fighting in South Korea. Now the prisoners were publicly identified as collaborators. Knowing that they had written their statements without strong coercion, the captives began to live up to the "collaborator" label, giving further aid to their jailers. Their small commitments had led to significant changes in their self-images.

Voluntary, public decisions increase the commitment of people who made the choice. They can't attribute their behavior to outside pressures. Consider the popularity of college hazing rituals, for example. Sorority and fraternity pledges (of their own free will) publicly commit themselves to a particular Greek affiliation. When they are subsequently subjected to strenuous—and perhaps dangerous—initiation ceremonies, they become even more committed. Despite the efforts of many college administrators, the new inductees continue the tradition and insist that future pledges go through similar initiation rites. Voicing concern about the initiation hazing could be interpreted as inconsistent with the previous commitment to the sorority or fraternity. Having endured an unpleasant experience, there is a desire to embrace the commitment even more strongly. Hazing isn't limited to Greek societies, however. A Florida A&M marching band drum major died of injuries suffered during a hazing ritual that took place despite previous hazing injuries and lawsuits as well as continual warnings from the university that hazing was illegal.[52]

Your best defense against the pull of commitment and consistency is listening to internal signals. Being trapped into complying with an undesirable request produces a tight, queasy stomach. Respond to these feelings by drawing the attention of the persuader to the tactic being used and to the faulty logic of being consistent for consistency's sake. Your heart can also signal when you are in danger of being taken advantage of. Ask yourself: "If I could go back in time, would I make the same choice again?" If you wouldn't make the same decision twice, then don't make it in the first place.

Moderation in temper is always a virtue,
but moderation in principle is always a vice.

—*Thomas Paine*

Social Proof (Validation)

Social proof refers to deciding how to act based on what others are doing. Television producers use laugh tracks, for example, to convince viewers that situation comedies are funny. Campaign managers hope to pick up additional support by trumpeting the fact that their candidates are leading in the polls. Publishers tout their books as best-sellers. Readers of Yelp online reviews consider the number of "friends" a reviewer has on the site when judging the credibility of the posting.[53] Social proof exerts the most influence when we observe others who are similar to us (the same age or social class, for example) and in ambiguous situations when observers don't know how to interpret information. Take the case of someone lying on a busy city sidewalk. This individual could be drunk, asleep, or sick. A drunk or sleepy person can be ignored; an individual with a medical emergency needs help. To determine how to respond, pedestrians look around and see how others react. If other passers-by stop to help, they are more likely to offer assistance as well. The influence exerted by social proof can be deadly. Members of Heaven's Gate (the Hale-Bopp cult) committed mass suicide in response to social pressure from other members of their group. Stories of homicides can stimulate copycat murders.

Social proof has less impact when you recognize that influencers are making false claims and/or creating false impressions. For instance, producers of infomercials pay actors to participate in "spontaneous" demonstrations designed to convince us that cosmetics and other products are effective and easy to use. Supporters of the president pack the gallery during the State of the Union address and applaud at every opportunity, hoping to make the chief executive look more popular. In addition to being on the lookout for misleading influence attempts, you can also increase your resistance to this shortcut by periodically testing the crowd's reactions against established facts as well as against your past experiences and personal judgments.

Liking

As targets of influence, we are more swayed by people we like. Celebrities take advantage of this fact by marketing to their Instagram followers. The Tupperware Corporation has representatives sell to friends and neighbors. The company has largely moved from the U.S. market to cultures in Latin America, Asia, and Europe where friends and family exert a stronger influence over behavior. Liking is based on a variety of factors, including: (1) physical attractiveness (attractive people are more likely to get elected, hired, and paid more money); (2) similarity (in appearance, attitude, nonverbal behavior, ethnic background); (3) compliments (flattery, praise); (4) familiarity and frequent cooperative contact; and (5) association with positive events and people (winning sports teams, celebrities).

Preventing liking is almost impossible. The key, according to Cialdini, is to determine if you like someone too much given the circumstances and to separate the merits of the proposal from the person. Ask yourself, for example: "Am I ignoring a lower bid just because I like another contractor better?" "Do I support an applicant for a job opening only because he or she shares the same ethnic background as me?" "Do I find it hard to say 'no' to a request when I've received compliments first?" If you say "yes" to any of these questions, you need to reconsider your choices.

Authority

Receivers frequently overlook the content of the message and respond instead based on status cues like titles, clothes, nice jewelry, and fine automobiles. The higher the perceived status of the persuader, the more likely it is that targets will comply. In one investigation, for example, hospital nurses were telephoned by a "doctor" (really an experimenter) they had never met who told them to administer a large amount of an unauthorized drug to a patient. Despite the fact that prescribing medications over the phone was expressly forbidden by hospital policy and the drug was not cleared for use, 95% of the nurses went straight to the patient's room to administer the dosage, only to be stopped by the researchers.[54]

The best way to undermine the influence of authority is to engage in critical thinking. Consider whether the person is truly an expert on the topic at hand. Consider too whether this person will likely be truthful in this situation (see our earlier discussion of trustworthiness). Be on guard against those who will benefit personally if you go along with their recommendations and be wary of those who appear to argue against their interests in order to secure your compliance.

Scarcity

Scarcity appeals are a staple of advertising. Television offers are good only if viewers call now, supermarket ads run for one week only, the most popular holiday toys always seem to be in short supply, and some furniture outlets always seem to be going out of business. Online travel sites also capitalize on the power of scarcity, noting that there are only a few airline seats or hotel rooms still available at a bargain price. Retailers recognize that items appear more valuable when they appear to be less available. Two principles underlie this mental shortcut. The first is the belief (often supported by experience) that opportunities in short supply are better than common ones. The second is that people react against any attempt to limit their freedoms, particularly when something is newly scarce or when competition develops. Notice how fast lines form at service stations at the first hint that supplies of gas will be running low before a major storm, for example, and how shoppers fight over limited supplies of the "hot" Christmas gift. Attempts to restrict information can have a similar effect. Censoring information makes it more desirable and believable. Further, influence targets are more persuaded by the thought of losing something than by the thought of gaining an advantage. For example, business managers making decisions are more concerned about what they might lose than what they might gain from their choices.

Scarcity generates physical arousal (i.e., increased blood pressure and adrenaline), making a rational response difficult. The best way to defend against physiological arousal is to calm the nervous system. Take a break in the negotiations or refuse to commit to a major decision until thinking about it overnight. Realize, too, that limited availability doesn't make an object any better. If you want the car, property, or service for its function to you or your organization, its ultimate usefulness should determine how much you pay for it, not its scarcity. Forgetting this principle has been costly to the owners of sports teams. Bidding against other owners for players encourages these leaders to pay too much for free agents. Often they lose sight of the fact that, despite the scarcity of good talent, no player is worth the cost if his or her signing means the franchise will lose money.

Unity

Considering someone to be part of our group makes us much more open to their influence.[55] These group relationships can be built on kinship or on physical proximity—place, home, or region. Consider, for example, how millions of viewers "cheer for the flag" at the Olympics. They root for the athletes representing their countries even though they know little about these individuals or the sports they are competing in. Acting together through song, chants, marches, prayers, and dances also creates a feeling of unity, fostering liking and the desire to support others. Creating with others (through group projects, for instance) increases collaboration and willingness to share credit. Giving advice links individuals to a brand or organization.

Life would be much poorer without kinship and geographical bonds. Acting in harmony with others by dancing at a concert, cheering at a sporting event, or kneeling for prayers at a religious service is an important element of the human experience. However, be alert to unscrupulous influencers who take advantage of the unity shortcut. Beware of businesses and nonprofits that use terms like "family," "brothers," "sisters," and "heritage" to create relationships with you where none exist. And relationships are no protection against deception. Affinity fraudsters take advantage of their group membership to sell useless investments to their friends, neighbors, professional colleagues, and fellow veterans. Guard against being swept up in illegal or unethical activities when acting in a group. Make sure an organization's request for advice is honest attempt to gather information and not a ploy to get you to buy a product or service.

∿ CHAPTER TAKEAWAYS

- Credibility, which is built on perceptions of our competence, trustworthiness, and dynamism, is the key to any successful influence attempt.

- Enhance your credibility through self-presentation behaviors that establish commonalities with your audience and distance yourself from untrustworthy groups. Avoid jargon and modify your nonverbal behaviors (appearance, voice, posture, eye contact). Build quality relationships with followers through discovering yourself, increasing your skills and confidence, appreciating constituents, affirming shared values, developing capacity, serving a purpose, and sustaining hope.

- Compliance-gaining strategies are the verbal tactics used to influence others in face-to-face encounters. In the interpersonal context, use "friendly persuasion"—positive strategies that put you and the other party in a positive frame of mind. As a leader in the organizational context, take a rational yet flexible approach. Offer reasons for compliance but switch tactics when appropriate.

- Avoid hard tactics like applying pressure or appealing to authority, whenever possible. These strategies may gain compliance but often at the expense of long-term commitment. Instead, use a combination of soft tactics (consulting with others, pointing out benefits, putting the other person in a good mood, arousing enthusiasm), which often work better together than alone. However, be careful not to mix incompatible strategies like applying pressure while trying to put the other person in a good mood.

- Argumentation involves controversy and extended discussion over issues. Never confuse argument with verbal aggression, which attacks the self-worth of others. Argumentation produces a wide array of positive outcomes; verbal aggression is destructive.

- In order to sway others to your point of view, you will need to avoid aggression and to develop argumentative competence. Argumentative competence consists of stating the controversy in propositional form, inventing arguments, presenting and defending your position, attacking other positions, and managing interpersonal relations.

- Negotiation is back-and-forth communication aimed at reaching a joint decision when people are in disagreement. The most effective negotiations generate solutions that benefit both parties. To reach integrative (win-win) agreements, build a cooperative atmosphere, take the perspective of the other person, and view the discussion as a problem-solving process.

- Joint problem-solving negotiation involves separating the people from the problem, identifying the interests of each party, brainstorming options for mutual gain, and basing the settlement on objective criteria.

- As a leader, you'll need to resist influence as well as exert it. Mental shortcuts can lead to poor choices. Be prepared to resist manipulative influence tactics that appeal to: the principle of reciprocation (give and take), the desire for consistency, social proof/validation (looking to others), liking, authority, the principle of scarcity, and the illusion of unity.

～ APPLICATION EXERCISES

1. **Evaluate Your Credibility**

   Rate your credibility on form 1 below. Place an X along the continuum between each pair of words. You may want to evaluate yourself based on your image in a particular situation. For example: how competent, trustworthy, and dynamic do you appear in class or at your job? Next, have someone else rate you on form 2, while you evaluate that person. After you have finished your evaluations, discuss your reactions to this exercise. Were you surprised at how your partner rated you? Pleased? Displeased? Why did you rate yourself as you did? Would others rate you the same way?

   ### Form 1: Self-Analysis[56]

   Competence

Experienced	__	__	__	__	__	__	__	Inexperienced
Informed	__	__	__	__	__	__	__	Uninformed
Skilled	__	__	__	__	__	__	__	Unskilled
Expert	__	__	__	__	__	__	__	Inexpert
Trained	__	__	__	__	__	__	__	Untrained

   Trustworthiness

Kind	__	__	__	__	__	__	__	Cruel
Friendly	__	__	__	__	__	__	__	Unfriendly
Honest	__	__	__	__	__	__	__	Dishonest
Sympathetic	__	__	__	__	__	__	__	Unsympathetic

   Dynamism

Assertive	__	__	__	__	__	__	__	Hesitant
Forceful	__	__	__	__	__	__	__	Meek
Bold	__	__	__	__	__	__	__	Timid
Active	__	__	__	__	__	__	__	Passive

   ### Form 2: Partner Rating

   Competence

Experienced	__	__	__	__	__	__	__	Inexperienced
Informed	__	__	__	__	__	__	__	Uninformed
Skilled	__	__	__	__	__	__	__	Unskilled
Expert	__	__	__	__	__	__	__	Inexpert
Trained	__	__	__	__	__	__	__	Untrained

Trustworthiness

Kind	— — — — — — —	Cruel
Friendly	— — — — — — —	Unfriendly
Honest	— — — — — — —	Dishonest
Sympathetic	— — — — — — —	Unsympathetic

Dynamism

Assertive	— — — — — — —	Hesitant
Forceful	— — — — — — —	Meek
Bold	— — — — — — —	Timid
Active	— — — — — — —	Passive

2. **Credo Memo**

   To help you develop your leadership philosophy, complete the following exercise developed by James Kouzes and Barry Posner.

   > Imagine that your organization has afforded you the chance to take a six-month sabbatical, all expenses paid. You will not be permitted to communicate to anyone at your office or plant while you are away. Not by letter, phone, fax, e-mail, or other means. But before you depart, those with whom you work need to know the principles that you believe should guide their decisions and actions in your absence. They need to know the values and beliefs that you think should steer the organization while you're away. After all, you'll want to be able to fit back in on your return.
   >
   > You are not to write a long report, however. Just a one-page "Credo Memo." Get a single sheet of paper and write that memo.
   >
   > It usually takes about five to ten minutes to write a Credo Memo. We do not pretend that this exercise is a substitute for more in-depth self-discovery, but it does provide a useful starting point for articulating your guiding principles. To deepen the clarification process, identify the values you listed in your memo (usually they appear as key words or phrases) and put them in order of priority. Or rank them from low to high. Or place them on a continuum. Forcing yourself to express preferences enables you to see the relative potency of each value.[57]

3. In a research paper, evaluate the credibility of a well-known leader. Rate this individual on each of the three dimensions of credibility. Support your evaluation with examples, experts, and other evidence. Draw conclusions about why this person succeeded or failed in establishing and maintaining her or his credibility. Identify insights that you can apply to building your credibility as a leader.

4. Provide an example of how you might use each of the 11 influence tactics (pp. 184–186) in your organization. Record your responses in the space provided:

   • Rational persuasion _____

   _____

   • Apprising _____

   _____

- Inspirational appeal _____

  _____

- Consultation _____

  _____

- Collaboration _____

  _____

- Ingratiation _____

  _____

- Personal appeal _____

  _____

- Exchange _____

  _____

- Coalition tactic _____

  _____

- Legitimating tactic _____

  _____

- Pressure _____

  _____

5. Analyze your effectiveness as a compliance gainer both in an interpersonal and in an organizational setting. Describe a recent situation in which you were the persuader in an interpersonal encounter and as an organizational leader or follower. Which strategy or combination of strategies did you use in each situation? Did they differ? Why did you choose those tactics? How successful were your efforts? Were you more effective in one context than the other? What would you do differently next time? As an alternative, analyze your efforts to express upward dissent.

6. Think of a time when you had an enjoyable argument with someone over a controversial issue, one that stimulated your thoughts and interest. Briefly describe that argument. Now think of a time when you had an unpleasant argument that resulted in hurt feelings and may have damaged the relationship. Briefly describe that situation. Was the first discussion an example of genuine argument and the second a case of verbal aggression? Why or why not?

7. Participate in a debate in class. Your instructor will give you the topic and ground rules. Use the inventional system presented in box 6.3 to construct your argument. When the debate is complete, evaluate your performance using the guidelines presented in the chapter.

8. Record a political talk show and then evaluate the evidence and reasoning of the host and callers. Identify examples of faulty evidence and reasoning and share your recording and analysis in class.

9. Prepare for a negotiation using material presented in the chapter. Outline specific steps for putting these strategies and skills into action.

10. Analyze an infomercial to identify its unethical, poorly reasoned persuasive appeals. As an alternative, identify similar appeals found in all the commercials that appear during a one-hour television broadcast.

∽ CULTURAL CONNECTIONS: NEGOTIATION IN INDIA[58]

The fact that India is a major trading partner of the United States and many European countries means that many American and European business people will find themselves negotiating with their Indian counterparts. Rajeesh Kumar and Kumar Sethi outline a number of key features of the Indian approach to negotiation—elements that can frustrate Western bargainers. For example, Indian managers see the negotiation process as a problem-solving exercise and seek the ideal solution. As a consequence, Indians spend a lot of time gathering information, which slows the negotiation down. The slow pace is troubling to Westerners but not so much to Indians who have a more relaxed (elastic) view of time. Driven by the desire to reach the highest quality solution, Indian negotiators are often highly critical of the position of the other party and can be reluctant to make concessions. Indian representatives, because they live in a society with scarce resources, are also very concerned with receiving their fair share of the settlement. They may also insist that the foreign partner take into consideration the poverty in India, arguing that they can't pay the asking price for, say, a new technology or a drug. Contracts aren't written as precisely as they are in Europe or North America because collectivist Indian society relies more on relationships when conducting business. Any attempt to enforce the terms of a contract is likely to get bogged down in the notoriously slow Indian legal system.

Kumar and Sethi offer some suggestions to Western negotiators doing business in India. First, to reduce the reluctance of the Indian party to yield, they should be as open as possible, remain humble, and try to establish good relationships with Indian business people who want to work with those they consider "friends." Second, Western managers shouldn't argue about high expectations but subtly work to reduce them and introduce a broader perspective by, for instance, comparing this project with other, similar projects. Third, Western bargainers should strive for fairness based not on adherence to a contract, but on the distribution of outcomes. This is particularly important in India where a great many factors are beyond the control of the Indian negotiator, such as poor infrastructure, power outages, and political instability. Flexibility in response to these issues will help build relationships with Indian managers.

∿ LEADERSHIP ON THE BIG SCREEN: *WOMAN IN GOLD*

Starring: Helen Mirren, Ryan Reynolds, Katie Holmes, Daniel Bruhl

Rating: PG-13 for mature themes

Synopsis: Sixty years after fleeing persecution in Austria, Maria Altman (played by Helen Mirren) wants to reclaim a portrait of her aunt stolen by the Nazis. She enlists the services of the grandson of a family friend to help her. The struggling young lawyer, Randy Schoenberg (Reynolds), has no experience in reclaiming art. Further, the painting, *Woman in Gold* by Gustav Klimt, is an Austrian cultural icon, described as the "Austrian Mona Lisa." Museum and government leaders have no intention of giving it back. Altman and Schoenberg, with the help of a Viennese journalist (Bruhl), build a case for restitution in Austria, only to be rebuffed. They then turn to the US legal system for help. Randy convinces the United States Supreme Court to allow Maria to sue the Austrian government for the painting's return. Later an Austrian arbitration board rules that the *Woman in Gold* should be returned to Altman, who then sells the painting for $135 million to a New York art gallery. An estimated 100,000 pieces of art taken by the Nazis, mostly from Jews, have yet to be returned to their rightful owners.

Chapter Links: credibility, compliance gaining, argumentative competence, negotiation

7

Leadership in Groups and Teams

The well-run group is not a battlefield of egos.

—*Lao Tzu*

Small groups play a major role in all of our lives. Every week we are members of planning committees, dorm councils, social clubs, condominium associations, and countless other groups. Often our most enjoyable memories are of group experiences like playing on a winning softball team or developing a new product on a task force. Yet, at the same time, some of our greatest frustrations arise out of group interaction. Many classroom project groups, for example, get low grades because group members dislike one another. In other instances, members fail to show up for meetings, leaving one person to do most of the work on the project at the last minute.

The purpose of this chapter is to improve your chances of having a productive group experience by building your understanding of group and team leadership. There are no formulas to guarantee that you will become a group leader or that your group will be successful. However, learning about how group leadership works can increase the likelihood that both will happen. We'll start by looking at some fundamentals of group behavior and then talk about emergent leadership, leading meetings, decision making, and team leadership.

Fundamentals of Group Interaction

As you read this book you may be learning a number of new terms, or you may be discovering new meanings for familiar terms. The symbols we master during our academic training focus our attention on some parts of the world and away from others. Kenneth Burke calls this focusing influence of language the "terministic screen."[1] Phillip Tompkins describes the following case of terministic screens in action:

> For example, suppose we assemble an economist, a psychologist, and a sociologist in the college cafeteria and ask each to give explanations of food choices made by a customer. Suppose further that the customer we observe happens to select custard rather than either cake or pie. The economist might explain that, because custard is less "labor intensive" and therefore cheaper than the other desserts, it was the only dessert the customer could afford. The psychologist might explain the choice by means of the customer's history; for instance, he or she might say that the customer's "past reinforcement schedule" provides the answer. The sociologist might explain the choice by pointing to the "ethno-social background" of the customer and showing how different classes of people favor different desserts. . . . Thus, the terministic screen of vocabulary causes each to focus on elements and interpretations of the situation to the exclusion of others.[2]

Viewing Groups from a Communication Perspective

The terministic screens of academic languages operate when scholars from different disciplines study groups. Psychologists, for example, are often interested in the personalities of group members and focus on how these characteristics shape group behaviors and outcomes. Sociologists pay attention to other factors like the social status of group members. Communication scholars are most interested in the communication that occurs within groups, which they label as interaction. They argue that group success or failure often rests most heavily on what group members say and do when the group is together rather than on what group members bring with them to the discussion.

Supreme Court decisions are good examples of how group outcomes can't necessarily be predicted by knowing the characteristics of members. Presidents try to influence Supreme Court decisions by appointing justices who favor either a conservative or liberal point of view. They are frequently surprised when their appointees violate their expectations after deliberating with other justices. In your own experience, there probably have been times when you went into a group meeting with your mind made up only to change your opinion as a result of the discussion. From a communication perspective, then, any definition of a group must take into account that communication is the essential characteristic of a group. A survey of small group communication texts reveals that the following elements define small groups.[3]

A common purpose or goal. A group is more than a collection of individuals. Several people waiting for a table at a restaurant would not constitute a group. Group members have something that they want to accomplish together, whether it is to overcome drug dependency, to decide on a new site for a manufacturing plant, or to study for an exam. As an outgrowth of this common goal and participation in the group, a sense of belonging or identity emerges. For example, in the cohort instructional model where the same students take all of their classes together, individuals start out as strangers but frequently develop deep relationships. They may buy shirts with the name of the class imprinted on the back, friend each other on Facebook, and stay in touch long after their academic program is over.

> *Cooperation can be set up, perhaps, more easily than competition.*
> —B. F. Skinner

Interdependence. The success of any one member of the group depends on everyone doing his or her part. When student group members fail to do their fair share of the work, the grade of even the brightest individual goes down. Interdependence is reflected in the roles that members play in the group. One person may gather materials for the meeting; another may take notes; a third may keep the group focused on the task.

Mutual influence. Not only do group members depend on each other, they influence each other through giving ideas, challenging opinions, listening, agreeing, and so on.

Ongoing communication. In order for a group to exist, members must engage in regular communication. For example, although employees working on an assembly line share the common goal of producing a product, they do not constitute a group unless they interact with one another.[4] Group members in the same location engage in face-to-face communication. Workers at different sites are linked through e-mail, online meetings, videoconferences, and telephone calls. (We'll have more to say about dispersed or virtual teams later in the chapter.)

Specific size. Groups range in size from 3 to 20 people. The addition of a third person makes a group more complex than a dyad. Group members must manage many relationships, not just one. They develop coalitions as well as sets of rules or norms to regulate group behavior. The group is also more stable than a dyad. While a dyad dissolves when one member leaves, the group (if large enough) can continue if it loses a member or two. Twenty is generally considered the maximum size for a group because group members lose the ability to communicate face-to-face when the group grows beyond this number.

John Cragan, Chris Kasch, and David Wright summarize the five elements described above in their definition of a small group: "A few people engaged in communication interaction over time, usually in face-to-face and/or computer-mediated environments, who have common goals and norms and have developed a communication pattern for meeting their goals in an interdependent manner."[5]

Group Evolution

Groups change and mature over time. A number of models that describe the evolution of groups have been offered. The Tuckman Model appears to be the most widely used.[6] According to Tuckman, groups of all types go through four phases. In each phase the group addresses both relational and task issues. In the initial *forming* stage, members are discovering what behaviors are acceptable and how much independence the group has. At the same time, they are getting oriented to the task and figuring out the ground rules for tackling the problem. The *storming* phase is marked by conflict as members express their individuality and may resist the formation of the group. They push back against demands the group's task will place on them. This resistance is overcome in the third stage—*norming*, Members begin to accept each other and develop norms or rules for interacting. They openly share information about themselves and the task. In the fourth stage, *performing*, they focus on addressing the assignment. Group structure is set, members take on roles to complete the work and solutions emerge. Tuckman later added a fifth stage—*adjourning*—that incorporates completion of the task and the end of the group.

Not everyone is convinced that groups develop through a single series of phases. For example, Marshall Scott Poole argues that groups go through multiple stages of development.[7] Poole suggests that at any given time a group may be at one point in its social development and at another in its task development. One group might start by proposing solutions and stop later to socialize, while another group might build relationships before tackling the task. Important moments of change in a group's development are called *breakpoints*. These breakpoints can involve naturally occurring topic changes, moments of delay, or, most seriously, disruptions caused by conflict or failure. Consensus about who the leader is will result in fewer delays and disruptions in the group's decision-making process.

Though scholars may describe the process in different ways, the concept of group evolution has important implications. First, timing is critical. It's not just what you say, it's when you say it. A good proposal made too early in the discussion, for instance, may not be accepted. Second, since groups take time to develop successfully, any attempt to rush a group's development is likely to meet with failure. Third, effective groups are characterized by a high degree of cohesion and commitment. Consensus both speeds the development of groups and is the product of effective group interaction. Finally, the evolution of groups suggests that group leadership also develops in stages or as a process.

Emergent Leadership

Ernest Bormann and others at the University of Minnesota studied emergent or "natural" leadership in small groups.[8] The researchers found that the group selects its leader by the *method of residues*. Instead of choosing a leader immediately, the group eliminates leader contenders until only one person is left. Although all members enter the group as potential leaders, contenders are disqualified until only one leader emerges.

According to Bormann and others, the elimination of potential leaders occurs in two phases. In the first phase, those deemed unsuitable for leadership are quickly removed from contention. Unsuitable candidates may be too quiet or they may be too rigid and aggressive. Many would-be leaders stumble because they appear to be unintelligent and uninformed. Once these cuts have been made, the group then enters the second phase. At this point, about half the group is still actively contending for leadership. Social relations are often tense during this stage. Communication behaviors that lead to elimination in phase two include dominating other group members and talking too much. Such factors as social standing outside the group may be used to eliminate other aspiring leaders.

Four major patterns of leader emergence were found in the Minnesota studies. In the first pattern, the ultimate winner recruits an ally or "lieutenant" who helps him or her win out over another strong contender. In the second pattern, each of the remaining contenders has a lieutenant and, as a result, the leadership struggle is prolonged, or no strong leader emerges. In the third pattern, a crisis determines leader emergence. The successful leader is the person who helps the group handle such traumatic events as unruly members or the loss of important materials. In the fourth pattern, no one emerges as a clear leader. The result is a high level of frustration. People find such groups to be "punishing."[9]

The Minnesota researchers seem to rule out the possibility that more than one person can act as a group leader or that leadership tasks can be shared among group members. While the emergence of a single leader may be the norm for most groups, there are times when two or more individuals share the functions of leadership, as described in chapter 3.

How *Not* to Emerge as a Leader

Since natural leaders emerge through the process of elimination, it can be useful to identify those behaviors that virtually guarantee you won't become the group's leader. B. Aubrey Fisher and Donald Ellis offered the following "rules" for those who want to secure a low-status position in the group.[10]

Rule 1: *Be absent from as many group meetings as possible.* Don't explain why you didn't attend.

Rule 2: *Contribute very little to the interaction.*

Rule 3: *Volunteer to be the secretary or the record keeper of your group's discussion.* This is an important role, but a recorder or secretary rarely ends up as the group's leader.

Rule 4: *Indicate that you are willing to do what you are told.* While disinterest guarantees avoiding leadership responsibilities, subservience is not perceived as a leadership quality.

Rule 5: *Come on [too] strong early in the group discussions.* Be extreme; appear unwilling to compromise.

Rule 6: *Try to assume the role of joker.* Make sure your jokes are off the topic and never let on that you are serious about anything.

Rule 7: *Demonstrate your knowledge of everything, including your extensive vocabulary of big words and technical jargon.* Be a know-it-all and use words that others in the group won't understand.

Rule 8: *Demonstrate a contempt for leadership.* Express your dislike for all kinds of leaders and the idea of leadership itself.

Avoiding the behaviors identified by Fisher and Ellis works in the reverse and increases the possibility of eventually emerging as the leader of a group.

Useful Strategies

Identifying negative behaviors that eliminate leader contenders is easier than isolating positive behaviors that are essential to leadership emergence. However, the following communication strategies can boost your chances of emerging as a group leader.

Participate early and often. The link between participation and leadership is the most consistent finding in small group leadership research.[11] Participation demonstrates both your motivation to lead and your commitment to the group. Impressions about who would and would not make a suitable leader begin to take shape almost immediately after a group is formed.[12] Begin contributing in the group's first session.

Focus on communication quality as well as quantity. Frequent participation earns you consideration as a leader. However, communicating the wrong messages—rigidity, contempt, irrelevance—can keep you from moving into the leadership position. Communication behaviors that are positively correlated with emergent leadership include: setting goals, giving directions, managing tension and conflict, and summarizing.[13] Not only is quality communication essential to becoming a leader, but effective leadership communication helps the group as a whole. Groups are most likely to make good decisions when their most influential members facilitate discussion by asking questions, challenging poor assumptions, clarifying ideas, and keeping the group on track.[14] (We'll have more to say about group decision making later in the chapter.)

Demonstrate your competence. Not surprisingly, the success of would-be leaders depends heavily on their ability to convince others that they can successfully help the group complete the job at hand. Doing your homework in preparation for a project, for example, gives your leadership bid a major boost. Along with competence, you will also need to demonstrate your character and dynamism. Group members want to know that the leader candidate has the best interests of the group in mind and is not manipulating the group for personal gain. Being enthusiastic and confident makes other members more receptive to your suggestions and ideas. As we noted in chapter 6, nonverbal communication plays an important role in building perceptions of all three dimensions of credibility. One study of the nonverbal behaviors of emergent small group leaders found that they gestured frequently, established good eye contact, and expressed agreement through nodding and facial expressions.[15]

Help build a cohesive unit. You must also demonstrate that you want to cooperate with others if you want to become a group leader. Successful leader candidates pitch in to help, work to build the status of others, and don't claim all the credit for decisions.

> *The path to greatness is along with others.*
> —*Baltasar Gracian*

Appointed vs. Emergent Leaders

In many cases, a leader is assigned to a group before it meets for the first time. As you might have discovered from personal experience, groups are often successful in spite of, not because of, their official leaders. Many appointed leaders fail to function as leaders; in addition, an incompetent leader slows group progress because members must spend time and energy developing alternative leadership. Groups spend less time on leadership issues if the appointed leader earns the leader label by doing an effective job.[16]

Researchers comparing the impact of assigning or choosing leaders have discovered that followers expect more from natural leaders than appointed leaders. Since they have more invested in leaders that they have selected for themselves, members have higher expectations and tolerate less failure. Yet, at the same time, group members give natural leaders more room to operate. Emergent leaders have greater freedom to make decisions on behalf of the group.[17]

Consultant Susan Wheelan encourages appointed leaders to adjust their leadership style to the group's stage of development.[18] In a new group, members haven't yet had time to organize so they expect the leader to provide structure. At this point leaders need to give direction and communicate that they are confident that the group will succeed. As group members become more comfortable, the leader should delegate more power to them, avoiding the temptation to take challenges to authority personally while opening up discussion about group conflicts. Many leadership functions (assigning tasks and reports, meeting with outsiders) ought to be shared with team members when the group is fully organized and functioning effectively. In mature groups, leaders can function as expert team members who continuously monitor collective performance.

One of the most common assignments for appointed group leaders is to plan and preside over meetings, the subject of the next section.

Leadership in Meetings

For many people, the thought of attending a meeting conjures up images of long, boring sessions spent doodling on a notepad while endless amounts of useless information are presented. The reason for this negative impression of meetings is simple: most meetings are poorly planned and ineptly led. That's unfortunate because U.S. workers spend lots of time in meetings. An estimated 11 million meetings take place each day; middle managers spent 35% of their time in meetings, upper management 50%.[19] Effective meeting leaders plan and prepare before a meeting to be certain that the content is both informative and useful. Adopting the following guidelines can help to ensure that your meetings are successful.

Determine if a meeting is necessary before calling people together. The first step before calling a meeting is to determine if you are justified in taking people away from other activities. Bert Auger, a supervisor with the 3M Corporation for over 30 years, provides a checklist outlining when you should and should not call a meeting.[20]

When to Call a Meeting

- Organizational goals need clarification.
- Information that may stimulate questions or discussion needs to be shared.
- Group consensus is required regarding a decision.
- A problem needs to be discovered, analyzed, or solved.
- An idea, program, or decision needs to be sold to others.
- Conflict needs to be resolved.
- It is important that a number of different people have a similar understanding of the same idea, program, or decision.
- Immediate reactions are needed to assess a proposed problem or action.
- An idea, program, or decision is stalled.

*When **Not** to Call a Meeting*

- Other communication networks, such as telephone, video conference, e-mail, letter, or memo will transmit the message as effectively.
- There is not sufficient time for adequate preparation by participants or the meeting leader.
- One or more of the key participants are not available.

- Issues are personal or sensitive and could be handled more effectively by talking with each person individually.

Have a clear agenda. A leader should outline the items he or she wishes to address before a meeting begins. Dividing a meeting into thirds is an effective way to structure an agenda. Devote the first third of the meeting, the warm-up phase, to announcements and items that are easy to decide. Tackle the most difficult issues during the middle third of the agenda, when the group is at peak functioning. During the final third of the session, "cool down" by addressing items that are up for discussion but not decision.[21] A copy of this agenda should be circulated well in advance of the meeting. Participants should be encouraged to add items to the agenda (within reason) that they feel are important. The agenda should be constructed with time constraints in mind. Additions that greatly increase the number of topics to be discussed should be tabled or scheduled for a separate meeting. Remember, it is the leader's responsibility to decide how much meeting time is available and to keep the meeting on schedule. As with writing a report or delivering a presentation, a meeting leader should always have a clear purpose and a plan for achieving his or her goals. Always ask: "Why are we having this meeting?"

Lay the groundwork. According to John Tropman of the University of Michigan's Meeting Master Research Project, meeting experts or masters put a great deal of effort into preparing for group sessions. In addition to marshalling the information that participants will need, meeting masters hold a series of "rehearsals" prior to the group "performance" (meeting). The goal of these rehearsals is to sharpen the performance of participants and to prevent surprises:

> The whole purpose of rehearsal is to bring to the front of consciousness skills, perspectives, and ideas that participants have and to allow them to freshen their own minds or explore their own minds with respect to these elements. What the meeting masters were anxious to avoid was any sense of trapping or capturing participants unaware in a meeting. . . . [Masters recognize] that many of us do not know how we are going to feel about something until we have had a chance to chew on it a bit. The informal setting allowed this to happen without a great deal of personal peril. Thus, it becomes a very important vehicle for moving ahead.[22]

Meeting masters meet one on one with group members to test out ideas and to gather feedback. In particular, they touch base with members who will be impacted by the group's decisions. Meeting masters also get together with subgroups preparing for a presentation or discussion and make sure subcommittees are carrying out their tasks. In some cases they hold a full dress rehearsal, a premeeting gathering with everyone present that highlights the key elements of the upcoming agenda.

Maintain focus on the agenda (and time limits) throughout the meeting. Unless leaders maintain sharp focus, meetings have a tendency to drift away from the intended agenda and take more than their scheduled time. When the meeting digresses significantly, the leader needs to redirect the group. Comments like, "I think we're getting away from the real issue here. Sam, what do you think about . . ." steer the discussion back to the original agenda. A meeting leader must engage in communication behaviors that help stimulate and maintain group interest and attention. Effective meeting leaders use language that is precise yet understandable. They speak loudly and clearly (not in a mumble), and they avoid distracting gestures or movements.

Guide the decision process. Meeting chairs need to manage ideas by (1) putting them in the right context, (2) considering problems in the right order, (3) setting and changing decision criteria, (4) setting the appropriate pace (not too fast or slow), and (5) crystallizing the decision (summarizing the discussion, offering action steps).

Listen to others. Effective meeting leaders are active, attentive listeners. Listening involves more than merely hearing what others say; it involves incorporating the meaning of messages. University of Minnesota professor Ralph Nichols pioneered the research on effective listening. Nichols suggests several strategies for improving listening skills.[23]

- *Focus on the content of the message, not the speaker's delivery.* Information is contained in the symbols the speaker uses. Although certain habits or mannerisms such as pacing, pushing up eyeglasses repeatedly, or the excessive use of powerless forms of language (see chapter 5) can be distracting, the content of the message should be the most important focal point. Effective listeners focus on the information that is important and useful while ignoring distracting elements of delivery.

- *Listen for ideas, not just facts.* Good listeners focus on the big picture. Effective listeners don't just collect facts; they listen for concepts. If you miss some of the facts but understand the main idea, it is easy to conduct research to fill in the missing details. On the other hand, a listener who tries to memorize all the facts may miss the larger and more important issues being addressed. It's always much more difficult to fill in the big picture later.

- *Don't let yourself get distracted.* Avoid distractions by any means possible. If you are distracted by a talkative group member, get up and move. If you are hungry, bring a snack with you to the meeting. Don't let external or internal distractions get in the way of your listening. One of the most common distractions experienced in meetings is complex or technical information. Many listeners simply tune out when information becomes difficult to comprehend, whereas effective listeners concentrate even harder. A good listener works to avoid all forms of distraction that interfere with effective listening.

- *Be open-minded.* Most of us respond instantly when someone says something with which we disagree. We may not blurt out our rebuttal immediately, but we almost always begin thinking of our response. The problem with this habit is that it interferes with our ability to listen intently to the other person's point of view. Effective listeners are open-minded and don't overreact to divergent points of view.

- *Use thought speed to your advantage.* Various researchers have suggested that we think from 4 to 20 times as fast as we speak.[24] This capability sometimes causes us to lose concentration while listening—everyone daydreams!

Effective listeners use the ability to think more rapidly to their advantage. They use internal thought processes to anticipate the next point, to summarize or paraphrase information that has already been presented, or to focus on nonverbal behaviors such as facial and body movements that illustrate key ideas. (For information on how to become a better listener by knowing your listening style, turn to box 7.1.)

We have been given two ears and but a single mouth
in order that we may hear more and talk less.

—Zeno of Citium

Box 7.1   Research Highlight   **Identifying Your Listening Style[25]**

According to listening experts Larry Barker and Kitty Watson, individuals have listening styles or preferences. While no one style is better than the others, knowing our particular style or blend of styles can help us become better listeners. That's because each preference has its own strengths and weaknesses.

People-Oriented. People-oriented listeners are most concerned about how their listening impacts their relationships with other people. If this is your style, you demonstrate care and concern while withholding judgment and are particularly skilled at recognizing emotional states and moods. However, as a people-oriented listener you can lose your objectivity and overlook the faults of others. You may find yourself taking on the negative emotional states—anger, sadness, depression—of others as well.

Action-Oriented. Action-oriented listeners concentrate on the task. If this is your pattern, you encourage others to stay focused on the topic at hand and want them to be organized and concise. Unfortunately, as an action-oriented listener, you likely get impatient with disorganized communicators and can jump ahead of speakers to draw the wrong conclusions. You also run the risk of appearing too critical.

Content-Oriented. Content-oriented listeners take in all the details and carefully evaluate what they hear. With this style you respect expert opinion, consider all sides of an issue, deal well with complexity, and enjoy interacting with ideas. On the down side, however, you can get bogged down in the details and take a long time making decisions.

Time-Oriented. Time-oriented listeners watch the clock and encourage others to present information in an efficient manner. As a time-oriented listener you let others know time limits and likely give your full attention during that period. The meetings you run seldom go long. Unfortunately, you frequently get impatient with others and tend to interrupt them. Speakers feel you cut them off and your clock watching means that there is little space for sharing creative ideas.

Barker and Watson go on to suggest that, in addition to knowing our own listening styles, we also need to understand the preferences of others in order to get them listen to us. To capture the attention of people-oriented listeners, tell human-interest stories, use first names, speak of "we" instead of "I," and employ self-effacing humor and illustrations. For action-oriented listeners, limit ideas to three main points or less, keep presentations short and focused, and speak at a rapid, controlled rate. For content-oriented listeners, provide hard data, quote experts, and use charts and graphs. For time-oriented listeners, keep under time limits, cut unnecessary examples and information, and respond immediately to nonverbal cues that signal impatience.

Involve all participants. Effective meeting leaders encourage the involvement of all participants. Meetings are designed as a forum for the exchange of information and ideas. Remember, a leader calls a meeting because he or she is eager to receive immediate information. Don't stifle participants. Always encourage an atmosphere in which discussion flourishes. When making particularly important decisions, you may want to poll each person individually to make sure the group hears from every member.

Keep a record. A written record serves as the group's memory. The minutes of a meeting should relate to the agenda and generally include: (1) when and where the session took place, (2) the names of those attending, and (3) a summary of the main points of the discussion (not what each person said) and important decisions.

Evaluate your performance. Stop periodically to reflect on your skills as a leader. You can use the self-assessment in box 7.2 to evaluate your performance.

> *A manager's ability to turn meetings into a thinking environment is probably an organization's greatest asset.*
>
> —Nancy Kline

Group Decision Making

Decision making and problem solving, as we noted earlier, are important reasons for calling group members together for a meeting. Groups are often charged with making choices because they have access to more information than do individuals. Members bring a variety of perspectives to the problem and challenge errors in thinking that might go unrecognized by a lone decision maker. Groups don't always make effective decisions, of course. But they are more likely to succeed when leaders and other members carry out important problem-solving functions, while avoiding the pitfalls that contribute to faulty solutions.

Functions and Formats

Group experts Dennis Gouran and Randy Hirokawa believe that high-quality solutions emerge from group deliberations when participants use communication to complete four tasks or functions: problem analysis, goal setting, identification of alternatives, and evaluation of possible solutions.[26] We'll use the example of a group made up of homeless shelter staff members to demonstrate the role that each of these functions plays in the decision-making process. The shelter team is meeting to discuss a year-long decline in the number of individuals and families seeking temporary housing at their facility.

Analysis of the problem. Clearly identifying the nature and extent of the dilemma is critical to resolving it. Analysis includes recognizing that there is a problem, determining its size and scope, isolating causes, figuring out who is impacted by

Box 7.2   Self-Assessment   **Meeting Leader Skills**[27]

Use this table to assess your skills as a meeting leader. You can also ask someone else to evaluate you on the same questions.

Organizing the meeting

Yes   No   Did you involve key participants in defining the purpose and outcomes of the meeting?

Yes   No   Was the meeting plan distributed well in advance of the meeting?

Yes   No   Did you ensure that people came to the meeting prepared?

Starting up the meeting

Yes   No   Did your opening remarks clarify the purpose, process, and boundaries for the meeting?

Yes   No   Did you clarify your role as chairperson, and how it relates to the outcomes being sought from the meeting?

Relating with meeting participants

Yes   No   Did you relate personally with each meeting participant?

Yes   No   Were you positive and enthusiastic?

Yes   No   Did you provide a comfortable setting for the meeting?

Yes   No   Did you negotiate, clarify, and adhere to ground rules with the group?

Yes   No   Did you create a protective climate in which it was safe for people to speak up?

Yes   No   Did you invite and support people's contributions to the meeting?

Yes   No   Did you keep a comfortable pace?

Yes   No   Did you start on time and end on time?

Facilitating the meeting

Yes   No   Did you divide the meeting into orderly steps?

Yes   No   Were discussions thought-provoking?

Yes   No   Did you invite and challenge meeting participants to think and innovate?

Yes   No   Did you offer your opinions?

Yes   No   Did you enable meeting participants to tap the resources of the group as a whole?

Yes   No   Did the discussion relate directly to the outcomes being sought from the meeting?

Yes   No   Did you provide opportunities for meeting participants to share information with each other?

Evaluating the meeting

Yes   No   Did you ask meeting participants what they achieved?

Yes   No   Did you work with meeting participants to evaluate the meeting?

Reflecting on your success as chairperson

Yes   No   Did you take care of yourself by being well prepared for your role as meeting chairperson?

Yes   No   Did you specifically state to meeting participants your responsibility to them?

Yes   No   Have you considered how to build on your achievements as a meeting chairperson, as well as improving where needed?

the problem, and so on. Analysis is a critical first step because initial decisions shape the rest of the group's deliberations. Our shelter team might decide that last year's decline in demand was a random occurrence, not a trend. If this is the case, then the situation doesn't need to be addressed for now. Even if the group determines that housing fewer residents poses a problem that must be solved, members could identify a variety of causes, each of which calls for a different solution. For example, low visibility in the community means more publicity is needed. If run-down facilities are discouraging potential clients, then the shelter house needs to be upgraded.

Goal setting. Outlining goals and objectives clarifies what the group wants to accomplish in addressing the problem. To succeed, members must formulate clear objectives and set goals that, if achieved, will produce a reasonable solution. Identifying criteria or standards for evaluating solutions is also part of goal setting. The group from the homeless shelter may agree that it wants to come up with a plan to rebuild numbers over the course of the next year, without a significant increase in the budget.

Identification of alternatives. The greater the number of potential solutions, the better the chances of coming up with a workable plan. Shelter staff members could consider a variety of options to draw more clients, including hiring outreach workers to reach out to those living on the street, building better relations with social service agencies and religious groups, renovation of facilities, and more staff training designed to improve service to residents.

Evaluation of solutions. In this function, decision makers evaluate the merits and demerits of each possible solution using the criteria developed earlier. Hiring outreach workers would probably bring more people to the homeless shelter, for instance, but would be expensive. Renovation of the facilities would also be too costly. On the other hand, establishing better relations with social service agencies and religious congregations who refer clients would likely increase occupancy rates without the high costs that are associated with advertising and remodeling.

Using a decision-making format is one way to encourage a group to carry out the functions described above. Following a set of predetermined steps increases the likelihood that members will carefully define the problem and develop criteria instead of rushing to potential solutions. There is no consensus as to which format is best, but evidence suggests that groups following a structure are generally more effective than those who don't.[28]

The oldest and most widely used decision-making format is the Standard Agenda. Originally developed by educator John Dewey to describe the process that individuals follow when making choices, the Standard Agenda consists of the following steps:[29]

1. *Identify the problem.* Formulate the problem in the form of a question. A question of fact addresses whether or not something is true (Is the defendant guilty?). A question of value asks for a judgment involving right or wrong, good or bad (Is it fair to allow only upperclassmen to live off campus?). A question of policy asks what course of action should be followed (Should taxes be raised to maintain public services?). Questions of policy

are the most common problems faced by groups. (See our earlier discussion of propositions of fact, value, and policy in chapter 6.)

2. *Analyze the problem.* Determine the cause(s), scope, and impact of the problem (number of people affected, costs to the organization or town, etc.).

3. *Develop criteria.* Criteria should be in place before entering the solution phase since these standards play a critical role in sorting through proposals.

4. *Generate possible solutions.* Strive for quantity. Produce a variety of alternatives without passing judgment.

5. *Evaluate and select a solution.* In this stage, apply the criteria generated earlier to eliminate options and to identify the best choice. The final solution may combine elements of several proposals.

6. *Implement the solution.* This seems like an obvious step but all too often groups make a decision only to fail to follow through on their choice. Before disbanding, determine who will take action (see our earlier discussion of action plans), if future meetings are needed, and so forth.

An alternative to the Standard Agenda is the Single Question Format. This procedure incorporates the communicative functions of effective group decision making by asking participants to formulate, analyze, and then solve the problem through a series of questions. A description of this procedure is found in box 7.3.

Box 7.3	**The Single Question Format**[30]

1. Identify the Problem
What is the *single question* to which the group needs to find an answer to accomplish its purpose for the meeting?

2. Create a Collaborative Setting

a. Agree on principles for discussion.
What principles should we agree on in order to maintain a reasonable and collaborative approach throughout the process?
Examples: We will:
1. Invite and understand all points of view.
2. Remain fact-based in our judgments.
3. Be tough on the issues, not on each other.
4. Put aside any personal agenda.

b. Surface any assumptions and biases.
What assumptions and biases are associated with the single question identified in step 1, and how might they influence the discussion?
Examples:
1. We tend to assume we know our customers' needs.
2. We believe we have efficient processes.
3. We think our level of customer service is acceptable.
4. We assume our past approach should be our future strategy.

(continued)

---

3. Identify and Analyze the Issues (Subquestions)
Before responding to the single question in step 1, what *issues*, or *subquestions*, *must be answered* in order to fully understand the complexities of the overall problem?
• Limit opinions by focusing on the facts.
• If facts are unavailable, agree on the *most reasonable* response to each subquestion.

4. Identify Possible Solutions
Based on an analysis of the issues, what are the two or three most reasonable solutions to the problem? Record the advantages/disadvantages of each.

	Advantages	Disadvantages
Solution 1		
Solution 2		
Solution 3		

5. Resolve the Single Question
Among the possible solutions, which one is *most desirable?*

Avoiding the Pitfalls

Using a format is the first step to effective problem solving; avoiding common decision-making pitfalls is the second. Groups make significant mistakes at every stage of the decision-making process. Members fail to recognize that there is a problem or come up with the wrong cause(s), for example. They set unclear or inappropriate goals that fail to adequately address the situation and misjudge the negative and positive consequences of alternative solutions. Faulty information and/or the faulty use of information also derail group deliberations. Problem solvers often ignore important details or rely on inaccurate information. Even if their information is sound, they may misinterpret or misapply the data.[31]

In light of the logical pitfalls of group decision making, Gouran and Hirokawa argue that counteractive influence—statements that highlight problems in reasoning and get the group back on track—are particularly important to group success. Leaders and followers exercising counteractive influence draw attention to faulty problem definitions, information, assumptions, and inferences. They challenge the group when it deviates from its mutually agreed upon procedures and aren't afraid to take issue with high-status members who are leading the rest of the participants astray.[32] Leaders and other group members also need to be able to correctly recognize and frame problems, make valid inferences or judgments based on available information, generate a variety of solutions, and make arguments.[33]

Poor logic isn't the only cause of faulty decision making. The relationships between members, referred to as the social or emotional dimension of the group, can also lead to poor choices.[34] Members who don't trust each other aren't likely to share important information, for instance, or to work hard on a project. On the other hand, too much emphasis on strong relationships (which puts cohesion above performance) can also be detrimental.

Social psychologist Irving Janis developed the label *groupthink* to characterize groups that put unanimous agreement above all other considerations.[35] Groups that suffer from this syndrome fail to: consider all the alternatives, reexamine a course of action when it doesn't seem to be working, gather additional information, weigh the risks of their choices, work out contingency plans, or discuss important ethical issues. Janis noted faulty thinking in groups of ordinary citizens but is best known for his analysis of major U.S. policy disasters like the failure to anticipate the attack on Pearl Harbor, the Bay of Pigs invasion of Cuba, and the invasion of North Korea. In each case, some of the smartest political and military leaders in U.S. history made poor choices.

Janis identified the following as symptoms or signs of groupthink:

Signs of Overconfidence

1. *Illusion of invulnerability.* Members are overly optimistic and prone to take extraordinary risks.

2. *Belief in the inherent morality of the group.* Participants ignore the ethical consequences of their actions and decisions.

Signs of Closed-Mindedness

3. *Collective rationalization.* Group members invent rationalizations to protect themselves from feedback that would challenge their assumptions.

4. *Stereotypes of outside groups.* Participants believe that members of other groups are evil, weak, or stupid; they underestimate the capabilities of others.

Signs of Group Pressure

5. *Pressure on dissenters.* Members coerce dissenting members to go along with the prevailing opinion in the group.

6. *Self-censorship.* Individuals keep their doubts about group decisions to themselves.

7. *Illusion of unanimity.* Group members mistakenly assume that the absence of conflicting opinions means that the entire group agrees on a course of action.

8. *Self-appointed mindguards.* Group members take it upon themselves to protect the leader from dissenting opinions that might disrupt the group's consensus.

A number of factors contribute to the emergence of groupthink, including failing to follow a decision-making procedure, group isolation, time pressures, homogenous members (same background and values), external threats, and low individual and group esteem caused by previous failures. However, leadership may be the most important influence contributing to groupthink.[36] Directive leaders who push for a particular solution cut off discussion and reduce the number of alternatives considered by the group.

Fortunately, leaders can prevent groupthink as well as promote it.[37] As a leader, don't express your preference for a particular solution; urge members to participate in the deliberations and to look at a variety of alternatives. Encourage every group member to be a critical evaluator and assign individual participants the role of "devil's advocate" to argue against prevailing opinion. Follow a set of decision-making guidelines like those outlined earlier. Divide regularly into subgroups and then come back to negotiate differences. Invite outside experts or colleagues to the group's meetings to challenge the group's ideas. Keep in regular contact with other groups in the organization. Role-play the reactions of rival organizations and groups to reduce the effects of stereotyping and rationalization. Visualize successful collective performance and eliminate negative talk and thought ("we can't succeed"; "the task is too difficult") within the group. Help members challenge the assumption that whatever they do is right and discuss the moral implications of choices.

After the decision has been made, give members one last chance to express any remaining doubts about the solution. The ancient Persians provide one example of how to revisit decisions. They made every major decision twice—once when sober and again when under the influence of wine!

In addition to poor logic and unhealthy relationships, the anxieties of individual members can undermine group problem solving. George Washington University management professor Jerry Harvey argues that it is often individual fears, not conformity pressures, that get groups in trouble.[38] He notes that we always have a choice about how to act in a group and must take responsibility for our behavior. Harvey introduces the concept of *mismanaged agreement* as an alternative to groupthink.

Mismanaged agreement refers to the tendency of group members to publicly support decisions that they oppose in private. As a result, groups continue to fund software installations that no one believes will ever become operational, for example, or engage in business practices that everyone in the group knows are illegal. Professor Harvey calls mismanaged agreement the Abilene Paradox based on an experience his family had many years ago. He, his wife, and his in-laws decided to drive 100 miles from Coleman to Abilene, Texas, in 100-degree-plus heat in a car without air conditioning. They made this trip to eat bad cafeteria food that "could serve as a first-rate prop in an antacid commercial." After arriving home, the family discovered that nobody had wanted to make the trip in the first place. Harvey believes that many groups and organizations also embark on needless excursions. They act in direct contradiction to their true desires and thereby undermine their goals.

Groups caught in the Abilene Paradox display several symptoms. Participants agree in private about the definition of the problem and the right course of action. However, they fail to accurately communicate their thoughts and feelings to others, which misleads their fellow members into thinking that a consensus exists. Members express support for the nonexistent consensus and make decisions that run contrary to their own beliefs. These decisions have negative consequences for the group and organization. The level of anger, frustration, and dissatisfaction skyrockets as a result. Members point the finger of blame at other groups, other members, and their leaders. If the cycle is not interrupted, it will repeat itself, resulting in even greater destruction.

The causes of the Abilene Paradox are rooted in fear. Individuals know what ought to be done but are too anxious to follow through (*action anxiety*). They would rather endure the negative consequences of going along (economic costs, moral failure, career damage) than speak up. Members have negative fantasies about what will happen if they do act on what they believe ("I'll be criticized for not being a 'team player.'" "I'll get a lower quarterly evaluation."). They also fear separation. Group members dread being cut off or separated from their colleagues. This drives them to accede to what they think is the collective will of the group even when they have serious reservations about the decision.

Diagnosis and confrontation are the keys to breaking out of the Paradox.[39] If you are on an unproductive "trip," take the initiative to challenge the group's direction. Call a meeting where you state your true opinion and invite feedback, discussion, and debate. Reward those who confront the group instead of, as is too often the case, "shooting the messenger." Create an organizational climate where group members feel free to express their opinions; where changing one's mind is seen as a sign of strength, not weakness; and where reaching shared goals is more important than pleasing the boss.

As noted above, continuing in a failed course of action is one of the products of mismanaged agreement. Researchers refer to this phenomenon as the *escalation of commitment*.[40] Instead of terminating a project and cutting their losses, groups double down, pouring in more resources. Costs continue to multiply until the moment when the group finally admits defeat. Escalating commitment has been used to explain why investors put more money into failing stocks, bankers continue to loan to problem borrowers, companies increase the advertising budgets for unpopular products, professional basketball teams keep underperforming draft picks on the court, and managers continue to support failing employees. Escalation of commitment played a role in the K2 case described in chapter 1. Once the climbers were near the summit, it was nearly impossible to convince some of them to turn around because they had invested so much money, time, and effort. Instead, they fell victim to "summit fever." Though they should have turned back after nearing the summit by 2 PM, they continued to climb, which stranded them without shelter during the night. Other prominent examples of the escalation of commitment include the automated baggage system at Denver International Airport (which delayed the airport's opening and never worked), and the failed Shoreham Nuclear Plant, which never produced a single kilowatt of electric power even though costs for the project ballooned from $75 million to over $5 billion over a 23-year period.

Teams stay the course for a number of reasons. They want to appear consistent and justify their earlier choices. (The organization may pressure them to continue as well.) Group members often have a personal stake in the project because their jobs and reputations are on the line. Many decision makers mistakenly hope to recoup their "sunk costs" or previous investments when they would be better off writing off their losses. Groups have a tendency to take more risks than individuals (risky shift), which prompts team members to devote more resources than they would on their own. Cognitive biases also come into play. Team members escalate because they (1) ignore negative feedback or interpret evidence so it supports their point of view (the process of selection perception), (2) are convinced they have more control over outcomes than they actually do (the illusion of control), (3) blame the bearers of bad news, and (4) become overconfident based on past successes.

De-escalation begins with acknowledging the problem. Don't ignore negative feedback or external pressure from outsiders who express doubts. Be alert to red flags like project delays and cost overruns. Bring in new group members who aren't as invested in the project, or hire an external auditor to help the group recognize the extent of the problem. Withhold additional funding when necessary. Look for opportunities to deinstitutionalize the project by separating it from the key goals of the organization or by isolating it physically. Corporations often spin off troubled units, for instance, or refer to risky programs as "experiments." To get the Denver International Airport up and running, city leaders de-emphasized the importance of the automated baggage system and used manual baggage conveyors instead.[41]

Team Leadership

We noted earlier that two of the distinguishing features of groups are commonality of purpose and interdependence. Members of every small group rely on each other as they work toward their objectives. Yet, some groups are more focused than others. Members of these groups are much more dependent on one another. Compare, for example, a task force designing a software product due on the market in six months to a board of directors that oversees a business. The task force has a narrow goal that cannot be achieved unless members coordinate their activities on a daily basis. The board can reach its broad objective by meeting a few times a year and by assigning ongoing tasks to individual members.

When Is a Group a Team?

In recognition of the fact that groups such as task forces and boards of directors function in different ways, some observers argue that we ought to differentiate between groups and teams. They suggest that while every team is a group, not every group is a team. Two leading proponents of this position are Jon Katzenbach and Douglas Smith. See table 7.1 for the contrasts they draw between working groups and teams.[42]

Katzenbach and Smith believe that the key difference between a working group and a team lies in what each produces. In a working group, members meet to share information, discuss ongoing projects, and make decisions. They don't produce anything collectively and are judged largely on their individual efforts. In a team, on the other hand, members work together to produce a joint product, such as an assigned class paper, a science experiment, or a marketing strategy. While the working group shares the overall mission of the organization and measures its effectiveness by how well the whole organization does, the team has a unique purpose and clearly defined performance goals ("cut working defects on the assembly line by 25%"; "recommend a new site for the plant by August"). Leaders of formal working groups often control the agenda and make most of the decisions and assignments. Team leaders share decision-making responsibilities, let team mem-

Table 7.1   Contrasts between Working Groups and Teams

Working Group	Team
Individual work products	Collective work products
Individual accountability	Individual and group accountability
Group's purpose is the same as the broader organizational mission	Specific team purpose
Measures performance indirectly by how it influences others (e.g., financial performance of the business)	Measures its effectiveness directly by assessing collective work products
Runs meetings and active problem-solving meetings	Encourages open-ended discussion
Discusses, decides, and delegates	Discusses, decides, and does real work together
Strong, clearly focused leader	Shared leadership roles

bers take the initiative in their areas of expertise, and are active participants in the work. (Turn to box 7.4 for an example of a team-based organization where employees group themselves according to their expertise and control the work they do.)

Common types of teams include (1) teams that recommend things (choosing a new computer system; planning a reorganization), (2) teams that make or do things (create, sell, or service products, for example), and (3) teams that run things (managing the development of a product line). There are many potential advantages to taking a team approach.

- Teams are more flexible than departments or organizations.
- Teams are more productive and fun than working groups.
- Teams help the organization adapt to change.
- Teams encourage individual learning and foster new behaviors.
- Teams build trust and confidence between members.
- Teams focus attention on the group agenda rather than on individual agendas.

Despite their many advantages, teams aren't the answer in every situation. Top-level executives are one category of employees who generally function in working groups. The director of a government agency, for instance, will likely take a group approach to running her organization, asking department heads to meet regularly to coordinate their activities. However, when she wants to make a major change in the structure or operations of the agency, a team approach will probably produce better results. The crucial decision for a leader, then, is to determine whether a group approach or a team approach is best. If performance levels can be met through individual activities, then stick with working groups. Make the shift from groups to teams only when the potential payoff outweighs the costs (effort, disruption, expense, etc.) of making the change. (The Leadership on the Big Screen feature at the end of the chapter describes one group that became a team.)

Box 7.4 Case Study	Team Leadership in the Video Game Industry: The Story of Valve

There are few industries more harsh, demanding, and competitive than the video game industry. Developing successful video games is a creative process, yet many large-scale game publishing companies subject employees to unstable work environments with heavy workloads (often more than 12 hours a day, 7 days a week before product release) that serve to stifle the creativity of developers and game designers.[43]

Under such stressful working conditions, it is no surprise the quality of products suffers—a costly situation for publishers competing for successful reviews and the attention of customers. Companies frequently fail and the job and financial security of developers is often at risk. One Seattle-based company, however, stands above the rest in terms of building successful teams and developing award-winning and popular games. Valve, a privately owned game development and publishing company with an estimated $2.5 billion in annual revenues, has been working since 1996 to create highly regarded video games in a unique team environment. They hold multiple "Game of the Year" awards for such popular games as Half-Life, Left 4 Dead, and Portal, and their Steam service has a 70% share of the video game online distribution market.

How does Valve consistently perform so well? By redefining the concept of team leadership. Valve has no formally assigned team leaders. Instead, power and the responsibility for developing and delivering games is placed solely on employees. As the employee handbook explains, "Valve is flat. It's our shorthand way of saying that we don't have any management, and nobody 'reports to' anybody else. . . . You have the power to green-light projects. You have the power to ship products."[44] At Valve, work gets done primarily through small, self-focused, self-structuring teams called "cabals." These cabals are fluid; employees can join or leave as they choose. All desks at Valve have wheels to make it easy to move team members closer to each other as cabals form. The employee handbook outlines these steps for moving: "Step 1. Unplug cords from wall. Step 2. Move your desk. Step 3. Plug cords back into wall. Step 4. Get back to work."

Groupings at Valve are generally unstructured. When structure arises, it is not because employees are assigned to join certain teams as an animator or programmer; rather, teams internally recruit employees who serve in the roles that fit the needs of the team. Sometimes, team leaders organically emerge. As the handbook says, "Most often, they're [leaders] primarily a clearinghouse of information. They're keeping the whole project in their head at once so that people can use them as a resource to check decisions."[45] The cabal team system means employees can select the place where they can be most valuable. New employee hiring and compensation are tied to the team system. Ad-hoc teams made up of interested parties do the hiring interviews. Employees working on the same project rank each other's contributions (technical skills, productivity, ability to work in a team). Those with the best ratings get the largest raises and highest salaries.

The cabal structure has its weaknesses. Co-founder Gabe Newell admits that there are few internal controls to spot mistakes. As a result, serious problems with Half-Life 2 went undetected for six months. One fired former employee noted that the lack of formal structure allowed a hidden power structure to emerge. "It felt a lot like high school," she complained. "There are popular kids that have acquired power in the company, then there's the trouble makers, and everyone in between."[46] Receiving low peer rankings is not an issue when the company is successful and everyone is well paid. However, there will likely be lots of hard feelings if Valve loses market share and can only give raises to a few people.

Discussion Questions

1. What do you see as the strengths of Valve's informal team structure? The weaknesses?

2. Would you prefer to be ranked by a supervisor or by your fellow team members?

3. Does the cabal system have application in other industries? Are there limits to how and where this type of team leadership might work?
4. Would you enjoy working for a company like Valve? Why? Why not?
5. Do you think people are more willing to work long hours when they have more choice in regard to their projects and assignments?
6. Can Valve's structure survive if the company loses market share and revenue?

Developing Team-Building Skills

Successful leaders are skilled at helping groups become teams when the situation calls for it. Carl Larson and Frank LaFasto spent nearly three years studying more than 75 diverse teams.[47] Larson and LaFasto interviewed key members of these teams, including the leader of the Boeing 747 project, a person who served on several presidential cabinets, members of cardiac surgery teams, the founder of the U.S. Space Command, a member of a Mount Everest climbing expedition, and several players from the 1966 Notre Dame championship football team. From their groundbreaking work, Larson and LaFasto identified eight strategies that they believe are essential to effective team performance.

Establish clear and inspiring team goals. Effective teams are clearly focused on goals that maximize team outcomes. Further, these goals inspire the team to perform at peak levels. The team leader is primarily responsible for defining and articulating goals and for motivating followers. Team failure can be caused by a lack of clarity in the identification of a team agenda, the loss of focus from the agenda, or from distractions associated with individual demands at the expense of the group.

Maintain a results-oriented team structure. Within effective teams, each member clearly understands his or her role in the overall successful functioning of the group. Further, team members are accountable for their behavior in all situations. Every member of a successful team knows what is expected and takes responsibility for making sure tasks are done correctly. Members of a surgical team, for example, all play an important role in the overall success of an operation. The anesthesiologist monitors the patient's breathing, the nurse prepares the instruments, and the surgeon performs the procedure. Each member of the team must perform his or her task in concert with others in order to achieve a successful outcome. Communication within results-oriented teams is open and honest. Effective team leaders communicate in a highly democratic manner. (You may want to refer back to chapter 2 to reacquaint yourself with the qualities of the democratic leadership communication style.) Information is easily accessible, and questions and comments are always welcomed from all members of the group. Successful team leaders also provide frequent evaluation and feedback to members. Identifying strengths and weaknesses of group members is necessary in order to reward excellence and to suggest strategies for improving deficiencies. Finally, results-oriented teams base their decisions on sound factual data. Although "gut" feelings and hunches may produce positive results on occasion, successful decision-making is based on objective criteria.

Assemble competent team members. Effective teams are comprised of competent team members. Both technical and interpersonal competencies are essential to team success. Technical competence refers to the knowledge, skills, and abilities relevant to the team's goals. Interpersonal competence relates to the ability of team members to communicate feelings and needs, to resolve conflict, and to think critically.

Strive for unified commitment. The members of successful teams are wholly committed. Leaders seeking this type of unified commitment must work to create a team identity. Team identity is enhanced when team members are involved in decision making, policy implementation, and analysis. Indeed, involvement begets commitment. Emergency response teams are examples of unified teams with a collective identity. Members of these groups feel such a strong sense of duty that they are literally on call to handle any crisis that may arise.

Provide a collaborative climate. Cooperation and teamwork are essential to allow teams to function smoothly. Teams that work well together perform most effectively. Trust is the key ingredient in teamwork. An open, honest environment in which team members trust and respect one another promotes collaboration. In such an atmosphere, team members feel free to express dissenting opinions, thus avoiding groupthink.

Encourage standards of excellence. Successful teams have high expectations regarding outcomes. These standards of excellence define acceptable performance. High standards mean hard work, and top performing teams spend a great deal of time preparing and practicing. They are ready for virtually any contingency. The cockpit crew of United Airlines Flight 232 performed an almost impossible task in July 1989 during a crash landing at Sioux City, Iowa. Although more than 100 passengers died, aviation experts lauded the crew for maneuvering the plane under the most extreme emergency—a complete failure of the hydraulic system. Fortunately for the surviving 185 passengers, crew members believed that they could do the impossible. (See chapter 13 for another example of a flight crew whose heroic efforts saved the lives of passengers.) Standards of excellence are found everywhere within successful teams. Individual team members expect excellence from themselves and others. Perhaps most importantly, the leaders of highly effective teams demand that a standard of excellence be upheld. They will accept nothing less from themselves or the team.

Furnish external support and recognition. External support in the form of material or social rewards is important to the success of teams. These rewards alone do not guarantee success, but the absence of any form of external recognition or support appears to be detrimental to a team's overall effectiveness. According to Larson and LaFasto, recognition and support are most critical when the team is performing either extremely well or extremely poorly.

Apply principled leadership. The leaders of effective teams employ transformational leadership techniques. As discussed in chapter 4, the transformational leader is creative, interactive, visionary, empowering, and passionate. Larson and LaFasto found that three qualities seemed most important to effective team leadership: (1) establishing a vision, (2) creating change, and (3) unleashing talent. Effective team leaders have a clear vision for the team. The specific actions required to achieve this vision are clearly presented to team members. Further, this vision represents an inspiring and desirable goal for the group. Effective leaders also create change. Change is essential to improving and progressing. Effective team leaders encourage team members to seek out new and better ways to perform tasks and solve problems. Successful team leaders are not completely satisfied with the present level of achievement; they are always looking to the next challenge. Finally, effective team leaders empower their followers by unleashing the talent of all members of the team.

> The most effective leaders, as reported by our sample, were those who subjugated the needs of their ego in favor of the team's goals. They allowed team members to take part in shaping the destiny of the team's effort. They allowed them to decide, to make choices, to act, to do something meaningful. The result of this approach was the creation of the "multiplier effect." It created a contagion among team members to unlock their own leadership abilities.[48]

It is not the individual but the team that is the instrument of sustained and enduring success in management.

—Anthony Jay

Project Leadership

Teams have been managing projects for thousands of years.[49] The Egyptian Pyramids, the Great Wall of China, the Taj Mahal, and Stonehenge are all the products of ancient project management. In more recent times, project teams have created everything from the atomic bomb to the personal computer and the iPhone. Thousands of people spend their careers working on political and advertising campaigns, films, defense systems, buildings, roads, new drugs, space launches, software implementations, and other projects. According to the Project Management Institute, which certifies project professionals, one-fifth of the world's Gross Domestic Product (GDP) or $12 trillion is spent every year on projects.[50]

Ongoing processes, such as manufacturing or bill processing, are repeated over and over again to produce the same results. In contrast, projects are temporary with a clear beginning and end. Project teams produce unique products while operating under time and budgetary constraints. They are generally accountable to organizational sponsors and outside clients. Team members are typically drawn from a variety of different organizational departments or functions.[51]

Unfortunately, an estimated 70% of all projects end in failure.[52] They go over budget, continue past deadlines, must be reworked, fall short of client expectations, and so on. Many of these failures can be traced back to ineffective leadership. To tilt the odds more in your favor as a project leader, experts suggest that you do the following.

Recognize the Demands of the Project Leadership Role

Project management is highly demanding, requiring leaders to master several different roles. Project management consultants Wendy Briner, Colin Hastings, and Michael Geddes use the term "lookings" to highlight the fact that the job of the project leader is multifaceted. They argue that the successful project manager must look in six different directions.[53]

Looking upwards. This refers to understanding and informing the project sponsor (usually the project manager's boss). The best leaders understand why their bosses want the project completed and keep them informed while managing the sponsors' concerns.

Looking outwards. A good project manager keeps the end user or client up to date and meets client expectations. Project leaders also meet the expectations of subcontractors and other outsiders.

Looking backwards and looking forwards. The project leader must ensure that the team meets its targets and learns from any mistakes.

Looking downwards. Effective leaders make sure that individuals and the group as a whole perform well.

Looking inwards. Successful project managers examine their personal performance to confirm that they are helping the team reach its objectives.

The first two tasks or lookings—upwards and outwards—involve the management of stakeholders. The keys to connecting with stakeholders include establishing who the stakeholders are, reconciling conflicting expectations for the project, building credibility through demonstrating competence, establishing networks of relationships, and marketing the project to the rest of the organization. The next two lookings (backwards and forwards) involve managing the work of the project. This requires anticipating possible problems, ongoing planning and reviewing, keeping the whole team informed, and seeking feedback from outsiders. The last two lookings—downwards and inwards—deal with the management of performance demands. Fulfilling these roles requires providing purpose and direction (explaining why the project is important to the organization and individual; being enthusiastic); setting clear goals and expectations of what is acceptable and what is not; being tough on quality or standards; expressing support of team members; setting time aside for stepping back to reflect on the group's progress (or lack thereof); and celebrating achievements along the way as well as at the completion of the project.

Acquire and Apply the Necessary Skill Sets

To carry out their roles, project managers must have the necessary skill sets. According to the Project Management Institute, these knowledge management areas include:[54]

- scope management: defining and staying within the boundaries of the project; breaking down the structure of the work
- time management: generating time estimates; setting and managing schedules
- cost management: estimating costs, setting a budget for labor and materials; monitoring expenses

- human resource management: determining personnel needs, recruiting team members; team building
- procurement management: identifying resources and services to be acquired outside the organization; soliciting bids and proposals; awarding contracts and monitoring vendor performance; closing out contracts
- communication management: identifying stakeholders; creating a communication plan for keeping stakeholders informed
- quality management: setting quality standards; sampling quality; improving quality assurance processes
- risk management: identifying risks and assessing the probability that each risk will occur; developing responses; monitoring risks
- integration management: tying all the other management skill areas together to develop the project plan, manage change, stay within the scope of the project, and so on

In addition to acquiring the necessary knowledge bases, leaders must also know when to apply them by understanding the project life cycle. Projects typically follow a five-stage pattern, beginning with initiation.[55] Box 7.5 identifies which management skill sets come into play during each stage of the product life cycle.

During the *initiating* stage, those interested in the project define what it is and get buy-in and approval from possible stakeholders. They make a case for the project and create an initial draft of the objectives, requirements, constraints, and success criteria. At this point they also appoint a project manager. During the *planning* process the project manager outlines project tasks, estimates needed

Box 7.5				**The Links Between** **Project Stages and Knowledge Areas**[56]	
Knowledge Areas	**Initiating**	**Planning**	**Executing**	**Controlling and Monitoring**	**Closing**
Scope		X		X	
Time		X		X	
Cost		X		X	
Quality		X	X	X	
Communication	X	X	X	X	
Human Resources		X	X		
Risk		X		X	
Procurement		X	X	X	X
Integration	X	X	X	X	X

time and resources, determines the total project cost, builds a schedule, and assembles the team. In the *executing* phase the team leader and team members get to work, setting the ground rules, outlining how the team will communicate, and carrying out tasks. During the *monitoring and controlling* process the team leader determines how well the plan is working by implementing changes as needed, monitoring performance, soliciting resources, solving problems, and ensuring that the scope of the project doesn't expand beyond original expectations. The *closing* stage brings the project to completion. The customer signs off and takes ownership of the product. The leader and team members meet to celebrate and to analyze what went well and what did not.

Adapt to Project Demands

Not all projects have clear objectives and outcomes.[57] Some teams may have well-defined goals but have no idea how to reach their objectives. For example, a consumer products manufacturer may ask a task force to increase market share, but team members may not be sure which product to produce in order to improve sales. Other teams lack both a clear goal as well as a clear solution. This is typical of many ongoing Research and Development department projects. Members of R & D teams work on developing new ideas but do not receive specific instructions about what they should create or a clear explanation of how their ideas will be used. Still other projects start with a solution and then ask the team to determine how to employ the idea. For instance, it took several years for employees at 3M to decide how to use the failed adhesive that produced the Post-it Note.

To succeed as a project manager, you will need to adapt your communication patterns and leadership style to the demands of the specific project (see the case study in box 7.6). Highly complex and uncertain projects require more "agile" project management that modifies the product life cycle described earlier.[58] Teams may repeatedly need to return to the planning stage, for instance, or release the product in increments for feedback and adaptation. Complexity also increases communication demands. Ill-defined projects change more frequently and rapidly so the project leader must interact more often with project sponsors and clients. Team leaders can no longer rely on one-way, written communication like status reports and updates but must interact person-to-person. They empower team members to make more decisions. The nature of the team changes as well. Instead of acting as a group of specialists, team members become generalists who organize themselves and their activities.

Leading Virtual Teams

Technological advances enable teams to function across space and time. No longer do members have to meet face-to-face. Now individuals working in different geographic locations and at different times of the day coordinate their efforts through *virtual teams*. Virtual teams use e-mail, videoconferencing, online bulletin boards, groupware, project management software, and other electronic means to carry out their work.[59] Large organizations like IBM, Sun Microsystems, SAP,

Box 7.6 **Case Study**	**Project Failure at Payton Financial Services**

Payton Financial Services (PFS) provides loan services for a variety of automobile and motorcycle dealerships throughout the southwestern United States. The computer systems at PFS are in need of an update as the current system is not able to manage the increasing customer volume generated through an aggressive sales campaign. Recently there have been several system failures including a major "crash" that took the entire loan-processing function offline for more than eight hours. Stephanie Bryant has been assigned to oversee the upgrade project at PFS. Her team consists of various customers from key business units, a half dozen IT developers, and two junior project managers.

The project is behind schedule and senior management is getting frustrated with the lack of progress. The initial difficulty focused on gaining clarity in regard to the specifications for the upgrade. Each business unit made requests for features that would fit their needs, but gave little thought to the impact these changes might have on other business units or the developers tasked with creating the functionality for these features. Stephanie was not able to broker an agreement and the debate over what needs to be done to improve the current system at PFS is still unclear to the team.

Further, the Chief Information Officer, Venkat Nair, has complained to Stephanie about the demands being made on the six IT staff assigned to the project. It seems one of the business unit leaders, Director of Consumer Operations Joe Moore, complained to Venkat that his IT employees are not used to working as hard as the staff in the Consumer Operations unit. Joe went on to tell Venkat that he had assigned employees with "poor skills and a bad work ethic" to the project team. These comments surprised and upset Venkat as he had personally selected the six IT employees working on the project. Venkat was so frustrated by his encounter with Joe that he asked Stephanie to reassign the IT developers back to him so that he could personally oversee their work. Stephanie was reluctant to make this shift in reporting structure, but she agreed anyway as she did not want to further anger Venkat or Joe. This change added a layer of communication complexity and made it more difficult for Stephanie to communicate with the IT staff assigned to her team. It also decreased the interaction between the IT developers and other members of the team as the IT staff insisted all communication be filtered through Venkat.

The current computer system at PFS is continuing to have problems and Stephanie and her team do not seem much closer to getting the updates completed than when the project started. Many of the business unit leaders are asking for a new leader to be appointed and Stephanie is feeling like she is losing control of the project.

Discussion Questions

1. Why do you think this project has derailed?

2. What advice would you have for Stephanie to get the project back on track?

3. How might Stephanie work to resolve the dispute between Venkat and Joe?

4. Have you ever been involved in a project where the team was not aligned? What caused this problem? How did you (or could you have) improve the situation?

5. Are the leadership challenges different in ad hoc project groups than in established long-term teams? What are the differences? How can these be managed?

TRW Automotive, Microsoft, Price Waterhouse Coopers, and General Electric rely on virtual teams to carry out marketing, consulting, project engineering, customer service, and other functions. Two-thirds of Intel's employees, for example, collaborate with team members at other locations. Virtual teams are used by a majority of global companies. Businesses and nonprofits want to draw on a wide variety of expertise from around the world without the expense of relocating employees or flying them to a central location. In addition, virtual global teams can respond more rapidly to changing international conditions than conventional teams, reducing product development times and costs.[60]

Experts agree that leading a virtual team is more challenging than leading a traditional team.[61] Virtual teams add a layer of complexity. Leaders must carry out all the functions we described earlier in the chapter—making effective decisions, building a collaborative climate, encouraging unified commitment, and so forth. At the same time, they also have to cope with the problems created by space, time, and cultural differences as well as by computer-mediated communication channels. Members often feel isolated and find it hard to stay committed to other team members they might never meet in person. It is easier for them to get distracted by competing demands in their immediate physical environments and to do less than their fair share of the team's work. Some in the group may have to get up early or stay up late to meet with those in other time zones. In virtual global teams, members have to manage cultural differences. Because electronic communication is not as "rich" (it doesn't carry as much information) as face-to-face communication, miscommunication is more likely. E-mail recipients have to decode messages without the benefit of verbal and nonverbal cues like tone of voice, facial expressions, and posture.

Investigators suggest that effective leaders meet the added challenges of virtual teams through the following strategies.[62] You can draw on these tactics if you find yourself in charge of a dispersed team.

Task-Oriented Team Building

In traditional groups, cohesion comes in large part from the informal interaction between group members, like gathering after work or impromptu discussions in the hallway. In virtual teams, team collaboration is more dependent on task performance—consistently carrying through on promises and assignments, responding quickly to requests, and so on. Effective virtual team leaders don't ignore the social dimension of group work. They may devote a good portion of initial e-mails and meetings to informal interaction about hobbies, work background, and family, for instance. However, the social component of team building complements the task dimension.

Perceptions of trustworthiness of other members form within "the first few keystrokes."[63] Brusque comments, ambiguous messages, and other credibility-reducing behaviors undermine trust. Leaders can help build a trusting climate by rallying the group around a common project or task and expressing their commitment and enthusiasm. They can also create an "expertise directory" which contains photos of members along with information on their training, skills, and experience. (We'll have more to say about trust building in the next chapter.)

How leaders and members respond to messages is particularly important to fostering collaboration in the virtual environment. Timely e-mail responses signal involvement, attraction, and attachment. Often the responder can provide information to help clarify the original message. Delayed responses frustrate communicators, can be interpreted as a signal of disinterest or dislike, and deprive senders of vital information needed to interpret earlier communication. The leaders of successful virtual teams encourage team members to respond quickly to messages. Predictability, like promptness, also plays a significant role in building cohesion. Group members don't always need to communicate often but they should do so in a consistent fashion (such as at the same time every week). They ought to notify others if they are going to be gone and can't participate in an upcoming discussion.

A Proactive Approach to Creating and Maintaining Structure

While structure is necessary for on-site teams, it takes on added importance in virtual teaming. Dispersed teams need clear guidelines and structure to help overcome the barriers of distance, diverse backgrounds, and competing demands on their time. Effective leaders are proactive, outlining the group's purpose and member roles before the team is formed. They provide detailed instructions in writing, describe workflow, and outline operating rules (e.g., members should respond to all e-mails within 24 hours). They also set forth clear performance standards related to such metrics as growth of market share, profitability for each transaction, process improvements (cycle time, installation time), and customer satisfaction. Once the group is underway, successful leaders make an ongoing effort to maintain and improve structure. They continuously monitor group interaction as well as individual and collective performance, providing ongoing feedback to members on how well they are fulfilling their roles and meeting objectives. In addition, they create a virtual workspace for posting progress reports, meeting agendas and minutes, action item lists, and other vital information.

Mastery of Communication Technology and Channels

Since virtual groups are linked through computer-mediated communication, skillful use of technology is critical. Members must have access to the right technology and know how to use it. Leaders of productive teams ensure that followers have the necessary equipment and software and provide training. They also abandon technologies that are no longer working. Yet, equipping and training are just the beginning. Effective leadership involves matching message content with the proper technology or format. To succeed, virtual team leaders must accurately determine which form of communication—e-mail, videoconferencing, online meetings—should be used in which situation. E-mails sent at different times (*asynchronous* messages) work well for routine communication. However, as the need for information and coordination increases, real-time forums (*synchronous* communication) are required. These include online chats, regularly scheduled online meetings, and phone calls. Managing conflicts, reinforcing group cohesion, and dealing with the most complex project issues requires even richer channels—videoconferencing and, whenever possible, face-to-face meetings.

Enhancing Visibility, Recognition, and Rewards

Virtual team members often operate "out of sight, out of mind." Much of the work they do is invisible to coworkers and, more importantly, to supervisors. They don't get the notice that physically present employees get from coming to work early and leaving late, for instance. As a consequence, bosses are less likely to recognize the contributions of virtual team members during performance reviews and less likely to make supportive comments. Effective virtual leaders make sure that local leaders are aware that their employees are engaged in important work. They may conduct status briefings for other managers, act as advocates for team members, set up virtual steering committees comprised of local supervisors, or require that individuals report out to their closest bosses. The best virtual team leaders also make sure that team members are rewarded for their efforts through hosting virtual reward ceremonies, acknowledging the successes of individual members at the beginning of meetings, praising team members to outside executives, and assuring that virtual work is seen as a path to career success.

Team Coaching

Teams of all types are more likely to succeed if they receive skilled coaching. Coaching refers to direct interventions or interactions with a team designed to help improve its collective performance.[64] Unlike individual coaching, which addresses the performance of a leader or individual group member (see chapter 11), team coaching is directed at the group as a whole. In some cases, the coach is an outside observer (someone from human resources, for instance) or an organizational consultant. In other cases, the team leader takes on this role.

Harvard University small group experts Richard Hackman and Ruth Wageman argue that coaches should set aside the belief that better interpersonal relationships are the key to better performance and focus instead on how groups can better complete their tasks.[65] Further, coaching needs to be offered at the right stage of the group's development. Hackman and Wageman outline three coaching functions to be carried out at different points in the group's evolution. *Motivational coaching* addresses the effort the team needs to put into the task and should be offered when the group is starting out. A new group is grappling with task requirements and has little capacity for developing a performance strategy. Instead, members need to commit themselves to the group and doing their share of the workload. *Consultative coaching* addresses the strategy the group uses to complete its work. It is best offered at the midway point, when group members may have discovered that their usual ways of interacting aren't effective and are looking to try new tactics. *Educational coaching* addresses the development and use of knowledge and skill. This type of coaching is best done at end of the project. Members may recognize that they paid too much attention to some members while undervaluing the contributions of others, for instance. The knowledge they capture at this point can be used to make the team more effective in future projects. (Turn to box 7.7 for more information on effective debriefing strategies.)

Box 7. 7 Research Highlight	**The Power of the Debrief[66]**

A debrief or "after-action review" is a simple, quick, low cost, and efficient way to improve group effectiveness. In one analysis of 46 studies of debriefs, researchers found that groups that systematically paused for reflection and goal setting saw an increase of 20–25% in individual and group performance. (The average debrief took only 18 minutes.) Debriefing not only helps the group identify what went well or what fell short in the current project but also helps the group better tackle the next assignment.

The researchers identified four characteristics of effective debriefs. First, they involve active learning. Instead of telling participants what the group did well or poorly and how to improve, leaders ask group members to share their thoughts and reflections through ratings, questions, and surveys. Second, effective debriefs are developmental, not administrative. Instead of using debriefs to evaluate group members, the focus is on helping the group learn and develop. Third, the best debriefs focus on specific events. Rather than addressing overall strengths and weaknesses, the leader or facilitator highlights specific events or situations that happened in the life of the group. This allows the group to develop specific action plans going forward. Fourth, information from multiple sources is more effective than from a single source. Hear from multiple team members and, when possible, from an outside observer.

Unfortunately, many groups fail to learn from their work together because they fail to debrief. Consider the experience of the many student groups, for instance. Once they complete a class assignment together, members immediately move on to tackle the next one without reflecting on their performance on the previous project. The same is true of flight crews. Few pilots and co-pilots pause to discuss how a flight went, for example, before heading home or on to the next route.

British consultant Peter Hawkins offers an approach to team coaching that is particularly well suited to project groups.[67] He urges team leaders and outside consultants to help teams develop the following five disciplines, which focus not only on how group members function with each other but also on how the team relates to outside stakeholders.

Discipline 1: Commissioning and re-commissioning. Commissioning coaching addresses elements of the team's formation (see our earlier discussion of the stages of the project life cycle). The team needs to understand why it was formed and the task it is commissioned to do. Targets need to be set, contracts drawn, and team members selected. The commissioning individual or body should outline the support it will provide to the team.

Discipline 2: Clarifying. Clarifying coaching helps the group tie its purpose to that of the larger organization. Team members need to develop their own mission and values as well as the unique strategy they will use to accomplish their work. They also need to identify the roles and expectations of group members while setting performance objectives and benchmarks.

Discipline 3: Co-Creation. Co-creation coaching is focused on how the group creates and carries out its work in formal meetings and when members interact between meetings. Interventions address work strategies and processes as well as how the group deals with conflict.

Discipline 4: Connecting. Connecting coaching provides feedback to the team on how well it is relating to important stakeholders. The team may need help developing effective strategies for communicating with outside groups and assign specific members to keep in touch with specific stakeholders.

Discipline 5: The core learning. Core-learning coaching helps individuals and the team as a whole perform and learn. Coaches help teams develop a positive supportive climate which promotes personal and collective development.

∼ CHAPTER TAKEAWAYS

- From a communication viewpoint, a small group has five essential elements: (1) a common purpose or goal, (2) interdependence, (3) mutual influence, (4) ongoing communication, and (5) a size of 3 to 20 members.

- Groups evolve over time. Both group decisions and group leaders emerge as the group changes and matures. Emergent group leaders (leaders who aren't appointed by someone outside the group) are selected through a process of elimination called the *method of residues*. Leader contenders are eliminated until only one remains.

- To emerge as a leader, avoid actions that eliminate you from contention like being silent, constantly joking around, or trying to impress others with your knowledge. Instead, participate frequently in the group discussion, make constructive contributions, demonstrate your competence, and help build a cohesive unit.

- To provide effective leadership in meetings: (1) determine if a meeting is necessary before calling people together; (2) have a clear agenda; (3) lay the groundwork; (4) maintain focus on the agenda throughout the meeting; (5) listen to others; (6) involve all participants; (7) keep a record; and (8) evaluate the group's performance.

- Groups charged with making decisions are more likely to succeed when they use communication to fulfill key problem-solving functions—analysis of the problem, goal setting, identification of alternatives, and evaluation of solutions—through the use of such formats as the Standard Agenda and Single Question Format.

- Avoid logical pitfalls that undermine group decision making through counteractive influence. Highlight problems in reasoning and get the group back on track.

- Combat groupthink, which is the tendency to put cohesion above performance, by soliciting input rather than pushing for your own choices. Encourage diverse opinions and constructive group thought patterns.

- Be alert to the danger of mismanaged agreement, the tendency for members to support in public what they oppose in private. Mismanaged agreement (the Abilene Paradox) causes groups to make choices that undermine their goals. To break the Paradox, publicly challenge the direction of the group and encourage others to do likewise.

- A working group meets to share information and ideas, but members are judged on their individual efforts. In contrast, in a team members work together to produce a joint product, and the team as a whole is accountable for achieving its objectives. One of your key responsibilities as a leader is to decide whether your members should function as a working group or as a team.

- Eight characteristics essential to effective team performance include: clear and inspiring team goals; results-oriented team structure (clear roles and responsibilities, an effective communication network, frequent feedback, objective criteria); competent team members; unified commitment; a collaborative climate; standards of excellence; external support and recognition; and principled (transformational) leadership.

- Project teams produce unique products while operating under time and budgetary constraints. Functioning as an effective project team leader means recognizing the multifaceted nature of the project management role. Acquire and apply the necessary skills sets (scope, time, cost, human resource, procurement, communication, quality, risk, integration) and adapt their communication patterns to the demands of the specific project.

- Virtual teams consist of members who work at different locations (often around the globe) and at different times who coordinate their efforts though e-mail, online meetings, videoconferencing, and other forms of electronic communication. To meet the challenges posed by spatial, time, and cultural differences, as a virtual team leader you will need to: (1) engage in task-oriented team building; (2) take a proactive approach to providing and maintaining team structure; (3) master communication technology and channels, and (4) enhance team members' visibility, recognition, and rewards.

- Team coaching describes interventions designed to help the group as a whole improve its performance. Motivational coaching delivered when the group is beginning encourages team members to put forth their best effort. Consultative coaching delivered at the mid-point of a project helps a group adjust its working strategies. Knowledge coaching at the end of the project enables the group to capture its learning. Coaching to improve group disciplines (clarifying, commissioning, connecting, co-creating, co-learning) is aimed at improving relationships with outside stakeholders in addition to improving group processes.

APPLICATION EXERCISES

1. Brainstorm a list of possible group norms. Which norms do leaders always have to follow? Which can they violate?

2. Discuss the pattern of leadership emergence in a group to which you belong. First, describe the communication patterns that eliminated members from leadership contention. Next, describe the communication behaviors of the leader (if one emerged) that contributed to that person's success. Evaluate your own performance. Why did you succeed in your attempt to become the leader or why did you fail?

3. Add to the list of reasons why you should or should not hold a meeting. What happens if you have a meeting when there isn't a valid reason for doing so?

4. Develop an agenda for an upcoming meeting using the guidelines provided in the chapter.

5. Form a group and use the Standard Agenda or Single Question Format to solve one of the following problems.

   • Due to a budget shortfall, one of your college or university's sports teams must be cut. The president of the school will act on the recommendation of your student panel. Decide which sport will be eliminated.

   • A wealthy donor has given $5 million to your institution "to be spent by students for the benefit of students." As members of student government, come up with recommendations for spending this gift.

   • Your college/university task force has been charged with developing a plan for improving relationships with the surrounding community. Outline a strategy for achieving this goal.

6. Determine if your group or organization is suffering from groupthink, mismanaged agreement, or escalation of commitment. Develop a plan for confronting the problem.

7. Analyze the performance of a team using the eight characteristics of effective teams presented in the chapter. Which elements are present? Which are missing? What can the team do to become more productive?

8. Describe a high performing team of which you have been a member. What made this team so successful? Did your group receive any coaching? Why do you think other teams you were on were less successful?

9. Interview someone who has been a member of a project management team or virtual team. Report your findings in class.

10. Write a research paper on virtual team leadership. What do you identify as the behaviors of effective virtual team leaders and members?

⌒ CULTURAL CONNECTIONS: AMERICAN AND ASIAN STUDENT GROUPS[68]

American and Asian students working in classroom-project groups in the United States can get frustrated with each other. American students sometimes complain that their Asian counterparts don't participate enough, and Asian students may feel like their opinions don't matter. To determine why these frustrations develop, University of Southern California professors Jolanta Aritz and Robyn Walker analyzed the attitudes and communication patterns of US and East Asian business professionals enrolled in an MBA program. First, they surveyed students to determine (1) their level of satisfaction with the group decision-making process, (2) their sense of being included and valued, and (3) their preferred leadership styles. The investigators then coded the transcripts of team meetings to determine how these leadership styles were reflected in the team's talk.

While the US born native English speakers and East Asians didn't differ on their overall satisfaction with the teams' decision-making process, the East Asians did not feel as included, valued, or supported. The cultural groups also differed in their leader style preferences. US team members favored "decisive and task oriented" as the most important quality of a leader, while Chinese, Japanese, and Korean respondents put much more value in being conscious of status; involving others in the deliberations; and being modest, compassionate, and supportive. (Modesty ranked last in importance to the Americans.) These preferences were reflected in the group discussions. In one group with a directive American leader, native English speakers took five times as many turns as East Asian members, spoke for more than twice as long per turn, and used an average of 1,170 words as compared to 127 for nonnative speakers. In a group led by a more collaborative American leader, the leader spent more time asking Asian members for their opinions, tied her thoughts into theirs, and demonstrated more listening behaviors. As a result, the contributions of both the Asian and American participants were roughly equal. American speakers took more turns during the discussion but the average number of words per turn and the total number of words of both the American (870) and Asian (843) speakers were similar.

Aritz and Walker conclude that US students ought to adopt a more cooperative and inclusive leadership style when working with their East Asian classmates in small groups. Directive leadership lowers participation and satisfaction. This style comes across as too aggressive and makes it harder for nonnative speakers to take their turn. In addition, the cooperative style is a better fit with the Asian cultural values of consideration and being respectful of others.

∿ LEADERSHIP ON THE BIG SCREEN: *THE WAY*

Starring: Martin Sheen, Emilio Estevez, Deborah Kara Unger, Yorick van Wageningen, James Nesbitt

Rating: PG-13 for mature themes, drug use, and smoking

Synopsis: California ophthalmologist Thomas Avery (Martin Sheen) travels to France to identify the body of his estranged adult son Daniel (Estevez), killed in the Pyrenees while walking the Camino de Santiago, a Catholic pilgrimage to Spain. Avery decides to honor his son by completing the 500-mile journey, scattering his son's ashes along the way. He sets out alone but reluctantly becomes part of a small group of pilgrims, including a Dutchman (van Wageningen) who is hoping to lose weight, a Canadian (Unger) who is fleeing an abusive husband, and an Irish writer (Nesbitt) who wants to publish a travel article about the trip. As the miles go by the group bonds, with members supporting each other in their efforts to finish the pilgrimage. The film was directed by Estevez, who wrote the role of Thomas Avery for his father, Sheen.

Chapter Links: elements of small groups, group evolution, emergent leadership, groups vs. teams

Leadership in Organizations

We view leadership as a verb, not a job.
                    —Ronald Heifetz, Alexander Grashow, Marty Linsky

OVERVIEW

The Leader as Culture Maker
    Elements of Organizational Culture
    Shaping Culture
    Creating a Learning, Trusting Culture
The Leader as Strategist
The Leader as Sensemaker
Intergroup Leadership
The Power of Expectations: The Pygmalion Effect
    The Communication of Expectations
    The Galatea Effect
    Putting Pygmalion to Work

Leaders and organizations: it's hard to talk for very long about either topic without mentioning the other. Although this chapter is devoted to a discussion of leadership in organizations, we've already talked at length about organizational leadership in this book. For example, many of the leadership theories presented in chapters 3 and 4 were developed by organizational scholars. Interest in organizational leadership is not surprising when you consider that leaders are extremely important to the health of organizations and that we spend a good deal of our time in organizations. Amitai Etzioni sums up the importance of organizations this way:

> We are born in organizations, educated by organizations, and most of us spend much of our lives working for organizations. We spend much of our leisure time paying, playing, and praying in organizations. Most of us will die in an organization and when the time comes for burial, the largest organization of all—the state—must grant official permission.[1]

In the pages that follow we will focus, first of all, on the important communication tasks of leaders. Then we'll explore the ways that leader expectations can either increase or decrease follower performance.

The Leader as Culture Maker

Earlier we noted that humans have the ability to create reality through their use of symbols, and this is readily apparent in the organizational context. Organizations are formed through the process of communication. As organizational members meet and interact, they develop a shared meaning for events. Communication is not contained within the organization. Instead, communication *is* the organization.

Communication scholars and others have borrowed the idea of culture from the field of anthropology to describe how organizations create shared meanings.[2] From a cultural perspective, the organization resembles a tribe. Over time, the tribe develops its own language, hierarchy, ceremonies, customs, and beliefs. Because each organizational tribe shares different experiences and meanings, each develops its own unique way of seeing the world or culture. Anyone who joins a new company, governmental agency, or nonprofit group quickly recognizes unique differences in perspectives.

New employees often undergo culture shock as they move into an organization with a different language, authority structure, and attitude toward work and people. Even long-term members can feel out of place if they change positions within the same organization. Each department or branch office may represent a distinct subculture. Salespeople, for example, generally talk and dress differently than engineers employed by the same firm.[3]

Elements of Organizational Culture

Dividing organizational culture into three levels—assumptions, values, and symbols—provides important insights into how culture operates. Members of every organization share a set of assumptions that serve as the foundation for the group's culture. Assumptions are unstated beliefs about: human relationships (are relationships between organizational members hierarchical, group oriented, or individualistic?); human nature (are humans basically good or evil or neither?); truth (is it revealed by authority figures or discovered on one's own through testing?); the environment (should we master the environment, be subjugated to it, or live in harmony with it?); and universalism/particularism (should all organizational members be treated the same, or should some individuals receive preferential treatment?).[4] How an organization answers these questions will determine the way it treats employees and outsiders, whether or not members will respond favorably to directives from management, what sorts of products a company manufactures, and so on.

Values make up the next level of organizational culture. Frequently (but not always) recognized and acknowledged by members, values reflect what the organization feels it "ought" to do. They serve as the yardstick for judging behavior. One way to identify important values is by examining credos, vision and mission statements, and advertising slogans. Words like "concern," "quality," and "corporate responsibility" articulate the official goals and standards of the organization. At times, however, the official or espoused values conflict with what people actually do, as in the case of an organization that touts its commitment to the environment but engages in illegal dumping.

Symbols and symbolic creations called artifacts make up the top level of an organization's culture. By analyzing these visible elements, used in everyday interaction, we gain insights into an organization's assumptions and values.[5] Common organizational symbols and artifacts include:

language	buildings
stories and myths	products
rites and rituals	technology
written materials	heroes
metaphors	logos
dress and physical appearance	office decor

While there are far too many symbols to examine each in detail, experts pay particularly close attention to the first three symbols when they analyze organizational culture. We will review them briefly.

A good way to determine how an organization views itself and the world is by listening carefully to the *language* that organizational members use. Word choices reflect and reinforce working relationships and values. The selection of the word "we" is revealing. It reflects a willingness to share power and credit and to work with others (see chapter 5). The choice of terms to describe followers also provides important insights into organizational life. For example, using the term "associates" rather than "employees" suggests that all organizational participants are important members of the team. Workers at Disney theme parks are called "cast members" to emphasize that they have significant roles to play in the overall performance for visitors who are, in turn, called "guests." Unfortunately, language also can reflect poor attitudes, as was the case at Goldman Sachs, where employees used the label "muppets" to refer to customers they thought were dumb or stupid.

Language is a powerful motivator that focuses attention on some aspects of experience and directs it away from others. Those who speak of innovation or quality workmanship ("BMW—The Ultimate Driving Machine") are generally more likely to provide creative and well-crafted products. In addition, a common language binds group members together. To demonstrate this fact, brainstorm a list of terms that you use frequently at school and on the job. Many verbal symbols like "student union" or "pull an all-nighter" that you take for granted as a student might not be familiar to those at your workplace. On the other hand, some of the terms you use at work might be new to other students.

Organizational *stories* carry multiple messages. They reflect important values, inspire, describe what members should do, and provide a means to vent emotions. In many cases, organizational members are more likely to believe the stories they hear from coworkers than the statistics they hear from management.[6] For example, workers at Intel tell the story of a manager who was fired after receiving an average performance evaluation. She was dismissed because "there are no average employees at Intel." This story makes it clear that the company has high expectations of its members. (Turn back to chapter 1 for more information on types of stories and storytelling.)

> *The key to effective leadership in corporations is reading and responding to cultural cues.*
>
> —*Terrence Deal*

Rituals, rites, and *routines* involve repeated patterns of behavior: saying "hello" in the morning to everyone on the floor; an annual staff retreat; or disciplinary procedures. Harrison Trice and Janice Beyer identify some common organizational rites:[7]

- *Rites of passage.* These events mark important changes in roles and statuses. When joining the army, for instance, the new recruit is stripped of his or her civilian identity and converted into a soldier with a new haircut, uniform, and prescribed ways of speaking and walking.

- *Rites of degradation.* Some rituals are used to lower the status of organizational members, such as when a coach or top executive is fired. These events are characterized by degradation talk aimed at discrediting the poor performer. Critics may claim, for example, that the coach couldn't get along with the players or that the executive was overly demanding.

- *Rites of enhancement.* Unlike rites of degradation, rites of enhancement raise the standing of organizational members. Giving medals to athletes and soldiers, listing faculty publications in the college newsletter, and publicly distributing sales bonuses are examples of such rituals.

- *Rites of renewal.* These rituals strengthen the current system. Many widely used management techniques like management by objectives and organizational development are rites of renewal because they serve the status quo.

Such programs direct attention toward employee evaluation, goal setting, long-range planning, and other areas that need improvement.

- *Rites of conflict reduction.* Organizations routinely use collective bargaining, task forces, and committees to resolve conflicts. Even though committees may not make important changes, their formation may reduce tension since they signal that an organization is trying to be responsive.

- *Rites of integration.* Rites of integration tie subgroups to the large system. Annual stockholder meetings, professional gatherings, and office picnics all integrate people into larger organizations.

- *Rites of creation.* These rites celebrate and encourage change, helping organizations remain flexible in turbulent environments marked by rapid shifts in markets and technology. Some groups rotate individuals in and out of the role of devil's advocate to challenge the status quo, for example. One company went so far as to appoint a "vice-president for revolutions." Every four years he made dramatic changes in the organization's structure and personnel in order to introduce new perspectives.

- *Rites of transition.* Meetings, speeches, and other strategies can help organizational members accept changes that they didn't plan, as in the case of an unexpected merger. Addressing what the group has lost—past values, symbols, heroes—can ease the transition to a new culture.

- *Rites of parting.* When organizations die (go bankrupt, disband), parting ceremonies are common. Members meet to reminisce and to say goodbye, often over meals. These events help participants understand and accept the loss and provide them with emotional support.

Those who give voice and form to our search for meaning,
and who help us make our world purposeful,
are leaders we cherish, and to whom we return gift for gift.

—Margaret Wheatley

Shaping Culture

Notable leaders concern themselves with much more than organizational charts, information management systems, and all the other traditional subjects of management training. They pay close attention to the assumptions, values, and symbols that create and reflect organizational culture. Organizational psychologist Edgar Schein highlights the significant role that leaders play in the creation of organizational culture:

> Neither culture or leadership, when one examines each closely, can really be understood by itself. In fact, one could argue that the only thing of real importance that leaders do is to create and manage culture and that the unique talent of leaders is their ability to understand and work with culture.[8]

Schein notes that the responsibilities of symbolic leaders shift as the organization matures. The founder/owner, in addition to determining the group's purpose, imparting values, and recruiting followers, provides stability and reduces the anxiety people feel when an organization is just starting out.[9] A new organization often struggles with meeting its payroll, developing a market niche, and managing growth. The seeds of future problems are often sown during the organization's initial stage of development. For example, the founder/leader might emphasize teamwork but continue to make all major decisions. Other founders do not perform as effectively as leaders once the organization has been firmly established. Founders/leaders often lay the groundwork for future change by promoting people who will share some, but not all, of their values. Once the organization reaches mid-life and maturity, leaders (frequently someone other than the founder) become change agents who intervene to challenge cultural assumptions, reinforce key values, or create new symbols. (Turn to box 8.1 to read about a founder who wants to keep his company's culture true to its roots.)

Box 8.1 Case Study	Caring for Employees at The Container Store[10]

Few companies treat their employees as well as The Container Store. The average sales associate at the company, which sells containers and storage units, makes $48,000 a year (twice the retail industry average). All workers receive health care coverage (even part timers), generous maternity and paternity leave, and free snacks. Valentine's Day is celebrated as "We Love Our Employees Day." New hires receive 263 hours of training in their first year; part timers 177 hours. Continuing employees receive 31 hours of training annually. (This compares to the retail industry average of 8 hours.)

The Container Store's "employee first" culture has paid off. The company expanded from its original store in Dallas in 1978 to 79 locations around the US with annual revenues of $795 million. In addition, it consistently ranks as one of America's most admired companies. For 17 straight years it has been one of *Fortune*'s 100 Best Companies to Work For. In 2015 it was also named to the following lists: Best Workplaces for Camaraderie, Best Workplaces for Diversity, Best Workplaces for Women, and Best Workplaces in Retail.

Co-founder, past CEO, and current chairman Kip Tindell is the driving force behind The Container Store's employee focus. Tindell is an advocate of "conscious capitalism," a business philosophy based on the premise that firms should meet the needs of all stakeholders (not just company owners and shareholders), and seek to benefit humanity as a whole. (Whole Foods and Starbucks are two other companies that follow this model.) Tindell believes that he can best serve company stockholders by making workers the top priority: "If you're lucky enough to be somebody's employer, you have a huge moral obligation to make sure they want to get of bed and come to work in the morning."[11]

CEO Tindell's relational focus is reflected in the Foundation Principles he created to shape the company's culture as it grew.

Principle #1: 1 Great Person = 3 Good People. One excellent sales associate is significantly more productive than three less productive employees, which is why the company pays its workers well above the industry average and provides generous benefits. Employees are compensated not based on commission but on such qualities as commitment, professionalism, problem solving, and teamwork. Tindell wants to employ people who excite their coworkers and make them eager to come to work.

Principle #2: Fill the Other Guy's Basket to the Brim. Making Money Then Becomes an Easy Proposition. This principle promotes win-win relationships with vendors. Container Store leaders work with suppliers by helping them develop products, placing orders during slow periods to keep their factories running, inviting them to company events, and paying all invoices on time (or even early). As a result, many Container Store products are exclusive and buyers are able to negotiate favorable prices.

Principle #3: Man in the Desert Selling. Sales associates focus on meeting the needs of customers, which can generate a large volume of sales. They never greet visitors by asking, "Can I help you?" but instead initiate conversations.

Principle 4: Communication IS Leadership. Container Store leaders build trust by sharing information about all aspects of company operations from goals and objectives to daily sales results and expansion plans to product information. Employees can provide feedback by speaking to anyone in the firm, not just their immediate supervisors.

Principle 5: The Best Selection, Service, and Price. Good relationships with vendors improve selection and lowers prices. Before opening a new store, top executives do a song and dance routine featuring hats that reflect the new community. They select one customer to be Super Fan, who gets to shop first and receives a gift card.

Principle 6: Intuition Does Not Come to an Unprepared Mind. You Need to Train Before It Happens. No guidebook can cover every situation so Tindell encourages employees to generate creative solutions. Well-trained employees are better equipped to meet the needs of customers, which is why the organization provides extensive training. Container Store employees are trained to work in every department of the store.

Principle 7: Air of Excitement! Happy employees attract and excite customers, while wide aisles and neatly shelved products reflect the company' focus on organization. Company efforts to maintain employee excitement include an annual chili cook-off and soap box derby. The company also established an Employee First Fund that provides financial assistance to employees facing emergencies.

Not surprisingly, employees respond well to the company's philosophy. More than 90% of employees say they are proud "to tell others I work here," believe that management is honest and ethical, and report that the firm is a great place to work. Only 4% of job applicants are hired after an extensive set of interviews and, at 10%, turnover is well below most other retailers, where it can be as high as 100%.

Despite the company's track record of success, Tindell was forced to step down as CEO in 2016 as sales dipped in the face of competition from Walmart, Ikea, and e-commerce sites. Analysts and critics wanted Tindell to cut labor costs in order to raise the stock price but he refused to do so, asserting: "A good capitalist will see the value of what we're doing. We would not be as profitable if we did less for our employees and vendors."[12] However, the new leadership team may not be able to resist the pressure to focus less on employees and more on the bottom line.

Discussion Questions

1. Have you ever shopped at The Container Store? If so, how would you describe your experience? If not, are you more likely to shop at the retailer after learning more about its culture?

2. Do you agree with Tindell's assertion that the company's success is based on its employee-first mentality? Would sales drop if the firm treated its employees like other retailers?

3. Can you think of other firms that seem to put people first?

4. How important is it for organizations to have fun? To create an air of excitement?

5. Should businesses serve a higher purpose than making money?

6. Will The Container Store be able to resist the pressure to change its corporate culture?

Your effectiveness as a leader will depend in large part on how well you put your "stamp" on an organization's culture or subcultures either as a founder or as a change agent. Perhaps you want to introduce more productive values and practices or encourage innovation as part of your vision or agenda. Cultural change, while necessary, is far from easy. Some organizational consultants sell programs that promise to modify organizational culture in a quick and orderly fashion. Such claims, which treat culture as yet another element housed in the organizational container, are misleading.

> *Nothing is inevitable until it happens.*
>
> —*A. J. P. Taylor*

Change is difficult because cultures are organized around deeply rooted assumptions and values that affect every aspect of organizational life. Current symbols and goals provide organizational and individual stability, so any innovation can be threatening. Nonetheless, knowing how culture is embedded and transmitted can help you guide the cultural creation and change process. According to Edgar Schein, there are six primary and six secondary mechanisms you can use to establish and maintain culture. Primary mechanisms create the organization's "climate" and are the most important tools for shaping culture. Secondary mechanisms serve a supporting role, reinforcing messages sent through the primary mechanisms.[13]

Primary Mechanisms

1. *Attention.* Systematically and persistently emphasize those values that undergird your organization's philosophy or plan. If your vision emphasizes customer service, for instance, then you need to focus the organization's attention on service activities. Your claim that service should be the company's first priority will not be taken seriously unless you as a leader perform service, honor good service, and penalize those who fail to respond to customer needs. In this way, others are encouraged to act as you do, to share your meaning that good service is important, and to believe service activities are critical. Some, like Ren McPherson of the Dana Corporation, argue that paying attention is the key activity of leader/managers. In McPherson's words: "When you assume the title of manager, you give up doing honest work for a living. You don't make it, you don't sell it, you don't service it. What's left? Attention is all there is."[14] Focused attention takes on even more importance when undertaking major transformation efforts.

2. *Reactions to critical incidents.* The way you respond to stressful events sends important messages about underlying organizational assumptions. Compare the way that organizations handle financial crises, for example. Some use layoffs as an efficient way to balance the books. Others, who put cooperation ahead of efficiency, cut costs by asking everyone to work fewer hours. (See chapter 13 for more information on how to prepare for crisis situations.)

3. *Resource allocation.* How an organization spends its money is a key indicator of where it is headed. Looking at projected expenses reveals whether a company will invest in new product lines, for example. Further, the process of budgeting reveals a great deal about organizational values and assumptions. The greater the organization's faith in the competence of its employees, for instance, the more likely it is to involve people from all levels of the organization in setting financial targets. Because budgeting sends such strong cultural signals, think carefully about what you want to communicate when deciding how to create the departmental or organizational spending plan.

4. *Role modeling.* Effective leaders work to develop others who share their vision. Become a coach and teacher to followers, particularly to those who are directly underneath you on the organizational ladder. Like The Container Store, you can also instill organizational philosophy through formal training programs.

5. *Rewards.* Rewards and punishments go hand in hand with the mechanism of attention described earlier. If service is your goal, then honor those who provide good service (through expanded job responsibilities, pay raises, etc.) and discipline those who don't.

6. *Selection.* Since organizations tend to perpetuate existing values and assumptions by hiring people who fit into the current system, reform the culture by recruiting members who share your new perspective rather than the old one. Promote those who support your vision; if necessary, help those who won't or can't change find employment at another organization.

Secondary Mechanisms

1. *Structure.* Organizational design and structure affect how leaders divide up such things as product lines, markets, and work responsibilities. Some structures emphasize the interdependence of organizational units, for example, while others encourage each department or branch to operate as independently as possible. With this in mind, determine what your current structure says about your underlying premises and make changes when appropriate.

2. *Systems and procedures.* Quarterly reports, monthly meetings, work routines, and other recurring tasks occupy much of our time in organizations. You can use these organizational routines to reinforce the message that you care about certain activities. For example, requiring a weekly sales report is a reminder that you are concerned about marketing results. Performance reviews that ask about an employee's honesty and integrity are a reminder that results need to be generated by ethical means.

3. *Rites and rituals.* To encourage change, nonessential rituals (those with little meaning for participants) can be dropped, essential rituals can be adapted to new purposes, and new rituals can be created. For instance, the annual Christmas party that has been a source of discomfort can become an annual banquet at which the organization promotes cooperation and teamwork. Harrison Trice and Janice Beyer suggest that rites of passage and

enhancement are the best ways to encourage change.[15] Develop new ways to help organizational members pass from one status to the next and publicly celebrate the accomplishments of those who meet the new standards. One college, for example, decided to officially welcome freshmen during the first week of school. Campus leaders instituted an all-campus assembly designed to reinforce the school's academic mission and to honor faculty achievement. Faculty members attend in their academic regalia and the student body president and college president greet the new students. Both incoming and returning students pledge to support one another. The recipients of the previous school year's faculty research and teaching awards are announced. The undergraduate professor of the year speaks to the gathering.

4. *Physical space.* The physical layout of your organization's facilities can transmit your values, but only if you pay close attention to the messages you send through these elements. Restaurants are good examples of how physical settings can communicate important themes. The harsh lights, stainless steel counters, bright colors, and uncomfortable seats of fast-food restaurants invite customers in for a cheap, pleasant, and quick meal. The muted lighting, plush carpeting, and linen tablecloths at fancy restaurants encourage customers to linger over expensive dinners complete with drinks and dessert. Determine what type of message you want to send through your use of physical space (collegiality, stability, familiarity) and design accordingly.

5. *Stories.* Consider creating new stories and changing old ones. If you are faced with a negative story that is already part of the organizational culture (perhaps a tale of how management is insensitive to worker needs), work to change the behaviors that made the story believable.

6. *Formal statements.* Most of what an organization believes never makes it into a formal statement. Nonetheless, as we noted earlier, credos and mission statements do reflect important values. Writing such statements can help you and your constituents clarify your thinking. If members understand the philosophy of the organization and have a statement of its goals, they can quickly make decisions about what actions will help their company or nonprofit group.

We must be the change we wish to see in the world.

—*Mahatma Gandhi*

Creating a Learning, Trusting Culture

The cultures of successful organizations take a variety of forms based on group history and membership, the environment, goals, values, and other factors. However, effective organizations generally share these cultural distinctives: a commitment to learning and a trusting organizational climate. In this section we'll outline ways you can promote organizational learning, and build trust.

Leading the Learning Organization

Learning is key to organizational adaptability and survival. Effective leaders build learning organizations that are skilled at generating and acquiring knowledge and then using that information to modify behavior.[16] They model learning by reading, attending workshops, visiting customers, touring factories, and so on. Learning leaders also function as teachers who challenge the assumptions of the group, ask probing questions, and allow others to experiment and fail.[17] (Box 8.2 describes one strategy for challenging assumptions.) They recognize the factors that inhibit learning. Common learning barriers include a lack of curiosity; inertia (it's easier to continue old ways of doing things); defensiveness that supports the status quo; fear of new ideas; organizational silos that separate groups; a lack of time and resources

---

Box 8.2	**Challenging Mental Models through Scenarios**[18]

Scenarios are stories about what might happen in the future. Shell Oil has used scenarios for decades and credits scenario planning for helping it anticipate the oil crisis of 1973 and to cut back on production before the oil glut of 1981. Scenarios challenge the assumptions of managers and force them to consider other alternatives, thus fostering learning. They also provide a common language for addressing problems, creating strategy and, in some cases, changing reality.

One example of the power of scenarios comes from the 1992 Mount Fleur Scenario exercise held during negotiations to end apartheid in South Africa. A diverse group of leaders—blacks, whites, liberals, conservatives, businesspeople, union members, academics, politicians—applied the Shell scenario method to make a successful transition to democracy. They developed four stories in response to this question: "How will the South African transition unfold and will the nation succeed going forward?" The first three scenarios were negative and were to be avoided: (1) Ostrich—the minority white government sticks its head in the sand and avoids a settlement with the black majority; (2) Lame Duck—a lengthy transition with a weakened government that satisfies no group; and (3) Icarus—the new black government embarks on a huge public spending program that bankrupts the country. The one ideal scenario to be pursued was Flight of the Flamingos, where everyone works together and all groups slowly prosper. Icarus got the most focus because it ran counter to the assumption of Nelson Mandela's ANC party that money should be redistributed from whites to blacks and that the economy would continue to prosper if it did so. However, Mandela and his top economic advisors changed their stance when they realized that the economy might be destroyed, undermining democratic government. After Mandela came to power, South Africa exercised fiscal discipline and observers gave credit to the Mount Fleur scenarios.

Effective scenarios need to capture the interest of readers and highlight different assumptions and outcomes. Before writing a scenario, interview key organizational members and gather information from outside sources. Develop a coherent story line and give each scenario a memorable name or title. Explain the use of scenarios to the leadership team and decide how they will be used by the organization. Shell scenario makers suggest that four scenarios are ideal. Offering three tempts leaders to choose the one they consider to be in the middle. More than four adds too much complexity.

dedicated to gathering and sharing information; and inability to act on learning.[19] Learning leaders seek to overcome these obstacles by, for example:

- promoting a recognition of the gap between current and desired performance
- rewarding creative ideas and innovation
- fostering open communication about problems, errors, or lessons learned
- making a commitment to continuous education
- honoring diverse ideas and approaches
- recognizing that the organization is a system with interdependent groups and units[20]

Further, learning leaders ensure that their organizations make effective use of three types of learning: intelligence, experience, and experimentation.[21]

Intelligence consists of the collection and interpretation of information gathered from sources outside and inside the organization. **Search intelligence** involves scanning and analyzing data that already exist or are readily available through public sources like newspapers, patent filings, information databases, social media, and Internet websites. Searching can reveal cultural or industry trends or market growth, for instance. (We'll have more to say about identifying important trends or issues in the next chapter.) **Inquiry intelligence** must be used when existing information is incomplete or unavailable. For example, an auto dealer may want to discover why car buyers chose its dealership over others in the area. Managers might use interviews, questionnaires, and/or focus groups to gather this information, asking closed-end questions like "How many dealerships did you visit before choosing this one?" or posing open-ended queries like "Why did you choose to buy a car from us?" **Observation intelligence** is appropriate when respondents have trouble communicating their real needs or feelings. Most employees can describe their formal job duties, for instance. However, by observing their behavior, you might discover that they spend much of their time on responsibilities not spelled out in their job descriptions.

Experience learning is based on doing—entering a new overseas market, acquiring a competitor, surviving a crisis, solving an ethical dilemma. Learning organizations analyze their successes and, more importantly, their failures. Learning leaders develop case studies based on organizational experiences, or they draw side-by-side comparisons between average and superior products. Boeing used the comparison strategy to make sure that problems with the 737 and 747 airplanes weren't repeated. These models were contrasted to the 707 and 727 rollouts, which were highly successful. You can also conduct reviews to determine why individuals (engineers, leaders), groups (project development teams), and entire organizations are effective.

Experimentation comes into play when organizations enter unfamiliar territory. Through experiments, learners introduce changes, observe, and then draw conclusions. They may test different explanations or interpretations to account for why sales are down or customer complaints are up, for example. Exploration is a form of experimentation that introduces prototype products (clothing lines, soft drinks, software) and processes (automated assembly lines) and then refines them based on feedback. Demonstration projects test significant changes in one location before they are rolled out to the rest of the organization. GE took this approach when it created an entirely new manufacturing plant to produce an advanced refrigerator compressor. At the facility, engineers developed a new manufacturing process and modified existing machines to meet more rigorous specifications. Employees received extensive training in order to master additional responsibilities and to succeed in newly created work teams. Many of the lessons learned at the plant were then adopted by managers and workers in other divisions of the company.[22]

The leaders of learning organizations effectively manage the knowledge gained through intelligence, experience, and experimentation.[23] They realize that information has little value unless it is shared or disseminated. In fact, failing to share knowledge can be expensive. A department at AT&T, for example, spent $79,449 to collect information that was already available to the public in a Bell Lab technical document priced at $13.[24] To encourage knowledge sharing rather than knowledge hoarding, knowledge management experts William Ives, Ben Torrey, and Cindy Gordon argue that you will need to address all of the following elements.[25]

- *Business context.* Link knowledge sharing to shared goals and the success of the organization. The greatest dissemination of knowledge occurs when employees are highly committed to the mission and values of the group, are informed of the organization's strategy, and understand the challenges and opportunities posed by the organizational environment.

- *Organizational structure and roles.* Create a competent staff of knowledge management professionals (IT staff, corporate librarians, chief knowledge officers) who can assist employees. Within business units, identify and encourage those who sponsor and reward knowledge-sharing activities, serve as experts in content areas, integrate new information into daily operations, and train employees.

- *Organizational processes.* Knowledge sharing should become part of the average job description. Specify how new knowledge is to be contributed and captured. Examples of knowledge-sharing processes include open forums, team debriefings, recording best practices, and knowledge fairs.

- *Organizational climate.* Knowledge sharing should become an organizational priority. Emphasize this behavior in orientation and training sessions, reward it, promote open communication between individuals and units, and include questions on knowledge sharing in project reviews.

- *Physical environment.* Create quiet spaces where employees can reflect and record their insights as well as attractive spots—kitchens, cafes, lobbies— where they can meet to share ideas. (Google, as we saw in chapter 4, provides lunch in order to encourage employees to share information.) Install network connections to allow interaction with those located off-site.

- *Direction.* Guide the knowledge-sharing process. Create guidelines and processes; focus on action steps; provide structured questions for analysis and reflection.

- *Measurement.* Assess individual and group knowledge-sharing behavior by measuring contributions (participation in online discussions, submissions to databases) and through cost-benefit analyses (reduced product development time, improved efficiency). Texas Instruments estimates that it retained $1.5 billion in business by improving its delivery times through knowledge management; Dow Chemical saved over $40 million in patent maintenance fees.

- *Means.* Facilitate knowledge sharing through technologies like e-mail, the Internet, groupware, and videoconferencing.

- *Ability.* Help followers develop information-sharing skills (networking, relationship building) and tools for capturing knowledge (logs, computer programs). Support their attempts to reflect on and to record their learning as they perform on the job.

- *Motivation.* Emphasize the intrinsic rewards of sharing data—saving time and money, completing a project, interacting with others, pride in being recognized as an expert. External rewards should not undermine team efforts or pit individuals against each other. Pay particular attention to the interpersonal dimension of information sharing by creating learning communities made up of groups of employees with similar tasks and interests. Demonstrate respect for the ideas of every follower.

> *Power comes from transmitting information*
> *to make it productive, not hiding it.*
>
> —*Peter Drucker*

Building a Trusting Climate

Trust, like learning, is essential to organizational success. Organizations with trusting climates are generally more productive, innovative, competitive, profitable, and effective.[26] Trust boosts collective performance by (1) fostering teamwork, cooperation, and risk taking; (2) increasing the flow and quality of information; and (3) improving problem solving. Those who work in a trusting environment are more productive because they have higher job satisfaction, enjoy better relationships, stay focused on their tasks, feel committed to the group, sacrifice for the greater organizational good, and are willing to go beyond their job descriptions to help out fellow employees.

Organizational trust is defined as the collective level of positive expectations that members have about others and the group as a whole. Trusting cultures are marked by high expectations of (1) collective competence, (2) openness and honesty, (3) concern for employees and other stakeholders, (4) reliability, and (5) identification.[27]

Competence is belief in the effectiveness of coworkers, leaders, and the entire organization. Members are convinced that the organization can survive through generating new products, meeting competitive pressures, and locating new markets. Leaders help foster perceptions of competence by creating a compelling and relevant purpose and vision. In addition, they promote competent individuals into leadership positions, design organizational structure to focus on results, focus the organization on its core capabilities, and manage change. Kia and Hyundai are two organizations that have moved from incompetent to competent. Once derided for their inferior products, the companies ranked second and fourth in the *2015 JD Powers Initial Quality Survey*.[28] (The Cultural Connections feature at the end of the chapter describes how Hyundai was able to improve so rapidly.)

Openness and honesty refers to the perception that people, both inside and outside the organization, get the information they need and that what they hear is truthful. The organization operates on a "need to share" basis by providing information in a timely fashion. Leaders foster openness and honesty by assessing and improving both current organizational communication practices and their own communication competencies. Volkswagen is one company that faltered because of its closed culture. The firm admitted to installing software that could defeat emissions tests (and improve results) in more than 15 million vehicles. Observers note that the firm has a "cutthroat and insular" culture which discouraged employees from speaking up about the scam for fear of punishment. Members of the board of directors say they didn't learn about the emissions cheating until two weeks after top executives acknowledged the deceit to American officials.[29]

Concern for employees and other stakeholders describes genuine caring for employees and other groups. Caring organizations communicate respect, are supportive, and try to correct mistakes and missteps. They listen to every stakeholder group with whom they come into contact—clients, vendors, neighbors, donors, investors, and customers. Policies and practices are consistent with a "stakeholder first" mentality. Employees, the most important stakeholders, feel fairly treated. Global engineering firm CH2M Hill (which is employee owned) demonstrates concern for workers by actively recruiting and advancing women, investing heavily in training and development programs, and providing employees with opportunities to work on interesting projects that benefit local communities.

Reliability describes organizational dependability. Reliable organizations act consistently. They can be counted upon to carry through on their commitments and their actions align with their words. Leaders build a culture of high reliability by making sure they follow through on their promises to purchase new equipment, raise salaries, change manufacturing processes, and so on. In addition, reliable leaders provide explanations for changes and refuse to overcommit or overpromise. They also communicate expectations and hold individuals at all levels of the organization accountable for results.

Identification is the degree to which members and other stakeholders identify with (connect with) the organization's goals, values, and culture. Leaders foster identification by (1) connecting employees to organizational mission and values through orientation and training programs, (2) continually emphasizing that employees, customers, and other stakeholders are important to the organization, and (3) modeling high character and courage.

Unfortunately, trust is fragile.[30] Untrustworthy acts can quickly undermine attempts to build a trusting culture. The reputation of Wells Fargo took a serious hit after it opened accounts without the permission of customers and then charged fees on some of those fraudulent accounts. Employees felt betrayed because they opened the accounts after being pressed to meet impossible sales goals; those who complained about the fraud were harassed or fired. CEO John Stumpf was forced to resign, though he left with millions in pay, which added to the sense of betrayal.[31]

To preserve trust, we need to remove those factors that destroy it. Listed below are some common "trust busters" to eliminate.[32]

inconsistent messages and behavior	dishonesty
unjust rewards	"us" versus "them" mentality
incompetence and low standards	restricted social interaction
inconsistent rules and procedures	negative moods (anger, frustration)
secrecy	finger pointing; blaming
concentration of power	micromanaging
hierarchy	failure to delegate
monitoring and surveillance	high turnover
unclear priorities and vision	unmet expectations and promises
organizational underperformance	

> *Trust has rightly moved from a bit player to center stage in contemporary organizational theory and research.*
>
> —*Roderick Kramer*

It isn't always possible to preserve trust. For example, you may promise extra vacation time only to be overruled by your supervisor, or employees may be bitter about the organization's pay structure. When trust has been significantly damaged, you will need to engage in trust repair. Following these four steps can help rebuild trust after it has been breached.[33]

Step 1. *Determine what happened.* The causes may not be as obvious as you think. Ask yourself:

- How fast did trust break down? If the deterioration was gradual, study the process to try to prevent similar failures in the future. However, don't expect to recover quickly from any breach of trust, slow or rapid.

- When did the violation of trust become known to you and to the larger organization? A significant gap between when the problem was recognized and when it was addressed will intensify feelings of betrayal.

- Was there a single cause? Responding to an isolated event is easier than dealing with a series of events, but don't ignore the possibility that several factors—poor performance, inconsistent standards, unfair rewards—could be at work.

- Was the loss of trust reciprocal? If both parties feel betrayed, then it is likely that neither side will respond objectively. Avoid retaliation and start a conflict resolution process if needed.

Step 2. *Determine the depth and breadth of the loss of trust.* Adjust your response to each affected group. In the case of layoffs, for example, some locations and departments will feel the impact more than others. More effort will need to be expended to restore the trust of these groups.

Step 3. *Own up to the loss (don't ignore or downplay it).* Acknowledge that trust has been broken as soon as possible. Promise to address the problem even if you don't have action steps in mind yet. Set a time when you will return with more specifics about how the issue will be addressed.

Step 4. *Identify what you must accomplish in order to rebuild trust.* Rebuilding trust may require providing more information, reconciling competing departments, or reducing pay inequities. List the changes that need to occur to reach these objectives. You may need to hold monthly informational meetings, merge work units, or form a compensation task force. Be careful not to overlook the details. Determine the extent of your involvement in the changes, for example; decide who else will be engaged in the process; and set a timeline for implementation.

> *Whatever matters to human beings,*
> *trust is the atmosphere in which it thrives.*
>
> —*Sissela Bok*

The Leader as Strategist

Setting the overall direction of the enterprise is an important responsibility for many organizational leaders, whether small business owners, entrepreneurs, senior corporate officers, managers of business units, board members, or nonprofit executives. Setting the wrong direction is the cause of many organizational miscues. The Digital Equipment Company (DEC) was once the second-largest computer company in the world with over 100,000 employees. However, the company no longer exists after being sold to Compaq, which was purchased, in turn, by Hewlett-Packard. DEC leaders decided to make products that were only compatible with other DEC products and believed that superior engineering meant it didn't have to advertise. When some of its products ran into trouble and competitors began offering similar items at lower prices, DEC was forced to lay off employees. IBM, on the other hand, remained successful because it made a strategic shift from selling computers and other hardware to providing software (technology services and consulting). Netflix is another firm that has prospered through a series of strategic choices. At first it sent DVDs to customers through the mail, offering a wider variety of films than could be found at Blockbuster or other video stores.

Then the company developed an algorithm that suggested related DVDs to users. Later the firm moved into streaming video both nationally and internationally and began providing original content.

Strategic leadership is concerned with the performance and future of the entire organization over an extended period of time.[34] According to research done at the Wharton School and with 20,000 executives, strategic leaders have six skills that enable them to think strategically. The investigators also make suggestions for improving each skill.[35]

1. *Anticipate.* Many leaders are poor at picking up on unclear threats and opportunities. Executives at Coors, for instance, failed to see the trend toward low-carb beers and Lego management didn't recognize the danger posed by electronic toys and games. Anticipatory leaders are continually scanning the environment for changes. Improve the ability to anticipate by talking to current customers and suppliers as well as lost customers. Try to gauge the response of competitors to new products and industry developments.

2. *Challenge.* Strategic leaders challenge their own assumptions and those of the organization while encouraging divergent points of view. Ways to develop the ability to challenge include, for example, focusing on the root causes of a problem, listing and examining long-term assumptions of the organization, encouraging debate, and getting input from outsiders who might be able to anticipate the negative outcomes of a choice.

3. *Interpret.* Thinking strategically means sorting through and synthesizing complex and often contradictory information. To sharpen interpretation skills, list three possible explanations for what is happening, actively look for information that disconfirms current hypotheses, and periodically step away to clear the mind.

4. *Decide.* Decisions often have to be made with incomplete information and involve trade-offs, but strategic leaders don't get locked in too soon to either/or choices. Build decision-making abilities by asking for other options, break down big decisions into parts, and balance short-term and long-term objectives when coming to a conclusion.

5. *Align.* Strategic success depends on getting buy-in from colleagues and stakeholders. Build the ability to align by communicating early and often, addressing key stakeholders, and reaching out to those who might resist the strategic plan.

6. *Learn.* Learning is key to strategic thinking. Promote a learning culture (see the discussion above) and continue to develop the ability to learn by documenting lessons from failure. (Information on debriefs can be found in chapter 7.) Reward managers who make good faith efforts but fail.

Strategic leaders use a variety of styles (described in box 8.3) to set direction. Whatever style they use, however, they begin by anchoring the strategic plan in the organization's vision and mission. With the vision and mission clearly in mind, the first step is to engage in internal and external analysis. Many organizations conduct a SWOT analysis to create a portrait of the group's current standing.[36] Draw four quadrants and then identify the following: organizational strengths (S), organizational weaknesses (W), opportunities (O), and potential threats (T). Strengths are factors that contribute to success—experienced staff, location, quality products,

---

Box 8.3 **Research Highlight**	**The Four Types of Strategic Leadership**[37]

British researchers Aaron Olson and Keith Simerson identified types of strategic leaders using interviews and focus groups made up of graduate students, experts, academics, and practitioners. They then talked to 300 leaders from 10 countries to further develop the characteristics of each type. According to the researchers, leaders take four approaches to the strategy process, each with its strengths, weaknesses, and unique behaviors. While there is no one best style, leaders need to carefully consider elements of the situation. In particular, they must decide if they should provide direction or solicit participation. Entrepreneurs generally have the freedom to direct the strategy. Leaders in other contexts, such as higher education, creative projects, and city planning, will need to involve followers in setting direction.

Visionary leaders (strategy through vision)

Examples: Steve Jobs, George Lucas, Nelson Mandela, Lee Kuan Yew (Singapore's first prime minister)

Strengths: insightful, inspirational, future oriented

Weaknesses: impatient and difficult to work with

Unique behaviors/actions: monitor trends, develop new insights, design solutions to address changing environments, move rapidly to change and evolve, enroll others to support the strategy

Directive (strategy through structure and process)

Examples: Jack Welch, Lou Gerstner, Dwight Eisenhower

Strengths: confident, decisive, fair

Weaknesses: controlling, remote, fail to execute the plan

Unique behaviors/actions: set direction through process, establish governance roles and systems, motivate others, monitor performance, intervene and adjust when necessary

Incubating (strategy through empowering others)

Examples: Ron Howard, Dr. Dre, Warren Buffett, venture capitalists

Strengths: experienced, perceptive, encouraging, nurturing, curious

Weaknesses: fail to provide clear direction, ineffective when put in positions of authority

Unique behaviors/actions: build networks, assess opportunities, diversify bets/investments, lend assets, create support systems

Collaborative (strategy though co-creation)

Examples: Phil Jackson, Lyndon Johnson, Tony Hsieh

Strengths: engaging, trustworthy, unleash creative energy, possess relational skills

Weaknesses: indecisive, slow to make decisions or fail to make decisions

Unique actions/behaviors: build relationships/connections, listen, find common interests, share power, demonstrate trust in others

reputation, etc. Weaknesses are any elements that hold you back—what your organization can't do or doesn't do well, or doesn't have. For example: high prices, poor quality, slow delivery times, and lack of technical savvy. Divide each category further and identify the strengths and weaknesses that will have the greatest impact—positive and negative—on future performance. Focus on those items. Then move onto opportunities and threats. Both opportunities and threats describe what is happening outside the organization. Opportunities are favorable developments that increase the chances of success. These could include the collapse of a competitor, new markets, increasing demand, or lower raw material costs. Threats are changes in the environment that could have a detrimental impact on the organization, such as new competitors, additional government regulations, and higher interest rates. Once again, concentrate on the most significant items. Use this information for determining the next steps your organization should take.

The Five Forces tool is another popular strategy for determining the strength of your current position and the possible consequences of adopting a new strategy.[38] The competitive forces include:

1. *Supplier power.* Assess how easy it is for suppliers to raise their prices based on the uniqueness of the product. The fewer the number of suppliers, the more powerful they are.

2. *Buyer power.* An organization's power is greater if it has lots of customers who would find it hard to switch from its products and services. Companies reliant on a few buyers (such as the public relations firm that has one major client) have little power. Walmart reportedly tells some of its suppliers how much they can charge for their products, refusing to let them raise prices even when their costs increase. Walmart can do so because these suppliers depend on the company for the vast majority of their business.[39]

3. *Competitive rivalry.* An organization loses power when customers can go to competitors for roughly equal products and service. The organization gains power if its product or service is unique. Netflix now faces fierce rivalry from Amazon, Hulu, and other companies that also offer streaming video services. Some of these competitors offer their own original television shows and movies and make their own deals with movie producers and television networks.

4. *Threat of substitution.* A company's power diminishes if customers can substitute for what the company provides. For instance, many travel agencies disappeared after travelers began to book their own flights and hotels on the Internet. Uber and Lyft offer alternatives to the traditional taxi and limousine businesses.

5. *Threat of new entry.* The easier it is for competitors to enter the market, the lower the organization's power. For example, the relative low cost and ease of online education has encouraged many colleges and universities to offer online programs. The high cost of offering degrees like engineering, nursing, and physical therapy (which require lots of equipment and have strict certification requirements) has discouraged many colleges from offering these programs.

Plans are nothing, planning is everything.

—Dwight D. Eisenhower

The analysis becomes the basis for the next stage in the planning process—designing a strategy. Selecting a strategy typically involves trade-offs. One major trade-off is between cost and differentiation (being different). Attempts to differentiate products and services from those of competitors (by improving quality or offering luxury features, for instance) drives up costs. As a result, firms usually favor one approach over the other.[40] The strategy takes shape through a host of decisions made throughout the organization about, for example, product design, marketing, research budgets, pricing, suppliers, staffing, and outsourcing.

Implementation or execution is the final step in strategic planning. Planners should keep three questions in mind to make sure their strategy is grounded in reality.[41] First, can we do it? The organization must have the resources and skills it needs to do what it plans. Second, does it make sense? External threats outside the control of the organization should be carefully considered. Third, does anyone care? No strategy can succeed if audiences—buyers, clients of nonprofits—don't think that the plan is important. For example, some consumers only adopt new technologies when they are forced to do so. They will not be willing to pay more for the latest cell phone or smart watch.

If you don't know where you're going, you might end up somewhere else.

—Casey Stengel

The Leader as Sensemaker

Strategic plans act as maps, identifying possible routes for the organization to follow as it travels forward. However, a number of scholars argue that leaders should navigate by a compass instead of a map.[42] Because the organizational environment is turbulent, they contend that leaders have to interpret conditions while on the go, making adjustments as events unfold.[43] Compasses are therefore more useful than maps because they provide leaders, like travelers, with a general sense of direction in the face of ambiguity. Leaders using compasses act as sensemakers, helping followers interpret or make sense of events and conditions.

We believe that leaders need to engage in **BOTH** strategic planning and sensemaking, to be guided by both maps and compasses. Leaders must give careful thought to the overall direction of their organizations since, as noted earlier, planning can be the key to success. Working toward fulfilling a mission and vision and meeting objectives engages and energizes followers and channels the energy of the group. Nevertheless, at the same time, plans are always tentative and subject to continuous revision. In many cases they need to be discarded. Unpredictable events like new technologies and competitors, recessions, natural disasters, and unanticipated opportunities can quickly render them useless. As a consequence, leaders need to be in constant touch with their environments and recognize that they are entering unknown territory. They will also need to provide explanations for what is happening in and around the group or organization. (The case study in box 8.5 introduces an organization that needs to plan as well as make sense of its environment.)

Social psychologist Karl Weick argues that sensemaking begins by admitting: "I don't know."

> The effective leader is someone who searches for the better question, accepts inexperience, stays in motion, channels decisions to those with the best knowledge of the matter at hand, crafts good stories, is obsessed with updating, encourages improvisation, and is deeply aware of personal ignorance. People who act this way help others make sense of what they are facing. Sensemaking is not about rules and options and decisions. . . . Instead, sensemaking is about how to stay in touch with context.[44]

A vivid example of sensemaking comes from fighting wildfires. Forest fire crew chief Paul Gleason, considered one of the world's best firefighters, puts a premium on staying in touch with the environment. If the danger level appears high, he might assign as many as 16 members of his team as lookouts, leaving only four individuals to actually fight the fire. At one fire Gleason worked without gloves to keep in better touch with weather conditions. When he felt a few drops of rain on the back of his hands, he knew he was feeling condensation from a huge column of smoke that was about to collapse. He quickly moved his firefighters to safety. Unfortunately, six people from another crew that didn't anticipate the danger were killed when the column collapsed.

Leading by the compass requires leaders to focus on animation, improvisation, lightness, authentication, and learning. *Animation* is keeping followers in motion. Often we don't really know the obstacles we face or really know what we think until we take action. Successful sensemakers take steps to engage followers through change programs that provide direction, get follower attention, and help members interact in a respectful way. *Improvisation* is reshaping or reworking previous experiences, practices, and knowledge. Previous material is adapted to fit current conditions. Jazz musicians are known for their improvisation. They continually introduce variations around a common theme. In the same way battlefield commanders begin the fight in order to discover the strength of the enemy. They then adapt their tactics in response to what they learn. *Lightness* means letting go of the belief that the leader has all the answers. This frees leaders and followers to keep listening and exploring. *Authentication* occurs when leaders admit they don't know but then ask followers to help them discover what is going on. *Learning* is the outcome of sensemaking. Leaders and followers collectively determine what they have learned because they admitted their doubts and navigated by compass instead of with a map.

Framing is one strategy that leaders can use to make sense or meaning and thus help create organizational reality.[45] In framing, leaders create a mental picture of the world and then encourage followers to accept their frame or interpretation of events. Leaders can't always control what happens in organizations, but they can exert significant influence over how events are understood. Helping followers interpret events like mergers, market shifts, and new programs is an important task of organizational leadership. Leaders must encourage constituents to adopt one particular interpretation or frame instead of alternative explanations. To translate a new corporate vision into action, for example, lower level leaders must: (1) help followers understand the new concepts associated with the vision, (2) show followers how the new vision is relevant to their jobs, (3) demonstrate enthusiasm for the vision, (4) relate new ideas with established programs and practices, and (5) help stakeholders see the next steps in implementing the vision.

> *Life can only be understood backwards; but it must be lived forwards.*
> —*Søren Kierkegaard*

Skillful leaders know how to design a framing response that is appropriate to the leadership context.[46] First, they determine the specific task at hand. They may be faced with leading change, increasing sales, or attracting investors and donors. They then identify aspects of the situation that might help or hinder their ability to succeed. A track record of success means that a leader will likely be more effective in convincing followers to accept his/her frame. Conversely, if followers are cynical about the latest reorganization plan, the leader will have more difficulty in persuading them to buy in to the changes. Third, effective framers determine who is making attributions about leadership in this situation. A financial analyst may judge a company leader according to one set of expectations; a union leader will use another set of criteria. Finally, they determine what frame to use in a particular setting. Common frames include simplifying complex or chaotic events, outlining gains and losses when making arguments, and establishing believability (truthfulness, objectivity, legitimacy).

Our communication style can help or hinder our efforts to frame reality. Expressive communicators struggle with framing because their goal is to express themselves, saying pretty much what they think no matter what the consequences. President Donald Trump is one well-known example of an expressive communicator. He says what he thinks (often through tweets), commenting on everything from restaurants and Broadway plays to election results and the actions of foreign countries. Conventional communicators are more sensitive to framing because they track what is appropriate to the situation and follow social norms. However, a conventional approach may blind communicators to better, more creative options. Strategic communicators are most likely to be skillful framers because they are very aware of the situation and alternatives for responding. They are highly sensitive to language and choose their words carefully. You can determine your communication style by completing the self-assessment in box 8.4.

Box 8.4   Self-Assessment   **Communication Style Inventory[47]**

Directions: There are fifteen pairs of statements in this inventory. For each pair, read both statements and quickly decide which statement best fits your communication style. Even if both statements are partially true, select the one that is true more often than not. **Circle either "a" or "b," not both.** There is no right or wrong answer in this survey.

1a. I pretty much say what I'm thinking most of the time.	1b. I try to be honest, but within the bounds of politeness.
2a. When communicating with another person, you have to respond to what the situation calls for.	2b. I focus on the situation, but I look for room to maneuver within it.
3a. I am sensitive to the context in which I communicate with others.	3b. When communicating with others, I try to seize the moment.
4a. I consider myself to be a straight-shooter. My communication is pretty transparent most of the time.	4b. When communicating with others, you have to really consider their thoughts and feelings.
5a. If my employees failed on an assignment that they are more than capable of handling, I would not be afraid to deliver a harsh message to them.	5b. If my employees failed on an assignment that they are more than capable of handling, I would try to couch a harsh message in a polite way.
6a. In difficult situations, I do what's right.	6b. In difficult situations, I try to redefine the context in ways that are more suitable to a beneficial resolution to the conflict at hand.
7a. People around me are shocked at times with things that I say.	7b. I try to keep most of my conversations from veering into unnecessary conflict.
8a. I am concerned about hurt feelings in a conflict.	8b. I try to seek consensus in conflict situations.
9a. I am careful in my use of language on the job.	9b. In general, I understand the power of language and the possibilities it affords, especially at work.
10a. My conflicts sometimes end with hurt feelings.	10b. Hurt feelings can usually be avoided in a conflict.
11a. I might be blunt at times, but people generally trust that I am telling them the truth.	11b. There is always a "proper" way to communicate truthfully that I try to follow.
12a. I try to persuade with the other person in mind.	12b. I've been told that I am very verbal; I could sell cars to a used-car salesman.
13a. I have one goal when I communicate, and that is to express myself.	13b. I try to communicate with an awareness of others' feelings about a given subject.
14a. I don't usually play games when I communicate.	14b. I can be subtly manipulative at times, but not unethical.
15a. If someone is really angry and potentially hostile, I'll back off. Otherwise, I express myself pretty freely.	15b. I try to prevent conflict as much as possible.

Scoring: When your response matches the letter "b," score one point. All answers matching the letter "a" are to be scored zero. The scale ranges from 0 to 15, with these approximate ranges:

    0–8 = Expressive   9–12 = Conventional   13–15 = Strategic

    Most leaders are Conventionals.

Becoming aware of the importance of framing is one step toward becoming a more strategic communicator. You can also prepare or "prime" yourself for framing opportunities. Engage in mental rehearsal before you present your frame, just as you would study for a test or repeat a person's name over and over in your head so you will remember it when you meet that individual again. Set aside time to reflect upon your mental images of your job and your organization. Constantly be on the lookout for opportunities to frame, such as when faced with a conflict about policies, a change initiative, or a crisis. Prime your language use by noting how words are used in conversation, literature, and news stories. Analyze arguments made in government and in the media. Create a story file to use in future framing contexts and constantly expand your vocabulary (learn a new word each day, for instance). Consciously avoid offensive words and reflect on your verbal missteps to learn from them.

Box 8.5 Case Study	**Facing Uncertainty at Airbnb**[48]

Few companies deal with as much uncertainty as Airbnb. For starters, the firm is operating under a new business model. Airbnb started in 2007 when friends Brian Chesky and Joe Gebbia (two unemployed Rhode Island School of Design graduates) decided to put out air mattresses and sell sleeping space to design show attendees in San Francisco. In 2008 another friend, Nathan Blecharczyk, joined Chesky and Gebbia and they created the website AirBedandBreakfast (air referring to the air mattresses and breakfast being pop tarts) for travelers who wanted to rent space in private residences. The firm got venture capital funding and expanded to listing entire apartments and homes as well as castles, boats, and tree houses for rent. Airbnb (the company shortened its name) operates with 2000 employees in 21 offices in 190 countries with service to 34,000 cities. In 2015, 35 million visitors booked accommodations on the site.

Airbnb's business model faces significant opposition, which also generates uncertainty. Hotel industry leaders argue that governments should level the playing field, making sure Airbnb follows the same guidelines and regulations as hoteliers. For example, hotels and motels typically carry liability coverage in case guests are hurt or become the victims of crime during their stay. Airbnb currently indemnifies property owners up to a million dollars for liability claims. But this coverage doesn't include claims for assault, sexual abuse, or terrorist acts. San Francisco and New York City prevented Airbnb from doing business in their cities. City officials complain that some property owners, instead of occasionally renting to visitors, operate unregulated and untaxed hotels by renting space nearly every day. They are also concerned that renting to visitors reduces the number of rental units available to local residents, contributing to a housing shortage. In addition to opposition from municipal officials, Airbnb faces the risk posed by the fact that "tens of thousands of individuals renting homes are interacting with people who they have never met."[49] There are stories of hosts welcoming guests clad only in towels. Moreover, visitors could damage rentals or attack homeowners.

CEO Chesky turned to a number of other leaders like Warren Buffet and former CIA director George Tenet for advice about how to navigate Airbnb's turbulent environment. Facebook COO Sheryl Sandberg and eBay executive John Donahoe advised him to quickly boost Airbnb's international presence. Taking their advice, Chesky expanded Airbnb's presence into Europe, also opening a dozen international offices with representatives in 30 languages and nearly every

(continued)

global time zone. (Airbnb now covers 99% of the world, compared to 52% for Intercontinental and Starwood hotels.) He hired Chip Conley, who developed a chain of boutique hotels, to be head of global hospitality and to help chart strategy. Chesky also drew on the insights of 60 employees who took five months to boil down the company's strategic plan to four major goals that fit on a single sheet of paper. (Chesky jokingly referred to this document as "the infamous paper to take over the world.")

Chesky, Conley, and others have determined that growth is in hospitality, not in renting space. To this end, the company has begun offering Airbnb tours and providing services like clean sheets and towels to hosts. In order to attract more business travelers, Airbnb sends traveler expenditure data to employers who can then track the spending of employees and now offers "business-travel-ready" rentals. Business-travel-ready rentals must have high customer ratings, not be shared by the owner, and provide Wi-Fi, laptop workspace, irons, hair dryers, and other amenities. The company has moved to attract more meeting attendees by embedding software in event websites to direct them to local Airbnb rentals. Company officials have also tested an airport-transportation service that could go head to head with Uber.

Airbnb faces continued uncertainty going forward. The battle over regulations continues. In an apparent shift of strategy, Airbnb agreed to comply with regulations in San Francisco and London that put a 90-day cap on the number of nights a whole apartment or home can be rented out. According to a professor of real estate at The Wharton School, "This is an example of how Airbnb may have to be flexible in order to expand its market share. Its potential is extraordinary but in the end it's going to have to deal with local regulatory bodies. Regulation is inevitable."[50] However, the company is still contesting New York City regulations that limit hosts to one apartment listing and prohibit short-term rentals in public housing. Airbnb also has to be careful not to alienate its loyal customer base as it pursues new sources of income. The decision to let businesses monitor the expenditures of employees who book through the platform may be seen as a violation of privacy by some travelers. Expanding hospitality services may make Airbnb seem like a travel agency or just another booking site like Trip Advisor or Expedia.

No matter what direction Airbnb takes as it navigates an uncertain environment, it needs to maintain the trust of customers—what global strategist Conley describes as a friendship with users:

> What I would want people to think, what we would want people to think about the Airbnb personality or the brand, is that it's like your local friend, the local friend who helps you to find the hidden treasures in the place you are going to.[51]

Discussion Questions

1. Have you used Airbnb? If so, what has been your experience? If you haven't stayed at an Airbnb property, would you be interested in doing so? Why or why not?

2. Should Airbnb continue to fight local regulations or comply with them?

3. What does Airbnb need to learn to continue to be successful?

4. What strategic leadership style does Chesky use? Is it the right approach for his company's situation?

5. Airbnb wants to be in the hospitality business. Is this the right strategy?

6. How should Airbnb balance strategic planning with sensemaking? How much should it rely on a map or a compass when moving forward?

Intergroup Leadership

Organizational success depends in large part on the coordinated efforts of groups and units. Doctors and nurses must work together to care for patients; faculty in different academic disciplines must coordinate their efforts to create new majors and programs; workers in newly merged manufacturing units must integrate their production lines and products. That makes intergroup leadership—promoting positive relations among subgroups—one of a leader's most important communication tasks.[52] Intergroup leadership is becoming even more critical as organizations become more team based.[53] In the past, coordinating group activities was the responsibility of top leaders. Now lower level leaders must coordinate patient care and curriculum decisions, redesign work processes, share information, gather resources, and so on.

Intergroup leadership is as challenging as it is important. Often the units being asked to work together have previously been in competition with each other for money, staff, facilities, and other organizational resources. The groups may differ in status as well. Take the case of a business acquisition, for instance. Members of the newly acquired firm are at a significant disadvantage when compared to members of the parent company. They may feel alienated as the dominant group tries to impose its values on them. Group identities pose the biggest barrier to intergroup collaboration, however.[54] When asked to define ourselves, we typically refer to our group memberships, describing ourselves as communication majors, students, accountants, union members, or managers (see chapter 3). Such group identifications make it easy to favor our in-groups at the expense of out-groups. We excuse the behavior of our group members while condemning the same behavior by members of other groups. We are "assertive," for example, but they are "pushy." Further, we prefer leaders who put the interests of our group over those of outside groups.[55]

Leaders who want to promote collaboration can start by encouraging interaction between units. Contact with outsiders can break down stereotypes and foster liking between individuals on different teams. Yet, contact by itself is not enough to guarantee that group members will develop positive feelings about their counterparts in other groups.[56] Negative interaction, such as when one group threatens the existence of another group, reinforces stereotypes and generates further hostility. Try to set the groundwork for positive contacts by emphasizing that the groups need to work together to achieve a superordinate or shared objective like instituting a new change initiative. Emphasize important universal values like equality and respect for others. Provide opportunities for various teams to interact informally through shared hobbies, social activities, and meals.[57]

Since differing group identities are the most significant obstacle to cooperation, the leader's primary task is creating an **intergroup relational identity**. Effective intergroup leaders encourage followers to see themselves as members of teams that function in relationship with other teams. Intergroup identity is dual identity.[58] Group members recognize that they are part of a larger organization but, at the same time, continue to identify themselves as members of their subgroups.

Successful intergroup leaders help create dual identities through their rheto-ric.[59] They outline a shared vision and a collective identity for all units while con-tinually emphasizing the importance of coordination. They also note how collaborating helps each group achieve its distinctive goals and retain its unique values. These leaders then back up their rhetoric by acting as boundary spanners. They bridge or span groups by having frequent contact with each team and devel-oping quality relationships with individuals from every group. They are careful not to favor one group over the other. Ultimately, they come to embody intergroup relational identity because they are seen as leading both teams, not one group or the other. In so doing, they serve as role models for cooperation and lay the groundwork for future collaboration.

Coalitions of boundary-spanning leaders can be more effective than bound-ary-spanning leaders acting on their own. When members of one group see posi-tive relations between team leaders, their attitude toward members of the other group improves as well. Combining leaders from low- and high-status units into the same coalition reduces the negative impacts of power differences by recogniz-ing that lower status groups—nurses, students, assembly workers—are valued members of the combined effort.

Transference is an important outcome of successful intergroup leadership. When intergroup relational identities have been established, they are more likely to transfer to new relationships. For example, doctors who have established intergroup identities with current nurses will probably transfer these collaborative relation-ships to new nurses. Nurses who share collective identities with doctors tend to extend their collaborative efforts to hospital administrators and patients as well.[60]

> *Organizations are collections of interrelated groups*
> *more than collections of separate individuals.*
> —Michael Hogg, Daan van Knippenberg, David Rast

The Power of Expectations: The Pygmalion Effect

What a leader expects is often what a leader gets. This makes the communica-tion of expectations one of a leader's most powerful tools. Our tendency to live up to the expectations placed on us is called the Pygmalion effect. Prince Pygmalion (a figure in Greek mythology) created a statue of a beautiful woman whom he named Galatea. After the figure was complete, he fell in love with his creation. The god-dess Venus took pity on the poor prince and brought Galatea to life. The Pygma-lion effect has been studied in a number of settings. Consider the following examples of the power of expectations in action.

- Patients often improve when they receive placebos because they believe they will get better.

- Nursing home residents are less depressed and go to hospitals less often when nurses and aides are told that the patients are expected to progress more quickly.[61]

- Clients labeled as "motivated" by their therapists are less likely to drop out of alcohol treatment programs than those described as "unmotivated."[62]

- Disabled Taiwanese college graduates who believe that society and employers accept disabilities are twice as likely to get jobs after graduation than those disabled students who don't perceive that disabilities are accepted. [63]

- The expectations of teachers can influence the test and IQ scores of students. The most widely publicized investigation of the Pygmalion effect in education was conducted by Robert Rosenthal and Lenore Jacobson, who randomly assigned students in a San Francisco area elementary school to a group labeled as intellectual "bloomers." These investigators told teachers to expect dramatic intellectual growth from these students during the school year. The "bloomers" made greater gains on intelligence tests and reading scores than the other children.[64]

- Military personnel perform up to the expectations of their superiors. At an Israeli army training base, for example, instructors were told that trainees had high, regular, or unknown command potential. The high-potential soldiers (who really had no more potential than the other trainees and who were not told that they were superior) outperformed the members of the other groups, were more satisfied with the training course, and were more motivated to go on for further training.[65] In an investigation conducted in the U.S. Navy, the performance of problem sailors improved significantly after they were assigned to mentors and given a special training seminar designed to promote personal growth.[66]

- Employees perform better when their leaders believe that the prototypical follower is industrious, enthusiastic, and a good citizen. Employee performance dips when their leaders believe that the typical follower is conformist, insubordinate, and incompetent.[67]

Patterns created through expectations tend to persist. One long-term study of 500 students revealed that their standardized math test scores in the twelfth grade were influenced, in part, by the expectations that teachers had of their mathematical abilities in the sixth grade.[68] David Berlew and Douglas Hall examined the careers of two groups of AT&T managers and found that new managers performed best if they worked for supervisors who had high but realistic expectations.[69] These new employees internalized positive attitudes and standards and were entrusted with greater responsibilities. Six years later, they were still highly productive. On the other hand, managers who worked for bosses who expected too much or too little performed poorly throughout the test period. These workers either failed to develop high standards or didn't get recognition for the work that they did complete. As a result, they may have decided to perform at minimal levels.

Berlew and Hall conclude that the first 12–18 months are critical to the career success of any new employee. Patterns set during this initial period often continue throughout a worker's tenure at a company.

There can be little doubt that leader expectations exert a long-lasting influence on performance. Yet, it would be a mistake to conclude that the Pygmalion effect has a dramatic impact on all followers. Disadvantaged groups (those stereotyped as low achievers) tend to benefit most from positive expectations, as do those who lack a clear sense of their abilities or find themselves in a novel situation (new hires, for example). Men seem to be more influenced by the expectancies of their managers than are women.[70]

Two characteristics of leaders moderate the impact of their expectations. The first is their level of self-esteem. Even when placed with subordinates with superior abilities, some leaders fail to communicate positive expectations because they lack confidence in their own abilities. One study of sales managers at a Metropolitan Life Insurance agency demonstrates the important relationship between leader self-confidence and the Pygmalion effect. Sales agents were randomly divided into high, average, and poor performance groups. Sales of the high performer unit dramatically increased, while sales of the weakest unit declined and members dropped out. Significantly, the performance of the "average" group went up because the leader of this group refused to accept the fact that he and his sales force were any less capable than the supposedly outstanding sales unit. The superior manager's confidence in his or her ability to develop and stimulate high levels of performance reaffirms the belief that expectations will be met. Doubts about one's ability lead to lowered expectations and less confident interactions.[71]

A second characteristic of leaders that moderates the influence of the Pygmalion effect is the level of expectations. As we saw in the case of the AT&T managers, expectations must be high but also realistic. Setting standards too low does not challenge the abilities of followers, since there is little satisfaction to be gained by fulfilling minimal expectations. Yet, setting expectations too high guarantees failure and may start a negative self-fulfilling prophecy. Having failed once, the organization member expects to fail again. Goal-setting theorists argue that high performance comes from setting specific, challenging objectives, not vague, easy ones. (Being told to "try your best" is not very motivating, for instance.)[72]

We are not only our brother's keeper;
in countless large and small ways, we are our brother's maker.
—*Bonaro Overstreet*

To summarize, followers often perform up to expectations, whether in the nursing home, the classroom, the military, or the corporation. Leaders must have confidence in their own abilities and set realistic goals for followers in order for the positive Pygmalion effect to operate. However, the confidence that leaders have in themselves and their followers will have no impact on group behavior unless group members know that this confidence exists. Leaders must clearly communicate their expectations to followers. With this in mind, we turn now to a description of how expectations are communicated.

The Communication of Expectations

Telling others that they have ability, offering them compliments, and saying that you expect great things from them communicates high expectations. Subordinates also get the message that leaders have high or low expectations of them even when expectancies are not explicitly stated. Expectations are communicated through four important channels.[73]

1. *Climate.* Climate refers to the type of social and emotional atmosphere leaders create for followers. When dealing with people whom they like, leaders act in a supportive, accepting, friendly, and encouraging manner. Nonverbal cues play a major role in creating climates. Communication experts John Baird and Gretchen Wieting recommend that organizational managers use nonverbal behaviors that emphasize concern, respect, equality, and warmth—while avoiding behaviors that communicate coolness, disinterest, superiority, and disrespect.[74] (See box 8.6 for a summary of nonverbal cues that communicate positive expectations.)

2. *Input.* In an organizational setting, positive expectations are also communicated through the number and type of assignments and projects given employees. Those expected to perform well are given more responsibility, which creates a positive performance spiral. As employees receive more

Box 8.6	Nonverbal Cues that Communicate Positive Expectations[75]
Nonverbal Category	**Positive Behaviors**
Time	Don't keep employees waiting, give adequate time, make frequent contacts.
Setting	Meet in pleasant, attractive surroundings and avoid using furniture as a barrier.
Physical Proximity	Sitting or standing close to an employee promotes warmth and decreases status differences.
Gestures	Make frequent use of open palm gestures.
Head Movements	Use head nods, but do not indicate suspicion by cocking the head or tilting it backward while the other person is speaking.
Facial Expression	Smile frequently.
Eye	Make frequent, direct eye contact.
Voice	Combine pitch, volume, quality, and rate to communicate warmth. Avoid sounding bored or disinterested.

tasks and complete them successfully, they gain self-confidence and the confidence of superiors. These star performers are then given additional responsibilities and are likely to meet the new challenges as well.

3. *Output.* Those expected to reach high standards are given more opportunities to speak, to offer their opinions, or to disagree. Superiors pay more attention to these employees when they speak and offer more assistance to them when they need to come up with solutions. This is similar to what happens in the classroom when teachers call on "high achievers" more than "low achievers," wait less time for low achievers to answer questions, and provide fewer clues and follow-up questions to low achievers.[76]

4. *Feedback.* Supervisors give more frequent positive feedback when they have high expectations of employees, praising them more often for success and criticizing them less often for failure. Managers also provide these subordinates with more detailed feedback about their performance. In contrast, superiors are more likely to praise minimal performance when it comes from those labeled as poor performers. This reinforces the perception that supervisors expect less from these followers.

A leader's job is not to put greatness into people, but rather to recognize that it already exists, and to create an environment where that greatness can emerge and grow.

—Brad Smith

The Galatea Effect

Our focus so far has been on the ways that leaders communicate their expectations to followers. Once communicated, these prophecies can have a significant impact on subordinate performance. The same effects can be generated by expectations that followers place on themselves, however. Earlier we noted the example of Israeli army trainees who performed up to instructor expectations. In a follow-up experiment, a psychologist told a random group of military recruits that they had high potential to succeed in a course. These trainees did as well as those who had been identified as high achievers to their instructors. In this case, the trainees became their own "prophets."[77] The power of self-expectancies has been called the Galatea effect in honor of Galatea, the statue who came to life in the story of Pygmalion.

Figure 8.1 depicts the relationship between supervisor and self-expectations. In the positive Pygmalion effect, the chain starts with the manager's expectations (box A), which causes him/her to allocate (arrow 1) more effective leadership behavior (box B). These leadership behaviors then positively influence (arrow 2) the expectations that followers have of themselves, particularly their sense of self-efficacy or personal power (box C). This increases motivation (arrow 3), leading to

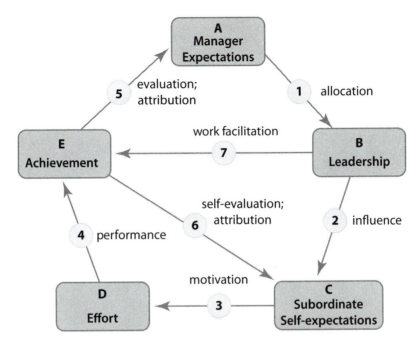

Figure 8.1   A Model of the Self-Fulfilling Prophecy at Work[78]

more effort (box D), greater performance (arrow 4), and higher achievement (box E). Subordinate performance then completes the chain because employee behavior raises or lowers the manager's expectations for future assignments (arrow 5). High expectations may also help the manager structure the subordinate's job to facilitate performance by eliminating obstacles, shielding him/her from outside interference (arrow 7). This leads to higher achievement without necessarily impacting follower motivation. Boxes A and B and arrows 1 and 2 are eliminated in the Galatea effect. Subordinates perform better if they set high standards for themselves (boxes C, D, and E). When they reach their goals, they expect to achieve even more in the future (arrow 6).

> *We usually see only the things we are looking for—*
> *so much that we sometimes see them where they are not.*
>
> *—Eric Hoffer*

Putting Pygmalion to Work

Since expectations can have a powerful influence on performance, we need to know how to put the power of Pygmalion to work. As leaders, we often aren't conscious of the expectations we have for others, or we don't realize how we communicate these expectations. We may assume that we treat all followers alike. Nevertheless, we've already noted that there are significant differences in how managers, teachers, and others treat high and low performers. Take inventory of how you communicate expectations using the four channels we discussed earlier: climate, input, output, and feedback. Analyze your nonverbal communication: do you engage in the behaviors described in box 8.6? Examine how assignments are distributed, how frequently some employees are given the opportunity to offer their opinions, whom you help most often, and the type of feedback you provide. Finally, identify the steps that you can take to communicate high expectations to your subordinates; try to put these behaviors into action.

In addition to taking steps as an individual leader to "harness" the power of Pygmalion, there are strategies that your organization can use to institute a positive expectation/performance cycle.[79] Eliminate organizational labels ("low performers," "fast trackers") that reflect low expectancies or suggest that only a few individuals are capable of outstanding performance. All supervisors should learn about the power of expectations and develop confidence in their ability to foster improvement in *all* of their subordinates. Because the patterns of high expectations/high success and low expectations/low success are established early in organizational careers, try to ensure that new employees work under effective managers. Often new subordinates are exposed to the worst leadership the organization has to offer—inexperienced supervisors or those who are trapped in low-level management positions because of poor past performance. Try instead to place new workers with the best leaders in the organization—those with high self-confidence who set challenging, yet realistic, goals. The positive patterns new subordinates establish under the guidance of these managers will pay off for both the individual and the organization for years to come. Consider moving established low performers to new situations where they can break the influence of old, negative self-fulfilling prophecies.

Use guided mastery to build skill levels and foster confidence through a series of "small wins."[80] In guided mastery the task is broken down into its component parts. Trainees practice each component with the help of an instructor. They then put the sub-processes together to complete the process. Managers provide positive role models for newcomers to observe and "persuade" trainees that they can succeed by outlining exactly why they as leaders believe that the followers will master the assignment.

Keep in mind that groups, like individuals, are shaped by the power of expectations. "Group efficacy" and "group potency" are terms that describe a team's level of confidence in itself.[81] Groups with high efficacy believe that they can complete the specific task set before them; groups with a high level of potency believe that they can achieve their goals no matter what tasks they have to tackle. In groups that have this "we can" attitude, members work together more effectively and enjoy greater success. As a leader, foster group efficacy and potency by being confident in your ability to lead and by practicing transformational leadership behaviors.

Emphasize the importance of working together, link group effort to outcomes, promote collaboration, communicate appreciation for the efforts of members, and express confidence that together the team can achieve its goals.[82]

We can also put the power of Pygmalion to work as followers. Dov Eden argues that as subordinates we can protect ourselves from the force of negative leadership expectations by being aware of how such expectancies operate. We can also encourage supervisors to have high expectations of us by meeting and exceeding standards. In essence, this approach uses the Galatea effect to create positive expectations in leaders. Eden summarizes subordinate use of expectations this way:

> Subordinates could be taught how to behave in a manner that would evoke more effective leadership from their supervisors. This would be harnessing Pygmalion in reverse, subordinates "treating" their supervisors in such a way that they mold their supervisory behavior in accordance with subordinate desires. Similarly, awareness of interpersonal expectancy effects might help immunize certain subordinates against the debilitating effects of poor leadership from supervisors who harbor low expectations toward them.[83]

∼ CHAPTER TAKEAWAYS

- Organizations are the product of communication. As organizational members communicate, they develop shared meanings that form the organization's unique way of seeing the world—an organization's culture. Cultures are made up of underlying assumptions, values, symbols, and symbolic creations called artifacts.

- You can embed and transmit culture by primary and secondary mechanisms. Primary mechanisms are the most important elements for shaping culture: what you pay attention to; how you react to critical incidents; the way you spend budgeted monies; how you role model; the criteria you select for allocation of rewards; and the criteria you use for selection. Secondary mechanisms reinforce primary messages: how you mold the organizational structure; how you utilize organizational systems and procedures; your use of rites and rituals; how you design physical space to reinforce key values; the stories you tell about important events and people; and the way you communicate organizational philosophy.

- Effective leaders build cultures that are committed to learning. Learning organizations are skilled at generating and acquiring knowledge and then using that information to modify their behavior. You will need to function as a learner/teacher who overcomes obstacles to learning and promotes information gathering through intelligence (collection of data), collective experience, and experimentation. Then make sure that this knowledge is widely shared or disseminated.

- Trust is critical to the success of any organization. Organizational trust is the collective level of positive expectations that coworkers, work units, and organizations will honor their commitments. Trusting organizational cultures are marked by high expectations of collective competence, openness and honesty, concern for employees and other stakeholders, reliability, and identification with the organization.

- When trust is broken, you will need to (1) determine what happened, (2) determine the depth and breadth of the loss of trust, (3) own up to the loss (don't ignore or downplay it), and (4) identify what you must accomplish in order to rebuild trust.

- Leaders play a key role in setting the overall direction of the organization through strategic planning. Strategic plans are grounded in the organization's mission and vision and the planning process involves internal and external analysis, strategy design, and implementation.

- To act as a strategic leader you will need to build your ability to anticipate, challenge, interpret, decide, align, and learn. You may practice strategic leadership in a visionary, directive, incubating, or collaborative style.

- Organizational leaders function as sensemakers who help followers interpret or make sense of events and conditions. Skillful sensemakers keep followers in motion, improvise, let go of the belief that they have all the answers, ask followers for help, and determine what the organization has learned through the sensemaking process.

- Framing, which is creating a mental picture of the world and then encouraging followers to accept this frame or interpretation, is one important sensemaking tool. Adopt a strategic communication style to become more successful at framing reality; consciously prepare or prime yourself for framing opportunities.

- Organizational success depends on getting units and groups to work together. Create an intergroup relational identity by encouraging team members to define themselves as both organizational and subgroup members. Act as a boundary spanner, developing quality relationships with individuals from every team.

- Expectations shape motivation and performance. The Pygmalion effect refers to our tendency to live up to the expectations of others. Generally, the higher the expectancy, the higher the performance. Leaders communicate expectations through climate (social and emotional atmosphere), input (the number and type of assignments they give to employees), output (the number of opportunities that followers have to voice opinions), and feedback (the frequency of praise or criticism).

- To create a high expectations/high performance cycle, eliminate labels, assign new employees to effective managers, and use guided mastery to build skills levels

- Self-expectations (called the Galatea effect) also influence performance. Protect yourself from the power of negative leadership expectations by setting high standards for yourself.

∽ APPLICATION EXERCISES

1. For a major research paper, conduct your own organizational culture analysis. Be sure to identify the following:
   - the role of the founder and current leadership
   - assumptions

- values
- important symbols, such as myths and stories, rituals, and language
- important artifacts, such as buildings, products, and technology
- efforts at change

2. In a group, identify important rites at your college or university and categorize them using the framework presented on pp. 254–255. What messages do these rituals send? How could they be modified to encourage cultural change?

3. Framing Scenario
Imagine that you work for the public relations office of Lake Okiboji University (L.O.U.). Your college is merging with a smaller school that was just about to close its doors for good. Your frame is that the merger will help both schools. The student body at L.O.U. will grow (increasing tuition revenue), and the merger will create an attractive new branch campus. Students at the smaller college (who would have been forced to transfer) can now finish their degrees without leaving town. The presence of a stronger university will also benefit the community as a whole. In addition to offering classes and cultural and athletic events, L.O.U. will become the area's largest employer when the merger is complete. Not everyone agrees with your perspective, however. You've heard the following comments from students, faculty, donors, and others in the community:

- L.O.U. is getting too big and impersonal.
- The leaders of L.O.U. are "empire builders."
- The needs of students have been ignored in the rush to merge.
- L.O.U. is more interested in collecting more tuition and acquiring property than in meeting the needs of the community.

Generate some possible responses to these competing frames and then pair off with a classmate. Take turns playing the role of the public relations professional and a stakeholder who is critical of the merger. When you're done, evaluate how well each of you constructed and communicated the university's frame to the hostile stakeholder.

4. Identify your communication style based on the self-assessment in box 8.4. How does your style help or hinder your ability to frame?

5. Conduct a SWOT analysis and Five Forces analysis of Airbnb (box 8.5). What strengths, weaknesses, opportunities, or threats are most significant? How might they shape the strategy of the company going forward? What is the competitive strength of the company? As an alternative, conduct these analyses on your college or university.

6. Develop a case study based on a learning organization. Describe how leaders overcome learning barriers, and how the group learns and shares knowledge. Identify any scenarios that the organization uses to promote learning and planning. Generate a list of best practices that other organizations could adopt.

7. Identify a situation in your organization that calls for trust repair. Outline a strategy for restoring trust based on the process described in the chapter. Write up your findings.

8. Evaluate the quality of intergroup leadership in your organization. How well do leaders create intergroup relational identity through their rhetoric and boundary-spanning activities?

9. Form a small group and brainstorm ways that teachers, managers, and others communicate both low and high expectations. Report your findings during class discussion.

10. Develop a strategy for creating positive expectations in those who lead you.

∿ CULTURAL CONNECTIONS: PLAYING CATCH-UP IN KOREA[84]

In order to compete in the global marketplace, Samsung, Hyundai, and other Korean companies had to play catch-up, quickly narrowing the technological and innovative gap with established multinationals in electronics, automobiles, semiconductors, shipbuilding, and machinery. They succeeded by reversing the typical learning process, which might serve as a model for other developing countries. Instead of first conducting research and development followed by engineering, Korean firms started with engineering and then began developing unique products. Hyundai, for example, started by manufacturing cars for Ford Motor Company, which gave it access to production manuals, blueprints, and technical specifications provided by Ford as well as access to engineers who knew about procurement, welding, painting, marketing, and other aspects of auto manufacturing. Suppliers also sent representatives to set up equipment and to train Hyundai employees. Later the firm was directed by the Korean government to develop a "Korean" car under very specific guidelines. The national government provided tax concessions, scholarships to foreign universities, and other incentives while supporting a country-wide effort to industrialize by building technological capacity.

Hyundai developed its first car model, the Pony, by partnering with firms in Japan, Italy, the United Kingdom, and Germany. The company sent a team of engineers to absorb all they could from Italian designers. This group spent a year and a half living together, recording what they learned during the day and holding learning reviews in the evening. In addition, Hyundai hired British and Japanese technological experts. Later the company rolled out the Excel, the first subcompact designed entirely in Korea. Initial quality was low but improved when the firm brought in experts who had previously worked with car producers as well as expatriates with doctoral degrees from US universities. Then it came out with the Accent, the first subcompact car designed entirely by Hyundai. At this point the automaker established its own research and development arm—the Advanced Engineering and Research Institute, completing the shift from imitation to innovation.

～ LEADERSHIP ON THE BIG SCREEN: *ALL THINGS MUST PASS*

Starring: Russ Solomon, Michael Solomon, Elton John, Bruce Springsteen

Rating: Not rated but probably PG-13 for sex, drinking, and drug references

Synopsis: This documentary tells the story of the rise and fall of Tower Records, the Sacramento record chain that grew to 200 stores and $1 billion in sales before going bankrupt in 2006. Founder Russ Solomon's vision was to create a record supermarket and a community for music lovers (particularly young fans). He oversaw a family-like corporate culture that tolerated employee drinking, drug use, and sex as long as the workers did their jobs. Most of the firm's senior leadership started as retail or shipping clerks and were promoted though the ranks. Individual store managers were left to run their outlets as they wanted. Tower Records began to falter when it expanded too rapidly, lost a key executive, and took on debt. Solomon and his team didn't respond to the threat of Napster, iTunes, and other online music services. The chain closed after bank-ordered reorganization plans failed to revive the company's fortunes, though Tower Records still thrives in Japan. "All Things Must Pass" was the message posted on one of the last Tower locations to close.

Chapter Links: organizational founders, organizational culture, failure of strategic planning, sensemaking, Pygmalion and Galatea effects

9

Public Leadership

OVERVIEW

The Power of Public Leadership

Public leadership is one of the most visible and dynamic forms of social influence. Religious and political authorities, educators, social activists, and other public leaders attempt to modify the attitudes and behaviors of mass audiences. It is important to note that public leadership is not limited to nationally known political, religious, or social figures. John Gardner, former secretary of Health, Education, and Welfare in the Lyndon Johnson administration and the founder of Common Cause, used the term "dispersed leadership" to describe how leaders are found at all levels, including social agencies, universities, the professions, businesses, and minority communities.[1] Gardner believed that dispersed leadership is essential to the health of complex organizations and societies. Lower-level leaders can deal more effectively with local problems. When local leaders take initiative, they encourage higher-level leaders to do the same. At times the efforts of lower-level leaders trigger events that change society as a whole. For example, Lech Walesa (an electrician) and Vaclav Havel (a writer) mobilized public sentiment against communist regimes in Poland and the Czech Republic and were later elected as the democratic leaders of those two nations. (Box 9.1 describes how sharing a common purpose can motivate leaders of all kinds.)

Every public leader, from the president of the United States down to the president of a local chamber of commerce, must influence the attitudes and behaviors of groups within a social system. This process of influence is called *opinion leadership*. Since public leaders deal with large audiences, they often use different tactics than leaders in other contexts. In an interpersonal encounter, a leader can target a persuasive message to the special needs of one follower using face-to-face communication. In a public setting, a leader must address messages to what groups of people have in common—health and financial worries, political beliefs, age, ethnic heritage—through both mediated and interpersonal channels.[2] Effective public leaders shape public opinion through public relations activities and relationships, public speaking, and persuasive campaigns.

Leading Public Opinion through Public Relations

Communication professionals use the term public relations to describe how groups and organizations influence important audiences (publics) through a cluster of coordinated activities. Sparked by the growth of the mass media, the development of computer-mediated communication channels, and the rising importance of public opinion, the practice of public relations has become a multibillion-dollar industry. Common public relations tasks include:[3]

- working with media representatives
- creating and maintaining websites
- monitoring and interacting on social media
- researching public attitudes

- disseminating financial information
- lobbying government agencies
- publicizing company events
- creating internal communication programs aimed at organizational members
- supporting marketing programs
- maintaining positive relationships with community groups
- responding to activists
- advising top management
- dealing with customer concerns and complaints
- fund-raising
- planning promotional events
- writing and delivering speeches and presentations
- organizing persuasive campaigns

Box 9.1 Research Highlight	**Invisible Leadership: The Power of Purpose[4]**

Passionate commitment to a common purpose energizes people to join social movements, form neighborhood associations, start nonprofits, act as public servants, and work for businesses that serve the common good. Leadership experts Gill Robinson Hickman and Georgia Sorenson use the term "invisible leadership" to refer to leaders and followers drawn together by dedication to a common purpose. Under invisible leadership, individuals focus more on the mission than on recognition or personal ego. They are willing to act as leader or follower in order to get the work done and don't worry about getting credit. Others recognize and acknowledge their contributions, but those driven by mission are willing to take either visible or background roles. Examples of highly visible, purpose driven leaders are Cherokee nation chief Norma Mankiller, social entrepreneur Bela Hatvany, and Jo Ann Robinson, a leader of the Montgomery Bus Boycott. Examples of invisible leaders who serve out of the limelight include members of the conductorless Orpheus orchestra, anonymous civil servants, and the black women who joined the boycott of the Montgomery bus system.

To test their invisible leadership model, Hickman and Sorenson surveyed 21 businesses and nonprofits from the WorldBlu List of Most Democratic Workplaces. They found plenty of evidence of invisible leadership from the results of their survey: 90% of participants agreed that they were committed to their organization's purpose; 87% accepted the common purpose as their own purpose and agreed that this shared mission motivated them to do their best work; 93% were willing to work in either a leader or follower role to accomplish the purpose, and 79% said that a strong relational bond formed as employees worked toward the mission.

The investigators conclude with suggestions for putting invisible leadership into practice. Leaders need to create groups centered on purpose and facilitate the work of the group (not control it). Leaders and members should continually dialogue about the purpose. To maintain the invisible leadership culture, leaders need to (1) carefully select and socialize new members, (2) build the collective capacity of the group by encouraging members to take on a variety of roles and responsibilities, (3) engage members in meaningful work, (4) foster strong bonds and relationships between members, and (5) facilitate change through an open and inclusive decision-making process.

The mix of activities that leaders use to influence public opinion will vary depending on the needs of the group. The leader of a private charity may concentrate on fund-raising and attracting donors. The leader of a publicly held corporation will likely devote attention to marketing and, by law, must provide information about the company's financial condition to important news sources.

Whatever their differences, the best public relations programs have a number of elements in common, according to a major research project commissioned by the International Association of Business Communicators (IABC). Researchers James Grunig, Larissa Grunig, and David Dozier surveyed public relations directors, CEOs, and employees at 300 organizations in the United States, Canada, and Great Britain.[5] They report that excellent public relations efforts—those that increase organizational effectiveness and benefit society as a whole—share the following characteristics.

Empowered. To be excellent, public relations functions must be valued and promoted by top management. The IABC researchers found that the most effective efforts are housed in a single department that functions separately from marketing. Top organizational leaders see public relations as a "critical management function." Public relations officials serve on the senior management team, often reporting directly to the CEO.

A strategic management role. The leaders of excellent public relations departments are managers, not technicians. Their success depends more on their ability to set policy, solve problems, and administer budgets than on writing, media production, event planning, and other technical skills. These leaders play a significant role in determining organizational strategy, one of the responsibilities of leaders described in the last chapter. They shape the organization's direction, in part, through **issues management**. Issues management is the ongoing process of (1) monitoring the environment for societal developments that pose threats or opportunities to the organization, and (2) responding in a way that reduces the threats and builds on the opportunities.[6] Thanks to issues managers, SC Johnson eliminated fluorocarbons from its aerosol sprays three years before federal regulations were passed. Sears recognized the dangers of flammable sleepwear and quickly removed these products from its shelves before they were outlawed. Other organizations have not been as successful at issues management. McDonald's failed to recognize rising interest in healthy foods, which cut into its market share and drew fire for promoting childhood obesity through advertising featuring Ronald McDonald.[7] The meat industry underestimated concerns about food safety. It was blindsided when media sources and bloggers led a successful effort to end the use of "pink slime" (lean finely textured beef) in restaurants, grocery stores, and in some school lunches.[8]

Issues management begins with scanning the environment—reading a wide variety of publications, monitoring news outlets, surfing the Web, surveying social media sites, tracking legislation—to identify potential issues, which are defined as differences of opinion or concerns that could impact the organization. PR managers monitor the issues to determine their trajectory (some issues disappear, others get national attention) and to determine if they are a concern to key organizational publics. The most pressing and important issues get top priority, and leaders outline a potential plan of action. Initiating a persuasive campaign is one option. (We'll have more to say about persuasive campaigns later in the chapter.) Instead of launching a campaign, an organization may need to take steps to repair its reputation. It may apologize to the public, change policies, fire unethical employees, support community projects, and so on. (See chapter 13 for more information on image restoration.)

Two-way communication, symmetrical relationships. In the popular imagination, public relations is viewed as a form of one-way communication. PR specialists, according to this view, craft messages and develop strategies designed to benefit the group or organization by shaping public attitudes. Little thought is given to the desires and needs of external audiences. As a result, the organization often gets its way at the expense of employees, neighbors, local governments, small businesses, unions, and other groups. The IABC researchers discovered, however, that outstanding public relations programs engage in two-way, not one-way, communication. Leaders of these programs still craft and deliver messages designed to shape public opinion, but they make an active effort to identify and to respond to the needs of important publics. They conduct ongoing research—using focus groups, surveys, community meetings, and other means—to determine the attitudes and behaviors of audiences. Just as important, they are willing to adjust their goals to develop collaborative or symmetrical relationships with outside groups. Consider the siting of a new county prison, for instance. An asymmetrical approach would be to identify a site, announce the location, and then ask county public relations personnel to develop a strategy to win over opponents. A symmetrical approach would be to solicit public input before making a final decision and then tailor the plan to meet local concerns. Officials might, for example, select an alternative site or change the building design.

Ethical. Engaging in two-way communication and building symmetrical relationships encourages ethical behavior. Excellent practitioners disclose accurate information to publics whom they treat as partners. As noted above, they listen and respond to the concerns of outsiders. These experts engage in dialogue, which seeks mutual benefit, rather than in monologue, which serves the interests of the organization at the expense of outsiders. The community as a whole benefits from the ethical, symmetrical relationships. Grunig, Grunig, and Dozier report that excellent public relations departments often become ethics counselors to management. They serve as advocates of social responsibility, which is doing business in a way that benefits society as well as the organization.

Supportive structure. Excellent public relations programs are nurtured by, and reflect, a supportive organizational structure. Supportive structure is organic: decentralized, less formal, less stratified into organizational layers, and more complex. Such structure facilitates participation by empowering employees, delegating responsibility, and soliciting input and feedback. Employees and managers engage in two-way communication and develop symmetrical relationships based on openness and trust. Women and minorities have more opportunities for advancement, and workers report a high degree of job satisfaction.

A growing number of scholars believe that public relations professionals should focus less on the short-term impact of specific public relations activities, programs, and events (the kinds of tasks described earlier) and more on the long-term relationships organizations establish with their publics. Drawing on the notion of two-way communication and symmetry described above, they define public relations as **relationship management**.[9] It is the "function that establishes and maintains mutually beneficial relationships between an organization and the public on whom its success or failure depends."[10] Public relations activities are still important but they should always be directed at the larger goal of relationship building. High quality organization-public relationships are marked by:[11]

1. *control mutuality*—both organizations and publics have some control over each other

2. *trust*—confidence in the other party and willingness to open up to the other party

3. *satisfaction*—the belief that benefits of the relationship outweigh the costs

4. *commitment*—the conviction that the relationship is worth continuing

5. *exchange relationship*—giving benefits because the other party has given benefits in the past or will do so in the future

6. *communal relationship*—parties provide benefits out of concern for the other, with no expectation of receiving anything in return

7. *community involvement*—the organization benefits from being in the community and the community benefits from the organization's investment in its local area

8. *reputation*—the public perceives the organization as effective, financially sound and innovative

Quality relationships greatly enhance an organization's ability to lead public opinion.[12] Consumers and donors are more likely to buy from and to give to organizations they have positive relationships with. They are willing to recommend these organizations to others and are less likely to defect to other businesses and nonprofits. (Keeping customers and donors is much less expensive than finding new ones.) Shareholders who feel a positive connection to management are more likely to support their initiatives. Employees (an important internal public) are more satisfied with their jobs. When dealing with government, organizations with relational support find it easier to pass legislation and to avoid regulation. Good relationships also reduce the dangers of lawsuits, pressure campaigns, and boycotts and serve as an early warning system for potential crises. If crisis does strike, a strong organization-public relationship often reduces reputational damage and allows the organization to recover more quickly. (Complete the self-assessment in box 9.2 to determine your relationship with an organization of your choice.)

The newest communication channels—Facebook, Twitter, Google+, YouTube, blogs, and other forms of social media—can be critical tools for building organization-public relationships.[13] These computer-mediated channels encourage rapid, two-way communication that is under the control of both parties. Companies can quickly deal with problems and adjust to the needs of their publics. Concerns expressed on social media alert the organization to emerging issues and problems. People trust those in their social networks so recommendations and positive comments on Facebook and Twitter can increase sales and donations while creating a

---

Box 9.2   Self-Assessment   Organization-Public Relationship Instrument[14]

Instructions: This questionnaire asks about your relationships with and perceptions of an organization of your choice. You do not have to have direct contact with this organization to answer these questions. Your perceptions of this organization's relationship with the general public can be your answers too. Rate each item on a scale of 1–7 with 1 being strongly disagree and 7 being strongly agree.

_____ 1. (The organization) treats people like me fairly and justly.

_____ 2. Whenever (the organization) makes an important decision, I know it will be concerned about people like me.

_____ 3. I believe that (the organization) takes the opinions of people like me into account when making decisions.

_____ 4. Sound principles seem to guide (the organization's) behavior.

_____ 5. I can see that (the organization) wants to maintain a relationship with people like me.

_____ 6. There is a long-lasting bond between (the organization) and people like me.

_____ 7. Both (the organization) and people like me benefit from their relationship.

_____ 8. Generally speaking, I am pleased with the relationship (the organization) has established with people like me.

_____ 9. I feel people like me are important to (the organization).

_____ 10. (The organization) seems to be the kind of company that invests in the community.

_____ 11. I am aware that (the organization) is involved in my community.

_____ 12. I think (the organization) is very dynamic in maintaining good relationships with the community.

_____ 13. (The organization) has the ability to attract, develop, and keep talented people.

_____ 14. (The organization) uses corporate visible and invisible assets very effectively.

_____ 15. (The organization) is financially sound enough to help others.

_____ 16. (The organization) is innovative in its corporate culture.

Scoring: Add up the scores for each dimension and then come up with a total by adding the dimensional scores. The higher the scores, the better the perceived relationship between the organization and its publics.

Trust: Items 1–4 _____ total

Commitment: Items 5–9 _____ total

Local or community involvement: Items 10–12 _____ total

Reputation: Items 13–16 _____ total

Total score _____ (range 16–112)

positive reputation. Social media can also boost engagement with the organization. Some firms, for example, sponsor sites where users share tips and experiences. Apparel company Saucony connects to its running audience through its Find Your Strong Program, where runners post comments and pictures about why they run. This program helped the company become the fastest-growing running brand.

Unfortunately, social media can be used to destroy organization-public relationships as well as to build them. Any individual (including those with malicious intent) can lodge a complaint against a company, share bad experiences with friends, or post a negative review. If negative messages go viral, even the strongest organization can be threatened. Domino's Pizza, for example, had to issue apologies after two employees filmed themselves doing disgusting things with food and posted the video. Slow responses can mean trouble, as in the case of the "United Breaks Guitars" song posted on YouTube. Dave Carroll wrote a ballad about how United Airlines refused to reimburse him for damaging his $3,500 guitar after he repeatedly contacted the airline for nine months. A number of news outlets like CNN, *The Wall Street Journal*, and the BBC picked up on the story. The company finally reimbursed him after his posting received 3 million views in one week and United's stock price dropped by 10%.

Influencing Audiences through Public Address

A Key Leadership Tool

Public speaking is a significant tool for all types of public leaders—from student body officers to environmental activists to religious figures. (The Leadership on the Big Screen case demonstrates just how important speech making can be.) As a matter of fact, it is hard to think of effective leaders who don't have at least some public speaking ability.[15] The president makes a steady stream of speeches announcing policy decisions and cabinet appointments, signing bills, responding to tragedies and disasters, announcing agreements with foreign leaders, and so on. School board members announce budgets and school boundary changes at public meetings. Protest leaders speak at rallies. CEOs address shareholder and employee meetings. University presidents speak to groups of parents, donors, students, and graduates. Law enforcement officials make public statements about ongoing investigations.

TED (Technology Entertainment Design) talks provide vivid evidence of the impact of public speaking. The first six of these 18-minute presentations were posted in 2006. By the end of 2009 there were 200 million views. By 2013 the number of views had reached one billion with new viewing starting 17 times a second (1.5 million times a day). In 2015 the 2,000th talk was posted.[16] The most-viewed TED talks reflect the variety of topics covered by speakers: (1) Ken Robinson: Do schools kill creativity? (40 million views), (2) Amy Cuddy: Your body language shapes who you are (36 million views), (3) Simon Sinek: How great leaders inspire action (28 million views), and (4) Brené Brown: The power of vulnerability (26 million views). (Box 9.3 outlines the strategies that contribute to the success of TED Talks.)

*Of all the talents bestowed upon men [women], none is so precious
as the gift of oratory. . . . Abandoned by his [her] party,
betrayed by his [her] friends, stripped of his [her] offices,
whoever can command this power is still formidable.*

—*Winston Churchill*

Box 9.3 **Research Highlight**	**Speaking Like TED**[17]

Communication coach Carmine Gallo conducted an in-depth analysis of successful TED talks and found nine elements that made them so engaging. According to Gallo, these strategies can be used in other settings, helping speakers better sell themselves and their ideas. Inspirational TED talks are:

Emotional—they touch the heart of listeners.

- Secret 1: Be passionate about your topic, something you just have to share with others. Passion is central to your identity.

- Secret 2: Master the art of storytelling. TED presenters tell personal stories related directly to the theme of the presentation, stories about others who have learned lessons that the audience can relate to, and stories about the success or failure of brands or products.

- Secret 3: Have a conversation. Internalize the content; deliver the talk like speaking with a friend. Strive to be natural and authentic through speech rate, volume, pitch, and effective pauses, and "talk, walk, and look like a leader" through movement, gestures and body language.

Novel—they teach something new.

- Secret 4: Reveal information that is new to the audience or arranged differently, or offers a fresh way to solve an old problem or issue. Boil down what you want the audience to know to a Twitter-friendly headline (140 characters or less).

- Secret 5: Deliver jaw-dropping moments. Do something surprising, impressive, moving, and memorable that will be remembered well after the presentation is over.

- Secret 6: Lighten up. Offer the audience something to smile about; don't take yourself too seriously. Have some good-natured fun at the expense of yourself and your topic.

Memorable—they present content in ways audiences will never forget.

- Secret 7: Stick to the 18-minute rule. Longer presentations overload audiences. Keep to three major points (which is all hearers can remember).

- Secret 8: Paint a mental picture with multisensory experiences. Engage more than one of the senses—sight, sound, touch, taste, and smell—through pictures, videos, vivid descriptions, and objects.

- Secret 9: Stay in your lane. Don't try to be something you aren't. Strive for openness and transparency. Represent yourself as best you can.

Developing Effective Public Speeches

Because public address is such an important skill for leaders, we need to understand the key elements that go into effective public messages. Regardless of where you speak—whether in the classroom, at a political rally, on television, on YouTube, or in a business meeting—you will discover that the delivery of an effective public speech enhances audience perceptions of your personal power and leadership potential. The effectiveness of a public speech depends on six primary elements: prespeech planning, organization, language, rehearsal, delivery, and responding to questions.

Prespeech Planning

Planning is essential in the development of successful public messages. The following factors should be considered before delivering a public presentation. In particular, think carefully about possible modes of delivery and audience analysis.

The principal modes of delivery are *impromptu, extemporaneous*, and *manuscript*. Impromptu speeches are delivered "off the cuff," with little advance preparation. Situations that might require an impromptu presentation include responding to an unexpected disaster or crisis or participating in a meeting. One of President George W. Bush's most memorable speeches was an impromptu message delivered to rescue workers through a bullhorn at Ground Zero in New York City. When speaking in the impromptu mode, try to maintain a clear focus or theme. Always avoid long, rambling impromptu messages.

Speaking from a prepared outline or set of notes is known as extemporaneous speech. This is the most common mode of public address. Extemporaneous speech gives you an opportunity to develop a clear presentational purpose or goal and adequate reasoning and support. The extemporaneous speech also offers you freedom in the construction of the message. Since your notes consist of an outline or a few key phrases, you have greater flexibility.

Working from a manuscript—a written transcript of the speech—allows for the greatest control of subject matter. Many political leaders use the manuscript mode of delivery. Manuscripts are most effective when the content of the message must be very precise, such as when the president announces the details of a treaty or when law enforcement officials reveal the results of an investigation. Because the manuscript mode does not allow a speaker to be spontaneous, it is advisable to use a teleprompter or similar mechanical device in order to maintain eye contact with the audience.

Regardless of the delivery style chosen, it is essential that you have an understanding of the attitudes and expertise of your listeners. Although audience size may vary from a small group to a worldwide conference, an understanding of the needs, aspirations, experiences, and intellectual abilities of listeners helps to create a more effective message. For example, a political candidate addressing a group of union employees will be more effective if he or she is aware of the issues that have the greatest impact on union members. A well-prepared speaker will seek information about the audience from a variety of sources. The speaker might research the previous positions of audience members; observe the group's current actions; or question, interview, or survey selected audience members as a means of uncovering information. In addition, he or she will have a clear grasp of the demands of the speaking situation (see box 9.4).

Box 9.4	**Leading through Special Occasion Speeches[18]**

Leaders are often called on to speak at special occasions like funerals, dedications, conventions, award ceremonies, and banquets, either as invited guests or as representatives of the group. On these occasions, speakers must pay particular attention to the requirements of the situation. Leaders who violate audience expectations for the setting, such as the CEO who delivers an off-color toast at an employee's wedding reception or the politician who delivers a campaign speech at a graduation ceremony, do significant damage to their credibility. They also diminish the occasion as well as those gathered to celebrate it. You can avoid the same fate by following the guidelines outlined below.

Type	Purpose	Techniques
Speech of Introduction	To prepare the audience for the speech to follow To build the speaker's credibility To make the speaker feel welcome	Be brief Be accurate Don't exaggerate by overstating the speaker's qualifications
Speech of Presentation	To present a gift, award, or honor	Adapt remarks to the audience Create a sense of anticipation Explain the background of the award Acknowledge the achievements of the recipient
Acceptance Speech	To accept or respond to an award	Express gratitude Acknowledge others Focus on the values represented in the award
Commemorative Speeches (eulogies, dedications, testimonials)	To pay tribute	Provide information about the subject of the tribute
After-Dinner Speeches	To entertain and celebrate	Arouse and heighten appreciation for the person, group, institution, or idea Be positive and light hearted Communicate a central theme or idea Use humor (but cautiously)
Speech of Inspiration	To arouse the audience to pursue common goals or values	Incorporate vivid descriptions and imagery Be enthusiastic Review shared experiences Focus on shared values

Organization

The logic and structure of the ideas presented within a public speech are critical. Successful presentations are organized around a central theme with supporting points. Developing a thesis, arranging ideas, linking primary points, and crafting a beginning and ending are the four most important factors in organizing a public speech.

The purpose or objective of a speech is known as the thesis. In general terms, the thesis identifies your goal—to inform, persuade, or entertain. More specifically, the thesis outlines exactly what you hope to achieve in your presentation. A thesis statement is prepared in the initial stages of speech organization and usually consists of one declarative sentence. The thesis statement itself should be as specific as possible in identifying the feelings, knowledge, or understanding you wish to convey to your audience. For instance, "My speech is on John F. Kennedy," is ineffective. This thesis provides no explanation regarding the specific purpose of the speech. A better thesis would be, "John F. Kennedy was one of the most effective public communicators of the twentieth century." This thesis statement provides a detailed description of the argument you wish to make.

> *Many leaders, in all fields, are too quick to patronize their public, assuming that people are selfish, dull, or uninterested in global or universal questions. Quite the contrary, the public is eager to hear, eager to engage, and eager to act when called to contribute to just causes that are larger than themselves.*
>
> —Terry Pearce

After the thesis has been developed, arrange the main points you have selected to support your thesis. The number of main points should be kept to a minimum, and each main point should be supported with statistics, examples, illustrations, anecdotes, or other forms of evidence. Main points can be arranged (1) in chronological order (from the earliest to the most recent event), (2) in spatial order (by some physical or geographical relationship), (3) in order of size or impact (from largest to smallest or vice versa), (4) in a problem-solution format (a problem definition followed by a resolution), or (5) in a cause-effect arrangement (based on a causal connection between two elements or events). When no other logical pattern seems appropriate, a topical arrangement may work best. Topical arrangement involves creating an organizational pattern that fits the ideas presented. For example, a persuasive speech describing the benefits of a particular university would be difficult to organize chronologically, spatially, in relation to size, or in a problem-solution or cause-effect format. Developing a series of arguments strung together in a topical pattern would be more effective. Topics could include tuition and housing costs, location, and the quality of the faculty. (Other organizational patterns may be more appropriate in other cultures—see the Cultural Connections feature at the end of the chapter.)

Statements that link ideas together are known as transitions. Be careful to include transitions in your presentation so that audience members can follow your message. Statements such as, "Now that we have discussed the affordable housing at State University, let's focus on the desirability of the surrounding area," help to shift an audience's attention from one main point to the next.

> *A bad beginning makes a bad ending.*
>
> *—Euripedes*

Once you've planned the body of your speech, then it is time to consider how you will introduce and conclude your presentation. An effective introduction serves four purposes.[19] First, it captures the attention of audience members and identifies the topic. Many speakers launch into their speeches by announcing their subject. For example: "Today I'm going to talk about empowerment" or "Hi, I'm Karen and I will explain the reorganization plan." While such statements leave no doubt as to the subject of the presentation, they do little to pique the interest of audience members. To create an effective introduction, begin with a memorable quotation or startling statistic, refer to a current event, tell a story, use an audiovisual aid, or ask a question. Give your audience a reason to listen. This can be done by establishing how the topic relates to the everyday lives of listeners as well as to their needs and motivations. An activist promoting stricter industry pollution standards will be more successful if she can establish that pollution poses a danger to local residents and lowers property values. Next, establish your credibility on this particular topic by describing your experience, research, and/or interest in the subject. Finally, preview the main points of the speech, generally in the form of a short statement that summarizes your thesis and transitions into the body. For example: "Today I will describe the personal and organizational benefits of empowering your employees."

A memorable conclusion leaves audience members with a positive impression of you and your topic and provides a sense of closure. Summarize your major points or thesis when informing an audience; ask for agreement and action when persuading. Make sure that the audience knows you are done by tying back to your introduction, posing a challenge or question, or using a quotation.

> *Always leave them wanting more.*
>
> *—Helen Hayes*

Language

The effective use of language is the key to producing memorable and moving public speeches. We remember Martin Luther King, Jr.'s "I Have a Dream" speech as one of the greatest of the twentieth century primarily because of the way King used words to create dramatic images. King spoke of coming to cash in on the promise of equal rights at the "bank of justice" and urged followers to refuse to drink from "the cup of bitterness and hatred." At one point he declared his hope that his children would "one day live in a nation where they will not be judged by the color of their skin, but by the content of their character." Successful speakers follow the example set by King by using language that is clear, vivid, and appropriate.

The best rule of thumb in a presentation is to use clear, specific, understandable language. Technical and complicated words should be used sparingly, particularly when dealing with mass audiences. Further, avoid the use of jargon and euphemisms. Government officials often try to create pleasant descriptions for unpleasant events, referring to missiles as "peace-keepers," taxes as "revenue enhancements," and death as "exceeding survivability."[20] This type of "doublespeak" confuses and distracts audience members. The more you complicate your message by using technical or convoluted language, the more likely it is that your message will be misunderstood.

Clear language does not have to be dull. Public speeches should be descriptive and distinctive. The use of affect and imagery enliven public address. Affective language sparks emotion, while imagery creates visual connections for the audience. Franklin Roosevelt's Declaration of War following the Pearl Harbor attack of 1941 began as follows:

> Yesterday, December 7, 1941—a date which will live in infamy—the United States was suddenly and deliberately attacked by naval and air forces of the Empire of Japan.

Roosevelt's words expressed the shock of a nation. Every year, on December 7, Americans remember the attack because of Roosevelt's speech, portions of which are rebroadcast. The mark of effective public speakers is their ability to create vivid, stirring representations for audiences. While a picture may paint a thousand words, it is equally true that a gifted speaker can fashion a word into a thousand pictures. (See box 9.5 for other examples of vivid language.)

Avoid using language that might offend members of the audience. The use of profane, obscene, or inappropriate language can irreparably damage a speaker's image. Mississippi Senator Trent Lott offended many and lost his position as majority leader of the Senate when he claimed that the United States might have been better off if the racist segregation policies outlined in the 1948 presidential campaign of Strom Thurmond had been adopted.

Some types of humor lower a speaker's credibility. One type of humor that can be detrimental involves making oneself or others the brunt of a joke. Disparagement focusing on personal shortcomings (such as height, weight, complexion, or social skills) does not enhance a speaker's image. Speakers who belittle themselves are rated as less competent, less expert, and less likable, while speakers who belittle others are rated as having lower character.[21] Other research suggests that a speaker's use of milder forms of disparaging humor aimed at one's occupation or profession are not as harmful.[22] Most evidence suggests that public speakers should generally avoid using disparaging humor.

Box 9.5   **Vivid Speech Samples**[23]

We're an army going out to set other men free. . . . Here you can be *something*. Here's a place to build a home. It isn't the land—there's always more land. It's the idea that we all have value, you and me, we're worth something more than the dirt. . . . What we're fighting for, in the end, is each other.
—Joshua Lawrence Chamberlain, 2nd Maine regiment,
prior to the Battle of the Little Round Top at Gettysburg

At the stroke of the midnight hour, when the world sleeps, India will awake to life and freedom. A moment comes, which comes but rarely in history, when we step out from the old to the new, when an age ends, and when the soul of a nation, long suppressed, finds utterance. It is fitting that at this solemn moment we take the pledge of dedication to the service of India and her people and to the still larger cause of humanity.
—Jawaharlal Nehru, speaking at the granting of
Indian independence following World War II

Let us treat others with the same passion and compassion with which we want to be treated. Let us seek for others the same possibilities which we seek for ourselves. Let us help others to grow as we would like to be helped ourselves. In a word, if we want security, let us give security; if we want life, let us give life; if we want opportunities, let us provide opportunities.
—Pope Francis speaking to
the United States Congress

The truth is that people are right to be angry. Angry that wages have been stagnant for a generation, while basic costs like housing, health care, and child care have skyrocketed. . . . Angry that while Washington dithers and spins and does the backstroke in an ocean of money, while the American Dream moves further and further out of reach for too many families. Angry that working people are in debt. Angry that seniors can't stretch a Social Security check to cover the basics.
—Senator Elizabeth Warren
speaking to the AFL-CIO

Remembering that I'll be dead soon is the most important tool I've ever encountered to help me make the big choices in life. Because almost everything—all external expectations, all pride, all fear of embarrassment or failure—these things just fall away in the face of death, leaving only what is truly important. Remembering that you are going to die is the best way I know to avoid the trap of thinking you have something to lose. You are already naked. There is no reason not to follow your heart.
—Steve Jobs speaking at
a Stanford University graduation ceremony

It was we, the people; not we, the white male citizens, nor yet we, the male citizens, but we, the whole people, we formed the Union. And we formed it, not to give the blessings of liberty, but to secure them; not the half of ourselves and the half of our posterity, but to the whole people—women as well as men.
—Susan B. Anthony
speaking for women's suffrage

Indifference elicits no response. Indifference is not a response. Indifference is not a beginning; it is an end. And, therefore, indifference is always the friend of the enemy, for it benefits the aggressor—never his victim, whose pain is magnified when he or she feels forgotten. The political prisoner in his cell, the hungry children, the homeless refugees—not to respond to their plight, not to relieve their solitude by offering them a spark of hope is to exile them from human memory. And in denying their humanity, we betray our own.
—Concentration camp survivor Elie Wiesel,
speaking on behalf of oppressed peoples of the world

> *The difference between the right word and the almost-right words*
> *is the difference between lightning and the lightning bug.*
>
> —*Mark Twain*

Rehearsal

Practicing gives you the opportunity to simulate a public presentation. This experience helps you refine content and increase your confidence level. Just as a dress rehearsal makes a marriage ceremony or theater production less confusing and stressful, a speech rehearsal helps polish a public presentation.

The most important thing to remember when rehearsing a speech is that you must practice out loud. We think more rapidly than we speak. As a result, internal thought and external speech operate differently. Thought is characterized by condensed grammar and syntax, which makes the structure of internal thought incomplete. Our thoughts are composed of fleeting images and words. External speech, on the other hand, is grammatically and syntactically complete. Speech consists of fully constructed messages that follow a distinctive organizational pattern. Since presentations are delivered in external speech, the external form of communication must be used during rehearsal. Rehearsing only in internal thought (just thinking about what you will say without saying it out loud) may contribute to the same feelings of anxiety that are associated with inadequate speech preparation.[24]

Delivery

Delivery refers to the physical aspects of speech making. A speaker's delivery should not be awkward or distracting. The delivery of a message is most effective when it appears natural. Physical appearance, gestures, movement, eye contact, and voice quality all directly affect the delivery of public messages.

Public speakers should be appropriately groomed and clothed. Audience expectations regarding hygiene and dress vary from one situation to another. For example, it is usually acceptable to deliver a classroom presentation dressed in jeans and a T-shirt, but this casual attire would not be acceptable for a speech to a group of civic leaders. In general, it is best to tailor your appearance to the situation, region, or culture in which you will be speaking. Your audience analysis should help you decide what will be acceptable.

Gestures occur naturally in conversation, and that tendency should be followed in public address. When did you last worry about gesturing while conversing casually with your best friend? Unfortunately, many speakers are uncomfortable about body language during their presentations. Instead of allowing the natural tendency to gesture to operate, they plan where to insert gestures in the speech. As a result, their movements are awkward and distracting. Pay attention to your natural pattern of gestures. When rehearsing, include natural gestures in your presentation. You'll then be more relaxed and natural when you make your appearance in front of an audience.

Movement can be used to heighten interest in a speech. Movement that minimizes physical distance between speaker and audience also creates a sense of psychological closeness that communication scholars call "immediacy." Audiences are more receptive to speakers who signal warmth, liking, and friendliness through movement and other nonverbal behaviors. You can assess how well you communicate a sense of immediacy as a public speaker by completing the self-assessment exercise in box 9.6.

Box 9.6   Self-Assessment   **Nonverbal Immediacy Scale[25]**

Directions: Originally developed to assess the nonverbal immediacy of teachers, this scale has been revised to reveal nonverbal immediacy in all types of public presentations. For each item, indicate how likely you would be to engage in the nonverbal behaviors while speaking before a large group. Use the following scale:

5—extremely likely   4—likely   3—maybe/unsure   2—unlikely   1—extremely unlikely

_____ 1. I would sit behind a table or desk while speaking.

_____ 2. I would use a lot of purposeful gestures while talking to the group.

_____ 3. I would use a monotone/dull voice when speaking.

_____ 4. I would look directly at my audience while presenting.

_____ 5. I would smile at the group while talking.

_____ 6. My entire body would feel tense and rigid while giving my speech.

_____ 7. I would approach or stand beside individual audience members.

_____ 8. I would move around the room while speaking.

_____ 9. I would avoid looking at individual audience members during my speech.

_____ 10. I would look at my notes frequently during my presentation.

_____ 11. I would stand behind a podium or desk while giving my speech.

_____ 12. I would have a very relaxed body position while talking to the group.

_____ 13. I would smile at individual members in the audience.

_____ 14. I would use a variety of vocal expressions while talking.

_____ 15. I would engage in a lot of nervous gestures or body movements, such as shuffling my note cards or switching my weight from one foot to the next.

Calculating Your Score

Step 1: Total your responses to items 1, 3, 6, 9, 10, 11, and 15 _____.

Step 2: Total your responses to items 2, 4, 5, 7, 8, 12, 13, and 14 _____.

Complete the following formula:

42 minus total from step 1 =   _____

Plus total from step 2 =   _____

YOUR TOTAL SCORE   _____

Interpreting Your Score: Your score should fall between 15 and 75. The average or midpoint is around 45. If your score totals 50 or higher, you are high in nonverbal immediacy and are likely to be seen as approachable and likable. If your score falls below 40, you might want to learn and practice the specific immediacy behaviors reflected in the items listed in step 2. Nonimmediate speakers are perceived as cold and distant and are more likely to bore their audiences.

In Western culture, looking others in the eyes is a sign of respect and honesty. Effective public speakers maintain eye contact with audience members. Staring at your notes or letting your eyes dart around leads to the perception that you are not trustworthy. Use your notes sparingly. Maintain focus for a few seconds on individuals seated in one section of the audience, and then sustain eye contact with another section. Avoid monotonous or strident tones. An expressive voice conveys emotion and interest without being harsh. Most unpleasant vocal patterns can be improved with training and practice.

Responding to Questions

The delivery of a speech is often followed by a question and answer session. Responding to questions can be stressful; speakers must "think on their feet." The advantage of taking questions is that it provides immediate feedback about how the audience reacted to the presentation and gives the speaker an opportunity to clarify misunderstandings. Effective responses can help a leader establish a stronger bond with the audience and build commitment to her or his message.[26]

Try to anticipate possible questions when preparing a speech and learn to distinguish between types of questions. Some questions are really statements of support that elaborate on points you made in your speech. They're easy to handle— just agree when the response is appropriate to what you've said. Other questions ask for additional information and clarification and should be acknowledged and answered as directly as possible. The most difficult queries are disputes or challenges offered in the form of a question. In these cases, listen to the questioner's words, tone of voice, and body language to determine her/his true intent. The question "When will we get our next raise?" might really be a criticism of the fact that employees in some departments got pay increases while members of other departments did not. Try to address both the stated question and the questioner's intention, acknowledging the feelings behind the dispute or challenge. Find commonalities between the challenger's position and yours if possible; differentiate your position when appropriate. In response to the question about raises, a corporate executive might answer:

> Linda, you've asked about upcoming raises, but I also sense that you have some frustration about unequal pay. Let me speak to both your question and other concerns you might have. It's true that union employees recently received pay increases even though we instituted a hiring and wage freeze in January. We were legally obligated to pay those increases to union employees under the previous contract. However, like many of you, I don't think that's fair. Now that the freeze has been lifted, the next round of raises is scheduled for July 1. At that time, we will give top priority to increasing the salaries of nonunion staff.

Persuasive Campaigns

As we've seen, public speaking is an important tool for public leaders. However, much like a single television advertisement or a single newspaper editorial, a single speech does not always change the attitudes or behaviors of large numbers of people. For this reason, public leaders frequently put together persuasive campaigns in order to influence public opinion.

Characteristics of Successful Campaigns

Persuasion expert Herbert Simons defines campaigns as "organized, sustained attempts at influencing groups of people . . . through a series of messages."[27] Campaigns use the mass media, social media, and interpersonal communication networks to achieve their goals. There are five types of persuasive campaigns: (1) product/commercial (selling goods and services), (2) public relations (building public awareness, providing information, educating the public, modifying behavior), (3) political (electing candidates to office), (4) issue (changing or implementing government or corporate policy), (5) and social movements (proposing or opposing change in societal norms and/or values).[28]

Not all campaigns are successful. The failure of many heavily promoted Hollywood movies, websites, and political candidates demonstrates how even well-planned and well-financed commercial campaigns can go astray. Other types of campaigns often suffer a similar fate. For example, the popular DARE (Drug Abuse Resistance Education) program for elementary school children has had no measurable long-term effect on drug usage. Teens who participated in campaign activities when they were younger are just as likely to take illegal substances as those who didn't go through the program.[29] One survey of health campaigns found that, on average, there was a 7% increase in adoption of new behaviors like safe sex and 5% for cessation of current behaviors like smoking.[30]

While many campaigns fail, others meet their objectives. The Centers for Disease Control sponsored a three-month, anti-smoking campaign featuring graphic images and stories of ex-smokers. Some 1.6 million people tried to quit as a result of the ads; 100,000 succeeded in kicking the habit.[31] Another successful campaign encourages the use of designated drivers. At one time, people used to joke about driving when drunk. In 1964, President Lyndon Johnson gave reporters a tour of his Texas ranch while driving 90 miles an hour and sipping beer from a cup. The number of drinkers who choose designated drivers has risen dramatically since the program began in 1988. The belief that drivers should not drink has now become a widely accepted norm in society.[32] (Box 9.7 describes how social norms are used to reduce drinking on college campuses.) The ALS society received $115 million in donations in one year through its Ice Bucket Challenge, where participants raised money by getting soaked in ice water. (Total donations were a little over $24 million in the year before the challenge.)[33]

Why do some campaigns have a significant impact on public attitudes and behavior while others have little influence at all? In order to answer this question, researchers have identified the following as characteristics of successful campaigns.[34]

Pretest messages and identify market segments. Organizers of effective campaigns rely on research to help them shape their messages. Doing market research prior to a campaign reveals what audiences currently believe, if receivers understand

Box 9.7 Case Study	Campus Drinking and Social Norms Marketing Campaigns[35]

Alcohol abuse is a serious problem on college campuses. The National Institute on Alcohol and Alcoholism reports that alcohol consumption contributes annually to 1,800 student deaths, 696,000 assaults on other students, and 97,000 sexual assaults. Heavy drinkers miss more class and get lower grades. College students are much more likely to binge drink than nonstudents in the 18–24 age group.

To reduce excessive drinking, many colleges and universities in the United States sponsor social norms marketing campaigns. (The National Social Norms Center at the Michigan State University is one resource for these efforts.) Social norms marketing (SNM) campaigns are based on changing widely held perceptions of social behavior. When it comes to drinking, students overestimate how much their fellow students drink, which encourages them to binge drink themselves. Campaign organizers hope to reduce alcohol consumption by convincing students that their peers drink less than they think. An effort known as the "0–4 drinks" campaign often asks students to estimate how many of their peers consume five or more alcoholic beverages in one sitting and then to report how much they drink at parties. Respondents generally overestimate how many of their peers consume five or more drinks but report that they typically drink less than four alcoholic drinks. The results of the surveys are then reported out to the campus as a whole.

Do SNM drinking campaigns work? Yes and no. Campaigns at Northern Illinois University, the University of Arizona, and the University of Virginia succeeded in reducing binge drinking. Investigators at the Boston University School of Public Health compared nine colleges without and nine universities with social norms marketing campaigns. Drinking levels went up at the control group colleges but not at the campaign schools. However, a follow-up project found that SNM efforts worked only in campus communities with few bars and other alcohol outlets. Studies on other US campuses reported no relationship between perceptions of social norms and intention to drink. These mixed results suggest that anti-drinking campaigns can reach their goals but their success likely depends on a number of intervening variables.

Researchers continue to identify factors that contribute to SNM success or failure. First, the type of norm can make a difference. Descriptive norms (knowing the popularity of drinking) may not be as influential as injunctive norms (knowing whether the behavior is socially acceptable). Students may accurately perceive how much other students drink but still binge drink if they believe that peers think the behavior is acceptable. Second, receivers must believe the campaign ads. Researchers at Rutgers discovered that only a minority of students believed the message that "0–4" drinks was the norm. Those who believed the message were more concerned about the risks of drinking and consumed less alcohol. Hard-core drinkers—those whom school officials would most like to reach—were least likely to believe the message. They had little concern for what others thought. Third, messages must be clear. The failure of one drinking-prevention campaign was linked to the primary print advertisement used in the campaign. Students liked the ad but failed to make the connection between the image in the ad and drinking norms. Fourth, perceptions of the alcohol use of friends (and communication about alcohol use with this group) have a greater impact on personal drinking than perceptions of alcohol use by students in general. This limits the effectiveness of campaigns that only provide information about national or university norms. Fifth, those who like to drink are least likely to change their attitudes and behaviors, though they may reduce their estimates of how much other students drink based on the campaign.

Discussion Questions

1. Why do you think college students are much more likely to binge drink than nonstudents of the same age?

2. What are the social norms about drinking on your campus? Do you think these norms accurately reflect the actual drinking behaviors of students? Is binge drinking socially acceptable?

3. What efforts have been made to prohibit or reduce drinking on your campus? Have any of these involved social norms marketing?

4. How do you respond to anti-drinking campaigns? Do they change your behavior? Why or why not?

5. Evaluate the drinking campaigns on your campus. Have they been successful? Why or why not? What accounts for their success or failure based on the characteristics of successful campaigns described in the chapter or the SNM factors identified in the case?

6. What suggestions would you make to those who want to reduce drinking through social norms campaigns or other strategies on your campus?

campaign advertisements and themes, and which messages are best suited to particular segments of the market. Soul City, a nonprofit health organization in South Africa, is one group that uses research to identify issues and audiences. The group's leaders conduct focus groups, interviews, and pretesting to identify important national health concerns—HIV prevention, alcohol abuse, domestic violence—and public attitudes about these issues. The mix of campaign media activities and materials is then adapted to target audiences. Soul City offers a popular television soap opera series to reach urban audiences while radio programs are directed at rural listeners. To reach 8–12 year-olds, it sponsors television and radio series, offers print materials, and hosts Soul Buddyz clubs which focus on such issues as trauma, road safety, nutrition, and disability. To reach young women 15–24, Soul City sponsors Rise Young Women's clubs, hosts a television talk show, and holds marches and other events that promote education and HIV prevention and other causes.[36]

Use the most accessible media for target groups. Successful campaigns utilize those media that are most accessible to audiences. In some countries few people have access to either television or digital media. In these situations, campaign organizers must rely on radio and other media. The Indian Healthy Highways Project, directed at truck drivers at high risk for getting and spreading AIDS, placed workers with flip charts at truck stops. The flip charts depicted an experienced driver showing his helper how to use a condom. The virus was depicted as a spiny round object with an evil face located in the body.[37] The timing of messages is also critical. Effective campaigns reach audiences when they are most receptive. For example, when the Olympic Games are in progress (and public interest in the Olympics is at its peak), corporations use media spots to trumpet the fact that their products are endorsed by the US Olympic Committee. When choosing communication channels, other important considerations include, for example, the *reach* of the media (the proportion of the audience exposed to the content), how easy it is to decode the message, and the cost of using the channel.

Use the media to raise awareness. The media are most effective when they are used to provide important information, stimulate interpersonal conversations, and recruit additional people to participate in the campaign. Media messages raise awareness and get people talking about the merits of politicians, products, organizations, and causes. In addition, many people volunteer for food drives, fund-raisers, clean-up campaigns, and other projects after hearing about them through advertisements or news stories.

Rely on interpersonal communication, particularly communication between people of similar social backgrounds, to lead to and reinforce behavior change. Interpersonal communication networks play a particularly important role in persuasive campaigns designed to change people's behaviors. Behavioral change is more likely when others model the desired behaviors. The long-running national crime prevention campaign that urges listeners and viewers to "Take a bite out of crime" is one example of how media and interpersonal channels can complement each other. Although many people learn about crime prevention behaviors through the campaign's media spots, listeners often put these behaviors into action only after they become involved in neighborhood watch groups. The groups reinforce the message and demonstrate that crime prevention activities are socially acceptable. Soul City's children's and young women's clubs also reinforce media messages.

Certain individuals—called opinion leaders—play a major role in convincing others to adopt new products, techniques, or ideas. Enlisting the participation of these individuals greatly increases a campaign's chances for success; failure to do so undermines the chances of success. For example, one attempt to persuade Peruvian villagers to boil their water to reduce illness failed because the public health worker ignored local opinion leaders and worked instead with housewives who weren't respected by their neighbors. Opinion leaders share four characteristics: (1) they have greater exposure to the media, outside change agents, and other key external communication sources; (2) they participate in a variety of social networks and rapidly spread new ideas to others; (3) they generally have a higher socioeconomic status than opinion followers; and (4) they are more innovative when the norms of the social system favor change.[38]

Use high credibility sources. Successful campaigns use highly credible representatives. (Refer to chapter 6 for more information on the dimensions of credibility.) One survey of global health communication projects found that high credibility was the most important factor determining whether new practices were adopted or rejected.[39] In Pakistan, villagers swaddling babies switched to talcum powder from cow dung, not because they understood the medical principles, but because trusted leaders advocated for the change. In Nigeria, trust in traditional leaders was the key to getting citizens to get smallpox vaccinations. In the United States, members of a religious sect rejected diphtheria immunizations because their leaders told them to do so. Audiences keep the motives of sources in mind when evaluating their credibility. An actor who promotes AIDS prevention as a public service is generally seen as more credible than an actor paid to promote a product.

Direct messages at the individual needs of the audience. Audiences are most influenced by messages aimed directly at personal needs. Effective political campaigns emphasize how the candidate will help the voter by lowering taxes, providing more jobs, building better roads, lowering crime, and so on. Campaigns for popular products link the purchase of the item with a specific need felt by the audience (e.g., smoke detectors for safety, cosmetics to enhance physical appearance, frozen dinners for convenience).

Vary message types. Campaign messages generally fall into three categories. *Awareness* messages "tell people what to do, specify who should do it, and provide cues about when and where it should be done."[40] They arouse interest and prompt listeners to seek more information about, for instance, a new product or recommended medical tests. *Instruction* messages focus on knowledge and skills acquisition. They offer training and encouragement to carry out the behavior. For example: how to select the right car seats for children and how to install them. These messages sometimes teach resistance to peer pressure or inoculate audiences against messages that might counter campaign messages, such as smoking is "cool" and "real men" don't wear motorcycle helmets. *Persuasive* messages advocate adopting or avoiding a behavior. It is easier to sway audiences who already have a positive attitude toward an action or to get them to continue to do what they are doing. Awareness messages are generally used more frequently at the beginning of campaigns, though the type of message will vary depending on the audience and the situation. Whenever possible, offer positive incentives for adopting the behavior, like making friends, being a good parent, losing weight, or appearing knowledgeable. Use a variety of appeals to these positive outcomes.

Campaign Stages

Even with an understanding of the factors that contribute to successful campaigns, organizing a campaign can seem like an overwhelming task. Successful campaigns involve research, the careful construction of messages, and effective use of both the media and interpersonal networks. To make the campaign process more manageable, Gary Woodward and Robert Denton suggest that you follow the six steps described in box 9.8.[41]

Box 9.8		Campaign Implementation Overview[42]	
Stage	**Components**	**Stage**	**Components**
1. Situation analysis	target audience product/issue/idea competition or opponent	4. Budget	labor material media talent production
2. Objectives	mission goals outcomes	5. Implementation	timing follow-up
3. Strategies	messages media presentation activities	6. Evaluation	what people say what people think what people do

Situation analysis is the foundation for the rest of the campaign. In this first stage, begin by identifying key audience characteristics. These include: (1) demographic variables (age, education, occupation); (2) geographic variables (urban versus suburban, West versus Midwest); and (3) psychographic variables (lifestyle, interests, activities, and opinions). If your campaign is product oriented, then size up the competition and determine attitudes toward your product. Your research can be both informal and formal. Informal research is the process of gathering information from libraries, personal contacts, industry publications, and other sources. Formal research is based on the statistical analysis of data collected through surveys and interviews.

Once the preliminary research is complete, goals should be set in stage two. *Objectives* can center on increased awareness, attitude change, or changes in behavior. Many campaigns fail because they are too ambitious. When you seek significant behavioral change, set more modest goals. For example, you might be able to convince a large percentage of your audience that recycling reduces our dependence on landfills. Yet, only a portion of those who believe in recycling will actually participate in recycling programs.

The hierarchy of effects model demonstrates why some campaign goals are harder to reach than others.[43] According to this model, there are intermediate steps that must be met before producing higher (more complex, demanding) effects. Breakdowns can occur at any step on the hierarchy.

1. *Exposure*—getting the message out is the first and easiest step. However, campaigns falter if audiences don't hear the message because they don't own computers, watch television, haven't joined Facebook, and so on.

2. *Attention*—a message has no impact if it is ignored. Audiences have more ways to ignore messages than ever before. Take television commercials for example. Viewers have hundreds of television channels to switch to during commercials or, if they record shows, they can fast forward through the ads. If they want to avoid commercials altogether, they binge watch television series on Netflix or through another streaming video service.

3. *Involvement (liking or interest)*—people quickly turn off messages they see as irrelevant, uninteresting, or offensive (not meeting their needs, for politicians they oppose, and so on).

4. *Comprehension (learning what)*—messages can be misinterpreted. For example, Mitt Romney's 2012 presidential campaign slogan "Believe in America" was confusing. Were audiences supposed to believe in the country or the candidate?

5. *Skill acquisition (learning how)*—audiences may want to follow through on a suggestion but can't. For instance, they can't attend a meeting because they don't have child care or they can't vote because they don't have transportation to the polls.

6. *Persuasion (attitude change)*—attitude change doesn't always lead to action, as in the case of those who say they will vote but don't, or know smoking is bad but won't quit.

7. *Memory storage*—to act on the message people must remember the message, which can be difficult given the multiple messages they receive every day. When the right time comes, individuals need to remember to make a call, go to a website, or buy a ticket.

8. *Information retrieval*—stored information must be retrieved at the appropriate time. This can be a problem when, for instance, someone remembers when the event is to take place but not where it is occurring.

9. *Motivation (decision)*—follow through only occurs when the benefits outweigh the costs. Incentives like reduced prices for products prompt people to act.

10. *Behavior*—success is often measured by sales, attendance, voting, and other actions. But securing a customer, attendee, donor, or voter is no guarantee that the individual will carry out the same behavior again.

11. *Reinforcement of behavior, attitude, or both*—those having doubts about their decision to purchase a certain product, for instance, need reassurance through good customer service, evidence of product quality, etc.

12. *Postbehavior consolidation*—in this final, highest stage individuals incorporate the campaign messages into their worldview. Take the case of those who take up exercising through a campaign, for example. They may engage in this behavior for the rest of their lives, making physical fitness a central personal value.

The third stage of the campaign is concerned with **strategies** to get things done. Structure messages to appeal to market segments, determine how you will use the media to reach audiences, and plan presentational activities like press conferences, rallies, and conventions. (See box 9.9 for a list of communication channels or vehicles commonly used in persuasive campaigns.)

In the fourth stage, prepare a **budget**. Financial resources will frequently determine the scope of your campaign. Labor, material, media, talent, and production costs must all be taken into consideration.

Implementation is the fifth stage. The campaign goes into action during this phase. Monitor your progress and determine the timing of messages through ongoing research. Poll voters to test attitudes; check and recheck reactions. By periodically gathering data, you will know if your campaign is on target or if you should modify your campaign messages and strategies.

The **evaluation** stage completes the ongoing campaign and lays the groundwork for future projects. In order to determine if you reached the campaign objectives you set earlier, you will need to survey target audiences, measure sales, and determine if favorable attitudes translate into desired action. What you learn from the successes and failures of one persuasive campaign can serve as the foundation for the next.

Box 9.9	Campaign Communication Channels[44]
Issues advertising	Placed and commissioned articles
Sponsored books, editorials	Employee communication
Negotiation	Internal and external newsletters
Executive comments	Speakers bureaus
Public affairs programming	Annual financial or special topic reports
Press releases, media relations	Videos mailed to key audiences and on request
Personal contact with opinion leaders by key staff and management personnel	Op-eds placed on editorial pages
Video and satellite presentations to internal and external audiences	Talk show appearances
	Electronic mail and bulletin boards
Congressional testimony, public hearings	Billboards
Mailings to constituencies	Special issue documents
Bill stuffers	Scholarly papers (commissioned)
Conference paper presentations	Citizens advisory committees
Trials	Lobbying
Open houses, issue workshops	Websites
Education information relevant to activist, government, or industry issues that can be distributed through schools	Social media
	Legislative position papers
	Collaborative decision making
	Joint research efforts

Collaborative (Integrative) Leadership

In a pluralistic society such as ours, encouraging groups to cooperate on behalf of the common good is often a public leader's greatest challenge.[45] Attempts to restore salmon and steelhead runs in the Pacific Northwest are a case in point. Billions of dollars have been spent to bolster these fish populations, but their numbers continue to decline due to dams, overgrazing, urban pollution, logging, irrigation, fishing, and other factors. Reversing this trend will take the cooperative efforts of biologists, government agencies, power companies, ranchers, barge owners, water districts, tribes, city councils, environmental activists, governors, and congressional representatives. Unless these groups look beyond their individual interests and work together, many species (which used to return to the region's rivers by the millions) will become extinct.

Fortunately, collaborative efforts can succeed if led effectively. Collaborative or integrative public leaders bring diverse groups together from various sectors of society, integrating their efforts to address community problems and to promote the common good.[46] Examples of successful collaborations range from creating a regional educational broadband service in North Carolina, to forming a planning and coordinating agency in Minneapolis-St. Paul, to improving the quality of the local workforce and lowering teen pregnancy rates in rural Oregon.

> *Treat every connection, communication and collaboration*
> *as part of a continuous relationship.*
> —*Kim Chandler McDonald*

Successful collaborative leadership takes a different set of competencies that overlap yet go beyond those needed for organizational leadership. Public administration professor Ricardo Morse surveyed research on collaborative leadership and identified important collaborative leadership competencies that divide into three subsets: attributes, skills and behaviors.[47]

Attributes

- *Collaborative mind-set*: seeing beyond organizational boundaries, having a vision for what collaboration can accomplish; seeing connections and possibilities instead of barriers.
- *Passion toward outcomes*: recognizing the need to bring about change, to make a positive difference.
- *Systems thinking*: thinking beyond the organization to the community as a whole; crossing specialties and disciplines.
- *Openness and risk taking*: willingness to take risks; being comfortable with uncertainty; willingness to change strategies.
- *A sense of mutuality and connectedness*: recognition of being part of the whole; understanding others and being concerned for others.
- *Humility*: satisfaction in sharing accomplishments and credit.

Skills

- *Self-management*: ability to prioritize and manage time effectively; proactively working across organizational boundaries.
- *Strategic thinking*: defining problems; identifying desired results rather than deficiencies; keeping the focus on goals; assessing stakeholder interest; seeing connections and interrelationships.
- *Facilitation skills:* helping the group generate new ideas; coping with conflict; helping groups get unstuck; forging agreements.

Behaviors

- *Stakeholder identification and stakeholder assessment*: locating a broad range of stakeholders, determining their interests, and deciding how to involve them.
- *Strategic issue framing*: advocating for issues; creating a sense of urgency; focusing attention on specific problems.

- *Relationship development with diverse stakeholders*: bringing groups together through establishing personal relationships with members of many different groups.

- *Convene working groups*: getting stakeholders together in a safe location; assuring that the discussion is transparent, without hidden agendas.

- *Facilitating mutual learning processes*: setting the standards for the tone of the group's communication; setting rules, values, and norms; focusing on learning together.

- *Inducing commitment*: soliciting commitment at the beginning of the process and throughout; getting buy in from key decision makers and other "champions" of the project.

- *Facilitating trusting relationships among partners*: ensuring that group members have good relationships with each other.

Collaborative leaders act as catalysts.[48] Like agents that speed up chemical reactions without being consumed, catalytic leaders foster integration. They recognize when the situation calls for joint action and bring the right organizations and individuals together to tackle the problem. (The case study in box 9.10 will provide you with some practice in identifying stakeholders.) They then initiate the process and make sure the stakeholders work together effectively and put the right structure in place to reach objectives. In the end, those involved in the collaborative effort achieve more than they could have acting on their own. Catalytic leaders don't dominate the process but share power. They are generally more interested in the process of decision making rather than on any particular outcome. They facilitate integration in different ways at different times. While they may not always be the most visible leaders or get the most credit, they play the most critical role in the success of the project.

Box 9.10 Case Study	**Building the Bypass: Identifying the Stakeholders**

For nearly 25 years, residents of Bloomburg have talked about the need for a bypass to carry traffic around their small city. Currently a major highway, which connects the state's major population center to the coast, runs through downtown. On week days the road is clogged with semis, logging trucks, and commuters. On summer weekends, traffic backs up for miles as vacationers head for the beach. Local residents find it difficult to get from one side of town to the next, frustrated travelers blame the city for their lengthy delays, and downtown businesses are fleeing to the neighboring community. City officials and the local chamber of commerce want to launch a downtown revitalization effort but there is little chance of success unless the highway is relocated.

Tom Hirokawa was recently hired as Bloomburg's first full-time planning director. One of his major responsibilities is to start work on the bypass project. He knows that a number of earlier bypass efforts failed. Local farmers and orchard growers viewed the bypass as a threat to their livelihoods, and highway funds weren't available. Hirokawa realizes that the farmers and growers still object to the bypass, but he has been told by local legislators and the area's congressional representative that the state and federal government will now pay for the project. According to plans drawn up earlier, the proposed route would not only cut across farmland and orchards but would also border a federally protected wetland. A small manufacturing facility and several homes would have to be relocated to accommodate the new road.

Tom knows that the critical first step in the project is identifying all the important stakeholder groups. Groups left out of the deliberations could later undermine the collaborative process. He also realizes that it is important to identify the interests and perspectives of stakeholders before he gathers them together to meet for the first time.

Discussion Questions

1. Who are the important stakeholder groups for the bypass project?
2. What are the needs and interests of each group?
3. Are there any groups that Tom shouldn't invite to participate in the discussions? Why?
4. Which groups have conflicting interests? How should Tom respond to these conflicts?
5. Based on your analysis of the stakeholder groups, how difficult is it going to be to reach consensus? Do you think the bypass will ever be built?

∼ CHAPTER TAKEAWAYS

- Public leaders influence the attitudes and behaviors of large audiences at all levels of society through the use of public relations activities, public address, and persuasive campaigns.

- Excellent public relations programs share the following characteristics: (1) empowered (valued and promoted by top management); (2) a strategic management role that helps shape organizational policy and direction; (3) two-way communication and symmetrical relationships that identify and respond to the needs of publics while fostering collaboration with outside groups; (4) ethical behavior that discloses accurate information, engages in dialogue, and advocates social responsibility; and (5) supportive structure that encourages participation and fosters the advancement of women and minorities.

- Public relations activities should be directed at building positive long-term relationships with publics. These quality relationships greatly enhance your organization's ability to lead public opinion.

- Your speech will be effective if it is based on careful prespeech planning (deciding on a mode of delivery, audience analysis); clear organization (developing a thesis statement, arranging and linking ideas, crafting a memorable introduction and conclusion); clear, vivid, and appropriate language; extensive rehearsal; delivery that appears natural and creates a sense of immediacy; and skillful anticipation and response to questions after the presentation is over.

- A persuasive campaign consists of a series of messages aimed at changing the beliefs and behaviors of others. To create a campaign with significant impact, pretest messages and identify market segments; use the media most accessible to target groups; rely on the media to raise awareness; utilize interpersonal commu-nication to bring about behavior change; employ high credibility sources; direct messages at individual needs; and vary message types.

- There are six steps or stages to any type of persuasive campaign: (1) situation analysis, which identifies key audience characteristics and possible competitors; (2) objectives, which vary in difficulty; (3) strategies, which identify types of mes-sages and communication activities; (4) budget, which determines the resources available to pay for labor, material, media, talent, and production costs; (5) implementation, which puts the campaign into action and evaluates progress; and (6) evaluation, which gathers feedback and measures outcomes.

- Collaborative (integrative) leaders bring diverse groups together in order to address community problems and to promote the common good. In order to be a successful collaborative leader, you must demonstrate these competencies: (1) attributes (collaborative mind-set, passion towards outcomes, systems thinking, openness and risk taking, a sense of mutuality and connectedness, humility); (2) skills (self-management, strategic thinking, facilitation skills); and (3) behaviors (stakeholder identification and stakeholder assessment, strategic issue framing, relationship development with diverse stakeholders, convening working groups, facilitating mutual learning processes, inducing commitment, facilitating trust-ing relationships among partners).

- Collaborative leaders act as catalysts that speed up the collaboration process and help group members achieve more than they could have on their own. To act as a catalytic leader, you must share power and be more interested in the process of decision making than in any particular outcome.

∼ APPLICATION EXERCISES

1. Pair off with someone and share your scores on the self-assessment in box 9.2. What do your scores reveal about your relationship with this organization and how has this relationship impacted your attitudes and behavior? What factors contribute to your perceptions? How could the organization build a better relationship with you?

2. As a research project, examine the public relations efforts of a large organiza-tion. Does the program meet the standards of excellence outlined in the chap-ter? How effective is the organization in building relationships with its publics?

3. In a small group, identify emerging issues that will likely have an impact on your college or another organization of your choice. How should the organiza-tion respond in order to lead public opinion?

4. Locate all the items related to public speaking from digital or traditional news sources on one day. Classify the news stories as local, regional, national, or international. What conclusions can you draw about the relationship between public address and public leadership based on your sample?

5. Practice your ability to deliver impromptu speeches. Your instructor will provide you with a list of topics and set time limits.

6. Use the techniques discussed in the chapter to prepare a speech. Concentrate on prespeech preparation, organization, language, rehearsal, and delivery. After the speech, evaluate your performance and record ways that you can make your future presentations more effective.

7. Evaluate a speech delivered by someone else based on concepts presented in the chapter. Write up your analysis.

8. In a research paper, describe the public speaking techniques of a well-known historical figure (e.g., Abraham Lincoln, Winston Churchill, Margaret Thatcher, Martin Luther King, Jr., or Eleanor Roosevelt). What made this individual an effective speaker? What can we learn about public address from this person?

9. Analyze a recent persuasive campaign based on the characteristics of successful campaigns presented in the chapter. Based on these elements, why did the campaign succeed or fail? Write up your findings. Or as an alternative, evaluate the effectiveness of a campus drinking campaign (see box 9.7).

10. Analyze the effectiveness of a collaborative/integrative public venture. How did the leader(s) demonstrate (or fail to demonstrate) collaborative competencies? How did the leader(s) act as catalysts for the collaborative effort? Report your findings in a class presentation.

～ CULTURAL CONNECTIONS: PUBLIC SPEAKING IN KENYA[49]

Culture has a significant impact on public-speaking patterns. The qualities that characterize an effective speaker in the United States and Canada often do not translate to other cultures. Consider the contrast between public address in Kenya, East Africa, and in the United States, for example. Ann Neville Miller, a professor at Daystar University in Nairobi, discovered that Americans and Kenyans view the prospect of speaking very differently. While a majority of Americans say they fear speaking in public, Kenyans expect to give speeches as part of everyday life.

> For most Kenyans public speaking is an unavoidable responsibility. Life events both major and minor are marked by ceremonies which occasion multiple public speeches. The normal procedure at wedding receptions, for example, is to include not only a speech by the best man and the parents of both bride and groom, but also addresses by the grandparents, various uncles and aunts, representatives of the bridal party's respective workplaces, and any of a host of other individuals and groups. Even the woman selected to cut the cake expects to give a brief word of advice before performing her duty.

North Americans give lots of persuasive and informative speeches that are supported by expert testimony and statistics. Kenyans, for the reasons described above, deliver more special occasion speeches that are supported with personal stories, parables that leave the audience to infer the main point, and proverbs. They may break out into song and encourage audience participation by leading chants or by having listeners fill in the end of sentences. East African speakers establish their credibility by virtue of their status (wealth, social standing, age, education, tribal affiliation) instead of through their expertise, as is the case in North America. Linear organizational patterns, like those outlined earlier in the chapter, are less common in African speeches. Instead, presenters often use a circular pattern that resembles a bicycle wheel. The main point serves as the hub. Personal stories, proverbs, and parables radiate out like spokes to the rim and then return to the hub or thesis.

∿ LEADERSHIP ON THE BIG SCREEN: *BRAVEHEART*

Starring: Mel Gibson, Angus Macfadyen, Patrick McGoohan, Sophie Marceau, Catherine McCormack, Brendan Gleeson

Rating: R for brutal medieval violence and brief nudity

Synopsis: Mel Gibson (who also directed the film) stars as William Wallace, the Scottish commoner who rallies his countrymen to overthrow the harsh rule of England's King Edward "Longshanks" (McGoohan). Wallace and his supporters succeed in driving out many of the English occupiers. Wallace delivers several stirring speeches, most notably one to lead his troops to victory in the face of overwhelming odds. Later he is defeated, captured, and killed after several Scottish lords betray him. However, a few years later one of his betrayers, Robert the Bruce (Macfadyen), now the Scottish king, invokes the name of Wallace to drive out the English and to secure Scottish freedom. The film won five Academy awards—including best picture—but had to tone down the violence to avoid an NC-17 rating. Viewers may want to fast forward through or skip particularly graphic scenes.

Chapter Links: dispersed leadership, invisible leadership, public opinion, the importance of public address, vivid language, collaboration

10

Leadership and Diversity

There are truths on this side of the Pyrenees which are falsehoods on the other.

—Blaise Pascal

OVERVIEW

Managing Diversity—The Core of Leadership

Understanding Cultural Differences
    Defining Culture
    Classifying Cultures
    Cultural Intelligence (CQ)
    Cultural Synergy

Fostering Diversity
    The Benefits of Diversity
    Obstacles to Diversity
    Promoting Diversity: Overcoming the Barriers

The Gender Leadership Gap: Breaking the Glass Ceiling, Avoiding the Glass Cliff, and Navigating the Labyrinth
    Male and Female Leadership Behavior: Is There a Difference?
    Creating the Gap
    Narrowing the Gap

Managing Diversity—The Core of Leadership

Cultural diversity is a growing force both at home and abroad. The nonwhite birth rate has surpassed the white birth rate in the United States. Minorities make up more than 37% of the total US population and the nation is expected to become "majority-minority" by 2043. Similarly, most of the growth in the workforces of other industrialized nations is coming from immigrants or groups currently underrepresented in the workplace. Along with these demographic trends, four main forces—known as the four Ts—have brought the world into a global age: *technology*, *travel*, *trade*, and *television*. Members of different cultures have more frequent contact and exposure to one another through: the Internet, satellite hookups, and fiber optic lines; increased international travel with millions of people visiting other nations each year; rapidly expanding broadcasting bandwidth; and multinational organizations and open markets. Nestlé, for example, has 97% of its employees working outside its headquarters in Switzerland, and US companies like Ford, General Electric, and IBM have more than 50% of their staff outside the United States.[1] (Box 10.1 introduces important historical figures behind globalization.)

Taylor Cox concludes that managing diversity is the "core" of modern organizational leadership.[2] To Cox and others, diversity management means taking advantage of the benefits of a diverse labor force while coping with the problems (conflict, misunderstandings) that arise when people from different backgrounds work together.[3] The goal is to enable all employees, regardless of ethnicity, gender, age, or physical ability, to achieve their full potential and to contribute to organizational goals and performance. While most experts focus their attention on the organizational work setting, diversity management is essential to leaders in group and public contexts as well. In this chapter we will explore the topic of leadership and diversity by (1) identifying important cultural differences, (2) examining the impact of culture on leadership behavior, (3) outlining ways to take advantage of cultural differences, (4) describing strategies for fostering diversity, and (5) discussing the gender leadership gap.

Understanding Cultural Differences

In chapter 8 we defined an organization's culture as a unique way of seeing the world, based on particular assumptions, values, rituals, stories, practices, artifacts, and physical settings. These same elements make up the cultures of larger groups.

Defining Culture

Everett Rogers and Thomas Steinfatt define culture as "the total way of life of a people, composed of their learned and shared behavior patterns, values, norms, and material objects."[4] Because cultures are human (symbolic) creations, they take many different forms. Cultural teachings result in very different assumptions, expectations, and rules for interaction. If we are not aware of these cultural differences, we can ascribe meanings to behaviors that are inaccurate and divisive.

Communication patterns are the verbal and nonverbal codes used to convey meanings in face-to-face encounters; these patterns vary from culture to culture. One important ingredient is language. Languages help people organize their perceptions and shape their worldviews. The grammar of Spanish, for instance, reflects a number of levels of respect that reinforces status distinctions. English reinforces individualism by being the only language that capitalizes the pronoun "I" in writing.

Nonverbal codes help individuals interpret the meaning of gestures, posture, facial expressions, time, touch, and space. Again, culture teaches the meanings of nonverbal behaviors. A simple action like sticking out the tongue can be interpreted many different ways. Tongue protrusion can signal everything from polite deference (Tibet), to embarrassment (south China), negation (Marquesa Islands), and contempt (United States).[5]

Patterns of relationships are strongly influenced by the culture in which one was raised. A son or daughter in the United States has much more freedom than his or her counterpart in South Korea. In traditional Korean families, the oldest male relative has the right to determine where children go to school, what careers they pursue, and whom they marry.

Formal organizations structure the activities of significant numbers of people. Important institutions include governments (which sponsor schools to teach cultural knowledge and values), social and professional organizations, work organizations, and religions. Religious faiths organize people differently. In Christianity or Judaism, adherents attach themselves to a particular church or synagogue, which sponsors a program of worship activities. Followers of Hinduism, on the other hand, worship whenever they want at the most convenient temple. Religions hold conflicting views about the meaning of existence, salvation, sin, and other questions.

Cultures create or borrow inventions necessary to maintain or enhance day-to-day functions. The term *artifacts* is frequently used to describe the tools used by a culture. The personal computer is one technological creation that has greatly impacted US culture. PCs, smartphones, and tablet devices have increased office productivity, encouraged more people to work at home, changed reading habits, increased the flow of information, linked users from around the world, and introduced new terms and phrases like "Google it," "hackers," "spam," the "cloud," and "Kindle" into the national vocabulary.

The *collective wisdom* of a culture is shaped by historical events such as immigration, invasions, wars, economic crises, legal decisions, legislative acts, and the decisions of prior leaders. For example, the rise of communism in Vietnam was spurred by the oppression of French colonialism. In the United States, the Social Security system and other entitlement programs are a legacy of the Great Depression.

A culture's external *environment*, including climate, geographical features, and natural resources, influences a wide variety of cultural elements, such as interaction patterns and population density. People from warm climates (the Middle East or the Mediterranean, for example) are typically more involved with each other, maintain closer distances, and engage in more touch than individuals from cold-weather climates like Scandinavia and Great Britain. In the United States, most major cities are located near lakes and rivers because they provide drinking water, serve as sources of hydroelectric power, and act as transportation corridors. The most sparsely populated regions of the country (portions of the Dakotas, Nebraska, Nevada, Oregon, Kansas, and Texas) generally receive very little rainfall.

Classifying Cultures

Researchers group cultures according to common characteristics. These commonalities help leaders recognize and respond to the needs of diverse groups.

Five cautions should be kept in mind when studying cultural categories. First, cultures change over time, so older groupings may not be as accurate as newer ones. Second, scholars disagree about how to categorize some nations and have not studied some regions (such as Africa and the Middle East) as thoroughly as others. Third, not every member of a cultural group will respond the same way. Statements about cultural patterns are generalizations that don't account for the behavior of every individual on every occasion. Americans are generally regarded as highly individualistic, but some groups in the United States—religious orders, small military units—are much more collectively oriented. Fourth, political and cultural boundaries are not always identical, as in the case of the Basque people, who live in both Spain and France. Fifth, Westerners have developed most of the cultural category systems and may have overlooked values that are important to non-Western societies.

Box 10.1 Research Highlight	**The Top Ten Global Leaders[6]**

Experts who study globalization often ignore the role that individuals play in making our world a smaller, more interconnected place. They focus instead on major trends like migration, technology, and trade; or examine international industries; or dissect major events like the recent global financial crisis. Yale economist Jeffery Garten argues that overlooking the role of leaders in globalization is a serious mistake, akin to studying war without looking at the actions of the top generals. To make his case, he points to the impact of ten historical leaders. According to Garten, these leaders "... opened doors to a broad array of possibilities for progress. They changed the prevailing paradigm of how society was organized. They raised the hopes of broad swaths of civilization. They opened highways on which many others could travel" (p. xiii).

Each of the nine men and one woman selected by Garten inaugurated a new phase of globalization. They were primarily doers, not thinkers. Each had a dark side, some leaving a trail of destruction—war, brutality, slavery, colonization, exploitation—in their wake. Garten's globalization leaders include:

Genghis Khan (1162–1227). Mongolian emperor Genghis Kahn and his descendants used war to build an empire that ranged from China to the Middle East. Political unity promoted cultural exchange and international trade, including the establishment of the Silk Road.

Prince Henry (1394–1460). This Portuguese prince played a key role in European exploration and expansion. He created the model that other adventurers followed and set in motion the Age of Exploration, which led to the colonization of Asia, Africa, and the Americas. Continuous trade then opened up between all the regions of the world.

Robert Clive (1725–1774). Clive led the expansion of Britain's East India Company in Asia. He promoted British rule and ideas like the rule of law, modern education, and market oriented economies.

Mayer Amschel Rothschild (1744–1812). German Mayer Rothschild founded the most powerful bank in the world and laid the groundwork for global financial markets, including the international bond trade. International banking enabled the world economy to grow faster.

Cyrus Field (1819–1892). A retired American paper industry executive, Field led the effort to lay telegraph cable between Newfoundland and England. The transatlantic cable led to almost instantaneous communication between Europe and the United States. The radio, telephone, and other communication breakthroughs soon followed. Currently 95% of all communication between continents, including email and phone calls, travels via nearly a million miles of underwater fiber-optic cable.

John D. Rockefeller (1839–1937). Rockefeller was the driving force behind the creation of the global petroleum industry. Standard Oil controlled every aspect of the oil business from extraction to delivery. Many also consider Rockefeller to be the father of international philanthropy. His Rockefeller Foundation was the first global philanthropic organization, working to improve health and nutrition in developing nations.

Jean Monnet (1888–1979). Frenchman Jean Monnet played a key role in the establishment of the European Union (EU). The EU reduced the threat of war and created an economic unit which accounts for around 20% of all global trade.

Margaret Thatcher (1925–2013). Thatcher served as the first woman prime minister of Britain from 1979–1990. During her term in office she instituted a series of austerity and free market measures, such as selling off government-controlled companies. Her efforts helped revive the British economy and encouraged other nations to reduce the role of government in the private sector.

Andy Grove (1936–2016). As Intel's CEO and board chair, Grove was at the forefront of the development of microprocessors. Microprocessors are the engines of the current technological age, powering computers, smartphones, machines, robots, and other devices.

Deng Xiaoping (1904–1997). Deng sparked China's economic boom after Mao's death. He encouraged the growth of private business, which helped lift hundreds of millions out of poverty, and expanded the country's economic and political ties with other nations. China is now the second largest economy in the world.

Professor Garten notes several common traits in his ten leaders, traits that future global leaders will need to handle crisis and turmoil. His leaders were, first of all, "hedgehogs." Unlike the fox that knows many things, the hedgehog focuses on one big idea and pursues that idea for decades. Robert Clive, for instance, kept his focus on conquering more territory and Jean Monnet spent his life fostering cooperation between countries. Second, these leaders were able to capitalize on the major trends of their times. Prince Henry benefitted from growing interest in exploration and Rockefeller discovered oil when the industrial revolution greatly increased demand. Third, while their efforts were transformational, the leaders in Garten's analysis looked to solve immediate problems rather than implement global visions. Fourth, each was also able to master the details of complex projects and to work effectively with others. Genghis Khan oversaw the day-to-day operation of a vast kingdom. Cyrus Field coordinated the efforts of technological and scientific experts, investors on different continents, and two governments.

Some fear that growing complexity will make it impossible for future individuals to wield as much global influence as past leaders. However, Garten points out that the world was as scary to his historical figures as it appears to us today. If past leaders met the challenges, then future leaders can as well. Further, thanks to the leaders on his list, "future hedgehogs" have much more powerful tools—modern communication, global finance and trade, digital technology—to use in reshaping the world.

To lead the people, walk behind them.

—Lao-tzu

There are a number of cultural classification systems; Edward Hall, Geert Hofstede, and Robert House and his colleagues developed three of the most notable.

High- and Low-Context Cultures

Hall, an anthropologist and nonverbal communication expert, categorizes cultures as high or low context based on the way people in the culture communicate.[7] In high-context cultures such as Japan, China, and South Korea, most of the information about the meaning of a message is contained in the context or setting. Group members assume that they share common meanings and prefer indirect or covert messages that rely heavily on nonverbal codes. In low-context cultures such as Germany and Great Britain, much more meaning is embedded in the words that make up the verbal message, and speakers are more direct. Other differences between high- and low-context cultures center on group membership, interpersonal relationships, and orientations toward time. A summary of the differences between high- and low-context cultures is found in box 10.2.

Leaders can run into serious difficulties when dealing with followers who prefer a different communication style. Take the case of the German manager who deals with conflict by confronting his Japanese employees directly. The supervisor's low-context culture encourages him to be honest and straightforward. However, his followers, who have been raised in a high-context society, would rather ignore tensions or deal with them indirectly through hints and nonverbal cues like making less eye contact.

Box 10.2	**Characteristics of High- and Low-Context Cultures[8]**
High-Context Cultures	**Low-Context Cultures**
Covert and implicit	Overt and explicit
Messages internalized	Messages plainly coded
Much nonverbal coding	Details verbalized
Reactions reserved	Reactions on the surface
Distinct in-groups and out-groups	Flexible in-groups and out-groups
Strong interpersonal bonds	Fragile interpersonal bonds
Commitment high	Commitment low
Time open and flexible	Time highly organized

> *Keep off the grass.*
>
> *—Lawn sign in the United States*

> *The grass is delicate and well cared for.*
>
> *—Lawn sign in China*

Programmed Values Patterns

Geert Hofstede of the Netherlands conducted a massive study of cultural patterns. In order to determine important values that are "programmed" into members of various cultures, Hofstede surveyed 116,000 IBM employees in 72 countries. He then validated his findings by correlating his results with data collected by other investigators in many of the same nations.[9] In his original research, Hofstede found four values dimensions that characterize cultures. With Michael Harris Bond, he later identified a fifth category that has its roots in Eastern culture.[10] Since then hundreds of studies have been conducted using the programmed values framework.[11] These dimensions and some of their implications for leader/follower relations are described below.[12]

Power distance. The first value dimension identified by Hofstede looks at the importance of power differences in a culture. "All societies are unequal," Hofstede states, "but some are more unequal than others."[13] In high power-distance cultures, inequality is considered to be a natural part of the world. Superiors are a special class of people who deserve special privileges. However, at the same time, they are obligated to take care of their less fortunate subordinates. High-status individuals try to look as powerful as possible and exert influence through coercive and referent power bases. In contrast, low power-distance cultures are uncomfortable with differences in wealth, status, power, and privilege; they promote equal rights. Members of these groups emphasize interdependence and rely on reward, legitimate, and expert power. Superiors are similar to subordinates and may try to appear less powerful than they actually are. Citizens of the Philippines, Mexico, Venezuela, India, and Singapore ranked among the highest in power distance; residents of New Zealand, Denmark, Israel, Austria, and Sweden the lowest. Power distance has a number of implications for leadership.

- The larger the power distance between leaders and followers, the greater the fear of disagreeing with a superior and the closer the supervision of follower activities.
- Followers in high power-distance countries expect managers to give direction and feel uncomfortable when asked to participate in decision making.
- Coercive, authoritarian leadership is more common in high power-distance countries; democratic leadership is more often the norm in low power-distance cultures.

- Organizations operating in low power-distance countries are less centralized and distribute rewards more equally.

Individualism-collectivism.   The second of Hofstede's value dimensions distinguishes cultures by their beliefs about individuals and groups. Individualistic cultures emphasize that the needs and goals of the individual and his or her immediate family are most important. Decisions are based on what benefits the person rather than the group. Collectivist cultures emphasize group identity. Individuals do not function as independent agents; rather, they define themselves and make decisions on the basis of their connection to an extended family, tribe, clan, or organization. The United States ranked as the most individualistic culture in Hofstede's sample, followed by Australia, Great Britain, Canada, and the Netherlands. Among the most collectivistic cultures were Colombia, Mexico, Pakistan, Taiwan, and South Korea. The following are implications for leadership along the individualism-collectivism continuum.

- Followers in individualistic societies generally respond well to material rewards that honor individual effort (commissions, bonuses for winning sales contests). Followers in collectivistic cultures don't feel comfortable with individual recognition and prefer team rewards instead.

- Members of collectivist societies expect mutual loyalty between organizational leaders and followers and feel betrayed when companies furlough or fire employees.

- To be accepted, new ideas in collectivist countries must come from the group as a whole rather than from any individual.

- Decision making is identified with a single leader in individualistic societies. Leaders in collectivist groups rely more heavily on group norms and social values to manage the behavior of followers.

- The ideal leader for individualists is someone who provides autonomy and opportunities for personal growth. The ideal leader for collectivists takes an active role in nurturing followers and fostering the growth of the group as a whole.

- Followers with a collectivist orientation prefer indirect criticism, while followers with individualistic values expect to be confronted directly about poor performance and conflicts.

Masculinity-femininity.   The third value dimension looks at roles assigned to the sexes. In masculine cultures, men are thought to be assertive, decisive, competitive, ambitious, and dominant. They are concerned with material success and "respect whatever is big, strong, and fast." Women are encouraged to serve; their responsibilities include nurturing interpersonal relationships and caring for the family and weaker members of society. In feminine cultures, sex roles overlap. Neither sex is expected to be competitive, ambitious, or caring at all times. These cultures stress intuition, interdependence, and concern; there is respect for the small, weak, and slow. Japan, Austria, Venezuela, and Italy were the most masculine cultures surveyed, while Sweden, Norway, the Netherlands, and Denmark were the most feminine. The masculinity-femininity implications for leadership include the following.

- Females in masculine cultures have a harder time emerging as leaders and are more likely to be segregated into a few specialized occupations.

- Decision makers in feminine cultures put a greater emphasis on intuition and consensus.

- Leaders and constituents in masculine cultures put a higher priority on work (they "live to work"); leaders and constituents in feminine cultures put more emphasis on the quality of life (they "work to live").

- Leaders in feminine societies are more likely to demonstrate an interpersonally oriented leadership style.

- Members of masculine cultures are more motivated by achievement, recognition, and challenge.

> *If a [hu]man can be gracious and courteous to strangers,*
> *it shows he[she] is a citizen of the world.*
>
> —*Francis Bacon*

Uncertainty avoidance.   The fourth dimension measures (1) the extent to which people feel uncomfortable in unstructured or unpredictable situations, and (2) the lengths to which they will go to avoid ambiguity by following strict codes of behavior or by believing in absolute truths. Members of high uncertainty-avoidance cultures view uncertainty as a threat, are less tolerant, face high stress, seek security, believe in written rules and regulations, and readily accept directives from experts and those in authority. Individuals in low uncertainty-avoidance cultures accept uncertainty as a fact of life, are more contemplative, experience less stress, take more risks, are less concerned about rules, are more likely to trust their own judgments or common sense rather than experts, and believe that authorities serve the citizens. Citizens of Greece, Portugal, Belgium, and Japan reported some of the highest uncertainty-avoidance ratings; residents of Jamaica, Denmark, Sweden, and Ireland among the lowest. Uncertainty-avoidance has several implications for leadership.

- High uncertainty-avoidance cultures give more weight to age and seniority when selecting leaders.

- Managers in low uncertainty-avoidance societies emphasize interpersonal relations and are more willing to take risks. Managers in high uncertainty-avoidance countries seem unapproachable and are more likely to try to control the activities of followers.

- Organizational constituents in high uncertainty-avoidance cultures prefer clear instructions, are more willing to follow orders, disapprove of competition between employees, and are more loyal than their low uncertainty-avoidance counterparts.

Long-term–short-term orientation. The fifth value dimension is concerned with how citizens view the past, present, and future. Cultures with a long-term orientation (LTO) encourage norms and behaviors that lead to future rewards. Members of these societies sacrifice immediate gratification (leisure time, luxuries, entertainment) for long-term benefits. They put a high value on persistence and perseverance, spend sparingly, and save a lot. Status relationships—teacher-student, manager-worker, parent-child—are clearly defined and honored. Feelings of shame come from violating social contracts and commitments. Cultures with a short-term orientation (STO) focus on the past and the present, respecting tradition and expecting quick results. Members of these groups put much less importance on persistence, spend freely, and have lower savings rates. China, Hong Kong, Taiwan, Japan, and South Korea ranked highest on long-term orientation; Pakistan, Nigeria, the Philippines, Canada, and Zimbabwe ranked lowest. Long-term or short-term orientations have the following implications for leadership.

- Leaders in LTO cultures can expect greater sacrifice from followers on behalf of long-term goals. Leaders in STO societies are under greater pressure to demonstrate immediate progress.

- Feelings of shame can be powerful motivational tools to encourage follower compliance in LTO nations.

- Short-term orientation, with its emphasis on spending instead of saving, interferes with economic development in emerging countries, making the task of national leaders and aid agencies more difficult.

The GLOBE Studies

More recently a cultural classification system related specifically to leadership was developed. The GLOBE studies, short for Global Leadership and Organizational Behavior Effectiveness, were initiated by Robert House. Working with more than 160 colleagues around the world, House and his research team have published a series of articles and books focusing on the relationship between culture and leadership.[14] The GLOBE research is based on analysis of the responses of 17,300 managers in more than 950 organizations across 62 cultures. The GLOBE studies produced a cultural classification system consisting of nine dimensions. In addition to the dimensions previously identified by Hofstede, the GLOBE investigators added the following:[15]

Assertiveness is the degree to which individuals in organizations or societies are assertive, confrontational, and aggressive in social relationships. The most assertive individuals in the GLOBE studies were found in Albania, Nigeria, Hungary, Germany, Hong Kong, Austria, El Salvador, South Africa, Greece, and the United States. Those in Sweden, New Zealand, Switzerland, Japan, Kuwait, Thailand, Portugal, Russia, and India were the least assertive, valuing modest and tender behavior over assertive and competitive stances.

Performance orientation is the degree to which an organization or society encourages and rewards group members for performance improvement and excellence. High performance-orientation scores were noted among GLOBE subjects in Switzerland, Singapore, Hong Kong, New Zealand, Canada, and the United States. Citizens in these societies value training and development opportunities and take initiative to improve performance. Those in Greece, Venezuela, Russia, Hungary, Qatar, Italy, Portugal, and Argentina had low performance-orientation scores. In these countries, individuals focus more on family background and group membership, as opposed to performance, as a means for achieving success.

Humane orientation is the degree to which individuals in organizations or societies encourage and reward individuals for being fair, altruistic, friendly, generous, caring, and kind to others. Those in Zambia, the Philippines, Ireland, Malaysia, Thailand, Egypt, India, Canada, and Denmark were high on this dimension, reflecting a focus on sympathy and support for the weak. Citizens of Germany, Spain, Greece, Hungary, France, Singapore, Switzerland, Poland, Italy, and Brazil were low on humane orientation, reflecting more importance given to power, material possessions, and self-interest.

Since the GLOBE studies were specifically concerned with the impact of culture on leadership, the researchers were interested in the specific leader characteristics and actions that were considered to be effective in different cultures. To this end, the GLOBE researchers identified six global leadership behaviors and the cultural contexts in which these behaviors are most positively viewed.[16]

Charismatic/value-based leadership.   This broadly defined leadership dimension reflects the ability to inspire and motivate and expects high performance from others based on shared core values. This type of leadership involves being visionary, inspirational, self-sacrificing, trustworthy, decisive, and performance oriented. Such leadership is viewed most positively in, for example, Finland, Sweden, the Netherlands, Australia, the United Kingdom, Ireland, and the United States.

Team-oriented leadership.   This leadership dimension emphasizes team building and a common purpose among team members; it includes characteristics such as being collaborative, integrative, diplomatic, and administratively competent. This type of leadership is viewed most positively in, for example, Finland, Sweden, the Netherlands, Portugal, Spain, Argentina, and Colombia.

Participative leadership.   This leadership dimension reflects the degree to which leaders involve others in decision making and implementation and thus includes being participative and nonauthoritarian. This type of leadership is viewed most positively in, for example, Austria, Germany, Greece, Switzerland, the United States, France, and Argentina.

Humane-oriented leadership.   This leadership dimension reflects supportive, considerate, compassionate, and generous behavior; it also includes modesty and sensitivity to the needs of others. This type of leadership is viewed most positively in, for example, Georgia, Canada, China, South Africa, Nigeria, and Iran.

Autonomous leadership.   This leadership dimension refers to independent and individualistic leadership. This type of leadership is viewed most positively in, for example, Russia, Indonesia, Germany, and Egypt.

Self-protective leadership.   This leadership dimension reflects behavior that ensures the safety and security of the leader and the group. Such leadership is leader-focused, status conscious, face saving, and procedural. This type of leadership is viewed most positively in, for example, Albania, Taiwan, Indonesia, and Iran.

Cultural Intelligence (CQ)

Understanding cultural differences lays the groundwork for leading groups in a variety of cultures as well as for leading groups made up of diverse members. The successful leader recognizes and responds to cultural differences; the leader who fails to appreciate cultural influences is doomed to frustration and failure. Consider these examples of failed intercultural communication:[17]

- A top American technology sales representative loses a sale because he rushes to close a deal with Mexican executives who first want to establish connections before doing business.

- An American human resource manager rejects a qualified Samoan job candidate because he misinterprets the applicant's behavior during a job interview. The manager is offended when the candidate comes in, sits down without being invited to do so, says nothing, and stares at the floor rather than making eye contact. However, the Samoan is treating the manager as an authority figure who deserves respect. The applicant demonstrates respect by only speaking when spoken to and by avoiding eye contact. He sits because standing while the authority figure is sitting (which puts the subordinate in a physically higher position) is a serious sign of disrespect.

- A Norwegian appointed to head a Russian subsidiary introduces Management by Objectives (MBO) to his new followers. Used to authoritarian leadership, they don't accept the notion that they or their subordinates should be setting their own goals.

- A New Zealand food-processing company executive tries to find out if the company's Japanese joint-venture partner had been fishing illegally within New Zealand's 20-mile zone. He asks directly but only gets vague responses like "when you beat a mat, the dust will rise." Only later does he realize that the Japanese would have lost face by admitting wrongdoing publicly. Instead, their obscure replies are an indirect acknowledgement of guilt.

Developing cultural intelligence is key to avoiding the kinds of mistakes described above. **Cultural intelligence (CQ)** is defined as he ability to function effectively in culturally diverse settings.[18] Those with high CQ are more successful in overseas assignments, short-term business travel, cross-cultural negotiation, and multicultural team and organizational leadership. They are more effective communicators and experience less anxiety in these contexts.[19] Cultural intelligence is made up of four factors. *Metacognitive CQ* refers to the level of cultural awareness when interacting with people from other cultures. Those with high metacognitive CQ are aware of their own cultural assumptions and can adjust to the cultural assumptions of others. *Cognitive CQ* describes knowledge of the norms and practices of a particular culture. *Motivational CQ* reflects the desire or drive to both learn about and then interact in cross-cultural settings. Strong motivation encourages communicators to interact with those from other cultures. *Behavioral CQ* describes the ability to communicate appropriately, both verbally and nonverbally, in cross-cultural settings. High behavioral competence includes understanding which behaviors are required, permitted, or forbidden; knowing how to interpret the words and behaviors of others; and being flexible, adjusting behaviors as needed. (Complete the self-assessment in box 10.3 to determine your level of cultural intelligence.)

The most effective way to develop cultural intelligence is through a long-term overseas experience like a semester abroad or overseas job assignment. However, if these options aren't available, enrolling in a cross-cultural communication or international business course; participating in a cross-cultural simulation; taking an educational, service, or business trip; and interacting with international students or colleagues can also boost your cultural intelligence.[20]

A [hu]man's feet must be planted in his[her] country,
but his[her] eyes should survey the world.

—*George Santayana*

Box 10.3 **Self-Assessment**	**Cultural Intelligence Scale—Short Version[21]**

Directions: Read each statement and select the response that best describes your capabilities. Select the answer that BEST describes you AS YOU REALLY ARE (1 = strongly disagree; 7 = strongly agree).

_____ I enjoy interacting with people from different cultures.

_____ I am sure I can deal with the stresses of adjusting to a culture that is new to me.

_____ I know the cultural values and religious beliefs of other cultures.

_____ I know the legal and economics systems of other cultures.

_____ I know the rules (e.g. vocabulary, grammar) of other languages.

_____ I am conscious of the cultural knowledge I use when interacting with people with different cultural backgrounds.

_____ I check the accuracy of my cultural knowledge as I interact with people from different cultures.

_____ I change my verbal behavior (e.g. accent, tone) when a cross-cultural interaction requires it.

_____ I change my nonverbal behavior when a cross-cultural situation requires it.

Scoring: Scores range from 9 to 63. The higher the score, the higher your perceived level of cultural intelligence.

Cultural Synergy

Cultural synergy is the ultimate goal of recognizing and responding to cultural variations. Synergy refers to the production of an end product that is greater than the sum of its parts. In cultural synergy, decision makers draw on the diversity of the group to produce a new, better-than-expected solution. According to cross-cultural management expert Nancy Adler, culturally synergistic problem solving is a four-step process.[22] (Turn to box 10.4 for an alternate perspective on how to make the most of cultural differences.)

The first step is identifying the dilemma or conflict facing the dyad or group. Due to differing cultural perspectives, some communicators may not realize that there is a problem. In the case of the Norwegian manager introducing MBO to his Russian subordinates, this leader likely didn't think goal setting would cause difficulties. After all, setting personal and collective objectives is what a "good" leader would do in Norway. This executive can't begin the synergistic process until he recognizes that soliciting participation is problematic for his followers. Further, he needs to identify the conflict without making negative value judgments. The Russians will need to approach him in the same nonjudgmental fashion.

In step two, communicators try to determine why members of other cultures think and act as they do. The underlying assumption is that all people act rationally from their culture's point of view. Communicators identify both similarities and differences in cultural perspectives and recognize that cultural values can cluster together in different ways. For instance, some collectivist societies are low in power distance. Others, such as Malaysia, are characterized by "vertical collectivism"—a combination of collectivism and high power distance.[23] Constituents in all collectivist cultures expect to work in groups, but vertical collectivists try to ensure that group decisions are acceptable to people in authority.[24]

Step three begins by asking the question: "What can people from one culture contribute to people from another culture?" Problem solvers then generate alternatives and come up with a creative answer that incorporates the cultural assumptions of all group members but also transcends them.

Consider the dilemma faced by American and Japanese sales representatives of a US-based freight company that promised customers specific flight arrival times.[25] American customers would accept delays with adequate explanation, but Japanese customers would not. As a result, company officials in Japan refused to promise delivery times until they were certain they would be kept, thus saving face. American customers wanted specific delivery times and began to lose faith in the freight business. The firm needed to come up with a "promising" system that was appropriate for both cultures. It had to be definite for the Americans and close enough to actual arrival times to satisfy the Japanese. The sales representatives from both countries came up with a creative, synergistic solution. They began to promise delivery within a time range rather than at specific times. For example: "late Wednesday morning" instead of "at 11:30 AM." The Americans were able to keep making promises and the Japanese were able to save face by never promising something they couldn't deliver.

Effective implementation of a solution in step four also requires synergistic thinking based on cultural awareness. Synergistic implementation of a sales reward system at a multinational corporation, for example, would give managers in host countries plenty of leeway in distributing awards appropriate for the specific cultural settings.[26] As we noted earlier, stakeholders in individualistic societies expect

---

Box 10.4   Research Highlight   **Reconciling Universal Dilemmas[27]**

Cross-cultural communication experts Fons Trompenaars and Charles Hampden-Turner believe that humans the world over face the same set of value choices, what they label as universal dilemmas. They identify six universal dilemmas based on their surveys of 46,000 managers from more than 40 countries:

- *Universalism* (focus on rules, codes, laws, and generalizations) or *particularism* (focus on exceptions, special circumstances, unique relations)
- *Individualism* (personal freedom, human rights, competitiveness) or *communitarianism* (social responsibility, harmonious relations, cooperation)
- *Specificity* (reality is viewed through an atomistic, reductive objective lens) or *diffusion* (reality is viewed through a holistic, elaborative, relational lens)
- *Achieved status* (social standing is based what you've done, your track record) or *ascribed status* (social standing is based on who you are, your potential and connections)
- *Inner direction* (virtue comes from inside us) or *outer direction* (virtue comes from outside—nature, beauty, and relationships)
- *Sequential time* (time is seen as a race along a set course) or *synchronous time* (time is seen as a dance involving coordination)

Cultures make different determinations when responding to these dilemmas. The job of the leader, then, is to reconcile these perspectives. Reconciliation is based on the realization that what appear to be opposites should be seen as part of the same circle. For example, decision making requires both specificity (breaking the problem into smaller parts) and diffusion (seeing the big picture). Hampden-Turner and Trompenaars point out that dwelling at one extreme or the other is dangerous. Achieved status promotes excellence but can lead to a "winner take all" society. Ascribed status, on the other hand, can encourage recipients to give back to society but can also lead to dictatorship. Communitarian societies need to protect and foster the individual and individualist societies need to promote community interests and the common good.

The researchers provide an example from their personal experience to demonstrate cultural reconciliation. Samsung (headquartered in particularistic South Korea) sent a letter thanking them for their book, which the company had translated and provided to its executives. Trouble is, the authors (from a more universalistic background) hadn't given their permission for the translation and could have sued for violation of copyright law. The authors speculated that perhaps Samsung thought a warm relationship should come before legality and discovered that the company spent $18,000 to translate the work. Nevertheless, the duo wanted to get paid for their labor. Trompenaars and Hampden-Turner decided that rather than sue they would instead write their own letter warmly thanking Samsung and asking for help in locating a Korean commercial publisher. Soon they had a Korean publisher and a legal contract protecting their copyright. Samsung's endorsement was displayed on the front cover of their book and sales were brisk. The value of lost royalties from Samsung was less than what it would have cost the authors to translate the work themselves.

to be compensated for their personal efforts, but a greater share of the rewards will go to the group in collectivistic cultures. One oil company took the collectivist orientation of its employees into account when it rewarded a group of workers by building a well in their African village. The new water system helped the community and, at the same time, raised the status of the employees. (The Leadership on the Big Screen feature at the end of the chapter provides another example of cultural synergy in action.)

Fostering Diversity

So far we've highlighted the importance of responding to cultural differences. We've seen that leaders improve their effectiveness if they recognize and incorporate differences into their problem solving. However, the best leaders go beyond simply responding to cultural differences; they actively promote diversity in the groups they lead. In this section of the chapter we provide a rationale for fostering diversity, discuss some of the obstacles that keep members of minority groups from reaching their full potential, and suggest ways to promote diversity in the organizational context.

The Benefits of Diversity

Perhaps the best reason for encouraging diversity is that it is the right thing to do. Fostering diversity reduces inequities and gives everyone a chance to make a meaningful contribution. While ethical considerations alone should be sufficient motivation for promoting diversity, there are also a number of practical benefits that come from making maximum use of the members of various constituencies. Taken together, these make the "business case" for promoting organizational diversity.[28]

- *Cost savings.* Absenteeism and turnover rates in organizations are often higher for women and ethnic minorities than they are for white males. Finding temporary substitutes and permanent replacements is expensive. Addressing diversity concerns lowers the number of absences and resignations and reduces the likelihood of sexual harassment and racial discrimination lawsuits.

- *Resource acquisition and utilization.* Organizations with reputations for managing diversity will attract the best personnel out of an increasingly diverse population. They will also help talented minority employees break out of low-level positions.

- *Keeping and gaining market share.* Diverse organizations are in the best position to take advantage of markets both at home and abroad. Such organizations understand the needs of a variety of target audiences and have minority representatives who can appeal to members of many different cultural groups. The Avon Company illustrates how diversity can boost the bottom line. The corporation gave African American and Hispanic managers authority over unprofitable inner-city markets. These territories are now among the company's most productive.

- *Better decision making.* Earlier we argued that cultural differences can be the basis for higher quality solutions. Forming heterogeneous groups is one way to stimulate cultural synergy. Members of diverse groups are also less likely to succumb to groupthink (see chapter 7). Having a variety of opinions forces group members to pay more attention to all aspects of an issue, consider more viewpoints, and use a wider variety of problem-solving strategies.[29]

- *Greater innovation.* Nurturing a variety of cultural perspectives makes an organization more open to ideas. Innovative organizations employ more women and minorities and work harder at eliminating racism and sexism.[30]

- *Higher performance.* Companies with the best diversity practices often (though not always) perform better. They are generally more profitable, having higher profit margins as well as better return on equity and assets.[31]

Organizations experience more of the benefits of diversity when their senior leaders strive for the cultural synergy we described earlier. These executives adopt a *learning-and-effectiveness* approach that recognizes cultural differences as valuable organizational assets.[32] Drawing on the insights of diverse members can dramatically improve how organizations carry out their tasks—helping them to think in new ways about markets, products, goals, and organizational structures. (See box 10.5 for more information on what diverse communities can bring to the understanding of leadership.) This synergistic approach stands in sharp contrast to the diversity paradigms adopted by the leaders of most organizations. Executives in some groups view diversity initiatives solely as a way to provide equal opportunity; they strive to treat everyone the same way and try to ignore cultural differences rather than building on them. Executives in other groups value minorities solely as marketing agents who can sell to their ethnic groups. Diversity in these two situations has little impact on the way that these organizations conduct their core businesses.

Box 10.5 Research Highlight	**Salsa, Soul, and Spirit**[33]

Diversity consultant Juana Bordas interviewed prominent Latino, African American, and American Indian leaders to determine what communities of color contribute to mainstream (white, male, Western) leadership theory. She highlights points of convergence from all three traditions, which she describes as bringing energy and vitality (Latina salsa), hope and resilience in the midst of hardship (African American soul), and recognition of the interconnectedness and sacredness of all life (American Indian spirit). From these communities of color she identifies eight principles of multicultural leadership divided into three categories.

A New Social Covenant

- *Principle 1: Sankofa—learn from the past.* The Sankofa is a mythical West African bird that has its feet planted forward while its head faces backward. Leaders need to understand how past events have kept some groups from participating fully in organizations and society. They should recognize that the dominant culture promotes individualistic, materialistic values that can be destructive.

(continued)

- *Principle 2: I to we—from individualism to collective identity.* Communities of color acknowledge the importance of connections to other group members. They focus on the "we" instead of the "I." Multicultural leaders also need to embrace social responsibility and concern for the common good.

- *Principle 3: Mi casa es su casa—a spirit of generosity.* Generosity, inclusiveness, and sharing are part of the history of the indigenous peoples of the Americas and Africa. Drawing from these traditions, leaders should focus on creating community wealth, not individual wealth, and act as good stewards of the environment for future generations.

Leadership Styles

- *Principle 4: A leader among equals—community-conferred leadership.* In collectivist cultures, the leader's authority is granted by the group. Reputation or character plays a key role in being selected as a leader and continuing in this role. The multicultural leader also needs to remain humble and be willing to do hard work alongside followers. She or he should focus on serving a greater cause rather than on money and privilege.

- *Principle 5: Leaders as guardians of public values—a tradition of activism.* The Civil Rights movement demonstrated the importance of looking beyond personal virtues to address public values and institutions that stand as barriers to diversity. Multicultural leaders need to follow the example of leaders in communities of color and bring people together to address unjust social and economic conditions.

- *Principle 6: Leaders as community stewards—working for the common goal.* Leaders in communities of color are servants, putting the needs of followers first. But they go beyond personal service to practice community stewardship. Following their example, multicultural leaders need to build the capacity of followers by, for example, encouraging participation and building consensus, establishing partnerships, and creating a community of leaders. They ought to see themselves as leaders among equals and as guardians of important public values.

Creating the Circle of Leadership

- *Principle 7: All my relatives—la familia, the village, the tribe.* Kinship is central to Latino, African American, and Native American societies. Effective leadership in these cultures is inclusive, recognizing the intrinsic value of people and treating them like family. Relationships come with the responsibility to care for others by meeting their basic needs for food and shelter. Kinship should also drive multicultural leaders, encouraging them to recognize the dignity of all followers and to take responsibility for their welfare.

- *Principle 8: Gracias—gratitude, hope, and forgiveness.* Gratitude, hope, and forgiveness have helped Black, Indian, and Latino leaders survive and overcome oppression. Multicultural leaders can draw from this tradition, focusing on what they have rather than what they lack, encouraging followers to have hope, and bringing reconciliation in the face of conflict. Collective spirituality sustains communities of color and brings with it a moral obligation to help others and serve the common good. This emphasis on leadership as spiritual activism can inform leaders of all ethnic backgrounds.

Obstacles to Diversity

While the benefits of fostering diversity are substantial, so too are the barriers that prevent leaders and followers from reaching cultural synergy. Diversity barriers can be found at every level of society—personal, group, and institutional. Barriers found at the individual level include prejudice, discrimination, stereotyping, and perceptual bias.[34] The term *prejudice* refers to negative attitudes toward people from other backgrounds. Despite improvements in racial attitudes over the past decades, many white respondents continue to rate blacks as less hardworking and intelligent than whites.[35] These negative attitudes produce discriminatory behavior, which likely accounts for the fact that minorities receive fewer organ transplants, are underrepresented in the media, serve on fewer corporate boards, earn less money than whites, and so on. *Stereotyping* is the process of classifying group members according to their perceived similarities, either good or bad. According to widely held stereotypes in US culture, disabled workers are seen as less productive, and Asian Americans are seen as excelling at technical but not managerial skills. As a consequence of these stereotypes, organizations are reluctant to hire disabled people and hire Asian Americans primarily for technical positions. (Asian Americans hold only 1–4% of upper management positions in the United States.)[36]

Perceptual biases reinforce the power of stereotypes. Individuals generally attribute their failings to external factors and their successes to internal factors. The opposite is true when it comes to evaluating the behavior of members of marginalized groups. When we fail, outside forces (other people, chance, bad weather) are to blame. When members of low-status groups fail, internal forces (laziness, poor character, low intelligence) are to blame. Our success is based on our skills and motivation. When marginalized individuals perform well, we attribute their success to help from others rather than to their individual abilities and efforts.

What is repugnant to every human being is to be reckoned as a member of a class and not an individual person.

—*Dorothy Sayers*

On a group level, *ethnocentrism*—the attitude (conscious or unconscious) that regards one's own culture as the measure by which all others should be judged—is a significant barrier to incorporating diversity. Ethnocentrism is less hostile than prejudice, but it still leads to preferential treatment for insiders. Most of us would rather socialize with people from similar backgrounds and prefer to recruit, promote, and reward those who share our values. Intergroup conflicts also serve as diversity obstacles. Religious, social, political, and economic differences generate tensions that tear groups and societies apart.

At the institutional level, large power differences between cultural groups reduce the motivation of minority group members and make it more difficult for them to be perceived as leaders. Many organizations (often without meaning to do so) engage in practices that keep minority groups from fully participating. These include: (1) 50-hour plus workweeks with weekend and evening meetings that increase stress on working mothers, (2) self-promotion which is uncomfortable for employees from cultures that value modesty, (3) exclusion of women, minorities, and others from informal ("old boy" networks) that are important sources of information, and (4) inaccessible facilities that make it difficult for disabled workers.[37]

Promoting Diversity: Overcoming the Barriers

Strategies for promoting diversity must address the obstacles described above. Applying cultural intelligence, particularly metacognitive CQ, is an excellent place to start. We can greatly reduce the power of stereotypes, prejudice, biased perceptions, and ethnocentrism if we are aware of our cultural assumptions and those of other communicators. In other words, we need to engage in *mindful* communication. Mindfulness refers to focused attention, which stands in sharp contrast to the *mindlessness* that characterizes our typical interactions. Most of the time, we operate mechanically without giving much conscious thought to our behaviors and to the behaviors of the other person. This mind-set, which relies on the scripts we've learned through experience, characterizes such routine encounters as chatting with a fellow student before class or discussing the latest online game with friends. Mindlessness can be dangerous when interacting with individuals of diverse backgrounds, however. Scripted responses make us susceptible to prejudice, stereotypes, and perceptual biases. If we do not engage in mindful communication, we are less likely to challenge the assumption that our culture is best or work to create cultural synergy.

A mindful state consists of three intrapersonal processes.[38] The first is the creation of new categories. Breaking old categories increases sensitivity to differences. We are then able to make finer distinctions within broad categories based on age, disabilities, race, gender, sexual orientation, and other factors. For instance, we recognize that not all older people find it difficult to learn new skills. In a mindful state, we are less likely to stereotype individuals or to act in a prejudiced manner. The second intrapersonal process is welcoming new information. In a mindless state, we are closed off to new data, which blinds us to potential cultural differences and prevents us from adjusting our behavior to meet the demands of the situation. In a mindful state, we monitor our actions and the actions of others. Heightened awareness enables us to modify our responses and to reach better conclusions. The third component of mindfulness is openness to different points of view. Recognizing that there are different perspectives on events and behaviors reduces the likelihood of cultural misunderstandings and opens the way for solutions that combine the insights of a variety of cultures. (See the Cultural Connections feature at the end of the chapter to see how mindless use of language can cause significant misunderstandings.)

Dignity, integrity, and inclusion are also important tools for overcoming personal and group barriers to diversity.[39] We need to recognize the dignity of others by respecting their views, even when we disagree. We need to retain our integrity by confronting others who demonstrate prejudice (e.g., use a racial slur, discriminate against a person of color). We need to include, not exclude, those of different backgrounds, applying the same rules of fairness to them as we apply to members of our group. Acting with dignity, integrity, and inclusion encourages followers to do the same, creating a more ethical and accepting group climate.

Organization-wide strategies for promoting diversity incorporate leadership, research and measurement, education, alignment of management systems, and follow up.[40] (Complete the self-assessment in box 10.6 to determine your perceptions of the current diversity climate of your work organization.)

Promoting diversity is nearly impossible without the *buy-in of leadership*. Top leaders must be committed but their efforts alone will not be enough. Department heads, diversity officers, diversity staff members, human resource personnel, union leaders, and others must also be involved. Defining the vision of what it means to be a diverse organization is key, as is modeling desired behaviors (e.g., conducting feedback sessions with underrepresented groups; attending diversity training). The executive leadership team needs to create a structure for fostering change (setting up steering teams, for example) and to ensure that diversity efforts fit with the overall strategy of the organization.

All diversity efforts must be *data driven*. Build the case for fostering diversity (see the earlier discussion of the benefits of diversity); identify the current diversity profile of the organization; measure progress on important diversity metrics (turnover, absenteeism, diversity profile, accommodation for persons with disabilities).

Education is key to any change effort, including diversity initiatives. Introduce employees to important cultural concepts and customize the content to the organization. For example, Ford Motor Company developed a training curriculum that provided an overview of the topic of diversity and then moved to modules on different types of identity, such as gender and persons with disabilities. Supplement formal training sessions with coaching and mentoring.

Systems should be aligned to support diversity goals. Pay particular attention to time, space, and people process factors, examining how each can be adjusted to better accommodate diverse groups. More liberal time-off policies like flex time generally attract diverse employees. Remove work environment barriers that reinforce existing hierarchies, like limited restroom facilities for women and executive dining rooms. When hiring, look for cultural intelligence in applicants, make sure recruiting teams are diverse, and include diversity material in new orientation sessions. Monitor performance appraisal procedures to eliminate biases against particular groups. Publicize job openings to all employees; incorporate underrepresented groups in the promotion and succession-planning process.

Follow up is critical to ensure that diversity isn't seen as the latest management fad and to ensure that the effort continues. Establish accountability by reviewing the diversity plan and "keep score" by monitoring progress toward goals. Reward progress by providing financial incentives for leaders reaching objectives, recognizing personal and group achievement, and making the ability to deal with diversity a key criteria for advancement. Apply the principles of knowledge management described in chapter 8 so that important diversity learning is not lost.

> *Leadership has a harder job to do than just choose sides.*
> *It must bring sides together.*
>
> —*Jesse Jackson*

Box 10.6 Self-Assessment	**The Diversity Perceptions Scale[41]**

Directions: Respond to each item by circling the appropriate number.
1 = strongly disagree ◄———► 6 = strongly agree

1. I feel that I have been treated differently here because of my race, gender, sexual orientation, religion or age.
   1   2   3   4   5   6

2. Managers here have a track record of hiring and promoting employees objectively, regardless of their race, gender, sexual orientation, religion, or age.
   1   2   3   4   5   6

3. Managers here give feedback and evaluate employees fairly, regardless of employees' race, gender, sexual orientation, religion, age, or social background.
   1   2   3   4   5   6

4. Managers here make layoff decisions fairly, regardless of factors such as employees' race, gender, age, or social background.
   1   2   3   4   5   6

5. Managers interpret human resource policies (such as sick leave) fairly for all employees.
   1   2   3   4   5   6

6. Managers give assignments based on the skills and abilities of employees.
   1   2   3   4   5   6

7. Management here encourages the formation of employee network support groups.
   1   2   3   4   5   6

8. There is a mentoring program in use here that identifies and prepares all minority and female employees for promotion.
   1   2   3   4   5   6

9. The "old boys network" is alive and well here.
   1   2   3   4   5   6

10. The company spends enough money and time on diversity awareness and related training.
    1   2   3   4   5   6

11. Knowing more about the cultural norms of diverse groups would help me be more effective in my job.
    1   2   3   4   5   6

12. I think that diverse viewpoints add value.
    1   2   3   4   5   6

13. I believe diversity is a strategic business issue.

    1   2   3   4   5   6

14. I feel at ease with people from backgrounds different from my own.

    1   2   3   4   5   6

15. I am afraid to disagree with members of other groups for fear of being called prejudiced.

    1   2   3   4   5   6

16. Diversity issues keep some work teams here from performing to their maximum effectiveness.

    1   2   3   4   5   6

Scoring: This scale measures two dimensions—the organizational and the personal—which each contain two factors as follows:

I. Organizational dimension

    a. Organizational fairness factor (items 1–6)

    b. Organizational inclusion factor (items 7–10)

II. Personal dimension

    c. Personal diversity value factor (items 11–13)

    d. Personal comfort with diversity (items 14–16)

Reverse scores on items 1, 9, 15, and 16 (1 = 6, 2 = 5, 3 = 4, 4 = 3, 5 = 2, 6 = 1). Then add up your responses to all 16 items (maximum score 96). The higher your total score, the more positive your view of the diversity climate. Similarly, the higher your score on each of the item subsets described above, the more positive your perceptions are on that factor.

The Gender Leadership Gap: Breaking the Glass Ceiling, Avoiding the Glass Cliff, and Navigating the Labyrinth

In recent decades, the number of women occupying leadership positions has risen dramatically. In 1900, women held only 4 out of 100 managerial positions. Now females hold a little over half of all managerial and professional positions in the US workforce. Few women, however, have moved into the highest level of government or business positions. They hold 84 seats in the House of Representatives and 21 seats in the Senate. These 105 legislators represent 19.6% of the total seats in the US Congress. (Rwanda has the highest percentage of female legislators at over 64%.) At last count 18 of the 192 member states of the United Nations are headed by women. (The first female presidential nominee of a major party in the United States was defeated.) In 2016, only 20% of board members of *Fortune* 500 companies were women and only 21 of the *Fortune* 500 companies had a female CEO.[42] Many have called this barrier to top-level leadership roles *the glass ceiling*.[43] The argument is that while women are represented more proportionately at lower levels of leadership, there is a barrier to women's advancement to higher-level leadership positions. Other researchers point out that those women who break the glass ceiling face another challenge—*the glass cliff*. Top women leaders often fill highly precarious positions (cliffs) that have a high risk of failure, such as managing organizations in crisis. (See box 10.7 for more information on what researchers have discovered about glass cliffs and how organizations can help women avoid them.)

Alice Eagly and Linda Carli propose a different metaphor instead—*the labyrinth*. As they explain:

> With continuing change, the obstacles that women face have become more surmountable, at least by some women some of the time. Paths to the top exist, and some women find them. The successful routes can be difficult to discover, however, and therefore we label these circuitous paths a labyrinth.[44]

The glass ceiling metaphor and related metaphors like the glass door and glass cliff remain popular. However, the labyrinth may be a more accurate depiction of the challenges that most women face. The existence of the gender leadership gap, and the labyrinth it creates for women, raises three significant questions: (1) Are there differences in how males and females lead? (And do women make better leaders?) (2) What factors hinder the emergence of women as leaders? (3) Can the gender leadership gap be narrowed? To answer these questions, we'll begin by taking a look at what researchers have discovered about female and male leadership behavior.

Box 10.7 Research Highlight	**Working on the Edge of the Glass Cliff[45]**

British researchers Michelle Ryan and Alexander Haslam are credited with identifying the glass cliff. They initially studied the biggest 100 companies on the London Stock Exchange and found that women were more likely to be appointed to the boards of poor-performing companies. They also discovered that women were more likely to be selected to run for hard-to-win Parliamentary seats. Subsequent experiments confirmed the existence of a "think crisis-think female" association. Respondents consistently chose the woman over the man when asked to select a leader for a troubled organization, believing that the qualities associated with the female stereotype—intuition, awareness of the feelings of others—are better suited for crisis situations. On the other hand, subjects preferred a male leader for a stable organization, believing that the stereotypical qualities of men—self-confidence, assertiveness—are better suited for successful companies.

Political commentators, journalists, and others point to a number of prominent examples of female leaders who appear to be teetering on the edge of glass cliffs. Marissa Mayer at Yahoo and Meg Whitman at Hewlett Packard were selected to head troubled companies. British Prime Minister Theresa May assumed her position following the country's decision to leave the European Union, a vote that generated a lot of tension and uncertainty. Two male contenders (former Prime Minister David Cameron who called for the Brexit vote and Boris Johnson who led the anti-EU forces) declined to run for the post.

Working on the glass cliff is dangerous for women. The risks are great and if the group fails, the female leader is likely to get the blame, even if the failure was caused by events that took place long before she came onto the scene. Organizations can lessen the dangers by providing support networks, getting women the information they need, and acknowledging their efforts. Groups can also provide more leadership opportunities for females—in stable situations as well as perilous ones. Redefining what it means to be an ideal leader will lessen the strength of the think crisis-think female association. If the ideal organizational leader is defined as empathetic, collaborative, and relational (stereotypical attributes of women), then women are more likely to be selected for all types of leadership roles, not just high risk ones.

Male and Female Leadership Behavior: Is There a Difference? (And Do Women Make Better Leaders?)

There has been much debate about whether there are differences between male and female leadership behaviors and whether, because of these differences, women make more effective leaders. Judy Rosener, for instance, argues that female leaders are more likely to use an interactive style of leadership that encourages participation, shares power and information, and enhances the self-worth of others.[46] These differences, Rosener contends, make women better leaders who are more interpersonally skilled and empowering.

To determine if there really is a difference between how men and women lead, Eagly and her colleagues used a statistical process called meta-analysis. In meta-analysis, investigators combine the results of many different studies to identify patterns of findings. Eagly and her colleagues report:[47]

- Men are more likely to emerge as leaders in short-term groups and in task-oriented teams; women are more likely to emerge as social leaders in small groups.

- Male leaders tend to adopt a more task-oriented style based on gender norms while female leaders tend to have a more interpersonally oriented style.

- Women adopt a more participative or democratic leadership style than men, reflecting a greater openness to collaboration and sharing power. When in top positions, though, women very often lead like their male counterparts by acting in a more autocratic fashion.

- The differences between male-female leadership styles, while present, are small. Nonetheless, even small differences can have a significant cumulative impact on perceptions and behaviors when enacted on a daily basis in organizational settings.

- Male and female leaders are rated as equally effective across organizational and laboratory studies. However, men are rated as more effective in roles defined as "masculine" (the military, for example) while women were rated as more effective in less masculine roles, such as in the fields of education and social service.

- Females are slightly more likely to engage in transformational leadership behaviors, specifically by providing individualized consideration (focusing on the needs of individual followers). They are also more likely to reward performance. Men are more likely to be laissez-faire leaders who are uninvolved and let problems reach a critical state. They also demonstrate a greater tendency to engage in management by exception, punishing those who fail to meet standards.

In sum, the research suggests that there are small differences in male and female leadership behaviors. Because there is significant overlap between styles between women and men, it is hard to predict how a leader will behave solely based on gender. Evidence does suggest, however, that females have the potential to be better leaders because they are more likely to engage in transformational leadership behaviors as well as to collaborate and share power.

Creating the Gap

The gender leadership gap is the product of the obstacles to diversity identified earlier in this chapter. One way to visualize the development of the gender leadership gap is to think of women and men competing against each other on a track. Both are running in a 440-yard race. However, women run the 440 hurdles while men run the 440 dash. With each hurdle, more women fall behind, and the gap between male and female leadership aspirants widens. These hurdles have eliminated most of the female competitors by the time both contenders reach the finish line. Common hurdles include (1) denying women experience in important business functions like operations, manufacturing, or marketing; (2) failure to receive mentoring and performance-based feedback; (3) family demands; (4) fear of powerful women; (5) old boy networks that exclude women; (6) discrimination against females; (7) social isolation; and (8) stereotyping.[48]

Of all the barriers to diversity, stereotyping has the greatest negative impact on female leaders. Gender stereotypes are based on cultural definitions of what it means to be male or female. In the United States (which ranks toward the masculine end of Hofstede's masculine-feminine typology), masculine characteristics are equated with strength, aggression, ambition, independence, stoicism, and rationality. Feminine characteristics are associated with sensitivity to the needs of others, concern for family and relationships, emotionality, and nurturing. Gender expectations are communicated to us from the moment we're born. Girl babies are dressed in pink, boy babies in blue. Parents engage in more rough-and-tumble play with their toddler sons than with their toddler daughters. Boys are encouraged to engage in adventurous activities and to avoid tears while girls are encouraged to be careful, to share, and to look pretty.

These expectations shape the roles we play in society. Despite a recent shift to greater role flexibility, women remain the primary caregivers (in a dual-career family, for instance, the mother is the parent who generally leaves work to pick up a sick child). Men are still considered the primary breadwinners and are most likely to build their identities around their careers.

Unfortunately, cultural expectations work against women who aspire to leadership. Not only are women and men viewed in different ways, but those characteristics defined as masculine are given higher status. As a culture, we put more value on decisiveness, assertiveness, competition, and other characteristics traditionally associated with males.[49] Compounding the problem of gender bias is the notion that the prototypical leader is masculine, which has been labeled as the "think manager, think male" effect.

The damaging impact of gender typing can be seen at every step in leadership development. Many women never seriously consider becoming leaders because the process of socialization has taught them that leadership is the province of males or that some professions are open to men but not to women (the "glass door" effect). Negative stereotypes and discrimination lower the self-confidence of some females, making them reluctant to take risks and to strive for leadership positions.[50] Because our culture highlights the nurturing role of women, most females enter service professions (teaching, nursing) or work in departments (such as human resources) that support the larger organization.[51] Female-dominated careers like clerical support, day care, and library science have less status than comparable male-dominated fields.

Women who do enter departments or professions that are overwhelmingly male, like software development, face difficulties common to all who act as token representatives of their social groups.[52] Female tokens often find themselves treated as mothers or daughters. They may turn against other women as a result of the perceived need to adopt the attitudes of the dominant male culture. There is also a more narrow range of acceptable behavior for female leaders. Women who act "too aggressive," for example, risk being criticized for behaving in an unfeminine manner.[53] (The case study in box 10.8 describes one influential female leader who is urging women to overcome self-doubts to assert themselves.)

In her book *Beyond the Double Bind*, Kathleen Jamieson explores a number of the traps and restrictions women confront. She describes a double bind as a rhetorical concept "that posits two and only two alternatives, one or both penalizing the person being offered them. . . . The strategy defines something 'fundamental' to women as incompatible with something the woman seeks—be it education, the ballot, or access to the workplace."[54] Thus, for example, it is often assumed that women cannot be both female and competent.

Other examples of double binds are plentiful. Historically, women were forbidden to speak, yet are now criticized for not producing great oratory. In the mid-

---

Box 10.8 **Case Study**	**Sheryl Sandberg: Leaning In through Tragedy[55]**

Sheryl Sandberg is out to change the way women think about work and leadership. Sandberg, the COO of Facebook and one of the world's richest corporate executives, believes that women hold themselves back, which keeps them from reaching their potential and filling top leadership roles. Instead of harboring doubts about their abilities, they need to "lean in," taking their place at the corporate table.

Sandberg first championed her ideas in a 2010 TED talk followed by a commencement address at Barnard College, where she ended her speech by urging the female graduates to close the ambition gap between men and women by overcoming their insecurities:

> . . . I hope that you—yes, you—have the ambition to lean in to your career and run the world. Because the world needs you to change it. Women all around the world are counting on you. So please ask yourself: What would I do if I weren't afraid? And then go do it.[56]

In 2013 she published a best-selling book entitled *Lean In: Women, Work, and the Will to Lead* in which Sandberg describes her own struggles with insecurities and offers advice, particularly to younger women. She acknowledges the tension between likability and success but reminds readers that they can't please everyone. For example, like men, women should not settle for the first offer but negotiate for better terms. (She admits that when she left Google for Facebook she had to be urged by her husband to strike a better deal with Facebook's Mark Zuckerberg.)

Sandberg cautions females to not "leave before you leave" by turning down attractive job assignments for fear that a future marriage or children will interfere. (Those issues may never

(continued)

arise or can be dealt with later.) She encourages women to be careful in their selection of a life partner and then to truly partner with that individual, sharing household and child-rearing duties. Sandberg describes career paths as a "jungle gym, not a ladder," noting that there are many different directions to the top of the jungle gym—sideways, downwards, on, off, and up. But whatever direction they choose, women should be willing to take risks and apply for promotions. Hoping to create a movement, Sandberg founded the Lean In organization to promote women's peer groups. (There are 30,000 such groups in 154 countries according to the LeanIn.org website.) A related organization—Lean In Together—encourages men to share domestic duties and to support their female partners and colleagues.

Sandberg's Lean In effort has generated significant pushback. Critics point out that her advice is impractical for disadvantaged women (the poor and single moms, for example). They often don't have supportive partners and may lose their low-wage jobs if they try to negotiate with their bosses. As a privileged woman, Sandberg can hire household help if needed, and arrange her work hours to be with her children. Disadvantaged women cannot. Others resent the fact that she appears to be blaming females for their failure to move into leadership positions. Feminists claim that Sandberg is offering self-help advice that doesn't address the fact that corporations are patriarchal systems dominated by males who discriminate against women. Improving the standing of a few women at the top won't necessarily "trickle down" to help women at lower levels of the organization.

In 2015 Sandberg's husband, Survey Monkey CEO Dave Goldberg, died suddenly of cardiac arrest. Sandberg admits that becoming a single mother made her realize that she wasn't as sensitive to the needs of single moms as she should have been when writing her book. She notes that losing her husband helped her find "deeper gratitude" for friends, family, and children. As a result of the tragedy, she started a new initiative called Option B, which is designed to help grieving families. The name for the group comes from an incident Sandberg described to Berkeley graduates a year after Dave's death.

> A few weeks after Dave died, I was talking to my friend Phil about a father-son activity that Dave was not here to do. We came up with a plan to fill in for Dave. I cried to him, "But I want Dave." Phil put his arm around me and said, "Option A is not available. So let's just kick the s—out of option B."[57]

Sandberg has dedicated a significant portion of her wealth (estimated at $1.2 billion) to both Lean In and Option B. She contributed $110 million in Facebook stock in honor of her husband to support both organizations as well as anti-poverty groups. She has pledged to give away at least half of her fortune upon her death.

Discussion Questions

1. Do you think doubts and insecurities are keeping women from seeking leadership roles? Do you think men harbor some of the same doubts?

2. How can women be encouraged to "lean in?" How can men "lean in together" with their partners and colleagues?

3. Do you agree with some or all of the advice she offers to female readers? Why or why not?

4. Can disadvantaged women take her advice?

5. Do you think that Sandberg is blaming women when the blame should focus on men and the systems they have created?

6. Does the fact that Sandberg suffered a personal tragedy change the way that you view her as a leader and the counsel she gives to others?

7. What needs do grieving families have that Option B might meet?

twentieth century (and continuing in moderated form), the trap was that women could choose either parenting or intellectual/economic pursuits. Discussions of similarities and/or differences between men and women use men as the standard, skewing the discussion from the start or, at a minimum, assuming that a "gain" for one "side" is a "loss" for the other. Jamieson points out that the double bind is "durable, but not indestructible."[58] She urges us to examine the binds as rhetorical forms to understand them, to manipulate them, and then to dismantle them.

> *The test of whether or not you can hold a job*
> *should not be the arrangement of your chromosomes.*
>
> —*Bella Abzug*

Narrowing the Gap

The best practices for fostering diversity outlined earlier in this chapter address many of the barriers generated by negative gender stereotypes. Aggressive recruitment, greater accountability for developing female leaders, formation of advocacy groups, mentorship, and executive development programs can help bridge the gender leadership gap. At the individual level, Alice Eagly and Linda Carli suggest two key principles that are critical in allowing women to ease their route through the labyrinth—thus narrowing the gap.[59] First, women must *blend agency with communion.* As Eagly and Carli explain, most people believe that leaders should be agentic— tough, decisive, and action oriented. Similarly, women are often viewed as being more communal—warm, friendly, and caring. These two perceptions create a conflict for female leaders. Nice, friendly female leaders may be criticized for not being assertive and decisive enough while strong, action-oriented female leaders may seem too harsh. For women, establishing both agency and communion can be challenging. To succeed in these dual demands, a woman must first establish an exceptional level of competence. This competence can be demonstrated, for example, by mastering job-relevant knowledge or being highly prepared for meetings. As Eagly and Carli suggest, although it isn't fair, women often need to be exceptionally good to be credited with the abilities of less-competent men. Once competence is established, a woman can finesse the agency/communion conflict by combining assertive task behavior with kindness, niceness, and helpfulness. Secondly, Eagly and Carli note that it is critical for women to *build social capital.* Those who create social capital through good relationships with colleagues, both within and outside their organization, are more likely to rise to positions of authority. This social capital can be earned through a variety of means, including developing informal relationships, participating in social networks, and establishing a mentor/protégé relationship.

British linguist Judith Baxter argues that the use of language is the key to overcoming barriers blocking women from their career objectives.[60] She introduces individual linguistic strategies that senior women can use to achieve their goals as well as tactics that corporations and other organizations can employ to counter negative evaluations of women. Females are much more likely to succeed when their organizations support their efforts.

Baxter encourages senior female leaders to become role models for their junior women colleagues. As role models, they need to demonstrate the following:

- *Doing authority.* Authority can be demonstrated in a variety of ways from demonstrating "a light touch to strong control." Female leaders need to avoid the stereotypical command style of the male leader and the co-cooperative, consensual strategies of the stereotypically female leader. Instead, they need to be flexible, adopting their tactics to the situation. To enact authority, women also need to develop their public voice by giving speeches (see chapter 9) and leading meetings and training sessions. Such activities help the female leader get noticed and recognized, providing "linguistic visibility." In addition, women should be skilled using both cold and warm language. Cold authority is based on rank and involves giving instructions, telling people what to do and pointing out misunderstandings or errors. This type of speech gains respect but can be potentially risky for women who are expected to be more supportive. In contrast, warm authority, which is expressed through a friendly manner, politeness, and indirect commands, fosters inclusion and encourages team ownership.

- *Doing politeness.* Politeness lets people go about their tasks without interference and also meets others' needs for approval and recognition. There are "cold" and "warm" kinds of politeness just as there are cold and warm expressions of authority. Cool politeness, such as using proper titles and saying please and thank you, are important to use in more formal settings. These formal terms signal respect for female leaders and their respect for others. Warm politeness expresses genuine interest in others and demonstrates respect for their viewpoints. Warm politeness is an effective way of generating support for collective projects.

- *Doing humor.* Humor performs a number of functions in the workplace, including releasing tension, promoting group solidarity, and providing transitions. Humor is essential for leaders because it establishes what employees have in common while downplaying status differences. Humor interacts with both authority and politeness. It can lessen the sting of commands and criticism and allow subordinates to challenge their leaders without appearing too direct. Humor can soften remarks that might appear impolite— blunt, personal, critical. Females (and males) should be careful to avoid negative humor like teasing and sarcasm, which can hurt others. Instead, use humor that fosters good relationships. Such humor includes telling funny stories or anecdotes, and using puns and other forms of wordplay.

Baxter encourages corporations to support the attempts of senior female leaders to act as role models by adopting the following tactics, which are specifically designed to challenge discrimination against women:

- *Contesting use of sexist language.* Adopt the use of nonsexist language. For example, replace "he" with "he/she" or substitute "Ms." for "Miss" or "Mrs." Use gender-neutral terms for occupations (chairperson). Policies encouraging such nonsexist speech are already in place at many public institutions. Despite being derided as "politically correct," these guidelines have raised awareness that words can reinforce stereotypes.

- *Contesting use of terms to describe women.* Draw attention to how women are often referred to in negative terms like tough, mean, difficult, shrill, hysterical, moody, or lesbian. Encourage corporate communication personnel to be alert to gendered speech. In one company newsletter, for example, the headline "the girls on the front desk" made the women seem trivial when a picture on the same page described a group of male employees as "men with a mission."

- *Contesting masculinized use of metaphors.* War/fighting metaphors are common in the business context. Company leaders speak of "rallying the troops" to go to "battle" against their corporate "enemies." Since war has traditionally been considered a masculine activity, repeated use of war imagery reinforces the notion that leaders are males and alienates females. Introduce alternative, nonviolent metaphors instead. For instance, replace war talk with language associated with dancing. The dance metaphor highlights the fact that business can be a collaborative activity.

- *Contesting the use of generalizations.* Challenge seemingly harmless statements such as "Like all men, he never listens" or "She's an emotional female." Such language builds and reinforces the stereotypes that serve as the primary barrier to women leaders. Encourage members to be alert to such statements and address the effects of these generalizations in training sessions. Light-hearted humor can also be used to draw attention to sweeping gender-based statements.

- *Contesting gossip and "mean talk."* Encourage women (who may have more difficulty accepting directive leadership from other women) to be supportive of the efforts of female leaders, avoiding gossip or other negative statements. Contest the myths and stereotypes of top female leaders as tough or scary by relying on evidence, not hearsay.

If you want it said, ask a man. If you want it done, ask a woman.
—*Margaret Thatcher*

Kathleen Kelley Reardon also urges women to challenge communication patterns that keep females from advancing to the top levels of many organizations.[61] She notes that men are more comfortable with self-promotion, verbal sparring, and the language of team sports. The contrasting male/female communication styles have created a number of dysfunctional communication patterns (DCPs) that belittle women and reinforce male bias. Common DCPs include (1) excluding women from the decision-making process; (2) dismissing their contributions by interrupting, talking over, or ignoring ideas expressed; (3) retaliation based on male fear of female competence; and (4) patronizing responses such as treating female participation as unimportant or as an afterthought. Reardon encourages

---

Box 10.9 Case Study	**Downsizing at Simtek[62]**

Karen Jacobs-McKinney is the manager of a group of 10 sales representatives at Simtek, a large computer components manufacturer. The company was founded by President and CEO John Simmons and has grown from a small, privately held start-up company to a publicly held corporation.

Simtek has been known for fair treatment of its nonunion employees and for employee relations policies that are above average. Pay and benefits are in the top fourth of the industry. The only major criticism leveled at Simtek was a charge that the company was not committed to its stated pro-diversity policy. Of its 400 employees, women and minorities represent less than 2%.

Jacobs-McKinney was the first woman of color hired by Simtek and is the only female manager in the company. She has been employed for five years and has worked very hard to be recognized as a fair and capable manager in a white, male-dominated organization. Karen has just been faced with an extremely difficult task. Her immediate supervisor has told her that Simtek is reengineering and her unit will have to downsize by two or three people. There will be a moderate severance package. Karen has to decide who will be released. She has both flexibility and responsibility for selecting among employees who have roughly equal work histories, skills, and potential.

The employees in Ms. Jacobs-McKinney's unit consist of seven white males, one white female, one African American male, and one Asian American female. When she compares the work performance of the 10, she finds that all have performed equally well. All have similar knowledge of the products, and their sales levels are also very similar. The white female, the African American male, and the Asian American female have all been hired in the past two years in an effort to increase diversity within the organization. The white males have all been employed there at least five years. If Karen relies on seniority to determine who should be laid off, then the department will lose all of the diversity that the company has tried to increase in the past two years. However, she also knows that if she decides to keep any of the new employees, then most likely she will be involved with the company in a reverse discrimination suit. White males have threatened legal action, complaining that Simtek now hires almost exclusively women and minorities.

The personnel manager has just called Karen requesting the names of the employees who will be terminated. She has one week to decide what to do.

Discussion Questions

1. What will be the likely impact if the three minority employees are terminated?

2. What will be the likely impact if more senior employees are terminated?

3. What criteria should Karen use in making her decision?

4. Who should Karen terminate? Why?

5. How should Karen announce her decision to those who are laid off? How should she explain her decision to others in the department?

6. Can you think of other leaders and organizations that have faced similar decisions? How did they respond? What happened as a result of their choices?

women managers (who often opt for silence) to confront these patterns head on. They should draw attention to the fact that they've been excluded from important meetings, claim credit for good proposals, challenge retaliatory statements, refuse to honor patronizing comments, and so on.

Finally, keep in mind that leaders perceived as transformational, whether male or female, exhibit gender balance—displaying characteristics traditionally regarded as masculine and feminine. Transformational leaders are emotional and nurturing as well as independent and ambitious—cooperative as well as competitive. The most effective leaders narrow the gender gap by combining the talents traditionally thought of as masculine and feminine to create a well-balanced leadership style.

> *The new leader is a facilitator, not an order giver.*
> —*John Naisbitt*

∿ CHAPTER TAKEAWAYS

- To be an effective organizational leader in an increasingly global society, you will need to manage diversity. Managing diversity means taking advantage of a diverse labor force while coping with the problems that arise when people of different backgrounds work together. The goal of diversity management is to help all employees reach their full potential.

- Culture refers to the total way of life of a group of people. Key cultural elements include communication patterns, patterns of relationships, formal organizations, artifacts, collective wisdom, and external environment.

- As human (symbolic) creations, cultures vary widely. However, recognizing cultural commonalities can help you respond to the needs of diverse groups.

- In high-context cultures, members prefer indirect or covert messages and determine meaning based largely on the context or setting. In low-context cultures, members communicate through overt messages and embed much more information in the language used to construct the message.

- Hofstede identified five values dimensions to analyze cultures: power distance (how societies deal with inequities); individualism-collectivism (the relative emphasis on the individual or the group); masculinity-femininity (the definition and differentiation of sex roles); uncertainty avoidance (the extent to which people feel uncomfortable in unstructured situations); and long-term–short-term orientation (the extent to which societies sacrifice immediate gratification).

- The GLOBE studies produced a cultural classification system consisting of Hofstede's five dimensions along with assertiveness, future orientation, performance orientation, and humane orientation.

- Cultural intelligence is the ability to perform effectively in cross-cultural settings and consists of four dimensions: metacognitive CQ, cognitive CQ, motivational CQ, and behavioral CQ. You can develop your CQ though both long-term and short-term overseas experiences, global courses, and interactions with those from other cultures taking courses at your college or university.

- Successful leaders recognize and respond to cultural differences, adapting their behaviors to meet cultural expectations. They also strive for cultural synergy. In cultural synergy, decision makers draw on the diversity of the group and cultural awareness to produce and implement a better-than-expected solution.

- The benefits of fostering diversity include cost savings, improved resource acquisition and utilization, greater market share, better decision making, higher creativity, and enhanced organizational performance.

- Obstacles to diversity operate at the personal, group, and institutional levels. Individuals engage in prejudice, discrimination, stereotyping, and perceptual bias. Group members often suffer from ethnocentrism and experience conflicts based on cultural differences. Institutions sponsor practices that limit the progress of women and minorities.

- Organization-wide strategies that promote diversity include: (1) getting the buy-in of leadership; (2) using data to drive diversity decisions; (3) diversity education; (4) aligning systems with diversity goals; and (5) follow-up to ensure accountability and progress.

- While women are represented more proportionately at lower levels of leadership, there is a barrier to women's advancement to, and success in, high-level leadership positions. This barrier has been described as the glass ceiling, the glass cliff, and the labyrinth.

- Evidence suggests that there are small differences in how men and women lead and that women are slightly more likely to exhibit transformational leadership behaviors.

- Two key principles are critical in allowing women to ease their route through the labyrinth. First, women must blend agency with communion. Second, it is critical for women to build social capital.

- Language strategies are key to overcoming barriers blocking women from their career objectives. Senior female leaders can become role models for junior women by demonstrating how to do authority, politeness, and humor. Organizations can support their efforts by contesting: the use of sexist language, negative terms used to describe women, the use of masculine metaphors, the use of gender generalizations, and gossip. As a woman, challenge dysfunctional communication patterns like being excluded from the decision-making process and having your contributions dismissed.

∽ APPLICATION EXERCISES

1. In a research paper, compare and contrast the cultural classification systems described in the chapter with others not mentioned in the text. What common

themes and differences do you note? What generalizations can you draw? How do your conclusions relate to leaders and followers?

2. Review the GLOBE research. Take a particular culture (or set of cultures) you are familiar with and analyze how effectively you believe the GLOBE research captures the nuances of this culture(s). What advice would you give to a leader from another society assigned to work in this culture? Share your reactions in class.

3. What does your cultural tradition contribute to our understanding of the theory and practice of leadership?

4. Develop a strategy for increasing your cultural intelligence (CQ) based on your response to the Cultural Intelligence assessment in box 10.3.

5. Create your own list of organizational practices that serve as barriers to diversity either on your own or in a small group. Share your findings with the rest of the class.

6. Share your scores from the Diversity Perceptions Scale in box 10.6 with a partner or in a small group. What do your responses reveal about your perceptions of your organization's fairness and inclusiveness? The value you put on diversity and your comfort with diversity issues in your organization? How do your answers compare with those of your partner or other members of the group?

7. Analyze the current diversity efforts of your college or work organization. What is the composition of the membership? The surrounding area? What steps have been taken to promote diversity? How effective have they been? Write up your findings.

8. Divide into debate teams and argue for or against each of the assertions listed below. Your instructor will determine the debate format.
   • Prejudice and discrimination are a natural part of the human condition.
   • Leaders should focus on cultural similarities instead of on cultural differences.
   • Women make better leaders than men.
   • Females are less ambitious than males.
   • Gender stereotypes will change significantly in the next 10 years.

9. Interview a successful female leader. Share your findings with the rest of the class.

10. Discuss whether you believe the challenges women face in obtaining top-level leadership roles are best described by the metaphor of the glass ceiling/glass cliff or the labyrinth.

⌒ CULTURAL CONNECTIONS: THE NOT SO UNIVERSAL LANGUAGE OF SPORTS[63]

American business executives (particularly male executives) are in love with sports jargon. They lace their speech with terms from baseball, football, basketball, and other sports. Here are some of the sports phrases used by US corporate leaders and what they mean in the business setting:

- *Step up to the plate.* Baseball: take your turn at bat, often in an important situation. Business: confront a problem; make a critical decision.
- *Ducks on the pond.* Baseball: runners on base. Business: a situation where the organization has a good chance at succeeding.
- *Curve.* Baseball: A pitch that breaks before it gets to the plate. Business: anything that happens that is unexpected.
- *All the bases covered.* Baseball: all fielders in the right position to get an out. Business: being prepared for every contingency.
- *Red zone selling.* Football: being inside the opponent's 20-yard line. Business: stakes get higher as the sale is about to close.
- *Hail Mary pass.* Football: desperate, last-second pass with little chance of being completed. Business: a desperate attempt to turn a situation around with little chance of success.
- *Calling an audible.* Football: quarterback changing the play at the line of scrimmage. Business: changing an agenda or plan at the last minute.
- *Jump ball scenario.* Basketball: throwing the ball up between two players to determine possession. Business: neither side has an advantage.
- *Slam dunk.* Basketball: a shot in which a player thrusts the ball forcefully down through the basket. Business: a can't-miss opportunity.
- *Under par.* Golf: scoring better than average. Business: exceeding the target.

While such jargon may make sense to many American executives, it confuses their counterparts from other cultures (India, Europe, Great Britain) where these sports are not played and can confuse their coworkers from the US who aren't as interested in athletics. On the other hand, sports terminology from other nations can puzzle US residents. Latin Americans may talk about "parar la pelota" (or "stop the ball") from soccer, which refers to pausing and taking stock before the next move. The use of sports metaphors leads to misunderstanding and may slow down the communication process. (One British executive reports that he spent 45 minutes trying to explain cricket terms like "sticky wicket" and "hitting a six" to his American audience without success.) Further, leaders in some nations, like the Czech Republic, apparently don't use sports jargon in business.

American leaders and their colleagues from other nations should limit the use of sports terminology. Such jargon should only be used with cross-cultural audiences who share the same sports (baseball is popular in Japan and the United States, for instance), and when sports language is considered appropriate for the business context. Even then, they ought to refrain from such talk if coworkers from their own country (female or male) are not interested in athletics.

∼ LEADERSHIP ON THE BIG SCREEN: *THE HUNDRED-FOOT JOURNEY*

Starring: Manish Dayal, Helen Mirren, Om Pirie, Charlotte Le Bon

Rating: PG for brief scenes of violence

Synopsis: After their restaurant is burned down in Mumbai, India, the Kardam family, led by patriarch Papa Kardam (played by Pirie), decides to introduce Indian cooking to a small town in France. Problem is, their new location is right across the road (a hundred feet away) from a traditional upscale French restaurant run by Madame Mallory (Mirren). Madame does her best to run her new competition out of town and soon a cross-cultural "food war" breaks out, culminating in a graffiti and arson attack on the Kardams' property. Mirren fires the chef responsible for the fire and scrubs off the anti-immigrant slogans herself. Young Hasan Kardam (Dayal), who has a unique gift for cooking, agrees to work at Madame's restaurant to reduce hostilities and to expand his knowledge of French food. His culinary genius leads to an additional Michelin star rating for the restaurant and a job offer from a top dining spot in Paris. There, Hasan becomes one of the country's best known chefs, known for fusing Indian and French flavors. He then decides to return home to reunite with his family, Madame Mallory, and Marguerite, a fellow chef and love interest.

Chapter Links: collectivism, individualism, power distance, assertiveness, long-term orientation, performance orientation, stereotypes, ethnocentrism, cultural synergy

Ethical Leadership and Followership

Most people wish to be good, but not all of the time.

—George Orwell

The Importance of Ethics

As we have suggested throughout this book, effective leadership is the product of the creation and delivery of inspiring and compelling messages. Humans, unlike other species, are capable of shaping reality through the manipulation of symbols. We do not passively react but rather *act* to change the world around us.

The power of human communication means that the question of ethics, in the words of Gerald Miller, is "inextricably bound up with every instance of human communication."[1] Ethics refer to standards of moral conduct, to judgments about whether human behavior is right or wrong.[2] The investigation of ethics is critical when focusing on leadership. A leader communicates a plan of action to his or her followers. The ethical implications of a leader's plans must be considered, since the exercise of unethical leadership can have devastating results. If you consider, for example, the negative impact of leaders such as Adolph Hitler and Joseph Stalin, you begin to appreciate the importance of the relationship between leadership and ethics.

Whether a leader is guiding a problem-solving group, a small business, a multimillion-dollar organization, or a national government, he or she exerts significant influence. Leaders must weigh the impact they have on their followers as well as on others external to the group, organization, or society.

Educational writer and consultant Parker Palmer introduces a powerful metaphor to highlight the importance of leadership ethics and to dramatize the difference between moral and immoral leadership. According to Palmer, the distinction between ethical and unethical leaders is as sharp as the contrast between light and darkness, between heaven and hell.

> A leader is a person who has an unusual degree of power to create the conditions under which other people must live and move and have their being—conditions that can be either as illuminating as heaven or as shadowy as hell. A leader must take special responsibility for what's going on inside his or her own self, inside his or her consciousness, lest the act of leadership create more harm than good.[3]

The Ethical Challenges of Leadership: Casting Light or Shadow

Functioning as a leader means taking on a unique set of ethical challenges in addition to a set of tasks and expectations. These dilemmas involve issues of information, responsibility, power, privilege, loyalty, and consistency. How leaders respond to these ethical challenges will determine if they cast more light than shadow.[4]

The Challenge of Information Management

Leaders typically have access to more information than do followers. They participate in decision-making groups, receive financial data, keep personnel files, network with managers from other units, and so on. Being "in the know" raises a number of complicated ethical dilemmas. One such dilemma is deciding whether or not to tell the truth. Sissela Bok, in her book *Lying: Moral Choice in Public and Private Life*, defines lies as messages designed to make others believe what we ourselves don't believe.[5] We have all probably told a lie (even if it was merely "little" or "white"). Leaders also practice deception, either to further their own interests or to promote the interests of the group. Only recently did we learn that former President Nixon undermined Vietnam War peace talks in order to better his chances of being elected. Yahoo CEO Scott Thompson stepped down after being accused of falsifying his résumé. NBC evening news anchor Brian Williams lost his post after falsely claiming that the helicopter he was riding in had nearly been shot down while covering the war in Iraq. Officials at the Veterans Administration altered wait lists to cover up the fact that patients weren't getting timely care.[6]

Most ethical experts agree that lying is wrong because it (1) damages the character of the liar by supplanting such virtues as honesty and consistency; and (2) damages organizational performance by destroying trust, lowering employee job satisfaction, driving out ethical workers, undermining the group's reputation, and corrupting the flow of information required for making decisions and coordinating activities.[7] However, there appear to be justified exceptions to the adage that states that honesty is the best policy. For example, we admire informants who infiltrate terrorist cells or criminal gangs. Reporters who go underground to uncover fraud and corruption win journalism awards.

Determining whether to tell or conceal the truth is not the only dilemma surrounding access to data. Leaders also must choose when to release information and to whom and whether to reveal that they possess important knowledge. Law enforcement officials wrestle with both these issues when solving major crimes. Citizens have a right to know what their officials are doing, and tips from the public are instrumental in bringing many offenders to justice. However, releasing too much information too soon can jeopardize cases by alerting perpetrators to hide incriminating evidence. Revealing details about the crime to the media disperses knowledge previously known only to the perpetrator—and investigators lose one of their tools for assessing guilt.

How leaders get information can be a concern too. For example, civil libertarians oppose antiterrorism measures like eavesdropping on conversations between suspected terrorists and their lawyers and opening the mail of US citizens. Watchdog agencies accuse the operators of children's apps and websites of collecting kids' names and email addresses and then sharing that information with third parties. Some employers secretly monitor worker behavior through hidden video cameras and recording systems as well as through spyware that records computer keystrokes. More law enforcement officers are wearing body cameras in order to increase transparency and accountability; but police video could violate the privacy of civilians who don't want to be recorded.

When it comes to the challenge of information management, leaders cast more shadow than light when they:

- lie, particularly for selfish ends
- use information solely for personal benefit
- deny having knowledge that is in their possession
- gather data in a way that violates privacy rights
- withhold information that followers legitimately need
- share information with the wrong people
- put followers in moral binds by insisting that they withhold information that others have a right to know

The Challenge of Responsibility

Followers are largely responsible for their own actions, but leaders are held accountable for the actions of others. They must answer for the performance of the entire group, whether an academic department, a business, a nonprofit, a government agency, or a sports franchise. This challenge is particularly important given the fact that leaders set the ethical tone for an entire organization. The commitment of senior-level executives determines whether or not a corporation takes its moral responsibilities seriously. To provide ethical leadership, executives must act as moral persons and as moral managers. As moral managers, they behave ethically while carrying out their leadership duties. They are viewed as honest, concerned, and principled individuals who make fair decisions. As moral managers, they promote ethical conduct in followers by modeling desired behavior, putting equitable policies in place, and reinforcing moral behavior through rewards and punishments (ethical performance becomes part of evaluation and promotion decisions, for example).[8]

While few would disagree with the fact that leaders are responsible for the actions of followers, determining the extent of a leader's responsibility is far from easy (see box 11.1). For example: Can we hold the editor of a school newspaper responsible for the racist comments of a guest writer? Are university administrators liable for what faculty members say off campus? Should clothing manufacturers be held accountable for working conditions in overseas factories run by subcontractors? Can we blame professional football coaches when their players commit crimes on their days off or during the off-season? Should military officers receive the same or harsher penalties when their subordinates are punished for following their orders? Answers to these questions can vary depending on the particular situation. Nonetheless, there are some general expectations of leaders. Responsible leaders:

- acknowledge and try to correct ethical problems
- admit that they have duties to followers
- promote ethical standards and behaviors
- take responsibility for the consequences of their orders and actions
- take reasonable steps to prevent crimes and other abuses by followers
- hold themselves to the same standards as their followers

Box 11.1 Case Study	**Uber Drivers: Independent Contractors or Employees?[9]**

Uber, the ride-hailing service, has the dubious distinction of being sued more often than any other start-up valued at $10 billion or more, which includes such other firms as Snapchat, SpaceX, Pinterest, and Dropbox. A great many of the Uber lawsuits allege that drivers should be treated as employees. The company currently treats them as independent contractors, noting that they use their own vehicles, set their own hours, have the right to turn down rides, and can also drive for other ride-sharing apps. Further, Uber officials point to the fact that nearly 90% of its drivers drive for the company because "they love being their own boss." Being classified as employees would take away their flexibility.

Treating drivers as contractors means that the ride-sharing platform doesn't have to pay minimum wage or overtime, reimburse business expenses, provide unemployment benefits, or to obey federal law that requires companies to provide 60-day notice to employees when closing a business enterprise. (Both Uber and its competitor Lyft are being sued for failing to provide such notice when they pulled out of Austin, Texas.) Uber's business model keeps costs down, which helps account for its popularity. Using the service is 25–50% cheaper than taking a taxi or limo. Redefining drivers as employees would raise fares for riders.

The largest employment-classification suit was brought on behalf of 350,000 drivers in California and Massachusetts. It came after an Uber driver filed a successful wage complaint with the California Labor Commissioner. The Commissioner ruled that drivers should be considered employees because they are essential to Uber's core business and noted that the firm supplies iPhones to drivers, closely monitors their performance, and deactivates inactive accounts. Uber settled the California and Massachusetts suit for $84 million (for $100 million if the firm goes public). Under the agreement, the drivers would remain independent contractors. However, claimants would receive $8,000 or more depending on miles driven and, in the future, can solicit tips. They no longer could be terminated without warning and can appeal suspensions. As soon as this settlement was announced, however, additional employment lawsuits were filed.

Uber's battle over the status of its workers could have far-reaching implications, with the outcome setting the precedent for the millions of workers in the gig or sharing economy. Gig economy jobs in delivery, transportation, rental, and other businesses are being created faster than traditional payroll jobs. According to one estimate, 40% of American workers will be independent contractors by 2020, unless the courts rule otherwise.

Discussion Questions

1. If you drove for Uber, would you want to be classified as an independent contractor or as an employee? Why?

2. Would you be willing to pay more for Uber rides if the company is forced to treat drivers as employees?

3. Are leaders at Uber shirking their responsibilities to drivers by treating them as independent contractors instead of employees? Are leaders at other companies in the gig economy doing the same?

4. What rights should Uber drivers have if they remain independent contractors? What rights do other workers have in the sharing economy if they remain independent contractors?

5. Can companies in the gig economy survive if they must operate under the traditional employee-employer model?

6. If you were a judge or a labor commissioner, would you rule that Uber drivers are contractors or employees? What would you base your decision on?

The Challenge of Power

A leader must decide when to employ power, what types of power to use, and how much power she or he wishes to exert over followers. These decisions have moral implications. Is it ethical, for instance, to use power to pursue personal objectives as well as organizational goals? Is it ethical to dominate followers and demand action, or should power be distributed? Is it ethical for a leader to demand compliance when a follower has a moral objection to the leader's request? The US government, for instance, allows those with a moral objection to war to register as conscientious objectors. Those who register for military service in this category are not assigned to combat units but serve in noncombat environments, such as hospitals. What if an employee finds a particular task morally objectionable or physically dangerous? Can a leader ethically insist that a follower perform the task? Some medical practitioners, for instance, refuse to participate in the performance of certain medical procedures such as abortions, sterilization, or euthanasia. Should these practitioners be punished for their views? Of course, followers who choose not to perform certain tasks must live with the consequences of their convictions: a demotion, a narrowing of responsibility, or reassignment to another unit. Under what conditions should a leader respect a follower's right to determine his or her own behavior?

How leaders respond to ethical questions surrounding the use of power will go a long way to determining if they cast light or shadow over the lives of followers. As we noted in chapter 5, power can exert a corrupting influence over those who possess it—the greater the power, the greater the potential for abuse. Impulsive, self-centered individuals more often seize powerful positions.[10] They then wield their influence to further their own interests (like accumulating more power or wealth) at the expense of the group.

Powerful leaders frequently protect their status by attacking those they view as threats and justify their lofty positions by assuming that powerless people aren't as qualified or valuable to the organization as they are. They are tempted to use subordinates as means to achieve their ends and employ coercion to get their way.[11] Without checks and balances, those in power are free to project their inner demons on larger and larger groups. For example, Amazon CEO Jeff Bezos has a reputation for pushing employees hard, expecting them to work 80–85 hours a week and to check in via text or email on vacations and holidays. Intolerant of mistakes, he rebukes subordinates with such "Jeffisms" as: "Are you lazy or just incompetent?" "Does it surprise you that you don't know the answer to that question?" and "Why are you ruining my life?"[12] On a global scale, history's most infamous leaders—Nero, Mao, Pol Pot, Idi Amin, Saddam Hussein—used their absolute power to imprison, torture, and murder millions.

Lust for power is the most flagrant of all passions.

—*Cornelius Tacitus*

The Challenge of Privilege

Positions of leadership are associated with social and material rewards. Leaders may reap social benefits such as status, privilege, and respect, as well as material benefits such as high salaries and stock options. Most would agree that leaders deserve additional privileges because they have a broader range of responsibilities than followers, but just how far should these benefits extend? Is it ethical for a leader to take advantage of his or her position to achieve personal power or prestige? Should a leader's concern always be for the good of the collective? What should be the relative difference in pay between employees and top management? How can societies address the growing gap between the haves and have-nots?

Abuse of privilege can have far reaching consequences. In Brazil, oil company Petrobras is embroiled in a multi-billion dollar kickback scandal. Contractors funneled cash and gifts—expensive wine, yachts, prostitutes—to company officials in return for lucrative contracts and shared some of the money with political parties and elected officials. At one point Petrobras was the sixth largest corporation in the world, accounting for 10% of the country's gross domestic product. Brazilians took great pride in the company and their nation's economic growth, which was fueled in large part by Petrobras. When the scandal broke, the firm lost half of its value while helping to plunge the nation into a major recession. Brazilians felt betrayed and angry, which contributed to the ouster of Brazilian president Dilma Rousseff, former CEO of Petrobras. One prosecutor estimated that the money lost to this one corruption scheme could have lifted 10 million Brazilians out of poverty.[13]

Abuse of privilege appears to be a universal phenomenon. For instance, corporate executives in the United States often live like royalty; they are the highest paid in the world and enjoy such perks as chauffeur driven limousines, private jets, and executive dining rooms. In 2015 the median CEO pay at the nation's largest companies was $16.6 million. Average CEO pay has skyrocketed while the wages of the average worker have remained stagnant.[14] Soaring executive compensation packages might be justified if there was a consistent correlation between CEO pay and performance. There isn't.[15] To make matters worse, some failed executives have been richly rewarded. Fired Pfizer CEO Henry McKinnell received $83 million in pension benefits even though Pfizer stock declined nearly 37% during his tenure. Equifax CEO Richard Smith resigned with $18.4 million in benefits after hackers stole the private information of 143 million Americans from the firm. Wells Fargo CEO John Stumpf retired with a final payout of $133.1 million after the fake-account scandal at the bank was uncovered.[16]

When it comes to executive excess, few can match former Tyco CEO Dennis Kozlowski. Kozlowski looted money from his company to buy art for his apartment (which cost $16.8 million to buy and $3 million to renovate) and then tried to avoid paying New York state income taxes on his purchases. He also threw a lavish $2.1 million birthday party for his wife and collected such accessories as a $6,300 sewing basket, a $6,000 shower curtain, a $2,200 metal wastebasket, $2,900 coat hangers, and a $445 pin cushion.[17]

Extravagant CEO pay packages reflect a larger economic divide. The top 1% of Americans makes approximately 22% of all income. This exceeds the share made by the bottom 50% of the population. Worldwide, the richest 1% own 50% of the wealth.[18] Hope for reducing economic disparity comes from some of the world's richest leaders, however. Warren Buffett, Mark Zuckerberg, Sheryl Sandberg, Paul Allen, and Bill and Melinda Gates have pledged to give away the vast majority of their wealth to philanthropic organizations and causes.

The Challenge of Loyalty

Leaders have to balance a variety of loyalties or duties when making decisions. Officers of a publicly held corporation, for instance, must weigh their obligations to stockholders, employees, suppliers, other businesses, local communities, the societies where the company does business, and the environment. These loyalties often conflict with one another. For example, moving manufacturing jobs overseas often lowers costs and increases profits. While this decision benefits stockholders, it comes at the expense of workers, local communities, and suppliers.

Admirable leaders put the needs of others above selfish concerns. Executives at Tom's of Maine (a consumer products company) and Patagonia (see chapter 2) draw praise for giving to deserving causes, supporting local communities, and protecting the environment. In contrast, trial attorneys were criticized for keeping their suspicions about the safety of Firestone ATV tires to themselves in order to increase their chances of winning lawsuits against the company. Their silence delayed the recall of the defective tires and may have resulted in additional injuries and deaths.[19] Investment bank Goldman Sachs "bet" against its own clients. The firm hedged against the very investments it was selling customers. It then profited when its customers lost money.

Broken loyalties can also cast shadows. Employees at Enron felt betrayed by the firm's president, Kenneth Lay. He assured workers that the company was prospering even as he sold large quantities of his own stock. When the value of Enron stock evaporated, the retirement savings of many workers disappeared along with their jobs. On the other hand, well-placed loyalty can make a powerful moral statement. This happened in the case of Pee-Wee Reese, the Brooklyn Dodger who publicly demonstrated loyalty to Jackie Robinson, the first black player in the major leagues. In one particularly vivid display of support, Reese put his arm around Robinson's shoulders in front of an extremely hostile crowd in Cincinnati.[20] More recently, Chilean President Sebastián Piñera demonstrated admirable loyalty. He decided to go forward with rescue efforts for 33 trapped miners even after being told that there was only a 2% chance of finding anyone alive. "We made a commitment to look for the miners as if they were our sons," he said. "Even if there's less than one tenth of one percent chance, it's our duty to keep searching." The search paid off with all 33 miners successfully rescued after spending 69 days 2,000 feet underground.[21]

The Challenge of Consistency

Leaders deal with a variety of followers, relationships, and situations, making it difficult to behave consistently. In fact, the situational and relational approaches discussed in chapter 3 are based on the premise that a leader's behavior will vary depending on such factors as the readiness levels of followers, the nature of the task, and whether subordinates are members of the in-group or out-group. Nonetheless, acting inconsistently raises significant ethical dilemmas. Those in a leader's in-group probably have no problem with the leader's favoritism; those in the out-group probably resent the preferential treatment. Deciding when to bend the rules and for whom is also problematic. A strict policy about being on time for work, for instance, may need to be relaxed during bad weather. Some coaches let their star players skip practices to rest up for big games. Resident assistants are tempted to overlook infractions of the rules committed by friends who live on their dormitory floors.

Wrong is wrong, no matter who does it or says it.

—*Malcolm X*

Some degree of inconsistency appears inevitable, but leaders cast shadows when they appear to act arbitrarily and unfairly. Leaders should try to be equitable with followers, making exceptions only after careful thought. In addition, they need to be evenhanded in their dealings with those outside the organization. Concerns about favoritism continue to plague the US political system. "Buying" access to political officials means that those who make large campaign contributions and pay for meals and trips for lawmakers generally receive better treatment in the form of favorable legislation. The financial industry used generous contributions to convince lawmakers to loosen restrictions on banks. This enabled lenders to package mortgages into unregulated and highly risky derivatives, which helped burst the housing bubble and triggered an international financial crisis.[22] In Britain, a phone-hacking scandal, in which journalists illegally tapped into private phone messages, raised concerns about the influence of media mogul Rupert Murdoch on the country's prime ministers.[23]

Inconsistency can also arise between what a leader advocates and his or her behavior, such as when religious leaders have extramarital affairs at the same time they are urging their congregations to remain faithful to their spouses. Bill Cosby allegedly drugged and sexually assaulted women even as he chastised the African American community for its low moral standards. Josh Duggar of the reality show *19 and Counting* (which promoted religious values) admitted to molesting girls when he was a teen, being addicted to pornography, and cheating on his wife. Former Speaker of the House Dennis Hastert promoted legislation supporting stronger punishment for sex crimes and sexual abuse of children while paying hush money to a man he molested when employed as a high school wrestling coach.

Meeting the unique ethical challenges of leadership is difficult, and we may disagree on what courses of action are appropriate. However, because moral judgments are critical to the practice of leadership, we have a responsibility to make reasoned, ethical decisions and to act on those choices. We can better fulfill this responsibility if we understand the components of ethical behavior and study some widely accepted ethical perspectives for guidance.

Components of Ethical Behavior

James Rest at the Center for the Study of Ethical Development at the University of Minnesota believed that ethical behavior is the product of four intrapersonal and interpersonal communication processes. Ethical failure occurs when one of these processes malfunctions. By taking a closer look at each of these components, we can improve our performance and help our followers do the same.[24]

Component 1: Moral Sensitivity (Recognition)

Moral sensitivity is identifying the existence of ethical problems. We can't solve a moral problem unless we first recognize that one exists. This component involves acknowledging that our behavior impacts others, identifying possible courses of action, and determining the consequences of each possible strategy. Empathy and perspective-taking skills are essential if we are to predict the possible consequences of our actions and to evaluate the effectiveness of various options. We need to imagine how others might feel or react. However, we can be victimized by moral tunnel vision when our mental scripts don't include ethical considerations. When buying clothes, for example, we may focus solely on getting a good deal, ignoring the fact that the retailer treats its employees poorly or that our purchase might help keep a sweatshop operating in the developing world. Ford Motor Company failed to fix the Pinto after rear-end collisions ruptured the vehicle's gas tank and set some vehicles and passengers on fire. The company's recall committee decided not to issue a recall after determining that the costs of fixing all the cars (at $11 a vehicle) were more than the costs in human life. Committee members defined the defective tanks as a business, not a moral, problem. Their mental scripts didn't include ethical considerations. Ford was later indicted for criminal negligence, the first time that a major firm had faced criminal, not civil, charges for manufacturing faulty products. (The firm was later acquitted.)[25]

Moral muteness is also a problem. All too often leaders are reluctant to use ethical terminology when describing situations, perhaps because they want to avoid conflict or believe that their silence will make them appear in control.[26]

You can increase your moral sensitivity if you: (1) engage in active listening to learn about the possible ethical consequences of your choices; (2) challenge your schemas to make sure that you're not overlooking important moral considerations; and (3) use ethical terms like *right, wrong, values, fairness*, and *immoral* when describing problems and solutions. You can also alert others to moral issues by increasing their moral intensity. Followers are more likely to note ethical problems if you can demonstrate their significance. Describe how an ethical decision will impact lots of other people, have serious consequences, pose an immediate threat, violate laws, and so on.[27]

Component 2: Moral Judgment

Moral judgment is deciding which course of action identified in the first component is the right one to follow. Decision makers determine what is the right or wrong thing to do in this particular situation. Moral judgment is the most studied component of Rest's model. Researchers have conducted more than a thousand studies of moral judgment using an instrument called the Defining Issues Test. Respondents read moral dilemmas (Should a model escaped prisoner be reported to the police? Should a doctor help a dying patient take her own life?) and then rank a series of items that reveal what they take into consideration when making ethical choices. According to Rest, the highest form of ethical reasoning is based on broad principles like justice, cooperation, and respect for others.[28]

Results from the Defining Issues Test indicate that we can increase our ethical competence. There is a strong link between higher education and reasoned decision-making.[29] People in college and graduate school demonstrate the greatest gains in moral development. However, insecurities, greed, and ego can subvert the reasoning process, contributing to the downfall of such prominent leaders as former South Korean President Park Geun-Hye. Due to loneliness and self-doubts, she allowed a close friend to exercise undue influence over her and her government. Martha Stewart risked her billion-dollar empire to avoid $45,000 in losses through insider trading on a stock deal.

To improve your moral judgment, maximize the ethical benefits of your college education by taking courses on ethics and by participating in internships that raise real-life ethical dilemmas. Base your decisions on widely accepted ethical principles (see the discussion of ethical perspectives to follow). Be alert to the possibility of faulty reasoning—consult with others to check your perceptions against reality and stay close to people who will tell you the truth and hold you accountable. Remember that we are all susceptible to unconscious distortions or *ethical blind spots*.[30] Studies consistently demonstrate that we overestimate how ethical we are, forgive our own immoral behavior, favor our own group, and fall victim to the prejudices and stereotypes described in the last chapter.

Finally, pay attention to your feelings. Neuroscientists, psychologists, and others have discovered that, contrary to previous thinking, emotions enhance rather than undermine moral decision making. Both emotional and cognitive areas of the brain are activated during ethical problem solving; damage to the emotional centers undermines moral reasoning. Instead of using logic to justify choices, we often make quick, intuitive decisions and then justify our choices using reason.[31] To draw upon both reason and emotion when facing an ethical dilemma, write down your initial reaction. Then use the ethical perspectives in the next section of the chapter to test your response. Compare your final decision to your immediate reaction. You may also want to test your conclusion to see if it "feels" right.

Component 3: Moral Motivation

Moral motivation refers to following through on choices. The desire to do the right thing generally comes into conflict with other values like security, wealth, and social acceptance. Ethical behavior results if moral values take precedence over other considerations.

Leaders and followers are more likely to follow through when they are rewarded for doing so. Some companies, for example, encourage ethical behavior by evaluating ethical performance as part of the review process. On the other side of the coin are organizations whose employees are encouraged to inflate sales figures, lie to investors, produce shoddy products, and take kickbacks from suppliers. Germany's Deutsche Bank has a "rap sheet" that includes collaborating with the Nazis, tax evasion, selling toxic mortgages, hiding losses, and helping Russians evade economic sanctions.[32]

Emotions influence ethical motivation just as they do moral judgment. In general, positive feelings like happiness, joy, and optimism encourage individuals to follow through while negative emotions like anger, frustration, stress, and depression lower motivation and instead encourage aggression and other antisocial behaviors.[33]

You can increase your moral motivation and that of your followers by creating an ethically rewarding environment and managing your emotions. Catch people doing good. That is, reward moral behavior that might otherwise go unappreciated, like providing outstanding customer service or eliminating wasteful spending. Don't focus solely on the bottom line but develop other measures of performance, such as community involvement and support of corporate mission and values. Evaluate based on processes as well as on results. Provide incentives for those who reach their goals in an ethical manner and punish those who don't. (Turn to box 11.2 for more information on how to create an ethical environment.) Monitor your emotions and regulate them to bring them in line with your goals. Note your destructive feelings and shift into a more positive frame of mind.

Component 4: Moral Character (Implementation)

Moral character is the implementation stage of the model. Opposition, fatigue, distractions, and other factors are formidable barriers to ethical action. Overcoming these obstacles takes persistence. Those with a strong will are more likely to persist as well as those with an internal locus of control. (See our discussion of leader traits in chapter 4 for more information on internal and external locus of control.) Internals are more likely to take personal responsibility for their actions and therefore try to do what is right. Externals are more likely to give in to situational pressures and to give up rather than to carry on.[34]

Duty orientation is another characteristic tied to moral behavior.[35] Those driven by duty to colleagues (fellow soldiers, small-group members), duty to mission (work and purpose), and duty to codes (formal rules and unofficial norms) make and follow through on ethical decisions based on their loyalty to the group. They willingly give up some of their free choice to fulfill their obligations. Duty orientation promotes such prosocial behaviors as donating unused vacation time to a sick coworker or defending a team member from gossip. At the same time, a sense of obligation limits deviant acts like stealing company property or sharing proprietary information with a competitor.

Successful implementation requires competence as well as persistence. Consider the high-tech manager who believes it is wrong to release the latest software update before it has been tested thoroughly. To delay the release, she'll need to

Box 11.2	**Creating an Ethical Environment: Defensive and Proactive Strategies[36]**

Ethical leaders increase the motivation to behave morally by shaping the group or organizational context through defensive and proactive strategies. Defensive tactics are designed to prevent unethical, destructive behaviors, including incivility (rude or discourteous actions like ignoring a coworker or stealing someone else's work), aggression aimed at hurting others or the organization, sexual harassment, and discrimination. Proactive tactics intentionally promote a positive moral atmosphere or climate.

Defensive Tactics

- Create zero-tolerance policies for antisocial behaviors
- Personally adhere to policies; model compliance
- Confront offenders at the first sign of trouble
- Punish those who break the rules
- Address the root causes of destructive behaviors: oppressive supervision, injustice, stress, unpleasant working conditions, extreme competitiveness
- Set up reporting systems (e.g., ethics hotlines) for ethical violations and create disciplinary procedures
- Design performance evaluation systems that detect unethical behavior

Proactive Tactics

- Create codes of ethics
- Appoint ethics officers
- Establish clear lines of accountability
- Honor ethical heroes
- Model moral behavior
- Continually communicate the organization's core values and core purpose
- Incorporate values into every organizational decision
- Equip constituents to make their own moral decisions; empower them to do so
- Build ethical criteria and standards into performance reviews
- Reward ethical behavior (e.g., honesty, fair treatment of vendors, courtesy, excellent service)
- Evaluate based on processes (how goals are reached) as well as on outcomes
- Support, don't punish, whistle-blowers
- Select employees based on their character and values
- Integrate discussion of ethics and values into socialization processes (employment interviews, orientation, training)
- Provide ongoing ethics training
- Periodically audit the ethical culture of the organization

marshal her evidence, enlist the help of her fellow managers, engage in constructive argument with her supervisors, negotiate with other departments, and so on.

You can boost the probability that you'll take moral action by (1) assessing your personal history (How well do you manage obstacles? What can you do to improve your track record?); (2) believing that you can make a difference; (3) recognizing your obligations to colleagues, purpose, and professional and organizational codes; (4) mastering the context (organizational policies, informal networks, key decision makers) so that you can respond effectively when needed; and (5) building your communication competence so that can put your choice into action.

Ethical Perspectives

Over the centuries philosophers and other scholars have developed a variety of theories or approaches that can be applied to ethical issues. These perspectives impact all four of the components of ethical behavior described earlier. They can raise our ethical awareness, guide our decision making, help us prioritize our values, and strengthen our moral character. In this section of the chapter we'll look at six ethical approaches that are particularly relevant to leadership.

Kant's Categorical Imperative

German philosopher Immanuel Kant (1724–1804) argued that individuals ought to do what is morally right, no matter what the consequences. The term *categorical* means *without exception*.[37] This approach to moral reasoning is the best known example of deontological ethics. Proponents of deontological ethics believe that we ought to base our choices on our duty (*deon* is the Greek word for duty) to follow universal truths that we discover through our intuition or reason. Kant's standard can be applied by asking a simple question: Would we want everyone to make the same decision we did? If the answer is "yes," the choice is ethical. If the answer is "no," the decision is wrong. Based on this reasoning, behaviors like treating employees fairly and keeping commitments are always right. Such behaviors as cheating, lying, and abusive behavior are always wrong. For instance, if we're tempted to make up statistics to boost donations to the nonprofit group we lead, we need to ask ourselves what would happen if every charity lied in order to raise funds. A climate of suspicion and hostility might be created that would bankrupt many worthy organizations. Our duty, then, is to present accurate information—even if misleading statistics might convince people to give more to our particular cause.

Kant also advocated respect for people, which has become one of the most influential ideas in Western moral philosophy.[38] According to Kant: "Act so that you treat humanity, whether in your own person or that of another, always as an end and never as a means only." We need followers to help us reach our objectives as leaders. However, we should never treat subordinates merely as tools. Our duty is to respect the right of followers to choose for themselves. Based on this principle, it is unethical to subject them to dangerous chemicals in the workplace or to gather personal information about them without their knowledge or consent.

Coercing or threatening followers is wrong because it violates their freedom of choice. Similarly, denying assistance to them is immoral because refusing help limits their options.

There are two major difficulties with Kant's system of thinking. One, it is hard to agree on universal principles that apply in every situation. We can almost always think of exceptions. For instance, as we noted earlier, there are cases when deception seems justified. Or we may oppose killing but believe that war is justified. Two, duties often contradict each other in complex moral dilemmas. Take the case of conflicting loyalties. Loyalty to customers and coworkers are both important. Yet, being loyal to customers and the public may mean breaking our loyalty to our peers, such as when we blow the whistle when our firm markets an unsafe product.

Utilitarianism

In sharp contrast to Kant, British philosophers Jeremy Bentham (1748–1832) and John Stuart Mill (1806–1873) argued that ethical choices should be based on their consequences rather than on individual duty. The best decisions are those that (1) generate the most benefits as compared to their disadvantages, and (2) benefit the largest number of people. The end result is that utilitarianism attempts to do the greatest good for the greatest number of people.[39]

Leaders commonly weigh outcomes when making decisions. Franklin Roosevelt, for instance, lied to Congress and the American people in order to help Great Britain in World War II. He began to send ships and materials to the embattled nation before he received congressional approval, judging that saving England justified his deceit. Harry Truman decided to drop the atomic bomb on Japan after determining that the benefits of shortening the war in the Pacific outweighed the costs of destroying Hiroshima and Nagasaki and ushering in the nuclear age.

Identifying and evaluating possible consequences can be difficult. Take the debate over wind power, for instance. At first, wind energy appeared to be a "no brainer." Increasing the number of giant wind turbines reduces dependence on foreign oil as well as pollution, since wind is a clean energy source. After the turbines were installed, however, a number of problems emerged. These mechanisms are noisy, which disturbs nearby residents; they kill birds, including endangered species; and they mar the view, particularly in scenic areas.

Based on the difficulty of determining potential costs and benefits in situations like the one described above, utilitarian decision makers sometimes reach different conclusions when faced with the same dilemma. Some historians, for example, criticize Truman for his decision to drop the atomic bomb. They argue that the war would have ended soon without the use of nuclear weapons and that no military objective justifies such widespread destruction.

Justice as Fairness

Justice or fairness is an important consideration for leaders. The ethical challenges of leadership described earlier—information management, power, privilege, responsibility, consistency, and loyalty—all raise questions about what is just. Is it fair to withhold information from employees? Should pharmaceutical companies be allowed to raise drug prices as high as they want despite the consequences to the poor and sick? How should power and privileges be distributed? How can leaders treat workers equitably despite their differences?

Harvard philosopher John Rawls (1921–2002) addressed questions like these in a series of articles and books during the last third of the twentieth century.[40] Rawls set out to identify a set of operating principles that could be used in democratic societies to distribute benefits and costs while fostering cooperation. These principles, in turn, would guide the decision making of individual citizens. Rawls recognized that democracies must deal with a fundamental tension. On the one hand, all citizens are free and equal. On the other hand, citizens are unequal because they vary in socioeconomic standing, status, talents, and abilities. To reconcile these competing realities, Rawls's standards honor individual freedom but also encourage more equitable allocation of resources. While designed to address the political structure of the nation as a whole, they can also apply to organizations and leaders operating within democratic societies.

Rawls rejected the use of utilitarian principles to distribute goods because generating the greatest good for the greatest number can seriously disadvantage particular groups and individuals. Deciding to construct a new reservoir, for example, may ensure a region's future water supply and provide new recreational opportunities. Yet, the farms and homes of those who live in the area will be submerged under water.

As an alternative to balancing costs and benefits, Rawls urged us to follow these principles of justice:[41]

> Principle 1: Each person has an equal right to the same basic liberties that are compatible with similar liberties for all.

> Principle 2: Social and economic inequalities are to satisfy two conditions: (a) they are to be attached to offices and positions open to all under conditions of fair equality of opportunity, and (b) they are to be the greatest benefit to the least advantaged members of society.

The first principle, the "principle of equal liberty," has priority over the second principle. It asserts that all citizens have certain rights and that these rights apply equally to everyone. These liberties include freedom of speech, the right to vote, freedom to own property, and freedom from arbitrary arrest. Pressuring employees to contribute to a particular political candidate and invading their privacy would violate this standard, as would arbitrary police searches and seizures.

Principle 2a, "the equal opportunity principle," asserts that every individual should have the same chance to qualify for offices and jobs. Job discrimination based on gender, race, or ethnic origin is thus forbidden. Equal opportunity is only the first step. All citizens should have access to the training and education that they need to qualify for these positions. Principle 2b, "the difference principle," recognizes the reality of inequality but argues that priority should go to meeting the needs of disadvantaged groups.

Rawls went on to introduce the concept of the **veil of ignorance** to back up his claim that his moral principles should serve as the foundation for democratic societies like the United States, Great Britain, Australia, and New Zealand. Imagine, he says, a group of people who are asked to develop a set of guidelines to govern society. These group members are ignorant of their personal characteristics and societal position. Faced with this uncertainty, individuals would likely act on the *maximin rule*. This rule states that the best option is the one whose worst outcome is better than the worst outcomes of all the other options available. In other words, the best choice is the alternative that guarantees everyone a minimum level of benefits. Citizens operating under the veil of ignorance would adopt Rawls's ethical guidelines because they would ensure the most favorable outcomes in the worst of circumstances. They would select (1) equal liberty, because they would be guaranteed freedom even if they were at the bottom of society, (2) equal opportunity, because if they discovered they were the most talented members of society, they likely would land the best jobs and be elected to office, and (3) the difference principle, because they would want to be sure they were cared for if they turned out to be disadvantaged.

Stepping behind the veil of ignorance does more than justify the difference and equal opportunity principles; it can also serve as a useful strategy for making ethical choices. Setting aside status and power differences, at least temporarily, generally produces more just decisions. The least advantaged usually benefit when status differences are excluded from the decision-making process. Classical orchestras provide one case of how screening out differences can help marginalized groups. Orchestras began to hire a much higher percentage of female musicians after they erected screens that prevented judges from seeing the gender of players during auditions.[42]

It should be noted that justice as fairness theory, like utilitarianism, can lead to different conclusions. Definitions of justice and fairness vary widely, for example. What seems just to one group or individual can seem grossly unfair to others. Granting Native Americans special fishing rights can be seen as a way to redress past abuses, honor important cultural traditions, and help raise the economic standing of a disadvantaged population. Caucasians and other groups often see these regulations as unfair special privileges that deny them equal opportunities.

Virtue Ethics

As we've seen, there are significant differences between the categorical, utilitarian, and justice as fairness perspectives. However, all three theories involve the application of universal rules or principles to specific situations. Dissatisfaction with rule-based approaches to ethical decision making is growing. Some ethicists complain that these guidelines are applied to extreme situations, not the types of choices we typically make.[43] Few of us will be faced with the extraordinary scenarios—stealing to save a life or lying to the secret police to protect a fugitive—that are frequently used to illustrate Kantian decision making, for instance. Our dilemmas are generally less dramatic. For instance: Should we lie to protect someone's feelings? Tell my employer about another job offer? Confront a coworker about a sexist joke? Ethical decision makers also deal with time pressures and uncertainty. In crisis situations they don't have time to carefully weigh consequences or to determine which abstract principle to apply.[44]

Recognizing the limitations of the utilitarian, justice as fairness, and categorical approaches, some scholars are turning back to one of the oldest ethical traditions— virtue ethics. Virtue ethicists highlight the role of the person or actor in ethical decision making. They argue that individuals with high moral character are more likely to make wise ethical choices. Virtue theorists seek: (1) to develop a description of the ideal person, (2) to identify the virtues that make up the character of this ethical prototype, and (3) to outline how individuals can acquire the required virtues.[45] Let's take a closer look at each of these objectives as they apply to leadership.

Definitions of **the ideal leader** will differ to some degree depending on the context. We may value kindness and consideration in a religious figure but want toughness in a military leader. Nevertheless, descriptions of the ideal leader show a high degree of consistency, no matter the setting. The most admired leadership characteristics (honesty, forward looking, inspiring, competent) that emerged in the study of 15,000 managers described in chapter 6 bear a striking resemblance to the things we look for in political leaders. We want elected officials who act with integrity, exercise good judgment, restrain their impulses, respect others, rally followers, persist in the face of strong opposition, and so forth.[46] (See the self-assessment in box 11.3 for one tool designed specifically to measure the honesty and consistency of those in leadership roles.)

The **virtues of the ethical leader** are "deep-rooted dispositions, habits, skills, or traits of character that incline persons to perceive, feel, and act in ethically right and sensitive ways."[47] Aristotle provided one of the first comprehensive lists of virtues in Western culture. He described the ideal citizen/leader as someone who possesses characteristics such as courage, moderation, justice, generosity, hospitality, a mild temper, truthfulness, and proper judgment. Most, if not all, of these virtues appear on the lists of contemporary ethicists and leadership scholars. Other common virtues include love, empathy, compassion, and strength.[48] Box 11.4 on p. 380 introduces one widely used list of virtues developed by social scientists.

Love is the virtue of the heart. Sincerity the virtue of the mind.
Courage the virtue of the spirit. Decision the virtue of the will.

—*Frank Lloyd Wright*

Exemplars or role models play a critical role in the **development of high moral character**. Virtues are more "caught than taught" in that they are acquired through observation and imitation. We learn what it means to be just, generous, and honest by seeing these qualities modeled in the lives of exemplary leaders. Exemplary leaders can be people we work for; political, religious, or military leaders; historical figures; and even fictional characters. Any story about leaders, whether it is an

Box 11.3   Self-Assessment   **Perceived Leader Integrity Scale (PLIS)**[49]

The following items concern your immediate supervisor—the person who has the most control over your daily work activities. Use the following numbers to indicate how well each item describes your immediate supervisor.

1 = Not at all   2 = Somewhat   3 = Very much   4 = Exactly

The higher the total score on the scale (31 is the lowest possible score, 124 the highest), the lower the perception of integrity of the person being rated. You can also use this instrument to assess the image others have of your character. You might distribute the survey to a group of followers and ask for anonymous responses or estimate how you think others would rate you on each item.

_____ 1. Would use my mistakes to attack me personally

_____ 2. Always gets even

_____ 3. Gives special favors to certain "pet" employees, but not to me

_____ 4. Would lie to me

_____ 5. Would risk me to protect himself/herself in work matters

_____ 6. Deliberately fuels conflict among employees

_____ 7. Is evil

_____ 8. Would use my performance appraisal to criticize me as a person

_____ 9. Has it in for me

_____ 10. Would allow me to be blamed for his/her mistake

_____ 11. Would falsify records if it would help his/her work situation

_____ 12. Lacks high morals

_____ 13. Makes fun of my mistakes instead of coaching me as to how to do my job better

_____ 14. Would deliberately exaggerate my mistakes to make me look bad when describing my performance to his/her superiors

_____ 15. Is vindictive

_____ 16. Would blame me for his/her own mistake

_____ 17. Avoids coaching me because (s)he wants me to fail

_____ 18. Would treat me better if we belonged to a different ethnic group

_____ 19. Would deliberately distort what we say

_____ 20. Deliberately makes employees angry at each other

_____ 21. Is a hypocrite

_____ 22. Would limit my training opportunities to prevent me from advancing

_____ 23. Would blackmail an employee if (s)he thought (s)he could get away with it

_____ 24. Enjoys turning down my requests

_____ 25. Would make trouble for me if we got on his/her bad side

_____ 26. Would take credit for my ideas

_____ 27. Would steal from the organization

_____ 28. Would risk me to get back at someone else

_____ 29. Would engage in sabotage against the organization

_____ 30. Would fire people just because (s)he doesn't like them if (s)he could get away with it

_____ 31. Would do things that violate organizational policy and then expect his/her subordinates to cover for him/her

---

Box 11.4 Research Highlight	Virtues as Personality Traits[50]

Positive psychologists believe that it is better to identify and promote the strengths of people rather than to address their weaknesses (which is the traditional approach of psychologists). They treat virtues as morally valued personality traits, ones that are considered desirable and recognized across cultures. Under this definition, some personality traits, such as extroversion or introversion, would not be virtues because they are not considered either ethical or unethical.

Under the direction of the Values in Action Institute, led by Christopher Peterson and Martin Seligman, positive psychologists identified the following as character strengths.

Wisdom and Knowledge—**cognitive strengths involving the acquisition and use of knowledge. These strengths include:**
- creativity: originality that makes a positive contribution to the individual and/or to others
- curiosity: intrinsic desire for experience and knowledge
- love of learning: motivation to value and acquire knowledge
- open-mindedness: willingness to search for and to weigh opposing viewpoints and evidence
- perspective: wisdom; self-knowledge; broad viewpoint; ability to advise and help others

Courage—**the exercise of will to accomplish goals in the face of opposition. Courage encompasses:**
- bravery: overcoming fear to do the right thing
- persistence: continuing to pursue a goal in spite of difficulties or discouragement
- integrity (honesty, authenticity): being true to the self; owning thoughts and feelings; consistent moral behavior
- vitality: energetic and alive, enthusiastic

Humanity—**strengths that involve tending to and befriending others in interpersonal relationships. Humanity is reflected in:**
- love: capacity to give and receive affection and care
- kindness: compassion, nurture
- social intelligence: ability to make accurate judgments about emotions and social situations

Justice—**strengths that underlie healthy groups and communities. Justice is made up of:**
- citizenship: identification with and an obligation to the common good; a strong sense of duty
- fairness: commitment to equitable arrangements; sensitivity to injustice
- leadership: motivation to seek out leadership roles and the capacity to carry them out

Temperance—**strengths that protect against excess, which include:**
- forgiveness and mercy: developing more positive feelings toward the transgressor; offering kindness or leniency
- humility and modesty: accurate self-assessment, openness to the ideas of others, moderate evaluation of achievements
- prudence: long-term perspective, careful consideration of consequences, self-management
- self-regulation: self-control of emotions and behaviors; overriding initial impulses

Transcendence—**character strengths that forge connection to the larger universe and provide meaning. These include:**
- appreciation of beauty and excellence: recognizing and taking pleasure in the goodness of the natural world and others; aesthetic sensitivity
- gratitude: thankfulness and joy in receiving a tangible or intangible gift
- hope: expecting good outcomes in the future
- humor: recognition of what is funny; cheerful view of adversity; ability to make others smile and laugh
- spirituality: belief in the transcendent (nonphysical); concept of the sacred

item in the morning newspaper, a segment on CNN, a novel, a play, a biography, or a movie, can provide insights into ethical (and unethical) leader behavior. (Turn to box 11.5 for a closer look at a leader and followers who demonstrate positive character traits.) Communities encourage the formation of moral character by telling

---

Box 11.5   Case Study   **Persisting for Peace[51]**

For 52 years Marxist guerillas with the Revolutionary Armed Forces of Colombia (FARC) battled against the government of Colombia and right-wing militia groups. The war took the lives of 220,000 and displaced eight million Colombians. There were plenty of atrocities committed on both sides during the conflict, including massacres, torture, executions, attacks on combatants' families, kidnappings, and assassinations of elected officials.

In 2012 Colombian President Juan Manuel Santos announced that his government was beginning negotiations with FARC to end the conflict. For four years the two sides talked in Havana, Cuba. To reach an agreement Santos had to assure FARC rebels that they wouldn't be arrested or extradited to another country to stand trial. They would also be allowed to run for office. In return, they would lay down their weapons, admit their guilt, and undertake community service.

The treaty was submitted to a national referendum but was narrowly defeated. Many citizens believed that the agreement was too lenient because it allowed rebels to escape jail. The previous president called Santos a "traitor" for excusing FARC crimes in order to strike a deal. For his part, President Santos argued that government negotiators had achieved the right balance between justice and achieving peace. He admitted, though, that it was hard to overcome the misgivings of opponents: "Making peace is much more difficult than making war because you need to change sentiments of people, people who have suffered, to try to persuade them to forgive."[52] Santos took comfort in the fact that those who had suffered most were most willing to forgive. Shortly after the referendum defeat, he visited a town where dozens of people had been killed at a church during a gun battle. The referendum was supported by 96% of this village. (The measure passed by a 67% margin in the 81 cities hardest hit by the war.) He told village residents, "The victims have taught me that the capacity to forgive can overcome hatred and rancor."[53] And he vowed to persist in his peace efforts. "I'm not going to falter a single minute. I'm not going to give up a single second" in searching for peace.[54]

Santos' attempts to broker a peace treaty got a boost when he was awarded the Nobel Peace Prize for his "resolute efforts" to end the conflict. The Norwegian Nobel Committee hoped that the peace prize would "give him strength to succeed in this demanding task." And it did. The Colombian Congress approved a revised deal shortly thereafter. In his Nobel acceptance speech, Santos described the award as a "gift from heaven" that made the "impossible dream" of ending the decades-long civil war possible. He told the Nobel gathering, "Ladies and gentlemen, there is one less war in the world, and it is the war in Colombia."[55]

Discussion Questions

1. What character traits enabled Santos to continue his pursuit of peace?
2. Why do you think so many victims of the war are able to forgive?
3. Do you agree that it is harder to make peace than to make war? Why or why not?
4. Do you think this peace agreement is too lenient?
5. What are the advantage and disadvantages of trying to reconcile and restore offenders rather than punishing them?
6. Would the treaty have been signed if Santos hadn't been awarded the Nobel Peace Prize?

and retelling stories that illustrate and reinforce ethical values.[56] Habits—repeated routines or practices—also build character. Every time we engage in a positive habit like working hard, standing up to peer pressure, and always turning in original work for school assignments, it leaves a trace or residue.[57] Over time, these residual effects become part of our character. (We'll take a closer look at key habits in the next chapter.) By the same token, engaging in unethical habits like cheating and lying also leave traces that eventually corrupt our character.

Altruism

Altruism makes concern for others the ultimate ethical standard. Proponents of altruistic behavior argue that we ought to help others regardless of whether we get any benefit from doing so. Altruism appears to be a universal value promoted in cultures around the world. For instance, the major world religions, those that have lasted and expanded over the centuries, emphasize love for all humanity. Well-known religious altruists include Tibet's Dalai Lama, South African bishop Desmond Tutu, India's Mahatma Gandhi, social activist Dorothy Day, Martin Luther King, Jr., hospice advocate Dame Cicely Sanders, and former UN Secretary Dag Hammarskjold.[58]

Altruistic behavior appears to be common in everyday life. Social scientists from such fields as psychology, economics, sociology, and political science report that altruism is an integral part of human nature.[59] We comfort our friends and family members, send money to tsunami victims, rebuild homes after hurricanes, push strangers' cars out of snow banks, provide free dental and medical care, volunteer for mountain rescue teams, and so on. Altruistic behavior not only benefits the recipients but also pays dividends for society as a whole. (See the Leadership on the Big Screen case for an example of altruism in action.) Such actions build bonds between people and nurture the cooperation and trust necessary to take collective action (e.g., form a political party, operate a business, educate students). In sum, society functions more effectively when people act on behalf of others. (Turn to box 11.6 for examples of altruistic behaviors that can boost organizational productivity.)

Doing good is one of the wonderful mysteries of the human universe.

—*Jeffrey Kottler*

While altruism is a significant ethical consideration for all citizens, concern for others may be more important for leaders than for followers. By definition, leaders serve group goals, not their selfish interests (see chapter 1). A number of effective leadership practices described in this text—team building, listening, transformational leadership, empowerment, mentoring—have an altruistic component. Many of the qualities of virtuous leaders described earlier, like generosity, hospitality, empathy, and compassion, reflect a focus on others rather than a self-focus. Management professors Rabindra Kanungo and Manuel Mendonca argue that "organizational leaders are only effective when they are motivated by a concern for others."[60] They contrast the motives of self- and other-motivated leaders. Self-focused leaders pursue their own agenda at the cost of the organization. They seek personal achievement, want to control followers, and make heavy use of legitimate,

---

Box 11.6	Organizational Altruistic Behaviors[61]

Directed to Benefit Individuals

- Consideration of others' needs
- Technical assistance on the job
- Job orientation in new jobs
- Buddy system of induction for new employees
- Training to acquire new skills
- Empowerment practices including mentoring and modeling for others to gain competence

Directed to Benefit Groups

- Team building
- Participative group decision making
- Protecting people from sexual harassment
- Minority promotion and advancement programs
- Counseling programs
- Educational support programs
- Interdepartmental cooperation

Directed to Benefit the Organization

- Organizational commitment and loyalty
- Work dedication
- Equitable compensation programs
- Whistle-blowing to maintain organizational integrity
- Protecting and conserving organizational resources
- Presenting a positive image of the organization to outsiders
- Sharing of organizational wealth through profit-sharing programs

Directed to Benefit Society

- Contributions to social welfare and community needs in the areas of health, education, the arts, and culture
- Lobbying for public interest legislation
- Affirmative action programs for minorities
- Training and employment for handicapped and hard-core unemployed
- Environmental pollution control
- Economic sanctions against oppressive social control
- Assuring product safety and customer satisfaction

reward, and coercive power bases. In the process they destroy loyalty and trust and put their organizations at risk. Other-focused leaders pursue institutional goals. They seek collective achievements, empower followers, and rely on referent and expert power bases. Altruistic leaders foster collaboration and their self-sacrifice demonstrates commitment to the group and its mission. When followers emulate the example of altruistic leaders, higher performance often results.

Taoism is one non-Western leadership philosophy that emphasizes altruism. In the *Tao te Ching*, Taoism's major text, Lao-tzu encourages leaders to demonstrate character and integrity by following natural principles that come from the Dao—the "way" or underlying power of the universe.[62] Lao-tzu draws upon a number of images from nature to illustrate these principles, including uncarved blocks, valleys, saplings and, most importantly, water. The following five qualities (the "Daoist Big Five") make up the water-like leadership personality or leadership style:[63]

Water is altruistic. All plants and animals depend on water, which expects nothing in return:

> The highest value (or the best) is like water,
> The value in water benefits ALL Things
> And yet it does not contend,
> It stays in places that others despise,
> And therefore is close to *Dao*. (ch 8)[64]

Good leaders, like water, are selfless, seeking to serve followers instead of competing with them.

Water is modest and humble. Instead of pursing authority and power like many Western leaders, the ideal Taoist leader maintains a low profile, being humble, modest, and helpful to others. Yet, these qualities can lead to great influence, as in the case of the sea, which occupies a low position but takes in the water of many rivers. According to Lao-tzu, "He/she who knows how to motivate people acts humble. This is the virtue of no rival and uses the strength of others" (ch. 68).

Water is very adaptable and flexible. Water can take the shape of any container. In the same way, ethical leaders are flexible and adaptable and can follow the path laid out before them.

Water is transparent and clear. Effective leaders, like clear water, should be honest and transparent. Lao-tzu believed that people are naturally transparent unless "muddied" by competition and outside pressure: "Who can (make) the muddy water clear? Let it be still, and it will gradually become clear" (ch. 15).

Water is soft and gentle, but also persistent and powerful. Water may be soft but, given enough time, it can cut through the hardest rock, creating canyons and valleys and wearing down mountains.

⌒

*To reveal someone's beauty is to reveal their value
by giving them time, attention, and tenderness.*

—*Jean Vanier*

Leaders as Servants

Contemporary interest in leaders as servants was sparked by Robert Greenleaf (1904–1990). He coined the term "servant leader" in 1970 to describe a leadership model that puts the concerns of followers first. Greenleaf later founded a center to promote servant leadership. His ideas have been adopted by businesses (Southwest Airlines, SAS, AFLAC, REI), nonprofit organizations, and community and service-learning programs.[65] Servant leaders put the needs of followers before their own needs. Because they continually ask themselves what would be best for their constituents, servant leaders are less tempted to take advantage of followers, act inconsistently, or accumulate money and power for themselves.

For decades support for servant leadership was largely anecdotal, consisting of descriptions of servant leaders and lists of servant characteristics. Recently, however, investigators have been able to subject servant leadership to empirical testing. Scholars have discovered that servant leadership is effective as well as ethical. Subordinates working under servant leaders indicate that they are more satisfied, believe that their needs are being met, declare that they will stay with their organizations, think their organizations are more effective, put forth extra effort, and report that they are justly treated. Employees, in turn, spend more time building relationships with customers and responding to consumer needs. Servant leadership also contributes to a more positive ethical organizational climate.[66]

While lists of servant leader traits vary between scholars, four principles appear to serve as the foundation for servant leadership. For a summary of the differences between traditional bosses and those who seek to serve, see box 11.7.

The first principle is a concern for people—an extension of the ethical principle of altruism. Servant leaders believe that healthy societies and organizations care for their members. They use such terms as *love, civility,* and *community* to characterize working relationships. Servant leaders argue that the measure of a leader's success lies in what happens in the lives of followers—not in what the leader has accomplished. Greenleaf suggests that we gauge a leader's effectiveness by asking the following questions: "Do those served grow as persons? Do they, while being served, become healthier, wise, freer, more autonomous, more likely themselves to become servants?"[67]

The second principle of servant leadership is stewardship. Servant leaders hold their positions and organizations in trust for others. They act on behalf of followers who have entrusted them with leadership responsibilities; they act on behalf of society by making sure that their organizations serve the common good. Stewards are accountable for results but reach their goals by serving others, not by controlling or coercing them.[68]

Indebtedness is an important component of stewardship. For those who view leadership as a form of service, leaders have certain responsibilities to their followers. According to Max DePree, former chairman of the board of furniture maker Herman Miller, constituents can expect the following rights from their leaders.[69]

- *Right to be needed.* Followers have the right to use their gifts and be connected in a meaningful way to the mission of the organization.

- *Right to be involved.* Everyone has a right to participate and to have input. In addition, leaders must respond to suggestions and work with followers to meet the needs of customers.

- *Right to a covenantal relationship.* Contractual relationships are based on legal agreements that define pay, working conditions, vacations, etc. Covenantal relationships are based on a commitment to common goals and values; such relationships meet deeper needs and help provide meaning to work.

- *Right to understand.* Followers have a right to know and understand the following elements: organizational mission, personal career paths, the competition, the working environment, terms of employment.

Box 11.7	Traditional Bosses vs. Servant Leaders: A New Kind of Leadership[70]
Traditional Boss	**Servant as Leader**
Motivated by personal drive to achieve.	Motivated by desire to serve others.
Highly competitive; independent mind-set; seeks to receive personal credit for achievement.	Highly collaborative and interdependent; gives credit to others generously.
Understands internal politics and uses them to win personally.	Sensitive to what motivates others and empowers all to win with shared goals and vision.
Focuses on fast action. Complains about long meetings and about others being too slow.	Focuses on gaining understanding, input, and buy-in from all parties.
Relies on facts, logic, or proof.	Uses intuition and foresight to balance facts, logic, or proof.
Controls information in order to maintain power.	Shares big-picture information generously.
Spends more time telling and giving orders. Sees too much listening or coaching as inefficient.	Listens deeply and respectfully to others— especially to those who disagree.
Feels that personal value comes from individual mentoring.	Feels that personal value comes from one's own talents and working collaboratively with others.
Sees network of supporters as power base and titles as a signal to others.	Develops trust across a network of constituencies; breaks down hierarchy.
Eager to speak first; feels his/her ideas are more important; often dominates or intimidates opponents.	Most likely to listen first; values others' input.
Uses personal power and intimidation to leverage what he/she wants.	Uses personal trust and respect to build bridges and do what's best for the "whole."
Accountability is more often about who is to blame.	Accountability is about making it safe to learn from mistakes.
Uses humor to control others.	Uses humor to lift others up and make it safe to learn from mistakes.

- *Right to affect one's own destiny.* Followers should always be involved in their performance evaluations and in promotion and transfer decisions that impact their careers.

- *Right to be accountable.* Accountability includes contributing to the achievement of group goals and sharing ownership in group problems and risks. Contributions should be evaluated according to clear, acceptable criteria.

- *Right to appeal.* Everyone should have the right to appeal decisions that might threaten one or more of the rights described earlier.

- *Right to make a commitment.* In order to make a commitment, followers must know that they can do their best and not be held back by leaders, particularly leaders who act in an irrational manner.

The highest of distinctions is service to others.

—George VI

The third principle of servant leadership is equity or justice. Servant leaders make a concerted effort to create a level playing field by distributing resources fairly. For example, former Costco CEO Jim Sinegal earned a salary of $350,000 a year. This is a sharp contrast to the typical CEO salaries noted earlier in this chapter. The principle of equity extends to the distribution of power. Servant leaders view followers as partners. They practice empowerment by giving followers the space to develop and exercise their talents, by delegating authority for important tasks, and by sharing information. DePree urges organizational leaders to engage in "lavish" communications, sharing information about every aspect of the operation. "Information is power," says DePree, "but it is pointless power if hoarded. Power must be shared for an organization or a relationship to work."[71] When DePree was CEO of Herman Miller, top executives reported monthly to employees on company profits and productivity.

One thing we know: The only ones among you who will be truly happy are those who have sought and found how to serve.

—Albert Schweitzer

The fourth principle of servant leadership is high moral character. Servant leaders possess such virtues as integrity, empathy, honesty, and wisdom. They model exemplary moral behavior. Self-understanding plays an important role in the character development of servant leaders. They analyze their motives, seek out opportunities for personal growth, and regularly take time to examine their attitudes and values. They continually strive to be trusting, insightful, open to new ideas, strong, and courageous.[72]

Following servant leadership principles can have a significant impact on how organizational leaders think and act, which helps produce the positive outcomes described earlier. To determine if your leader acts like a servant, complete the Servant Leader Questionnaire in box 11.8.

Box 11.8 Self-Assessment   **Servant Leadership Questionnaire**[73]

Instructions: You can use this questionnaire to rate the servant leadership behaviors of one of your leaders or ask someone else to rate you. Respond to each question on the following scale: 1 = strongly disagree, 2 = somewhat disagree, 3 = somewhat agree, 4 = strongly agree. The scale rates five dimensions of servant leadership, which are described below. Add up the item ratings to come up with the total score for each component. Add the component scores to come up with a total servant leadership rating (range 24–96).

_____ 1. This person puts my best interests ahead of his/her own.

_____ 2. This person does everything he/she can do to serve me.

_____ 3. This person is one we would turn to if we had a personal trauma.

_____ 4. This person seems alert to what's happening.

_____ 5. This person offers compelling reasons to get me to do things.

_____ 6. This person encourages me to dream "big dreams" about the organization.

_____ 7. This person is good at anticipating the consequences of decisions.

_____ 8. This person is good at helping me with my emotional issues.

_____ 9. This person has great awareness of what is going on.

_____ 10. This person is very persuasive.

_____ 11. This person believes that the organization needs to play a moral role in society.

_____ 12. This person is talented at helping me to heal emotionally.

_____ 13. This person seems in touch with what's happening.

_____ 14. This person is good at convincing me to do things.

_____ 15. This person believes that our organization needs to function as a community.

_____ 16. This person sacrifices his/her own interests to meet my needs.

_____ 17. This person is one who could help me mend my hard feelings.

_____ 18. This person is gifted when it comes to persuading me.

_____ 19. This person is talented at helping me to heal emotionally.

_____ 20. This person sees the organization for its potential to contribute to society.

_____ 21. This person encourages me to have a community spirit in the workplace.

_____ 22. This person goes above and beyond the call of duty to meet my needs.

_____ 23. This person seems to know what is going to happen.

_____ 24. This person is preparing the organization to make a positive difference in the future.

Scoring:

Altruistic Calling (Deep-rooted desire to make a positive difference)

Item 1 _____	Item 21 _____
Item 2 _____	Item 22 _____
Item 16 _____	Total _____ out of 20

Emotional Healing (Fostering spiritual recovery from hardship or trauma)

Item 3 _____	Item 17 _____
Item 8 _____	Item 19 _____
Item 12 _____	Total _____ out of 20

Wisdom (Awareness of surroundings and anticipation of consequences)

Item 4 _____	Item 13 _____
Item 7 _____	Item 23 _____
Item 9 _____	Total _____ out of 20

Persuasive Mapping (Use of sound reasoning and mental frameworks)

Item 5 _____	Item 14 _____
Item 6 _____	Item 18 _____
Item 10 _____	Total _____ out of 20

Organizational Development (Making a collective, positive contribution to society)

Item 11 _____	Item 21 _____
Item 15 _____	Item 24 _____
Item 20 _____	Total _____ out of 20

Overall score _____ out of 100

Meeting the Ethical Challenges of Followership

So far we have focused our attention on the ethical responsibilities of leaders. However, followers also make moral choices. Followers are charged with doing the work and implementing the decisions of leaders. They also have less status and power. Their special ethical challenges center around the following.[74]

Obligation. Followers are obligated to their leaders and their organizations, which provide them with paychecks, health insurance, friendships, training, meaningful work, and other benefits. Yet, they must decide how far those obligations extend. Followers should meet minimal responsibilities by showing up to work on time, faithfully carrying out job duties, and respecting company property. However, some organizations ask too much of their members, as in the case of technology firms that require their employees to work 70–80 hours a week or religious cults that demand total obedience. The challenge for followers lies in determining whether they are meeting their ethical obligations or giving too little or too much.

Obedience. Obeying orders and directives (even unpopular ones) is routine for followers. The challenge comes when they have to decide when to disobey. Obedience is essential if organizations are to function smoothly. Yet, time and time again, followers blindly follow authority with devastating consequences, as in the case of the mass genocide in Nazi Germany and more recently in Rwanda and Darfur. However, being a follower does not justify unethical behavior. At the Nuremberg trials held after World War II the international tribunal rejected the argument that Nazi officials should be exempt from punishment because they were "following orders." American soldiers are punished for obeying illegal orders. Followers need to exercise *intelligent obedience.*[75] This term comes from guide dog training. These service animals obey the commands of their owners except when doing so would put the person in danger (such as crossing a street when a car is coming). Followers need to intelligently disobey when the leader's commands would endanger the group by pausing to clarify and examine the directive, choosing to comply or resist (offering an alternative when possible), and being accountable for their choices.

Cynicism. Cynicism is a common trait of many followers, and it is easy to see why. Followers enjoy less information, power, and privilege than leaders. They get left out of important decisions. At times, the actions of their superiors seem to defy logic. Far too many hard-working, loyal employees have lost their jobs and pension plans at places like Enron, American Airlines, United, and Delta. Nonetheless, cynicism acts like acid, lowering personal commitment and effort, destroying trust, and cutting off communication. The challenge is to maintain a level of healthy skepticism (which prevents exploitation) while avoiding unhealthy cynicism, which poisons the organizational atmosphere while eroding performance.

Dissent. Followers can't change policies, procedures, salary schedules, working conditions, and other factors themselves so they have to express their disagreement to those who can. To begin, they have to decide when to speak up and when to keep their objections to themselves. Followers who raise too many issues earn the "whiner" label. On the flip side, silence can be immoral, as in the case of the accountant who discovers that her company is lying to investors. Followers who decide to protest face the additional challenge of determining how to dissent, whom to contact with their concerns, how to respond to rejection, and when to go outside the organization with complaints.

Bad news. Delivering bad news is risky. Followers who tell their leaders what they don't want to hear can incur their wrath and retribution. The risk is greatest when the bearer of bad news is at fault. Not surprisingly, subordinates routinely keep negative information to themselves, even feedback about leader behaviors that could be keeping the group from achieving its goals.[76] Organizations suffer when followers cover up or hide bad news or try to blame others. Serious deficiencies, like financial or product quality problems, may remain undetected and uncorrected. Members focus on defending themselves instead of on resolving issues. Leaders remain blind to their ineffective habits.

Understanding the components of moral action and major ethical perspectives can help us meet the moral demands of followership just as they can help us master the ethical challenges of leadership. However, to close out this chapter we'll look at two approaches—servant followership and courageous followership—that are specifically designed to help us act ethically in a follower role.

Servant Followership

Servant followership is the flip side of servant leadership. According to Robert Kelley, servant followership is more important than servant leadership because most people spend most of their time in follower roles and followers contribute more to organizational success.[77] Kelley defines a servant-follower as someone who wants to remain in a follower role rather than to seek a leadership position. This reduces the likelihood of destructive competition and conflict and keeps the focus on organizational goals.

Servant-followers demonstrate the exemplary behaviors described in chapter 2. They take initiative and think for themselves. In particular, they know how to "disagree agreeably" about policies and procedures by employing seven strategies. One, servant-followers are proactive, assuming that their leaders want the best outcomes. They provide leaders with the information they need to change course. Two, they gather their facts and try to educate their superiors. Three, servant-followers seek wise counsel from trusted advisors who understand the organization and its leadership. Four, they play by the rules, signaling that they want to be part of the community by using the system. Five, they speak the language of the organization, tying their arguments to the group's values and vision. Six, servant-followers prepare themselves to go to top leaders if lower-level managers ignore their concerns. Seven, they either enlist others to stand with them or make contingency plans (saving plans, other job offers) if they must stand alone.

Max DePree argues that servant-followers have responsibilities to their leaders just as servant leaders have responsibilities to their followers. Followers owe the following to their leaders and institutions:[78]

- understand the institution and its goals, customers, limitations, etc.
- take responsibility for reaching personal goals
- be loyal to the idea behind the organization even when not in agreement with all of the organization's goals and procedures
- resist fear of the new and unknown
- understand the value of others as members of the group and their contributions
- make a personal commitment to be open to change
- build constructive relationships
- ask a great many questions of leaders, including what they believe, how they have prepared themselves for leadership, and whether they can help followers reach their potential

Courageous Followership

Ira Chaleff believes that courage is the most important virtue for followers. He defines courage as accepting a higher level of risk.[79] It is risky, for instance, for a student to confront a professor about an unfair grading policy, for a vice president to oppose the pet project of the CEO, or for a congressional chief of staff to challenge the position of a member of the House or Senate. Exhibiting courage is easier if followers recognize that their ultimate allegiance is to the purpose and values of the organization, not to the leader. Chaleff outlines five dimensions of courageous followership.

The Courage to Assume Responsibility

Followers must be accountable both for themselves and for the organization as a whole. Taking responsibility utilizes many of the strategies outlined in our discussion of self-leadership in chapter 5. Courageous followers take stock of their skills and attitudes, seek feedback and personal growth, maintain a healthy private life, and care deeply about the organization's goals. They take initiative to change organizational culture by challenging rules and mind-sets and by improving processes.

The Courage to Serve

Courageous followers support their leaders through hard, often unglamorous, work. This labor takes a variety of forms, including:

- helping leaders conserve their energies for their most significant tasks
- organizing the flow of information from and to the leader
- controlling access to the leader
- defending the leader from unjust criticism
- relaying a leader's messages in an accurate, effective manner
- acting in the leader's name when appropriate
- shaping a leader's public image
- helping the creative leader focus on the most useful ideas generated
- presenting options during decision making
- encouraging the leader to develop a variety of relationships
- preparing for crises
- helping the leader and the group cope if the leader becomes ill
- mediating conflicts between leaders
- promoting performance reviews for leaders

The Courage to Challenge

Inappropriate behavior damages the relationship between leaders and followers and threatens the purpose of the organization. Leaders may break the law; scream at or use demeaning language with employees; display an arrogant attitude; engage in sexual harassment; abuse drugs and alcohol; and misuse funds. Courageous followers need to confront leaders acting in a destructive manner. In some situations, just asking questions about the wisdom of a policy decision is sufficient to bring about change. In more extreme cases, followers may need to disobey unethical orders.

Courage is being scared to death—and saddling up anyway.

—Cowboy actor John Wayne

While challenge is a critical element of courageous followership, Chaleff notes that support is just as important.[80] The most ethical followers function as *partners* with leaders by demonstrating both the courage to support and the courage to challenge. They back their leaders (which makes leaders more open to feedback) and, at the same time, they raise questions about the leaders' behaviors and policies when needed. Other types of followers fall short when it comes to one or both of these dimensions. The *resource follower* provides little support or challenge. This type of follower does the minimum required and little more. The *individualist follower* provides low support but high challenge. These constituents speak up (even when others are silent) but are frequently marginalized as chronic complainers. The *implementer follower* is very supportive but provides little challenge. Leaders love these subordinates because they get the job done without much supervision. However, implementers generally don't caution the leader against missteps, which puts the organization at risk.

Followership is a discipline of supporting leaders
and helping them to lead well.

—Ira Chaleff

Chaleff offers a number of suggestions for those who must stand up to their leaders. First, recognize that leaders are particularly prone to self-delusion because they have strong egos and their strategies have been successful in the past. The very traits that elevated them to positions of responsibility—decisiveness, independence, and attention to detail—may now be weaknesses in light of current organizational realities. Next, confront destructive behavior when it first occurs—before it becomes a habit that undermines the organization and the leader. Defuse defensiveness by prefacing comments with statements of support and respect. Finally, aim negative feedback at a behavior or policy, not at the person. Be specific about what the problem behavior is, its negative consequences, and the potential long-term impact if it continues.

The Courage to Participate in Transformation

Negative behavior, when unchecked, often results in a leader's destruction. Yet overcoming ingrained habits and communication patterns is a long, difficult process. Leaders may deny the need to change, or they may attempt to justify their behavior. They might claim that whatever they do for themselves (embezzling, enriching themselves at the expense of stockholders, etc.) ultimately benefits the organization. To succeed in modifying their behavior patterns, leaders must admit they have a problem and acknowledge that they should change. They need to take personal responsibility and visualize the outcomes of the transformation—better health, more productive employees, higher self-esteem, restored relationships. Followers can aid in the process of transformation by: drawing attention to what needs to be changed, providing honest feedback, suggesting resources; creating a supportive environment, modeling openness to change and empathy, and providing positive reinforcement for positive new behaviors.

The Courage to Leave

When leaders are unwilling to change, courageous followers may take principled action by resigning from the organization. Departure is justified when the leader's behaviors clash with the leader's self-proclaimed values or the values of the group, or when the leader degrades or endangers others. Sometimes leaving is not enough. In the event of serious ethical violations, the misbehavior of the leader must be brought to the attention of the public by going to the authorities or the press. Such a response would be justified when police commanders order the torture of suspects, corporate executives ask employees to ignore serious safety problems, or the founders of activist groups call for acts that endanger the lives of citizens.

Expect to pay a high price for blowing the whistle on wrongdoing. Whistle-blowers are frequently attacked, criticized, or humiliated by superiors; abandoned by coworkers; relegated to meaningless tasks or demoted; shunned by neighbors, and so on. As one expert observed, "Most whistle-blowers discover that exposing organizational misconduct is a low-reward and high-risk activity."[81] Consider the experience of Tyler Schultz who worked for Theranos, the laboratory that claimed to have developed a revolutionary new method for testing blood. Schultz discovered that the laboratory was doctoring results and repeatedly failed quality control tests.[82] He wrote a memo to Theranos founder Elizabeth Holmes expressing his concerns. Holmes forwarded his memo to the company president who scoffed at Schultz's grasp of mathematics and laboratory science. Schultz quit and then went to New York authorities and the *Wall Street Journal* with his allegations. Since then he has rung up $400,000 in legal fees and his grandfather, former Secretary of State George Schultz who serves on the board of Theranos, sided with the company and ended their relationship. The younger Schultz ultimately was vindicated. Holmes was banned from running a lab for two years and the company had to restate many test results. Walgreens (which had partnered with the company) ended its relationship with Theranos and sued the lab for $150 million.

Those who decide to leave can reduce the risks by setting contingency funds aside, by having written references on file should the need to change jobs arise, by developing good relations with the media in case they need to go public, and by building support groups.

The brave carve out their own fortune.

—*Cervantes*

⌒ CHAPTER TAKEAWAYS

- Standards of moral judgment are critical to the practice of leadership because unethical leaders can do significant damage to groups, organizations, and societies.

- When you take on the role of leader, you take on ethical challenges in addition to a set of tasks and expectations. The moral demands of the leadership role include: (1) issues related to truthfulness and the release and collection of information; (2) the extent of responsibility for the actions of followers; (3) use of power; (4) accumulation of social and material rewards; (5) conflicting and broken loyalties; and (6) inconsistent treatment of subordinates and outsiders. How you respond to these challenges will determine if you cast light or shadow over the lives of your followers.

- Four processes or components lead to ethical behavior: moral sensitivity, moral judgment, moral motivation, and moral action.

- Moral sensitivity (recognition) is the identification of the existence of moral problems. This component involves acknowledging that our behavior impacts others, identifying possible courses of action, and determining the consequences of each possible strategy. You can build your moral sensitivity through: listening to others and working on perspective-taking skills; including moral considerations in decision-making processes; and using moral terminology when discussing problems.

- Moral judgment is deciding which course of action is best. The highest form of ethical reasoning employs widely held moral standards. You can improve your moral judgment by focusing on ethics during your college education, basing your choices on ethical principles, paying attention to your feelings, and being alert to the possibility of faulty reasoning.

- Moral motivation refers to following through on ethical choices, which requires putting moral values ahead of competing values. Rewards and positive emotions increase the likelihood of ethical follow through. Boost the moral motivation of your organization by creating an ethically rewarding environment. Boost your personal moral motivation by regulating your emotions and setting aside destructive feelings for more constructive ones.

- Moral character (implementation) is the action stage of the ethical behavior model. Opposition, fatigue, distractions, and other obstacles must be overcome through persistence. Competence—knowing whom to influence and how—is also essential to successful implementation. You are more likely to put your decisions into action if you assess your personal history, believe that you can make a difference, master the context, and build your communication competence.

- Kant's categorical imperative argues that leaders ought to do what is morally right no matter what the consequences (without exception). Such behaviors as exaggeration, lying, stealing, and murder are always wrong because we wouldn't want others to engage in them. Respect for people is an important corollary to

Kant's imperative. Never treat followers as a means to an end. They have a right to choose for themselves.

- The premise of utilitarianism is that ethical choices should be based on their consequences. The best decisions are those that generate the most advantages as compared to disadvantages and that benefit the greatest number of people.

- Justice as fairness balances the need to honor the equality of all citizens with the recognition that people differ in economic standing, status, and abilities. Ensure that all followers have the same equal right to basic liberties, guarantee that every individual has an equal chance to qualify for jobs and offices, and give priority to meeting the needs of disadvantaged groups. When making decisions, step behind a veil of ignorance, setting aside the characteristics and societal position of those involved to come to the most just conclusion.

- Virtue ethics highlights the role of the person making ethical choices. Leaders with high moral character—who display virtues such as courage, integrity, justice, wisdom, and generosity—are more likely to behave in an ethical manner.

- Altruism makes concern for others the ultimate standard. Altruistic behavior is critical for leaders who must pursue group goals rather than selfish interests. Many effective leadership practices have an altruistic component. To be an effective leader, you will need to promote collective achievements while empowering followers and engaging in self-sacrificing behavior.

- Servant leaders put the needs of followers before their own needs. Four principles serve as the foundation of servant leadership: (1) concern for people; (2) stewardship (holding your position and organization in trust for followers and society and recognizing that leaders and followers "owe" each other certain responsibilities); (3) equity or justice created by distributing rewards fairly and treating your followers as partners; and (4) high moral character fostered by self-understanding.

- The ethical challenges of followership involve obligation, obedience, cynicism, dissent, and communicating bad news.

- Servant-followers want to remain followers rather than compete for leadership positions. In so doing, they reduce destructive conflict and build trust. They are highly engaged, independent thinkers who know how to "disagree agreeably" with their leaders.

- Courage (accepting a higher level of risk) is critical for those in the follower position. As a follower you must: take responsibility for yourself and the organization; serve your leaders through hard work; challenge leaders when they engage in destructive behaviors; help leaders overcome destructive patterns and habits; and leave when a leader's behaviors clash with important values or when the leader degrades or endangers others. But remember that serving your leader is as important as challenging her or him.

∿ APPLICATION EXERCISES

1. Look for examples of unethical leadership behavior in the media and classify them according to the six ethical challenges. Which challenge(s) did the leader fail to meet? What shadows did she/he cast? Do you note any patterns? Are there additional ethical dilemmas unique to leadership beyond those discussed in the chapter?

2. Which challenge of ethical leadership poses the most danger to leaders? Defend your choice.

3. Think of an ethical dilemma you have faced and analyze your response based on Rest's four-component model. Why did you identify this problem as an ethical issue? What considerations played a part in your decision about what to do? What values impacted your motivation to implement your choice? Did you follow through on your decision and take the action you had determined to be appropriate? Why or why not? Write up your analysis in a 4–5 page paper.

4. Form a small group and analyze the Uber Drivers case study in box 11.1 using each of the major ethical perspectives described in the chapter. Record the group's answers. Then answer the following questions: Did the group reach different solutions based on the perspective it used? Do some perspectives apply better than others? Did employing a variety of perspectives improve deliberations? How did the group's conclusions compare to the initial response of each member before beginning the discussion? How does each group member feel about the group's answers?

5. What is the most important virtue for leaders? Defend your choice.

6. Use the chart of defensive and proactive strategies for creating an ethical environment in box 11.2 to evaluate your organization. Does your organization have a positive moral climate? Why or why not?

7. Find a partner and discuss your scores on the Perceived Leader Integrity Scale or the Servant Leadership Questionnaire. How did you rate your leader and why?

8. Conduct a class debate concerning whether or not leaders should act as "servants" to their followers. As an alternative, debate whether altruism is part of human nature or whether more societal and organizational benefits should go to the least advantaged.

9. Interview someone you would consider to be a servant-follower to determine how this individual manages the moral demands of followership. Write up your findings.

10. Evaluate yourself as a courageous follower. What steps can you take to improve?

11. Practice confronting leaders by role-playing the following scenarios in class:
    • You have been at your new job for six months and really enjoy it. However, you are becoming increasingly uncomfortable with the way that your supervisor touches you. At first he gave you brief pats on the shoulder and back.

Now his hand lingers for 2–3 seconds. You are concerned that he will become even more intimate, so you set up an appointment to talk about his behavior.

- Your supervisor at an advertising agency is a "hard charger" who has dramatically increased billings for new clients. Unfortunately, this highly competent and confident leader demeans employees who don't meet her high standards. In the most recent incident, she screamed obscenities at an account executive during a staff meeting. You decide to confront her in private.

- You admire your supervisor, who is kind and generous with all employees. However, she can't seem to stay focused on important tasks. As a result, you get stuck with a lot of last minute details that aren't in your job description. You worry that your supervisor and your department will suffer if she doesn't start finishing projects on time and paying attention to the overall direction of your group. Your weekly appointment with your supervisor is about to begin.

- You are assistant director at a nonprofit organization that serves the developmentally disabled. The director founded the agency 25 years ago. He recently suffered a series of strokes and cannot carry out many of his responsibilities, including raising money and setting the budget. He refuses to step down or even to take a temporary leave. You decide to discuss his future with him.

- You are the manager of a bakery that makes breads, bagels, and other goods for supermarket chains. Your company's vice president of operations has ordered significant cuts in maintenance staff at your plant in order to cut costs and boost profits. Staff reductions will mean a dirtier production facility, which will increase the likelihood that dirt and bacteria could contaminate your products. You decide to protest this directive. To do so you will need to speak directly to the VP of operations. The VP is one organizational level above the district manager, who is your immediate supervisor.

∼ CULTURAL CONNECTIONS: MORAL TASTE BUDS[83]

Psychologist Jonathan Haidt believes that all human are equipped with ethical predispositions or "moral taste buds." These mental foundations, which are part of our genetic profile, developed to enable humans to live together in groups. Just as nearly everyone is born with the same set of taste receptors, everyone has the same set of moral taste buds. But much like each culture develops its own cuisine—which highlights different tastes—every culture shapes how ethical systems are employed, emphasizing some values over others. Haidt originally identified five moral taste buds but recently added a sixth. These foundations of morality include:

Harm/care. All humans are sensitive to the suffering of those outside the family. Kindness and compassion appear to be valued in every society. However, cultures differ in how much they care for outsiders based on the influence of the other five factors described below.

Fairness/reciprocity. Fairness and reciprocity help make human cooperation possible. Anger, guilt, and gratitude are emotions that encourage us to repay others. Also, we want cheaters to be punished and good citizens to be rewarded in proportion to their actions. High concern for fairness and reciprocity leads to an emphasis on individual rights and equality.

In-group loyalty. People favor members of their in-group and are generally distrustful of members of other groups. They value those who sacrifice on behalf of the in-group and despise those who betray the group. In most cultures loyalty, patriotism, and heroism are considered admirable virtues but some societies put more value on loyalty than others. These cultures find it harder to value diversity. Their citizens consider dissent, particularly in wartime, disloyal or treasonous.

Authority/respect. All human societies are hierarchical and individuals may feel awe and respect for those in authority. Status can be based on anything from physical strength and appearance to family lineage and wealth. Some cultures are more concerned with status than others, however. Deference and obedience are virtues in some nations while other societies urge leaders to treat followers with respect.

Purity/sanctity. Only humans seem to feel disgust. Revulsion not only helps protect the body from the dangers posed by vomit, feces, and rancid meat but also has a social dimension. We tend to turn away from those who have physical deformities, for example, and may ostracize individuals who work in some professions, like crime scene clean up or grave digging. Religions often promote purity, believing that the soul is housed in the body. But even secular societies are critical of those who seem to be driven by lust, gluttony, or greed.

Liberty/oppression. This foundation triggers people to take note of, and resent, attempts at domination. They then band together to resist bullies or dictators. This dimension can manifest itself as antiauthoritarianism or as anger against government intrusion into the lives of ordinary citizens.

Haidt points out that Western societies typically privilege the first two moral tastes—harm/concern and fairness/reciprocity. These cultures emphasize the autonomy and freedom of the individual while reaching out to the less fortunate. The moral tastes of much of the rest of the world are very different. In Asia, for example, loyalty, stability, and hierarchy are more significant. Middle Eastern societies put a high value on purity, which is reflected in strict prohibitions about food and dress as well as emphasis on separation. There are strict barriers between men and women and between believers and infidels. Western leaders, then, need to be prepared to speak to all six moral systems when dealing with followers from other cultures. Further, recognizing that others have different central moral values can reduce hostility in ethical conflicts and serve as the first step toward mutual understanding.

∿ LEADERSHIP ON THE BIG SCREEN: *ANGELS IN THE DUST*

Starring: Marion Cloete, Con Cloete, orphans, students, volunteers, village residents

Rating: NR but likely PG-13 for frank discussion of sexual themes and death

Synopsis: This documentary tells the story of therapist Marion Cloete, her husband Con, and their two daughters who left their home in a wealthy Johannesburg, South Africa, suburb to establish a rural village and school for AIDS orphans.

Driven by their vow never to turn away anyone in need, their nonprofit Boikara-belo (formerly Bothsabelo) provides housing, food, and education for more than 550 children. Marion and Con act as house parents, nurses, therapists, AIDS activists, and advocates for children and the dying in the neighboring village. Marion, while respecting the rights of children and the sick, doesn't hold back her anger in the face of injustice. She confronts mothers who deny that their children have been molested or who force their girls into prostitution. She comforts orphans who have lost their parents through AIDS (or face death because they are infected with the disease) by asking them to imagine angels taking them and their loved ones home.

Chapter Links: altruism, servant leadership, servant followership, character, respect for persons, justice as fairness, character, meeting the challenge of responsibility

12

Leader and Leadership Development

You have to be careful if you don't know where you are going, because you might not get there.

—Yogi Berra

OVERVIEW

Leader Development: A Lifelong Journey

Every year millions of adult learners over the age of 25 return to college classrooms to complete their undergraduate and graduate degrees and to upgrade their job skills. According to one estimate, approximately 40% of the undergraduate population is made up of older students.[1] Adult learners (you may be one of them) believe in lifelong learning. We do, too. Developing leadership communication skills is an ongoing process or journey, not a single event. Like other journeys, leader development unfolds step by step. How far we go and how much we get out of the trip depends on us. We need to prepare for the journey and be open to new experiences. The moment we think we have "arrived" as leaders, our progress stops.

Ellen Van Velsor and Cynthia McCauley of the Center for Creative Leadership define the goal of the leader development journey as "the expansion of a person's capacity to be effective in leadership roles and processes."[2] Two elements are central to this definition:

1. Leadership can be learned. Individuals can expand their leadership capacities at any age. People do learn, grow, and change.

2. Leader development helps to make a person effective in a variety of formal and informal leadership roles. While developing leader abilities improves leadership effectiveness among those who serve in formal leadership roles such as supervisors, managers, and project leaders, it can be equally as important in developing competencies for those who play informal leadership roles in their campus, community, workplace, or religious organization.

Van Velsor and her colleagues make a distinction between *leader development* and *leadership development*.[3] Leader development promotes personal growth, helping individuals develop their abilities to manage themselves, to work effectively with others, and to ensure that the work gets done. (Complete the self assessment in box 12.1 to assess your current leadership skills.) Leadership development promotes organizational growth, helping the group as a whole develop the leaders it needs to carry out such tasks as securing the commitment of members and setting direction. In keeping with this distinction, we have titled this chapter "Leader and Leadership Development." Our primary focus will be on how you can continue your development as a leader. However, we'll also look at how organizations promote their collective leadership capacity.

A Proactive Approach to Leader Development

Satisfying journeys don't generally happen by accident. If you want to become an effective leader, you will need to be proactive, taking responsibility for your development. This proactive approach includes raising your leader developmental readiness level, an ongoing commitment to leadership learning, building developmental relationships, and taking advantage of developmental experiences.

Box 12.1 Self-Assessment	**Self-Perception of Leadership Skills[4]**

Directions: Rate the extent to which these 18 statements apply to you on the following scale: 5 = moderately strong, 4 = no opinion, 3= not applicable, 2 = moderately weak, 1 = very weak. When you've completed your responses, add up your scores for each of the leadership skill sets. The lower your score on a particular dimension, the more you believe you need to develop those skills.

_____ 1. I enjoy working on teams.

_____ 2. I enjoy relating to others on an interpersonal basis.

_____ 3. I could delegate work to others.

_____ 4. I want to take charge.

_____ 5. I could appraise and provide feedback to employees.

_____ 6. One of my greatest desires is to become a leader.

_____ 7. Giving directions is comfortable to me.

_____ 8. I am good at planning.

_____ 9. I can interpret rules and regulations.

_____ 10. I know how to develop goals and carry them out.

_____ 11. I am good at problem solving.

_____ 12. I enjoy collecting and analyzing data.

_____ 13. I am comfortable at implementing new techniques.

_____ 14. I am curious.

_____ 15. I am comfortable asking others for advice.

_____ 16. If I make a mistake, I would admit it and correct it.

_____ 17. I believe in workplace diversity.

_____ 18. I thrive on change.

Scoring

Interpersonal/Intrapersonal Skills: Items 1–7 (range 7–35) _____

Task-Specific Skills: Items 8–11 (range 4–20) _____

Cognitive Skills: Items 12–14 (range 3–15) _____

Communication Skills: Items 15–18 (range 4–20) _____

Raise Your Developmental Readiness Level

Readiness to change or develop will help determine how fast you expand your leadership capacities.[5] The higher the readiness level, the more you will benefit from leadership learning, relationships, and experiences. Leader development readiness is made up of motivation and ability. The drive to master new knowledge, skills, abilities, and attributes (KSAAs) starts with interests. Interest in a particular topic, such as environmental leadership or project management, sparks engagement in learning experiences and encourages leaders to expand their knowledge base. Those who benefit most from leadership tasks adopt a *learning goal orientation*. They don't view performance on tasks as a test of their abilities but, rather, as a chance to learn and develop incrementally, over time. Further, they demonstrate *leader self-efficacy*, confident that they can learn specific KSAAs— public speaking, project management, listening, framing—and apply them.[6] Effective leaders integrate these KSAAs into their habitual ways of thinking and acting.

In addition to the motivation to develop, leaders need the ability to do so. Ability to develop takes, first of all, *self-awareness* and *self-concept clarity*. Higher self-awareness and clearer self-concept make it easier to incorporate new skills and knowledge into existing knowledge structures (schemas) and identity (see chapter 2.) Those who practice positive self-reflection instead of highly critical self-examination develop more quickly. Ability development also takes *complexity*, the capacity to make cognitive and emotional associations. Complexity makes it easier to distinguish similarities and differences between cultures, for example, which, as we saw in chapter 10, is an important element of successful cross-cultural communication. Finally, leaders need to be able to "think about their thinking," to demonstrate *meta-cognitive ability*. They need to be able to reflect on whether they are overreacting to a critical comment from a colleague, how they might respond more effectively to a difficult subordinate, what they need to learn to get promoted, and so on.

There are several ways that you can prepare yourself to develop. First, enhance your motivation by tailoring your developmental experience (as much as you can) to your particular interests—your major, career path, athletics, the arts, and so forth. Second, concentrate on learning rather than performance. For instance, many students are so focused on getting a good grade that they overlook valuable learning. They dismiss or ignore feedback on papers and other assignments that could help them be more successful in other classes and in their careers. Third, build your leader efficacy by reflecting on your (a) past successes, (b) looking to role models, (c) learning from the experiences of others, and (d) communicating high self-expectations to yourself (the Galatea Effect described in chapter 9).

Fourth, take opportunities to reflect on who you are (your self-concept) and avoid unhealthy self-reflection focused on your failings. Fifth, continue to develop your cognitive complexity through education and challenging experiences (see the discussion to follow). Train yourself to think about your thinking by periodically stepping back mentally to examine what happened in a developmental event. Ask yourself such questions as: "What positive or negative emotions am I experiencing right now?" "How are those emotions influencing my thoughts and behaviors?" "How do these new knowledge and skills relate to how I define myself as a person?" "How does this experience help me grow toward my future leader self?"

Seek Out Leadership Learning Opportunities

There is no shortage of opportunities to learn about leadership. As a matter of fact, it would be hard to avoid hearing about leaders. We track their successes and failures online, in the newspaper, read about them in history books, and follow them at school and on the job. Some of the strategies and behaviors we witness are excellent models for our own attempts to lead. Unfortunately, we sometimes learn very little from the examples of other leaders because we merely observe them without understanding the reasons behind their successes and failures.

One way to become a more perceptive student of leadership is to keep current with leadership research. The explosion of leadership knowledge in recent years demonstrates why it is so important to view leadership learning as an ongoing process. A search on Amazon.com yielded more than 8,500 books related to leadership communication, while the word *leadership* produced more than 189,000 results.

> *Leadership and learning are indispensable to one another.*
>
> —*John F. Kennedy*

According to one estimate, there are approximately 1,000 leader development programs offered at institutions of higher education in the United States, ranging from small liberal arts colleges to major state schools and Ivy League universities.[7] In addition, leadership topics are integrated into the curriculum in many courses, including communication.[8] A rapidly increasing number of colleges and universities are offering minors, majors, and even graduate degrees in leadership studies.

Within work organizations, formal training programs are widely used to improve leadership effectiveness. Corporations around the globe have recognized that leadership skills can be developed. Companies like Disney, Southwest Airlines, Xerox, American Express, Ritz-Carlton, and PepsiCo, among others, spend millions of dollars each year on training. Much of this training is devoted to improving leadership effectiveness. The training consulting firm Bersin and Associates found that large corporations spent an average of $2,600 a year per first-level manager on leadership training, and double that amount for mid-level managers. At an estimated $15.5 billion, leadership development makes up a significant portion of the more than $70 billion spent each year on employee learning and development.[9] (Box 12.2 examines one widely used leadership development and appraisal tool.)

Chances are you'll participate in one or more of the following types of programs during your career.[10]

1. *Individual preparation.* Historically, training programs have focused on developing the individual leader in the belief that improving a leader's effectiveness will improve the organization as a whole. *Conceptual awareness* workshops develop cognitive understanding. Trainers use case studies, lecture, and discussion to present leadership models or to introduce participants to the differences between leadership and management. *Feedback sessions* provide information to participants about leadership behaviors. Armed with this knowledge, they can address their weaknesses and build on their strengths. Feedback comes from trainers who observe in-class exercises, from fellow trainees, and from self-assessment instruments like those

found in each chapter of this text. The Strengths Finder is one widely used self-assessment. Developed by researchers at the Gallup organization, it identifies common talents and domains of leadership strength. *Skills-based training* helps leaders master such skills as public speaking, listening, and conflict management through modeling and hands-on practice. *Personal growth* programs put leaders into challenging situations that encourage reflection about working relationships and personal priorities while building confidence. Completing a ropes course, white-water rafting, rappelling, and other strenuous activities are designed to get trainees thinking about teamwork, risk taking, creativity, and goal setting in hopes that they will take these insights back to their workplaces and homes.

2. *Socializing company vision and values.* Transmitting a group's culture, as we saw in chapter 8, is one of the most important responsibilities of organizational leaders. In recognition of this fact, Federal Express, The Container Store, Nordstrom, and the US Army use leadership training as a socialization tool. Their training programs highlight corporate vision and values, encourage commitment to organizational priorities, develop a shared interpretation of the group's culture, and provide a forum for dialogue between new and established leaders.

3. *Strategic leadership initiatives.* In this approach, participants learn how to lead change while working toward actual corporate objectives. Strategic programs involve leaders at every level of the organization, and concepts and knowledge covered in training sessions relate directly to the problem at hand. Often teams are assigned to conduct research and then report their findings and recommendations in presentations to management. At General Electric, for example, learning groups carry out consulting projects for business units. Teams have assessed the overall strategy of the European plastics division and helped the locomotive division identify markets for leasing engines.[11]

The strategic initiatives approach, based on action learning, has become the centerpiece of many corporate leadership programs.[12] Action learning benefits both the individual and the organization. Adults learn best when they immediately apply concepts to the problems they face at work, while companies see visible results from these initiatives. Nissan and IBM both used cross-functional teams as action learning and strategic tools to engineer turnarounds. Team members developed an in-depth understanding of problems, learned to tackle challenges under time pressure, and determined how to work with those in other functional areas. The solutions they developed enabled the two firms to survive.

Effective action learning programs involve: (1) careful selection of projects—significant ones that build the skills of individuals; (2) clearly defined objectives and results; (3) periodic opportunities for individuals and groups to discuss and reflect on what they are learning about the project and their personal strengths and weaknesses; (4) sponsorship, participation, and review by top management; and (5)

Box 12.2 **Research Highlight**	**Just How Effective Is 360-Degree Feedback?**[13]

The introduction of 360-degree or multisource feedback marked a major shift in employee performance appraisal. Traditional performance reviews consisted of one supervisor evaluating the work of a subordinate. In contrast, 360-degree reviews solicit feedback on a subordinate from a variety of sources—supervisors, followers, peers, customers, and clients. Originally designed to provide feedback to foster personal development, they are now widely used to evaluate the work of employees and managers.

There are a number of reasons for the popularity of multisource reviews. One, they have the potential to provide more accurate feedback. Input from a variety of sources should give a fuller picture of an individual's performance. Two, 360-degree numerical ratings appear to be less subject to supervisor bias. Three, multisource evaluations are easy to use. A number of vendors provide 360-degree instruments that are taken and scored online. Four, many 360-degree feedback systems provide comparison data, allowing employees to evaluate their performance against departmental and organizational norms.

Despite the popularity of multisource feedback, there is some question about its effectiveness. Approximately one-third of all feedback interventions, including 360-degree feedback, actually *lower* employee performance. Oftentimes, 360-degree data is flawed because of small sample sizes and poorly worded questions. Different feedback sources (peers, supervisors) may evaluate a leader's behaviors differently. Raters may inflate their scores in hopes that the person being evaluated will return the favor. Finally, 360-degree feedback was developed in the United States and may not be appropriate in cultures that put more emphasis on group achievement rather than individual performance.

Multisource feedback works best when the sample sizes are large enough to generate reliable data (at least three respondents for each ratee) and questions are carefully chosen. Moreover, giving individuals their results is not enough. Interpretation must be provided and managers need to follow up with each employee to discuss the results. Behavioral change is most likely when supervisors help employees set specific goals. High-quality (LMX) leader-follower relationships and communication quality, along with organizational support, improve the chances that the feedback will lead to improved performance.

expert facilitation and coaching, generally by outside consultants. Unfortunately, many action-learning formats fail to live up to their potential. Too often they require just one learning experience, not repeated experiences that reinforce learning. Little opportunity is provided for reflection, and participants don't get to implement their recommendations.[14]

> *The trouble with learning is that it's always about stuff you don't know.*
> —Dennis the Menace

Establish Developmental Relationships

Establishing connections with those who can help you achieve your goals will greatly increase your chances of emerging as a leader in an organizational context.

Some of these supportive relationships can be established with peers.[15] *Information peers* are casual acquaintances who provide useful information. *Collegial peers* help with career strategies and provide job-related feedback as well as friendship. *Special peers* act like best friends—giving confirmation, emotional support, and personal feedback. However, the most beneficial relationships will pair you with senior leaders. An established leader can help you by serving as an example that you can emulate from a distance or by taking an active role in your development through acting as your mentor.[16]

The term "mentor" originated from the character Mentor who was the friend of the ancient Greek king Ulysses in Homer's *Odyssey*. He watched the king's son while Ulysses was away, acting as a personal and professional counselor and guide. Modern mentors perform many of the functions of the original. Mentoring expert Kathleen Kram divides mentor functions into two types: career and psychosocial.[17] Career functions are aspects of the relationship that help protégés in their career advancement. Psychosocial functions build the sense of competence and self-worth of both mentors and protégés.

It is important to note that individuals can serve in a mentor role even if they carry out only one set of functions. Some men, for example, find it hard to provide emotional support to protégés but are eager to offer career advice.[18] The shifting needs of protégés will also have an impact on the functions that mentors perform. An inexperienced protégé may need more reassurance; a long-time protégé may want more advice about how to achieve career goals.[19] With this in mind, here is a brief description of the specific functions that fall into each category.

Career Functions

- *Sponsorship.* Mentors fight for their protégés by standing up for them in meetings, putting their names in for promotions, and so forth. Protégés also gain power and more chances for advancement through their association with powerful mentors.

- *Coaching.* Mentors help protégés learn the ins and outs of the organization, including how decisions are made, what the key values are, and who holds power. Mentors have been totally immersed in the corporate culture and can help acclimate the protégé. In addition, they make specific suggestions about how to get the work done, give advice about how to achieve career goals, and supply valuable feedback about job performance.

- *Protection.* Mentors shield their protégés when things aren't going well. They take the blame for slow progress on projects, talk to senior officials when their mentees aren't ready to do so, and step in when their junior partners aren't up to the task.

- *Challenging assignments.* As we noted in our discussion of the Pygmalion effect in chapter 8, the type of assignments that a new manager receives can determine whether that person becomes a low or a high performer. Low expectations communicated through unchallenging or overly demanding assignments can generate a negative performance cycle. Effective mentors set challenging yet realistic goals and work with protégés to help them achieve their objectives. Protégés learn key skills and develop a sense of accomplishment as they master challenges.

> *Simply put, mentors matter.*
>
> —*Suzanne de Janasz,*
> *Sherry Sullivan, and Vicki Whiting*

Psychosocial Functions

- *Role modeling.* Mentors are role models who demonstrate leadership skills. During their apprenticeships, protégés learn how to manage conflict, build teams, gather information, and make ethical choices by observing the behavior of their senior colleagues.
- *Acceptance and confirmation.* Positive regard develops in a healthy mentor/mentee relationship. Each side enjoys the feeling of respect and encouragement that comes from interacting with the other party. When a protégé feels accepted and affirmed, she or he is more willing to take risks and to explore new behaviors.
- *Counseling.* Mentors often become sounding boards for their protégés, helping them work through conflicts that detract from work performance. Three issues are particularly important for those just starting out in a career: (1) how to develop job competence and satisfaction, (2) how to relate to the organization without compromising values and individuality, and (3) how to balance work and family responsibilities.
- *Friendship.* In many successful mentor/protégé partnerships, the parties become friends who develop a mutual liking for one another and engage in informal interaction. The emergence of this function signals that the protégé has become more of a peer than a subordinate. Even when the original relationship ends because of a promotion, job transfer, or some other factor, the friendship often remains.

> *Make yourself necessary to someone.*
>
> —*Ralph Waldo Emerson*

Mentoring Strategies

Based on what mentors can do for their protégés, it's not surprising that those who have organizational sponsors are generally more successful. They typically earn higher salaries, get promoted more often, enjoy greater recognition, and experience higher job satisfaction—results replicated in a variety of cultures.[20] They also experience a boost in leader efficacy.[21] Mentoring programs can help women and those from diverse backgrounds move into senior leadership positions.[22] These advantages carry over into the university setting. Instructors who receive mentoring help have higher rank and pay, are more likely to be tenured, and feel more committed to their institutions.[23] Undergraduates who receive individual attention from a faculty member generally do better in school.[24]

Protégés aren't the only ones to profit from the establishment of mentor/protégé partnerships. The organization as a whole benefits because those who have been successfully mentored are more productive and more committed to the institution. Mentors benefit from the help they get with tasks as well as from the affirmation, confirmation, and friendship provided by protégés. They enjoy passing on their values and insights and seeing their protégés develop and, at the same time, learn from their mentees. Further, those managers who provide career-related mentoring to their employees are rated more favorably by their direct reports and receive higher performance ratings from their bosses.[25] (The film highlighted in the Leadership on the Big Screen feature at the end of the chapter describes a mentoring relationship where both parties profit from the friendship.)

While there are a great many advantages to mentoring, there are potential difficulties as well. Some mentors engage in distancing or manipulative behavior. Distant/manipulative mentors (1) sabotage the work of their protégés, (2) take credit for mentee work, (3) deceive their protégés, (4) abuse their power, and (5) deliberately neglect or distance themselves from their mentees (shut them out of important meetings and messages). In other cases there is a bad relational fit between mentor and protégé that undermines the mentoring relationship. For example, the personalities, values, and work styles of the parties don't match, one or both individuals lack technical or interpersonal skills, or one partner may have personal problems that keep him or her from developing a close relationship with the other person.[26] Protégés as well as mentors can behave in dysfunctional ways, as when mentees take advantage of their mentors by not providing assistance when needed or violating confidences.[27]

Ernst & Young, Pulte Homes, KPMG, and a number of other organizations sponsor mentorship programs to promote the benefits of mentoring while, at the same time, they try to reduce the risks associated with the mentor/protégé relationship. Well-designed programs generally include the following elements:[28]

- criteria and process for selecting both protégés and mentors
- tools for diagnosing the needs of protégés
- strategies for matching protégés with mentors
- formal, negotiated agreements between mentors and protégés
- a coordinator who trains participants, maintains the program, and monitors the mentor/protégé pairs
- periodic evaluation to make necessary adjustments and to determine outcomes for the protégés, mentors, and organization

Joining an organization that has a mentoring program will simplify your search for a mentor. However, many organizations do not have systematic mentoring efforts. In these cases, you'll need to identify the person or persons who might aid in your leadership development. This takes more effort on your part, but research suggests that informal mentor/protégé relationships are generally more productive than those established through formal mentoring programs. Unofficial partnerships last longer and are more supportive than those where protégés are assigned to mentors.

Experts also suggest that you build a mentor network. Establishing one stable mentor relationship is getting harder as more people work from home and individuals frequently change jobs and organizations.[29] Managers have had to take on more responsibilities as organizations downsize, which leaves them less time to mentor. In addition, it is less likely that one individual will possess all the knowledge that a mentee needs in an increasingly technical, global workplace. Begin to build a mentoring network by first considering who you are (your career interest or passion), what you can do (your level of expertise), and who you know (the relationships that can build your network). Then commit yourself to investing time and energy to making connections with multiple possible mentors of various skills, racial and educational backgrounds, industries, genders, and so on. A diverse network will allow you to tap into the knowledge and strengths of a variety of individuals as you take on new jobs and leadership roles.

Some corporations have developed innovative ways to promote mentor networks. Delta Airlines launched a new Innovation Class on some of its flights, where young professionals book a first-class seat next to a leader in their field and get advice for the duration of the trip. Rockwell Collins and IBM promote "speed mentoring" where protégés and senior leaders meet for 15 minutes either in person or online.[30]

Formal Coaching

In recent years, more and more leaders are turning to *formal coaches* to supplement or even to substitute for mentor relationships.[31] According to one estimate, there are 30,000 coaches worldwide.[32] (See the Cultural Connections feature at the end of the chapter for more information on cross-cultural coaching.) Managers, mentors, and peers can act as informal coaches, but formal coaches are outside experts hired to work one-on-one with leaders.[33] Coaching can address specific skills that an executive needs to develop, competencies that equip a leader to succeed in her or his current role, or competencies that the leader will need to fulfill a future, more demanding role.[34] Typically, a coaching program has three phases. In the preprogram phase, the coach meets with the client to determine his/her level of readiness and to design a development plan. A coachee might want help in leading a corporate turnaround, learning to delegate more effectively, or becoming more accessible to followers. The plan will include details on the length of the coaching relationship; how the pair will interact (online, in person) and how often; the release of information; and assessment tools. During the program implementation stage, the coach and coachee establish their relationship, collect and review data on the coachee's performance, and then construct and implement a personal learning agenda with goals, action steps, and measurable outcomes. In the postprogram phase, the participants review and evaluate the client's performance and the coach's input.

To benefit from coaching, you'll need to avoid the following pitfalls:[35]

1. *Failure to commit.* Coaching can only be productive if you are committed to the process. If you don't understand why you need coaching or resent being coached, you will only put in a half-hearted effort or rebel. At the same, the coach will focus his or her energies elsewhere.

2. *Unrealistic expectations.* Remember that it is hard to change ingrained behaviors or to address several behaviors at one time. Be realistic about what coaching can achieve. Recognize that improvement will not automatically lead to a promotion.

3. *Defensiveness.* Be honest about your strengths and limitations and be receptive to feedback. Avoid rationalizing failures, blaming others or denying problems.

4. *Passive role.* The more active you are in setting goals and seeking help, the more you will get out of the coaching process. Passivity undermines the coaching process.

5. *Failure to risk/playing it safe.* Don't play it safe but be willing to open up to the coach; avoid protecting your ego. Don't be afraid to address deeply rooted problems.

6. *Failure to involve others.* Don't hide the fact that you are being coached. Outsiders can help support your efforts to change. The more you involve others in the coaching process, the more likely you will be seen as having improved your performance.

Capitalize on Your Experiences

Any setting where you can master your communication skills—whether at home, at work, or at school—is preparation for leadership. The most useful experiences, though, are those that put you in the leader role. Since leadership experience is so vital, seek out chances to act as a leader. Volunteer to coordinate a campus or community activity, be a crew manager, teach a skill to a group, or offer to serve in any capacity to further your leadership skills. What you learn from your successes—and perhaps more importantly, from your failures—is preparation for future leadership assignments.

Experience is not what happens to a man [woman].
It is what a man [woman] does with what happens to him [her].

—*Aldous Huxley*

Certain kinds of experiences, called developmental job assignments, are extremely helpful in developing leadership abilities.[36] The key characteristic in all developmental job assignments is challenge. These ventures involve risk and require people to leave their comfort zones. There are five broad types of developmental job opportunities.

- *Job transitions.* Moving from one position to another puts people in new situations where job responsibilities are often unfamiliar. Transitions require people to alter their routines and to find new ways to frame and to solve problems. The greater the change in job function, the more opportunity for leadership development.

- *Creating change.* Job experiences that require a person to create change challenge individuals to find new ways to face ambiguous circumstances. A leader may be asked to develop a new product or process, reorganize a work unit, or develop a strategy for dealing with a crisis. Such situations provide fertile experiences for leaders to develop and enrich leadership skills.

- *High levels of responsibility.* Leadership assignments with high levels of responsibility provide potent learning opportunities. These jobs generally involve complex, strategic issues that have a significant impact on an organization. Although these assignments may be stressful, they offer an opportunity for greater visibility and can be a great boon to a leader's self-confidence.

- *Managing boundaries.* Most leaders are accustomed to managing downward. When they have to work with peers, clients, or others with whom they do not have direct authority, they must learn to work collaboratively. Leaders in these assignments need to develop skills in relationship building, problem solving, negotiation, and conflict resolution.

- *Dealing with diversity.* As noted in chapter 10, leaders must learn to work with and to manage those who have significantly different experiences, backgrounds, values, and needs. This requires them to understand diverse perspectives and to manage differences. (See box 12.3 for examples of each of the developmental job assignments.)

To make the most of your developmental job experiences, focus on learning, not just on having the experience (see our earlier discussion of learning orientation). Immediate bosses are often too busy to focus on your development, so you will need to take responsibility. You'll deliberately need to focus your attention on learning by asking: "What I have been doing" and "What, if anything, have I learned from it?" Focus, too, on mastering the demands of the leadership role. There is no one right way to meet the challenges of being a leader so concentrate instead on acquiring the skills and knowledge you need to help you succeed.[37]

Another type of developmental experience is **hardship.** Hardships differ from the other developmental opportunities because people encounter them with little or no warning. Popular author and speaker John Maxwell argues that the difference between average and exceptional leaders lies in their response to adversity and failure.[38] Typical leaders "fail backward" by blaming others, repeating their

Box 12.3	Developmental Challenges and Examples of Assignments Where They May Be Found[39]
Development Component	**Examples of Assignments**
Job transitions	Being the inexperienced member of a project team Taking a temporary assignment in another function Moving to a general management job Managing a group or discipline you know little about Moving from a line job to a corporate staff role Making a lateral move to another department
Creating change	Launching a new product, project, or system Serving on a reengineering team Facilitating the development of a new vision or mission statement Dealing with a business crisis Handling a workforce reduction Hiring new staff Breaking ground on a new operation Reorganizing a unit Resolving subordinate performance problems Supervising the liquidation of products or equipment
High levels of responsibility	Managing a corporate assignment with tight deadlines Representing the organization to the media or influential outsiders Managing across geographic locations Assuming additional responsibilities following a downsizing Taking on a colleague's responsibilities during his or her absence
Managing boundaries	Presenting a proposal to top management Performing a corporate staff job Serving on a cross-functional team Managing an internal project such as a company event or office renovation Working on a project with a community or social organization
Dealing with diversity	Negotiating with a union Managing a vendor relationship Taking an assignment in another country Managing a workgroup made up of people with racial, ethnic, or religious backgrounds different from your own Managing a group of employees from a different generation who seem to be motivated in different ways than you are Training in your organization's diversity program Leading an organizational effort to revise policies about harassment; or the development of the skills of people of different genders, races, sexual orientations, and so on Managing a group that consists largely of expatriates

errors, setting unrealistically high expectations, internalizing their disappointments, and quitting. Successful leaders "fail forward" by taking responsibility for their errors and learning from them, maintaining a positive attitude, taking on new risks, and persevering. To learn from adversity, Maxwell suggests that you ask yourself the following questions every time you encounter failures or mistakes.

What caused the failure: the situation, someone else, or myself? You must identify what went wrong before you can put it right. Don't confuse failure with being a failure. Instead, view what happened as a learning experience and start by locating the source of the problem.

Was this truly a failure, or did I just fall short? Some "failures" are really attempts to meet unrealistic expectations (generally those we put on ourselves). Falling short of an unrealistic goal is not a failure.

What successes are contained in the failure? Failures often contain the keys to future success. For example, Kellogg's Corn Flakes is the result of accidentally leaving boiled corn in a baking pan overnight, and Ivory soap floats because excess air was pumped into a batch when the mixer was left on too long.[40]

What can I learn from what happened? Failure can teach us more than success. When we succeed, we generally use the same approach again. When we fail, we look for different, better ways to proceed.

Am I grateful for the experience? Gratitude can be the key to a teachable mindset. If nothing else, falling short teaches us how to live with disappointments.

How can I turn this into a success? Mistakes teach us how to avoid future miscues and (as we saw above) can lead to important discoveries. Bernie Marcus provides one example of the principle of turning failure into success. After being fired from the Handy Dan hardware chain, Marcus and a partner opened their own home improvement store called The Home Depot. The Home Depot now generates approximately $88 billion in sales annually.

Who can help me with this issue? Learning from adversity is easier with the help of mentors, families, peers, and others. The best advice comes from those who have successfully dealt with their own failures.

Where do I go from here? You can't claim to have learned from an experience unless it leads to a change in behavior.

Research suggests that there are five primary types of hardship events.[41]

- *Business mistakes and failures.* These take the form of lost advertising clients, disgruntled employees, failed mergers, discontinued product lines, bankruptcies, and other organizational mishaps. They offer excellent opportunities for failing forward, teaching important lessons about how to manage others, coping with adversity, and the need for humility.

- *Career setbacks.* Career setbacks like being fired or getting stuck in a dead-end job should be viewed as a wake-up call. They offer the opportunity to see how others perceive you and your contributions. For those who are willing to learn, career setbacks can provide valuable information that can enhance readiness for future leadership endeavors. (See the case study in box 12.4.)

Box 12.4 Case Study	**Profile in Hardship: Abraham Lincoln**[42]

The leaders we admire the most are often the ones who have endured the greatest hardships. William Wilberforce, for example, fought for 46 years to eliminate slavery in Great Britain. Nelson Mandela, Alexander Solzhenitsyn, and Vaclav Havel served prison sentences. Mother Teresa lived in poverty in order to serve the poor. Franklin Roosevelt had to conquer the ravages of polio.

When it comes to rising above hardship, few can match the record of Abraham Lincoln. Lincoln was a small-town lawyer from Illinois who lost two bids for the Senate before his election to the presidency in 1860. He received only 40% of the popular vote in a field of four candidates. Assassination threats forced him to sneak into Washington DC to take his oath of office. He then presided over a war that cost the lives of one out of every five male citizens between the ages of 15 and 40. Some members of Lincoln's extended family fought for the South, and during his first term his beloved son Willie died from illness.

Instead of breaking under the strain, Lincoln grew in stature. He gained confidence and became more committed to the cause of maintaining the Union. The Emancipation Proclamation is one example of how Lincoln matured as a moral and political leader. He bypassed congressional opposition to freeing blacks by issuing the proclamation as a military order. Later, members of the House and Senate followed his example and passed the Thirteenth Amendment, the measure that permanently outlawed slavery in the United States. Few leaders can match Lincoln's generous spirit. He invited his political rivals William Seward, Salmon Chase, and Edward Bates to serve on his cabinet. He specifically instructed Ulysses S. Grant to offer lenient surrender terms to the Confederate army. On the very day he was shot, Lincoln urged his cabinet to welcome Robert E. Lee and other Confederate leaders back into the Union fold.

What was the secret of Lincoln's grace under pressure? No one can say for sure, but three factors seem particularly important. (1) Lincoln tried to understand the meaning underlying the tragic events around him. He was convinced that there was a moral pattern in history and that the suffering of the nation was its punishment for slavery. (2) Lincoln was committed to the cause of continuing the "American experiment" in democracy. He believed that the United States was a model for other nations. (3) Lincoln found a spiritual anchor, placing his confidence in God and seeing himself as an imperfect servant of God's will. Never a member of any particular religious group, he nonetheless devoted himself to prayer and to the study of scripture and has been described as the nation's most spiritual president. Lincoln's search for meaning, belief in the American cause, and spiritual understanding are reflected in his second inaugural address. This message, which is etched on his memorial, is considered by some to be the finest political statement of the 1800s. Lincoln concludes his address with these words:

> Fondly do we hope, fervently do we pray, that this mighty scourge of war may speedily pass away. Yet, if God wills that it continue until all the wealth piled by the bondsman's two hundred and fifty years of unrequited toil shall be sunk, and until every drop of blood drawn with the lash shall be paid by another drawn with the sword, as was said three thousand years ago, so still it must be said "the judgements of the Lord are true and righteous altogether."
>
> With malice toward none, with charity for all, with firmness in the right as God gives us to see the right, let us strive on to finish the work we are in, to bind up the nation's wounds, to care for him who shall have borne the battle and for his widow and his orphan, to do all which may achieve and cherish a just and lasting peace among ourselves and with all nations.

Discussion Questions

1. Can you think of other leaders, famous or not, who endured significant hardship?
2. What role has hardship played in your development as a leader?

3. Why do some people mature when faced with hardship, while others become bitter and disillusioned?

4. What can we learn from Lincoln's struggle with adversity?

5. Why don't contemporary political leaders follow Lincoln's example and reach out to their opponents?

6. How does Lincoln demonstrate the principle of failing forward?

- *Personal trauma.* In many instances a personal trauma such as an illness, death in the family, divorce, or difficulties with children can provide a powerful jolt to a leader. These traumas may prompt a leader to soften his or her behavior, focus more attention on a work-life balance, or learn the value of perseverance.

- *Problem employees.* Dealing with difficult employees offers an opportunity for leader development. Whether it is the employee who behaves in a fraudulent or unethical manner, has a poor work ethic, or is just difficult to get along with, problem employees teach a leader how to deal directly with problem situations.

- *Downsizing.* Being downsized is a hardship that offers a leader a chance to reflect on her or his current situation and to make choices for the future. Although many victimized by downsizing feel a powerful sense of anger, distrust, and loss, those who use the time to take stock and to consider anew what's important in life and their career can ultimately improve their effectiveness.

> *Never, never, never, never give up.*
>
> *—Winston Churchill*

As you can see, some developmental experiences are planned while others are not. Further, such experiences can take place both on and off the job. University of Washington professor Bruce Avolio argues that nearly every important event (moving to a new city, battling cancer) or person (parent, sibling, a favorite teacher or coach) in our "life stream" shapes our development as leaders. (Box 12.5 takes a closer look at how these events promote leadership development.) He notes that both the former president of Poland, Lech Walesa, and the former president of South Africa, Nelson Mandela, boxed when they were young. Skilled boxers know when to punch and when to cover up. This experience, in turn, shaped their leadership behavior: "Both of these men [Walesa and Mandela] stood toe to toe with awesome regimes that had all of the institutional power, and yet they took the punches and survived."[43]

The experiences of our life stream create a life model that contains our views of the world and our perspective on how we should lead others. In other words, how we lead can't be separated from who we are. That means we need to reflect on all the meaningful people and events in our lives to determine how they have impacted our development and to draw useful insights to improve our performance. You can begin to identify these significant relationships and circumstances

---

Box 12.5   Research Highlight   **The Power of Trigger Events**[44]

Authentic leadership scholars (see chapter 4) use the term "trigger events" to describe critical incidents that play an important role in the moral development of authentic leaders. These events, which can be positive or negative, promote introspection and reflection. Trigger experiences are often dramatic—facing near death, visiting a war-torn country, volunteering to rebuild after a hurricane. However, trigger events can also be more mundane, such as reading an important book or working with someone who challenges your point of view. Sometimes a series of small events, like several successes or failures, can have a cumulative effect, prompting significant thought and reflection while changing life direction. Leaders develop a clearer sense of self, including their standards of right or wrong, through these experiences. They also build a store of moral knowledge that they can draw on to make better choices when facing future ethical dilemmas.

In his book *The Road to Character*, author David Brooks describes the life-long moral development (and moral struggles) of a number of important historical figures.[45] Trigger events played a role for many of these leaders, determining their purpose and moral trajectory. They illustrate how these critical incidents can take many different forms.

- Frances Perkins witnessed the infamous Triangle Factory fire at a New York City sweatshop, watching as women burned to death or jumped to their deaths. She dedicated the rest of her life to improving the lives of the poor. Perkins served as labor secretary under FDR and pushed for many New Deal jobs programs, including the Civilian Conservation Corps and the Public Works Administration.

- Psychologist Victor Frankl used his concentration camp experience in Auschwitz to encourage others to develop purpose and meaning whatever the circumstances.

- Albert Schweitzer gave up a successful musical career to become a doctor to the poor in Africa after reading the following Bible passage: "Whosoever would save his life shall lose it and whosoever shall lose his life for my sake shall save it."

- General George Marshall was determined to succeed after he overheard his older brother telling his mother that she should not let George follow in his footsteps and enroll in the Virginia Military Institute (VMI). He believed that George would disgrace the family name. Marshall enrolled and learned that success for him would be the product of hard work and determination.

- Novelist George (Mary Anne) Eliot stopped going to church with her highly religious father, which caused a rift in their relationship and set her on an independent path. She subsequently developed her own philosophy based on empathy and sympathy, which is a central theme of *Middlemarch* and her other works.

- St. Augustine experienced a conversion experience that turned the course of his life from the pursuit of happiness to humble service to God and others.

- Katherine Graham, with no business or journalism experience, became publisher of the *Washington Post* after her husband's death. She then overcame her insecurities to stand up to the Nixon White House during the Watergate crisis and to become one of the most admired publishers in the United States.

by completing Application Exercise 6, which asks you to draw a map of your personal leader journey.

In sum, when it comes to our growth as leaders, we need to capitalize on our developmental experiences whenever and wherever they arise—structured or unstructured, at work or at home, painful or pleasurable. We need to reflect on them and discover what they can teach us. Rather than being trapped by our experiences, we can build on the past to anticipate and to shape future events.

> *What good is experience if you do not reflect?*
> —*Frederick the Great*

Leader Development as an Internal Process

The fact that how we lead (our doing) can't be separated from who we are (our being) means that we need to pay close attention to the inner dimension of leader development. In this section we'll examine leader development as a process that occurs *within* an individual. First, we'll review two acclaimed models that are based on the premise that a great deal of a leader's development happens internally. We will then probe the possible link between spirituality and leader development.

Stephen Covey: *The 7 Habits of Highly Effective People*

This has been one of most popular leadership development programs in the United States. The seven habits, developed by business consultant Stephen Covey, are described in the best-selling book by the same name. Thousands of businesses, nonprofit groups, and government agencies have participated in workshops offered by the Covey Leadership Center. In his book Covey argues that a leader's effectiveness is based on such character principles as fairness, integrity, honesty, service, excellence, and growth. (Refer to chapter 11 for more information on virtue or character ethics.) He defines a habit as a combination of *knowledge* (what to do and why to do it), *skill* (how to do it), and *motivation* (wanting to do it).[46] Leadership development is an "inside-out" process that starts within the leader and then moves outward to impact others.

Habit 1. Be proactive. Proactive leaders realize that they can choose how they respond to events. For instance, when insulted or unfairly criticized, they decide to remain calm instead of getting angry. Proactive individuals also take the initiative by opting to attack problems instead of accepting defeat. Their language reflects their willingness to accept rather than to avoid responsibility. A proactive leader makes such statements as "let's examine our options" and "I can create a strategic plan." A reactive leader makes such comments as "the organization won't go along with that idea," "I'm too old to change," and "that's just who I am."

> *No one can hurt you without your consent.*
>
> —*Eleanor Roosevelt*

Habit 2. Begin with the end in mind. Effective leaders always keep their ultimate goals in mind. Creating personal and organizational mission statements is one way to identify end results. Covey urges leaders to center their lives on inner principles rather than on external factors like family, money, friends, or work.

Habit 3. Put first things first. This principle is based on the notion that a leader's time should be organized around priorities. Too many leaders spend their time coping with emergencies and neglect long-range planning and relationships. They mistakenly believe that urgent items are always important. Effective leaders carve out time for significant activities by identifying their most important roles, selecting their goals, creating schedules that enable them to reach their objectives, and modifying these plans when necessary. They also know how to delegate tasks and have the courage to say "no" to requests that don't fit their priorities.

Habit 4. Think win/win. Those with win/win perspectives take a mutual gains approach to communication, believing that the best solution benefits both parties. The win/win habit is based on: character (integrity, maturity, and a willingness to share); trusting relationships committed to mutual benefit; performance or partnership agreements that spell out conditions and responsibilities; organizational systems that fairly distribute rewards; and principled negotiation that guarantees that the solution is generated by both parties and not imposed by one side or the other. (For an in-depth look at principled negotiation, turn to chapter 6.)

Habit 5. Seek first to understand, then to be understood. Effective leaders put aside their personal concerns to engage in empathetic listening. They seek to understand instead of evaluating, advising, or interpreting. Empathetic listening is an excellent way to build a trusting relationship. Covey uses the metaphor of the emotional bank account to illustrate how trust develops. Principled leaders make deposits in the emotional bank account by showing kindness and courtesy, keeping commitments, paying attention to small details, and seeking to understand. These strong relational reserves help prevent misunderstandings and increase the likelihood that leaders and followers will quickly resolve any problems that do arise.

Habit 6. Synergize. As we noted in our discussion of cultural differences in chapter 10, synergy creates a solution that is greater than the sum of its parts. Synergistic, creative solutions can only come out of trusting relationships (those with high emotional bank accounts) where participants value their differences.

Habit 7. Sharpen the saw. Sharpening the saw refers to continual renewal of the physical, social/emotional, spiritual, and mental dimensions of the self. Healthy leaders care for their bodies, nurture their inner values through study and/or meditation, encourage their mental development through reading and writing, and generate positive self-esteem through meaningful relationships with others.

Kevin Cashman: *Leadership from the Inside Out*

Korn Ferry consultant Kevin Cashman argues that too many leadership development books focus on the external act of leadership.[47] He believes that leadership comes from within and is an expression of who we are as people. Leadership is not something that one does; it comes from somewhere inside. Cashman defines leadership as "authentic self-expression that creates value."[48] This form of leadership can be found at all levels in organizations and can be exhibited by anyone.

> *A life without purpose is an early death.*
> —*Johann Wolfgang von Goethe*

To develop self-leadership skills, Cashman identifies seven pathways that allow a person to lead from the inside out. These pathways are not stages of development arranged in a sequential or hierarchical order. Rather, they are viewed holistically as integrated pieces of a collective framework.

Pathway One: Personal Mastery—Leading with Awareness and Authenticity. The ongoing commitment to exploring who you are is the key to personal mastery. This understanding allows a person to develop moral character and to lead through authentic self-expression. Learning what is important to you will impact how you lead, moving you from reacting (coping) to creating value (character) as a leader. Cashman suggests exploring such questions as:

- What is going on in these times?
- How can I challenge myself to move from coping to character more often?
- What fears do you have to face to lead from character?
- How can I lead from character in more situations in the future?

Questions such as these bring your beliefs to the forefront and help to guide your leadership efforts.

Pathway Two: Purpose Mastery—Leading on Purpose. Learning how you make a difference is key to the second pathway. Purpose mastery connects your gifts and talents to your values. Get in touch with what is important to you and commit yourself to acting "on purpose" in every area of life; focus on how your gifts can serve others.

> *The number one reason leaders are so unsuccessful is their inability to lead themselves.*
> —*Truett Cathy*

Pathway Three: Interpersonal Mastery—Leading through Synergy and Service. This pathway focuses on the development of interpersonal competencies.

Many leaders are not skilled in building relationships with others. A study of 6,403 middle and upper managers conducted by the Foundation for Future Leadership found that managers receive their highest evaluations for their intellect and technical expertise and their lowest marks for their interpersonal skills.[49] To develop interpersonal mastery, focus on building relationships with others that lead to collaborative efforts and seek to serve followers.

Pathway Four: Change Mastery—Leading with Agility. Letting go of old patterns and taking a fresh approach allows a leader to enhance his or her creativity. This pathway emphasizes the need to be adaptable and willing to change. Being open to change allows a leader to recognize the possibilities presented by each situation, whether it is the opportunity to start a business, go back to school, or simply try a new restaurant. Change challenges current reality and allows a leader to see a new reality. Change masters know how to live in the moment while maintaining a broad awareness of long term goals.

Pathway Five: Resilience Mastery—Leading with Energy. Taking time for self, family, and friends is critical to developing resilience. Without resilience, a leader can become irritable, uninspired, unfocused, and nervous. Resilient leaders focus on renewing their energy through exercise, rest, enjoyable activities, avoiding poor habits, nurturing close relationships, managing stress, and simplifying their lives.

Pathway Six: Being Mastery—Leading with Presence. Being is at the core of an individual. Being mastery involves using periods of peace and silence to understand one's innermost depths of character and being. Quiet moments, meditation, a favorite piece of music, a walk in the country, or inspirational reading can serve as a catalyst for exploring one's being and connecting with the inner self.

Pathway Seven: Action Mastery—Leading through Coaching. Action mastery is applying purpose and potential to increase impact. In this pathway, a leader coaches the self and others. Reaching full potential—for the leader and followers—takes self-awareness, commitment to growth, and learning and practicing new behaviors.

The Role of Spirituality in Leader Development

A number of leaders report that spirituality has played a critical role in their development, helping them to make and follow through on their moral choices, develop virtues and character, identify their values and purpose, reach out to others, and benefit from (rather than being overwhelmed by) challenging job assignments and hardships. The topic of spirituality, once relegated to the margins of organizational and leadership studies, has entered the academic mainstream. Researchers are studying the impact of spiritual beliefs and practices on organizational and leadership performance, examining the relationship between spirituality and job satisfaction, turnover, decision making, employee commitment, productivity, and other variables. Their findings are reported in a variety of journals (*Journal of Organizational Change Management, Journal of Managerial Psychology, Leadership Quarterly*) and books (*Handbook of Workplace Spirituality and Organizational Performance, Spiritual Intelligence at Work, Religion in the Workplace*). Investigators have discovered that spirituality fosters organizational learning and creativity, improves morale, generates higher productivity, encourages collaboration, and enhances commitment to the organizational mission, core values, and ethical standards.[50] Spirituality in the workplace has also attracted popular attention. Some organizations sponsor groups for spiritual seekers, and those interested in the subject can attend a variety of business and spirituality conferences and seminars. Tom's of Maine, TD Industries, Toro, and Medtronic are a few of the companies that put spiritual values at the center of their organizational cultures.

Connectedness is key to understanding the nature of spirituality in organizations. Workplace spirituality is about integration and connection, not separation and differentiation. According to one widely cited definition, for example, workplace spirituality is "a framework of organizational values evidenced in the culture that promotes employees' experience of transcendence through the work process, facilitating their sense of being connected to others in a way that provides feelings of completeness and joy."[51] Ian Mitroff and Elizabeth Denton describe organizational spirituality as "the basic feeling of being connected with one's complete self, others, and the entire universe."[52] Feeling connected with self means getting in touch with our inner longings and emotions while reintegrating thoughts and feelings. Feeling connected with others is lived out through concern for coworkers, respect, teamwork, and community involvement. Feeling connected to "the entire universe" describes developing relationships with larger forces like nature, a higher power, or God. Many scholars distinguish between religion and spirituality. While the two overlap, they are not identical. Religion involves belief systems and institutions (temples, meetings, churches) that nurture and structure spiritual experiences, but spiritual encounters can occur outside formal religious settings.

Spiritual leadership expert Laura Reave reviewed more than 150 studies and found a correlation between spiritual values and leader effectiveness.[53] Spiritual values play an important role in both leader and follower motivation. Leaders and followers alike want to serve worthy purposes, to view work as a calling that serves the needs of others and a higher power. Promoting spiritual values reduces stress, absenteeism, and turnover while improving morale and profitability. Spiritual values also promote leader integrity and humility. As we saw in our discussion of credibility in chapter 6, organizational trust in chapter 8, and character in chapter 11, these qualities are essential to personal and collective success.

Reave also found that the following common spiritual practices also promote leader effectiveness.

1. *Treating others fairly.* Fairness is an outcome of viewing others with respect, an important tenet in most belief systems and spiritual paths. Employees put a high priority on fairness at work. They are more likely to trust leaders who treat them fairly and to go beyond their job descriptions to help coworkers.

2. *Expressing caring and concern.* Spirituality often takes the form of supportive behavior. Those working for caring leaders are more satisfied and build better relationships with their supervisors. As we noted in our review of LMX theory in chapter 3, fulfilling relationships lead to increased productivity. Caring and concern for the community also pays off. Employees of

organizations known for corporate philanthropy rate their work environments as excellent and ethical, get a higher sense of achievement from their work, and take more pride in the company.

3. *Listening responsively.* Listening and responding to the needs of others is another practice endorsed by many spiritual traditions. Good listeners are more likely to emerge as group leaders, and organizational leaders who demonstrate better listening skills are rated as more effective. Successful leaders also respond to what they hear.

4. *Appreciating the contributions of others.* Most of the world's faiths view people as creations of God (or some other powerful force) who are worthy of praise. Praise for God's creation, in turn, expresses gratitude to God. In the workplace, recognizing and praising employee contributions generates goodwill toward the organization, creates a sense of community, and fosters continuing commitment and contribution.

5. *Engaging in reflective practice.* Spiritual practice doesn't end with demonstrating fairness, caring, and appreciation to others. It also has a self-reflective component. Meditation, prayer, journaling, and spiritual reading deepen spirituality and also pay practical dividends.[54] Leaders who engage in such practices improve their mental and physical health by reducing stress levels, becoming more productive, and developing stronger relationships with others. They are better equipped to rebound from crises and to discover the deeper meaning in the defining moments of their lives. Self-reflective leaders also have more control over their emotions and exercise more self-discipline.

Evidence that spiritual values and practices can improve leader effectiveness provides a link between spiritual development and leader development. As we develop spiritually, we can expand our capacity to function as leaders. Kazimierz Gozdz and Robert Frager offer the following model of spiritual development that measures both personal and organizational spiritual growth.[55] You can use this model to track your spiritual progress as well as the spiritual progress of your organization.

Stage I. Unprincipled. Unprincipled individuals are egocentric and narcissistic (focused on personal pleasure). They are unwilling to give up their needs for anyone or anything else. At this stage, people want to have their own way and seek to dominate and control others. At the same time, they refuse to admit that their actions are problematic. Such individuals break or bend the rules when they can and only obey out of fear of punishment. Stage I organizations "are dysfunctional for society and for the planet."[56] They are greedy and pursue selfish interests. To them, the world is a battleground. In the fight for survival, anything goes—cheating, lying, overcharging, polluting the environment. These dysfunctional institutions are frequently run by tyrannical bosses.

Stage II. Conventional. People in this stage have a good deal of self-doubt, so they turn to rules and organizational structure for comfort instead of relying on their own judgment. These individuals are often subservient to those above them and abusive to those below them. They rarely question the system and are more interested in getting on with the job. The Stage II institution (a family business, for example) promotes obedience to the system and the rules. The group is conservative, relying on strategies that have worked in the past. Hard work is more important than taking initiative. Leaders in these organizations are often autocratic and patriarchal, managing through detailed procedures and regulations as well as through threats of punishment.

Stage III. Self-Actualizing. Individuals in the third stage are committed to personal growth and demonstrate a high degree of self-awareness. They can articulate their values and are inner-directed. Stage III people are more willing to challenge assumptions and regulations than their Stage I and Stage II counterparts. However, they often experience burn out because they work long and hard to reach their goals. Egocentric, they may also lose sight of organizational and societal goals and interests as they compete with others. Organizations in this stage put a premium on growth and innovation. Like sports teams, they encourage teamwork while at the same time they strive to beat other "teams." Stage III groups are good at strategic planning and responding to change. They reward both individual initiative as well as teamwork. During his business career Bill Gates was an example of a Stage III leader. Now that he is working mostly with his foundation, Gates appears to have moved to the next stage. The organization he founded, however—Microsoft—appears to be still functioning at this third stage.

Stage IV. Integral. At this final stage, individuals move beyond their egos and demonstrate deeper levels of spirituality. They have experienced powerful feelings of connection to others and larger ("transcendent") forces outside themselves. These moments have made them more humble and compassionate, shifting them from self-concern to a willingness to surrender to greater, higher causes. People in this stage of development feel integration between their inner and outer selves. They are committed to questioning and challenging assumptions and realize that the world is always changing. As a result, they value change, growth, and flexibility. Stage IV institutions are learning organizations (see chapter 8). They anticipate change and respond quickly and effectively to threats and opportunities. Their structures are fluid, based more on functional and project groups than on hierarchy and authority. Such organizations make decisions based on what is good for society, the world, and the environment. These groups actively seek feedback and set aside competition for collaboration that produces win/win solutions. Leaders of Stage IV organizations have a clear vision that they articulate in an inspiring manner. Such leaders are servants (see chapter 11) who build others up rather than using them. As a result, followers also move to higher stages of spiritual development.

Leadership Transitions

Leadership transitions are critical to both personal and organizational success. Not only do we need to acquire the knowledge and skills necessary to carry out new leadership roles, we also need to help ensure that the group as a whole chooses the right successors when positions open up. Any transition is risky. Estimates are that 40% of newly promoted managers and two-thirds of senior leaders appointed from outside the organization have to be replaced within 18 months.[57] One survey found that 50% of large organizations have CEOs with tenure of five years or less. Another found that 60% of small to medium for-profit and nonprofit organizations have top leaders who have been in their roles less than five years.[58] A number of prominent CEOs like Mattel's Bryan Stockton, Reddit's Yishan Wong, and McDonald's Don Thompson were forced out after only a few years on the job. In this final section of the chapter, we will outline common leadership passages, describe ways to take charge as a new leader, and identify the characteristics of effective succession planning programs.

> *Nothing is permanent but change.*
>
> —*Heracleitus*

Leadership Passages

Leadership succession takes place at all levels of the organization, creating what Ram Charan, Stephen Drotter, and James Noel call a "leadership pipeline."[59] The leadership pipeline, in turn, contains six key leadership turns or passages. When leaders master each passage, the pipeline keeps flowing, building the leadership base of the organization. Trouble arises when leaders promoted to new roles continue to work at previous levels. Successfully navigating each passage means leaving behind old ways of thinking and behaving and adopting new ways of managing. Specifically, individuals must acquire new skills, adopt new time frames, and develop new values about what is important and should be the focus of their efforts. (Box 12.6 describes additional factors that derail executives.)

Here are the six key leadership pipeline turns along with suggestions for how you can navigate each turn.

Passage One: From Managing Self to Managing Others

Most young employees spend their initial years on the job as individual contributors, using their technical or professional skills in accounting, finance, sales, engineering, and other fields. They focus on getting their tasks done on time and on developing their individual skills. Punctuality, quality, and reliability are important values and getting tasks done on time is critical. If you demonstrate the ability to contribute on an individual level, chances are you will be promoted to a management position. Unfortunately, many newly minted managers take the title without making the necessary changes in their thinking and behavior. They still want to do the work themselves instead of learning how to plan work, motivate employees, assess the work of others, and so on. They fail to make the fundamental shift from doing the work to doing the work through other people. To avoid this trap, learn to value managerial work, and make time for planning, coaching, and other managerial tasks.

Box 12.6	Derailment Factors[60]

A number of bright, talented individuals fail to navigate the leadership passages. Instead of successfully making a transition, they are *derailed*. Derailed leaders apparently have the ability to be promoted but are instead fired, demoted, or plateaued (kept at the same level). Derailment also occurs to leaders who stay in their current networks. They may be punished for failing to adapt to changes in their jobs and workplaces (e.g., additional assignments, transfers, layoffs, mergers, new systems). Flaws that derail leaders include:

- *Problems with interpersonal relationships* (overly ambitious, isolated from others, authoritarian, poor working relations)
- *Failure to meet business objectives* (overpromising, lack of follow through, betrayal of trust)
- *Inability to build and lead a team* (poor selection of group members, putting personal achievement over team achievement, poor management)
- *Inability to change or adapt during a transition* (failure to handle a conflict or style differences with a boss; overdependence on one skill/failure to master new skills; failure to adapt to a new job, culture, or market changes)

Passage Two: From Managing Others to Managing Other Managers

In this passage leaders totally give up individual tasks and become pure managers. They choose the followers who will move to Passage One, assign work to these individuals, and then measure their progress. Passage Two leaders must look beyond their immediate roles and think about the overall direction of the business or organizations. As a Passage Two leader, it is particularly important to recognize when Passage One leaders are resisting doing managerial work, as in the case of the software designer who would rather create software than manage others. In some cases, you may need to return Passage One leaders to their individual contributor roles. Expect to spend time mentoring Passage One leaders.

Passage Three: From Managing Managers to Functional Manager

At stage three, managers are now two levels removed from individual contributors and must learn how to keep in touch with frontline workers without alienating Passage One and Two subordinates. Functional managers, as the name implies, oversee important organizational functions like managing, accounting, or engineering. To succeed in this role, you'll have to broaden your focus, managing those outside your areas of expertise. You will need to develop strategies that support the overall business strategy. Expect to spend a significant amount of your time in meetings with those from other functions and learn how to delegate responsibility for functional tasks to direct reports. This level requires a higher level of "managerial maturity." Functional leaders see the broader picture and think long term, developing new products and other strategies that put their organizations ahead of the competition.

Passage Four: From Functional Manager to Business Manager

This passage involves taking charge of an entire business, such as the printer unit of a computer company. Business managers have to integrate functions, determining whether or not a plan or proposal will be profitable and whether that profit can be sustained over the long term. If you become a Passage Four leader, you will be responsible for unfamiliar functions (those you don't know) and must work with a wider variety of people. Success in this role requires continually balancing short-term concerns like meeting payroll and profit goals with long-term objectives (3–5 years out). Take time for reflection, value staff functions like human resources and finance, and learn to trust lower level managers in charge of unfamiliar functions.

Passage Five: From Business Manager to Group Manager

While the business manager focuses on the success of her or his own business, the group manager must value the success of other people's businesses. This means setting aside the desire to get all the credit for success. To succeed as a group manager, you'll need to master four new critical skill shifts. One, learn how to evaluate strategy for deploying capital. Second, identify those who should become Passage Four leaders and then help develop these individuals for their roles. Third, become skilled at portfolio strategy. Determine if the enterprise has the right collection of businesses, selling or adding companies as necessary. Fourth, assess the organization to identify if it has the appropriate core competencies to carry out its strategies and reach its goals. Keep in mind that Passage Five leadership is holistic. To function at this level you will have to oversee multiple businesses, interact with the larger community and government agents, participate in ceremonial activities, take greater risks, assume greater responsibilities, and so on.

Passage Six: From Group Manager to Enterprise Manager

Many of the skills of the Passage Five leader carry over to Passage Six. (In smaller organizations, leaders may go directly from level 4 to level 6.) At this level, values take on added importance. The Passage Six leader must be visionary, know how to meet demands for immediate profit while fulfilling long-term strategy, and manage external constituencies and issues (see the discussion of issues management in chapter 9). Your success or failure in this role will be based on three or four important decisions every year, so focus on a handful of priorities. Assemble a top-level leadership team to assist you in running the enterprise.

Taking Charge

John Gabarro uses the term "taking charge" to describe how newly appointed managers become leaders.[61] Gabarro notes that new managers rely heavily on legitimate power, which is based on organizational position. If they want to become leaders, they must extend their influence by developing other power bases. Appointees take charge by developing an understanding of the leadership situation, gaining acceptance as leaders, and having an impact on organizational performance. To achieve these outcomes, they engage in three types of work or processes: *cognitive* (learning about the organization and its culture, acquiring technical knowledge, diagnosing problems, understanding issues); *organizational* (developing a set of shared expectations with followers, working out conflicts, and building a cohesive management team); and *interpersonal* (developing good working relationships with superiors, subordinates, and peers).

There are a number of variables that either facilitate or complicate the task of taking charge.[62] Some of these variables have to do with the characteristics of the successor. Those brought in from outside the organization generally make more changes and have more to learn. A close match between the successor's previous experience and the demands of the new position make for a smoother transition, but conflicts will likely develop if the successor's leadership communication style is inconsistent with her or his predecessor's. Other variables are situational in nature. Those faced with significant performance problems must make greater changes. A perceived need for change; a strong power base built on competence, position, and other factors; and a strong, supportive management team facilitates the process of taking charge. Disgruntled employees who were turned down for the leader's position make the successor's job harder.

The final cluster of variables involves the selection process itself and how the organization prepares for the arrival of the new leader. The successor who clearly understands the expectations of the organization and is given a mandate for change has the greatest chance of success. The new leader's superior can defuse the hostility of disappointed candidates by telling them why they weren't chosen for the position.

Management transition consultant Peter Fischer identifies seven building blocks that you can use as a new leader to facilitate the process of taking charge and promote the changes you'll want to implement.[63]

1. *Management of expectations.* Find out the expectations of your superior when coming into a new role. What are his or her most important goals, for example? Determine the expectations of employees as well as colleagues. Often these expectations are unstated ("We want our leader to be human"; "We expect you to go along with current procedures and respect our work"). Identifying expectations is critical since unmet expectations frequently derail new managers. (Conflicting expectations are at the heart of the transition crisis described in box 12.7.)

2. *Develop key relationships.* Try to bridge the gap with disappointed rivals who wanted your position; offer to cooperate with them. Recognize that colleagues will be concerned that you will be making significant changes. They may also resent your new ideas. As a consequence, it is important to build solid connections with your peers. Be careful not to disparage your predecessor, whether that person was a success or a failure. Resist the temptation to come in as the group's "savior." Establish a relational network with others throughout the organization in order to increase your power and influence.

3. *Constructively analyze the situation.* Start by discovering the assumptions and values of the organizational culture—see chapter 8. Sort through the issues facing the organization, deciding which deserve priority. Gather the facts (e.g., income statements, market developments, complaints). Deter-

mine the extent to which the organization is willing to innovate and change in order to address its problems and opportunities. Identify the resources or strengths of the group and decide whether they are adequate to achieve organizational objectives.

4. *Establish a set of motivating goals*. Create shared goals that emphasize both stability (i.e., maintaining market position and values) and change (expanding operations to new countries) as well as task and relationships. Be sure that the goals are specific and significant, and recognize that problems are interrelated. Create a motivating vision of what the organization will be like in the future.

Box 12.7 Case Study	**The President Who Would Be Provost**

Tom Peterson thought he had found the perfect place to wind up his career as a college administrator. After previously serving as a dean at two other schools, he was hired several months ago as provost at Tyree University, a public liberal arts college in British Columbia. The provost is second only to the university president on the organizational chart and oversees all academic programs and the faculty. Tom looked forward to putting his "stamp" on the college's academic culture. He saw some weaknesses in the university's core curriculum and thought he could introduce new majors to make Tyree more attractive to prospective students. He was also eager to improve the quality of the faculty and to act as a strong voice for faculty members who have complained of being left out of many important decisions.

Tom was hired shortly after Bert Behrens, the previous provost, was promoted to president. The university's board of trustees thought that Peterson's lengthy experience would be helpful to the younger Behrens as he transitioned to his new role. College presidents traditionally spend much of their time representing the university to outside groups and fund-raising.

Unfortunately, the president-provost relationship is off to a rocky start. Behrens so far refuses to relinquish his former role and seems determined to act as both provost and president. He continues to interject himself into academic decision-making while spending little time raising money. The president, not the provost, launched an initiative to restructure the college's core curriculum. Behrens vetoed a hiring decision supported by both the faculty and Peterson in favor of a candidate he favored. So far it appears as if Behrens expects Peterson to act in a supportive role, implementing his plans and policies and enforcing his decisions.

Unless the situation changes, Tom doesn't think he will remain at Tyree.

Discussion Questions

1. What are the expectations of President Behrens, Provost Peterson, the board of trustees, and faculty?

2. Should Peterson modify his expectations and focus more on implementing the plans of the president rather than on developing his own initiatives? What might be the consequences if he did so?

3. Why do you think the president continues to act as provost?

4. What steps could the board of trustees take to encourage Behrens to fully transition to the president role?

5. Who is to blame for this difficult transition?

6. Is this transition doomed to fail or can it be salvaged?

5. *Foster a positive climate for change.* Ask appreciative questions that focus on gathering information and that recognize the strengths of employees. Get followers to think, inquire about the resources they have or need, and ask what they believe will happen in the future. Surface and acknowledge skepticism about proposed projects. (Doing so will reveal potential problems.) Build trust with employees and utilize their strengths in change initiatives.

6. *Initiate change effectively.* Send strong signals that change is needed. Present a theme that captures the change strategy and follow up with specific action steps. Involve others in the process. Build momentum by successfully completing a series of small steps. Small victories build momentum for greater changes. Monitor success or failure. Knowing when to start the change is a key element of this building block. Don't start until followers are prepared for change, key relationships are in place, and the initial steps are clear.

7. *Use symbols and rituals.* Establish your identity as a new leader through your language and actions. You may want to demonstrate that you have a different style than your predecessor, encourage cooperation, reassure followers that their jobs are secure, change the culture, and so on. For example, if you want to communicate that you are responsive, then take telephone calls personally and respond quickly to e-mail inquiries. Add rituals that reinforce the message you want bring. To signal that the team is important, for instance, celebrate achievements with team members.

Succession Planning

A growing number of large organizations are developing succession-planning programs that take a systematic approach to identifying and developing future leaders. Anticipating leadership transitions makes sense for several reasons. As we saw earlier, the importance of leadership changeover and the high failure rate of new leaders suggest that succession planning should not be left to chance. The demand for future leaders is likely to increase as baby boomers reach retirement age at the same time that there are fewer younger workers to replace them. Corporate layoffs may also contribute to a leader shortfall by reducing the number of middle management positions that have traditionally served as training grounds for executives. Further, a systematic approach to leadership transitions reduces the likelihood of a mismatch between the person and the position as well as the tendency for job incumbents (who are often white males) to choose successors who resemble themselves (other white males). In recognition of the importance of succession planning for publicly traded companies, the Securities and Exchange Commission has identified CEO succession planning as a key responsibility of boards of directors. Shareholder groups are beginning to demand that companies disclose their written succession plans.[64] (Complete the self-assessment in box 12.8 to determine if your organization has a systematic process for leadership succession.)

| Box 12.8   Self-Assessment | | | Succession Planning Survey[65] |

Complete the following survey to determine the status of your work group or organization's succession-planning process. "No" responses indicate potential weaknesses. Outline steps that your work group or organization can take to address these problem areas.

Question	Yes	No	Your Comments
A. Is there a systematic means to identify possible replacement needs stemming from retirement or other predictable losses of people?			
B. Is there a systematic approach to performance appraisal so as to clarify each individual's current performance?			
C. Is there a systematic approach to identifying individuals who have the potential to advance one or more levels beyond their current positions?			
D. Is there a systematic approach by which to accelerate the development of individuals who have the potential to advance one or more levels beyond their current positions?			
E. Does a means by which to keep track of possible replacements by key positions exist?			

Experts report that effective succession-planning programs share the following characteristics:[66]

- *Participation and support of top management.* When top leaders are involved, others are more likely to devote time and effort to succession concerns. The board of directors should also be included in the process from the start.
- *Include all leadership levels.* Succession planning is important for low-level management positions as well as for executive ones.
- *Organizational needs assessment.* Organizations must decide on the direction in which they are headed before they know what types of skills their future leaders must develop.
- *Competency focused.* Focusing on competencies means equipping people to take a variety of positions, not just the next one up the organizational ladder.
- *Accountability.* Accountability comes from appointing one person to oversee the succession program as well as from evaluating current leaders on how well they are preparing potential replacements.
- *Development.* Future leaders must be developed. Development tools include job rotation, training programs, and mentoring. While organizations provide development opportunities, every employee is ultimately responsible for acquiring the competencies she or he needs to move into new leadership positions.

∽ CHAPTER TAKEAWAYS

- Leader development promotes individual growth, helping a person expand his/her capacity to be effective in a variety of formal and informal leadership roles.

- Leadership development promotes organizational growth, helping the group as a whole develop the leaders it needs to be successful.

- Leader development is a lifelong journey. To become an effective leader, you will need to be proactive, raising your level of developmental readiness, seeking out leadership learning opportunities, building developmental relationships, and capitalizing on your experiences.

- Developmental readiness is made up of motivation (learning goal orientation, leader efficacy) and ability (self-awareness, self-concept clarity, complexity, meta-cognitive ability). To build your readiness, tailor your experiences to your interests, focus on learning, build your self-efficacy, reflect on who you are, participate in education and challenging experiences, and train yourself to "think about your thinking."

- Leadership learning can be achieved through reading, attending college or university courses, and training. Three common types of training programs include: (1) individual preparation, (2) socializing company vision and values, and (3) strategic leadership initiatives.

- Establishing connections with those who can help you achieve your goals will greatly increase your chances of emerging as a leader in an organizational context. The most beneficial relationships are with mentors. Mentors act as sponsors, provide coaching, protect protégés, give challenging assignments, serve as role models, supply acceptance and confirmation, function as counselors or sounding boards, and become friends.

- Build a network of mentors if possible. Consider who you are, what you can do, and who you know. Then invest time and energy in making connections with mentors from a variety of backgrounds.

- Formal coaches can be used to supplement or even to substitute for mentor relationships. Coaches help clients design, implement, and evaluate personal development plans. To benefit from coaching, be a committed and active participant in the process and be open to change and risk.

- Leadership experiences enable us to expand our leadership skills. The richest experiences occur in developmental job assignments. These experiences fall into five categories: job transitions, creating change, taking on a high level of responsibility, managing boundaries, and dealing with diversity. Another type of developmental experience is hardship. Successful leaders "fail forward" by learning from adversity. The most common hardships are business mistakes and failures, career setbacks, personal trauma, problem employees, and downsizing.

- Unstructured experiences also contribute to your development as a leader. Reflect on and learn from all the important events and relationships in your life stream.

- Two models view leadership development as an internal process. Stephen Covey prescribes seven habits for effective leadership: (1) be proactive; (2) begin with an end in mind; (3) put first things first; (4) think win/win; (5) seek first to understand, then to be understood; (6) synergize; and (7) sharpen the saw. Kevin Cashman's *Leadership from the Inside Out* offers a holistic approach consisting of seven pathways to leadership: (1) personal mastery; (2) purpose mastery; (3) interpersonal mastery; (4) change mastery; (5) resilience mastery; (6) being mastery; and (7) action mastery.

- Spiritual development can be tied to leader development. Common spiritual practices that promote leadership effectiveness include treating others fairly, expressing caring and concern, listening responsively, appreciating the contributions of others, and engaging in reflective practice (meditation, prayer, journaling, spiritual reading). There are four stages of personal and organizational spiritual development: Stage I: Unprincipled (egocentric, self-centered); Stage II: Conventional (bound by rules and structure); Stage III: Self-Actualizing (committed to individual and collective growth, inner-directed); and Stage IV: Integral (deeply spiritual, connected, other-focused).

- Important leadership passages include: (1) from managing self to managing others, (2) from managing others to managing managers, (3) from managing managers to functional manager, (4) from functional manager to business manager, (5) from business manager to group manager, and (6) from group manager to enterprise manager.

- Taking charge as a new leader means developing an understanding of the leadership context, gaining acceptance as a leader, and having an impact on organizational performance. To successfully take charge, you should manage expectations, develop key relationships, analyze the situation, establish motivating goals, foster a positive change climate, initiate change effectively, and use symbols and rituals to establish your identity as a new leader.

- Succession plans are systematic approaches to identifying and developing future leaders. Effective plans take the participation of top management, involve all leadership levels, are competency focused, demand accountability, and include leader development.

∽ APPLICATION EXERCISES

1. Evaluate your readiness to develop as a leader. How can you improve your readiness level? What do your scores on the Self-Perceptions of Leadership Skills assessment in box 12.1 reveal about your current level of leader skill development?

2. Talk with someone who is employed in a company that offers leadership training to its workers. Compare your experiences in this course to the training received in the organization. Share your findings in class.

3. Read a book on leadership. Give a presentation to your classmates outlining the major concepts in the book and your evaluation of the strengths and weaknesses of the book you selected.

4. Profile a famous leader and identify hardships she/he has suffered. Discuss these examples in class, and try to determine if these experiences were valuable in the leader's development.

5. Pair off with someone and discuss developmental relationships. Describe peer relationships that have been most helpful to you at work or at school. Have you served as a mentor or protégé? Been a part of a formal mentoring program? Tried to establish a mentor network? Received leadership coaching? How would you evaluate these experiences?

6. Create a leader journey map following these instructions.

   Step 1: Create a map of your journey as a leader to this point in your life. Draw your leadership path or road. Put in important twists and turns as well as highs and lows. Mark important events or experiences that have shaped who you are and how you think and act as a leader. Identify important people who played a role along the way. Note any trigger events. Then share your map with a partner or small group. Describing your drawing will deepen your self-understanding and provide others with important insights into your leader behavior.

   Step 2: Extend your map 5–10 years out into the future. Identify the learning opportunities, experiences, and relationships you want to have to become a more effective leader. Describe your map and the action steps you will take to reach your goals.

7. Read either *The 7 Habits of Highly Effective People* by Stephen Covey or *Leadership from the Inside Out* by Kevin Cashman. Attempt to use either of these models to develop your internal approach to leadership. Report your experiences to your classmates.

8. Write a research paper on spirituality and leadership. What do you conclude about the relationship between spiritual development and leader development?

9. Attend a leadership-training seminar and measure its effectiveness based on material covered in this text and in class. Write up your findings.

10. Develop a taking-charge case study based on the experiences of a new leader. What challenges did this leader face? How did he/she accomplish the three tasks of taking charge? Did she/he employ the building blocks outlined in the chapter? How successful was the leadership transition? Write up your findings.

11. Evaluate your organization's succession-planning process. Share your findings with the organization's leadership team.

∽ CULTURAL CONNECTIONS: COACHING ACROSS CULTURES[67]

The growth of multinational corporations means that more coaches and clients come from different cultural backgrounds. A Swiss coach might be paired with a Turkish executive, for example, or an Australian with a Chinese supervisor. Cultural differences can undermine the coaching process. Consider the conflicting values of a US manager assigned to work with a Saudi Arabian manager. The US manager, coming from the individualistic, equalitarian culture that developed executive coaching, is focused on the personal development of the Saudi. He believes that clients should be internally motivated and take responsibility for their own development. The Saudi manager, coming from a more authoritarian culture, may be reluctant to set his own goals, relying more on what his supervisor wants. He could be more passive, perhaps convinced that whatever happens is the will of Allah. This may make him reluctant to follow through on coaching assignments. He might also take any negative feedback as a personal attack. Interviews with German cross-cultural coaches highlight the types of issues faced by coaches and clients. Communication problems caused a number of difficulties. The German coaches reported incidents where clients feared loss of face for admitting problems, would only talk about the positive, were uncommunicative, or rejected critical feedback. Coaches and clients often struggled with defining their relationship—whether it should become a friendship, how to establish trust, and how to overcome reservations about the coach's gender, culture, or religion. Issues also arose about where the coaching should take place and how to define the coach's role. (Some clients asked their coaches to act as a mediator or as a messenger to their bosses.)

Effective cross-cultural coaching begins with cultural understanding. Successful coaches try to understand the background of the client using Hofstede's programmed values, the GLOBE dimensions, or another cultural classification system. They draw upon their cultural intelligence (see chapter 10) and discover how they can assist the other party in the most culturally appropriate manner. (They also accept coaching from their coachees about cultural matters.) Competent coaches take the time they need to build relationships with their clients, which often takes longer in cross-cultural settings. They pay close attention to the language they use, check frequently for understanding, and become comfortable with silence (which is valued in some societies) when necessary.

∽ LEADERSHIP ON THE BIG SCREEN: *THE INTERN*

Starring: Robert De Niro, Anne Hathaway, Rene Russo, Anders Holm, Adam Devine

Synopsis: Seventy-year-old widower Ben Whittaker (Robert De Niro) comes out of retirement to take a senior intern position at an e-commerce women's clothing company started by Jules Ostin (Anne Hathaway). Ben, who dresses in a suit and tie and hardly knows how to turn on a computer, is initially out of place. Soon, however, the senior intern becomes a mentor to his younger coworkers and a trusted advisor to Jules, who is being urged to bring in an outside CEO to run the firm. Jules and Ben's colleagues, in turn, provide technical advice to Ben and give him a reason to get up in the morning. Ben helps Jules navigate the CEO decision as well as a marriage crisis. Along the way Ben finds romance with the company masseuse (Russo).

Rating: PG-13 for sexual content and language.

Chapter Links: mentors/protégés, coaching, peer relationships, hardships, leading from the inside out, leadership transitions, succession planning

13

Leadership in Crisis

There can't be a crisis next week. My schedule is already full.

—Henry Kissinger

OVERVIEW

The Crucible of Crisis

We live in an age of crisis. Stories of terrorist attacks, hurricanes, tornados, corporate and political scandals, school shootings, epidemics, tsunamis, earthquakes, and other crises headline the news. Evidence suggests that some types of crises are happening with greater frequency. Significant industrial accidents (those with 50 or more deaths) are more common, and deliberate attacks (bombings, kidnappings, cyber attacks, sabotage) have risen sharply.[1] At the same time, global warming disrupts weather patterns, increasing the number and strength of hurricanes while raising sea levels, endangering coastal regions.

The proliferation of crises means that leaders must act as crisis managers. They have to be alert to dangers, prepare their groups and organizations for trouble, and respond quickly and effectively when a crisis breaks out. Crisis management may be the most demanding task of leadership. In the crucible of a crisis, the organization is threatened and comes under media and public scrutiny. Jobs and property are lost, and lives may be at stake. Events move at lightning speed, requiring quick decisions even though vital information may be missing. As a result, crises often bring out the worst in organizations and their leaders.[2]

The 2010 BP Gulf Oil spill—the largest in US history—is rapidly becoming a textbook case of how *not* to handle a crisis. The company claimed that only 1,000–5,000 barrels of oil were being released every day when the actual amount was as high as 62,000 barrels. BP CEO Tony Hayward was criticized for declaring that he "wanted his life back" in the midst of the Gulf Oil spill. This made him appear insensitive to the families of the 11 victims who died when the Deepwater Horizon rig exploded. Later he further alienated Gulf Coast residents by declaring that the spill was "a drop in the ocean" and taking a break from his crisis management duties to attend a yacht race. During testimony before Congress, Hayward stonewalled by obstructing and delaying information. He claimed that he wasn't involved in the decisions that went into drilling the faulty well, saying at one point, "I can't answer that question, I'm not a cement engineer I'm afraid." Hayward's attempts to stonewall made it appear as if he was hiding something, particularly since he had a doctorate in geology, had spent 28 years in the oil business, and was an experienced exploration manager.[3]

Fortunately, some organizations respond quickly and forcefully when a crisis strikes and emerge stronger than ever. A case in point is the Johnson & Johnson Company, the makers of Tylenol. When six people died in the 1980s after taking extra-strength Tylenol capsules laced with cyanide, the firm, led by CEO James Burke, immediately recalled the capsules and later replaced them with caplets. Company officials cooperated fully with the press and government authorities. Public confidence in Johnson & Johnson was restored, and Tylenol sales are higher now than they were before the tampering incident. When McDonald's CEO James Cantalupo died of a heart attack while attending a meeting of the firm's owner-operators, the company implemented its succession plan within a few hours, naming his replacement. Its quick action calmed the stock market and reassured franchisees.

The goal of this chapter is to help you, your followers, your organization, and your community manage crises rather than fall victim to them. In the first section of the chapter, we'll dissect crises in order to understand them better. In the second section of the chapter, we will examine the communication strategies essential to successful crisis leadership. In the final section we'll identify the successful strategies of leaders who voluntarily put themselves and their followers into dangerous situations.

> *There is nothing quite like a crisis to test your leadership.*
> *It will make or break you.*
>
> —*Bill George*

Anatomy of a Crisis

"Know your enemy" is the first step to effective crisis leadership. We can't prepare for or manage crises until we have a better understanding of what they are and how they unfold. Crises can be categorized by type and by stages of development.

Crisis Types

A crisis is any major unpredictable event that has the potential to damage an organization and, in extreme cases, to threaten its survival.[4] There is no single universally accepted list of all potential crises. However, a number of investigators divide crises into types. Here is one typology that identifies ten types of crises.[5]

1. *Public perception:* negative stories about the organization's products, personnel, or services; negative rumors, blogs, Facebook groups, and websites

2. *Natural disasters:* tornadoes, hurricanes, mudslides, wildfires, blizzards, earthquakes, volcano eruptions

3. *Product or service:* product recalls, food-borne illnesses, concern about products and services generated by the media

4. *Terrorist attacks:* bombings, hijackings, abductions, poisonings

5. *Economic:* cash shortages, bankruptcies, hostile takeovers, accounting scandals

6. *Human resource:* workplace violence, strikes, labor unrest, discrimination, sexual harassment, school and workplace shootings, theft, fraud

7. *Industrial:* mine collapses, nuclear accidents, fires, explosions

8. *Oil and chemical spills:* tanker and railway spills, pipeline and well leaks

9. *Transportation:* train derailments, plane crashes, truck accidents, multi-vehicle pileups

10. *Outside environment:* collapse of financial systems, rising fuel prices, deregulation, nationalization of private companies, mortgage crisis

Ian Mitroff, former director of the Center for Crisis Management at the University of Southern California, offers an alternative crisis typology based on the intentions of those involved in the crisis event.[6] He differentiates between *abnormal accidents* and *normal accidents*. Abnormal accidents are deliberate acts designed to disrupt or destroy systems. The attacks of 9/11, the Boston Marathon bombing, and cyber attacks on business, government, and the military are examples of abnormal accidents. Massive chemical explosions in Tianjin, China, plane crashes, fire on a Carnival cruise ship, and mining disasters are normal accidents that reflect problems with routine procedures. Abnormal accidents are more challenging to prepare for but leaders must do so. Mitroff points out that most terrorist acts are directed at private businesses, not the government. He also notes that even routine crises are becoming harder to manage in an increasingly interconnected, complex society. Consider, for example, how bad weather at just one major airport disrupts flights all around the world.

These classification systems and others like them can help leaders better prepare for emergency situations. Different types of crises call for different responses. Recovering from flood damage to corporate headquarters calls for one set of tactics; coping with a case of product tampering requires another. Classifying crises can also help leaders determine where their organizations are most vulnerable. A high school must be on guard against student violence, for example, while a software manufacturer must contend with computer hackers. In addition, no organization can prepare for every potential crisis. Crisis managers can, nonetheless, develop a plan that can be used for incidents that occur within each category.

Crisis Stages

While crises differ, they all appear to follow a similar pattern of development. Each passes through the same three stages: precrisis, crisis event, and postcrisis.[7]

Stage 1: Precrisis

Organizations spend most of their time between crises. During these periods of normalcy, leaders typically assume that the risks of a crisis occurring are low. Further, they believe that their organizations are adequately prepared for any potential contingency. The longer the period between crises, the more confident leaders become. They may cut back crisis-training programs as well as funding for backup operational sites and other crisis containment measures. Sadly, such overconfidence makes disaster more likely. Officials at NASA, for example, became overconfident about the safety of shuttle missions between the *Challenger* and *Columbia* disasters. Safety concerns were a priority after the *Challenger* crash. Seventeen years later, other goals, like keeping the shuttle program on schedule, took precedence. Top managers dismissed concerns that the *Columbia* had been damaged during its launch. However, a small hole opened by a debris strike shortly after liftoff allowed superheated gas to enter the craft when it returned to Earth. *Columbia* disintegrated, taking the lives of seven astronauts.[8]

As a leader, you'll need to fight the tendency to become complacent. Even during periods of relative calm, there are likely to be indications that another crisis is brewing. Crisis expert Steven Fink uses the term "prodomes" (taken from the Greek term meaning "running before") to describe the warning signs that something is seriously amiss.[9] BP had been fined for previous safety violations before the Gulf Coast oil spill. An engineer described the drilling platform where the accident occurred as a "nightmare well" before the fire and explosion. Similarly, computer simulations demonstrated that the levees in New Orleans wouldn't withstand the force of a hurricane as strong as Katrina.

In addition to battling complacency, leaders must also overcome: (1) *human biases* (errors in decision making and judgment); (2) *institutional failures* (organizational breakdowns in processing information); and (3) *special-interest groups* (resistance from groups that look out for the interests of their own members). Box 13.1 summarizes the ways in which these barriers can undermine crisis readiness.

Box 13.1	**Barriers to Crisis Prevention**[10]

Human Biases

- positive illusions that falsely convince decision makers that a problem doesn't exist or isn't severe enough to require action
- interpreting events in an egocentric manner that favors the leader and the organization while blaming outsiders
- discounting the future by ignoring possible long-term costs; refusing to invest resources now to prevent future crises
- maintaining the dysfunctional status quo by refusing to inflict any harm (such as higher social security taxes) that would address a mounting problem (the danger that the social security system will become insolvent)
- failure to recognize problems because they aren't vivid (they are not personally experienced as direct threats)

Institutional Failures

- failure to collect adequate data due to (a) ignoring certain problems and discounting evidence, (b) the presence of conflicting information, and (c) information overload
- information is not integrated into the organization as a whole because departments operate independently and managers maintain secrecy
- members lack incentive to take action because they are rewarded for acting selfishly or believe that everyone agrees with a course of action
- leaders fail to learn from experience or to disseminate lessons learned because information is not recorded or shared or because key organizational members are lost

Special-Interest Groups

- impose social burdens (higher taxes, water pollution, high drug prices) in order to benefit themselves
- blame complex problems on individuals rather than on systems that are at fault
- oppose reform efforts

A corporate crisis is a question of when rather than if.

—*John Deverel*

Max Bazerman and Michael Watkins use the term "predictable surprises" to describe situations where organizations have all the information they need to predict what will happen but fail to take action due to the decision barriers listed earlier.[11] The attacks of 9/11 are a case in point. Between 1987 and 2000, the General Accounting Office (GAO) and two presidential commissions issued reports warning of weaknesses in the airline industry's security systems and outlining steps for improvement. Further, government officials were aware of the growing hatred of Islamic extremists and that knives had been used in previous hijackings. Nevertheless, little was done to enhance security on the ground or in the air due to pressure from the airline industry (security is expensive) and inaction at the Federal Aviation Administration (FAA).

One of the extraordinary things about human events
is that the unthinkable becomes thinkable.

—*Salman Rushdie*

Stage 2: Crisis Event

This stage begins with a "trigger event" that initiates the crisis and ends when the crisis is resolved. Harm is done to people, property, and the environment. Organizational members experience strong emotions like surprise, fear, and anger. They are confused about how to respond and worried about what will happen to the organization and themselves. The crisis erupts into public consciousness.

During the crisis event, the focus shifts to damage control. The group implements its crisis management plans, communicates to internal and external publics, responds to outside pressures, and tries to resume normal operations. Containing the problem (preventing radiation leaks, rescuing villagers stranded by an earthquake) is an important component of this stage.

Stage 3: Postcrisis

The postcrisis stage begins when the immediate danger is past and the organization has been able to resume its normal operations. This is a period of evaluation, analysis, and restoration. Crisis-savvy leaders try to learn from their experiences. They make sure that the organization evaluates its response in order to determine the extent of the damage and to determine how well contingency plans worked. They record the results of the analysis to help ensure that the crisis lessons become part of the organization's memory and institute needed changes. Effective crisis managers also help their organizations recover from the trauma and move forward.

Crisis Leadership

The three-stage model of crisis development provides a useful framework for crisis leadership. Each crisis stage makes unique demands on leaders. Successful leaders must recognize and meet these challenges by shifting communication strategies as the crisis develops. They must also develop the leadership competencies described in box 13.2, some of which will be addressed in more detail later in the chapter.

Box 13.2   Research Highlight   **Crisis Leadership Competencies[12]**

Professors Lynn Perry Wooten and Erika Hayes James conducted an in-depth review of 20 business crises between 2000–2006. These crises involved accidents, scandals, product safety/health problems, and incidents involving employees. Included in the analysis were an Alaska Airlines crash, a class-action racial discrimination suit against Coca-Cola, a sex discrimination suit at Morgan Stanley Dean Witter, a Hepatitis A outbreak at Chi Chi's restaurants, and the recall of the drug Vioxx at Merck. The researchers discovered that firms generally handle one crisis phase well but stumble during another. They identified 11 competencies that are critical to crisis leadership. Each phase of a crisis calls for different abilities.

Precrisis

Sensemaking—leaders must be able to make sense of individual events and how seemingly unrelated events may pose a threat. In other words, they must note the warning signs and figure out what they mean to the organization. Leaders at Coke had been told repeatedly that the company needed more diversity but failed to address the issue, resulting in a class-action suit.

Perspective taking—leaders must tend to the needs of everyone impacted by a crisis, not just shareholders or those who are most vocal. Firestone focused on data rather than people, and, as a result, judged that its Explorer tires, which exploded at high temperatures, posed "acceptable risk." It came under heavy criticism for putting the needs of investors ahead of consumers who risked death and injury.

Issue selling—middle managers, in particular, must convince top executives to pay attention to issues that they would otherwise ignore. They must persuade their leaders to engage in crisis planning and to identify learning after a crisis has occurred. Effective issues selling occurred at Alaska Airlines. Alaska leaders developed a plan that not only dealt with managing operations during a crisis, but also addressed ways to help crash survivors deal with trauma and grief.

Organizational agility—effective crisis leaders have knowledge of all aspects of the business. This is critical because a crisis in one part of a business may soon involve all units. Walmart demonstrated such agility before Hurricane Katrina, stocking supplies that would be needed following the disaster. The CEO assembled a cross-functional emergency team to make decisions and set priorities during the disaster.

Creativity—to prepare for a crisis, leaders must be creative, identifying potential vulnerabilities and then planning imaginative ways to respond. Creation of disaster scenarios helps organizations respond more effectively when crisis strikes.

Crisis Event

Decision making under pressure—crises are typically viewed as threats, prompting leaders to engage in damage control. Focus on damage control encourages leaders to take short-term actions that may cause long-term damage. Negative emotions also interfere with the ability to make wise decisions.

(continued)

Communicating effectively—this is the competency that is most associated with crisis management. The most effective leaders know how to connect emotionally with audiences. They are transparent rather than defensive. Coca-Cola's leaders denied that they discriminated against minority employees even though there was mounting evidence to the contrary. As a result, the company's image suffered.

Risk taking—when threatened, decision makers tend to be more rigid. They share less information and tend to fall back on habitual behavior when they should be looking for novel ways to deal with the crisis. When Martha Stewart was imprisoned for insider trading, the Martha Stewart Omnimedia CEO took significant risk by taking Stewart off magazine covers, de-emphasizing her name on products, and reorganizing executive teams to manage core business functions. The company was then able to ride out the storm of negative publicity.

Postcrisis

Promoting organizational resiliency—the most effective leaders want to do more than return to "business as usual." They want to move the organization to a better place. In other words, they are resilient, demonstrating the capacity to absorb pain and keep functioning in adversity. United Airlines was resilient following the events of September 11, 2001. The company engaged in cost cutting and then emphasized a "Back to Business" fare sale to lure customers back.

Acting with integrity—rebuilding trust is critical after a crisis since, if the business is at fault, stakeholders see what happened as a form of betrayal. Leaders need to make sure that they act with integrity (matching words and deeds). They may need to restructure the organization as WorldCom did after a massive accounting scandal. The company selected a new board, instituted a new code of ethics, revamped corporate principles, and instituted a system of checks and balances.

Learning orientation—"exceptional" crisis management includes learning and reflection. Firms view crises as opportunities and try to learn from them. In so doing, they develop new, better ways to operate. New leaders at Tyco learned from the mistakes of past executives, instituting new financial controls and ethics initiatives.

Precrisis Leadership

During the precrisis stage, the leader's primary responsibility is to move the organization from crisis prone to crisis ready.[13] The crisis-ready organization is alert to warning signs, identifies potential trouble spots, develops a crisis management plan, and creates a reservoir of credibility and goodwill. You can determine your organization's crisis readiness by completing the self-assessment in box 13.3.

Recognize Danger Signs

Leaders can prevent many crises by being alert to prodomes, the warning signs that something is amiss. To pick up on these signals, they must encourage their organizations to continually scan the environment. Environmental scanning looks both outward and inward. In external scanning, the organization surveys the news media, blogs, trade journals, public opinion polls, online publications, websites, and other sources to identify potential dangers. Dell, for example, set up a center to track and respond to social media postings 24 hours a day. Thousands of employees have also been trained to monitor company related items on Twitter, Facebook, and other sites.

Warning signs often come from those who have an ongoing relationship with the organization, like customers, donors, and suppliers. Indicators of trouble include product returns, public criticism, complaints, and protests. Failure to respond to these signals can spell trouble, as Procter & Gamble (P&G) discovered in the "devil case." P&G initially dismissed phone inquiries that the company was connected to the Church of Satan. By not taking these calls seriously, the company soon found itself fielding 15,000 devil-related calls every month in the early 1980s, and rumors about its satanic connections still linger.[14] IKEA ignored consumer safety advocates who urged the Swedish firm to change the design of a line of children's dressers in

---

Box 13.3 Self-Assessment	Crisis Preparedness Scale[15]

To determine how ready your organization is to deal with a crisis, answer yes or no to the following questions.

Statement	Yes	No
1. Our organization has the necessary abilities to assess the potential numbers and types of injuries (to people, animals, the environment) associated with any crisis.		
2. Our organization has the capabilities required to treat whatever injuries might result.		
3. Our organization's values system or culture gives priority to treating injuries promptly.		
4. Our organization gives priority to covering up or denying a crisis.		
5. Legal considerations do not override ethical and human concerns.		
6. Our organization has a trained crisis management team (CMT) that can assemble quickly and make effective decisions.		
7. Our organization has the capabilities to investigate and determine		
a. the precise type or nature of whatever crisis could occur.		
b. the early warning signals that precede each type of crisis.		
c. whether such signals were blocked or ignored.		
d. the exact, human, organizational, and technical causes of a crisis.		
8. Our organization has properly designed, constantly maintained, and regularly tested damage containment systems in place.		
9. Our organization has backup manufacturing equipment and computers so that it can resume operations as quickly as possible.		
10. Our organization has recovery mechanisms to restore full site and organizational operations.		
11. Our organization has recovery mechanisms to restore the surrounding community and environment.		
12. Our organization has the capabilities to communicate effectively, notify the proper authorities, respond to the media, and reassure a wide array of stakeholders.		

If you answered no to two or more of these statements it is likely that your organization will have a crisis and that it will have difficulty handling it properly.

order to prevent the furniture from toppling over. Six toddlers died and others were injured when IKEA dressers (which were not anchored to the wall) fell over and crushed them to death. The firm was forced to recall the product and reached a $50 million settlement with three of the victims' families.[16]

Internal scanning looks for organizational deficiencies that could lead to crisis situations. These might include signs of overconfidence, inadequate safety procedures, decaying equipment, and overloaded transportation systems.[17] Unfortunately, obtaining accurate information about internal conditions is difficult. Warnings threaten the group's sense of well-being and whistle-blowers are often punished. Lower-level employees distort information by sending only positive messages to their superiors and by downplaying risks. As a consequence, leaders may be surprised by organizational crises while their employees are not. The flow of negative information generally increases if leaders create a trusting atmosphere, being particularly careful not to punish those who bring bad news. Both Penn State and Baylor ignored internal warning signs involving their football programs. Penn State University officials were told that assistant coach Jerry Sandusky was sexually abusing children but failed to act in hopes of protecting the reputation of the school and the team. Baylor's football coach, athletic director, president, campus police, and others apparently suppressed complaints by women who reported sexual assaults (including gang rapes) by players. According to the law firm that investigated Baylor's response to sexual violence, the school's football program "hindered enforcement of rules and policies, and created a cultural perception that football was above the rules."[18]

Prediction is very difficult, especially about the future.

—Niels Bohr

Look for Trouble

Looking for trouble means revealing weaknesses that could prove harmful or fatal to the organization. One trouble-shooting tactic is to brainstorm a list of possible crises. Here, for example, are some potential crises that might strike your college or university (see Application Exercise 1).

- student protests
- asbestos contamination
- murder
- dramatic decrease in enrollment
- earthquake
- explosion in the science lab
- faculty member or administrator accused of illegal or immoral conduct
- food poisoning in the cafeteria

- financial problems
- fire
- flood
- lawsuits against the university
- staff or faculty strike
- sexual assaults
- students arrested for serious crimes
- controversial speaker or art exhibit
- students hurt or killed while participating in school-sponsored activities

Ian Mitroff and Murat Alpasian offer four additional techniques that can be used along with brainstorming to help leaders highlight organizational vulnerabilities.[19]

Wheel of crises. Build a wheel complete with a spinner. List all the types of crises that a company or nonprofit can face. Take turns spinning the wheel. When the spinner stops, brainstorm all of the kinds of possible crises that might occur in that category. In a variation of this technique, combine two crises. This will drive home the point of the magnitude for potential disaster. New Orleans and the Gulf Coast were devastated by both high winds and high water during Hurricane Katrina, for example.

Internal assassins. Ask members of your organization to play the role of villains and to imagine ways to destroy products and processes. Have these teams of assassins think of ways to disrupt the manufacturing process, embezzle money, hide accounting losses, steal personal data, and so on. Then develop strategies for foiling such attacks.

Mixed metaphors. Look to other industries to determine if the dangers they face pose a threat to your type of organization. One large electronics manufacturer imagined itself as part of the food industry. Leaders at this company thought about how "bugs" and "microbes" might "infect" their products. They went so far as to hire an infectious disease specialist to help prevent such infections. Based on this analysis, executives determined that disgruntled employees could introduce pathogens (computer viruses or faulty parts, for example) into company products. They decided to quarantine suspect shipments until the items were inoculated (repaired).

Spy games. Hire journalists, private investigators, consumer experts, lawyers, and others to expose weaknesses. These impartial outsiders can visit plant facilities to determine security breaches, write investigative stories, or produce simulated videos attacking the organization, employees, or products.

A degree of paranoia helps protect organizations.

—*Yiannis Gabriel*

Create a Crisis Management Plan (CMP)

Once potential crises have been identified, develop an action plan to cope with each type of emergency. Every crisis management plan (CMP) should contain the following elements.[20] (The case study in box 13.4 describes how one company plans for natural disasters.)

Cover page. This cover sheet should identify the document, and, in many cases, state that it is confidential and not to be shown to those outside the organization. Be sure to include dates when the plan was written and revised to help readers determine how current the document is.

Introduction. The introduction generally should be written by the organization's top executive in order to highlight the importance of the CMP.

Acknowledgement form. This removable page is signed by employees and put on file with the human resources department. It serves as an official record that employees have read and understood the plan.

Rehearsal dates page. Record when the plan has been practiced. Responses to the most likely and most damaging crises should be practiced at least once a year. Hospitals, for example, hold disaster drills on a regular basis, complete with volunteers who play the role of patients.

First action page. Identify who is in charge during the incident and how this person can be reached. Describe when the CMP should be activated and by whom.

Box 13.4 Case Study	**Fighting Disaster with Waffles**[21]

Big-box retailers like Home Depot, Lowes, and Target get high marks for disaster preparedness and recovery. Each of these companies has an emergency command center where meteorologists and crisis personnel monitor possible storms. They have sophisticated delivery systems and can put supplies in place before major hurricanes and floods. Lowes, for example, stocks extra disaster supplies at stores in hurricane-prone communities, at regional distribution centers, and at a central warehouse. When a hurricane is on its way, the emergency command center is staffed with representatives from HR and public relations as well as with community relations and construction specialists. As Hurricane Matthew approached the southeastern US coast in 2016, the company had vendors send products directly to stores and converted a major distribution center from shipping appliances to shipping disaster supplies like generators, chain saws, buckets, and gas cans.

It's not surprising that big box retailers would be cited as good examples of crisis preparedness. Not only do they have sophisticated logistical systems already in place, they have a financial incentive to prepare and to recover. People turn to these stores for the supplies they need to get ready for storms and flooding. After natural disasters, big box stores supply the materials for rebuilding, which also boosts sales. However, it is surprising that the restaurant chain Waffle House is also cited as a model of disaster response. FEMA, the Federal Emergency Management Agency, uses the Waffle House Index as an informal measure of the severity of a disaster. FEMA director Craig Fugate came up with this measure. Authorities call a Waffle House restaurant in the stricken area. If it's open and serving a full menu with water and electricity, the index is green. If the restaurant is serving a limited menu, the index is yellow. If the restaurant is closed, the index is red and conditions are really bad.

Waffle House's commitment to keeping its restaurants open appears to be mission driven. Company officials believe that they are providing a vital service by providing hot meals for emergency responders, National Guard personnel, and community members. Many emergency personnel report that Waffle House is the first hot meal they get after arriving on scene. According to company president Bert Thornton:

> Our position is this: those customers and those associates are there for us in the good times, so it's our responsibility to be there when times are tough. We do not take a back seat; we don't subscribe to the theory that you just wait until everything is easy to do and then open the doors. We're always the first ones in.[22]

To fulfill its commitment, Waffle House has a well-defined hurricane response plan. (Five hundred of its 1650 stores are located in hurricane zones in the South and along the Atlantic Coast.) The leadership team, made up of senior managers from each functional area, holds an annual preparation meeting and reviews the disaster checklist in the spring. In May, right before the hurricane season (which runs from June 1 to November 30), the entire hurricane response team meets at headquarters to discuss lessons learned from the previous year, and to go over written procedures and policies. Team members send out safety information to Waffle House associates. They make arrangements to secure fuel and portable toilets, vehicles, communication equipment, and other items needed following a storm. They also determine the shortened menu each restaurant will serve following the disaster because of limited ingredients and time. (Bacon isn't on the hurricane menu because it takes up too much grill space and takes too long to cook.) They file the list of items and fixed prices with government authorities in each state. Prices are rounded down to the nearest nickel to make it easier to total bills in case the cash registers don't work.

When the storm is on the move, team members, under the direction of a commander-in-control, arrange for extra supplies and line up recreational vehicles and refrigerator trucks as necessary. The RVs are used to transport additional restaurant personnel to the affected area after the storm passes (generally within 12 hours) and the trucks are used to transport goods. After the storm is over, responders assess damage and determine which locations will open. The first truck brings "first-wave supplies"—ice, bottled water, canned soft drinks, to-go supplies, and cleaning products. The first restaurants opened use these items, whatever food they have on hand, and product from other outlets. All employees are given a key chain fob with a phone number to call to confirm both their location and the status of the restaurant. The company moves quickly to rebuild its restaurants during the recovery period.

Waffle House now has tropical storm tracking software that allows it to predict to the minute when any location will be affected and when it will reopen. The chain shares this information with FEMA ahead of landfall. According to Waffle House Vice President Pat Warner, "we're just glad to play a part" in the move toward greater cooperation between the private and public sector in disaster recovery.[23]

Discussion Questions

1. Do you think Waffle House would invest so much in crisis preparedness if it weren't driven by the company's core values and mission?
2. Does Waffle House have a financial incentive to respond quickly to disasters? Do you think it makes or loses money on its crisis preparation and disaster recovery efforts?
3. Does Waffle House provide a vital service to first responders and survivors?
4. Why don't other restaurant chains follow the example of Waffle House?
5. When it comes to crisis preparedness and disaster recovery, what can other organizations learn from the Waffle House and the big-box retailers?

Crisis management team (CMT). The composition of the crisis management team will vary depending on the exact nature of the crisis. However, the typical team for a large organization will consist of the following members:[24]

- Attorney to review messages, reduce legal risk, and outline legal requirements
- Public relations director or coordinator to manage internal and external communication strategies and media relations
- Operational managers to coordinate recovery
- Controller or another financial manager with knowledge of financial assets and insurance coverage
- Institutional technology manager to help keep communication channels open and to maintain databases
- Regulatory expert to coordinate with government agencies and represent the interests of the public
- The CEO or a representative from his/her office

List the names of team members, their organizational roles, and areas of expertise. Also include outsiders, like emergency personnel, insurance agents, key suppliers, and consultants, who should be contacted during an emergency. The contact sheet should make it easy to identify and reach members of the crisis management team.

Crisis risk assessment. This section incorporates the analysis done during the precrisis stage. Identify possible crises and evaluate risk based on probability (likelihood of occurring) and impact (potential damage). In addition to helping an organization prepare for crises, the risk assessment demonstrates that your group has engaged in due diligence to try to prevent these crises.

Incident report. Keep detailed records of your organization's activities during the crisis. Record when the incident started and where, what happened during the crisis, and who was contacted during the emergency. This documentation will help the group evaluate its crisis management efforts and to respond to lawsuits and government investigations.

Proprietary information. Some information should not be revealed during a crisis without the express consent of the CEO and legal counsel. This might include, for instance, certain manufacturing processes and product ingredients. Also, never release the names of victims before notifying their families.

CMP communication strategy worksheet. This element of the plan emphasizes that every message sent during a crisis needs to serve a clear purpose and documents crisis actions. Crisis managers should record the specific audiences they address as well as their goals and include copies of the messages they send. Communicators may need to be reminded to avoid technical jargon and to define organizational terms in a way that outsiders can understand.

Secondary contact sheet. On this contact sheet, identify other groups that should be notified during the crisis, either because they have important information or because they will be affected by the emergency. Identify the type of stakeholder and important contact information. Specify who should get in touch with each stakeholder and document who made the contact and when.

Stakeholder contact worksheet. Some stakeholders will contact the organization directly for information. The media, in particular, will demand a prompt response. Outline procedures for responding to calls from the press as well as from families, employees, and community leaders. Determine how to route these calls and who should speak on behalf of the organization. Document responses, including who contacted the organization and when, the communication channel used to make the contact, the nature of the inquiry, the response, and any required follow up.

Business continuity plan. Getting back to regular operations as soon as possible is an important organizational goal. The plan should spell out how your organization will respond when communications systems and facilities are damaged, data is lost, and so on.

Crisis control center description. Designate a place where crisis team members can gather and coordinate their efforts. Some larger organizations have developed permanent crisis command centers for use during emergencies.

Postcrisis evaluation forms. Develop an evaluation form to help the group learn from the crisis. Determine how well the CMP functioned, including its activation, contacts, message strategy, stakeholder relations, and business resumption measures.

Establish Credibility

Organizations with a reputation for integrity and competence in environmental concerns are better equipped to weather a crisis (for more information on the dimensions of credibility, see chapter 6). They create goodwill that encourages government officials and the public to treat them more leniently when they come under attack or make mistakes. The importance of establishing credibility can be seen in public responses to airline disasters. Delta recovered rapidly from the 1985 crash of a jet during a thunderstorm in part because it had an excellent service record at that time as well as a "family image." Two years later Northwest Airlines stock declined after a DC-9 crashed on takeoff. Prior to the crash, Northwest was embroiled in labor disputes and led the industry in customer complaints. The company's out-of-control image carried over into its recovery efforts. Observers criticized Northwest for not taking charge and for ignoring the needs of victims' families. Some relatives filed lawsuits less than a week after the crash.[25]

Work hard to build and maintain credibility by producing quality products, providing excellent customer service, keeping promises and commitments, and acting in a socially responsible manner. Treat employees well, support community programs, be a responsible steward of the environment, and so on. Stay close to stakeholders (see chapter 9) by engaging in regular two-way communication.

Leading during the Crisis Event

Leaders take charge of the organization's response when crises break out. They initiate action, serve as spokespeople, engage in vigilant decision making, and connect to core values.

Initiate Action and Coordinate Activities

The leader's first responsibility is to recognize that a crisis has occurred. However, some crises are subtle. Intel failed to recognize that it faced a crisis when it learned that its processor chip made mistakes when doing advanced calculations. The company decided to replace the chip only after the problem had been posted on the Internet and customers were angered.[26] Be prepared to engage in issue selling, convincing your organization that the event is very important (poses a great risk), is an immediate threat, and can't be solved through ordinary measures and procedures. This can be difficult even when natural disasters occur. Thirty thousand Swedes were vacationing on the beaches of Thailand when tsunamis hit in 2004. A low-ranking official on duty at Sweden's Foreign Ministry recognized the danger to Swedish citizens and notified her bosses. Unfortunately, they didn't see that there was a significant problem. When she persisted in her efforts to warn them, she was reprimanded and called hysterical.[27] (Later she was commended for speaking up.) Put the crisis management plan into action and mobilize the crisis management team. Focus on containing the threats to people, property, and the environment.

Crises intensify the need for coordination. For example, the quick thinking of Captain Chelsey Sullenberger is credited with saving all the lives aboard US Airways Flight 1549 when it was forced to land in the Hudson River. However, the "Miracle on the Hudson" would not have been possible without the coordinated efforts of nearby tugboats and ferries, the Coast Guard, and local police. (The movie described in Leadership on the Big Screen at the end of the chapter provides another example of successful crisis coordination.) Resources and group members often have to be redeployed in crisis situations, such as when transportation personnel normally assigned to routine road maintenance operate snowplows and sanding trucks during blizzards. New systems and safeguards may also have to be put into place. Johnson & Johnson developed new tamper-resistant packaging for Tylenol, for instance, and the Catholic Church adopted new guidelines for dealing with priests suspected of sexual abuse. (The Cultural Connections feature at the end of the chapter describes how putting safeguards in place generated significant opposition during one crisis.) In addition, leaders and their representatives have to contact and then coordinate with local government officials, emergency personnel, and the media.

Act as a Spokesperson

In case of an emergency, one person should take primary responsibility to speak on behalf of the entire organization in order to eliminate conflicting messages and to prevent the spread of misinformation. Contradictory and inaccurate messages undermined the crisis response to the mysterious disappearance of Malaysia Airlines Flight 370 over the Indian Ocean. Malaysian airline and government officials sometimes contradicted each other, as did military and civilian officials. Often the information they released was incomplete and inaccurate.[28] The Centers for Disease Control (CDC) faced a similar problem during a bioterrorism incident in which letters containing lethal anthrax spores were mailed to media outlets, government officials, and others. As many as 81 separate individuals acted as formal and informal spokespeople during the crisis, which added to the confusion surrounding how anthrax contamination spread. CDC officials assured the public that there was no danger from other mail being contaminated by anthrax spores, but later two people died from cross-contamination. Officials had to admit they were wrong but sent mixed messages to postal workers about whether they should take an anthrax vaccine.[29]

Generally the chief operating officer should fill the role of chief spokesperson, receiving assistance from others when needed. This leader's performance in front of the media will have a significant impact on public perceptions, for better or for worse. (See our discussion of public speaking in chapter 9.) Successful spokespeople communicate in a clear, succinct, and forthright manner under pressure and handle hostile questions without getting angry or flustered. Speaking with a lower voice pitch, making eye contact, expressive body movement and relaxed facial expression communicate power and competence, which is critical during the crisis. In the aftermath of the crisis, it is more important to communicate sincerity.[30] Recording and evaluating mock interviews and press conferences is one way to prepare for this role (see Application Exercise 7).

Those directly affected by the crisis have special information needs.[31] They should receive *instructing information* that tells them how to protect themselves. Neighbors downwind of a chemical leak will need to be told how to evacuate; those in the path of a tornado will need to take shelter; potential victims of a virus will need to receive vaccinations. They also need *adjusting information* that helps them cope psychologically by explaining what happened. Communicating to affected groups should be the top priority of the spokesperson and crisis management team. Modern technology can play an important role in reaching out to those directly impacted by events. Managers at Tokyo's transportation system used the Internet and social media to send messages and collect information after the 9.0 earthquake and tsunami. Jet Blue's president created a YouTube video to communicate to customers during a weather and operational crisis that trapped travelers in planes for hours on airport runways and snarled flights for days thereafter.[32]

Because leaders are the faces and voices of the organization, they need to respond quickly and forcefully when crisis breaks out. News of a disaster gets out fast and creates a demand for information. If your organization doesn't fill the information void, other groups (the media, critics) will, often supplying misinformation. A rapid response ensures that the public gets accurate data and signals that the organization is taking control of the situation. Slow moving organizations appear inept and incompetent. They allow others to define the crisis situation.

Leaders should appear before the media immediately even if they don't have the complete story. Spokespeople should never say "no comment," however. This statement is often taken as an admission of guilt. Instead, if you don't have information, admit that fact and promise to provide the data when it becomes available. Getting to the scene of the crisis is important as well. Then-mayor Rudolph Giuliani was praised for getting to Ground Zero shortly after the terrorist attacks of 9/11. Exxon CEO Lawrence Rawl was criticized for not immediately traveling to the scene of the Exxon *Valdez* oil spill.

Plan to cooperate with the media in order to encourage more accurate and favorable coverage. Make sure the spokesperson is available to the press at all times. Compile press kits that describe the organization and its officers. Set up a crisis center with additional phone lines, copiers, and fax machines. Conduct press conferences well before newspaper and television deadlines.

When it comes to a crisis, honesty is the best policy. If your organization is at fault, take responsibility. Don't try to hide damaging information (chances are it will be discovered anyway), and correct your mistakes when necessary. At the beginning of the Tylenol tampering crisis, the Johnson & Johnson Company stated that cyanide was not present in the manufacturing process. When the company later discovered that small amounts of the chemical were used, it admitted the error. Demonstrate genuine concern by acting as quickly as possible to repair the damage and by communicating your compassion for victims. Maple Leaf Foods CEO Michael McCain modeled such concern. When 21 people died in a listeria outbreak after eating the firm's sliced meat, he refused to claim success for the company's response, which was lauded as a model of crisis management. Instead, McCain reiterated that the incident was "just an outright tragedy."[33]

Engage in Vigilant Decision Making

The stress of a crisis puts incredible demands on organizational leaders. Lives may have been lost, property damaged, or products recalled from shelves. Mental and physical fatigue sets in. Under such conditions, both individual leaders and groups of decision makers are tempted to make quick decisions. Crisis thinking pathologies include:[34]

1. *Narrowing of cognitive processes*—fewer people are consulted, concentrating decisions at the top levels of the organization. Often decision makers are unable to consider the perspectives of others.

2. *Information distortion*—a small number of decision makers must cope with a high volume of information. In addition, information is filtered before it reaches top leaders; decision makers act on irrelevant or incorrect data.

3. *Group pathologies*—small tightly knit homogeneous groups of top leaders are highly susceptible to groupthink.

4. *Rigidities in programming*—standard operating procedures, which are designed to deal with normal conditions, cannot accommodate novel, threatening events.

5. *Lack of decision readiness*—surprise events overwhelm the ability to learn and adapt.

6. *Implementation failures*—organizational units fail to mobilize to implement decisions quickly.

Combating these pathologies takes vigilance.[35] Vigilant decision makers examine a wide variety of options and weigh the costs and benefits of each alternative. They seek out new information and reevaluate their choices in the face of what they discover. Be sure to carry out the decision-making functions described in chapter 7—analyze the problem, set goals, and then identify and evaluate alternatives—whether working alone or with others. Be alert to possible decision-making biases that can intensify the crisis. When deciding in a group, be particularly attuned to symptoms of groupthink and the tendency to escalate commitment.

> *I take it we are all in complete agreement on the decision here. . . .*
> *Then I propose we postpone further discussion of this matter*
> *until our next meeting to give ourselves time to develop disagreement*
> *and perhaps gain some understanding of what the decision is all about.*
>
> —*Alfred P. Sloan*

Connect with Vision and Values

One of a leader's major responsibilities during a crisis is to remind followers of the group's purpose and values, reinforcing their use as a set of operating principles. Guided by a clear mission and a set of operating principles, organizational members can respond quickly and effectively in emergency situations. Followers empowered to make decisions generally act decisively during a crisis.[36] If they are part of an organization with a commitment to people and society, their actions will likely be marked by integrity and compassion. During the Tylenol tampering crisis, for instance, employees of Johnson & Johnson were guided by the company's credo, which states that the firm is responsible to local communities as well as to the world community.

Postcrisis Leadership

During the postcrisis phase, the leader spearheads the organization's recovery. He or she helps the group restore its image, learn from the crisis experience, build resilience, and experience healing.

Rebuild the Organization's Image

An organization can make it through the crisis stage but ultimately be doomed if it cannot restore its image. Customers may boycott the company's products, lawmakers may call for stricter regulation, regulators may enforce stiff penalties, voters may desert the party, donors quit giving, and so on. Pan Am Airways went out of business in part because the company was seen as callous and uncaring after Flight 103 was blown up over Lockerbie, Scotland. Victims' families, the media, and the public blamed Pan Am for inadequate security and ignoring a bomb threat.[37] PTL (Praise the Lord) Ministries, once a highly successful and visible religious organization, collapsed after accusations of securities fraud and wasteful spending. Because public image is so critical, leaders must help the group repair its reputation when the immediate crisis is past. (Box 13.5 describes one company attempting repair its image and lure back customers.)

Box 13.5 Case Study	Food with Integrity Meets E-Coli[38]

Denver-based Chipotle Mexican Grill prides itself on serving "food with integrity." The chain rejects GMO products and is committed to family farms, the ethical treatment of animals, and sustainability. In contrast to McDonald's and other fast-food companies, which prepare many ingredients in central kitchens and then freeze them, most of Chipotle's ingredients are prepared fresh in the store. Customers go through a food assembly line, choosing the meats, cheeses, vegetables, and other ingredients that go into four items—burritos, burrito bowls, tacos, and salads. Chipotle has been a favorite of diners and investors alike. Started in 1993, the firm now has 2000 locations. One hundred shares of the company purchased for $2,200 at its initial public stock offering in 2006 were worth $75,700 at the stock's highest point, a 3,340% increase.

In the fall of 2015, Chipotle had to temporarily close 43 locations in Washington and Oregon after an outbreak of *E. coli-26* was linked to dining at the restaurants. This strain of *E. coli* causes vomiting and diarrhea and can be life threatening if toxins are released into internal organs. A total of 60 people were sickened in 14 states. Just as the *E. coli* outbreak was subsiding, Chipotle had to close a store in Massachusetts after 143 people, many of them Boston College students, came down with norovirus after eating at a Chipotle. Health officials cited the restaurant for improper handling of poultry and letting an employee work while sick. Norovirus struck yet another Massachusetts location shortly thereafter. Company sales declined 30% and the firm's stock price dropped a third, losing $10 billion in value. Some returning customers joked, "Can I have my burrito without *E. coli*?"

Co-CEOs Steve Ells and Monty Moran reported being caught "off guard" by the outbreaks. According to critics, however, the outbreak shouldn't have come as a complete surprise. Rapid expansion (the company once hired 4,000 people on one day) and high turnover (as much as 130% a year) make it hard to maintain safety standards. "They're trying to be local and serve food with integrity, but as you grow, it becomes incredibly complex and difficult and challenging," said the president of one industry research firm. "When you look at what's going on, how they're expanding, the outbreak was almost bound to happen."[39] Only four people were assigned to oversee quality assurance, prompting a food safety expert to declare, "there is no way a team that small could properly manage all the food coming into that system."[40] Then, too, preparing the food on site at thousands of locations increased the danger. Even Ells and Moran admitted that the firm was at risk. In the company's 2013 and 2014 annual reports they noted: "We may be at a higher risk for foodborne-illness outbreaks than some competitors due to our use of fresh produce and meats rather than frozen, and our reliance on employees cooking with traditional methods rather than automation."[41]

Ells and Moran (who later resigned his post) brought in a food safety expert to oversee thousands of tests on Chipotle food, which found no signs of contamination. (The tainted food was likely gone since it takes a while for the bacteria to take effect in the body.) Company officials then accused the Centers for Disease Control and Prevention (CDC) of raising alarm about an outbreak that had been contained. The CDC fired back, pointing out that it had treated this outbreak like all others, announcing new cases when they occurred.

Ells went on national television to express his regret for what had happened: "I'm sorry for the people who got sick, they're having a tough time and I feel terrible about that. We're doing a lot to rectify that so this won't happen again."[42] The company also took out full-page ads in 61 newspapers to apologize and to identify new safety measures. Company leaders instituted a series of changes designed to create a "near zero" risk of foodborne illness. They closed all locations on one day to introduce staff to a series of new protocols that included, for example, DNA testing of fresh produce and meats, preparing high-risk items like tomatoes and lettuce in central kitchens, and blanching other items like citrus and avocados to kill pathogens. Managers now receive bonuses based on food safety audit scores as well as on customer service.

After the new measures went into effect, customers complained about the taste of the lettuce and bell peppers prepared in central kitchens so those ingredients are once again prepared on site. Nonetheless, more reliance on central kitchens to prepare meats and other ingredients alters Chipotle's business model, bringing it closer to the way that McDonald's and Taco Bell operate. The brand may suffer as a result. Why pay more for Chipotle food if you can get the same quality food at Taco Bell?

To lure customers back to its stores, Chipotle sent free meal coupons to 20 million households, offered a $50 discount for catering orders of 20 or more burritos during the Super Bowl, introduced a summer rewards program, and created an animated film short that played in more than 10,000 theaters. These efforts appear to be paying off as both sales and the stock price are up.

Discussion Questions

1. What has been your experience with Chipotle? If you are a customer, why do you eat there?
2. As a current or prospective diner, are you less likely to eat at Chipotle after the outbreak? What would it take to get you into (or back into) their restaurants?
3. What steps should Chipotle have taken to prevent this crisis?
4. In responding to the crisis, what did company leaders do right? Do wrong?
5. Do you think that Chipotle suffered more reputational damage because of its commitment to food with integrity? How can Chipotle restore its image?
6. Do the new safety measures weaken Chipotle's business model? If so, how should company leaders respond?
7. What can other restaurant chains and food suppliers learn from this crisis?

Communication professor William Benoit offers one widely used typology of image restoration strategies that can be used in crisis situations.[43]

Denial. Organizational leaders try to avoid blame by (1) denying they were responsible, or (2) shifting the responsibility to someone else. PepsiCo is one organization that successfully used denial to avoid blame. The public accepted its claim that it was not responsible for syringes in cans of its diet cola. On the other hand, BP and the operator of the Deepwater Horizon Well, Transocean Corporation, tried to shift blame to each other for the oil rig explosion and spill. Both companies appeared more interested in avoiding accountability than in helping the victims of the disaster.

Evading responsibility. Those who can't deny that they contributed to a crisis can try instead to lessen their responsibility for what happened. First, leaders may claim that they were provoked into action (provocation). The Bush administration, for example, argued that its controversial invasion of Iraq was justified because Saddam Hussein refused to stop his weapons program. Second, officials may claim that they can't be held accountable because of lack of information or factors like strikes or market forces beyond their control (defeasibility). Third, leaders may offer excuses—freak weather conditions, time pressures, lack of resources—to lower accountability. Fourth, leaders may evade responsibility by claiming good intentions. Actors might admit to a wrongdoing but claim that they were acting out of honorable intentions (they were trying to prevent a larger problem, help others, etc.).

Reducing offensiveness. There are several variations of this strategy, which is designed to reduce the audience's negative feelings toward the act and/or actor. *Bolstering* is attempting to boost the audience's positive affect for the leader and organization. Listeners may still be angry about what happened but these feelings may be offset in part by reminding them of the organization's past service to the community, excellent products, contributions to the local economy, and so on. *Minimization* reduces the damage caused by the crisis by convincing publics that what happened wasn't as bad as it seemed. There weren't as many injuries as first feared, for example, or that the damage caused by an oil spill will soon dissipate. *Differentiation* distinguishes the act in question from other similar but more damaging actions. A company might point out, for instance, that a misstatement of earnings does not equate to widespread accounting fraud. *Transcendence* places a harmful act in a broader context to justify behavior. For example, a police officer accused of shooting an unarmed suspect may claim that all traffic stops are potentially dangerous and that the suspect appeared to be holding a gun. *Attacking the accusers* turns the tables by reducing the credibility of the critics. Such attacks can deflect attention away from the speaker and reduce damage to his/her image. Cyclist Lance Armstrong used this approach for years to fend off allegations that he used performance-enhancing drugs, before finally admitting his guilt. He successfully sued a newspaper for defamation, turned on former associates who claimed he had cheated, and mocked skeptics from the 2005 Tour de France victor's stand. *Compensation* attempts to reduce the damage of an action by offering payments to those, for instance, who were hospitalized after eating tainted food or lost their loved ones in a plant explosion.

Corrective action. In corrective action, organizational leaders pledge to correct the problem by restoring conditions to what they were before the crisis or by taking steps to make sure that the problem doesn't reoccur. Often this strategy is combined with an apology, but an organization can take corrective action without admitting guilt. Corrective action differs from compensation. While compensation is designed to counterbalance the damage, corrective action promises to rectify the situation. General Motors took corrective action after it failed to replace a defective ignition switch for over a decade. CEO Mary Barra promised to create a "new GM" more transparent and focused on safety. She then instituted a series of changes, including integrating engineering units and forming a department to oversee product safety.[44]

Mortification. Mortification consists of admitting responsibility and asking for forgiveness. If the apology is seen as sincere, stakeholders often pardon the organization. Amtrak CEO Joe Boardman took this approach after a speeding train crashed in Philadelphia, killing eight and injuring 200. In an email to everyone who had registered an email address with the railroad, he declared, "Amtrak takes full responsibility and deeply apologizes for our role in this tragic event." He made this statement even before the cause of the crash had been completely determined.[45]

Benoit applies his typology to a number of significant crises, such as the Exxon *Valdez* oil spill, the Bhopal tragedy, the Sears auto repair scandal, and court battles over the safety of Dow Corning breast implants. Based on his analysis, he offers several suggestions for leaders engaged in image restoration. First, if you and your organization are at fault, acknowledge that fact right away. Credibility can be severely damaged if an organization initially denies responsibility but then is forced to accept blame later. Second, denial, if backed by solid evidence, can restore a tarnished reputation. Third, shifting blame generally is only effective when attention shifts away from the organization and onto a plausible scapegoat or when there does appear to be factors beyond the organization's control. (Exxon was unable to shift blame to the captain of the *Valdez* oil tanker, for example.) Fourth, outline plans to correct the immediate effects of the crisis and to prevent a recurrence in the future.

Fifth, minimizing the damage can backfire if the organization is seen as trying to trivialize a significant problem. Sixth, a combination of image-restoration strategies (mortification and corrective action, bolstering and defeasibility) often works better than one tactic alone. Seventh, employing several groups to reinforce the message—top management, customers, employees, suppliers—is generally more effective than one group speaking on its own. Eighth, the more important or salient a disaster is to an audience, the harder it will be to restore the image of the organization linked to the crisis. Ninth, the power of image restoration is limited. If your group has made serious mistakes, it can expect to suffer serious consequences.

Professor Timothy Coombs offers an alternative image-restoration strategy based on the level of reputational threat posed by the crisis.[46] According to his Situational Crisis Communication Theory (SCCT), managers should select a communication strategy based on three factors: (1) who is responsible for the crisis, (2) the organization's crisis history, and (3) the organization's reputation prior to the crisis event. Attributions about responsibility, in turn, fall into three clusters. In the victim cluster, which would include natural disasters, product tampering, false rumors, and workplace violence, there is very little responsibility placed on the organization. In the accidental cluster, there is minimal attribution of blame because the event (like a computer glitch that shuts down airline flights) is considered unintentional or uncontrollable. In the intentional cluster, the organization is blamed for the crisis, such as when banks order loan officers to mislead borrowers or when auto manufacturers try to fool emissions tests.

The first step in evaluating reputational threat is determining initial responsibility using the three clusters. The second step is to consider the crisis history of the organization and its prior relationship with its publics. If the organization has suffered a similar crisis in the past, as in the case of repeated chemical spills or electrical failures, it receives more blame and reputational damage. Similarly, if the organization has a reputation for treating stakeholders poorly in the past, it will also receive more blame and suffer more damage, as we noted earlier. Riots broke out after police shootings in Baltimore and in Ferguson, Missouri, in part because these police departments had poor relationships with minority communities.[47]

Deny strategies claim there is no crisis or that the crisis was caused by some outside force in an attempt to eliminate any possible connection between the organization and the crisis. They work best with victim-cluster crises. *Diminish* strategies minimize the organization's responsibility for the amount of damage caused by the crisis or claim inability to control the events leading up to the crisis. These are generally most effective in responding to accidental events. *Rebuild* strategies involve refurbishing the organization's image by taking full responsibility, asking forgiveness, and offering compensation to victims. They are most successful in intentional crisis situations. However, past history and reputation also come into play when selecting strategies. Audiences will be less likely to accept denial or diminish tactics if the organization has repeated violations. The organization will then need to focus its communication on rebuilding its reputation. Deny, diminish, and rebuild strategies can all be bolstered by attempting to build positive connection with publics through reminding them of the organization's past good works and pointing out that the organization is also a victim of events.

> *Never waste the opportunities offered by a good crisis.*
> —*Niccolò Machiavelli*

Learn from the Experience

Image restoration must be coupled with learning or the crisis is likely to repeat itself. That's why detailed record keeping and evaluation are built into the crisis management plan. Three forms of organizational learning should take place in the postcrisis phase.[48] In *retrospective sensemaking*, organizational members look back to identify what they previously overlooked and to highlight faulty assumptions that contributed to the emergency. Such self-reflection can lead to greater understanding and improve crisis planning and response. The *Columbia* Accident Investigation Board, for instance, put much of the blame for the disaster on the organization's culture, which, as we've seen, became overconfident about safety and prevented communication between the agency departments and levels. Faulty assumptions led engineers to believe that all materials covering the spacecraft were equally durable when they were not.

Reconsidering structure addresses the structural problems. Crisis disrupts the current organizational structure and provides opportunity for change. In many cases, changes in leadership, practices, and processes are required in order for the group to regain its legitimacy. One major organizational restructuring took place after the events of 9/11 when the Department of Homeland Security (DHS) was created. The DHS combined the Coast Guard, FEMA, the Transportation Safety Agency, and other departments into one unit.

Since crises are so public, organizations can often learn from the examples of others. *Vicarious learning* consists of observing models of crisis management or mismanagement and then applying the insights learned. Take the case of Hurricane Katrina, which is considered to be an example of failed crisis management. We can learn from the mistakes of local, state, and national officials to prepare for the next major natural disaster. (Read about some of the positive lessons that can be learned from the events of 9/11 in box 13.6.)

> *Adversity is the first path to truth.*
>
> —*Lord Byron*

The ultimate goal of crisis learning is to rebuild the organization so that it rarely fails even though it may face lots of unexpected events. According to University of Michigan business professors Karl Weick and Kathleen Sutcliffe, high-reliability organizations (HROs) have mindful cultures.[49] They are very sensitive to even the weakest signs that trouble is brewing and respond forcefully. Weick and Sutcliffe use the nuclear aircraft carrier as the prototypical HRO. A carrier's deck has been called "the most dangerous four and one-half acres in the world." This small space is filled with jet aircraft (armed with lethal weapons) that are constantly launching and landing. It is covered with a slippery mix of seawater and oil. There are few safe places to stand, and vocal communication is difficult. Those who run the ship's operations are generally 19- and 20-year-olds who may never have seen a jet close up or who have never been on a large, ocean-going vessel.

Despite the dangers, mishaps on aircraft carriers are rare. Weick and Sutcliffe argue that adopting the practices of this high-reliability organization can help other complex groups (health care facilities, railroads, nuclear power plants) reduce their odds of crisis.

Carrier captains build a high-reliability culture that is *preoccupied with (mindful of) failure.* Every landing is filmed and graded, and near misses require detailed debriefings. Any deviation is seen as a potential sign of a larger, more significant problem. Crew members of every rank routinely walk the deck to spot any object (a bolt, a wrench) that could get sucked into a fighter engine and cause a crash. Carrier crews are *reluctant to simplify,* taking nothing for granted. Every plane is inspected several times, and responsibilities are clearly communicated through uniform color, hand signals, and voice signals. The entire ship is *concerned with operations.* Officers engage in continuous communication during flight operations. The captain who is in charge of the ship and the commander of the Air Wing (who directs the aircraft) are positioned to observe every step of the operation. Crews are *committed to resilience* (see the following discussion). They know the importance of routines but can improvise in the face of surprises. For example, the first captain of the nuclear carrier *Carl Vinson* drove the ship at 10 knots in reverse during an intense storm. This reduced wind speeds across the deck to allow planes to land safely. Finally, team members *defer to expertise.* A lower-level officer may override a superior if he or she has more knowledge about, for example, how to land an aircraft with mechanical problems.

Box 13.6 Research Highlight	**The Communication Lessons of 9/11**[50]

The terrorist attacks on September 11, 2001, marked one of the most significant crises in the history of American business. Companies located in and near the World Trade Center lost employees, offices, records, and communication systems. Other corporations were unable to fill orders, airlines were grounded, stock trading was suspended, and business activity declined dramatically. Even companies not directly or indirectly impacted by the crisis had to respond to employees traumatized by these events.

Paul Argenti, a professor of management and corporate communication at Dartmouth College, interviewed managers and executives after 9/11 to identify guideposts for future leaders who find themselves in crisis situations. He discovered that internal communications take priority in extreme circumstances. Employee morale and confidence must be restored before an organization can take any constructive action (serving customers, covering news stories, resuming flights, managing investments). Professor Argenti identifies five crisis communication lessons from 9/11.

Lesson 1: Get on the scene. During the crisis, the most effective leaders maintained a high profile. New York City Mayor Rudolph Giuliani rushed to the World Trade Center (WTC) after the first attack, held several press conferences near Ground Zero, and attended many funerals and memorial services for victims. Top officials at Verizon visited thousands of employees near the WTC. At *The New York Times,* the president, CEO, and publisher formed a crisis management team that walked through the building every day to answer questions and to thank employees. According to Argenti, followers needed to hear the voices of their leaders:

> Written statements have their place, but oral statements and the sound of an empathic human voice communicate sincerity. And if the voice belongs to a company leader, the listener has reason to think that the full weight of the company stands behind whatever promises and assurances are being made.

Lesson 2: Choose your channels carefully. The terrorist attacks disrupted normal channels of communication. Morgan Stanley, for example, lost the voicemail system that served 3,700 employees in the Two World Trade Center and Five World Trade Center buildings. Leaders had to become creative about how they communicated with followers. Workers at Morgan Stanley confirmed that they were safe by calling one of the toll-free lines at the firm's Discover Card call center. This number was broadcast by the television networks and placed on the ticker display on the Times Square building. American Airlines president Don Carty updated his labor force through the SABRE machines that print itineraries and tickets as well as through e-mail and the Internet.

Lesson 3: Stay focused on the business. Concentrating on work provides an outlet to employees, provides a sense of normalcy, builds pride in the company, and creates bonds with suppliers and customers. The Dell Corporation, headquartered in Texas, wasn't a target of the attacks. Yet its customers were. Dell employees (who had records of what customers had lost) worked overtime to ship replacement products. At the same time, corporate communications officials provided regular updates on the crisis to personnel.

Lesson 4: Have a plan in place. Crisis plans need to be backed by alternate work sites. The New York Board of Trade established two backup sites after the truck bombing at the WTC in 1993. These contingency locations enabled the organization to quickly resume trading in 2001. While operations can be scattered among several sites, decision making and communication should be centralized. American Airlines operated out of a specially designed crisis command center. Messages at Oppenheimer Funds came directly from the corporate affairs director and CEO. Many respondents told Argenti that having experienced communications professionals on hand was essential to coping with the crisis. These professionals didn't panic and could be used in a variety of jobs.

Lesson 5: Improvise, but from a strong foundation. When a crisis strikes, managers and employees have to think on their feet. However, they are more likely to make the right choices if they are prepared. Preparation extends beyond training to include instilling corporate values. One of the key values in the Starbucks mission statement is, "Contribute positively to our communities and our environment." Driven by this precept, managers at several undamaged stores near Ground Zero kept their locations open even though all other stores around the country were ordered shut. Starbucks employees provided coffee and pastries to medical personnel and rescue workers and also pulled pedestrians to safety.

Like many other tragedies, the trauma of 9/11 brought people closer together. Many of the executives interviewed by Professor Argenti reported that their companies sustained a sense of community by keeping the communication lines open long after the immediate danger had passed.

The fatal error is not the commission of errors, for all of us are prone to mistakes. Rather, the fatal error is not to learn from our previous mistakes.

—*Ian Mitroff and Gus Anagnos*

Foster Resilience

Organizational resilience describes the collective ability to weather and then bounce back from crisis events.[51] For some, this means returning to the status quo. However, a number of scholars argue that resilient groups come out of a crisis stronger than before. Those who take this more proactive approach treat collective resilience as a capacity that groups can develop. Leaders play a critical role in expanding this capacity by fostering the resilience of followers while, at the same time, helping to create resilient organizational and community cultures.

Transformational leadership behaviors are particularly effective in building constituent resilience.[52] Idealized influence shifts the focus of group members from their fears to shared purpose and values. Inspirational motivation communicates optimism and vision, which energizes followers to move beyond feelings of hopelessness and to overcome obstacles. Intellectual stimulation encourages group members to engage in problem solving, critical thinking and the generation of alternatives, all of which are essential to vigilant decision making. Individualized consideration builds followers' sense of self-efficacy, equipping them to respond more effectively in a crisis. Because they feel valued by their leaders, they are more likely to invest themselves in responding to the threat.

In addition to fostering follower resilience, leaders help create resilient organizational cultures. Resilient organizational cultures demonstrate:[53]

1. *Psychological safety.* To feel safe, members must feel free to ask questions, seek help, admit mistakes, and experiment without being seen as ignorant or incompetent. They must also be free to offer critical feedback to others and to seek honest feedback. Feeling safe encourages people to take interpersonal risks, which is essential in emergency situations.

2. *Deep social capital.* Deep social capital evolves over time from respectful, ongoing face-to-face interactions based on honesty and trust. These interactions foster the sharing of information and resources in a crisis and build collaboration. Deep social capital sets the stage for long-term partnerships after the immediate danger is over.

3. *Diffused power and responsibility.* Resilient organizations aren't organized hierarchically but disperse influence and accountability. Each component of the organization is designed to learn and change. Every member has the discretion along with the responsibility to reach organizational objectives. These elements help organizations adapt quickly to changing crisis conditions.

4. *Access to broad resource networks.* Resilient organizations, like resilient individuals, develop relationships they can draw upon for support. The partnerships they build with suppliers, neighboring businesses, governments, and other groups provides them with more options in the crisis and maintains social capital beyond the boundaries of the organization.

Leaders can also help communities, as well as organizations, develop their resilience. The "dividend" for building resilience is both immediate and long term.[54] Resilience lessens the impact of a disaster and speeds recovery. At the same time, community members build new relationships, take on new initiatives, and seize new opportunities that emerge from the crisis. Inspired by the example of New Orleans, which has undergone a renaissance since Hurricane Katrina destroyed portions of the city in 2005, the nonprofit Rockefeller Foundation provided funding to 100 cities to help them better prepare and recover from crises.[55] With this money each city hired a chief resilience officer (CRO) to develop resilience projects, coordinate stakeholders, and remind citizens of the importance of disaster preparedness. In New Orleans (which received the first Rockefeller grant), the city installed sculptures to mark evacuation bus stops and trained 300 volunteers to heighten awareness of hurricane threats and to oversee evacuations. Each CRO focuses on the specific threat facing her or his city. The emphasis in New York City is on strengthening infrastructure—sewer, water, communication, energy—to better withstand flooding. In earthquake-prone Christchurch, New Zealand, the CRO identified areas called green zones in which it is safe to build. Haiyan, China, home of the world's largest nuclear reactor, faces the threat of a nuclear accident. Calgary, Canada, must deal with blizzards and flooding. Addis Ababa, Ethiopia, faces challenges from disease, collapsing infrastructure, and terrorism.

According to Rockefeller Foundation president Judith Rodin, the resilient community framework is made up of five characteristics.[56]

1. *Aware.* Resilient communities have a good grasp of their strengths and vulnerabilities. They also demonstrate "situational awareness," taking in new information by talking to constituents, surveying the condition of infrastructure, and so on.

2. *Diverse.* Resilient communities have a variety of resources to draw on when disaster strikes. Even if one element breaks down (one computer center is

flooded), there are other systems in place (backup computer centers). They also have diverse populations from which to draw ideas.

3. *Integrated.* Resilient communities, while diverse, are also well coordinated. Government agencies, private companies, community groups, disaster response teams, and other groups share information, people, and other resources both during and between disasters.

4. *Self-regulating.* In resilient communities the failure of one part of the system (i.e., a power plant, building) doesn't disrupt other parts of the system. Other power plants remain on line, other buildings remain standing during the earthquake, and so on.

5. *Adaptive.* Resilient communities adjust to changing conditions by coming up with new plans, trying new strategies, and changing behaviors. They're flexible, putting resources and people to work in new ways in order to respond to the crisis.

Promote Healing

Taking corrective action is an important step to healing. Addressing vulnerabilities (reinforcing flood levees, tighter security measures) reduces stress and promotes recovery. In addition to correcting problems, carefully shape the memories of what happened. Honor heroes, like the firefighters who died while rescuing the victims of 9/11 or students and professors who barricaded classroom doors during the shootings at Virginia Tech. Remember the bravery and sacrifice of those touched by the tragedy. Observe the anniversary of the crisis. In some cases, plaques, trees, and other memorials are appropriate.

Crisis communication experts Robert Ulmer, Timothy Sellnow, and Matthew Seeger believe that organizations can emerge from crises stronger than before if they engage in a *discourse of renewal*.[57] Renewal discourse looks beyond the immediate crisis event and is concerned about more than restoring the organization's image. Instead, leaders provide an inspiring vision for the future. There are four elements related to renewing discourse. First, renewing discourse focuses on organizational learning. Leaders highlight what they, their organizations, and their followers can learn from the event. Second, renewing discourse is based on an ethical foundation laid before disaster strikes. Leaders establish positive relationships with stakeholders; respond instinctively based on values and virtues (rather than on strategic communication designed to protect the group's image); and provide accurate, complete information that allows stakeholders to make rational choices. Third, the discourse of renewal is prospective not retrospective. Leaders focus on the future and see opportunities in the crisis. Fourth, renewal rhetoric is effective, helping followers to adopt the leader's view or frame of the crisis. Renewing leaders communicate that the organization can reshape itself and convince stakeholders to stay with the organization.

Ulmer, Sellnow, and Seeger point to the 2006 Red River Valley flood as an example of the power of renewal discourse. In 1996–97 the Red River flooded this region between northern Minnesota and North Dakota, displacing 50,000 residents and causing $5 billion in damage. In 2006 the region flooded again but thanks to renewal, very little damage was done. Leaders had learned from earlier events, installing new measuring devices and dikes and removing homes from low-lying areas. Open and honest communication during the 1996 flood earned the Fargo mayor and others a good deal of credibility, which they drew upon to recruit volunteers to fight the 2006 flooding. Community leaders continually made comparisons to the earlier event, pointing out the progress that had been made. Residents kept a sense of humor, joking about the inconveniences they experienced. Both local and state leaders struck a balance between reassurance and alarm. They didn't heighten the fears of residents but were quick to provide warnings and precautions, urging residents to complete their flood preparations as rapidly as possible as the river rose. The governors of North Dakota and Minnesota offered assistance.

In sum, healed or renewed organizations focus on the future, on how they can explore new opportunities. They put aside blame to tell stories about support and rebuilding. Former FEMA Director James Lee Witt argues that, when it comes to natural disasters at least, crisis can be turned into triumph:

> I'm taken by the fact that I meet people all the time who start their stories about surviving a crisis with words along the lines of "I think the storm was a blessing." Their tales usually turn to the ways that the disaster forced them to work with people they didn't know beforehand, or to find out how they or their neighbors could be heroes, or to realign the priorities in their life, or to make their town a safer place. A crisis gives your people a chance to demonstrate leadership that can be valuable not just in a crisis. It allows you to solidify relationships with suppliers, clients, or partners. It forces you to see the weaknesses in the way you do business and turn them into strengths.[58]

Extreme Leadership

Extreme leaders provide direction in dangerous, highly stressful situations. Extreme leadership shares much in common with crisis leadership. Both involve threat, danger, and rapidly changing conditions. However, while crisis leaders respond to unexpected events that threaten the group, extreme leaders continually operate in crisis environments. They voluntarily put themselves in danger. Extreme organizational contexts include (1) trauma organizations (first responders, hospital emergency rooms), (2) critical action organizations (military combat teams, fire fighters, search and rescue teams, SWAT teams, disaster response teams), and (3) high-reliability organizations that try to contain or control extreme events (forest fire smoke jumpers, medical teams).[59] (Box 13.7 describes leadership in a unique extreme setting.) A significant number of people work in extreme contexts. There are 4 million police officers in the ten largest countries, for example, and 89 million people serve in the military around the world.[60]

Retired Colonel Thomas Kolditz of the West Point Military Academy uses the term "in extremis" to describe leaders who operate in life and death situations.[61] Examples of in extremis leaders include soldiers, law enforcement officers, parachutists, wildlife photographers, and mountain-climbing guides. He conducted interviews with in extremis leaders and participated in high-risk activities to determine the characteristics of leaders who operate "in the shadow of death." Successful in extremis leaders help their teams emerge healthy and alive. They share the following attitudes and behaviors:

1. *Inherently motivated.* Dangerous situations are inherently motivating because they can result in injury and death. Leaders don't have to be concerned about motivating themselves or followers because the context provides the impetus to act.

2. *Continuous learning.* The threat of the extreme situation demands that leaders look outward to make sense of the environment and to adapt to changing conditions.

3. *Share risk with followers.* In extremis leaders share the risks with followers rather than standing back. They fight with their platoons, join in sky dives, rope up with other climbers, and so on.

4. *No elitism.* In extremis leaders focus on values like saving human lives rather than on money or material goods. They live modestly, like their followers.

5. *Have and inspire high competence, trust, and loyalty.* Leader competence is critical in life-and-death situations. In extremis leaders are quick to take control and to demonstrate their abilities. They also assume responsibility for outcomes. Their competence inspires trust and loyalty in followers. High mutual trust and loyalty between leaders and followers is essential for the success of teams in high-risk activities.

Authenticity appears to be essential for in extremis leadership (see the discussion of authentic leadership in chapter 4).[62] In dangerous situations, followers are quick to spot phony or fake leaders. They want leaders who can offer them hope. Authentic leaders meet these expectations by being self-aware, consistent, transparent, and positive. They have a clear sense of their abilities and live out their values. They are open with followers and communicate confidence and optimism.

Kolditz believes we can apply lessons drawn from in extremis leadership to other contexts. For example, if followers are already motivated, focus the team on new problems and unresolved issues; help the group work smarter. Build credibility by sharing risk with followers; put the needs of others before your own comfort and safety. Demonstrate humility and selflessness through a modest lifestyle. Make sure you are passionate about leading your team.

In-extremis leaders can expect to lose team members to death. How leaders treat the dead is critical.

> People watch leaders in the presence of the dead very carefully, because the dead are the most vulnerable members of any organization: they can't defend themselves, and they project the innocence of the human soul. They no longer have the ability to contribute, so there is no transactional purpose associated with their treatment. Therefore, how the leader treats them and the surviving members carries important transformational messages that can't be driven home in other contexts. You reach every member of your organization by the way you treat your dead.[63]

Box 13.7 Case Study	**Leadership at the Bottom of the World**[64]

Antarctica is the driest, coldest, windiest continent on Earth. Temperatures can fall below –129 Fahrenheit with blizzard wind speeds reaching 200 miles per hour. Some months are spent in complete darkness. A number of countries operate scientific stations on the continent. Station personnel are made up of visiting scientists and technical personnel who support the research mission—heating and venting engineers, vehicle mechanics, medical staff, radio operators, and so forth. Support personnel can spend up to two years at a time at a station.

Ian Lovegrove studied 26 station managers assigned to the two British scientific stations to determine the leader characteristics needed to effectively operate in this physically extreme and isolated environment. Not only are station personnel (called sojourners) faced with danger, they are separated from family and friends. They experience "forced togetherness" in confined spaces with people who were previously strangers; they endure long periods of inactivity. Lovegrove divides the attitudes of successful station managers into three categories: relating to others, emotions and self-attitude, and style of thinking. He believes that the qualities of these station managers could apply to other leaders in extreme settings as well as to corporate leaders in rapidly changing environments that produce mental as well as physical isolation.

Relating to Others

Trust. Trust takes on more importance in extreme environments because the consequences of failure are so much greater. Station managers generally extend trust to sojourners who respond in kind.

Communication. Communication between station managers and sojourners is open and honest, particularly when dealing with "near misses." Personnel must be open about their mistakes to reduce the likelihood that others will be exposed to the same risks.

Reserved warmth. Effective station managers are friendly and easy going, but generally more reserved than leaders is less extreme environments. They have to display empathy but provide discipline when needed (provide "tough love").

Reduced sensitivity. Station managers are more objective and self-reliant than non-extreme leaders. They recognize that sojourners spend as much as 60% of their time alone, so acknowledge their need for privacy and solitude. Station leaders also have to be more tough-minded when dealing with death. Such losses are tough on these close-knit communities, and empty chairs and beds serve as visual reminders of the loss of colleagues. Station leaders objectively analyze the situation and focus on how to move forward after the tragedy.

Emotions and Self-Attitude

Self-awareness, stability, and self-control. Station managers score significantly higher than non-extreme leaders on measures of self-awareness. They demonstrate emotional stability and self-control while conscientiously carrying out their duties.

Low anxiety or neuroticism. Sojourners want managers who calm and relaxed, have a higher tolerance for stress, and remain confident and composed in the face of crisis events.

Optimism and humor. Optimism (which reflects low apprehension) is particularly important in confined environments. Humor serves as a tension-releaser.

Integrity and leading by example. In the small world of an Antarctic station, managers must act with integrity, leading by example. Lovegrove notes: "Within the close social and physical confines of an Antarctic station there are, quite literally, few places for the station manager to hide." Sojourners look to station managers to act justly and fairly. The station manager must obey the same rules as followers.

Style of Thinking

Openness to change. Compared to non-extreme leaders, station managers are much more open to change. They need to respond to challenges and their openness contributes to the accomplishment of the station's mission.

Grounded and consistent approach. Effective station managers are more practical than imaginative. Their consistent thinking and performance engenders trust. They appear to strike a balance between planning, organization and precision (which are needed to launch a scientific mission in an isolated locale with limited resources), and flexibility, which helps them respond quickly when needed.

Discussion Questions

1. What would be the most difficult challenge of working at an Antarctic station?

2. What types of people would be best suited to working in this environment? Do you think you could work in this setting?

3. What two or three characteristics of station managers do you think are most important for their success?

4. What characteristics do sojourners need in order to be successful followers?

5. What similarities do you see between leading at an Antarctic station and other types of extreme leadership?

6. Would any of the characteristics of effective station managers be important for you as a leader in a non-extreme setting?

Leaders of all kinds need to prepare for death events by making sure that they are notified when anyone in the organization is killed or injured. (This applies even to leaders of large military units and corporations.) The CEO or a designated representative should recognize any death or hospitalization, from janitor to executive vice president. Leaders need to remain humble throughout the tragedy, keeping the focus clearly on the injured person, decedent, and her/his family. After meeting the needs of survivors, they should provide some form of recognition, which helps the organization grieve and move on. Financial services company Cantor Fitzgerald CEO Howard Lutnick, for instance, addressed the needs of surviving families and honored each of the firm's 658 employees who died during the 9/11 attacks. The firm paid 25% of profits to families for five years and continued paying health insurance for ten years. Executives established a website with photographs and postings of each victim; employees and survivors gather every September 11 to read the names of the dead and to honor their memory. In sum, followers expect their leaders to be deeply involved on a personal, emotional level during tragic situations. Leaders who meet these expectations bring hope and help to reestablish a sense of order.

∽ CHAPTER TAKEAWAYS

- A crisis is any major unpredictable event that threatens an organization. Common types of crises include economic, informational, physical, human resource, reputational, psychopathic acts, and natural disasters.

- Regardless of type, crises pass through the same series of stages. The precrisis stage is a period of normalcy when the group should be alert to warning signs (prodomes) that signal that a crisis is developing. The crisis event stage begins when trouble breaks out and ends when the immediate danger is over. The post-crisis phase of evaluation and analysis starts when the immediate danger is past and the organization has resumed normal operations.

- Each stage of the crisis process requires different communication skills and strategies. Your duty as a leader in the precrisis stage is to move the organization from crisis prone to crisis ready. Crisis readiness requires (1) recognizing danger signs through scanning the external and internal environments; (2) identifying trouble spots or vulnerabilities; (3) developing a crisis management plan (including a crisis management team); and (4) building organizational credibility.

- During the crisis event, you will need to initiate action by convincing the organization that a crisis exists, by implementing the crisis management plan, and by mobilizing the crisis management team. Coordinate such activities as redeploying resources and group members, instituting new systems and safeguards, containing the damage, and working with outside agencies. Act as a spokesperson during the crisis, appearing before the media and providing information to protect victims. Effective spokespeople respond quickly and forcefully by getting to the scene of the crisis whenever possible, cooperating with media outlets, and expressing honesty and compassion.

- In the midst of the emergency, engage in vigilant decision making. Resist the temptation to reach decisions quickly and seek out new information instead, reevaluating your choices based on what you discover. In addition, connect with the organization's ethical foundation, encouraging followers to use shared vision and values as operating principles during the crisis.

- After the immediate threat is past, help your organization restore its reputation, learn from the experience, build resilience, and promote healing. Commonly used image-restoration strategies include: (1) denial (denying or shifting responsibility); (2) evading responsibility (lessening the degree of responsibility for what happened); (3) reducing offensiveness (minimizing the audience's negative feelings toward the act and actor); (4) corrective action to repair the damage and to prevent a reoccurrence of the problem; and (5) mortification (admitting guilt and apologizing). When at fault, acknowledge that fact right away and outline plans for correcting the immediate problem and for preventing a recurrence in the future.

- According to Situational Crisis Communication Theory, base your image-restoration strategy on the level of organizational threat. Deny strategies are most effective when the organization is the victim of events. Diminish strategies work best when the crisis is accidental or unintentional. Rebuild strategies should be used when the organization is blamed for the crisis.

- Learning is facilitated by thorough record keeping during the crisis event and takes place through retrospective sensemaking (reflecting on past events), organizational restructuring, and through observing the examples of other organizations. The ultimate goal of crisis learning is to create a high-reliability organization. High-reliability organizations are mindful of failure, taking nothing for granted while improvising in the face of surprises.

- Resilience describes the ability to bounce back after a crisis, to become better than before. As a leader you can foster the reliance of followers through transformational leadership behaviors. Build a resilient organizational culture marked by psychological safety, deep social capital, diffused power and accountability, and access to broad resource networks. Foster community resilience by helping towns, cities, and regions become aware, diverse, integrated, self-regulating, and adaptive.

- Corrective action promotes healing, as does shaping the memories of events, focusing on the future, engaging in renewing discourse, and recognizing that triumph can come out of tragedy.

- Extreme leaders provide purpose and direction to followers in dangerous situations. Successful in extremis leaders are inherently motivated, engage in continuous learning, share risks with followers, live modestly, and have and inspire high competence, trust, and loyalty. They make special effort to treat dead team members with respect.

~ APPLICATION EXERCISES

1. In a group, create your own list of possible crises that could strike your college or university. Place these potential crises in the categories outlined in the chapter.

2. Choose one crisis from your list in exercise 1 and develop a response plan.

3. Use one of the trouble-shooting tactics in the chapter to prepare your organization for a crisis.

4. Share your response to the self-assessment in box 13.3 with a partner. What does your score reveal about the crisis preparedness of your organization? What steps should it take to better prepare for potential crisis events?

5. Describe a time when you and/or your organization were in a crisis situation. Identify what you learned from the experience.

6. Create a crisis case study based on an organization or community. Describe the type and development of the crisis and how it was managed. Evaluate the effectiveness of the leader and organization or community. Determine the long-term effects of the crisis event and the organization or community's learning, healing, and renewal. Identify a set of lessons you can draw from this event.

7. Write a reaction paper in response to one of the research highlights in the chapter. What do you learn from the research results? How do these findings reinforce or challenge your current thinking? How can you apply this information as a leader in a crisis or extreme setting?

8. Role-play a crisis press conference. Choose 6–8 class members to be the crisis team and assign a specific organizational role—CEO, public relations director,

chief engineer—to each. The rest of the class will be the reporters. Separate the groups to prepare for the news conference. Begin with a statement from the crisis management team, followed by questions from the reporters. Make sure that the entire CMT participates. Film the proceedings and debrief, evaluating the performance of both sides.

9. As a class, brainstorm a list of the ways that groups, organizations, and communities can promote healing after a crisis.

10. In a group, share any experiences group members have had as leaders or followers in a life-or-death situation—mountain climbing, sky diving, combat. What does it take to be a successful leader or follower in extreme situations? How does your list of in extremis leadership characteristics compare to that provided in the chapter?

⌒ CULTURAL CONNECTIONS: BATTLING EBOLA AND CULTURE[65]

The 2014–2015 Ebola epidemic in West Africa highlights the impact of culture on crisis response. Ebola is a particularly frightening disease, causing severe vomiting, diarrhea, and headaches; bleeding; and uncontrollable hiccups. These symptoms can put the body into shock and result in death in 25–90% of those infected. The disease spreads through contact with the bodily fluids of patients.

Liberia, Sierra Leone, and Guinea are some of the poorest countries in the world. When crisis responders from Doctors Without Borders, the World Health Organization, the United States government, and other groups arrived, there were few hospitals and clinics and even these lacked such basics as hand soap and running water. In addition to dealing with the lack of medical facilities, responders also confronted cultural beliefs that complicated their battle against Ebola. After years of civil war and unrest in the region, a great many local residents don't trust their governments. Some believed that government officials created the epidemic to attract funds from international donors. There were claims that the disease was a curse or a plot to sell the body parts of those who died. Local authorities raised fear levels by communicating inaccurate health messages, such as contracting Ebola is an automatic death sentence. Angry mobs threatened health workers who tried to identify victims and enforce quarantines. A Doctor Without Borders treatment center was ransacked. Patients resisted going for medical care because clinics and hospitals were viewed as places where victims went to die, surrounded by medical personnel dressed head to toe in protective clothing resembling moon suits.

The biggest cultural barrier was traditional treatment of the sick and the dying. In West Africa, animists, Christians, and Muslims all provide hands-on treatment of the ill and prepare the bodies of loved ones for burial. Caregivers came down with the illness themselves after coming into contact with the sick and the dead. In one case a village healer infected with Ebola died surrounded by her extended family and neighbors, who pulled back the covers and touched the body to say goodbye. Later she was washed and wrapped for burial by a group of women, and relatives stayed in her infected bedroom for several days after her death. Soon after her husband died from Ebola along with a grandson, several of the women who had prepared her body for burial, and others exposed to those women.

To help stop the spread of the disease, government authorities finally banned traditional burial practices. But these measures were difficult to accept. According to former Liberian President Ellen Johnson Sirleaf: "The messages about don't touch the dead, wash your hands, if somebody is sick, leave them—these were all strange things, completely contrary to our tradition and culture."[66]

⌒ LEADERSHIP ON THE BIG SCREEN: *PATRIOTS DAY*

Starring: Mark Wahlberg, John Goodman, J. K. Simmons, Michelle Monaghan, Kevin Bacon, Rachel Brosnahan, Jimmy O. Yang, Alex Wolff, Themo Melikidze

Rating: R for violence, disturbing images, and language

Synopsis: A fictionalized account of the 2013 Boston Marathon bombing and subsequent manhunt. Introduces key players—law enforcement officials, victims, bombers—and then follows the events as they unfold. Composite character Boston police officer Tommy Saunders (Wahlberg) is present at key moments in the drama. Following the two blasts at the finish line, the FBI and local authorities work quickly to identify and locate the two suspects, brothers who later kill an MIT policeman and hijack a car on their way to carry out further attacks. Authorities must determine whether or not to release photos of the bombers and how to best protect the city when one of the brothers remains on the loose. Bostonians rally around the slogan "Boston Strong" following the crisis. Interviews with victims at the end of the film reveal their determination to overcome the tragedy despite the loss of their legs and feet.

Chapter Links: abnormal accidents, crisis stages, warning signs, discourse of renewal, transparency, crisis management teams, in extremis leaders

Endnotes

 **CHAPTER ONE**

[1] For more information on the history of leadership study, see: Bass, B. M. (Ed.). (1990). *Bass and Stogdill's handbook of leadership* (3rd ed., ch. 1). New York: Free Press.

[2] Fairhurst, G. T., & Sarr, R. A. (1996). *The art of framing: Managing the language of leadership*. San Francisco: Jossey-Bass.

[3] Adapted from Tichy, N. M. (1997). *The leadership engine*. New York: HarperBusiness, pp. 215–216.

[4] Case based on: Bowley, G., & Kannapell, A. (2008, August 6). Chaos on the "mountain that invites death." *The New York Times*, p. A1; Power, M. (2008, November). K2: The killing peak. *Men's Journal*; Ramesh, R. (2008, August 5). K2 tragedy. *The Guardian* (London), p. 2; Taylor, J. (2008, August 5). What makes K2 the most perilous challenge a mountaineer can face? *The Independent* (London), Comment, p. 30; Viesturs, E., & Roberts, D. (2009). *K2: Life and death on the world's most dangerous mountain*. New York: Broadway Books; Zuckerman, P., & Padoan, A. (2012*). Buried in the sky: The extraordinary story of the Sherpa climbers on K2's deadliest day*. New York: Norton.

[5] Dance, F. E. X. (1982). A speech theory of human communication. In F. E. X. Dance (Ed.), *Human communication theory* (pp. 120–146). New York: Harper & Row, p. 126.

[6] White, L. A. (1949). *The science of culture*. New York: Farrar, Strauss and Cudahy, p. 25.

[7] Information concerning differences among human and animal communication systems is extensive. The following sources serve as a good starting point for reading in this area: Adler, J. J. (1967). *The difference of man and the difference it makes*. New York: Holt, Rinehart and Winston; Pearce, W. B. (1989). *Communication and the human condition*. Carbondale: Southern Illinois University Press; Sebeok, T. A., & Rosenthal, R. (Eds.). (1981). *The clever Hans phenomenon: Communication with horses, whales, apes, and people*. Annals of the New York Academy of Sciences, Vol. 364. New York: New York Academy of Sciences.

[8] Barnlund, D. C. (1962). Toward a meaning-centered philosophy of communication. *Journal of Communication, 12*, 197–211.

[9] Burns, J. M. (1978). *Leadership*. New York: Harper & Row, p. 2.

[10] Rost, J. C. (1991). *Leadership for the twenty-first century*. New York: Praeger.

[11] Bogardus, E. S. (1934). *Leaders and leadership*. New York: Appleton-Century.

[12] Bingham, W. V. (1927). Leadership. In H. C. Metcalf, *The psychological foundations of management*. New York: Shaw.

[13] Hersey, P. (1984). *The situational leader*. Escondido, CA: Center for Leadership Studies, p. 14.

[14] Bass, B. M. (1960). *Leadership, psychology, and organizational behavior*. New York: Harper & Row, p. 90.

[15] Alvesson, M. (2002). *Understanding organizational culture*. Thousand Oaks, CA: Sage, p. 105.

[16] Hemphill, J. K. (1949). The leader and his group. *Journal of Educational Research, 28*, 225–229.

[17] Stogdill, R. M. (1950). Leadership, membership and organization. *Psychological Bulletin, 47*, p. 4.

[18] Rost, J. C. (1993). Leadership in the new millennium. *The Journal of Leadership Studies*, 91–110, p. 99; Rost, *Leadership for the twenty-first century*.

[19] See, for example: Block, P. (1993). *Stewardship: Choosing service over self-interest*. San Francisco: Berrett-Koehler; Greenleaf, R. K. (1977). *Servant leadership*. New York: Paulist Press.

[20] Northouse, P. (2013). *Leadership: Theory and practice* (6th ed.). Thousand Oaks, CA: Sage, p. 5.

[21] Yukl, G. (2013). *Leadership in organizations* (8th ed.). Upper Saddle River, NJ: Prentice-Hall, p. 7.

[22] Nahavandi, A. (2006). *The art and science of leadership* (4th ed.). Upper Saddle River, NJ: Prentice-Hall, p. 4.

[23] Hughes, R. L., Ginnett, R. C., & Curphy, G. J. (2009). *Leadership: Enhancing the lessons of experience* (6th ed.). Boston: McGraw-Hill Irwin.

[24] Manning, G., & Curtis, K. (2015). *The art of leadership* (5th ed.) Boston: McGraw-Hill, p. 2.

[25] Pierce, J. L, & Newstrom, J. W. (2011). *Leaders & the leadership process: Readings, self-assessments & applications* (6th ed.). New York: McGraw-Hill Irwin, p. 10.

[26] Dubrin, A. J. (2013). *Leadership: Research findings, practice, and skills* (7th ed.). Mason, OH: South-Western, p. 1.

[27] Kouzes, J. M., & Posner, B. Z. (1987). *The leadership challenge: How to get extraordinary things done in organizations*. San Francisco: Jossey-Bass, pp. 31–32.

[28] Kotter, J. P. (1990). *A force for change: How leadership differs from management*. New York: Free Press.

[29] Dutch Bros (2016). Company information. Retrieved from dutchbros.com/AboutUs/

[30] See, for example: Kellerman, B. (2004). *Bad leadership*. Boston: Harvard University Press; Lipman-Blumen, J. (2005). *The allure of toxic leaders*. New York: Oxford University Press; Schyns, B., & Hansbrough, T. (Eds.). (2010). *When leadership goes wrong: Destructive leadership mistakes and ethical failures*. Charlotte, NC: Information Age.

[31] Pfeffer, J. (2015). *Leadership BS: Fixing workplaces and careers one truth at a time*. New York: Harper-Business.

[32] This notion of making a distinction between leaders and power wielders comes from Burns.

[33] Keltner, D., Langner, C. A., & Allison, M. L. (2006). Power and moral leadership. In D. L. Rhode (Ed.), *Moral leadership: The theory and practice of power, judgment, and policy* (pp. 177–194). San Francisco: Jossey-Bass.

[34] Thoroughgood, C. N, Padilla, A., Hunter, S. T., & Tate, B. W. (2012). The susceptible circle: A taxonomy of followers associated with destructive leadership. *Leadership Quarterly, 23*, 897–917.

[35] Lubit, R. (2002). The long-term organizational impact of destructively narcissistic managers. *Academy of Management Executive, 16*(1), 127–138; Higgs, M. (2009). The good, the bad and the ugly: Leadership and narcissism. *Journal of Change Management, 9*(2), 165–178.

[36] Brunell, A. B., Gentry, W. A., Campbell, W. K., Hoffman, B. J., Kuhnert, K. W., & DeMarree, K. G. (2008). Leader emergence: The case of the narcissistic leader. *Personality and Social Psychology Bulletin, 34*(12), 1663–1676.

[37] Christie, R., & Gies, F. L. (1970). *Studies in Machiavellianism*. New York: Academic Press; Paulus, D. L., & Williams, K. M. (2002). The dark triad of personality: Narcissism, Machiavellianism, and psychopathy. *Journal of Research in Personality, 36*, 556–563.

[38] Teven, J. J., McCroskey, J. C., & Richmond, V. P. (2006). Communication correlates of perceived Machiavellianism of supervisors: Communication orientations and outcomes. *Communication Quarterly, 54*(2), 127–142.

[39] Hunter, S. T., Tate, B. W., Dzieweczynski, J. L., & Cushenbery, L. (2010). Understanding the antecedents of unintentional leader errors: A multilevel perspective. In B. Schyns & T. Hansbrough (Eds.), *When leadership goes wrong: Destructive leadership mistakes and ethical failures* (pp. 405–443). Charlotte, NC: Information Age.

[40] Mulvey, P. W., & Padilla, A. (2010). The environment of destructive leadership. In B. Schyns & T. Hansbrough (Eds.), *When leadership goes wrong: Destructive leadership mistakes and ethical failures* (pp. 49–71). Charlotte, NC: Information Age.

[41] Definitions come from Kellerman, *Bad leadership*. Examples have been updated.

[42] Einarsen, S., Aasland, M. S., & Skogstad, A. (2007). Destructive leadership behaviour: A definition and conceptual model. *Leadership Quarterly, 18*, 207–216; Einarsen, S., Skogstad, A., & Aasland, M. S. (2010). The nature, prevalence, and outcomes of destructive leadership: A behavior and conglomerate approach. In B. Schyns & T. Hansbrough (Eds.), *When leadership goes wrong: Destructive leadership mistakes and ethical failures* (pp. 145–171). Charlotte, NC: Information Age.

[43] Blygh, M. C. (2011). Followership and follower-centered approaches. In A. Bryman, D. Collinson, K. Grint, B. Jackson, & M. Uhl-Bien (Eds.), *The Sage handbook of leadership* (pp. 425–436). Los Angeles: Sage.

[44] Kellerman, B. (2008). *Followership: How followers are creating change and changing leaders.* Boston: Harvard Business Press; Stengel, R. (2011, December 26). 2011 Person of the year: The protester. *Time*, pp. 53ff.

[45] Pearce, C. L., & Conger, J. A. (2003). All those years ago: The historical underpinnings of shared leadership. In C. L. Pearce & J. A. Conger (Eds.), *Shared leadership: Reframing the hows and whys of leadership* (pp. 1–16). Thousand Oaks, CA: Sage; Pearce, C. L. (2004). The future of leadership: Combining vertical and shared leadership to transform knowledge work. *Academy of Management Review, 18*, 47–57.

[46] Hollander, E. P. (1992, April). The essential interdependence of leadership and followership. *Current Directions in Psychological Science*, 71–75.

[47] Kelley, R. (1992). *The power of followership: How to create leaders people want to follow and followers who lead themselves.* New York: Doubleday/Currency, p. 41.

[48] Summaries of the development of the Willingness to Communicate construct can be found in: McCroskey, J. C., & Richmond, V. P. (1998). Willingness to communicate. In J. C. McCroskey, J. A. Daly, M. M. Martin, & M. J. Beatty (Eds.), *Communication and personality: Trait perspectives* (pp. 119–131). Cresswell, NJ: Hampton Press; Morreale, S. P. (2007). *Assessing motivation to communication: Willingness to communicate and personal report of communication apprehension* (2nd ed.). Washington, DC: National Communication Association.

[49] McCroskey, J. C., & Richmond, V. P. (1996). *Fundamentals of human communication: An interpersonal perspective.* Long Grove, IL: Waveland Press, pp. 53-54. Used by permission.

[50] McCroskey, J. C., & Richmond, V. P. (1990). Willingness to communicate: Differing cultural perspectives. *Southern Communication Journal, 56*, 72–77.

[51] Teven, J. J., Richmond, V. P., McCroskey, J. C., & McCroskey, L. L. (2010). Updating relationships between communication traits and communication competence. *Communication Research Reports, 27*(3), 263–270; Miczo, N. (2004). Humor ability, unwillingness to communicate, loneliness, and perceived stress: Testing a security theory. *Communication Studies, 55*(2), 209–226.

[52] Kassing, J. W. (1997). Development of the intercultural willingness to communicate scale. *Communication Research Reports, 14*(4), 399–407.

[53] Gilchrist-Petty, E., & Folk, Z. D. (2014). "Suck it up": The relationship between willingness to communicate and reduced soldier stress. *The Northwest Journal of Communication, 42*, 87–116.

[54] Johnson, C. E., Dixon, B., Hackman, M. Z., & Vinson, L. (1995). Willingness to communicate, the need for cognition and innovativeness: New Zealand students and professionals. In J. E. Aitken & L. J. Shedletsky (Eds.), *Intrapersonal communication processes* (pp. 376–381). Plymouth, MI: Midnight Oil and the Speech Communication Association; Hackman, M. Z., & Johnson, C. (1994). *A cross-cultural investigation of innovativeness, willingness to communicate and need for cognition.* Paper presented at the Speech Communication Association convention, New Orleans, LA.

[55] Hodis, G. M., Bardhan, N. R., & Hodis, F. A. (2010). Patterns of change in willingness to communicate in public speaking contexts: A latent growth modeling analysis. *Journal of Applied Communication Research, 38*(5), 248–267.

[56] Marquardt, M. (2005). *Leading with questions.* San Francisco: Jossey-Bass.

[57] Harvey, M. (2006). Leadership and the human condition. In G. R. Goethals & G. L. J. Sorenson (Eds.), *The quest for a general theory of leadership* (pp. 39–45). Northampton, MA: Edward Elgar, p. 42.

[58] Denning, S. (2005). *The leader's guide to storytelling.* San Francisco: Jossey-Bass.

[59] Mirvis, P. (1996, March). Can you teach your people to think smarter? *Across the Board*, 26–27.

[60] Definitions and examples from Denning.

[61] Fisher, S. (2007, October). Telling tales: The art of corporate story telling. *The Costco Connection*, pp. 22–23.

[62] Freiberg, K., & Freiberg, J. (1996). *Nuts! Southwest Airlines' crazy recipe for business and personal success.* New York: Broadway Books, p. 290.

[63] Ashkanasy, N. M, & Jordan, P. J. (2008). A multilevel view of leadership and emotion. In R. H. Humphrey (Ed.), *Affect and emotion: New directions in management theory and research* (pp. 19–41). Charlotte, NC: Information Age; Ashkanasy, N. M., & Humphrey, R. H. (2011). A multi-level view of leadership and emotion: Leading with emotional labor. In A. Bryman, D. Collinson, K. Grint, B. Jackson, & M. Uhl-Bien (Eds.), *The Sage handbook of leadership* (pp. 365–379). Los Angeles: Sage.

[64] For an overview of the development of the field of emotional intelligence, see Mayer, J. D. (2001). A field guide to emotional intelligence. In J. Ciarrochi, J. P. Forgas, & J. D. Mayer (Eds.), *Emotional intelligence in everyday life: A scientific inquiry* (pp. 3–24). Philadelphia: Psychology Press.

[65] Walter, F., Cole, M. S., & Humphrey, R. H. (2011). Emotional intelligence: Sine qua non of leadership or folderol? *Academy of Management Perspectives*, 45–59.

[66] Cherniss, C. (2000). Social and emotional competence in the workplace. In R. Bar-On & J. D. A. Parker (Eds.), *The handbook of emotional intelligence: Theory, development, assessment, and application at home, school, and in the workplace.* San Francisco: Jossey-Bass; Goleman, D. (1998). *Working with emotional intelligence.* New York: Bantam Books; Cooper, R. K., & Sawat, A. (1996). *Executive EQ: Emotional intelligence in leadership and organizations.* New York: Grosset/Putnam.

[67] Johnson, C. (2002). Evaluating the impact of emotional intelligence on leadership performance: Resonance or dissonance? *Selected Proceedings of the 2002 International Leadership Association convention.* Available from http://www.academy.umd.edu/ILA.

[68] Salovey, P., Bedell, B. T., Detweiler, J. B., & Mayer, J. D. (2000). Current directions in emotional intelligence research. In M. Lewis & J. M. Haviland-Lewis (Eds.), *Handbook of emotions* (2nd ed., pp. 504–520). New York: Guilford Press.

[69] Tee, E. Y. J. (2015). The emotional link: Leadership and the role of implicit and explicit emotional contagion processes across multiple organizational levels. *Leadership Quarterly, 23*, 654–670.

[70] Stretcher Sigmar, L., Hynes, G. E., & Hill, K. L. (2012). Strategies for teaching social and emotional intelligence in business communication. *Business Communication Quarterly, 75*(3), 301–317. Used by permission of Sage Publications.

[71] Goffman, E. (1959). *The presentation of self in everyday life.* Garden City, NY: Doubleday; Brissett, D., & Edgley, C. (2005). The dramaturgical perspective. In D. Brissett & C. Edgley (Eds.), *Life as theater: A dramaturgical sourcebook* (2nd ed., pp. 1–46). New York: Aldine de Gruyter.

[72] Gardner, W. L., & Cleavenger, D. (1998). The impression management strategies associated with transformational leadership at the world-class level: A psychological assessment. *Management Communication Quarterly, 12*, 3–41; Griffith, J., Connelly, S., Thiel, C., & Johnson, G. (2015). How outstanding leaders lead with affect: An examination of charismatic, ideological, and pragmatic leadership. *Leadership Quarterly, 26*, 502–517.

[73] Ladkin, D. (2008). Leading beautifully: How mastery, congruence and purpose create the aesthetic of embodied leadership practice. *Leadership Quarterly, 19*, 31–41.

[74] Anderson University (Producer) & Biggs, D. (Director). (2008). *A ripple of hope.* (Documentary film).

[75] Goethals, G. R. (2005). Nonverbal behavior and political leadership. In R. E. Riggio & R. S. Feldman (Eds.), *Applications of nonverbal communication* (pp. 95–115). Mahwah, NJ: Lawrence Erlbaum.

[76] Gardner, W. L., & Martinko, M. J. (1988). Impression management in organizations. *Journal of Management, 14*, 321–338.

[77] Rosenfeld, P., Giacalone, R. A., & Riordan, C. A. (1995*). Impression management in organizations: Theory, measurement, practice.* New York: Routledge, p. 133.

[78] Julien, M., Wright, B., & Zinni, D. M. (2010). Stories from the circle: Leadership lessons learned from aboriginal leaders. *Leadership Quarterly, 21*, 114–126.

∿ CHAPTER TWO

[1] Lewin, K., Lippitt, R., & White, R. K. (1939). Patterns of aggressive behavior in experimentally created "social climates." *Journal of Social Psychology, 10,* 271–299.

[2] See, for example: Bass, B. M. (1990). *Bass & Stogdill's handbook of leadership* (3rd ed., ch. 25). New York: Free Press.

[3] Wasden, M., & Guzley, R. (2004, November). *Guided freedom leadership: Competent and capable individuals in the 21st century.* Paper presented at the International Leadership Association Conference, Washington, DC.

[4] Lewin et al., Patterns of aggressive behavior.

[5] White, R., & Lippitt, R. (1968). Leader behavior and member reaction in three "social climates." In D. Cartwright & A. Zander (Eds.), *Group dynamics* (pp. 318–335). New York: Harper & Row.

[6] Shaw, M. E. (1955). A comparison of two types of leadership in various communication nets. *Journal of Abnormal and Social Psychology, 50,* 127–134; Hise, R. T. (1968, Fall). The effect of close supervision on productivity of simulated managerial decision-making groups. *Business Studies, North Texas University,* pp. 96–104.

[7] Argyle, M., Gardner, G., & Ciofi, F. (1958). Supervisory methods related to productivity, absenteeism, and labor turnover. *Human Relations, 11,* 23–40.

[8] Farris, G. F. (1972). The effect of individual roles on performance in innovative groups. *R & D Management, 3,* 23–28.

[9] Cammalleri, J. A., Hendrick, H. W., Pittmen, W. C., Jr., Blout, H. D., & Prather, D. C. (1973). Effects of different leadership styles on group accuracy. *Journal of Applied Psychology, 57,* 32–37.

[10] Mohr, L. B. (1971). Organizational technology and organizational structure. *Administrative Science Quarterly, 16,* 444–459; Bass, B. M., Burger, P. C., Doktor, R., & Barrett, G. V. (1979). *Assessment of managers: An international comparison.* New York: Free Press.

[11] Aspegren, R. E. (1963). A study of leadership behavior and its effects on morale and attitudes in selected elementary schools. *Dissertation Abstracts, 23,* 3708.

[12] Vroom, V. H., & Mann, F. C. (1960). Leader authorization and employee attitudes. *Personnel Psychology, 13,* 125–140.

[13] Hespe, G., & Wall, T. (1976). The demand for participation among employees. *Human Relations, 29,* 411–428.

[14] Baumgartel, H. (1957). Leadership style as a variable in research administration. *Administrative Science Quarterly, 2,* 344–360.

[15] Rudin, S. A. (1964). Leadership as psychophysiological activation of group members: A case experimental study. *Psychological Reports, 15,* 577–578.

[16] Ziller, R. C. (1954). Four techniques of group decision making under uncertainty. *American Psychologist, 9,* 498.

[17] Muringham, J. K., & Leung, T. K. (1976). The effects of leadership involvement and the importance of the task on subordinates' performance. *Organizational Behavior and Human Performance, 17,* 299–310.

[18] Day, R. C., & Hamblin, R. L. (1964). Some effects of close and punitive styles of supervision. *American Journal of Sociology, 69,* 499–510.

[19] Farris, G. F. (1972). The effect of individual roles on performance in innovative groups. *R & D Management, 3,* 23–28.

[20] Weschler, I. R., Kahane, M., & Tannenbaum, R. (1952). Job satisfaction, productivity, and morale: A case study. *Occupational Psychology, 26,* 1–14; Meltzer, L. (1956). Scientific productivity in organizational settings. *Journal of Social Issues, 12,* 32–40.

[21] Ley, R. (1966). Labor turnover as a function of worker differences, work environment, and authoritarianism of foremen. *Journal of Applied Psychology, 50,* 497–500.

[22] Meyer, H. H. (1968). Achievement motivation and industrial climates. In R. Tagiuri & G. H. Litwin (Eds.), *Organizational climate: Explorations of a concept* (pp. 151–166). Boston: Division of Research, Harvard Business School.

[23] Skogstad, A., Einarsen, S., Torsheim, T., Shanke Aasland, M., & Hetland, H. (2007). The destructiveness of laissez-faire leadership behavior. *Journal of Occupational Health Psychology, 12*, 80–92.

[24] Information in this case from: Chouinard, Y. (2005). *Let my people go surfing*. New York: Penguin Press; Wright, M. (2011, November 7). Success means telling people to buy less. *Guardian Unlimited*; Martin, H. (2012, May 25). Clothier's products all come in green. *Los Angeles Times*, p. B1; Mackinnon, J. B. (2015, May 21). Patagonia's anti-growth strategy. *The New Yorker*; Don of the dirtbags: An interview with Yvon Chouinard. (2016, February 26). *The Usual.*

[25] Chouinard, *Let my people go surfing*, p. 178.

[26] Chouinard, *Let my people go surfing*, p. 181.

[27] Stech, E. L. (1983). *Leadership communication*. Chicago: Nelson-Hall, ch. 4.

[28] See: Katz, D., Maccoby, N., Gurin, G., & Floor, L. (1951). *Productivity, supervision, and morale among railroad workers*. Ann Arbor: University of Michigan, Institute for Social Research; Katz, D., Maccoby, N., & Morse, N. (1950). *Productivity, supervision, and morale in an office situation*. Ann Arbor: University of Michigan, Institute for Social Research.

[29] Although the one-dimensional view of leadership communication has been criticized as being overly simplistic, some one-dimensional models are still routinely discussed in leadership courses. For an example of a commonly cited one-dimensional model see: Tannenbaum, R., & Schmidt, W. H. (1958). How to choose a leadership pattern. *Harvard Business Review, 36*, 95–101.

[30] Kahn, R. L. (1956). The prediction of productivity. *Journal of Social Issues, 12*, 41–49.

[31] Stogdill, R. M., & Coons, A. E. (1957). *Leader behavior: Its description and measurement*. Columbus: Ohio State University, Bureau of Business Research.

[32] Stogdill, R. M. (1965). *Managers, employees, organizations*. Columbus: Ohio State University, Bureau of Business Research.

[33] Northouse, P. (2013). *Leadership: Theory and Practice* (6th ed.). Thousand Oaks, CA: Sage, pp. 93–94. Used by permission of Sage Publications.

[34] Eckvall, G., & Arvoven, J. (1991). Change-centered leadership: An extension of the two-dimensional model. *Scandinavian Journal of Management, 7*, 15–26; Gil, F., Rico, R., Alcover, C. M., & Barrasa, A. (2005). Change-oriented leadership, satisfaction and performance in work groups: Effects of team climate and group potency. *Journal of Managerial Psychology, 20*, 312–328; Ortega, A., Van den Bossche, P., Sanchez-Manzanares, M., Rice, R., & Gil, F. (2014). The influence of change-oriented leadership and psychological safety on team learning in healthcare teams. *Journal of Business Psychology, 29*, 311–321.

[35] Yukl, G., Gordon, A., & Taber, T. (2002). A hierarchical taxonomy of leadership behavior: Integrating a half century of behavior research. *Journal of Leadership & Organizational Studies, 9*, 15–32.

[36] McGregor, D. (1960). *The human side of enterprise*. New York: McGraw-Hill.

[37] Blake, R. R., & McCanse, A. A. (1991). *Leadership dilemmas—grid solutions*. Houston: Gulf; Blake, R. R., & Mouton, J. S. (1985). *The managerial grid III: The key to leadership excellence*. Houston: Gulf.

[38] The Leadership Grid Figure for *Leadership Dilemmas—Grid Solutions* by Robert R. Blake and Anne Adams McCanse (formerly the Managerial Grid Figure by Robert R. Blake and Jane S. Mouton). Austin, TX: Grid International, p. 29. © 1991 by Grid International. Used by permission.

[39] See: Blake & McCanse, *Leadership dilemmas*; Blake, R. R., Mouton, J. S., Barnes, L. B., & Greiner, L. E. (1964). Breakthrough in organization development. *Harvard Business Review, 42*, 133–155.

[40] Kelley, R. (1992). *The power of followership: How to create leaders that people want to follow and followers who lead themselves*. New York: Doubleday/Currency; Kelley, R. (1988, November–December). In praise of followers. *Harvard Business Review, 66*, 142–148.

[41] Kellerman, B. A. (2008). *Followership: How followers are creating change and changing leaders*. Boston: Harvard Business Press.

[42] Kelley, *The power of followership*.

[43] From *The power of followership* (pp. 89–97) by Robert E. Kelley, copyright © 1992 by Consultants to Executives and Organizations, Ltd. Used by permission of Doubleday, a division of Penguin Random House LLC. All rights reserved.

[44] Adair, R. (2008). Developing great leaders, one follower at a time. In R. Riggio, I. Chaleff, & J. Lipman-Blumen (Eds.), *The art of followership: How great followers create great leaders and organizations* (pp. 137–153). San Francisco: Jossey-Bass.

[45] Pina e Cunha, M., Rego, A., Clegg, S., & Neves, P. (2013). The case for transcendent followership. *Leadership, 9*, 87–196.

[46] Brown, D. J., Scott, K. A., & Lewis, H. (2004). Information processing and leadership. In J. Antonakis, A. T. Cianciolo, & R. J. Sternberg (Eds.), *The nature of leadership* (pp. 125–147). Thousand Oaks, CA: Sage.

[47] Brown et al., Information processing and leadership, p. 126.

[48] See, for example: Vygotsky, L. (1986). *Thought and language* (Trans. A. Kozulin). Cambridge, MA: MIT Press; Luria, A. R. (1982). *Language and cognition*. J. V. Wertsch (Ed.). New York: John Wiley & Sons; Johnson, J. R. (1984). The role of inner speech in human communication. *Communication Education, 33*, 211–222.

[49] Connelly, M. S., Gilbert, J. A., Zaccaro, S. J., Threlfall, K. V., Marks, M. A., & Mumford, M. D. (2000). Exploring the relationship of leadership skills and knowledge to leader performance. *Leadership Quarterly, 11*, 65–86.

[50] Carsten, M. K., Uhl-Bien, M., West, B. J., Patera, J. L., & McGregor, R. (2010). Exploring social constructions of followership: A qualitative study. *Leadership Quarterly, 21*, 543–562; Carsten, M. K., & Uhl-Bien, M. (2012). Follower beliefs in the co-production of leadership: Examining upward communication and the moderating role of context. *Journal of Psychology, 220*, 210–220; Carsten, M. K., & Uhl-Bien, M. (2013). Ethical followership: An examination of followership beliefs and crimes of obedience. *Journal of Leadership & Organizational Studies, 20*, 49–61.

[51] Lord, R. G., & Maher, K. J. (1991). *Leadership and information processing: Linking perceptions and performance*. Boston: Unwin Hyman.

[52] Derr, C. B., Roussillon, S., & Bournois, F. (2002). Conclusion. In C. B. Derr, S. Roussillon, & F. Bournois (Eds.), *Cross-cultural approaches to leadership development* (pp. 289–303). Westport, CT: Quorum Books, pp. 290–292.

[53] Lord & Maher, *Leadership and information processing*.

[54] van Knippenberg, D., van Knippenberg, B., De Cremer, D., & Hogg, M. A. (2004). Leadership, self, and identity: A review and research agenda. *Leadership Quarterly, 15*, 825–856; Lord, R. G., & Brown, D. J. (2004). *Leadership processes and follower self-identity*. Mahwah, NJ: Lawrence Erlbaum; Shamir, B., House, R. J., & Arthur, M. B. (1993). The motivational effects of charismatic leadership: A self-concept based theory. *Organization Science, 4*, 577–594.

[55] Hogg, M. A. (2001). A social identity theory of leadership. *Personality and Social Psychology Review, 5*, 184–200; Haslam, S. A., & Platow, M. J. (2001). The link between leadership and followership: How affirming social identity translates vision into action. *PSPB, 27*, 146–147; Tee, E. Y. J., Paulsen, N., & Ashkanasy, N. M. (2013). Revisiting followership through a social identity perspective: The role of collective follower emotion and action. *Leadership Quarterly, 24*, 902–918.

[56] Misumi, J., & Peterson, M. F. (1985). The Performance-Maintenance theory of leadership: Review of a Japanese research program. *Administrative Science Quarterly, 30*, 198–223; Smith, P. B., Misumi, J., Tayeb, M., Peterson, M., & Bond, M. (1989). On the generality of leadership style measures across cultures. *Journal of Occupational Psychology, 62*, 97–109.

∾ CHAPTER THREE

[1] Stogdill, R. M. (1948). Personal factors associated with leadership: A survey of the literature. *Journal of Psychology, 25*, 35–71.

[2] Stogdill, Personal factors, p. 64.

[3] Stogdill, R. M. (1974). *Handbook of leadership*. New York: The Free Press.

[4] Stogdill, *Handbook*, p. 72.

[5] Kenny, D. A., & Zaccaro, S. J. (1983). An estimate of variance due to traits in leadership. *Journal of Applied Psychology, 68*, 678–685 (a reanalysis of Barnlund's consistency of emergent leadership in groups with changing tasks and members published in *Speech Monographs* in 1962); Lord, R. G., De Vader, C. L., & Alliger, G. M. (1986). A meta-analysis of the relation between personality traits and leadership perceptions: An application of validity generalization procedures. *Journal of Applied Psy-*

chology, 71, 402–410 (a reanalysis of Mann's review of the relationships between personality and performance in small groups published in *Psychological Bulletin* in 1959); Hoffman, B. J., Woehr, D. J., Maldagen-Youngjohn, R., & Lyons, B. D. (2011). Great man or great myth? A quantitative review of the relationship between individual differences and leader effectiveness. *Journal of Occupational and Organizational Psychology 84,* 347–381.

6   Zaccaro, S. J., Kemp, C., & Bader, P. (2004). Leader traits and attributes. In J. Antonakis, A. Cianciolo, & R. J. Sternberg (Eds.), *The nature of leadership* (pp. 101–124). Thousand Oaks, CA: Sage.

7   Rotter, J. B. (1966). Generalized expectancies for internal versus external control of reinforcement. *Psychological Monographs, 80,* 1–28.

8   Goodstadt, B. E., & Hjelle, L. A. (1973). Power to the powerless: Locus of control and the use of power. *Journal of Personality and Social Psychology, 27,* 190–196; Miller, D., Kets De Vries, M. F. R., & Toulouse, J-M. Top executive locus of control and its relationship to strategy-making, structure, and environment. *Academy of Management Journal, 25,* 237–253; Yukl, G. (2013). *Leadership in organizations* (8th ed.). Boston: Pearson.

9   Goldberg, L. R. (1990). An alternative "description of personality": The big-five factor structure. *Journal of Personality and Social Psychology, 59,* 1216–1229; McCrae, R. R., & Costa, P. T. (1987). Validation of the five-factor model of personality across instruments and observers. *Journal of Personality and Social Psychology, 52,* 81–90.

10 Judge, T. A., Bono, J. E., Ilies, R., & Gerhardt, M. W. (2002). Personality and leadership: A qualitative and quantitative review. *Journal of Applied Psychology, 87,* 765–780.

11 Howard, P. S., & Howard, J. M. (2001). *The owner's manual for personality at work.* Atlanta: Bard Press.

12 McClelland, D. C. (1975). *Power: The inner experience.* New York: Wiley. McClelland, D. C. (1982). Leadership motive pattern and long-term success in management. *Journal of Applied Psychology, 67,* 737–743; Yukl, *Leadership in organizations.*

13 Locke, E. A. (1991). *The essence of leadership: Four keys to leading successfully.* Lanham, MD: Lexington Books.

14 Chan, K. Y., & Drasgow, F. (2001). Toward a theory of individual differences and leadership: Understanding the motivation to lead. *Journal of Applied Psychology, 86,* 481–498; Luria, G., & Berson, Y. (2013). How do leadership motives affect informal and formal leadership emergence? *Journal of Organizational Behavior, 34,* 995–1015; Hendricks, J. W., & Payne, S. C. (2007). Beyond the Big Five: Leader goal orientation as a predictor of leadership effectiveness. *Human Performance, 20,* 317–343; Stehl, S. K., Felfe, J., Elprana, G., & Gatzka, M. B. (2015). The role of motivation to lead for leadership training effectiveness. *International Journal of Training and Development, 19,* 81–97.

15 Cain, S. (2012). *Quiet: The power of introverts in a world that can't stop talking.* New York: Crown; Kahnweiller, J. (2009). *The introverted leader: Building on your quiet strength.* San Francisco: Berrett-Koehler.

16 Walsh, B. (2012, February 12). The upside of being an introvert (and why extroverts are overrated). *Time,* pp. 40–45.

17 Chan, K. Y., & Drasgow, F. (2001). Toward a theory of individual differences and leadership: Understanding the motivation to lead. *Journal of Applied Psychology, 86,* p. 486. Used by permission of the American Psychological Association.

18 Case based on material from Gerber, R. (2002). *Leadership the Eleanor Roosevelt way: Timeless strategies from the first lady of courage.* New York: Prentice-Hall.

19 Gerber, *Leadership the Eleanor Roosevelt way,* p. 169.

20 Gerber, *Leadership the Eleanor Roosevelt way,* p. 7.

21 Gerber, *Leadership the Eleanor Roosevelt way,* pp. 4–5.

22 See, for example: Burns, T., & Stalker, G. M. (1961). *The management of innovation.* Chicago: Quadrangle Books; Lawrence, P. R., & Lorsch, J. W. (1967). *Organization and environment.* Cambridge, MA: Harvard University Press.

23 See, for example: House, R. J. (1971). A path-goal theory of leader effectiveness. *Administrative Science Quarterly, 16,* 321–338; House, R. J., & Mitchell, T. R. (1974). Path-goal theory of leadership. *Journal of Contemporary Business, 3,* 81–97.

24 House, R. J., (1996). Path-goal theory of leadership: Lessons, legacy, and a reformulated theory. *Leadership Quarterly, 7*, 323–352, p. 335.

25 See, for example: Veechio, R. P., Justin, J. E., & Pearce, C. L. (2008). The utility of transactional and transformational leadership for predicting performance and satisfaction within a path-goal theory framework. *Journal of Occupational and Organizational Psychology, 81*, 71–82; Djibo, I. J. A., Desiderio, K., & Price, N. M. (2010). Examining the role of perceived leader behavior on temporary employees' organizational commitment and citizenship behavior. *Human Resource Development Quarterly, 21*, 321–342.

26 Hersey, P., Blanchard, K. H., & Johnson, D. (2008). *Management of organizational behavior: Leading human resources* (9th ed.). Upper Saddle River, NJ: Prentice-Hall.

27 See, for example: Graeff, C. L. (1983). The situational leadership theory: A critical view. *Academy of Management Review, 8*, 285–291; Graeff, C. L. (1997). Evolution of situational leadership theory: A critical review. *Leadership Quarterly, 8*, 153–170; Johansen, B-C. P. (1990). Situational leadership: A review of the research. *Human Resource Development Quarterly, 1*, 73–85.

28 Barnard, C. I. (1938). *The functions of the executive.* Cambridge, MA: Harvard University Press.

29 Benne, K. D., & Sheats, P. (1948). Functional roles of group members. *Journal of Social Issues, 4*, 41–49.

30 Krech, D., & Crutchfield, R. (1948). *Theory and problems of social psychology.* New York: McGraw-Hill.

31 Bowers, D. G., & Seashore, S. E. (1966). Predicting organizational effectiveness with a four-factor theory of leadership. *Administrative Science Quarterly, 2*, 238–263.

32 Cartwright, D., & Zander, A. (1968). Leadership and performance of group functions: Introduction. In D. Cartwright & A. Zander (Eds.), *Group dynamics* (pp. 301–317). New York: Harper & Row.

33 Katz, R. L. (1955). Skills of an effective administrator. *Harvard Business Review, 33*, 33–42.

34 Van Velsor, E., & McCauley, C. D. (2010). Introduction: Our view of leadership development. In E. Van Velsor, C. D. McCauley, & M. N. Ruderman (Eds.), *The Center for Creative Leadership handbook of leadership development* (3rd ed., pp. 1–22). San Francisco: Jossey-Bass.

35 Mumford, M. D., Zaccaro, S. J., Harding, F. D., Jacobs, J. O., & Fleishman, E. A. (2000). Leadership skills for a changing world: Solving complex social problems. *Leadership Quarterly, 11*, 11–35; Connelly, M. S., Gilbert, J. A., Zaccaro, S. J., Threlfall, K. V., Marks, M. A., & Mumford, M. D. (2000). Exploring the relationship of leadership skills and knowledge to leader performance. *Leadership Quarterly, 11*, 65–86; Mumford, M. D., Marks, M. A., Connelly, M. S., Zaccaro, S. J., & Reiter-Palmon, R. (2000). Development of leadership skills: Experience and timing. *Leadership Quarterly, 11*, 87–114; Mumford, M. D., Zacarro, S. J., Connelly, M. S., & Marks, M. A. (2000). Leadership skills: Conclusions and future directions. *Leadership Quarterly, 11*, 155–170.

36 See, for example: Graen, G. (1976). Role-making processes within complex organizations. In M. D. Dunnette (Ed.), *Handbook of industrial organizational psychology* (pp. 1201–1246). Chicago: Rand-McNally; Graen, G. B., & Cashman, J. F. (1975). A role-making model of leadership in formal organizations: A developmental approach. In J. G. Hunt & L. L. Larson (Eds.), *Leadership frontiers* (pp. 143–165). Kent, OH: Kent State University Press; Duchon, D., Green, S. G., & Taber, T. D. (1988). Vertical dyad linkage: A longitudinal assessment of antecedents, measures, and consequences. *Journal of Applied Psychology, 71*, 56–60; van Breukelen, W., Schyns, B., & Le Blanc, P. (2006). Leader-member exchange theory and research: Accomplishments and future challenges. *Leadership 2*, 295–316.

37 Uhl-Bien, M. (2003). Relationship development as a key ingredient for leadership development. In S. E. Murphy & R. E. Riggo (Eds.), *The future of leadership development* (pp. 129–147). Mahwah, NJ: Lawrence Erlbaum.

38 Gerstner, C. R., & Day, D. V. (1997). Meta-analytic review of leader-member exchange theory: Correlates and construct issues. *Journal of Applied Psychology, 82*, 827–844; Walumbwa, F. O., Cropanzano, R., & Goldman, B. M. (2011). How leader-member exchange influences effective work behaviors: Social exchange and internal-external efficacy perspectives. *Personnel Psychology, 64*, 739–770; Ilies, R., Nahrgang, J. D., & Morgeson, F. P. (2007). Leader-member exchange and citizenship behaviors: A meta-analysis. *Journal of Applied Psychology, 92*(1), 269–277; Karanika-Murray, M., Bartholomew, K. J., Williams, G. A., & Cox, T. (2015). Leader-member exchange across two hierarchical levels of leadership: Concurrent influences on work characteristics and employee psychological health. *Work & Stress, 29*, 57–74.

[39] Adapted from Graen, G., & Uhl-Bien, M. (1998). Relationship-based approach to leadership: Development of leader-member exchange (LMX) theory of leadership over 25 years: Applying a multi-level multi-domain perspective. In F. Dansereau & F. J. Yammarino (Eds.), *Leadership: The multiple level approaches* (Vol. 24, p. 123). New York: Elsevier. Used by permission of Elsevier.

[40] Graen & Uhl-Bien, Relationship-based approach to leadership, pp. 103–158.

[41] Walumbwa, Cropanzano, & Goldman, How leader-member exchange influences effective work behaviors, p. 739.

[42] Bauer, T. N., & Erdogan, B. (2016). *The Oxford handbook of leader-member exchange*. Oxford, UK: Oxford University Press.

[43] Schriesheim, C. A., Castro, S. L., & Cogliser, C. C. (1999). Leader-member exchange (LMX) research: A comprehensive review of theory, measurement, and data-analytic practices. *Leadership Quarterly, 10*, 63–113; Northouse, P. (2013). *Leadership: Theory and practice* (6th ed., chapter 8). Thousand Oaks, CA: Sage; Hock-Peng, S., Nahrgang, J. D., & Morgeson, F. P. (2009). Understanding why they don't see eye to eye: An examination of leader-member exchange (LMX) agreement. *Journal of Applied Psychology, 94*, 1048–1057; Matta, F. K., Scott, B. A., Koopman, J., & Conlon, D. E. (2015). Does seeing "eye to eye" affect work engagement and organizational citizenship behavior? A role theory perspective on LMX agreement. *Academy of Management Journal, 58*, 1686–1708; Graen, G. B. (2006). To share or not to share leadership: New LMX-MMX network leadership or charismatic leadership on creative projects. In G. B. Graen (Ed.), *Sharing network leadership* (pp. 25–36). Greenwich, CT: Information Age.

[44] Pellegrini, E. K., & Scandura, T. A. (2008). Paternalistic leadership: A review and agenda for future research. *Journal of Management, 34*(3), 566–593; Pellegrini, E. K., Scandura, T. A., & Jayaraman, V. (2010). Cross-cultural generalizability of paternalistic leadership: An expansion of Leader-Member Exchange theory. *Group & Organization Management, 35*(4), 391–420.

～ CHAPTER FOUR

[1] Burns, J. M. (1978). *Leadership*. New York: Harper & Row.

[2] Maslow, A. H. (1970). *Motivation and personality*. New York: Harper & Row.

[3] See, for example: Bass, B. M. (1985). *Leadership and performance beyond expectations*. New York: The Free Press.

[4] Bass, B. M. (1990). *Bass & Stogdill's handbook of leadership* (3rd ed., p. 53). New York: The Free Press.

[5] Burns, *Leadership*, p. 4.

[6] Bass, *Leadership*; Bass, B. M., & Avolio, B. J. (1994). *Improving organizational effectiveness through transformational leadership*. Thousand Oaks, CA: Sage.

[7] Bass, *Leadership*; Bass, B. M. (1990). From transactional to transformational leadership: Learning to share the vision. *Organizational Dynamics, 18*, 19–31; Bass & Avolio, *Improving organizational effectiveness*.

[8] Bass, *Leadership*, p. 17.

[9] Zorn, T. E. (1991). Construct system development, transformational leadership and leadership messages. *Southern Communication Journal, 56*, 178–193.

[10] For evidence of the effectiveness of transformational leadership, see: Avolio, B. J., & Yammarino, F. J. (Eds.). (2002). *Transformational and charismatic leadership: The road ahead*. Boston: JAI; Lowe, K. B., & Kroeck, K. G. (1996). Effectiveness correlates of transformational and transactional leadership: A meta-analytic review. *Leadership Quarterly, 7*, 385–425; Bass, B. M., & Riggio, R. E. (2006). *Transformational leadership* (2nd ed.). Mahwah, NJ: Lawrence Erlbaum; Judge, T. A., & Piccolo, R. F. (2004). Transformational and transactional leadership: A meta-analytic test of their relative validity. *Journal of Applied Psychology, 89*, 755–768.

[11] Podsakoff, P. M., MacKenzie, S. B., Moorman, R. H. & Fetter, R. (1990). Transformational leader behaviors and their effects on followers' trust in leader, satisfaction, and organizational citizenship behavior. *Leadership Quarterly 1*, 107–142. Used by permission of Elsevier.

[12] Peters, T. J., & Waterman, R. H., Jr. (1982). *In search of excellence*. New York: Harper & Row. See also: Peters, T J. & Austin, N K. (1985). *A passion for excellence: The leadership difference*. New York: Warner Books; Peters, T. (1992). *Liberation management*. New York: Ballantine.

[13] Bennis, W. G., & Nanus, B. (1997). *Leaders: The strategies for taking charge* (2nd ed.). New York: Harper & Row.

[14] Kouzes, J. M., & Posner, B. Z. (2012). *The leadership challenge: How to get extraordinary things done in organizations*. (5th ed.). San Francisco: Jossey-Bass.

[15] Avolio, B. J., & Bass, B. M. (2002). *Developing potential across a full range of leadership: Cases on transactional and transformational leadership*. Mahwah, NJ: Lawrence Erlbaum.

[16] Snyder, N. H., & Graves, M. (1994). Leadership and vision. *Business Horizons, 37*, 1–7.

[17] Kriegel, R. J., & Patler, L. (1991*). If it ain't broke . . . break it!* New York: Warner Books.

[18] Parnes, S. J. (1975). "Aha!" In I. A. Taylor & J. W. Getzels (Eds.), *Perspectives on creativity* (pp. 224–248). Chicago: Aldine.

[19] Mednick, S. A. (1962). The associative basis of the creative process. *Psychological Review, 69*, 221.

[20] Wallas, G. (1926). *The art of thought*. New York: Harcourt.

[21] von Oech, R. (1986). *A kick in the seat of the pants*. New York: Harper & Row, pp. 30, 32.

[22] Orsag Madigan, C., & Elwood, A. (1983). *Brainstorms and thunderbolts*. New York: Macmillan.

[23] Johnson, C. E., & Hackman, M. Z. (1995). *Creative communication: Principles and applications* (ch. 2). Long Grove, IL: Waveland Press.

[24] Getzels, J. W. (1975). Problem-finding and the inventiveness of solutions. *Journal of Creative Behavior, 9*, 12–18; Getzels, J. W. (1973, November 21). Problem finding: The 343rd Convocation Address, the University of Chicago. *The University of Chicago Record, 9*, 281–283.

[25] Kriegel, R., & Brandt, D. (1996). *Sacred cows make the best burgers: Paradigm-busting strategies for developing change-ready people and organizations*. New York: Warner Books.

[26] Peters & Waterman, *In search of excellence*, p. 223.

[27] Garvin, D. A. (1993, July–August). Building a learning organization. *Harvard Business Review*, 86.

[28] Martin, F. (2002, April). So you failed . . . so what? *Unlimited*, p. 48.

[29] Elon Musk quotes that show his genius. (n.d.) *Business Insider India*.

[30] Bennis, W. G., & Nanus, B. (1985). *Leaders: The strategies for taking charge*. New York: Harper & Row.

[31] Govindarajan, V., & Srinivas, S. (2013, August 6). The innovation mindset in action: 3M corporation. *Harvard Business Review*; Arndt, M. (2006, May 9). 3M's seven pillars of innovation. *Bloomberg*.

[32] Auletta, K. (2009). *Googled: The end of the world as we know it*. New York: Penguin Press; Stross, R. (2008). *Planet Google: One company's audacious plan to organize everything we know*. New York: Free Press; Kotler, S. (2016, February 23). The eight principles that made Google the most innovative company on earth. *Observer*. Gersch, K. (2013, August 21). Google's' best new innovation: Rules around '20% time.' *Forbes*; Clifton, J. (n.d.). 10 failed Google projects. *HowStuffWorks*; Schmidt, E., Rosenberg, J, & Eagle, A. (2014). *Google: How Google works*. New York: Grand Central Publishing.

[33] Vise, D. A., & Malsee, M. (2005). *Google story*. Westminster, MD: Dell.

[34] Joyce, L. (2005, March 1). It's Google mania! *R and D*, p. 28.

[35] Claburn, T. (2006, August 28). Google revealed. *InformationWeek*, 34.

[36] Peters & Austin, *A passion for excellence*, ch. 2.

[37] Neff, T. J., & Citrin, J. M. (1999). *Lessons from the top*. New York: Doubleday.

[38] Neff & Citrin, *Lessons from the top*, pp. 39–40.

[39] Pasternack, B. A., & O'Toole, J. (2002, second quarter). Yellow light leadership: How the world's best companies manage uncertainty. *Strategy + Business*, 74–83.

[40] Guarrero, C. A. (1998, October). The leadership challenge. *Security Management*, 27–29.

[41] Masters, C. (2007, August 30). How Boeing got going. *Time*, pp. 1–6.

[42] Gumbel, P. (2007, July 5). BMW drives Germany. *Time*, 1–6.

[43] Bennis & Nanus, *Leaders* (1997).

[44] Nanus, B. (1992). *Visionary leadership*. San Francisco: Jossey-Bass.

[45] Collins, J. C., & Porras, J. I. (2004). *Built to last*. New York: Harper Business.

[46] Kotter, J. P. (1990). *A force for change: How leadership differs from management*. New York: Free Press, p. 36.

[47] The vision thing. (1991, November 9). *The Economist*, 89.

[48] These vision/mission statements came from company websites as well as the Panmore Institute at panmore.com/tag/vision-and-mission-statements.

[49] Baum, R. J., Locke, E. A., & Kirkpatrick, S. (1998). A longitudinal study of the relations of vision and vision communication to venture growth in entrepreneurial firms. *Journal of Applied Psychology, 83*, 43–54.

[50] From *The nature of human values* by Milton Rokeach. Copyright © 1973 by The Free Press. Copyright © renewed 2001 by Sandra Ball-Rokeach. Reprinted with the permission of The Free Press, a Division of Simon & Schuster Inc. All rights reserved.

[51] Hoffman, J. (2014, May 8). Secrets of the Ritz-Carlton's 'legendary' customer service. *PSA Perspective*; Solomon, M. (2013, September 18). A Ritz-Carlton caliber experience requires employee empowerment and customer service standards. *Forbes.*

[52] Spector, R., & McCarthy, P. (2012). *The Nordstrom way to customer service excellence: A handbook.* Hoboken, NJ: John Wiley & Sons, p. 30. More recent sources report that the card is no longer distributed and the statement has been streamlined. However, the one rule remains in place. See also: Solomon, M. (2014, March 15). Take these two steps to rival Nordstrom's customer service experience. *Forbes*; Nordstrom, Inc. (2016). *Great place to work reviews.* Retrieved from http://reviews.greatplacetowork.com/; Lutz, A. (2014, October 13). Nordstrom's employee handbook has only one rule. *Business Insider.*

[53] Neff & Citrin, *Lessons from the top*, p. 188.

[54] Spector & McCarthy, *The Nordstrom way.*

[55] Heskett, J. L., Sasser, W. E., Jr., & Hart, C. W. L. (1990). *Service breakthroughs.* New York: Free Press, pp. 13–14.

[56] Spector, R. (2001). *Lessons from the Nordstrom way.* New York: John Wiley & Sons, p. 68.

[57] Lundin, S. C., Paul, H., & Christensen, J. (2000). *Fish! A remarkable way to boost morale and improve results.* New York: Hyperion.

[58] Chang, R. (2001). *The passion plan at work.* San Francisco: Jossey-Bass, p. 5.

[59] Bass, *Leadership*, ch. 3. Some contemporary Christian groups also consider their leaders to be gifted by God. The term "charismatic" can also refer to a particular style of religious worship.

[60] Weber, M. (1947). *The theory of social and economic organization* (A. M. Henderson & T. Parsons, Trans.). Glencoe, IL: The Free Press, pp. 358–359.

[61] Trice, H. M., & Beyer, J. M. (1993). *The cultures of work organizations.* Englewood Cliffs, NJ: Prentice-Hall, p. 259.

[62] Bass, *Handbook*, p. 187. Bass summarizes the concerns regarding the centrality of crisis in the definition of charismatic leadership and provides an example of charisma without crisis. Bass notes that financial investment brokers often have devoted, unquestioning followers who perceive them as being charismatic even in times of financial calm.

[63] Conger, J. A., & Kanungo, R. N. (1987). Toward a behavioral theory of charismatic leadership in organizational settings. *Academy of Management of Management Review, 12*, 637–647.

[64] Barboza, D. (2014, September 7). The Jack Ma Way: At Alibaba, the founder is squarely in charge. *The New York Times*, p. BU1; Kaiman, J. (2014, September 19). Jack Ma profile—Alibaba's powerful but humble billionaire. *The Guardian*; MacLeod, C. (2014, September 19). Alibaba's Jack Ma: From 'crazy' to China's richest man. *USA Today;* Soki, A. (2015, May 25). How an English teacher conquered China: Wisdom of Jack Ma condensed into 33 quotes. Retrieved from alok@yourstory.com.

[65] D'Onfro, J. (2014, September 14). How Jack Ma went from being a poor school teacher to turning Alibaba into a $160 billion behemoth. *Business Insider.*

[66] Erisman, P. (2015). *Alibaba's world: How a remarkable Chinese company is changing the face of global business.* New York: PalgraveMacmillan, p. 8.

[67] Mellor, W, Chen, L. Y, & Wu, Z. (2014, November 9). Ma says Alibaba shareholders should feel love, not no. 3. *Bloomberg.com.*

[68] D'Onfro (2014).

[69] Richardson, R. J., & Thayer, S. K. (1993). *The charisma factor.* Englewood Cliffs, NJ: Prentice-Hall, p. 27.

[70] Geertz, C. (1977). Centers, kings, and charisma: Reflections on the symbolics of power. In J. Ben-David & T. Nichols (Eds.), *Culture and its creation: Essays in honor of Edward Shils* (pp. 150–171). Chicago: University of Chicago Press, p. 151.

[71] Gardner, W. L. (1992). Lessons in organizational dramaturgy: The art of impression management. *Organizational Dynamics, 21,* 33–46; Gardner, W. L., & Cleavenger, D. (1998). The impression management strategies associated with transformational leadership at the world-class level: A psychological assessment. *Management Communication Quarterly, 12,* 3–41; Gardner, W. L., & Avolio, B. J. (1998). The charismatic relationship: A dramaturgical perspective. *Academy of Management Review, 23,* 32–58.

[72] Dow, T. (1969). The theory of charisma. *Sociological Quarterly, 10,* 31.

[73] Huggins, N. (1987). Martin Luther King, Jr.: Charisma and leadership. *Journal of American History, 74,* 477–481.

[74] Yukl, G. (1999). An evaluation of conceptual weaknesses in transformational and charismatic leadership theories. *Leadership Quarterly, 10,* 285–305.

[75] Tourish, D. (2008). Challenging the transformational agenda: Leadership theory in transition? *Management Communication Quarterly, 21,* 522–528; Tourish, D., & Pinnington, A. (2002). Transformational leadership, corporate cultism and the spirituality paradigm: An unholy trinity in the workplace? *Human Relations, 55*(2), 147–172; Kelley, R. (1992). *The power of followership.* New York: Doubleday/Currency.

[76] Bass, B. M. (1995). The ethics of transformational leadership. In J. B. Ciulla (Ed.), *Ethics: The heart of leadership* (pp. 169–192). Westport, CT: Praeger; Bass, B. M., & Steidlmeier, P. (1999). Ethics, character and authentic transformational leadership. *Leadership Quarterly, 1,* 181–217.

[77] Johnson, C. E. (2018). *Meeting the ethical challenges of leadership: Casting light or shadow* (6th ed., p. 248). Thousand Oaks, CA: Sage. Used with permission of Sage Publications. See also: Bass, B. M. (1995). The ethics of transformational leadership. In J. B. Ciulla (Ed.), *Ethics: The heart of leadership* (pp. 169–192). Westport, CT: Praeger; Bass, B. M., & Steidlmeier, P. (1999). Ethics, character, and authentic transformational leadership behavior. *Leadership Quarterly, 1,* 181–217.

[78] Howell, J. M., & Avolio, B. J. (1992). The ethics of charismatic leadership: Submission or liberation. *Academy of Management Executive, 6,* 43–54; Howell, J. M. (1988). Two faces of charisma: Socialized and personalized leadership in organizations. In J. A. Conger & R. N. Kanungo (Eds.), *Charismatic leadership: The elusive factor in organizational effectiveness* (pp. 213–236). San Francisco: Jossey-Bass.

[79] Avolio, B. J., & Gardner, W. L. (2005). Authentic leadership development: Getting to the root of positive forms of leadership. *Leadership Quarterly, 16,* 315–338; Casa, A., & Jackson, B. (2016). Authentic leadership. In G. Hickman (Ed), *Leading Organizations: Perspectives for a new era* (pp. 414–429). Thousand Oaks, CA: Sage; Novicevic, M., Harvey, M. G., Buckley, H, R., Brown, J. A., & Evans, R. (2006). Authentic leadership: A historical perspective. *Journal of Leadership and Organizational Studies, 23,* 64–76; Avolio, B. J., & Luthans, F. (2006). *The high impact leader: Moments matter for accelerating authentic leadership development.* New York: McGraw Hill.

[80] Kernis, M. H. (2003). Toward a conceptualization of optimal self-esteem. *Psychological Inquiry, 14,* 1–26; Ilies, R., Morgeson, F. P., & Nahrgang, J. D. (2005). Authentic leadership and eudaemonic well-being: Understanding leader-follower outcomes. *Leadership Quarterly, 16,* 373–394.

[81] Walumbwa, F. O., Avolio, B. J., Gardner, W. L., Wernsing, T. S., & Peterson, S. J. (2008). Authentic leadership: Development and validation of a theory-based measure. *Journal of Management, 34,* 89–126, p. 94.

[82] Gardner et al. (2005); Harvey, P., Martinko, M. J., & Gardner, W. L. (2006). Promoting authentic behavior in organizations: An attributional perspective. *Journal of Leadership and Organizational Studies, 12,* 1–11; Zhu, W., May, D. R., & Avolio, B. J. (2004). The impact of ethical leadership behavior on employee outcomes: The roles of psychological empowerment and authenticity. *Journal of Leadership and Organizational Studies, 11,* 16–26; Avolio, B. J., Gardner, W. L., Walumbwa, F. O., Luthans, F., & May, D. R. (2004). Unlocking the mask: A look at the process by which authentic leaders impact follower attitudes and behaviors. *Leadership Quarterly, 15,* 801–823; Peus, C., Wesche, J. S., Streicher, B., Braun, S., & Frey, D. (2012). Authentic leadership: An empirical test of its antecedents, consequences, and mediating mechanisms. *Journal of Business Ethics, 107,* 331–348; Wang, H., Sui, Y., Luthans, F., Wang, D., & Wu, Y. (2014). Impact of authentic leadership on performance: Role of followers' positive psychological capital and relational processes. *Journal of Organizational Behavior, 35,* 5–12.

[83] Walumbwa et al (2008).

[84] Casa & Jackson, p. 425.

[85] Pfeffer, J. (2015). *Leadership BS: Fixing workplaces and careers one truth at a time.* New York: Harper-Business.

[86] Mumford, M. D. & Van Doorn, J. R. (2001). The leadership of pragmatism: Reconsidering Franklin in the age of charisma. *Leadership Quarterly, 12,* 274–309; Mumford, M. D. (2006). *Pathways to outstanding leadership: A comparative analysis of charismatic, ideological, and pragmatic leaders.* Mahwah, NJ: Lawrence Erlbaum; Mumford, M. D., & Antes, A. L., Caughron, J. J., & Friedrich, T. L. (2008). Charismatic, ideological, and pragmatic leadership: Multi-level influences on emergence and performance. *Leadership Quarterly, 19,* 144–160; Hunter, S. T., Cushenbery, L., Thoroughgood, C., Johnson, J. E., & Ligon, G. S. (2011). First and ten leadership: A historiometric investigation of the CIP leadership model. *Leadership Quarterly, 22,* 70–91.

[87] Bedell-Avers, K. E., Hunter, S. T., & Mumford, M. D. (2008). Conditions of problem-solving and the performance of charismatic, ideological, and pragmatic leaders: A comparative experimental study. *Leadership Quarterly, 19,* 89–106. Hunter, S. T., Bedell-Avers, K. E., & Mumford, M. D. (2009). Impact of situational framing and complexity on charismatic, ideological and pragmatic leaders: Investigation using a computer simulation. *Leadership Quarterly, 20,* 383–404.

[88] Bass, B. M. (1997). Does the transactional-transformational leadership paradigm transcend organizational and national boundaries? *American Psychologist, 52,* 130–139; Bass, B. M., & Avolio, B. J. (1993). Transformational leadership: A response to critiques. In M. M. Chemers & R. Ayman (Eds.), *Leadership theory and research: Perspectives and directions* (pp. 49–80). New York: Academic Press; Den Hartog, D. N., House, R. J., Hanges, P. J., & Ruiz-Quintanilla, S. A. (1999). Culture specific and cross-culturally generalizable implicit leadership theories: Are attributes of charismatic/transformational leadership universally endorsed? *Leadership Quarterly, 10,* 219–256; House, R. J., Hanges, P. J., Javidian, M., Dorfman, P. W., & Gupta, V. (2004). *Culture, leadership, and organizations: The GLOBE study of 62 societies.* Thousand Oaks, CA: Sage; House, R. J., Dorfman, P. W., Javidian, M., Hanges, P. J., & Sully de Luque, M. F. (2014). *Strategic leadership across cultures: The GLOBE study of CEO leadership behavior and effectiveness in 24 countries.* Thousand Oaks, CA: Sage.

[89] House et al, 2014, p. 23.

∾ CHAPTER FIVE

[1] Diamond, J. (2016). *Power: A user's guide.* Santa Fe, NM: Belly Song Press, p. 13. Rosabeth Moss Kanter refers to power as America's "last dirty word." See Kanter, R. M. (1979, July–August). Power failure in management circuits. *Harvard Business Review, 57,* 65–75.

[2] Pfeffer, J. (1992, Winter). Understanding power in organizations. *California Management Review,* 29–50.

[3] Gardner, J. (1990). *On leadership.* New York: Free Press, pp. 55–57.

[4] Galinsky, A. D., Jordan, J., & Sivanathan, N. (2008). Harnessing power to capture leadership. In J. B Ciulla, D. R. Forsyth, M. A. Genovese, G. R. Goethals, L. C. Han, & C. L. Hoyt (Eds.), *Leadership at the crossroads* (pp. 283–299). Santa Barbara, CA: ABC-Clio Greenwood.

[5] Bennis, W., & Nanus, B. (1985). *Leaders: The strategies for taking charge.* New York: Harper & Row, pp. 17–18.

[6] Yukl, G. (2013). *Leadership in organizations* (8th ed.). Upper Saddle River, NJ: Prentice-Hall, ch. 8.

[7] French, J. R. P., & Raven, B. (1959). The bases of social power. In D. Cartwright (Ed.), *Studies in social power* (pp. 150–167). Ann Arbor: University of Michigan, Institute for Social Research. Although there are a number of power typologies, this is the most widely used, generating research in such fields as management, communication, and education.

[8] Modified version of Hinken, T. R., & Schriesheim, C. A. (1989). Development and application of new scales to measure the French and Raven (1959) bases of social power. *Journal of Applied Psychology, 74,* 561–567. Used by permission of the American Psychological Association.

[9] Katzenbach, J. R. (2003). *Why pride matters more than money: The power of the world's greatest motivational force.* New York: Crown Business.

¹⁰ For one update on the French and Raven power bases, see: Raven, B. H. (2010). The bases of power: Origins and recent developments. *Journal of Social Issues, 49*, 227–251.

¹¹ The most popular social exchange theory is that of J. W. Thibault and H. H. Kelley: *Interpersonal relations: A theory of interdependence*. New York: John Wiley, 1978. For one application of social exchange theory to groups, see: Hollander, E. (1978). *Leadership dynamics: A practical guide to effective relationships*. New York: The Free Press.

¹² Information on the costs and benefits of power types is found in the following sources: Bass, B. (1990). *Bass and Stogdill's handbook of leadership* (3rd ed., ch. 13). New York: Free Press; Hersey, P., Blanchard, K. H., & Johnson, D. (2008). *Management of organizational behavior: Leading human resources* (9th ed.). Upper Saddle River, NJ: Prentice-Hall; Yukl, G., & Falbe, C. M. (1991). Importance of different power sources in downward and lateral relations. *Journal of Applied Psychology, 76*, 416–423; Baldwin, D. A. (1971). The costs of power. *Journal of Conflict Resolution, 15*, 145–155; Yukl, *Leadership in organizations*.

¹³ Nye, J. S. (2008). *The powers to lead*. Oxford, UK: Oxford University Press.

¹⁴ Drory, A., & Romm, T. (1990). The definition of organizational politics: A review. *Human Relations, 43*(11), 1133–1154.

¹⁵ Miller, B. K., Rutherford, M. A., & Kolodinsky, R. W. (2008). Perceptions of organizational politics: A meta-analysis. *Journal of Business Psychology, 22*, 209–222; Vigoda, E. (2003). *Developments in organizational politics: How political dynamics affect employee performance in modern work sites*. Cheltenham, UK: Edward Elgar.

¹⁶ Vigoda-Gadot, E., & Drory, A. (2006). Organizational politics, leadership and performance in modern public worksites: A theoretical framework. In E. Vigoda-Gadot & A. Drory (Eds.), *Handbook of organizational politics* (pp. 3–15). Cheltenham, UK: Edward Elgar.

¹⁷ Valle, M. (2006, May/June). The power of politics: Why leaders need to learn the art of influence. *Leadership in Action*, 8–12.

¹⁸ Vigoda, E. (2003). *Developments in organizational politics: How political dynamics affect employee performance in modern work sites*. Cheltenham, UK: Edward Elgar, p. 202. Used by permission.

¹⁹ Kurchner-Hawkins, R., & Miller, R. (2006). Organizational politics: Building positive political strategies in turbulent times. In E. Vigoda-Gadot & A. Drory (Eds.), *Handbook of organizational politics* (pp. 328–351). Cheltenham, UK: Edward Elgar.

²⁰ Butcher, D., & Clarke, M. (2008). *Smart management: Using politics in organizations* (2nd ed.). Houndmills, UK: Palgrave Macmillan.

²¹ Giles, H., & Powesland, P. F. (1975). *Speech style and social evaluation*. London: Academic Press.

²² O'Barr, W. (1984). Asking the right questions about language and power. In C. Kramarae, M. Schulz, & W. O'Barr (Eds.), *Language and power* (pp. 260–280). Beverly Hills, CA: Sage.

²³ Bradac, J., & Mulac, A. (1984). A molecular view of powerful and powerless speech styles: Attributional consequences of specific language features and communicator intentions. *Communication Monographs, 51*, 307–319.

²⁴ See, for example: Burell, N. A., & Koper, R. J. (1994). The efficacy of powerful/powerless language on persuasiveness/credibility: A meta-analytic review. In R. W. Preiss & M. Allen (Eds.), *Prospects and precautions in the use of meta-analysis* (pp. 235–255). Dubuque, IA: Brown & Benchmark; Johnson, C., Vinson, L., Hackman, M., & Hardin, T. (1989). The effects of an instructor's use of hesitation form on student ratings of quality, recommendations to hire, and lecture listening. *Journal of the International Listening Association, 3*, 32–43; Ruya, C. L., & Bryant, J. B. (2004). The impact of age, speech style, and question form on perceptions of witness credibility and trial outcome. *Journal of Applied Social Psychology, 34*, 1919–1944.

²⁵ Areni, C. S., & Sparks, J. R. (2005). Language power and persuasion. *Psychology and Marketing 22*(6), 507–525; Hosman, L. A., Huebner, T. M., & Siltanen, S. A. (2002). The impact of speech style, argument strength, and need for cognition on impression formation, cognitive responses, and persuasion. *Journal of Language and Social Psychology, 21*(4), 361–379; Blankenship, K. L., & Holtgraves, T. (2005). The role of different markers of linguistic powerlessness in persuasion. *Journal of Language and Social Psychology, 24*(1), 3–24.

[26] Johnson, C., & Vinson, L. (1987). Damned if you do, damned if you don't?: Status, powerful speech and evaluations of female witnesses. *Women's Studies in Communication, 10,* 37–44.

[27] Vinson, L., & Johnson, C. (1990). The relationship between the use of hesitations and/or hedges and listening: The role of perceived importance as a mediating variable. *Journal of the International Listening Association, 4,* 116–127.

[28] Hosman, Huebner, & Siltanen, The impact of speech style.

[29] Sorensen, R., & Pickett, T. (1986). A test of two teaching strategies designed to improve interview effectiveness: Rating behavior and videotaped feedback. *Communication Monographs, 35,* 13–22.

[30] Bass, *Handbook.*

[31] Kanter, R. M. (1977). *Men and women of the corporation.* New York: Basic Books, ch. 7; Kanter, R. M. (2010, July/August). Powerlessness corrupts. *Harvard Business Review, 36.*

[32] Kouzes, J. M., & Posner, B. Z. (2007). *The leadership challenge: How to get extraordinary things done in organizations* (4th ed.). San Francisco: Jossey-Bass, p. 20.

[33] Bennis, W. (1976). *The unconscious conspiracy: Why leaders can't lead.* New York: AMACOM, p. 167.

[34] Bies, R., & Tripp, T. M. (1998). Two faces of the powerless: Coping with tyranny in organizations. In R. M. Kramer & M. A. Neale (Eds.), *Power and influence in organizations* (pp. 203–219). Thousand Oaks, CA: Sage. See also: Hornstein, H. A. (1996). *Brutal bosses and their prey.* New York: Riverhead Books.

[35] Fiske, S. T. (1993, June). Controlling other people: The impact of power on stereotyping. *American Psychologist,* 621–628; Galinsky, Jordan, & Sivanathan, Harnessing power.

[36] Edwards, P., & Kraft, M. (2011). *Dumbemployed: Hilariously dumb and sadly true stories about jobs like yours.* Used by permission of Running Press, an imprint of Hachette Book Group.

[37] Yukl, G. A., & Becker, W. S. (2006). Effective empowerment in organizations. *Organization Management Journal, 3,* 210–231.

[38] Conger, J. (1989). Leadership: The art of empowering others. *The Academy of Management EXECUTIVE, 3,* 17–24, p. 22. Used by permission.

[39] Thomas, K. W., & Velthouse, B. A. (1990). Cognitive elements of empowerment: An "interpretive" model of intrinsic task motivation. *Academy of Management Review, 15,* 666–681; Spreitzer, G. M. (1995). Psychological empowerment in the workplace: Dimensions, measurement, and validation. *Academy of Management Journal, 38,* 1422–1465; Spreitzer, G. M. (1996). Social structural characteristics of psychological empowerment. *Academy of Management Journal, 39,* 483–504.

[40] Bandura, A. (1977). Self-efficacy: Toward a unifying theory of behavioral change. *Psychological Review, 84,* 191–215; Bandura, A., & Wood, R. (1989). Effect of perceived controllability and performance standards on self-regulation of complex decision making. *Journal of Personality and Social Psychology, 84,* 805–814.

[41] See: Conger, J. A., & Kanungo, R. N. (1988). The empowerment process: Integrating theory and practice. *Academy of Management Review, 13,* 471–482; Conger, Leadership, pp. 17–24.

[42] Kanter, Power failure.

[43] Charles Manz, Henry Sims, Jr., and Christopher Neck have described superleadership and self-leadership in a variety of sources. Material for this section was taken from: Sims, H. P., & Manz, C. C. (1996). *Company of heroes: Unleashing the power of self-leadership.* New York: John Wiley; Manz, C. C., & Sims, H. P., Jr. (2001). *The new superleadership: Leading others to lead themselves.* San Francisco: Berrett-Koehler; Neck, C. P., Manz, C. C., & Houghton, J. D. (2017). *Self-leadership: The definitive guide to personal excellence.* Los Angeles: Sage; Neck, C. P., & Houghton, J. D. (2006). Two decades of self-leadership theory and research: Past developments, present trends, and future possibilities. *Journal of Managerial Psychology, 21,* 270–295.

[44] Manz & Sims, *The new superleadership,* p. 69. Used by permission.

[45] Neck & Houghton, Two decades of self-leadership theory.

[46] Hsieh, T. (2010). *Delivering happiness: A path to profits, passion and purpose.* New York: Business Plus; Lam, B. (2015, January 15). Why are so many Zappos employees leaving? *The Atlantic*; Lashinsky, A. (2016, March 4). Why Amazon tolerates Zappos' extreme management experiment. *Fortune.com*; Michelli, J. A. (2012). *The Zappos experience: 5 principles to inspire, engage, and WOW.* New York: McGraw-Hill; Reston, L (2015, July 17). Tony Hsieh's workplace dream: Is holacracy a big failure?

Forbes; Feloni, R. (2014, April 15). Zappos CEO Tony Hsieh to employees: Embrace self-management or leave by the end of the month. *Forbes.*

47 Groth. A. (2013, December 30). Zappos is going holacratic: No job titles, no managers, no hierarchy. *Quartz.*

48 Reingold, J. (2016, March 15). How a radical shift left Zappos reeling. *Fortune.com.*

49 Reingold, How a radical shift left Zappos reeling.

50 Feloni, R. (2015, May 16). Inside Zappos CEO Tony Hsieh's radical management experiment that prompted 14% of employees to quit. *Business Insider.*

51 Dolnick, E. (2001). *Down the great unknown: John Wesley Powell's 1869 journey of discovery and tragedy through the Grand Canyon.* New York: HarperCollins; Stegner, W. (1954). *Beyond the hundredth meridian: John Wesley Powell and the second opening of the West.* New York: Penguin Books.

52 Belasco, J. A., & Stayer, R. C. (1994). *Flight of the buffalo.* New York: Warner Books.

53 Belasco & Stayer, *Flight of the buffalo,* p. 351.

54 Hough, J., & Neuland, E. W. (2000). *Global business.* Oxford: Oxford University Press; Louw, D. J. (2001). *Ubuntu and the challenges of multiculturalism in post-apartheid South Africa.* Retrieved from: http://www.phys.uu.nl/~unitwin/ubuntu.html; Munyaka, M., & Motlhabi, M. (2009). Ubuntu and its socio-moral significance. In M. F. Munyaradzi (Ed.), *African ethics: An anthology of comparative and applied ethics* (pp. 63–84). Scottsville, South Africa: University of KwaZulu-Natal Press.

∼ CHAPTER SIX

1 Kouzes, J. M., & Posner, B. Z. (2011). *Credibility: How leaders gain and lose it, why people demand it* (Rev. ed.). San Francisco: Jossey-Bass, p. 16.

2 Sattler, W. M. (1947). Conceptions of ethos in ancient rhetoric. *Speech Monographs, 14,* 55–65.

3 McCroskey, J. C., & Young, T. J. (1981). Ethos and credibility: The construct and its measurement after three decades. *Central States Speech Journal, 32,* 24.

4 Warren, I. D. (1969). The effects of credibility in sources of testimony and audience attitudes toward speaker and topic. *Speech Monographs, 36,* 456–458.

5 Strong, S. R., & Schmidt, L. D. (1970). Expertness and influence in counseling. *Journal of Counseling Psychology, 17,* 81–87; Strong, S. R., & Dixon, D. N. (1971). Expertness, attractiveness, and influence in counseling. *Journal of Counseling Psychology, 18,* 562–570.

6 Hovland, C. I., & Weiss, W. (1951). The influence of source credibility on communication effectiveness. *Public Opinion Quarterly, 15,* 635–650.

7 Dirks, K. T. (2000). Trust in leadership and team performance: Evidence from NCAA basketball. *Journal of Applied Psychology, 85,* 1004–1012.

8 Finn, A. N., Schrodt, P., Witt, P. L., Elledge, N., Jernberg, K. A., & Larson, L. M. (2009). A meta-analytical review of teacher credibility and its associations with teacher behaviors and student outcomes. *Communication Education, 58,* 516–537.

9 Brembeck, W. L., & Howell, W. S. (1976). *Persuasion: A means of social influence* (2nd ed.). Englewood Cliffs, NJ: Prentice-Hall.

10 Kouzes, J. M., & Posner, B. Z. (2007). *The leadership challenge: How to get extraordinary things done in organizations* (4th ed.). San Francisco: Jossey-Bass.

11 Carl Hovland, a pioneer in credibility research, was among the first to argue that a distinction should be made between competence and trustworthiness. He pointed out that a message from a competent source will be rejected if listeners believe that this person is lying. See: Hovland, C., Janis, I., & Kelley, H. H. (1953). *Communication and persuasion.* New Haven, CT: Yale University Press.

12 Strauss, G. (2012, January 24). More CEOs rake in $50M and up; Firms 'tone deaf' to spirit of times. *USA Today,* p. 1A.

13 Dirks, K. T., & Skarlicki, D. P. (2004). Trust in leaders: Existing research and emerging issues. In R. M. Kramer & K. S. Cook (Eds.), *Trust and distrust in organizations: Dilemmas and approaches* (pp. 21–40). New York: Russell Sage Foundation.

[14] Dirks, K. T., & Ferrin, D. L. (2002). Trust in leadership: Meta-analytic findings and implications for research and practice. *Journal of Applied Psychology, 87,* 611–628.

[15] Elsbach, K. D. (2004). Managing images of trustworthiness in organizations. In R. M. Kramer & K. S. Cook (Eds.), *Trust and distrust in organizations: Dilemmas and approaches* (pp. 275–292). New York: Russell Sage Foundation.

[16] O'Keefe, D. J. (1987). The persuasive effects of delaying identification of high and low-credibility communicators: A meta-analytic review. *Central States Speech Journal, 38,* 63–72; Kumkale, G. T., & Albarracin, D. (2004). The sleeper effect in persuasion: A meta-analytic review. *Psychological Bulletin, 130,* 143–172.

[17] Kelman, H. C., & Hovland, C. L. (1953). "Reinstatement" of the communicator in delayed measurement of opinion change. *Journal of Abnormal and Social Psychology, 48,* 327–335.

[18] Elsbach, Managing images; Leathers, D. G., & Eaves, M. (2008). *Successful nonverbal communication: Principles and applications* (4th ed.). New York: Macmillan; McMahan, E. M. (1976). Nonverbal communication as a function of attribution in impression formation. *Communication Monographs, 43,* 287–294.

[19] Whitener, E. M., Brodt, S. E., Korsgaard, J. A., & Werner, J. M. (1998). Managers as initiators of trust: An exchange relationship framework for understanding managerial trustworthy behavior. *Academy of Management Review, 23,* 513–530.

[20] Kouzes & Posner, *Credibility.*

[21] Yukl, G. (2013). *Leadership in organizations* (8th ed.). Upper Saddle River, NJ: Prentice-Hall; Yukl, G., Guinan, P. J., & Sottolano, D. (1995). Influence tactics used for different objectives with subordinates, peers, and superiors. *Group & Organization Management, 20,* 272–296.

[22] Yukl, *Leadership.*

[23] Yukl, G., Falbe, C. M., & Youn, J. (1993). Patterns of influence behaviors for managers. *Group & Organization Management, 18,* 5–28.

[24] Hunter, J. E., & Boster, F. J. (1987). A model of compliance-gaining message selection. *Communication Monographs, 54,* 63–84; Vinson, L. (1988, November). *An emotion-based model of compliance-gaining message selection.* Paper presented at the Speech Communication Association convention, New Orleans, LA; Grant, J. A., King, P. E., & Behnke, R. R. (1994). Compliance-gaining strategies, communication satisfaction, and willingness to comply. *Communication Reports, 7,* 99–108.

[25] Kassing, J. W. (2002). Speaking up: Identifying employees' upward dissent strategies. *Management Communication Quarterly, 16,* 187–209; Kassing, J. W. (2005). Speaking up competently: A comparison of perceived competence in upward dissent strategies. *Communication Research Reports, 22,* 227–234; Kassing, J. W. (2011). *Dissent in organizations.* Cambridge, UK: Polity Press.

[26] Kassing, J. W., & Kava, W. (2013). Assessing disagreement expressed to management: Development of the Upward Dissent Scale. *Communication Research Reports, 30,* 46–56. Used by permission of Taylor & Francis.

[27] Hill, T. A. (1976). An experimental study of the relationship between opinionated leadership and small group consensus. *Speech Monographs, 43,* 246–257; Schultz, B. (1982). Argumentativeness: Its effect in group decision making and its role in leadership perception. *Communication Quarterly, 30,* 368–375; Muscovici, S., Mugny, G., & Van Avermaet, E. (Eds.). (1985). *Perspectives on minority influence.* Cambridge, MA: Cambridge University Press.

[28] Infante, D. A., & Gorden, W. I. (1985). Superiors' argumentativeness and verbal aggressiveness as predictors of subordinates' satisfaction. *Human Communication Research, 12,* 117–125; Infante, D. A., & Gorden, W. I. (1991). How employees see the boss: Test of an argumentative and affirming model of supervisors' communicative behavior. *Western Journal of Speech Communication, 55,* 294–304; Infante, D. A., & Gorden, W. I. (1989). Argumentativeness and affirming communicator style as predictors of satisfaction/dissatisfaction with subordinates. *Communication Quarterly, 31,* 81–90.

[29] Infante, D. (1988). *Arguing constructively.* Long Grove, IL: Waveland Press; Infante, D., & Rancer, A. (1996). Argumentativeness and verbal aggressiveness: A review of recent theory and research. In B. Burleson (Ed.), *Communication Yearbook 19* (pp. 319–351). Thousand Oaks, CA: Sage.

[30] Infante, D. A., & Rancer, A. S. (1982). A conceptualization and measure of argumentativeness. *Journal of Personality Assessment, 46,* 72–80. Used by permission.

[31] Hample, D. (2003). Arguing skill. In J. O. Greene & B. R. Burleson (Eds.), *Handbook of communication and social interaction skills* (pp. 439–477). Mahwah, NJ: Lawrence Erlbaum; Infante, D. A. (1995). Teaching students to understand and control verbal aggression. *Communication Education, 44,* 51–63.

[32] Rancer, A. S., & Avtgis, T. A. (2006). *Argumentative and aggressive communication: Theory, research, and application.* Thousand Oaks, CA: Sage.

[33] Infante, *Arguing constructively,* pp. 33–81.

[34] Infante, *Arguing constructively,* p. 47. Used by permission.

[35] Inch, E. S., & Warnick, B. (2002). *Critical thinking and communication: The use of reason in argument* (4th ed.). Boston: Allyn & Bacon.

[36] Deutsch, M. (1973). *The resolution of conflict.* New Haven, CT: Yale University Press. Other scholars use the term "integrative" to describe cooperative negotiations. They use the term "distributive" to describe the competitive orientation toward negotiation.

[37] Deutsch, *The resolution of conflict.*

[38] Rubin, J. Z., & Brown, B. R. (1975). *The social psychology of bargaining and negotiation.* New York: Academic Press.

[39] See, for example: Axelrod, R. (1984). *The evolution of cooperation.* New York: Basic Books. Axelrod set up a tournament using a computerized version of the Prisoner's Dilemma game. The Tit for Tat strategy beat all other entries. Pruitt, D. G., & Carnevale, P. J. (1993). *Negotiation in social conflict.* Pacific Grove, CA: Brooks/Cole, ch. 4; Sheldon, K. (1999). Learning the lessons of Tit-for-Tat: Even competitors can get the message. *Journal of Personality & Social Psychology, 77,* 1245–1253.

[40] Isenhart, M. W., & Spangle, M. (2000). *Collaborative approaches to resolving conflict.* Thousand Oaks, CA: Sage, pp. 56–58.

[41] Neale, M. A., & Bazerman, M. H. (1983). The role of perspective-taking ability in negotiating under different forms of arbitration. *Industrial and Labor Relations, 36,* 378–388; Kemp, K. F., & Smith, W. P. (1994). Information exchange, toughness, and integrative bargaining: The roles of explicit cues and perspective-taking. *The International Journal of Conflict Management, 5,* 5–12.

[42] Roloff, M. E., Putnam, L. L., & Anastasiou, L. (2003). Negotiation skills. In J. O. Greene & B. R. Burleson (Eds.), *Handbook of communication and social interaction skills* (pp. 801–833). Mahwah, NJ: Lawrence Erlbaum.

[43] Fisher, R., Ury, W., & Patton, B. (2011). *Getting to yes* (Rev. ed.). New York: Penguin Books.

[44] Nielsen, R. P. (1998). Quaker foundations for Greenleaf's servant-leadership and "friendly disentangling" method. In L. Spears (Ed.), *Insights on leadership* (pp. 126–144). New York: John Wiley & Sons.

[45] Fisher, Ury, & Patton, *Getting to yes,* p. 43.

[46] Fisher, Ury, & Patton, *Getting to yes,* p. 40.

[47] Cialdini, R. B. (2009). *Influence: Science and practice* (5th ed.). Boston: Pearson; Rhoads, K. V. L., & Cialdini, R. B. (2002). The business of influence: Principles that lead to success in commercial settings. In J. P. Dillard & M. Pfau (Eds.), *The persuasion handbook: Developments in theory and practice.* Thousand Oaks, CA: Sage. Some of the examples in this section are drawn from these sources.

[48] Richard Petty and John Cacioppo's elaboration likelihood model is also based on the premise that receivers don't have the time, energy, or mental capacity to think carefully about (to elaborate on) all the persuasive messages they receive. Topics deemed important and relevant are carefully processed along the central route of persuasion. All others are processed along the peripheral route, which is heavily influenced by the mental shortcuts identified by Cialdini. See, for example: Petty, R. E., & Cacioppo, J. T. (1986). *Communication and persuasion: Central and peripheral routes to attitude change.* New York: Springer-Verlag; Petty, R., & Wegener, D. (1999). The elaboration likelihood model: Current status and controversies. In S. Chaiken & Y. Trope (Eds.), *Dual process theories in social psychology* (pp. 41–72). New York: Guilford.

[49] See, for example: Zuwerink Jacks, J., & Cameron, K. (2003). Strategies for resisting persuasion. *Basic and Applied Social Psychology, 25,* 145–161; Zuwerink Jacks, J., & Devne, P. G. (2000). Attitude importance, forewarning of message content, and resistance to persuasion. *Basic & Applied Social Psychology, 22,* 19–29.

[50] Sagarin, B. J., & Cialdini, R. B. (2004). Creating critical consumers: Motivating receptivity by teaching resistance. In E. S. Knowles & J. A. Linn (Eds.), *Resistance and persuasion* (pp. 259–282). Mahwah, NJ: Erlbaum.

[51] Cialdini, R., Vincent, J., Lewis, S., Catalan, J., Wheeler, D., & Darby, B. (1975). Reciprocal procedure for inducing compliance: The door-in-the-face technique. *Journal of Personality and Social Psychology, 31*, 206–213.

[52] Balona, D., (2012, March 29). FAMU hazing investigation: 2 faculty members suspended. *Orlando Sentinel*, p. A1.

[53] Lim, Y-S, & Van Der Heide, B. (2015). Evaluating the wisdom of strangers: The perceived credibility of online consumer reviews on Yelp. *Journal of Computer-Mediated Communication, 20*, 67–82.

[54] Hofling, C. K., Brotzman, E., Dalrymple, S., Graves, N., & Pierce, C. M. (1966). An experimental study of nurse-physician relationships. *Journal of Nervous and Mental Disease, 143*, 171–180.

[55] Cialdini, R. (2016). *Pre-suasion: A revolutionary way to influence and persuade*. New York: Simon & Schuster.

[56] Adapted from the credibility scales of: Berlo, D., Lemert, J., & Mertz, R. (1969). Dimensions for evaluation of the acceptability of message sources. *Public Opinion Quarterly, 33*, 563–576; McCroskey, J., & Young, T. (1981). Ethos and credibility: The construct and its measurements after two decades. *Central States Speech Journal*, 22–34.

[57] From *The leadership challenge*, 3rd ed., by James Kouzes and Barry Posner. Used by permission of John Wiley & Sons.

[58] Kumar, R., & Sethi, K. (2006). *Doing business in India: A guide for Western managers*. New York: Palgrave Macmillan, ch 9.

◠ CHAPTER SEVEN

[1] Burke, K. (1968). *Language as symbolic action*. Berkeley: University of California Press.

[2] Tompkins, P. K. (1982). *Communication as action: An introduction to rhetoric and communication*. Belmont, CA: Wadsworth, p. 8.

[3] Books surveyed include: Beebe, S. A., & Masterson, J. T. (2012). *Communicating in small groups: Principles and practices*. Boston: Allyn & Bacon; Patton, B. P., & Downs, T. M. (2003). *Decision-making group interaction: Achieving quality* (4th ed.). New York: Allyn & Bacon; Rothwell, J. D. (2013). *In mixed company: Small group communication* (8th ed.). Belmont, CA: Wadsworth; Engleberg, I. N., & Wynn, D. R. (2003). *Working in groups: Communication principles and strategies* (3rd ed.). Boston: Houghton Mifflin; Lumsden, G., Lumsden, D., & Wiethoff, C. (2010). *Communicating in groups and teams: Sharing leadership*. Boston: Wadsworth.

[4] Patton & Downs, *Decision-making*, p. 3.

[5] Cragan, J. F., Kasch, C. R., & Wright, D. W. (2009). *Communication in small groups* (7th ed., p. 9). Boston: Wadsworth.

[6] Tuckman, B. W., (1965). Developmental sequence in small groups. *Psychological Bulletin, 63*, 384–399; Tuckman, B. W., & Jensen, M. A. (1977). Stages of small-group development revisited. *Group & Organization Studies, 2*, 419–427.

[7] Poole, M. S. (1983). Decision development in small groups II: A study of multiple sequences in decision making. *Communication Monographs, 50*, 206–232; Poole, M. S. (1983). Decision development in small groups III: A multiple sequence model of group decision development. *Communication Monographs, 50*, 321–341.

[8] A summary of the results of these studies can be found in Bormann, E. G. (1975). *Discussion and group methods* (2nd ed., ch. 11). New York: Harper & Row. Leader emergence findings from this research program are also reported in Mortensen, C. D. (1966). Should the discussion group have an assigned leader? *The Speech Teacher, 15*, 34–41; and Geier, J. G. (1967). A trait approach to the study of leadership. *Journal of Communication, 17*, 316–323.

[9] Bormann, *Discussion and group methods*, p. 261.

[10] Fisher, B. A., & Ellis, D. G. (1994). *Small group decision making* (4th ed.). New York: McGraw-Hill, pp. 251–253.

[11] See, for example: Riggio, R. E., Riggio, H. R., Salinas, C., & Cole, E. J. (2003). The role of social and emotional communication skills in leader emergence and effectiveness. *Group Dynamics: Theory, Research, and Practice, 7*, 83–103; Regula, C. R., & Julian, J. W. (1973). The impact of quality and frequency of task contributions on perceived ability. *Journal of Social Psychology, 89*, 115–122; Daly, J. A., McCroskey, J. C., & Richmond, V. P. (1980). Relationship between vocal activity and perception of communication in small group interaction. *Western Journal of Speech Communication, 41*, 175–187.

[12] Schultz, B. (1980). Communicative correlates of perceived leaders. *Small Group Behavior, 11*, 175–191.

[13] Schultz, B. (1979). Predicting emergent leaders: An exploratory study of the salience of communicative functions. *Small Group Behavior, 9*, 109–114.

[14] Hirokawa, R., & Pace, R. (1983). A descriptive investigation of the possible communication-based reasons for effective and ineffective group decision making. *Communication Monographs, 50*, 363–379.

[15] Baird, J. E. (1977). Some nonverbal elements of leadership emergence. *Southern Speech Communication Journal, 42*, 352–361.

[16] Hollander, E. P. (1978). *Leadership dynamics: A practical guide to effective relationships*. New York: The Free Press.

[17] Poole, Decision development III.

[18] Wheelan, S. A. (2010). *Creating effective teams: A guide for members and leaders*. Thousand Oaks, CA: Sage.

[19] Russell, D. (2015, April 20). America meets a lot: An analysis of meeting length, frequency and cost. *Attentiv*; Dockweiler, S. (n.d.). How much time do we spend in meetings? (Hint: It's scary). *The Muse*.

[20] Auger, B. Y. (1972). *How to run better business meetings*. New York: AMACOM.

[21] Tropman, J. E. (2014). *Effective meetings: Improving group decision making*. Los Angeles: Sage; Tropman, J. E. (2003). *Making meetings work: Achieving high quality group decisions* (2nd ed.). Thousand Oaks, CA: Sage.

[22] Tropman, *Making meetings work*, p. 66.

[23] Nichols, R. G. (1961). Do we know how to listen? Practical helps in a modern age. *The Speech Teacher, 10*, 120–124.

[24] See, for example: Foulke, E. (1971). The perception of time compressed speech. In D. L. Horton & J. J. Jenkins (Eds.), *The perception of language* (pp. 79–107). Columbus, OH: Charles E. Merrill; Landauer, T. J. (1962). Rate of implicit speech. *Perceptual and Motor Skills, 15*, 646.

[25] Barker, L., & Watson, K. (2000). *Listen up: How to improve relationships, reduce stress, and be more productive by using the power of listening*. New York: St. Martin's Press.

[26] Gouran, D. S., Hirokawa, R. Y., Julian, K. M., & Leatham, G. B. (1993). The evolution and current status of the functional perspective on communication in decision-making and problem-solving groups. In S. Deetz (Ed.), *Communication yearbook 16* (pp. 573–600). Newbury Park, CA: Sage; Griffin, E. (2009). *A first look at communication theory* (7th ed., ch. 17). New York: McGraw-Hill.

[27] Hiebert, M., & Klatt, B. (2001). *The encyclopedia of leadership: A practical guide to popular leadership theories and techniques*. New York: McGraw-Hill, p. 345. Used by permission of Murray Hiebert and Bruce Klatt.

[28] Larson, C. E. (1969). Forms of analysis and small group problem-solving. *Speech Monographs, 36*, 452–455.

[29] Dewey, J. (1910). *How we think*. Boston: D.C. Heath. There are a number of variations of Dewey's original model. The version described in this chapter is found in Rothwell.

[30] LaFasto, F., & Larson, C. (2001). *When teams work best: 6000 team members and leaders tell what it takes to excel*. Thousand Oaks, CA: Sage, p. 85. Used by permission of the Sage Publications.

[31] Hirokawa, R. Y., & Scheerhorn, D. R. (1986). Communication in faulty group decision-making. In R. Y. Hirokawa & M. S. Poole (Eds.), *Communication and group decision-making* (pp. 63–80). Beverly Hills, CA: Sage.

[32] Gouran, D. S., & Hirokawa, R. Y. (1986). Counteractive functions of communication in effective group decision-making. In R. Y. Hirokawa & M. S. Poole (Eds.), *Communication and group decision-making* (pp. 81–90). Beverly Hills, CA: Sage.

[33] Gouran, D. S. (2003). Communication skills for group decision-making. In J. O. Greene & B. R. Burleson (Eds.), *Handbook of communication and social interaction skills* (pp. 835–870). Mahwah, NJ: Lawrence Erlbaum.

[34] Druskat, V. U., & Wolff, S. B. (2001, March). Building the emotional intelligence of groups. *Harvard Business Review,* 80–90.

[35] Janis, I. (1982). *Groupthink* (2nd ed.). Boston: Houghton Mifflin; Janis, I. (1989). *Crucial decisions: Leadership in policymaking and crisis management.* New York: The Free Press; Janis, I., & Mann, L. (1977). *Decision making.* New York: The Free Press. Groupthink has also been identified in other historical events, including the *Challenger* shuttle launch and the Iran–Contra Affair. See: Esser, J. K. (1998). Alive and well after 25 years: A review of groupthink research. *Organizational Behavior and Human Decision Processes, 73,* 116–141.

[36] Chen, Z., Lawson, R. B., Gordon, L. R., & McIntosh, B. (1996). Groupthink: Deciding with the leader and the devil. *Psychological Record, 46,* 581–590.

[37] Janis, *Groupthink*; Manz, C. C., & Neck, C. P. (1995). Teamthink: Beyond the groupthink syndrome in self-managing work teams. *Journal of Managerial Psychology, 10,* 7–15; Moorhead, G., Neck, C. P., & West, M. S. (1998). The tendency toward defective decision making within self-managing teams: The relevance of groupthink for the 21st century. *Organizational Behavior and Human Decision Processes, 73,* 327–351.

[38] Harvey, J. (1974, Summer). The Abilene Paradox: The mismanagement of agreement. *Organizational Dynamics,* 63–80; Harvey, J. (1988). *The Abilene Paradox and other meditations on management.* Lexington, MA: Lexington Books.

[39] Kanter, R. M. (2001). An Abilene defense: Commentary one. *Organizational Dynamics, 17,* 37–39.

[40] Keil, M., & Montealegre, R. (2000, Spring). Cutting your losses: Extracting your organization when a big project goes awry. *Sloan Management Review, 41,* 55–68; Ross, J., & Staw, B. M. (1993). Organizational escalation and exit: Lessons from the Shoreham nuclear power plant. *Academy of Management Journal, 36,* 701–732; Staw, B. M. (2001). The escalation of commitment to a course of action. *Academy of Management Review, 5,* 577–587.

[41] Keil & Montealegre, Cutting your losses.

[42] Katzenbach, J. R., & Smith, D. K. (1993, March–April). The discipline of teams. *Harvard Business Review,* 111–120; Katzenbach, J. R., & Smith, D. K. (1993). *The wisdom of teams.* Boston: Harvard Business School Press.

[43] *IGDA satisfaction survey.* (2015). International Game Developers Association. Retrieved from http://www.igda.org; Kelion, L. (2013, September 23). Valve: How going boss-free empowered the gamesmaker. *BBC News.*

[44] *Handbook for new employees.* (2012). Retrieved from http://www.valvesoftware.com/company/Valve_Handbook_LowRes.pdf

[45] *Handbook for new employees.*

[46] Warr, P. (2013, July 9). Former Valve employee: "It felt a lot like high school." *Wired.*

[47] Larson, C. E., & LaFasto, F. M. J. (1989). *Teamwork: What must go right/What can go wrong.* Newbury Park, CA: Sage.

[48] Larson & LaFasto, *Teamwork,* p. 128.

[49] Cleland, D. I. (1999). *Project management: Strategic design and implementation* (2nd ed.). New York: McGraw-Hill.

[50] Statistic retrieved from www.pmi.org/certification/what-are-PMI-certifications.aspx.

[51] Martin, P., & Tate, K. (2001). *Getting started in project management.* New York: Wiley; Sanghera, P. (2008). *Fundamentals of effective program management: A process approach based on the global standard.* Ft. Lauderdale, FL: J. Ross.

[52] Westland, J. (2007). *Project management life cycle: A compete step-by-step methodology for initiating, planning, executing and closing a project successfully.* London: Kogan.

[53] Briner, W., Hastings, C., & Geddes, M. (1996). *Project leadership* (2nd ed.). Aldershot, UK: Gower.

[54] Biafore, B., & Stover, T. (2012). *Your project management coach: Best practices for managing projects in the real world.* Hoboken, NJ: Wiley; Heagney, J. (2012). *Fundamentals of project management* (4th ed.). New York: AMACOM.

55 Biafore & Stover, *Your project management coach.*

56 Biafore, B., & Stover, T. (2012). *Your project management coach: Best practices for managing projects in the real world.* Hoboken, NJ: Wiley, p. 24. Used by permission of John Wiley & Sons.

57 Wysocky, R. K. (2009). *Effective project management: Traditional, agile, extreme.* Hoboken, NJ: Wiley.

58 Wysocky, *Effective project management.* See also: Cobb, C. G. (2011). *Making sense of agile project management: Balancing control and agility.* Hoboken, NJ: Wiley.

59 Zaccaro, S. J., Ardison, S. D., & Orvis, K. L. (2004). Leadership in virtual teams. In D. V. Day, S. M. Halpin, & S. J. Zaccaro (Eds.), *Leadership development for transforming organizations: Growing leaders for tomorrow.* Mahwah, NJ: Lawrence Erlbaum.

60 Jarvenpaa, S. L., & Leidner, D. E. (1999). Communication and trust in global virtual teams. *Organization Science, 10,* 791–815; Minton-Eversole, T. (2012, July 19). Virtual teams used by most global organizations. *Society for Human Resource Management.*

61 Kayworth, T. R., & Leidner, D. E. (2001–2002). Leadership effectiveness in global virtual teams. *Journal of Management Information Systems, 18,* 7–40; DeRosa, D. (2009, May/June). Improving performance by emulating the best. *Leadership in Action,* 17–19.

62 Bell, F. S. (2002). A typology of virtual teams: Implications for effective leadership. *Group & Organization Management, 27,* 14–49; Cascio, W. F. (2000). Managing a virtual workplace. *Academy of Management Executive, 14,* 81–90; Malhotra, A., Majchrzak, A., & Rosen, B. (2007). Leading virtual teams. *Academy of Management Perspectives, 21,* 60–70; Berry, G. R. (2011). Enhancing effectiveness on virtual teams: Understanding why traditional team skills are insufficient. *Journal of Business Communication, 48,* 186–206.

63 Jarvenpaa & Leidner, Communication and trust.

64 Clutterbuck, D. (2009). *Coaching the team at work.* London: Nicholas Brealey.

65 Hackman, J. R., & Wageman, R. (2006). A theory of team coaching. *Academy of Management Review, 30,* 269–287; Hackman, J. R., & Wageman, R. (2005). When and how team leaders matter. *Research in Organizational Behavior, 28,* 37–74; Hackman, J. R. (2002). *Leading teams: Setting the stage for great performances.* Boston MA: Harvard Business School Press.

66 Tannenbaum, S. I., & Cerasoli, C. P. (2013). Do team and individual debriefs enhance performance? A meta-analysis. *Human Factors, 55,* 231–245.

67 Hawkins, P. (2014). *Leadership team coaching: Developing collective transformational leadership.* London: Kogan-Page; Hawkins, P. (Ed.). (2014). *Leadership team coaching in practice: Developing high-performing teams.* London: Kogan-Page.

68 Aritz, J., & Walker, R. C. (2014). Leadership styles in multicultural groups: Americans and East Asians working together. *International Journal of Business Communication, 51,* 72–92.

∽ CHAPTER EIGHT

1 Etzioni, A. (1964). *Modern organizations.* Englewood Cliffs, NJ: Prentice-Hall, p. 1.

2 For an overview of the different ways that communication scholars approach the study of organizational culture, see: Eisenberg, E. M., & Riley, P. (2001). Organizational culture. In F. M. Jablin & L. L. Putnam (Eds.), *The new handbook of organizational communication: Advances in theory, research, and methods* (pp. 291–322). Thousand Oaks, CA: Sage.

3 The number of cultures an organization has is a matter of some debate. One group of researchers argues that there is only one culture per organization. Others argue that an organization consists of a series of cultural islands or subcultures. A third group contends that there are multiple cultures created by members as they interact. We think that there must be some common cultural elements in order for there to be an organization, but we acknowledge the presence of subcultures and that individuals shape and form culture as they coordinate their actions. For a description of the three perspectives and how each can provide useful insights into organizational behavior, see: Martin, J. (1992). *Cultures in organizations.* New York: Oxford University Press; Martin, J. (2002). *Organizational culture: Mapping the terrain.* Thousand Oaks, CA: Sage.

⁴ Dyer, W. G. (1985). The cycle of cultural evolution in organizations. In R. H. Kilmann, M. J. Saxton, & R. Serpa (Eds.), *Gaining control of the corporate culture* (pp. 200–229). San Francisco: Jossey-Bass.

⁵ Rafaeli, A., & Worline, M. (2000). Symbols in organizational culture. In N. M. Ashkanasy, C. P. M. Wilderom, & M. F. Peterson (Eds.), *Handbook of organizational culture and climate* (pp. 71–84). Thousand Oaks, CA: Sage.

⁶ Martin, J., & Powers, M. E. (1983). Truth or corporate propaganda: The value of a good story. In L. R. Pondy, P. J. Frost, G. Morgan, & T. C. Dandridge (Eds.), *Organizational symbolism* (pp. 93–107). Greenwich, CT: JAI Press.

⁷ Trice, H. M., & Beyer, J. M. (1984). Studying organizational cultures through rites and ceremonials. *Academy of Management Review, 9,* 653–669; Trice, H. M., & Beyer, J. M. (1993). *The cultures of work organizations.* Englewood Cliffs, NJ: Prentice-Hall, ch. 3.

⁸ Schein, E. H. (1992). *Organizational culture and leadership* (2nd ed.). San Francisco: Jossey-Bass, p. 5.

⁹ Schein, *Organizational culture,* ch. 10; Schein, E. H. (1983). The role of the founder in creating organizational culture. *Organizational Dynamics, 12,* 13–26.

¹⁰ Koch, J. (2001, March). Thinking outside the box at The Container Store. *Workforce,* pp. 34–38; Tindell, K. (2014). *Uncontainable: How passion, commitment and conscious capitalism build a business where everyone thrives.* New York: Grand Central; Wahba, P. (2016, May 19). Why Container Store's founder is quitting CEO job. *Fortune;* What we stand for. The Container Store, http://standfor.conatinerstore.com.

¹¹ Rohman, J. (n.d.). With an "employee-first" mentality, everyone wins. www.greatplacetowork.com

¹² Schawbel, D. (2014, October 7). Kip Tindell: How he created an employee-first culture at The Container Store. *Forbes.*

¹³ Schein, *Organizational culture,* ch. 11.

¹⁴ Peters, T., & Austin, N. (1985). *A passion for excellence: The leadership difference.* New York: Warner Books, p. 337.

¹⁵ Trice, H. M., & Beyer, J. M. (1985). Using six organizational rites to change culture. In R. H. Kilmann, M. J. Saxton, & R. Serpa (Eds.), *Gaining control of the corporate culture* (pp. 370–399). San Francisco: Jossey-Bass. See also: Knittel, R. E. (1974). Essential and nonessential ritual in programs of planned change. *Human Organizations, 33,* 394–396.

¹⁶ Garvin, D. A. (1993, July–August). Building a learning organization. *Harvard Business Review,* 78–91.

¹⁷ Senge, P. M. (1990). *The fifth discipline: The art and practice of the learning organization.* New York: Doubleday/Currency; Sadler, P. (2001). Leadership and organizational learning. In M. Dierkes, A. Berthoin Antal, J. Child, & I. Nonaka (Eds.), *Handbook of organizational learning and knowledge* (pp. 415–427). Oxford: Oxford University Press.

¹⁸ De Geus, A. (1988, February). Planning as learning. *Harvard Business Review,* 70–74; Kahane, A. (2010, March 14). Learning from experience: The Mont Fleur scenario exercise. *Reos Partners;* Wack, P. (1985, September). Scenarios: Uncharted waters ahead. *Harvard Business Review;* Wack, P. (1985, November). Scenarios: Shooting the rapids. *Harvard Business Review;* Ringland, G. (2016). *Scenario planning: Managing for the future* (2nd ed.). Chichester, UK: Wiley.

¹⁹ Antal, A. B., Lenhardt, U., & Rosenbrock, R. (2003). Barriers to organizational learning. In M. Dierkes, A. B. Antal, J. Child, & I. Nonaka (Eds), *Handbook of organizational learning and knowledge.* (pp. 865–88).Oxford, UK: Oxford University Press; Weir, D., & Ortenblad, A. (2013). Obstacles to the learning organization. In A. Ortenblad (Ed.), *Handbook of research on the learning organization* (pp. 68–85). Cheltenham, UK: Edward Elgar.

²⁰ DiBella, A. J., & Nevis, E. C. (1998). *How organizations learn: An integrated strategy for building learning capability.* San Francisco: Jossey-Bass.

²¹ Garvin, D. A. (2000). *Learning in action: A guide to putting the learning organization to work.* Boston: Harvard Business School Press. A number of examples of the three learning types come from Garvin's work.

²² Magaziner, I. C., & Patinkin, M. (1989). *The silent war: Inside the global business battles shaping America's future.* New York: Random House, ch. 3.

²³ For purposes of this discussion, we are distinguishing between knowledge generation (learning) and knowledge management (the dissemination and storage of information). Some scholars, however, treat learning as a subset of knowledge management. See, for example: Hult, G. T. M. (2003). An

integration of thoughts on knowledge management. *Decision Sciences, 34,* 189–195; Skyrme, D. J. (2000). Developing a knowledge strategy: From management to leadership. In D. Morey, M. Maybury, & B. Thuraisingham (Eds.), *Knowledge management: Classic and contemporary works* (pp. 61–83). Cambridge, MA: MIT Press.

24 Skyrme, Developing a knowledge strategy.

25 Ives, W., Torrey, B., & Gordon, C. (2000). Knowledge sharing is human behavior. In D. Morey, M. Maybury, & B. Thuraisingham (Eds.), *Knowledge management: Classic and contemporary works* (pp. 99–129). Cambridge, MA: MIT Press.

26 See, for example: Bruhn, J. G. (2001). *Trust and the health of organizations.* New York: Kluwer/Plenum; Dirks, K. T. (1999). The effects of interpersonal trust on work group performance. *Journal of Applied Psychology, 84,* 445–455; Kramer, R. M., & Tyler, T. R. (1996). *Trust in organizations: Frontiers of theory and research.* Thousand Oaks, CA: Sage; Mayer, R. C., & Gavin, M. B. (2005). Trust in management and performance: Who minds the shop while the employees watch the boss? *Academy of Management Journal, 48,* 874–888; Shockley-Zalabak, P., Ellis, K., & Winograd, G. (2000). Organizational trust: What it means, why it matters. *Organization Development Journal, 18,* 35–47.

27 Shockley-Zalabak, P., Morreale, S., & Hackman, M. Z. (2010). *Building the high-trust organization: Strategies for supporting the five key dimensions of trust.* San Francisco: Jossey-Bass; Shockley-Zalabak, Ellis, & Winograd, Organizational trust. See also: Mishra, A. K. (1996). Organizational responses to crisis: The centrality of trust. In R. M. Kramer & T. R. Tyler (Eds.), *Trust in organizations: Frontiers of theory and research* (pp. 261–287). Thousand Oaks, CA: Sage. Many of the examples in this section are from Shockley-Zalabak, Morreale, & Hackman.

28 West, E. (2015, October 16). 5 car quality myths, busted. *JD Powers.com.*

29 Ewing, J., & Bowley, G. (2015, December 14). Volkswagen sowed seeds of forceful ambition. *The New York Times,* p. B1; 3 directors say VW hid deceit from the board. *The New York Times,* p. A1.

30 Kramer, R. M. (1999). Trust and distrust in organizations: Emerging perspectives, enduring questions. *Annual Review of Psychology, 50,* 569–598.

31 Egan, M. (2016, September 9). 5,300 Wells Fargo employees fired over 2 million phony accounts. *CNNMoney*; Olen, H. (2016, October 13). Why the Wells Fargo scandal is different. *Slate.*

32 Trustbusting factors are drawn from a variety of sources, including: Bruhn, *Trust and the health of organizations*; Elangovan, A. R., & Shapiro, D. L. (1998). Betrayal of trust in organizations. *Academy of Management Review, 23,* 547–566; Galford, R., & Drapeau, A. S. (2003, February). The enemies of trust. *Harvard Business Review, 81,* 88–97; Prusak, L., & Cohen, D. (2001, June). How to invest in social capital. *Harvard Business Review,* 86–93; Simons, T. (2002, September). The high cost of lost trust. *Harvard Business Review,* 18–19; Whitener, E. M. (1997). The impact of human resource activities on employee trust. *Human Resource Management Review, 7,* 380–405.

33 Galford & Drapeau, The enemies of trust.

34 Hughes, R. L., Beatty, K. M., & Dinwoodie, D. (2005*). Becoming a strategic leader: Your role in your organization's enduring success.* San Francisco: Wiley.

35 Schoemaker, P. J. H., Krupp, S., & Howland, S. (2013, January-February). Strategic leadership: The essential skills. *Harvard Business Review.*

36 Lake, N. (2006). *The strategic planning handbook* (2nd ed.). London: Kogan-Page.

37 Olson, A. K., & Simerson, B. K. (2015). *Leading with strategic thinking: Four ways effective leaders gain insight.* Hoboken, NJ: Wiley.

38 Porter, M. E. (1979, March). How competitive forces shape strategy. *Harvard Business Review.* Porter, M. E. (1985). *Competitive advantage: Creating and sustaining superior performance.* New York: The Free Press.

39 Fishman, C. (2011). *The Wal-Mart effect* (rev. ed.). New York: Penguin.

40 Porter, *Competitive advantage.*

41 Forgang. W. G. (2004). *Strategy-specific decision making: A guide for executing competitive strategy.* Armonk, NY: Sharpe.

42 Weick, K. E. (1995). *Sensemaking in organizations.* Thousand Oaks, CA: Sage.

[43] Weick, K. E. (2001). Leadership as the legitimation of doubt. In W. Bennis, G. M. Spreitzer, & T. G. Cummings (Eds.), *The future of leadership: Today's top leadership thinkers speak to tomorrow's leaders* (pp. 91–102). San Francisco: Jossey-Bass.

[44] Weick, Leadership, p. 94.

[45] Fairhurst, G., & Sarr, R. A. (1996). *The art of framing: Managing the language of leadership.* San Francisco: Jossey-Bass.

[46] Fairhurst, G. T. (2011). *The power of framing: Creating the language of leadership.* San Francisco: Jossey-Bass.

[47] Fairhurst, *The power of framing*, pp. 15–17. Used by permission of John Wiley & Sons.

[48] Oates, G. (2016, June 29). Airbnb explains its strategic move into the meetings and events industry. *Skift*; Carr, A. (2014, March 17). Punk, meet rock. *Fast Company*; Levere, J. L. (2016, August 15). Airbnb for business travelers: More wi-fi, fewer hosts in towels. *The New York Times*; Weise, E. (2016, October 19). Airbnb and New York City go head to head. *USA Today.*

[49] Kriger, M., & Zhovtobryukh, Y. (2016). *Strategic leadership for turbulent times.* New York: Springer, p. 139.

[50] Weise, E. (2016, November 14). In shift, Airbnb agrees to San Francisco regs. *USA Today.*

[51] Ting, D. (2016, November 29). This is why Airbnb is doing what it's doing with trips and more. *Skift.*

[52] Pittinsky, T. L., & Simon, S. (2007). Intergroup leadership. *Leadership Quarterly, 18*, 586–605.

[53] Cross, R. L., Yan, A., & Louis, M. R. (2000). Boundary activities in "boundaryless" organizations: A case study of a transformation to a team-based structure. *Human Relations, 53*(6), 841–868.

[54] Pittinsky & Simon, Intergroup leadership; Hogg, M. H., van Knippenberg, D., & Rast, D. E. (2012). Intergroup leadership in organizations: Leading across group and organizational boundaries. *The Academy of Management Review, 37*(2), 232–255.

[55] Duck, J. M., & Fielding, K. S. (2003). Leaders and their treatment of subgroups: Implications for evaluations of the leader and the superordinate group. *European Journal of Social Psychology, 33*, 387–401.

[56] Pettigrew, T., & Tropp, L. (2006). A meta-analytic test of intergroup contact theory. *Journal of Personality and Social Psychology, 90*, 751–783.

[57] Ernst, C., & Yip, J. (2009). Boundary-spanning leadership: Tactics to bridge social identity in organizations. In T. L. Pittinsky (Ed.), *Crossing the divide: Intergroup leadership in a world of difference* (pp. 87–112). Boston: Harvard Business Press.

[58] Hogg et al., Intergroup leadership; Richter, A. W., West, M. A., Van Dick, R., & Dawson, J. F. (2006). Boundary spanners identification, intergroup contact, and effective intergroup relations. *Academy of Management Journal, 49*, 1252–1269; Dovidio, J. F., Gaertner, S. L., & Lamoreaux, M. J. (2009). Leadership across group divides: The challenges and potential of common group identity. In T. L. Pittinsky (Ed.), *Crossing the divide: Intergroup leadership in a world of difference* (pp. 3–15). Boston: Harvard Business Press.

[59] Hogg et al., Intergroup leadership.

[60] Example taken from Hogg et al., Intergroup leadership.

[61] Learman, L. A., Avorn, J., Everitt, D. E., & Rosenthal, R. (1990). Pygmalion in the nursing home: The effects of caregiver expectations on patient outcomes. *Journal of the American Geriatrics Society, 38*, 797–803.

[62] Jenner, H. (1990). The Pygmalion effect: The importance of expectancies. *Alcoholism Treatment Quarterly, 38*, 797–803.

[63] Chen, L. J. (2015). Effect of acceptance expectations on the employment development of individuals with disabilities: The self-fulfilling prophecy applied. *Journal of Employment Counseling, 42*, 98–109.

[64] Rosenthal, R., & Jacobson, L. (1968). *Pygmalion in the classroom.* New York: Holt, Rinehart and Winston. Many other researchers have verified the findings of Rosenthal and Jacobson's groundbreaking study. See, for example: Jussim, L., Madon, S., & Chatman, C. (1994). Teacher expectations and student achievement: Self-fulfilling prophecies, biases, and accuracy. In L. Heath, R. S. Tindale, J. Edwards, E. J. Posavac, F. B. Bryant, E. Henderson-King, Y. Suarez-Balcazar, & J. Myers (Eds.), *Applications of heuristics and biases to social issues* (pp. 303–334). New York: Plenum Press; Barad, E. (1993). Pygmalion—25 years after interpersonal expectations in the classroom. In P. D. Blanck

(Ed.), *Interpersonal expectations: Theory, research, and applications* (pp. 125–153). Cambridge, MA: Cambridge University Press.

[65] Eden, D., & Shami, A. B. (1982). Pygmalion goes to boot camp: Expectancy, leadership, and trainee performance. *Journal of Applied Psychology, 67*, 194–199.

[66] Crawford, K. S., Thomas, E. D., & Fink, J. J. (1980). Pygmalion at sea: Improving the work effectiveness of low performers. *Journal of Applied Behavioral Science, 16*, 482–505.

[67] Whiteley, P., Sy, T., & Johnson, S. K. (2012). Leaders' conceptions of followers: Implications for naturally occurring Pygmalion effects. *The Leadership Quarterly, 23*, 822–834; Sy, T. (2010). What do you think of followers? Examining the content, structure, and consequences of implicit followership theories. *Organizational Behavior and Human Decision Processes, 113*, 73–84.

[68] Smith, A. E., Jussim, L., & Eccles, J. (1999). Do self-fulfilling prophecies accumulate, dissipate, or remain stable over time? *Journal of Personality and Social Psychology, 77*, 548–565.

[69] Berlew, D., & Hall, D. (1966). The socialization of managers: Effects of expectations on performance. *Administrative Science Quarterly, 2*, 208–223.

[70] White, S. S., & Locke, E. A. (2000). Problems with the Pygmalion effect and some proposed solutions. *Leadership Quarterly, 11*, 389–416; McNatt, D. B. (2000). Ancient Pygmalion joins contemporary management: A meta-analysis of the result. *Journal of Applied Psychology, 85*, 314–322; Duir, T., Eden, D., & Banjo, M. L. (1995). Self-fulfilling prophecy and gender: Can women be Pygmalion and Galatea? *Journal of Applied Psychology, 80*, 253–270.

[71] Livingston, J. S. (1969). Pygmalion in management. *Harvard Business Review, 47*, 81-89. For another discussion of self-esteem and expectations, see: Hill, N. (1976, August). Self-esteem: The key to effective leadership. *Administrative Management, 51*, 24–25.

[72] Locke, E. A., & Latham, G. P. (1990). *A theory of goal setting & task performance.* Englewood Cliffs, NJ: Prentice-Hall.

[73] Rosenthal, R. (1993). Interpersonal expectations: Some antecedents and some consequences. In P. D. Blanck (Ed.), *Interpersonal expectations: Theory, research, and applications* (pp. 3–24). Cambridge, MA: Cambridge University Press.

[74] Baird, J., & Wieting, G. K. (1979, September). Nonverbal communication can be a motivational tool. *Personnel Journal*, 607–610.

[75] Baird & Wieting, Nonverbal communication.

[76] Good, T., & Brophy, J. (1980). *Educational psychology: A realistic approach.* New York: Holt, Rinehart and Winston.

[77] Eden, D., & Ravid, G. (1982). Pygmalion vs. self-expectancy: Effects of instructor and self-expectancy on trainee performance. *Organizational Behavior and Human Performance, 30*, 351–364.

[78] Eden, D. (1984). Self-fulfilling prophecy as a management tool: Harnessing Pygmalion. *Academy of Management Review, 9*, 64–73. Used by permission.

[79] Eden, D. (1990). *Pygmalion in management.* Lexington, MA: Lexington Books/D. C. Heath; Eden, D. (1993). Interpersonal expectations in organizations. In P. D. Blanck (Ed.), *Interpersonal expectations: Theory, research, and applications* (pp. 154–178). Cambridge, MA: Cambridge University Press.

[80] White & Locke (2000).

[81] See, for example: De Jong, A., de Ruyter, K., & Wetzels, M. (2005). Antecedents and consequences of group potency: A study of self-managing service teams. *Management Science, 51*, 1610–1625; Hecht, T. D., Allen, N. J., Klammer, J. D., & Kelly, E. C. (2002). Group beliefs, ability, and performance: The potency of group potency. *Group Dynamics: Theory, Research, and Practice, 6*, 143–152.

[82] Hoyt, C. L., Murphy, S. E., Halverson, S. K., & Watson, C. B. (2003). Group leadership: Efficacy and effectiveness. *Group Dynamics: Theory, Research, and Practice, 7*, 259–274; Sosik, J. J., Avolio, B. J., & Kahai, S. S. (1997). Effects of leadership style and anonymity on group potency and effectiveness in a group decision support system environment. *Journal of Applied Psychology, 82*, 89–103.

[83] Eden, Self-fulfilling prophecy.

[84] Rivera Vargas, M. I. (2011). Organizational learning model for sustainable innovation: Elements for a new innovation approach in developing countries. *Projectics/Proyectica/Projectique, 1*, 37–47; Kim, L. (1998). Crisis construction and organizational learning: Capability building in catching-up at Hyundai Motor. *Organization Science, 9*, 506–521.

∽ CHAPTER NINE

[1] Gardner, J. (1990). *On leadership*. New York: Free Press, p. xiii.

[2] For more information on the unique features of public communication, see: Asante, M. K., & Frye, J. K. (1977). *Contemporary public communication*. New York: Harper & Row.

[3] Newsom, D., Van Slyke Turk, J., & Kruckeberg, D. (2004). *This is PR: The realities of public relations* (8th ed.). Belmont, CA: Wadsworth/Thompson Learning; Wilcox, D. L., Cameron, G. T., Ault, P. H., & Agee, W. K. (2003). *Public relations: Strategies and tactics* (7th ed.). New York: Longman.

[4] Robinson Hickman, G., & Sorenson, G. J. (2014). *The power of invisible leadership: How a compelling common purpose inspires exceptional leadership*. Los Angeles, CA: Sage.

[5] Grunig, L. A., Grunig, J. E., & Dozier, D. M. (2002). *Excellent public relations and effective organizations: A study of communication management in three countries*. Mahwah, NJ: Lawrence Erlbaum. See also: Dozier, D. M., Grunig, L. A., & Grunig, J. E. (1995). *Manager's guide to excellence in public relations and communication management*. Mahwah, NJ: Lawrence Erlbaum.

[6] Bridges, J. A., & Nelson, R. A. (2000). Issues management: A relational approach. In J. A. Ledingham & S. D. Bruning (Eds.), *Public relations as relationship management: A relational approach to the study and practice of public relations* (pp. 95–115). Mahwah, NJ: Lawrence Erlbaum; Heath, R. L. (2002). Issues management: Its past, present and future. *Journal of Public Affairs, 2*, 209–214.

[7] Corporate Accountability International. (2011). Clowning with kids' health: The case for Ronald McDonald's retirement. Retrieved from http://www.RetireRonald.org; Teather, D. (2005, June 9). Fatboy Ronald McDonald downsizes to head off critics. *The Guardian*, City, p. 19.

[8] Boffey, P. M. (2012, May 13). What if it weren't called pink slime? *The New York Times*, p. SSR 12.

[9] Ledingham, J. A., & Bruning, S. D. (1998). Relationship management in public relations: Dimensions of an organization-public relationship. *Public Relations Review, 24*, 55–65.

[10] Cutlip, S. M., Center, A. H., & Broom, G. M. (1994). *Effective public relations*. Upper Saddle River, NJ: Prentice-Hall, p. 2.

[11] Hon, L. C., & Grunig, J. E. (1999). *Guidelines for measuring relationships in public relations*. Tallahassee, FL: Institute for Public Relations; Kim, Y. (2001). Searching for the organizational-public relationship: A valid and reliable instrument. *Journalism & Mass Communication Quarterly, 78*, 799–815.

[12] Hon & Grunig; Ki, E-J, & Hon L. C (2007). Testing the linkages among the organization-public relationship and attitude and behavioral intentions. *Journal of Public Relations Research 19*, 1–23; Bruning, S. D., Castle, J. D., & Schrepper, E. (2004). Building relationships between organizations and public: Examining the linkage between organization-public relationships, evaluations of satisfaction, and behavioral intent. *Communication Studies, 55*, 435–446; Watson, T., & Noble, P. (2014). *PR in practice: Evaluating public relations*. London UK: Kogan Page.

[13] Quesenberry, K. A. (2016). *Social media strategy: Marketing and advertising in the consumer revolution*. Lanham, MA: Rowman & Littlefield; Shih, C. (2011). *The Facebook era: Tapping online social networks to market, sell, and innovate*. Upper Saddle River, NJ: Prentice Hall.

[14] Kim, Y. (2001). Searching for the organizational-public relationship: A valid and reliable instrument. *Journalism & Mass Communication Quarterly, 78*, 799–815. Used by permission of Sage Publications.

[15] Whitman, R. F., & Foster, T. J. (1994). *Speaking in public*. New York: Macmillan, ch. 1.

[16] TED staff. (2012, November 13). TED reaches its billionth video View! *Ted Blog*; The most popular talks of all time (n.d.). *TED.com*.

[17] Gallo, C. (2014). *Talk like TED: The 9 public speaking secrets of the world's top minds*. New York: St. Martin's.

[18] Lucas, S. E. (2003). *The art of public speaking* (7th ed.). Boston: McGraw-Hill.

[19] Jaffe, C. (2007). *Public speaking: Concepts and skills for a diverse society* (5th ed.). Belmont, CA: Wadsworth/Thomson; Devito, J. (2000). *The elements of public speaking* (7th ed.). New York: Longman.

[20] For more examples of this kind of deceptive communication, see: Lutz, W. (1989). *Doublespeak*. New York: Harper & Row. Don Watson (2003) provides a number of additional examples of distorted verbiage from his country in *Death sentences: How clichés, weasel words, and managementspeak are strangling public language*. New York: Gotham Books.

[21] See: Hackman, M. Z. (1988). Audience reactions to the use of direct and personal disparaging humor in informative public address. *Communication Research Reports, 5,* 126–130; Hackman, M. Z. (1988). Reactions to the use of self-disparaging humor by informative public speakers. *Southern Speech Communication Journal, 53,* 175–183.

[22] Chang, M., & Gruner, C. R. (1981). Audience reaction to self-disparaging humor. *Southern Speech Communication Journal, 46,* 419–447.

[23] Speech samples taken from: Useem, M. (1998). *The leadership moment.* New York: Times Books; Montefiore, S. S. (2005). *Speeches that changed the world: The stories and transcripts of the moments that made history.* London: Author; The 10 greatest all time speeches by 10 inspired women. (n.d.). *Marieclaire.co.uk*; "You've got to find what you love," Jobs says. (2005, June 14). *Stanford News*; Top 10 Greatest Speeches. (2016). *Time.com*; Transcript: Read the speech Pope Francis gave to Congress. (2015, September 24). *Time.com.*

[24] For a more complete discussion of the importance of internal thought and external speech in public address, see: Hackman, M. Z. (1989). The inner game of public speaking: Applying intrapersonal communication processes in the public speaking course. *Carolinas Speech Communication Annual, 5,* 41–47. For more information on the importance or oral rehearsal, see: Theobald, T. (2013). *Creating Success: Develop your presentation skills.* London, UK: Kogan Page.

[25] Adapted from DeFleur, M. L., Kearney, P., & Plax, T. G. (1993). *Mastering communication in contemporary America.* Mountain View, CA: Mayfield, pp. 418–419. Used by permission of McGraw-Hill Education.

[26] Pearce, T. (2013). *Leading out loud: A guide for engaging others in creating the future* (3rd ed.). Hoboken, NJ: Wiley.

[27] Simons, H. W., & Jones, J. G. (2011). *Persuasion in society* (2nd ed.). New York: Routledge, p. 319.

[28] Persuasion experts categorize campaigns in different ways. These categories are adapted from: Woodward, G. C., & Denton, R. E. (2014). *Persuasion & influence in American life* (7th ed., ch. 9). Long Grove, IL: Waveland Press. For more information on social movements, see: Stewart, C. J., Smith, C. A., & Denton, R. E. (2012). *Persuasion and social movements* (6th ed.). Long Grove, IL: Waveland Press.

[29] Lynam, D. R., & Milich, R. (1999). Project DARE: No effects at 10 year follow up. *Journal of Consulting Clinical Psychology, 67,* 590–594.

[30] Snyder, L. & LaCroix, J. M. (2013). How effective are mediated health campaigns? A synthesis of meta-analyses. In R. Rice & C. Atkin (Eds.), *Public communication campaigns* (4th ed., pp. 181–190). Thousand Oaks, CA: Sage.

[31] Mitchell, E. S. (2013, September 10). The CDC's anti-smoking scare tactics prove effective. *Adweek.*

[32] Winsten, J. A., & DeJong, W. (2001). The designated driver campaign. In R. E. Rice & C. K. Atkin (Eds.), *Public communication campaigns* (3rd ed., pp. 290–294) Thousand Oaks, CA: Sage; Perloff, R. M. (2009). *The dynamics of persuasion: Communication and attitudes in the 21st century.* Hoboken, NJ: Routledge.

[33] Wolf-Mann, E. (2015, August 21). Remember the ice bucket challenge? Here is what happened to the money. *Money.*

[34] See, for example: Atkin, C. K., & Salmon, C. T. (2013). Persuasive strategies in health campaigns. In J. P. Dillard & L. Shen (Eds.), *The Sage handbook of persuasion* (2nd ed., pp. 278–295). Los Angeles: Sage; Atkin, C. K. (2001). Theory and principles of media health campaigns. In R. E. Rice & C. K. Atkin (Eds.), *Public communication campaigns* (3rd ed., pp. 49–68). Thousand Oaks, CA: Sage.

[35] New college students and risky alcohol behaviors. (2016). National Social Norms Center; Cameron, K. A., & Campo, S. (2006). Stepping back from social norms campaigns: Comparing normative influences to other predictors of health behaviors. *Health Communication, 20,* 277–288; DeJong, W. (2010). Social norms marketing campaigns to reduce campus alcohol problems. *Health Communication, 25,* 615–616; Park, H. S., Smith, S. W., Klein, K. A., & Martell, D. (2011). College students' estimation and accuracy of other students' drinking and believability of advertisements featured in a social norms campaign. *Journal of Health Communication, 16,* 504–518; Russell, C. A., Clapp, J. D., & DeJong, W. (2005). Done 4: Analysis of a failed social norms marketing campaign. *Health Com-*

munication 17, 57–65; Yanovitzky, I., Stewart, L. P., & Lederman, L. C. (2006). Social distance, perceived drinking by peers, and alcohol use by college students. *Health Communication, 19*, 1–10; Polonec, L. D., Major, A. M., & Atwood, L. E. (2006). Evaluating the believability and effectiveness of the social norms message "most students drink 0 to 4 drinks when they party." *Health Communication, 20*, 23–34; Paek, H. J., & Hove, T. (2012). Determinants of underage college student drinking: Implications for four major alcohol reduction strategies. *Journal of Health Communication, 17*, 659–676.

[36] Soul City target audience research reports are available at http://www.soulcity.org.za/research/target-audience-research. See also: Singhal, A., & Rogers, E. (1999). *Entertainment-education: A communication strategy for social change.* Mahwah, NJ: Lawrence Erlbaum, ch. 9.

[37] Singhal, A., & Rogers, E. M. (2003). *Combating AIDS: Communication strategies in action.* New Delhi: Sage.

[38] Rogers, E. M. (2003). *Diffusion of innovations* (5th ed.). New York: Free Press.

[39] Barker, K. (2004). Diffusion of innovations: A world tour. *Journal of Health Communication, 9*, 131–137.

[40] Atkin & Salmon (2010), p. 423.

[41] Woodward & Denton, *Persuasion and influence*, ch. 9.

[42] Woodward & Denton, *Persuasion and influence*, p. 250. Used by permission.

[43] McGuire, W. J. (1989). Theoretical foundations of campaigns. In R. E. Rice & C. K. Atkin (Eds.), *Public communication campaigns* (2nd ed., pp. 43–65). Newbury Park, CA: Sage.

[44] Heath, R. L. (1997). *Strategic issues management: Organizations and public policy challenges.* Thousand Oaks, CA: Sage, p. 231. Used by permission of Sage Publications.

[45] Gardner, *On leadership*, chs. 9 and 10.

[46] Crosby, B. C., & Bryson, J. M. (2010). Integrative leadership and the creation and maintenance of cross-sector collaborations. *Leadership Quarterly, 21*, 211–230.

[47] Morse, R. S. (2008). Developing public leaders in an age of collaborative governance. In R. S. Morse & T. F. Buss (Eds.), *Innovations in public leadership development* (pp. 79–100). Armonk, NY: M. E. Sharpe.

[48] Luke, J. S., (1998). *Catalytic leadership: Strategies for an interconnected world.* San Francisco: Jossey-Bass; Morse, R. S. (2010). Integrative public leadership: Catalyzing collaboration to create public value. *Leadership Quarterly, 21*, 231–245; Chrislip, D. D., & Larson, C. E. (1994). *Collaborative leadership.* San Francisco: Jossey-Bass.

[49] Miller, A. N. (2002). An exploration of Kenyan public speaking patterns with implications for the American introductory public speaking course. *Communication Education 51*, 168–182.

∽ CHAPTER TEN

[1] Data taken from: Yen, H. (2013, June 13). White majority in US gone by 2043. *Associated Press*; Cohn, D. (2016, June 23). It's official: Minority babies are the majority among the nation's infants, but only just. *Pew Research Center*; Osborn, K. (2015, September 15). General Electric is moving 500 U.S. jobs overseas. *Time*; Stutman, J. (2015, January 27). IBM could lay of every American employee (and then some). *Wealth Daily*; Workplace profile (n.d.). *Ford Sustainability Report* 2015/16; Hays-Thomas, R. (2004). Why now? The contemporary focus on managing diversity. In M. S. Stockdale & F. J. Crosby (Eds.), *The psychology and management of workplace diversity* (pp. 3–30). Malden, MA: Blackwell; Mor Barak, M. E. (2011). *Managing diversity: Toward a globally inclusive workplace* (2nd ed.). Thousand Oaks, CA: Sage.

[2] Cox, T. (1993). *Cultural diversity in organizations.* San Francisco: Berrett-Koehler, ch. 2; Cox, T. (2001). *Creating the multicultural organization: A strategy for capturing the power of diversity.* San Francisco: Jossey-Bass; Hays-Thomas, Why now?

[3] We will use the terms "managing diversity" and "diversity management" interchangeably. However, some scholars distinguish between the two phrases. See, for example: Pushkala, P., Pringle, J. K., & Konrad, A. M. (2006). Examining the contours of workplace diversity: Concepts, contexts and challenges. In A. M. Konrad, P. Prasad, & J. K. Pringle (Eds.), *Handbook of workplace diversity* (pp. 1–22). London: Sage.

[4] Rogers, E. M., & Steinfatt, T. M. (1999). *Intercultural communication*. Long Grove, IL: Waveland Press, p. 79.

[5] Larrabee, W. (1972). Paralinguistics, kinesics, and cultural anthropology. In L. Samovar & R. Porter (Eds.), *Intercultural communication: A reader* (pp. 172–180). Belmont, CA: Wadsworth.

[6] Garten, J. E. (2016). *From silk to silicon: The story of globalization through ten extraordinary lives*. New York: HarperCollins.

[7] Hall, E. (1977). *Beyond culture*. Garden City, NY: Anchor.

[8] Lustig, M. W., & Koester, J. (2006). *Intercultural competence: Interpersonal communication across cultures* (5th ed.). Boston: Allyn & Bacon. Used by permission of Pearson Education.

[9] Hofstede, G. (2001). *Culture's consequences: Comparing values, behaviors, institutions, and organizations across nations* (2nd ed.). Thousand Oaks, CA: Sage; Hofstede, G. (1991). *Cultures and organizations: Software of the mind*. London: McGraw-Hill.

[10] Hofstede, G., & Bond, M. H. (1988). The Confucius connection: From cultural roots to economic growth. *Organizational Dynamics, 14*, 483–503; Chinese Culture Connection. (1987). Chinese values and the search for culture-free dimensions of culture. *Journal of Cross-Cultural Psychology, 18*, 143–174.

[11] For a summary of the relationship between Hofstede's cultural value dimensions and organizational outcomes, see: Taras, V., Kirkman, B. L., & Steel, P. (2010). Examining the impact of *Culture's consequences*: A three-decade, multilevel, meta-analytic review of Hofstede's cultural value dimensions. *Journal of Applied Psychology, 95*, 405–439.

[12] See, for example: Erez, M., & Earley, P. C. (1993). *Culture, self-identity, and work*. New York: Oxford University Press, ch. 8; Hofstede, *Cultures and organizations*; Hofstede, *Culture's consequences*; Offermann, L. R., & Hellmann, P. S. (1997). Culture's consequences for leadership behavior: National values in action. *Journal of Cross-Cultural Psychology, 28*, 342–351; Triandis, H. C. (1993). The contingency model in cross-cultural perspective. In M. M. Chemers & R. Ayman (Eds.), *Leadership theory and research: Perspectives and directions* (pp. 167–188). San Diego: Academic Press.

[13] Hofstede, *Culture's consequences*, p. 390.

[14] House, R. J., Hanges, P. J., Javidan, M., Dorfman, P. W., & Gupta, V. (2004). *Culture, leadership, and organizations: The GLOBE study of 62 societies*. Thousand Oaks, CA: Sage; Chhokar, J. S., Brodbeck, F. C., & House, R. J. (2007). *Culture and leadership across the world: The GLOBE book of in-depth studies of 25 societies*. Mahwah, NJ: Lawrence Erlbaum; Javidan, M., Dorfman, P. W., Sully De Lugue, M., & House, R. J. (2006, February). In the eye of the beholder: Cross cultural lessons in leadership from Project GLOBE. *Academy of Management Perspectives*, 67–90; House, R. J., Dorfman, P. W., Javidian, M., Hanges, P. J., Sully de Luque, M. F. (2014). *Strategic leadership across cultures: The GLOBE study of CEO leadership behavior and effectiveness in 24 countries*. Thousand Oaks, CA: Sage.

[15] House et al., *Culture, leadership, and organizations*.

[16] House et al., *Culture, leadership, and organizations*; Chhokar et al., *Culture and leadership across the world*.

[17] Examples taken from Thomas, D. C., & Inkson, K. (2004). *Cultural intelligence: People skills for global business*. San Francisco: Berrett-Koehler.

[18] Ang, S., & Van Dyne, L. (2008). Conceptualization of cultural intelligence: Definition, distinctiveness, and nomological network. In S. Ang & L. Van Dyne (Eds.), *Handbook of cultural intelligence: Theory, measurement, and applications* (pp. 3–15). Armonk, NY: Sharpe.

[19] Ang & Van Dyne, *Handbook*; Bucker, J. J. L. E., Furrer, O., Poutsma, E., & Buyens, D. (2014). The impact of cultural intelligence on communication effectiveness, job satisfaction and anxiety for Chinese host country managers working for foreign multinationals. *The International Journal of Human Resource Management, 25*, 2068–2087; Rockstuhl, T., Seiler, S., Ang, S., Van Dyne, L., & Annen, H. (2011). Beyond general intelligence (IQ) and emotional intelligence (EQ): The role of cultural intelligence (CQ) on cross-border leadership effectiveness in a globalized world. *Journal of Social Issues, 67*, 825–840.

[20] See, for example: Wood, E. D., & St. Peters, H. Y. Z. (2014). Short-term cross-cultural study tours: Impact on cultural intelligence. *International Journal of Human Resource Management*, 558–570;

Eisenberg, J., Lee, H.-J., Bruck, F., Brenner, B., Claes, M-T., Mironski, J., & Bell, R. (2013). Can business schools make students culturally competent? Effects of cross-cultural management courses on cultural intelligence. *Academy of Management Learning & Education, 12*, 603–621.

21 Ang, S., & Van Dyne, L. (Eds.) (2008). *Handbook of cultural intelligence: Theory, measurement, and applications.* Armonk, NY: Sharpe, Appendix C, p. 391. Used by permission of Taylor & Francis.

22 Adler, N. J. (2002). *From Boston to Beijing: Managing with a world view.* Cincinnati, OH: South-Western; Adler, N. J. (1991). *International dimensions of organizational behavior* (2nd ed.). Belmont, CA: Wadsworth.

23 Singelis, T. M., Triandis, H. C., Bhawuk, D. S., & Gelfand, M. (1995). Horizontal and vertical dimensions of individualism and collectivism: A theoretical and measurement refinement. *Cross-cultural Research, 29*, 240–275.

24 Schermerhorn, R., & Bond, M. H. (1997). Cross-cultural leadership dynamics in collectivism and high power distance settings. *Leadership & Organization Development Journal, 18*, 187–193.

25 Adler, *From Boston to Beijing.*

26 Trompenaars, F. (1994). *Riding the waves of culture: Understanding diversity in global business.* Burr Ridge, IL: Irwin.

27 Hampden-Turner, C.,& Trompenaars, F. (2000). *Building cross-cultural competence: How to create wealth from conflicting values.* New Haven, CT: Yale University Press; Trompenaars, F., & Woolliams, P. (2009). Getting the measure of intercultural leadership. In M. A. Moodian (Ed.), *Contemporary leadership and intercultural competence: Exploring the cross-cultural dynamics with organizations* (pp. 161–174). Los Angeles: Sage.

28 Konrad, A. M. (2006). Leveraging workplace diversity in organizations. *Organization Management Journal, 3*, 164–189; Hays-Thomas, R., Kossek, E. E., Lobel, S. A., & Brown, J. (2006). Human resource strategies to manage workplace diversity: Examining "the business case." In A. M. Konrad, P. Prasad, & J. K. Pringle (Eds.), *Handbook of workplace diversity* (pp. 53–74). London: Sage; Cox, T. (1991). Managing cultural diversity: Implications for organizational competitiveness. *Academy of Management Executive, 5*, 45–56.

29 For summaries of research on minority influence processes, see: Moscovici, S., Mugny, G., & Van Avermaet, E. (Eds.). (1985). *Perspectives on minority influence.* Cambridge, MA: Cambridge University Press; Maas, A., & Clark, R. D. (1984). Hidden impact of minorities: Fifteen years of minority influence research. *Psychological Bulletin, 95*, 428–450.

30 Eisenberger, R., Fasolo, P., & Davis-LaMastro, V. (1990). Perceived organizational support and employee diligence, commitment, and innovation. *Journal of Applied Psychology, 75*, 57–59.

31 Moss, G. (2010). Introduction. In G. Moss (Ed.), *Profiting from diversity: The business advantage and the obstacles to achieving diversity* (pp. 3–18). Houndmills, UK: Palgrave Macmillan.

32 Thomas, D. A., & Ely, R. J. (1996, September–October). Making differences matter: A new paradigm for managing diversity. *Harvard Business Review*, 79–90.

33 Bordas, J. (2007). *Salsa, soul, and spirit: Leadership for a multicultural age.* San Francisco: Berrett-Koehler.

34 Cox, *Cultural diversity*, ch. 13; Brown, R. (1995). *Prejudice: Its social psychology.* Oxford, UK: Blackwell; Fiske, S. T. (1998). Stereotyping, prejudice, and discrimination. In D. T. Gilbert, S. T. Fiske, & G. Lindzey (Eds.), *The handbook of social psychology* (Vol. 2, pp. 357–411). Boston: McGraw-Hill.

35 Bobo, L. D., Charles, C. Z., Krysan, M., & Simmons, A. D. (2012). The *real* record on racial attitudes. In P. V. Marsden (Ed), *Social trends in American life: Findings from the General Social Survey since 1972* (pp. 38–83). Princeton, NJ: Princeton University Press.

36 Burris, K., Ayman, R., Che, Y., & Min, H. (2013). Asian Americans' and Caucasians' implicit leadership theories: Asian stereotypes, transformational and authentic leadership. *Asian American Journal of Psychology, 4*, 258–266.

37 Cox, *Cultural diversity*, ch. 13.

38 Langer, E. J. (1989). *Mindfulness.* Reading, MA: Addison-Wesley.

39 Gudykunst, W. B., Kim, Y. Y. (2003). *Communicating with strangers: An approach to intercultural communication* (4th ed.). New York: McGraw-Hill; See also: Opotow, S. (1990). Moral exclusion and injustice: An introduction. *Journal of Social Issues, 6*, 1–20.

40 Cox, *Creating the multicultural organization.* See also: Konrad, Leveraging workplace diversity; Agars, M. D., & Kottke, J. L. (2004). Models and practice of diversity management: A historical review and presentation of a new integration theory. In M. S. Stockdale & F. J. Crosby (Eds.), *The psychology and management of workplace diversity* (pp. 55–77). Malden, MA: Blackwell.

41 Mor Barak, *Managing diversity,* pp. 328–329. Used by permission of Sage Publications.

42 Statistics taken from: Simmons A. (2016, June 7). Clinton is set to make history, but female leaders are nothing new in other parts of the world. *Los Angeles Times*; Quick Take: Women in the workforce (2016, August 11). *Catalyst*; Warner, J. (2014, March 7). Fact sheet: The women's leadership gap. *Center for American Progress.*

43 The term *glass ceiling* was first used in a special issue of the *Wall Street Journal* in 1986. The corporate woman: A special report. (1986, March 24). *Wall Street Journal*, 32-page supplement.

44 Eagly & Carli, *Through the labyrinth,* p. 6.

45 Ryan, M. K., & Haslam, S. A. (2005). The glass cliff: Evidence that women are over-represented in precarious leadership positions. *British Journal of Management, 16*, 81–90; Ryan, M. K., Haslam, S. A., & Kulich, C. (2010). Politics and the glass cliff: Evidence that women are preferentially selected to contest hard-to-win seats. *Psychology of Women Quarterly, 34*, 56–64; Ryan, M. K., Haslam, S. A., Hersby, M. D., & Bongiorno, R. (2011). Think crisis-think female: The glass cliff and contextual variation in the think manager-think male stereotype. *Journal of Applied Psychology, 96*, 470–484; Smith, A. E. (2015, Fall). On the edge of a glass cliff: Women in leadership in public organizations. *Public Administration Quarterly.*

46 Rosener, J. B. (1990, November–December). Ways women lead. *Harvard Business Review, 119*–125.

47 Eagly, A. H., Karau, S. J., & Makhijani, M. G. (1995). Gender and the effectiveness of leaders: A meta-analysis. *Psychological Bulletin, 117*, 125–145; Eagly, A. H., Johannesen-Schmidt, M. C., & Engen, M. L. (2003). Transformational, transactional, and laissez-faire leadership styles: A meta-analysis comparing women and men. *Psychological Bulletin, 129*, 569–591; Eagly, A. H. (2007). Female leadership advantage and disadvantage: Resolving the contradictions. *Psychology of Women Quarterly, 31*, 1–12; Eagly & Carli, *Through the labyrinth.*

48 Oakley, G. (2000). Gender-based barriers to senior management positions: Understanding the scarcity of female CEOs. *Journal of Business Ethics, 27*, 321–334.

49 Zhang, S., Schmader, T., & Forbes, C. (2009). The effects of gender stereotypes on women's career choice: Opening the glass door. In M. Barreto, M. K. Ryan, & M. T. Schmitt (Eds.), *The glass ceiling in the 21st century: Understanding barriers to gender equality* (pp. 125–150). Washington, DC: American Psychological Association; Heilman, M. E., & Eagly, A. H. (2008). Gender stereotypes are alive, well, and busy producing workplace discrimination. *Industrial and Organizational Psychology, 1*, 393–398.

50 See: Andrews, P. (1984). Performance, self-esteem and perceptions of leadership emergence: A comparative study of men and women. *Western Journal of Speech Communication, 48*, 1–13.

51 Epstein, C. F. (1988). *Deceptive distinctions: Sex, gender, and the social order.* New Haven, CT: Yale University Press.

52 Kanter, R. M. (1977). Some effects of proportions on group life: Skewed sex ratios and responses to token women. *American Journal of Sociology, 82*, 969–990.

53 Morrison, A. M., White, R. P., & Van Velsor, E. (1987, August). Executive women: Substance plus style. *Psychology Today,* 18–26.

54 Jamieson, K. H. (1995). *Beyond the double bind: Women and leadership.* New York: Oxford University Press, pp. 13–14.

55 Sandberg, S. (2013). *Lean in: Women, work, and the will to lead.* New York: Alfred Knopf; Bruenig, E. (2015, March 9). Sheryl Sandberg's lean in philosophy doesn't just ignore disadvantaged women. It hurts their cause. *New Republic*; Garcia, V. (2013, July 19). Why I won't lean in. *The Huffington Post*; Slaughter, A-M (2013, March 7). Yes, you can. *The New York Times*; Hooks, B. (2013, October 28). Dig deep: Beyond lean in. *The Feminist Wire.*

56 Sandberg, *Lean in,* pp. 25–26.

57 Garcia, A. (2016, May 16). Sheryl Sandberg speaks publicly about her husband's death for the first time. *CNN Money.*

58 Jamieson, *Beyond the double bind*, p. 20.

59 Eagly & Carli, *Through the labyrinth*.

60 Baxter, J. (2010). *The language of female leadership*. Houndmills, UK: Palgrave Macmillan.

61 Reardon, K. K. (1995). *They just don't get it, do they?* New York: Little, Brown.

62 Adapted from: Hopkins, S. A. (1997). Case #1: Downsizing at Simtek. In W. E. Hopkins (Ed.), *Ethical dimensions of diversity* (pp. 119–121). Thousand Oaks, CA: Sage. Used by permission of Sage Publications.

63 Jones, D. (2007, May 30). Do foreign executives balk at sports jargon? *USA Today*, pp. B1, B2; Learn the lingo: 10 sports terms that became business terms. (2013, December 3). *Gal's Got Game*; Ryan, L. (2014, October 1). What business jargon says about us. *Forbes*.

∼ CHAPTER ELEVEN

1 Miller, G. R. (1969). Contributions of communication research to the study of speech. In A. H. Monroe & D. Ehninger (Eds.), *Principles and types of speech communication* (6th brief ed., pp. 334–357). Glenview, IL: Scott Foresman, p. 355.

2 Johannesen, R. L., Valde, K. S., & Whedbee, K. E. (2008). *Ethics in human communication* (6th ed.). Long Grove, IL: Waveland Press.

3 Palmer, P. (1998). Leading from within. In L. C. Spears (Ed.), *Insights on leadership: Service, stewardship, spirit, and servant-leadership* (pp. 197–208). New York: John Wiley, p. 200.

4 Material from this section is adapted from: Johnson, C. E. (2018). *Meeting the ethical challenges of leadership: Casting light or shadow* (6th ed.). Thousand Oaks, CA: Sage.

5 Bok, S. (1979). *Lying: Moral choice in public and private life*. New York: Vintage Books.

6 Shear, M. D., & Joachim, D. S. (2014, May 31). Shinseki apologizes for misconduct at V.A. hospitals. *The New York Times*.

7 Grover, S. L. (1997). Lying in organizations: Theory, research, and future directions. In R. A. Giacalone & J. Greenberg (Eds.), *Antisocial behavior in organizations* (pp. 68–84). Thousand Oaks, CA: Sage; Cialdini, R. B., Petrova, P. K., & Goldstein, N. J. (2004, Spring). The hidden costs of organizational dishonesty. *MIT Sloan Management Review*, 67–73.

8 Brown, M. E., & Trevino, L. K. (2006). Ethical leadership: A review and future directions. *Leadership Quarterly, 17*, 595–616.

9 Kelley, H. (2016, August 11). Uber's never-ending stream of lawsuits. *CNNMoney*; Associated Press (2016, May 11). Uber drivers welcome $100m settlement in employee status lawsuit. *The Times-Picayune*; Lien, T. (2016, May 2). Uber sued again over drivers' employment status. *Los Angeles Times*; Hicks, N. (2016, June 9). Lawsuits: Uber, Lyft violated labor law in Austin shutdown; Wells, N. (2016, October 13). The 'gig' economy' is growing—and now we know by how much. *CNBC*; Wigmore, I. (2016, May). What is gig economy? *WhatIs.com*.

10 Keltner, D., Langner, C. A., & Allison, M. L. (2006). Power and moral leadership. In D. L. Rhode (Ed.), *Moral leadership: The theory and practice of power, judgment and policy* (pp. 177–194). San Francisco: Jossey-Bass.

11 Fiske, S. T. (1993). Controlling other people: The impact of power on stereotyping. *American Psychologist, 48*, 621–628; Goodwin, S. A. (2003). Power and prejudice: A social-cognitive perspective on power and leadership. In D. van Knippenberg & M. A. Hogg (Eds.), *Leadership and power: Identity processes in groups and organizations* (pp. 138–152). London: Sage.

12 Kantor, J., & Streitfeld, D. (2015, August 15). Inside Amazon: Wrestling big ideas in a bruising workplace. *The New York Times*; Schwartz, T. (2015, August 21). Why Jeff Bezos should care more for Amazon's employees. *The New York Times*; Stone, B. (2013). *The everything store: Jeff Bezos and the age of Amazon*. New York: Little, Brown.

13 Segal, D. (2015, August 9). Petrobras oil scandal leaves Brazilians lamenting a lost dream. *The New York Times*, p. BU1.

14 200 highest-paid CEOs 2016. (2016, May 27). *Equilar/The New York Times*; Krantz, M., & Hansen, B. (2011, April 4). CEO pay soars while workers' pay stalls. *USA Today*.

[15] Adams, S. (2014, June 16). The highest paid CEOs are the worst performers, new study says. *Forbes*.

[16] Lublin, J. S. (2006, October 12). Executive pay soars despite attempted restraints. *Associated Press Financial Wire*; Surane, J., & Melin, A. (2017, September 26). Equifax CEO Richard Smith resigns after uproar over massive hack. *Bloomberg*; Shen, L. (2016, October 13). Here's how much Wells Fargo CEO John Stumpf is getting to leave the bank. *Fortune*.

[17] Jennings, M. M. (2006). The *seven signs of ethical collapse: How to spot moral meltdowns in companies . . . before it's too late*. New York: St. Martin's Press.

[18] Upper 1% of Americans are rolling in the dough. (December 12, 2012). *The Oregonian*, p. A2; Bentley, D. (2015, October 14). The top 1% now owns half of the world's wealth. *Fortune.com*.

[19] Bradsher, K. (2001, June 24). Firestone tire flaw unreported for 4 years. *The Oregonian*, p. A4.

[20] Ramperstad, A. (1997). *Jackie Robinson*. New York: Knopf.

[21] Fletcher, M. (2010, October 16). "We decided to look for the miners as if they were our sons." *The Times News* (London), pp. 4, 5.

[22] Weissman, R. (2011, May 25). Deregulation and the financial crisis. *The Huffington Post*; Chan, S. (2011). Financial crisis was avoidable, inquiry concludes. *The New York Times*, p. A1.

[23] Burns, J. F. (2012, May 12). Cameron stands to lose much as scandal wears on. *The New York Times on the Web*.

[24] Rest, J. R. (1986). *Moral development: Advances in research and theory*. New York: Praeger; Rest, J. R. (1994). Background: Theory and research. In J. R. Rest & D. Narvaez (Eds.), *Moral development in the professions: Psychology and applied ethics* (pp. 1–25). Hillsdale, NJ: Lawrence Erlbaum.

[25] Gioia, D. A. (1992). Pinto fires and personal ethics: A script analysis of missed opportunities. *Journal of Business Ethics, 11*, 379–389.

[26] Bird, F. B. (1996). *The muted conscience: Moral silence and the practice of ethics in business*. Westport, CT: Quorum Books.

[27] Jones, T. M. (1991). Ethical decision making by individuals in organizations: An issue-contingent approach. *Academy of Management Review, 16*, 366–395.

[28] Rest, *Moral development*.

[29] Rest, J. R. (1993). Research on moral judgment in college students. In A. Garrod (Ed.), *Approaches to moral development* (pp. 201–211). New York: Teachers College Press.

[30] Bazerman, M. H. (2011). *Blind spots: Why we fail to do what's right and what to do about it*. Princeton, NJ: Princeton University Press.

[31] See, for example: Boksem, M.A.S., & de Cremer, D. (2009). The neural basis of morality. In D. de Cremer (Ed.), *Psychological perspectives on ethical behavior and decision-making* (pp. 153–166). Charlotte, NC: Information Age; Haidt, J. (2012). *The righteous mind: Why good people are divided by politics and religion*. New York: Pantheon Books.

[32] Mattera, P. (n.d.) Deutsche Bank: Corporate rap sheet. *Corporate Research Project*; Caesar, E. (2017, August 29). Deutsche Bank's $10-billion scandal. *The New Yorker*.

[33] Eisenberg, N. (2000). Emotion, regulation, and moral development. *Annual Review of Psychology, 51*, 665–697; Guadine, A., & Thorne, L. (2001). Emotion and ethical decision-making in organizations. *Journal of Business Ethics, 31*, 175–187; Giacalone, R. A., & Greenbergh, J. (Eds.). (1997). *Antisocial behavior in organizations*. Thousand Oaks, CA: Sage.

[34] Trevino, L. K., & Weaver, G. R. (2003). *Managing ethics in business organizations: Social scientific perspectives*. Palo Alto, CA: Stanford University Press, ch. 7.

[35] Hannah, S. T., Jennings, P. L., Bluhm, D., Chunyan Peng, A., & Schaubroeck, J. M. (2014). Duty orientation: Theoretical development and preliminary construct. *Organizational Behavior and Human Decision Processes, 123*, 220–238.

[36] Johnson, C. E. (2007). Best practices in ethical leadership. In J. A. Conger & R. E. Riggio (Eds.), *The practice of leadership: Developing the next generation of leaders* (pp. 150–171). San Francisco: Jossey-Bass.

[37] Kant, I. (1964). *Ground work for the metaphysics of morals* (Trans. H. J. Ryan). New York: Harper & Row.

[38] Graham, G. (2004). *Eight theories of ethics*. London: Routledge, ch. 6.

[39] See, for example: Bentham, J. (1948). *An introduction to the principles of morals and legislation*. New York: Hafner Publishing; Gorovitz, S. (Ed.). (1971). *Utilitarianism: Text and critical essays*. Indianapolis: Bobbs-Merrill.

[40] Material on Rawls's Theory of Justice taken from the following sources: Rawls, J. (1971). *A theory of justice.* Cambridge, MA: Belknap Press; Rawls, J. (1993). Distributive justice. In T. Donaldson & P. H. Werhane (Eds.), *Ethical issues in business: A philosophical approach* (4th ed., pp. 274–285). Englewood Cliffs, NJ: Prentice-Hall; Rawls, J. (1993). *Political liberalism.* New York: Columbia University Press; Rawls, J. (2001). *Justice as fairness: A restatement* (E. Kelly, Ed.). Cambridge, MA: Belknap Press; Blocker, H. G., & Smith, E. H. (Eds.). (1980). *John Rawls' theory of justice: An introduction.* Athens: Ohio University.

[41] Rawls, *Justice as fairness*, p. 42.

[42] Gladwell, M. (2005). *Blink: The power of thinking without thinking.* New York: Little, Brown.

[43] Meilander, G. (1986). Virtue in contemporary religious thought. In R. J. Nehaus (Ed.), *Virtue: Public and private* (pp. 7–30). Grand Rapids, MI: Eerdmans; Alderman, H. (1997). By virtue of a virtue. In D. Statman (Ed.), *Virtue ethics* (pp. 145–164). Washington, DC: Georgetown University Press.

[44] Johannesen et al., *Ethics in human communication*, pp. 10–11.

[45] Solomon, R. (1988). Internal objections to virtue ethics. *Midwest Studies in Philosophy, 8,* 428–441.

[46] Johannesen, R. L. (1991). Virtue ethics, character, and political communication. In R. E. Denton (Ed.), *Ethical dimensions of political communication* (pp. 69–90). New York: Praeger.

[47] Johannesen et al., *Ethics in human communication*, p. 10.

[48] Luke, J. S. (1994). Character and conduct in the public service. In T. C. Cooper (Ed.), *The handbook of administrative ethics* (pp. 391–412). New York: Marcel Dekker; Hart, D. K. (1994). Administration and the ethics of virtue. In T. C. Cooper (Ed.), *The handbook of administrative ethics* (pp. 107–123). New York: Marcel Dekker.

[49] Bartholomew, C. S., & Gustafson, S. B. (1998). Perceived Leader Integrity Scale: An instrument for assessing employee perceptions of leader integrity. *Leadership Quarterly, 9,* 127–145. Used by permission of Elsevier Limited.

[50] Peterson, C., & Seligman, M. E. P. (2004). *Character strengths and virtues: A handbook and classification.* Washington DC: American Psychological Association/Oxford University Press.

[51] Reuters. (2016, November 24). "It's final!": Colombian president signs revised peace deal. *New York Post*; Farah, D. (n.d.). Colombia. *Crimes of war.*

[52] Casey, N. (2016, October 7). Colombia's president, Juan Manuel Santos, is awarded Nobel Prize. *The New York Times*, p. A8.

[53] Associated Press (2016, October 10). Colombia president will donate Nobel Peace Prize money to victims.

[54] Associated Press, Colombia president will donate Nobel Peace Prize money to victims.

[55] Associated Press (2016, December 16). Colombian president says Nobel peace prize win helped end civil war. *The Guardian.*

[56] MacIntyre, A. (1984). *After virtue: A study in moral theory* (2nd ed.). Notre Dame, IN: University of Notre Dame Press; Hauerwas, S. (1981). *A community of character.* Notre Dame, IN: University of Notre Dame Press.

[57] Aristotle. (1962). *Nichomachean ethics* (M. Ostwald, Trans: Book II). Indianapolis, IN: Bobbs-Merrill.

[58] Post, S. G. (2002). The tradition of agape. In S. G. Post, L. G. Underwood, J. P. Schloss, & W. B. Hurlbut (Eds.), *Altruism & altruistic love: Science, philosophy, & religion in dialogue* (pp. 51–64). Oxford: Oxford University Press.

[59] Piliavin, J. A., & Charng, H-W. (1990). Altruism: A review of recent theory and research. *Annual Review of Sociology, 16,* 27–65; Batson, C. D., Van Lange, P. A. M., Ahmad, N., & Lishner, D. A. (2003). Altruism and helping behavior. In M. A. Hogg & J. Cooper (Eds.), *The Sage handbook of social psychology* (pp. 279–295). London: Sage.

[60] Kanungo, R. N., & Mendonca, M. (1996). *Ethical dimensions of leadership.* Thousand Oaks, CA: Sage, p. 35.

[61] Kanungo, R. N., & Conger, J. A. (1990). The quest for altruism in organizations. In S. Srivastva & D. L. Cooperrider and Associates (Eds.), *Appreciative management and leadership: The power of positive thought and action in organizations* (pp. 248–249). San Francisco: Jossey-Bass. Used by permission.

[62] Johnson, C. E. (1997, Spring). A leadership journey to the East. *Journal of Leadership Studies, 4,* 82–88.

63 Lee, Y.-T., Haught, H., Chen, K., & Chan, S. (2013). Examining Daoist Big-Five leadership in cross-cultural and gender perspectives. *Asian American Journal of Psychology, 4*, 267–276; Lee, Y.-T., Chen, W., & Chan, S. X (2013). Daoism and altruism: China-USA perspective. In D. A. Vakoch (Ed.), *Altruism in cross-cultural perspective* (pp. 85–99). New York: Springer; Lee, Y.-T, Yang, H., & Ming M. (2009). Daoist harmony as a Chinese philosophy and psychology. *Peace and Conflict Studies, 16*, Article 5.

64 Chapter citations taken from the *Tao te ching*, which is available in a variety of translations, including, for example: Lao-Tzu. (1993). *Tao te ching* (Trans. S. Addiss & S. Lombardo). Indianapolis, IN: Hackett; Chan, W. (1963). *The way of Lao Tzu*. Indianapolis: Bobbs-Merrill.

65 Spears, L. (1998). Tracing the growing impact of servant-leadership. In L. Spears (Ed.), *Insights on leadership: Service, stewardship, spirit, and servant leadership* (pp. 1–15). New York: John Wiley & Sons; Lichtenwainer, B. (2011, March 1). *Fortune*'s best companies to work for with servant leadership. *Modern Servant Leader.*

66 McCuddy, M. K., & Cavin, M. C. (2008). Fundamental moral orientations, servant leadership, and leadership effectiveness: An empirical test. *Review of Business Research, 8*(4), 107–117; Walumbwa, F. O., Hartnell, C. A., & Oke, A. (2010). Servant leadership, procedural justice climate, service climate, and organizational citizenship behavior: A cross-level investigation. *Journal of Applied Psychology, 95*, 517–529; Mayer, D. M., Bardes, M., & Piccolo, R. F. (2008). Do servant-leaders help satisfy follower needs? An organizational justice perspective. *European Journal of Work and Organizational Psychology, 17*(2), 180–197; Barbuto, J. E., & Wheeler, D. W. (2006). Scale development and construct clarification of servant leadership. *Group & Organization Management, 31*, 300–326.

67 Greenleaf, R. (1977). *Servant leadership.* New York: Paulist Press, pp. 13–14.

68 Block, P. (1993). *Stewardship: Choosing service over self-interest.* San Francisco: Berrett-Koehler.

69 DePree, M. (1992). *Leadership jazz.* New York: Currency Doubleday.

70 McGee-Cooper, A., & Trammell, D. (2002). From hero-as-leader to servant-as-leader. In L. C. Spears & M. Lawrence (Eds.), *Focus on leadership: Servant-leadership for the twenty-first century* (pp. 145–146). New York: John Wiley & Sons. Used by permission.

71 DePree, M. (1989). *Leadership is an art.* New York: Doubleday, p. 92.

72 Fraker, A. (1996). Robert K. Greenleaf and business ethics: There is no code. In L. C. Spears (Ed.), *Reflections on leadership* (pp. 37–48). New York: John Wiley.

73 Adapted from Barbuto, J. E., & Wheeler, D. W. (2006). Scale development and construct clarification of servant leadership. *Group & Organization Management*, 300–326. Used by permission of Sage Publications.

74 Johnson, C. E. (2016). *Organizational ethics: A practical approach* (3rd ed.). Los Angeles: Sage, ch. 9.

75 Chaleff, I. (2015). *Intelligent disobedience: Doing right when what you're told to do is wrong.* Oakland, CA: Berrett-Koehler.

76 Roloff, M. E., & Paulson, G. D. (2001). Confronting organizational transgressions. In J. M. Darley, D. M. Messick, & T. R Tyler (Eds.), Social influences on ethical behavior in organizations (pp. 53–68). Mahwah, NJ: Lawrence Erlbaum.

77 Kelley, R. E. (1998). Followership in a leadership world. In L. Spears (Ed.), *Insights on leadership: Service, stewardship, spirit, and servant leadership* (pp. 170–184). New York: John Wiley & Sons.

78 DePree, *Leadership is an art.*

79 Chaleff, I. (2003). *The courageous follower: Standing up to & for our leaders* (2nd Ed.). San Francisco: Berrett-Koehler.

80 Chaleff, I. (2008). New ways of following. In R. E. Riggio, I. Chaleff, & J. Lipman-Blumen (Eds.), *The art of followership: How great followers create great leaders and organizations* (pp. 67–87). San Francisco: Jossey-Bass.

81 Miethe, T. D. (1999). *Whistleblowing at work: Tough choices in exposing fraud, waste, and abuse on the job.* Boulder, CO: Westview Press, p. 209.

82 Masnick, M. (2016, November 21). Theranos's insane campaign to punish whistleblower, who happened to be famous board member's grandson. *Techdirt.*

83 Haidt, J., & Graham, J. (2007). When morality opposes justice: Conservatives have moral intuitions that liberals may not recognize. *Social Justice Research, 40*, 98–116; Haidt, J. (2012). *The righteous*

mind: Why good people are divided by politics and religion. New York: Pantheon Books; Koleva, S. P., Graham, J., Iyer, R., Ditto, P. H., & Haidt, J. (2012). Tracing the threads: How the five moral concerns (especially purity) help explain culture war attitudes. *Journal of Research in Personality, 46*(2), 184–194.

∼ CHAPTER TWELVE

[1] National Center for Educational Statistics. (n.d.). Retrieved from http://nces.ed.gov/fastfacts/display/asp?id=98; Luzer, D. (2011, March 28). Nontraditional college students: America's most important group. *Washington Monthly.*

[2] Van Velsor, E., & McCauley, C. D. (2010). Introduction: Our view of leadership development. In C. D. McCauley & E. Van Velsor (Eds.), *The Center for Creative Leadership handbook of leadership development* (3rd ed., pp. 1–22). San Francisco: Jossey-Bass, p. 2.

[3] A number of experts make a similar distinction between leader and leadership development. See, for example: Day, D. V., & Halpin, S. M. (2004). Growing leaders for tomorrow: An introduction. In D. Day, S. J. Zaccaro, & S. M. Halpin (Eds.), *Leader development for transforming organizations* (pp. 3–22). Mahwah, NJ: Lawrence Erlbaum; Day, D. V., & O'Connor, P. M. (2003). Leadership development: Understanding the process. In S. E. Murphy & R. E. Riggio (Eds.), *The future of leadership development* (pp. 11–27). Mahwah, NJ: Lawrence Erlbaum.

[4] Adapted from Zula, K., Yarrish, K., & Christensen, S. D. (2010). Initial assessment and validation of an instrument to measure student perceptions of leadership skills. *Journal of Leadership Studies, 4,* 48–54. Used by permission of John Wiley & Sons.

[5] Avolio, B. J. (2008). Developmental readiness: Accelerating leader development. *Consulting Psychology Journal: Practice and Research, 60,* 331–347; Hannah, S. T., & Avolio, B. J. (2010). Ready or not: How do we accelerate the developmental readiness of leader? *Journal of Organizational Behavior, 31,* 1181–1187.

[6] Hannah, S. T., Avolio, B. J., Luthans, F., & Harms, P. D. (2008). Leadership efficacy: Review and future directions. *Leadership Quarterly, 19,* 669–692.

[7] Ayman, R., Adams, S., Fisher, B., & Hartman, E. (2003). Leadership development in higher education institutions: A present and future perspective. In S. E. Murphy & R. E. Riggio (Eds.), *The future of leadership development* (pp. 201–222). Mahwah, NJ: Lawrence Erlbaum; Riggio, R. E., Ciulla, J. B., & Sorenson, G. J. (2003). Leadership education at the undergraduate level: A liberal arts approach to leadership development. In S. E. Murphy & R. E. Riggio (Eds.), *The future of leadership development* (pp. 223–236). Mahwah, NJ: Lawrence Erlbaum.

[8] Johnson, C., & Hackman, M. (1993). The status of leadership coursework in communication. *The Michigan Association of Speech Communication Journal, 28,* 1–13. Leadership material is most often included in small group, organizational, and political communication courses.

[9] Meinert, D. (2014, July 22). Leadership development spending is up. *Society for Human Resource Management;* 2015 training industry report (n.d.). *Training.*

[10] Conger, J. A., & Benjamin, B. (1999). *Building leaders: How successful companies develop the next generation.* San Francisco: Jossey-Bass.

[11] Conger, J. A., & Toegel, G. (2003). Action learning and multirater feedback: Pathways to leadership development? In S. E. Murphy & R. E. Riggio (Eds.), *The future of leadership development* (pp. 107–125). Mahwah, NJ: Lawrence Erlbaum. See also: Day, D. V. (2001). Leadership development: A review in context. *Leadership Quarterly, 11,* 581–613.

[12] Brown, P. T. (1999–2000, Winter). New directions in leadership development: A review of trends and best practices. *The Public Manager,* 37–41.

[13] Rai, H., & Singh, M. (2013). A study of mediating variables of the relationship between 360 degree feedback and employee performance. *Human Resource Development International, 16,* 56–73; Nowack, K. M., & Mashihi, S. (2012). Evidence-based answers to 15 questions about leveraging 360-degree feedback. *Consulting Psychology Journal: Practice and Research, 64,* 157–182.

[14] Conger & Toegel, Action learning.

[15] Kram, K. E., & Isabella, L. A. (1985). Mentoring alternatives: The role of peer relationships in career development. *Academy of Management Review, 28,* 110–132.

[16] Crosby, F. J. (1999). The developing literature on developmental relationships. In A. J. Murrell, F. J. Crosby, & R. J. Ely (Eds.), *Mentoring dilemmas: Developmental relationships within multicultural organizations* (pp. 3–20). Mahwah, NJ: Lawrence Erlbaum. See also: Zachary, L. J. (2000). *The mentor's guide*. San Francisco: Jossey-Bass.

[17] Kram, K. E. (1985). *Mentoring at work: Developmental relationships in organizational life*. Glenview, IL: Scott, Foresman and Company; Ragins, B. R., & Kram. K. E. (2008). *The handbook of mentoring at work: Theory, research, and practice*. Los Angeles: Sage. See also: Hunt, D. M., & Michael, C. (1983). Mentorship: A career training and development tool. *Academy of Management Review, 8*, 475–485.

[18] Crosby, The developing literature; Mullen, E. J. (1998). Vocational and psychosocial mentoring functions: Identifying mentors who serve both. *Human Resource Development Quarterly, 9*, 319–331.

[19] Otto, M. L. (1994). Mentoring: An adult developmental perspective. In M. A. Wunsch (Ed.), *Mentoring revisited: Making an impact on individuals and institutions* (pp. 15–22). San Francisco: Jossey-Bass.

[20] See, for example: Gentry, W. A., Weber, T. J., & Sadri, G. (2008). Examining career-related mentoring and managerial performance across cultures: A multilevel analysis. *Journal of Vocational Behavior, 72*, 241–253; Ragins & Kram, *Handbook of mentoring*; Mullen, Vocational and psychosocial mentoring; Allen, T. D., Eby, L. T., Poteet, M. L., Lentz, E., & Lima, L. (2004). Career benefits associated with mentoring for protégés: A meta-analysis. *Journal of Applied Psychology, 89*, 127–136.

[21] Lester, P. B., Hannah, S. T., Harms, P. D., Vogelgesang, G. R., & Avolio, B. J. (2011). Mentoring impact on leader efficacy development: A field experiment. *Academy of Management Learning & Education, 10*, 409–429.

[22] Olson, D. A., & Jackson, D. (2009). Expanding leadership diversity through formal mentoring programs. *Journal of Leadership Studies, 3*, 47–60; Passmore, J., Peterson, D., & Freire, T. (Eds.). (2013). *The Wiley-Blackwell handbook of the psychology of coaching and mentoring*. Hoboken, NJ: Wiley & Sons.

[23] Kogler Hill, S. E., Bahniuk, M. H., & Dobbs, J. (1989). The impact of mentoring and collegial support on faculty success: An analysis of support behavior information adequacy, and communication apprehension. *Communication Education, 38*, 15–33; Schrodt, P., Cawyer, C. S., & Sanders, R. (2003). An examination of academic mentoring behaviors and new faculty members' satisfaction with socialization and tenure and promotion processes. *Communication Education, 52*, 17–29.

[24] Jacobi, M. (1991). Mentoring and undergraduate academic success: A literature review. *Review of Educational Research, 61*(4), 505–532.

[25] Jones, J. (2013). Factors influencing mentees' and mentors' learning throughout formal mentoring relationships. *Human Resource Development International, 16*, 390–408.

[26] Eby, L. T., & Allen, T. D. (2002). Further investigation of proteges' negative mentoring experiences: Patterns and outcomes. *Group & Organization Management, 27*, 456–479.

[27] Feldman, D. C. (1999). Toxic mentors or toxic protégés? A critical re-examination of dysfunctional mentoring. *Human Resource Management Review, 9*, 247–278.

[28] Murray, M. (1991). *Beyond the myths and magic of mentoring*. San Francisco: Jossey-Bass; Kram, K. E., & Bragar, M. C. (1992). Development through mentoring: A strategic approach. In D. H. Montross & C. J. Shinkman (Eds.), *Career development: Theory and practice* (pp. 221–254). Springfield, IL: Charles C. Thomas.

[29] de Janasz, S. C., Sullivan, S. E., & Whiting, V. (2003). Mentor networks and career success: Lessons for turbulent times. *Academy of Management Executive, 17*, 78–91.

[30] Begelson, M. (2014). Developing tomorrow's leaders: Innovative approaches to mentorship. *People & Strategy, 37*, 18–22.

[31] Ting, S., & Hart, E. W. (2004). Formal coaching. In C. D. McCauley & E. Van Velsor (Eds.), *The Center for Creative Leadership handbook of leadership development* (2nd ed., pp. 116–150). San Francisco: Jossey-Bass; Ting, S., & Scisco, P. (2006). *The CCL handbook of coaching: A guide for the leader coach*. San Francisco: Jossey-Bass.

[32] Carey, W., Philippon, D. J., & Cummings, G. G. (2011). Coaching models for leadership development: An integrative review. *Journal of Leadership Studies, 5*, 51–69.

[33] For more information on how managers can coach employees on an ongoing basis, see: Hunt, J. M., & Weintraub, J. R. (2011). *The coaching manager* (2nd ed.) Thousand Oaks, CA: Sage; Harvard Business School. (2004). *Coaching and mentoring: How to develop top talent and achieve stronger performance.* Boston: Harvard Business School Press.

[34] Witherspoon, R. (2000). Coaching smart: Clarifying coaching goals and roles. In M. Goldsmith, L. Lyons, & A. Freas (Eds.), *Coaching for leadership: How the world's greatest coaches help leaders learn* (pp. 165–188*).* San Francisco: Jossey-Bass/Pfeiffer.

[35] Grayson, D., & Larson, K. (2000). How to make the most of the coaching relationship for the person being coached. In M. Goldsmith, L. Lyons, & A. Freas (Eds.), *Coaching for leadership: How the world's greatest coaches help leaders learn* (pp. 121–130*).* San Francisco: Jossey-Bass/Pfeiffer.

[36] Ohlott, P. J. (2004). Job assignments. In C. D. McCauley & E. Van Velsor (Eds.), *The Center for Creative Leadership handbook of leadership development* (2nd ed., pp. 151–182). San Francisco: Jossey-Bass. See also: McCauley, C. D. (2001). Leader training and development. In S. J. Zaccaro & R. J. Klimoski (Eds.), *The nature of organizational leadership: Understanding the performance imperatives confronting today's leaders* (pp. 347–383). San Francisco: Jossey-Bass.

[37] McCall, M. W. (2010). Recasting leadership development. *Industrial and Organizational Psychology, 3,* 3–19.

[38] Maxwell, J. (2000). *Failing forward: Turning mistakes into stepping-stones for success.* Nashville: Thomas Nelson Publishers.

[39] From P. J. Ohlott, Job assignments, p. 157. Used by permission of John Wiley & Sons.

[40] Maxwell, *Failing forward,* p. 117.

[41] Moxley, R. S., & Pulley, M. L. (2004). Hardships. In C. D. McCauley & E. Van Velsor (Eds.), *The Center for Creative Leadership handbook of leadership development* (2nd ed., pp. 183–203). San Francisco: Jossey-Bass.

[42] Guinness, O. (Ed.). (1999). *Character counts: Leadership qualities in Washington, Wilberforce, Lincoln, and Solzhenitsyn.* Grand Rapids, MI: Baker Books; Goodwin, D. K. (2005). *Team of rivals: The political genius of Abraham Lincoln.* New York: Simon & Schuster.

[43] Avolio, B. J. (2005). *Leadership development in balance: Made/born.* Mahwah, NJ: Lawrence Erlbaum, p. 15.

[44] Avolio, *Leadership development.*

[45] Brooks, D. (2015). *The road to character.* New York: Random House.

[46] Covey, S. R. (1989). *The 7 habits of highly effective people.* New York: Simon and Schuster.

[47] Cashman, K. (2008). *Leadership from the inside out* (2nd ed.). San Francisco: Berrett-Kohler.

[48] Cashman, *Leadership,* p. 24.

[49] Cashman, *Leadership.*

[50] Giacalone, R. A., & Jurkiewicz, C. L. (2003). Toward a science of workplace spirituality. In R. A. Giacalone & C. L. Jurkiewicz (Eds.), *Handbook of workplace spirituality and organizational performance* (pp. 3–28). Armonk, NY: M. E. Sharpe; Duchon, D., & Plowman, D. A. (2005). Nurturing the spirit at work: Impact on work unit performance. *Leadership Quarterly, 16,* 807–833.

[51] Giacalone & Jurkiewicz, Toward a science, p. 13.

[52] Mitroff, I., & Denton, E. A. (1999, Summer). A study of spirituality in the workplace. *Sloan Management Review, 40,* 83–92. See also: Mitroff, I., & Denton, E. A. (1999). *A spiritual audit of corporate America: A hard look at spirituality, religion, and values in the workplace.* San Francisco: Jossey-Bass.

[53] Reave, L. (2005). Spiritual values and practices related to leadership effectiveness. *Leadership Quarterly, 16,* 655–687.

[54] For more information on self-reflective practices, see: Foster, R. J. (1998). *Celebration of discipline: The path to spiritual growth* (20th anniversary edition). San Francisco: Harper.

[55] Gozdz, K., & Frager, R. (2003). Using everyday challenges of business to transform individuals and organizations. In R. A. Giacalone & C. L. Jurkiewicz (Eds.), *Handbook of workplace spirituality and organizational performance* (pp. 475–492). Armonk, NY: M. E. Sharpe.

[56] Gozdz & Frager, Using everyday challenges, p. 486.

[57] Gale, S. F. (2001, June). Bringing good leaders to light. *Training*, 38–42; Caudron, S. (1999, September). The looming leadership crisis. *Workforce*, 72–76; Rothwell, W. J. (2016). *Effective succession planning* (5th ed.). New York: AMACOM.

[58] Cairns, T. D. (2011, Summer). Who's up next? Most companies fail to plan for leadership succession. *Employment Relations Today*, 27–34.

[59] Charan, R., Drotter, S., & Noel, J. (2010). *The leadership pipeline: How to build the leadership-powered company*. San Francisco: Jossey-Bass.

[60] Lombardo, M. M., & McCauley, C. D. (1988). *The dynamics of management derailment*. Technical Report No. 34. Greensboro, NC: Center for Creative Leadership; Leslie, J. B., & Van Velsor, E. (1996). *A look at derailment today: North America and Europe*. Greensboro, NC: Center for Creative Leadership.

[61] Gabarro, J. J. (1988). Executive leadership and succession: The process of taking charge. In D. C. Hambrick (Ed.), *The executive effect: Concepts and methods for studying top managers* (p. 258). Greenwich, CT: JAI Press.

[62] For further discussion of important variables in the succession process, see: Lord, R., & Maher, K. (1991). *Leadership and information processing*. Boston: Unwin Hyman, ch. 10; Giambatista, R. C., Rowe, W. G., & Riaz, S. (2005). Nothing succeeds like succession: A critical review of leader succession literature since 1994. *Leadership Quarterly, 16*, 963–991.

[63] Fischer, P. (2007). *The new boss: How to survive the first 100 days*. London: Kogan Page.

[64] Cairns, Who's up next?

[65] Rothwell, *Effective succession planning*, p. 112. Used by permission of the American Management Association.

[66] Rothwell, *Effective succession planning*; Gale, Bringing good leaders to light; Caudron, The looming leadership crisis.

[67] DeLay, L., & Dalton, M. (2006). Coaching across cultures. In S. Ting & P. Scisco (Eds.), *The CCL handbook of coaching: A guide for the leader coach*. San Francisco: Jossey Bass; Milner, J., Ostmeier, E., & Franke, R. (2013). Critical incidents in cross-cultural coaching: The view from German coaches. *International Journal of Evidence Based Coaching and Mentoring, 11*, 19–31; Peterson, D. B. (2007). Executive coaching in a cross-cultural context. *Consulting Psychology Journal: Practice and Research, 59*, 261–271.

∿ CHAPTER THIRTEEN

[1] Mitroff, I. I., & Anagnos, G. (2001). *Managing crises before they happen: What every executive and manager needs to know about crisis management*. New York: American Management Association; Schoenberg, A. (2005, Spring). Do crisis plans matter? A new perspective on leading during a crisis. *Public Relations Quarterly, 50*, 2–6; Perrow, C. (1999). *Normal accidents: Living with high-risk technologies*. Princeton, NJ: Princeton University Press.

[2] Fearn-Banks, K. (2007). *Crisis communications: A casebook approach* (3rd ed.). Mahwah, NJ: Lawrence Erlbaum.

[3] Steward, C. (2010, June 21). BP chief under fire for yacht trip. *The Herald (Glasgow) News*, p. 2; Smithson, J., & Venette, S. (2013, September-October). Stonewalling as an image-defense strategy: A critical examination of BP's response to the Deepwater Horizon explosion. *Communication Studies, 64*, 395–410.

[4] Fearn-Banks, *Crisis communications*.

[5] Coombs, W. T. (1999). *Ongoing crisis communication: Planning, managing, and responding*. Thousand Oaks, CA: Sage; Seeger, M. W., Sellnow, T. L., & Ulmer, R. R. (2003). *Communication and organizational crisis*. Westport, CT: Praeger.

[6] Mitroff, I. I. (2005). *Why some companies emerge stronger and better from a crisis*. New York: AMACOM.

[7] Coombs, W. T. (2012). *Ongoing crisis communication: Planning, managing, and responding* (3rd ed.). Thousand Oaks, CA: Sage; Seeger et al., *Communication and organizational crisis*.

[8] Mishra, R. (2003, August 27). Probe hits NASA in crash of shuttle. *The Boston Globe*, p. A1.

[9] Fink, S. (2000). *Crisis management: Planning for the inevitable.* New York: AMACOM.

[10] Bazerman, M. H., & Watkins, M. D. (2004). *Predictable surprises: The disasters you should have seen coming, and how to prevent them.* Boston: Harvard Business School Press.

[11] Bazerman & Watkins, *Predictable surprises.*

[12] Wooten, L. P., & Hayes James, E. (2008). Linking crisis management and leadership competencies: The role of human resource development. *Advances in Developing Human Resources, 10,* 352–379.

[13] Pauchant, T. C., & Mitroff, I. I. (1992). *Transforming the crisis-prone organization: Preventing individual, organizational, and environmental tragedies.* San Francisco: Jossey-Bass; Mitroff, I. I., & Pearson, C. M. (1993). *Crisis management: A diagnostic guide for improving your organization's crisis-preparedness.* San Francisco: Jossey-Bass.

[14] Coombs, *Ongoing crisis communication* (1999); Mikkelson, D. (2013, June 22). Trademark of the devil. *Snopes.com*; Stampler, L. (2013, May 21). In spite of old, false Satanist accusations, P&G put a moon back into its new logo. *Business Insider.*

[15] Mitroff, I. I., Pearson, C. M., & Harrington, L. K. (1996). *The essential guide to managing corporate crises: A step-by-step handbook for surviving major catastrophes.* New York: Oxford University Press, pp. 22–23. Copyright © 1996. By permission of Oxford University Press, USA.

[16] McPhate, M. (2016, June 28). Ikea recalls 29 million chests and dressers after 6 children die. *The New York Times*; Engle Bromwich, J. (2016, December 22). Ikea reaches $50 million settlement over deadly furniture accidents. *The New York Times.*

[17] Seeger et al., *Communication and organizational crisis.*

[18] Axon, R. (2016, October 28). Baylor regents reveal shocking information surrounding sexual assault scandal. *USA Today.*

[19] Mitroff, I. I., & Alpasian, M. C. (2003, April). Preparing for evil. *Harvard Business Review,* 109–115. See also: Mitroff, *Why some companies.*

[20] Coombs, Ongoing crisis communication. See also: Fearn-Banks, Crisis communications.

[21] Ergun, O., Heier Stamm, J. L., Keskinocak, P., & Swann, J. L. (2010). Waffle House restaurants hurricane response: A case study. *International Journal of Production Economics, 126,* 111–126; Green, E. (2016, October 16). As hurricane rages, Lowe's teams surge into action. *Inside Lowe's*; Horowitz, J. (2014, July 29). Home Depot's disaster preparedness initiatives set to boost retail sales. *TheStreet*; Pittman, E. (2011, November 11). What big-box retailers can teach government about disaster recovery. *Government Technology*; Stoneking, D. (n.d.). News of the day—what do Waffle Houses have to do with risk management? *FEMA.gov*; Tenney, G. (2012, May 2). When disaster strikes, FEMA turns to . . . Waffle House. *Fox News.*

[22] Dillow, C. (2013, November 11). How Waffle House became a disaster indicator for FEMA. *Popular Science.*

[23] Ergun, O., Heier Stamm, J. L., Keskinocak, P., & Swann, J. L. (n.d.). *Lessons in disaster supply chain management from Waffle House restaurant.* Georgia Tech College of Engineering.

[24] Barton, L. (2001). *Crisis in organizations II.* Cincinnati: South-Western.

[25] Ray, S. J. (1999). *Strategic communication in crisis management: Lessons from the airline industry.* Westport, CT: Quorum Books.

[26] Coombs, *Ongoing crisis communication* (2012). See also: Fearn-Banks, *Crisis communications.*

[27] Daleus, P., & Hansen, D. (2011). Inherent ethical challenges in bureaucratic crisis management: The Swedish experience with the 2004 tsunami disaster. In L. Svedin (Ed.), *Ethics and crisis management* (pp. 21–36). Charlotte, NC: Information Age.

[28] Denyer, S. (2014, March 12). Contradictory statements from Malaysia over missing airliner perplex, infuriate. *WashingtonPost.com.*

[29] Barrett, M. S. (2005). Spokespersons and message control: How the CDC lost credibility during the anthrax crisis. *Qualitative Research Reports in Communication, 6,* 59–68.

[30] Claeys, A-S., & Cauberghe, V. (2014). Keeping control: The importance of nonverbal expressions of power by organizational spokespersons in times of crisis. *Journal of Communication, 64,* 1160–1180.

[31] Coombs, W. T. (2007). Protecting organization reputations during a crisis: The development and application of situational crisis communication theory. *Corporate Reputation Review, 10,* 163–176.

[32] James, E. H., Crane, B., & Perry Wooten, L. (2013). Managing the crisis lifecycle in the information age. In A. J. Dubrin (Ed), *Handbook of research on crisis leadership in organizations* (pp. 177–192). Cheltenham, UK: Edward Elgar.

[33] Howell, G. V. J., & Miller, R. (2010). Organizational response to crisis: A case study of Maple Leaf Foods. *Northwest Journal of Communication, 39*, 91–108.

[34] Smart, C., & Vertinsky, I. (2006). Designs for crisis decision units. In D. Smith & D. Elliott (Eds.), *Key readings in crisis management: Systems and structures for prevention and recovery* (pp. 321–342). London: Routledge.

[35] Seeger, M. W., Sellnow, T. L., & Ulmer, R. R. (1998). Communication, organization, and crisis. In M. E. Roloff (Ed.), *Communication yearbook 21* (pp. 231–275). Thousand Oaks, CA: Sage.

[36] Olaniran, B. A., & Williams, D. D. (2001). Anticipatory model of crisis management: A vigilant response to technological crises. In R. L. Heath & G. Vasquez (Eds.), *Handbook of public relations* (pp. 487–500). Thousand Oaks, CA: Sage.

[37] Ray, *Strategic communication.*

[38] Beach, C. (2016, May 6). CDC to Chipotle: Public has a right to know about outbreaks. *Food Safety News*; Jennings, L. (2016, February 15). Chipotle's road to recovery. *Nation's Restaurant News.*

[39] Ferdman, R. A., & Bhattarai, A. (2015, December 10). Food illnesses test Chipotle's good-citizen calling card. *The Washington Post*, p. A01.

[40] Carr, A. (2016, October 16). Chipotle eats itself. *Fast Company.*

[41] Carr, Chipotle eats itself.

[42] Jennings, L. (2015, December 10). Experts unimpressed with Chipotle's crisis management. *Nation's Restaurant News.*

[43] Benoit, W. L. (1995). *Accounts, excuses and apologies.* Albany: State University of New York Press; Benoit, W. L. (2004). Image restoration discourse and crisis communication. In D. P. Millar & R. L. Heath (Eds.), *Responding to crisis: A rhetorical approach to crisis communication* (pp. 263–280). Mahwah, NJ: Lawrence Erlbaum.

[44] Priddle, A., & Bomey, N. (2014, April 2). GM restructures engineering team to better respond to safety problems. *Detroit Free Press.*

[45] Two surprisingly good corporate apologies. (2015, May 19). *SorryWatch.*

[46] Coombs, T. (2007). Protecting organization reputations during a crisis; Sellnow, T. L., & Seeger M. (2013). *Theorizing crisis communication.* Hoboken, NJ: Wiley.

[47] Lowery, W., Leoning, C. D., & Berman, M. (2014, August 13). Even before Michael Brown's slaying in Ferguson, racial questions hung over police. *The Washington Post*; Policing Baltimore's police. (2015, May 4). *Baltimore Sun.*

[48] Weick, K. E., & Sutcliffe, K. M. (2001). *Managing the unexpected: Assuring high performance in an age of complexity.* San Francisco: Jossey-Bass.

[49] Weick & Sutcliffe, *Managing the unexpected.*

[50] Argenti, P. (2002, December). Crisis communication: Lessons from 9/11. *Harvard Business Review*, 103–109.

[51] Sutcliffe, K. M., & Vogus, T. J. (2003). Organizing for resilience. In K. S. Cameron, J. E. Dutton & R. E. Quinn (Eds.), *Positive organizational scholarship: Foundations for a new discipline* (pp. 94–110). San Francisco: Berrett-Koehler; Lengnick-Hall, C. A., Beck, T. E., & Lengnick-Hall, M. L. (2011). Developing a capacity for organizational resilience through strategic human resource management. *Human Resource Management Review, 21*, 243–255.

[52] Rajah, R., & Arvey, R. D. (2013). Helping group members develop resilience. In A. J. Dubrin (Ed), *Handbook of research on crisis leadership in organizations* (pp. 149–173). Cheltenham, UK: Edward Elgar.

[53] Lengnick-Hall, Beck, & Lengnick-Hall, Developing a capacity.

[54] Rodin, J. (2014). *The resilience dividend: Being strong in a world where things go wrong.* New York: PublicAffairs.

[55] Toppo, G. (2013, June 11). At-risk cities ramp up disaster-response planning. *USA Today*; McKay, J. (2014, September 12). Chief resilience officers: Coming to your city? *Emergency Management*; Watts, J. (2014, January 13). Eleven U.S. cities to receive funds to increase resiliency. *Bond Buyer.*

[56] Rodin, *The resilience dividend.*

[57] Ulmer, R. R., Sellnow, T. L., & Seeger, M. (2008). Post-crisis communication and renewal: Understanding the potential for positive outcomes in crisis communication. In R. L. Heath & H. D. O'Hair (Eds.), *Handbook of risk and crisis communication* (pp. 302–322). Hoboken, NJ: Routledge; Ulmer, R. R., Seeger, M. W., & Sellnow, T. L. (2007). Post-crisis communication and renewal: Expanding the parameters of post-crisis discourse. *Public Relations Review, 33,* 130–134.

[58] Witt, J. L., & Morgan, J. (2002). *Stronger in the broken places: Nine lessons for turning crisis into triumph.* New York: Times Books/Henry Holt, p. 222.

[59] Hannah, S. T., Uhl-Bien, M., Avolio, B. J., & Cavarreta, F. L. (2009). A framework for examining leadership in extreme contexts. *Leadership Quarterly, 20,* 897–919.

[60] Hannah, S. T., & Parry, K. W. (2014). Leadership in extreme contexts. In D. V. Day (Ed.), *The Oxford handbook of leadership and organizations* (613-637). New York: Oxford University Press.

[61] Kolditz, T. A. (2007). *In extremis leadership: Leading as if your life depended on it.* San Francisco: Jossey Bass; Kolditz, T. A., & Brazil, D. M. (2005). Authentic leadership in extremis settings: A concept for extraordinary leaders in exceptional situations. In W. L. Gardner, B. J. Avolio, & F. O. Walumbwa (Eds.), *Authentic leadership theory and practice: Origins, effects and development* (pp. 345–356). Amsterdam: Elsevier.

[62] Kolditz, *In extremis leadership*; Kolditz & Brazil, Authentic leadership in extremis settings.

[63] Kolditz, *In extremis leadership*, p. 139.

[64] Lovegrove, I. (2013). Leaders in Antarctica: Characteristics of an Antarctic station manager. In C. M. Giannantonio & A. E. Hurley-Hanson (Eds.), *Extreme leadership: Leaders, teams and situations outside the norm* (pp. 47–61). Cheltenham, UK: Edward Elgar.

[65] von Drehle, D., & Baker, A. (2014, December 10). The Ebola fighters: The ones who answered the call. *Time.*

[66] Sack, K., Fink, S., Belluck, P., & Nossiter, A. (2014, December 29). How Ebola roared back. *The New York Times.*

Bibliography

Adair, R. (2008). Developing great leaders, one follower at a time. In R. Riggio, I. Chaleff, & J. Lipman-Blumen (Eds.), *The art of followership: How great followers create great leaders and organizations* (pp. 137–153). San Francisco: Jossey-Bass.

Adams, S. (2014, June 16). The highest paid CEOS are the worst performers, new study says. *Forbes*.

Adler, J. J. (1967). *The difference of man and the difference it makes*. New York: Holt, Rinehart and Winston.

Adler, N. J. (1991). *International dimensions of organizational behavior* (2nd ed.). Belmont, CA: Wadsworth.

Adler, N. J. (2002). *From Boston to Beijing: Managing with a world view*. Cincinnati, OH: South-Western.

Agars, M. D., & Kottke, J. L. (2004). Models and practice of diversity management: A historical review and presentation of a new integration theory. In M. S. Stockdale & F. J. Crosby (Eds.), *The psychology and management of workplace diversity* (pp. 55–77). Malden, MA: Blackwell.

Alderman, H. (1997). By virtue of a virtue. In D. Statman (Ed.), *Virtue ethics* (pp. 145–164). Washington, DC: Georgetown University Press.

Alexander, J. A., Comfort, M. E., Weiner, B. J., & Bogue, R. (2001). Leadership in collaborative community health partnerships. *Nonprofit Management & Leadership, 12*, 159–175.

Allen, T. D., Eby, L. T., Poteet, M. L., Lentz, E., & Lima, L. (2004). Career benefits associated with mentoring for protégés: A meta-analysis. *Journal of Applied Psychology, 89*, 127–136.

Alvesson, M. (2002). *Understanding organizational culture*. Thousand Oaks, CA: Sage.

Anderson University (Producer) & Biggs, D. (Director). (2008). *A ripple of hope*. (Documentary film).

Andrews, P. (1984). Performance, self-esteem and perceptions of leadership emergence: A comparative study of men and women. *Western Journal of Speech Communication, 48*, 1–13.

Ang, S., & Van Dyne, L. (2008). Conceptualization of cultural intelligence: Definition, distinctiveness, and nomological network. In S. Ang & L. Van Dyne (Eds.), *Handbook of cultural intelligence: Theory, measurement, and applications* (pp. 3–15). Armonk, NY: Sharpe.

Antal, A. B., Lenhardt, U., & Rosenbrock, R. (2003). Barriers to organizational learning. In M. Dierkes, A. B. Antal, J. Child, & I. Nonaka (Eds.), *Handbook of organizational learning and knowledge* (pp. 865–885). Oxford, UK: Oxford University Press:

Areni, C. S., & Sparks, J. R. (2005). Language power and persuasion. *Psychology and Marketing, 22*(6), 507–525.

Argenti, P. (2002, December). Crisis communication: Lessons from 9/11. *Harvard Business Review*, 103–109.

Argyle, M., Gardner, G., & Ciofi, F. (1958). Supervisory methods related to productivity, absenteeism, and labor turnover. *Human Relations, 11*, 23–40.

Aristotle. (1962). *Nichomachean ethics* (M. Ostwald, Trans: Book II). Indianapolis, IN: Bobbs-Merrill.

Aritz, J., & Walker, R. C. (2014). Leadership styles in multicultural groups: Americans and East Asians working together. *International Journal of Business Communication, 51*, 72–92.

Arndt, M. (2006, May 9). 3M's seven pillars of innovation. *Bloomberg.*

Asante, M. K., & Frye, J. K. (1977). *Contemporary public communication.* New York: Harper & Row.

Ashkanasy, N. M., & Humphrey, R. H. (2011). A multi-level view of leadership and emotion: Leading with emotional labor. In A. Bryman, D. Collinson, K. Grint, B. Jackson, & M. Uhl-Bien (Eds.), *The Sage handbook of leadership* (pp. 365–379). Los Angeles: Sage.

Ashkanasy, N. M, & Jordan, P. J. (2008). A multilevel view of leadership and emotion. In R. H. Humphrey (Ed.), *Affect and emotion: New directions in management theory and research* (pp. 19–41). Charlotte, NC: Information Age.

Aspegren, R. E. (1963). A study of leadership behavior and its effects on morale and attitudes in selected elementary schools. *Dissertation Abstracts, 23,* 3708.

Associated Press. (2016, May 11). Uber drivers welcome $100m settlement in employee status lawsuit. *The Times-Picayune.*

Associated Press. (2016, October 10). Colombia president will donate Nobel Peace Prize money to victims.

Associated Press. (2016, December 16). Colombian president says Nobel peace prize win helped end civil war. *The Guardian.*

Atkin, C. K. (2001). Theory and principles of media health campaigns. In R. E. Rice & C. K. Atkin (Eds.), *Public communication campaigns* (3rd ed., pp. 49–68). Thousand Oaks, CA: Sage.

Atkin, C. K., & Salmon, C. T. (2013). Persuasive strategies in health campaigns. In J. P. Dillard & L. Shen (Eds.), *The Sage handbook of persuasion* (2nd ed., pp. 278–295). Los Angeles: Sage.

Auger, B. Y. (1972). *How to run better business meetings.* New York: AMACOM.

Auletta, K. (2009). *Googled: The end of the world as we know it.* New York: Penguin Press.

Avolio, B. J. (2005). *Leadership development in balance: Made/born.* Mahwah, NJ: Lawrence Erlbaum.

Avolio, B. J. (2008). Developmental readiness: Accelerating leader development. *Consulting Psychology Journal: Practice and Research, 60,* 331–347.

Avolio, B. J., & Bass, B. M. (2002). *Developing potential across a full range of leadership: Cases on transactional and transformational leadership.* Mahwah, NJ: Lawrence Erlbaum.

Avolio, B. J., & Gardner, W. L. (2005). Authentic leadership development: Getting to the root of positive forms of leadership. *Leadership Quarterly, 16,* 315–338.

Avolio, B. J., Gardner, W. L., Walumbwa, F. O., Luthans, F., & May, D. R. (2004). Unlocking the mask: A look at the process by which authentic leaders impact follower attitudes and behaviors. *The Leadership Quarterly, 15,* 801–823.

Avolio, B. J., & Luthans, F. (2006). *The high impact leader: Moments matter for accelerating authentic leadership development.* New York: McGraw-Hill.

Avolio, B. J., & Yammarino, F. J. (Eds.). (2002). *Transformational and charismatic leadership: The road ahead.* Boston: JAI.

Axelrod, R. (1984). *The evolution of cooperation.* New York: Basic Books.

Axon, R. (2016, October 28). Baylor regents reveal shocking information surrounding sexual assault scandal. *USA Today.*

Ayman, R., Adams, S., Fisher, B., & Hartman, E. (2003). Leadership development in higher education institutions: A present and future perspective. In S. E. Murphy & R. E. Riggio (Eds.), *The future of leadership development* (pp. 201–222). Mahwah, NJ: Lawrence Erlbaum.

Baird, J. E. (1977). Some nonverbal elements of leadership emergence. *Southern Speech Communication Journal, 42,* 352–361.

Baird, J. E., & Wieting, G. K. (1979, September). Nonverbal communication can be a motivational tool. *Personnel Journal,* 607–610.

Baldwin, D. A. (1971). The costs of power. *Journal of Conflict Resolution, 15,* 145–155.

Bales, R. F. (1970). *Personality and interpersonal behavior.* New York: Holt, Rinehart and Winston.

Bales, R. F., & Cohen, S. P. (1979). *Symlog: A system for the multiple level observation of groups.* London: Collier.

Balona, D. (2012, March 29). FAMU hazing investigation: 2 faculty members suspended. *Orlando Sentinel*, p. A1.

Bandura, A. (1977). Self-efficacy: Toward a unifying theory of behavioral change. *Psychological Review, 84*, 191–215.

Bandura, A., & Wood, R. (1989). Effect of perceived controllability and performance standards of self-regulation of complex decision making. *Journal of Personality and Social Psychology, 84*, 804–814.

Barad, E. (1993). Pygmalion—25 years after interpersonal expectations in the classroom. In P. D. Blanck (Ed.), *Interpersonal expectations: Theory, research, and applications* (pp. 125–153). Cambridge: Cambridge University Press.

Barboza, D. (2014, September 7). The Jack Ma Way: At Alibaba, the founder is squarely in charge. *The New York Times*, p. BU1.

Barbuto, J. E., & Wheeler, D. W. (2006). Scale development and construct clarification of servant leadership. *Group & Organization Management, 31*, 300–326.

Barker, K. (2004). Diffusion of innovations: A world tour. *Journal of Health Communication, 9*, 131–137.

Barker, L., & Watson, K. (2000). *Listen up: How to improve relationships, reduce stress, and be more productive by using the power of listening.* New York: St. Martin's Press.

Barnard, C. I. (1938). *The functions of the executive.* Cambridge, MA: Harvard University Press.

Barnlund, D. C. (1962). Toward a meaning-centered philosophy of communication. *Journal of Communication, 12*, 197–211.

Barrett, M. S. (2005). Spokespersons and message control: How the CDC lost credibility during the anthrax crisis. *Qualitative Research Reports in Communication, 6*, 59–68.

Bartholomew, C. S., & Gustafson, S. B. (1998). Perceived Leader Integrity Scale: An instrument for assessing employee perceptions of leader integrity. *Leadership Quarterly, 9*, 127–145.

Barton, L. (2001). *Crisis in organizations II.* Cincinnati, OH: South-Western Publishing.

Bass, B. M. (1960). *Leadership, psychology, and organizational behavior.* New York: Harper & Row.

Bass, B. M. (1985). *Leadership and performance beyond expectations.* New York: Free Press.

Bass, B. M. (Ed.). (1990). *Bass and Stogdill's handbook of leadership* (3rd ed.). New York: Free Press.

Bass, B. M. (1990). From transactional to transformational leadership: Learning to share the vision. *Organizational Dynamics, 18*, 19–31.

Bass, B. M. (1995). The ethics of transformational leadership. In J. B. Ciulla (Ed.), *Ethics: The heart of leadership* (pp. 169–192). Westport, CT: Praeger.

Bass, B. M. (1997). Does the transactional-transformational leadership paradigm transcend organizational and national boundaries? *American Psychologist, 52*, 130–139.

Bass, B. M., & Avolio, B. J. (1993). Transformational leadership: A response to critiques. In M. M. Chemers & R. Ayman (Eds.), *Leadership theory and research: Perspectives and directions* (pp. 49–80). New York: Academic Press.

Bass, B. M., & Avolio, B. J. (1994). *Improving organizational effectiveness through transformational leadership.* Thousand Oaks, CA: Sage.

Bass, B. M., Burger, P. C., Doktor, R., & Barrett, G. V. (1979). *Assessment of managers: An international comparison.* New York: Free Press.

Bass, B. M., & Riggio, R. E. (2006). *Transformational leadership* (2nd ed.). Mahwah, NJ: Lawrence Erlbaum.

Bass, B. M., & Steidlmeier, P. (1999). Ethics, character and authentic transformational leadership. *Leadership Quarterly, 1*, 181–217.

Batson, C. D., Van Lange, P. A. M., Ahmad, N., & Lishner, D. A. (2003). Altruism and helping behavior. In M. A. Hogg & J. Cooper (Eds.), *The Sage handbook of social psychology* (pp. 279–295). London: Sage.

Bauer, T. N., & Erdogan, B. (2016). *The Oxford handbook of leader-member exchange.* Oxford, UK: Oxford University Press.

Baum, R. J., Locke, E. A., & Kirkpatrick, S. (1998). A longitudinal study of the relations of vision and vision communication to venture growth in entrepreneurial firms. *Journal of Applied Psychology, 83,* 43–54.

Baumgartel, H. (1957). Leadership style as a variable in research administration. *Administrative Science Quarterly, 2,* 344–360.

Baxter, J. (2010). *The language of female leadership.* Houndmills, UK: Palgrave Macmillan.

Bazerman, M. H. (2011). *Blind spots: Why we fail to do what's right and what to do about it.* Princeton, NJ: Princeton University Press.

Bazerman, M. H., & Watkins, M. D. (2004). *Predictable surprises: The disasters you should have seen coming, and how to prevent them.* Boston: Harvard Business School Press.

Beach, C. (2016, May 6). CDC to Chipotle: Public has a right to know about outbreaks. *Food Safety News.*

Bedell-Avers, K. E., Hunter, S. T., & Mumford, M. D. (2008). Conditions of problem-solving and the performance of charismatic, ideological, and pragmatic leaders: A comparative experimental study. *Leadership Quarterly, 19,* 89–106.

Beebe, S. A., & Masterson, J. T. (2012). *Communicating in small groups: Principles and practices.* Boston: Allyn & Bacon.

Begelson, M. (2014). Developing tomorrow's leaders: Innovative approaches to mentorship. *People & Strategy, 37,* 18–22.

Belasco, J. A., & Stayer, R. C. (1994). *Flight of the buffalo: Soaring to excellence, learning to let employees lead.* New York: Warner Books.

Belasen, A. T. (2008). *The theory and practice of corporate communication.* Los Angeles: Sage.

Bell, B. S. (2002). A typology of virtual teams: Implications for effective leadership. *Group & Organization Management, 27,* 14–49.

Benne, K. D., & Sheats, P. (1948). Functional roles of group members. *Journal of Social Issues, 4,* 41–49.

Bennis, W. (1976). *The unconscious conspiracy: Why leaders can't lead.* New York: AMACOM.

Bennis, W. G., & Nanus, B. (1997). *Leaders: The strategies for taking charge* (2nd ed.). New York: Harper & Row.

Benoit, W. L. (1995). *Accounts, excuses and apologies.* Albany: State University of New York Press.

Benoit, W. L. (2004). Image restoration discourse and crisis communication. In D. P. Millar & R. L. Heath (Eds.), *Responding to crisis: A rhetorical approach to crisis communication* (pp. 263–280). Mahwah, NJ: Lawrence Erlbaum.

Bentham, J. (1948). *An introduction to the principles of morals and legislation.* New York: Hafner Publishing.

Bentley, D. (2015, October 14). The top 1% now owns half of the world's wealth. *Fortune.com.*

Berlew, D., & Hall, D. (1966). The socialization of managers: Effects of expectations on performance. *Administrative Science Quarterly,* 208–223.

Berlo, D., Lemert, J., & Mertz, R. (1969). Dimensions for evaluation of the acceptability of message sources. *Public Opinion Quarterly, 33,* 563–576.

Berry, G. R. (2011). Enhancing effectiveness on virtual teams: Understanding why traditional team skills are insufficient. *Journal of Business Communication, 48,* 186–206.

Biafore, B., & Stover, T. (2012). *Your project management coach: Best practices for managing projects in the real world.* Hoboken, NJ: Wiley.

Bies, R., & Tripp, T. M. (1998). Two faces of the powerless: Coping with tyranny in organizations. In R. M. Kramer & M. A. Neale (Eds.), *Power and influence in organizations* (pp. 203–219). Thousand Oaks, CA: Sage.

Bingham, W. V. (1927). Leadership. In H. C. Metcalf (Ed.), *The psychological foundations of management.* New York: Shaw.

Bird, F. B. (1996). *The muted conscience: Moral silence and the practice of ethics in business.* Westport, CT: Quarum Books.

Blake, R. R., & McCanse, A. A. (1991). *Leadership dilemmas—grid solutions.* Houston, TX: Gulf Publishing.

Blake, R. R., & Mouton, J. S. (1985). *The managerial grid III: The key to leadership excellence.* Houston, TX: Gulf Publishing.

Blake, R. R., Mouton, J. S., Barnes, L. B., & Greiner, L. E. (1964). Breakthrough in organization development. *Harvard Business Review, 42,* 133–155.

Blankenship, K. L., & Holtgraves, T. (2005). The role of different markers of linguistic powerlessness in persuasion. *Journal of Language and Social Psychology, 24*(1), 3–24.

Block, P. (1993). *Stewardship: Choosing service over self-interest.* San Francisco: Berrett-Koehler.

Blocker, H. G., & Smith, E. H. (Eds.). (1980). *John Rawls' theory of justice: An introduction.* Athens: Ohio University Press.

Blygh, M. C. (2011). Followership and follower-centered approaches. In A. Bryman, D. Collinson, K. Grint, B. Jackson, & M. Uhl-Bien (Eds.), *The Sage handbook of leadership* (pp. 425–436). Los Angeles: Sage.

Boffey, P. M. (2012, May 13). What if it weren't called pink slime? *The New York Times*, p. SSR 12.

Bogardus, E. S. (1934). *Leaders and leadership.* New York: Appleton-Century.

Bok, S. (1999; updated edition). *Lying: Moral choice in public and private life.* New York: Random/Vintage Books.

Boksem, M.A.S., & de Cremer, D. (2009). The neural basis of morality. In D. de Cremer (Ed.), *Psychological perspectives on ethical behavior and decision-making* (pp. 153–166). Charlotte, NC: Information Age.

Bordas, J. (2007). *Salsa, soul, and spirit: Leadership for a multicultural age.* San Francisco: Berrett-Koehler.

Bormann, E. G. (1975). *Discussion and group methods* (2nd ed.). New York: Harper & Row.

Botkin, J. W., Elmandjra, M., & Malitza, M. (1979). *No limits to learning.* New York: Penguin Books.

Bowers, D. G., & Seashore, S. E. (1966). Predicting organizational effectiveness with a four-factor theory of leadership. *Administrative Science Quarterly, 2,* 238–263.

Bowley, G., & Kannapell, A. (2008, August 6). Chaos on the "mountain that invites death." *The New York Times*, p. A1.

Bradac, J., & Mulac, A. (1984). A molecular view of powerful and powerless speech styles: Attributional consequences of specific language features and communicator intentions. *Communication Monographs, 51,* 307–319.

Bradsher, K. (2001, June 24). Firestone tire flaw unreported for 4 years. *The Oregonian*, p. A4.

Brembeck, W. L., & Howell, W. S. (1976). *Persuasion: A means of social influence* (2nd ed.). Englewood Cliffs, NJ: Prentice-Hall.

Bridges, J. A., & Nelson, R. A. (2000). Issues management: A relational approach. In J. A. Ledingham & S. D. Bruning (Eds.), *Public relations as relationship management: A relational approach to the study and practice of public relations* (pp. 95–115). Mahwah, NJ: Lawrence Erlbaum.

Briner, W., Hastings, C., & Geddes, M. (1996). *Project leadership* (2nd ed.). Aldershot, UK: Gower.

Brissett, D., & Edgley, C. (2005). The dramaturgical perspective. In D. Brissett & C. Edgley (Eds.), *Life as theater: A dramaturgical sourcebook* (2nd ed.). New York: Aldine de Gruyter.

Brooks, D. (2015). *The road to character.* New York: Random House.

Brown, D. J., Scott, K. A., & Lewis, H. (2004). Information processing and leadership. In J. Antonakis, A. T. Cianciolo, & R. J. Sternberg (Eds.), *The nature of leadership* (pp. 125–147). Thousand Oaks, CA: Sage.

Brown, M. E., & Trevino, L. K. (2006). Ethical leadership: A review and future directions. *Leadership Quarterly, 17,* 595–616.

Brown, P. T. (1999–2000, Winter). New directions in leadership development: A review of trends and best practices. *The Public Manager,* 37–41.

Brown, R. (1995). *Prejudice: Its social psychology.* Oxford, UK: Blackwell.

Bruenig, E. (2015, March 9). Sheryl Sandberg's lean in philosophy doesn't just ignore disadvantaged women. It hurts their cause. *New Republic.*

Bruhn, J. G. (2001). *Trust and the health of organizations.* New York: Kluwer/Plenum.

Brunell, A. B., Gentry, W. A., Campbell, W. K., Hoffman, B. J., Kuhnert, K. W., & DeMarree, K. G. (2008). Leader emergence: The case of the narcissistic leader. *Personality and Social Psychology Bulletin, 34*(12), 1663–1676.

Bruning, S. D, Castle, J. D., & Schrepper, E. (2004). Building relationships between organizations and public: Examining the linkage between organization-public relationships, evaluations of satisfaction, and behavioral intent. *Communication Studies, 55*, 435–446.

Bucker, J. J. L. E., Furrer, O., Poutsma, E., & Buyens, D. (2014). The impact of cultural intelligence on communication effectiveness, job satisfaction and anxiety for Chinese host country managers working for foreign multinationals. *The International Journal of Human Resource Management, 25*, 2068–2087.

Burell, N. A., & Koper, R. J. (1994). The efficacy of power/powerless language on persuasiveness/ credibility: A meta-analytic review. In R. W. Preiss & M. Allen (Eds.), *Prospects and precautions in the use of meta-analysis* (pp. 235–255). Dubuque, IA: Brown & Benchmark.

Burke, K. (1968). *Language as a symbolic action.* Berkeley: University of California Press.

Burns, J. F. (2012, May 12). Cameron stands to lose much as scandal wears on. *The New York Times on the Web.*

Burns, J. M. (1978). *Leadership.* New York: Harper & Row.

Burns, T., & Stalker, G. M. (1961). *The management of innovation.* Chicago: Quadrangle Books.

Burris, K., Ayman, R., Che, Y., & Min, H. (2013). Asian Americans' and Caucasians' implicit leadership theories: Asian stereotypes, transformational and authentic leadership. *Asian American Journal of Psychology, 4*, 258–266.

Butcher, D., & Clarke, M. (2008). *Smart management: Using politics in organizations* (2nd ed.). Houndmills, UK: Palgrave Macmillan.

Caesar, E. (2017, August 29). Deutsche Bank's $10-billion scandal. *The New Yorker.*

Cain, S. (2012). *Quiet: The power of introverts in a world that can't stop talking.* New York: Crown.

Cairns, T. D. (2011, Summer). Who's up next? Most companies fail to plan for leadership succession. *Employment Relations Today*, 27–34.

Cameron, K. A., & Campo, S. (2006). Stepping back from social norms campaigns: Comparing normative influences to other predictors of health behaviors. *Health Communication, 20*, 277–288.

Cammalleri, J. A., Hendrick, H. W., Pittmen, W. C., Jr., Blout, H. D., & Prather, D. C. (1973). Effects of different leadership styles on group accuracy. *Journal of Applied Psychology, 57*, 32–37.

Carey, W., Philippon, D. J., & Cummings, G. G. (2011). Coaching models for leadership development: An integrative review. *Journal of Leadership Studies, 5*, 51–69.

Carr, A. (2014, March 17). Punk, meet rock. *Fast Company.*

Carr, A. (2016, October 16). Chipotle eats itself. *Fast Company.*

Carsten, M. K., & Uhl-Bien, M. (2012). Follower beliefs in the co-production of leadership: Examining upward communication and the moderating role of context. *Journal of Psychology, 220*, 210–220.

Carsten, M. K., & Uhl-Bien, M. (2013). Ethical followership: An examination of followership beliefs and crimes of obedience. *Journal of Leadership & Organizational Studies, 20*, 49–61.

Carsten, M. K., Uhl-Bien, M., West, B. J., Patera, J. L., & McGregor, R. (2010). Exploring social constructions of followership: A qualitative study. *Leadership Quarterly, 21*, 543–562.

Cartwright, D., & Zander, A. (1968). Leadership and performance of group functions: Introduction. In D. Cartwright and A. Zander (Eds.), *Group dynamics* (pp. 301–317). New York: Harper & Row.

Casa, A., & Jackson, B. (2016). Authentic leadership. In G. Hickman (Ed.), *Leading organizations: Perspectives for a new era* (pp. 414–429). Thousand Oaks, CA: Sage.

Cascio, W. F. (2000). Managing a virtual workplace. *Academy of Management Executive, 14*, 81–90.

Casey, N. (2016, October 7). Colombia's president, Juan Manuel Santos, is awarded Nobel Prize. *The New York Times*, p. A8.

Cashman, K. (2008). *Leadership from the inside out* (2nd ed.). San Francisco: Berrett-Koehler.

Castro, R. (2012). *OnLive acquired by Lauder Partners affiliate, restructures company.* Retrieved from http://www.lazytechguys.com/news/business/

Caudron, S. (1999, September). The looming leadership crisis. *Workforce,* 72–76.

Chaleff, I. (2008). New ways of following. In R. E. Riggio, I. Chaleff, & J. Lipman-Blumen (Eds.), *The art of followership: How great followers create great leaders and organizations* (pp. 67–87). San Francisco: Jossey-Bass.

Chaleff, I. (2009). *The courageous follower* (3rd ed.). San Francisco: Berrett-Koehler.

Chaleff, I. (2015). *Intelligent disobedience: Doing right when what you're told to do is wrong.* Oakland, CA: Berrett-Koehler.

Chan, K. Y., & Drasgow, F. (2001). Toward a theory of individual differences and leadership: Understanding the motivation to lead. *Journal of Applied Psychology, 86,* 481–498.

Chan, S. (2011). Financial crisis was avoidable, inquiry concludes. *The New York Times,* p. A1.

Chan, W. (1963). *The way of Lao Tzu.* Indianapolis: Bobbs-Merrill.

Chang, M., & Gruner, C. R. (1981). Audience reaction to self-disparaging humor. *Southern Speech Communication Journal, 46,* 419–426.

Chang, R. (2001). *The passion plan at work.* San Francisco: Jossey-Bass.

Charan, R., Drotter, S., & Noel, J. (2010). *The leadership pipeline: How to build the leadership-powered company.* San Francisco: Jossey-Bass.

Chen, L. J. (2015). Effect of acceptance expectations on the employment development of individuals with disabilities: The self-fulfilling prophecy applied. *Journal of Employment Counseling, 42,* 98–109.

Chen, Z., Lawson, R. B., Gordon, L. R., & McIntosh, B. (1996). Groupthink: Deciding with the leader and the devil. *Psychological Record, 46,* 581–590.

Cherniss, C. (2000). Social and emotional competence in the workplace. In R. Bar-On & J. D. A. Parker (Eds.), *The handbook of emotional intelligence: Theory, development, assessment, and application at home, school, and in the workplace* (pp. 433–458). San Francisco: Jossey-Bass.

Cherniss, C., & Goleman, D. (Eds.). (2001). *The emotionally intelligent workplace: How to select for, measure, and improve emotional intelligence in individuals, groups and organizations.* San Francisco: Jossey-Bass.

Chhokar, J. S., Brodbeck, F. C., & House, R. J. (2007). *Culture and leadership across the world: The GLOBE book of in-depth studies of 25 societies.* Mahwah, NJ: Lawrence Erlbaum.

Chinese Culture Connection. (1987). Chinese values and the search for culture-free dimensions of culture. *Journal of Cross-Cultural Psychology, 18,* 143–174.

Chouinard, Y. (2005). *Let my people go surfing.* New York: Penguin Press.

Chrislip, D. D., & Larson, C. E. (1994). *Collaborative leadership.* San Francisco: Jossey-Bass.

Christie, R., & Gies, F. L. (1970). *Studies in Machiavellianism.* New York: Academic Press.

Cialdini, R. B. (2009). *Influence: Science and practice* (5th ed.). Boston: Allyn & Bacon.

Cialdini, R. (2016). *Pre-suasion: A revolutionary way to influence and persuade.* New York: Simon & Schuster.

Cialdini, R. B., Petrova, P. K., & Goldstein, N. J. (2004, Spring). The hidden costs of organizational dishonesty. *MIT Sloan Management Review,* 67–73.

Cialdini, R., Vincent, J., Lewis, S., Catalan, J., Wheeler, D., & Darby, B. (1975). Reciprocal procedure for inducing compliance: The door-in-the-face technique. *Journal of Personality and Social Psychology, 31,* 206–213.

Claburn, T. (2006, August 28). Google revealed. *Information Week,* p. 34.

Claeys, A-S., & Cauberghe, V. (2014). Keeping control: The importance of nonverbal expressions of power by organizational spokespersons in times of crisis. *Journal of Communication, 64,* 1160–1180.

Cleland, D. I. (1999). *Project management: Strategic design and implementation* (2nd ed.). New York: McGraw-Hill.

Clifton, J. (n.d.). 10 failed Google projects. *HowStuffWorks.*

Cobb, C. G. (2011). *Making sense of agile project management: Balancing control and agility.* Hoboken, NJ: Wiley.

Cohn, D. (2016. June 23). It's official: Minority babies are the majority among the nation's infants, but only just. *Pew Research Center.*

Collins, J. (2001). *Good to great.* New York: HarperBusiness.

Collins, J. C., & Porras, J. I. (1996, September–October). Building your company's vision. *Harvard Business Review,* 65–77.

Collins, J. C., & Porras, J. I. (2004). *Built to last.* New York: HarperBusiness.

Conger, J. A. (1989). Leadership: The art of empowering others. *The Academy of Management Executive, 3,* 17–24.

Conger, J. A. (1991). Inspiring others: The language of leadership. *Academy of Management Executive, 5,* 30–45.

Conger, J. A., & Benjamin, B. (1999). *Building leaders: How successful companies develop the next generation.* San Francisco: Jossey-Bass.

Conger, J. A., & Kanungo, R. N. (1987). Toward a behavioral theory of charismatic leadership in organizational settings. *Academy of Management Review, 12,* 637–647.

Conger, J. A., & Kanungo, R. N. (1988). The empowerment process: Integrating theory and practice. *Academy of Management Review, 13,* 471–482.

Conger, J. A., & Toegel, G. (2003). Action learning and multirater feedback: Pathways to leadership development? In S. E. Murphy & R. E. Riggio (Eds.), *The future of leadership development* (pp. 107–125). Mahwah, NJ: Lawrence Erlbaum.

Connelly, M. S., Gilbert, J. A., Zaccaro, S. J., Threlfall, K. V., Marks, M. A., & Mumford, M. D. (2000). Exploring the relationship of leadership skills and knowledge to leader performance. *Leadership Quarterly, 11,* 65–86.

Coombs, W. T. (1999). *Ongoing crisis communication: Planning, managing, and responding.* Thousand Oaks, CA: Sage.

Coombs, W. T. (2007). Protecting organization reputations during a crisis: The development and application of situational crisis communication theory. *Corporate Reputation Review, 10,* 163–176.

Cooper, R. K., & Sawat, A. (1996). *Executive EQ: Emotional intelligence in leadership and organizations.* New York: Grosset/Putnam.

Corporate Accountability International. (2011). Clowning with kids' health: The case for Ronald McDonald's retirement. Retrieved from http://www.RetireRonald.org

Costa, P. T. (1987). Validation of the five-factor model of personality across instruments and observers. *Journal of Personality and Social Psychology, 52,* 81–90.

Covey, S. R. (1989). *The 7 habits of highly effective people.* New York: Simon and Schuster.

Cox, T. (1991). Managing cultural diversity: Implications for organizational competitiveness. *Academy of Management Executive, 5,* 45–56.

Cox, T. (1993). *Cultural diversity in organizations: Theory, research and practice.* San Francisco: Berrett-Koehler.

Cox, T. (2001). *Creating the multicultural organization: A strategy for capturing the power of diversity.* San Francisco: Jossey-Bass.

Cragan, J. F., Kasch, C. R., & Wright, D. W. (2009). *Communication in small groups: Theory, process, skills* (7th ed.). Boston: Wadsworth.

Crawford, K. S., Thomas, E. D., & Fink, J. J. (1980). Pygmalion at sea: Improving the work effectiveness of low performers. *Journal of Applied Behavioral Science, 16,* 482–505.

Crosby, B. C., & Bryson, J. M. (2010). Integrative leadership and the creation and maintenance of cross-sector collaborations. *Leadership Quarterly, 21,* 211–230.

Crosby, F. J. (1999). The developing literature on developmental relationships. In A. J. Murrell, F. J. Crosby, & R. J. Ely (Eds.), *Mentoring dilemmas: Developmental relationships within multicultural organizations* (pp. 3–20). Mahwah, NJ: Lawrence Erlbaum.

Cross, R. L., Yan, A., & Louis, M. R. (2000). Boundary activities in "boundaryless" organizations: A case study of a transformation to a team-based structure. *Human Relations, 53*(6), 841–868.

Cutlip, S. M., Center, A. H., & Broom, G. M. (1994). *Effective public relations.* Upper Saddle River, NJ: Prentice-Hall.

Daft, R. L. (2005). *The leadership experience.* Mason, OH: Thomson-Southwestern.

Daleus, P., & Hansen, D. (2011). Inherent ethical challenges in bureaucratic crisis management: The Swedish experience with the 2004 tsunami disaster. In L. Svedin (Ed.), *Ethics and crisis management* (pp. 21–36). Charlotte, NC: Information Age.

Daly, J. A., McCroskey, J. C., & Richmond, V. P. (1980). Relationship between vocal activity and perception of communication in small group interaction. *Western Journal of Speech Communication, 41,* 175–187.

Dance, F. E. X. (1982). A speech theory of human communication. In F. E. X. Dance (Ed.), *Human communication theory* (pp. 120–146). New York: Harper & Row.

Day, D. V. (2001). Leadership development: A review in context. *Leadership Quarterly, 11,* 581–613.

Day, D. V., & Halpin, S. M. (2004). Growing leaders for tomorrow: An introduction. In D. Day, S. J. Zaccaro, & S. M. Halpin (Eds.), *Leader development for transforming organizations* (pp. 3–22). Mahwah, NJ: Lawrence Erlbaum.

Day, D. V., & O'Connor, P. M. (2003). Leadership development: Understanding the process. In S. E. Murphy & R. E. Riggio (Eds.), *The future of leadership development* (pp. 11–27). Mahwah, NJ: Lawrence Erlbaum.

Day, R. C., & Hamblin, R. L. (1964). Some effects of close and punitive styles of supervision. *American Journal of Sociology, 69,* 499–510.

DeFleur, M. L., Kearney, P., & Plax, T. G. (1993). *Mastering communication in contemporary America.* Mountain View, CA: Mayfield.

De Geus, A. (1988, February). Planning as learning. *Harvard Business Review,* 70–74.

de Janasz, S. C., Sullivan, S. E., & Whiting, V. (2003). Mentor networks and career success: Lessons for turbulent times. *Academy of Management Executive, 17,* 78–91.

De Jong, A., de Ruyter, K., & Wetzels, M. (2005). Antecedents and consequences of group potency: A study of self-managing service teams. *Management Science, 51,* 1610–1625.

DeJong, W. (2010). Social norms marketing campaigns to reduce campus alcohol problems. *Health Communication, 25,* 615–616.

DeLay, L., & Dalton, M. (2006). Coaching across cultures. In S. Ting & P. Scisco (Eds.), *The CCL handbook of coaching: A guide for the leader coach* (pp. 122–148). San Francisco: Jossey Bass.

Den Hartog, D. N., House, R. J., Hanges, P. J., & Ruiz-Quintanilla, S. A. (1999). Culture specific and cross-culturally generalizable implicit leadership theories: Are attributes of charismatic/transformational leadership universally endorsed? *Leadership Quarterly, 10,* 219–256.

Denning, S. (2005). *The leader's guide to storytelling.* San Francisco: Jossey-Bass.

Denyer, S. (2014, March 12). Contradictory statements from Malaysia over missing airliner perplex, infuriate. *WashingtonPost.com.*

DePree, M. (1989). *Leadership is an art.* New York: Doubleday.

DePree, M. (1992). *Leadership jazz.* New York: Currency Doubleday.

DeRosa, D. (2009, May/June). Improving performance by emulating the best. *Leadership in Action,* 17–19.

Derr, C. B., Roussillon, S., & Bournois, F. (2002). Conclusion. In C. B. Derr, S. Roussillon, & F. Bournois (Eds.), *Cross-cultural approaches to leadership development* (pp. 289–303). Westport, CT: Quorum Books.

Deutsch, M. (1973). *The resolution of conflict.* New Haven, CT: Yale University Press.

Devito, J. (2000). *The elements of public speaking* (7th ed.). New York: Longman.

Dewey, J. (1910). *How we think.* Boston: D. C. Heath.

Diamond, J. (2016). *Power: A user's guide.* Santa Fe, NM: Belly Song Press.

DiBella, A. J., & Nevis, E. C. (1998). *How organizations learn: An integrated strategy for building learning capability.* San Francisco: Jossey-Bass.

Dillow, C. (2013, November 11). How Waffle House became a disaster indicator for FEMA. *Popular Science.*

Dirks, K. T. (1999). The effects of interpersonal trust on work group performance. *Journal of Applied Psychology, 84,* 445–455.

Dirks, K. T. (2000). Trust in leadership and team performance: Evidence from NCAA basketball. *Journal of Applied Psychology, 85,* 1004–1012.

Dirks, K. T., & Ferrin, D. L. (2002). Trust in leadership: Meta-analytic findings and implications for research and practice. *Journal of Applied Psychology, 87,* 611–628.

Dirks, K. T., & Skarlicki, D. P. (2004). Trust in leaders: Existing research and emerging issues. In R. M. Kramer & K. S. Cook (Eds.), *Trust and distrust in organizations: Dilemmas and approaches* (pp. 21–40). New York: Russell Sage Foundation.

Djibo, I. J. A., Desiderio, K., & Price, N. M. (2010). Examining the role of perceived leader behavior on temporary employees' organizational commitment and citizenship behavior. *Human Resource Development Quarterly, 21,* 321–342.

Dolnick, E. (2001). *Down the great unknown: John Wesley Powell's 1869 journey of discovery and tragedy through the Grand Canyon.* New York: HarperCollins.

D'Onfro, J. (2014, September 14). How Jack Ma went from being a poor school teacher to turning Alibaba into a $160 billion behemoth. *Business Insider.*

Don of the dirtbags: An interview with Yvon Chouinard. (2016, February 26). *The Usual.*

Dovidio, J. F., Gaertner, S. L., & Lamoreaux, M. J. (2009). Leadership across group divides: The challenges and potential of common group identity. In T. L. Pittinsky (Ed.), *Crossing the divide: Intergroup leadership in a world of difference* (pp. 3–15). Boston: Harvard Business School Press.

Dow, T. (1969). The theory of charisma. *Sociological Quarterly, 10,* 306–318.

Dozier, D. M., Grunig, L. A., & Grunig, J. E. (1995). *Manager's guide to excellence in public relations and communication management.* Mahwah, NJ: Lawrence Erlbaum.

Drory, A., & Romm, T. (1990). The definition of organizational politics: A review. *Human Relations, 43*(11), 1133–1154.

Druskat, V. U., & Wolff, S. B. (2001, March). Building the emotional intelligence of groups. *Harvard Business Review,* 80–90.

Duchon, D., Green, S. G., & Taber, T. D. (1988). Vertical dyad linkage: A longitudinal assessment of antecedents, measures, and consequences. *Journal of Applied Psychology, 71,* 56–60.

Duchon, D., & Plowman, D. A. (2005). Nurturing the spirit at work: Impact on work unit performance. *Leadership Quarterly, 16,* 807–833.

Duck, J. M., & Fielding, K. S. (2003). Leaders and their treatment of subgroups: Implications for evaluations of the leader and the superordinate group. *European Journal of Social Psychology, 33,* 387–401.

Duir, T., Eden, D., & Banjo, M. L. (1995). Self-fulfilling prophecy and gender: Can women be Pygmalion and Galatea? *Journal of Applied Psychology, 80,* 253–270.

Dutch Bros. (2016). Company information. Retrieved from dutchbros.com/AboutUs/

Dyer, W. G. (1985). The cycle of cultural evolution in organizations. In R. H. Killmann, M. J. Saxton, & R. Serpa (Eds.), *Gaining control of the corporate culture* (pp. 200–229). San Francisco: Jossey-Bass.

Eagly, A. H. (2007). Female leadership advantage and disadvantage: Resolving the contradictions. *Psychology of Women Quarterly, 31,* 1–12.

Eagly, A. H., & Carli, L. L. (2007). *Through the labyrinth: The truth about how women become leaders.* Boston: Harvard Business School Press.

Eagly, A. H., Johannesen-Schmidt, M. C., & Engen, M. L. (2003). Transformational, transactional, and laissez-faire leadership styles: A meta-analysis comparing women and men. *Psychological Bulletin, 129,* 569–591.

Eagly, A. H., Karau, S. J., & Makhijani, M. G. (1995). Gender and the effectiveness of leaders: A meta-analysis. *Psychological Bulletin, 117,* 125–145.

Eby, L. T., & Allen, T. D. (2002). Further investigation of proteges' negative mentoring experiences: Patterns and outcomes. *Group & Organization Management, 27,* 456–479.

Eckvall, G., & Arvoven, J. (1991). Change-centered leadership: An extension of the two-dimensional model. *Scandinavian Journal of Management, 7*, 15–26.

Eden, D. (1984). Self-fulfilling prophecy as a management tool: Harnessing Pygmalion. *Academy of Management Review, 9*, 64–73.

Eden, D. (1990). *Pygmalion in management.* Lexington, MA: Lexington Books/D. C. Heath.

Eden, D. (1993). Interpersonal expectations in organizations. In P. D. Blanck (Ed.), *Interpersonal expectations: Theory, research, and applications* (pp. 154–178). Cambridge: Cambridge University Press.

Eden, D., & Ravid, G. (1982). Pygmalion vs. self-expectancy: Effects of instructor and self-expectancy on trainee performance. *Organizational Behavior and Human Performance, 30*, 351–364.

Eden, D., & Shani, A. B. (1982). Pygmalion goes to boot camp: Expectancy, leadership, and trainee performance. *Journal of Applied Psychology, 67*, 194–199.

Edwards, P., & Kraft, M. (2011). *Dumbemployed: Hilariously dumb and sadly true stories about jobs like yours.* Philadelphia: Running Press.

Egan, M. (2016, September 9). 5,300 Wells Fargo employees fired over 2 million phony accounts. *CNNMoney.*

Einarsen, S., Aasland, M. S., & Skogstad, A. (2007). Destructive leadership behaviour: A definition and conceptual model. *Leadership Quarterly, 18*, 207–216.

Einarsen, S., Skogstad, A., & Aasland, M. S. (2010). The nature, prevalence, and outcomes of destructive leadership: A behavior and conglomerate approach. In B. Schyns & T. Hansbrough (Eds.), *When leadership goes wrong: Destructive leadership mistakes and ethical failures* (pp. 145–171). Charlotte, NC: Information Age.

Eisenberg, E. M., & Riley, P. (2001). Organizational culture. In F. M. Jablin & L. L. Putnam (Eds.), *The new handbook of organizational communication advances in theory, research, and methods* (pp. 291–322). Thousand Oaks, CA: Sage.

Eisenberg, J., Lee, H-J., Bruck, F., Brenner, B., Claes, M-T., Mironski, J., & Bell, R. (2013). Can business schools make students culturally competent? Effects of cross-cultural management courses on cultural intelligence. *Academy of Management Learning & Education, 12*, 603–621.

Eisenberg, N. (2000). Emotion, regulation, and moral development. *Annual Review of Psychology, 51*, 665–697.

Eisenberger, R., Fasolo, P., & Davis-LaMastro, C. (1990). Perceived organizational support and employee diligence, commitments, and innovation. *Journal of Applied Psychology, 75*, 57–59.

Elangovan, A. R., & Shapiro, D. L. (1998). Betrayal of trust in organizations. *Academy of Management Review, 23*, 547–566.

11 Elon Musk quotes that show his genius. (n.d.). *Business Insider India.*

Elsbach, K. D. (2004). Managing images of trustworthiness in organizations. In R. M. Kramer & K. S. Cook (Eds.), *Trust and distrust in organizations: Dilemmas and approaches* (pp. 275–292). New York: Russell Sage Foundation.

Engleberg, I. N., & Wynn, D. R. (2003). *Working in groups: Communication principles and strategies* (3rd ed.). Boston: Houghton Mifflin.

Engle Bromwich, J. (2016, December 22). Ikea reaches 450 million settlement over deadly furniture accidents. *The New York Times.*

Epstein, C. F. (1988). *Deceptive distinctions: Sex, gender, and the social order.* New Haven, CT: Yale University Press.

Erez, M., & Earley, P. C. (1993). *Culture, self-identity, and work.* New York: Oxford University Press.

Ergun, O., Heier Stamm, J. L., Keskinocak, P., & Swan, J. L. (2010). Waffle House restaurants hurricane response: A case study. *International Journal of Production Economics, 126*, 111–126.

Ergun, O., Heier Stamm, J. L., Keskinocak, P., & Swan, J. L. (n.d.). *Lessons in disaster supply chain management from Waffle House restaurant.* Atlanta: Georgia Tech College of Engineering.

Erisman, P. (2015). *Alibaba's world: How a remarkable Chinese company is changing the face of global business.* New York: PalgraveMacmillan.

Ernst, C., & Yip, J. (2009). Boundary-spanning leadership: Tactics to bridge social identity in organizations. In T. L. Pittinsky (Ed.), *Crossing the divide: Intergroup leadership in a world of difference* (pp. 87–112). Boston: Harvard Business Press.

Esser, J. K. (1998). Alive and well after 25 years: A review of groupthink research. *Organizational Behavior and Human Decision Processes, 73,* 116–141.

Etzioni, A. (1964). *Modern organizations.* Englewood Cliffs, NJ: Prentice-Hall.

Ewing, J., & Bowley, G. (2015, December 14). Volkswagen sowed seeds of forceful ambition. *The New York Times,* p. B1.

Fagenson, E. A. (1989). The mentor advantage: Perceived career/job experiences of protégés versus non-protégés. *Journal of Organizational Behavior, 10,* 309–320.

Fairhurst, G. T. (2011). *The power of framing: Creating the language of leadership.* San Francisco: Jossey-Bass.

Fairhurst, G. T., & Sarr, R. A. (1996). *The art of framing: Managing the language of leadership.* San Francisco: Jossey-Bass.

Farah, D. (n.d.). Colombia. *Crimes of war.*

Farris, G. F. (1972). The effect of individual roles on performance in innovative groups. *R & D Management, 3,* 23–28.

Fearn-Banks, K. (2002). *Crisis communications: A casebook approach* (2nd ed.). Mahwah, NJ: Lawrence Erlbaum.

Feldman, D. C. (1999). Toxic mentors or toxic protégés? A critical re-examination of dysfunctional mentoring. *Human Resource Management Review, 9,* 247–278.

Feloni, R. (2014, April 15). Zappos CEO Tony Hsieh to employees: Embrace self-management or leave by the end of the month. *Business Insider.*

Feloni, R. (2015, May 16). Inside Zappos CEO Tony Hsieh's radical management experiment that prompted 14% of employees to quit. *Business Insider.*

Ferdman, R. A., & Bhattarai, A. (2015, December 10). Food illnesses test Chipotle's good-citizen calling card. *The Washington Post,* p. A01.

Fink, S. (2000). *Crisis management: Planning for the inevitable.* New York: AMACOM.

Finn, A. N., Shrodt, P., Witt, P. L., Elledge, N., Jernbers, K. A., & Larson, L. M. (2009). A meta-analytical review of teacher credibility and its associations with teacher behaviors and student outcomes. *Communication Education, 58,* 516–537.

Fischer, P. (2007). *The new boss: How to survive the first 100 days.* London: Kogan Page.

Fisher, B. A., & Ellis, D. G. (1994). *Small group decision making* (4th ed.). New York: McGraw-Hill.

Fisher, R., Ury, W., & Patton, B. (2011). *Getting to yes* (Rev. ed.). New York: Penguin Books.

Fisher, S. (2007, October). Telling tales: The art of corporate story telling. *The Costco Connection,* pp. 22–23.

Fishman, C. (2011). *The Wal-Mart effect* (Rev. ed.). New York: Penguin.

Fiske, S. T. (1993, June). Controlling other people: The impact of power on stereotyping. *American Psychologist,* 621–628.

Fiske S. T. (1998). Stereotyping, prejudice, and discrimination. In D. T. Gilbert, S. T. Fiske, & G. Lindzey (Eds.), *The handbook of social psychology* (Vol. 2, pp. 357–411). Boston: McGraw-Hill.

Fletcher, M. (2010, October 16). "We decided to look for the miners as if they were our sons." *The Times News* (London), pp. 4, 5.

Forgang, W. G. (2004). *Strategy-specific decision-making: A guide for executing competitive strategy.* Armonk, NY: Sharpe.

Foster, R. J. (1998). *Celebration of discipline: The path to spiritual growth* (20th anniversary edition). San Francisco: HarperSanFrancisco.

Foulke, E. (1971). The perception of time compressed speech. In D. L. Horton & J. J. Jenkins (Eds.), *The perception of language* (pp. 79–107). Columbus, OH: Charles E. Merrill.

Fraker, A. (1996). Robert K. Greenleaf and business ethics: There is no code. In L. C. Spears (Ed.), *Reflections on leadership* (pp. 37–48). New York: John Wiley.

French, J. R. P., & Raven, B. (1959). The bases of social power. In D. Cartwright (Ed.), *Studies in social power* (pp. 150–167). Ann Arbor: University of Michigan, Institute for Social Research.

French, M. M. (2013, July 8). Valve's "perfect hiring" hierarchy has "hidden management" clique like high school. *Develop on-line.*

Gabarro, J. J. (1988). Executive leadership and succession: The process of taking charge. In D. C. Hambrick (Ed.), *The executive effect: Concepts and methods for studying top managers* (pp. 237–268). Greenwich, CT: JAI Press.

Gale, S. F. (2001, June). Bringing good leaders to light. *Training,* 38–42.

Galford, R., & Drapeau, A. S. (2003, February). The enemies of trust. *Harvard Business Review, 81,* 88–97.

Galinsky, A. D., Jordan, J., & Sivanathan, N. (2008). Harnessing power to capture leadership. In J. B Ciulla, D. R. Forsyth, M. A. Genovese, G. R. Goethals, L. C. Han, & C. H. Hoyt (Eds). *Leadership at the crossroads* (pp. 283–299). Santa Barbara, CA: ABC-Clio Greenwood.

Gallo, C. (2014). *Talk like TED: The 9 public speaking secrets of the world's top minds.* New York: St. Martin's.

Garcia, A. (2016, May 16). Sheryl Sandberg speaks publicly about her husband's death for the first time. *CNN Money.*

Garcia, V. (2013, July 19). Why I won't lean in. *The Huffington Post.*

Gardner, J. W. (1990). *On leadership.* New York: The Free Press.

Gardner, W. L. (1992). Lessons in organizational dramaturgy: The art of impression management. *Organizational Dynamics, 21,* 33–46.

Gardner, W. L., & Avolio, B. J. (1998). The charismatic relationship: A dramaturgical perspective. *Academy of Management Review, 23,* 32–58.

Gardner, W. L., Avolio, B. J., Luthans, F., May, D. R., & Walumbwa, F. (2005). "Can you see the real me?" A self-based model of authentic leader and follower development. *Leadership Quarterly, 16,* 343–372.

Gardner, W. L., & Cleavenger, D. (1998). The impression management strategies associated with transformational leadership at the world-class level: A psychological assessment. *Management Communication Quarterly, 12,* 3–41.

Gardner, W. L., & Martinko, M. J. (1988). Impression management in organizations. *Journal of Management, 14,* 321–338.

Garten, J. E. (2016). *From silk to silicon: The story of globalization through ten extraordinary lives.* New York: HarperCollins.

Garvin, D. A. (1993, July–August). Building a learning organization. *Harvard Business Review,* 86.

Garvin, D. A. (2000). *Learning in action: A guide to putting the learning organization to work.* Boston: Harvard Business School Press.

Geertz, C. (1977). Centers, kings, and charisma: Reflections on the symbolics of power. In J. Ben-David & T. Nichols (Eds.), *Culture and its creation: Essays in honor of Edward Shils* (pp. 150–171). Chicago: University of Chicago Press.

Geier, J. G. (1967). A trait approach to the study of leadership. *Journal of Communication, 17,* 316–323.

Gentry, W. A., Weber, T. J., & Sadri, G. (2008). Examining career-related mentoring and managerial performance across cultures: A multilevel analysis. *Journal of Vocational Behavior, 72,* 241–253.

Gerber, R. (2002). *Leadership the Eleanor Roosevelt way: Timeless strategies from the first lady of courage.* New York: Prentice-Hall.

Gersch, K. (2013, August 21). Google's best new innovation: Rules around "20% time." *Forbes.*

Gerstner, C. R., & Day, D. V. (1997). Meta-analytic review of leader-member exchange theory: Correlates and construct issues. *Journal of Applied Psychology, 82,* 827–844.

Getzels, J. W. (1973, November 21). Problem finding: The 343rd Convocation Address, the University of Chicago. *The University of Chicago Record, 9,* 281–283.

Getzels, J. W. (1975). Problem-finding and the inventiveness of solutions. *Journal of Creative Behavior, 9,* 12–18.

Giacalone, R. A., & Greenbergh, J. (Eds.). (1997). *Antisocial behavior in organizations.* Thousand Oaks, CA: Sage.

Giacalone, R. A., & Jurkiewicz, C. L. (2003). Toward a science of workplace spirituality. In R. A. Giacalone & C. L. Jurkiewicz (Eds.), *Handbook of workplace spirituality and organizational performance* (pp. 3–28). Armonk, NY: M. E. Sharpe.

Giambatista, R. C., Rowe, W. G., & Riaz, S. (2005). Nothing succeeds like succession: A critical review of leader succession literature since 1994. *Leadership Quarterly, 16*, 963–991.

Gil, F., Rico, R., Alcover, C. M., & Barrasa, A. (2005). Change-oriented leadership, satisfaction and performance in work groups: Effects of team climate and group potency. *Journal of Managerial Psychology, 20*, 312–328.

Gilchrist-Petty, E., & Folk, Z. D. (2014) "Suck it up": The relationship between willingness to communicate and reduced soldier stress. *The Northwest Journal of Communication, 42*, 87–116.

Giles, H., & Powesland, P. F. (1975). *Speech style and social evaluation*. London: Academic Press.

Gioia, D. A. (1992). Pinto fires and personal ethics: A script analysis of missed opportunities. *Journal of Business Ethics, 11*, 379–389.

Gladwell, M. (2002). *The tipping point: How little things can make a big difference*. Boston: Little, Brown.

Gladwell, M. (2005). *Blink: The power of thinking without thinking*. New York: Little, Brown.

Godzicki, J., & Varma, A. (2011). A comparative study of the impact of leader-member exchange in two samples: U.S.A. and Poland. *Organizations and Markets in Emerging Economies, 2*, 9–23.

Goethals, G. R. (2005). Nonverbal behavior and political leadership. In R. E. Riggio & R. S. Feldman (Eds.), *Applications of nonverbal communication* (pp. 95–115). Mahwah, NJ: Lawrence Erlbaum.

Goffman, E. (1959). *The presentation of self in everyday life*. Garden City, NY: Doubleday.

Goldberg, L. R. (1990). An alternative "description of personality": The big-five factor structure. *Journal of Personality and Social Psychology, 59*, 1216–1229.

Good, T., & Brophy, J. (1980). *Education psychology: A realistic approach*. New York: Holt, Rinehart and Winston.

Goodstadt, B. E., & Hjelle, L. A. (1973). Power to the powerless: Locus of control and the use of power. *Journal of Personality and Social Psychology, 27*, 190–196.

Goodwin, D. K. (2005). *Team of rivals: The political genius of Abraham Lincoln*. New York: Simon & Schuster.

Goodwin, S. A. (2003). Power and prejudice: A social-cognitive perspective on power and leadership. In D. van Knippenberg & M. A. Hogg, *Leadership and power: Identity processes in groups and organizations* (pp. 138–152). London: Sage.

Gorovitz, S. (Ed.). (1971). *Utilitarianism: Text and critical essays*. Indianapolis: Bobbs-Merrill.

Gouran, D. S. (2003). Communication skills for group decision-making. In J. O. Greene & B. R. Burleson (Eds.), *Handbook of communication and social interaction skills* (pp. 835–870). Mahwah, NJ: Lawrence Erlbaum.

Gouran, D. S., & Hirokawa, R. Y. (1986). Counteractive functions of communication in effective group decision-making. In R. Y. Hirokawa & M. S. Poole (Eds.), *Communication and group decision-making* (pp. 81–90). Beverly Hills, CA: Sage.

Gouran, D. S., Hirokawa, R. Y., Julian, K. M., & Leatham, G. B. (1993). The evolution and current status of the functional perspective on communication in decision-making and problem-solving groups. In S. Deetz (Ed.), *Communication Yearbook 16* (pp. 573–600). Newbury Park, CA: Sage.

Govindarajan, V., & Srinivas, S. (2013, August 6). The innovation mindset in action: 3M corporation. *Harvard Business Review*.

Gozdz, K., & Frager, R. (2003). Using everyday challenges of business to transform individuals and organizations. In R. A. Giacalone & C. L. Jurkiewicz (Eds.), *Handbook of workplace spirituality and organizational performance* (pp. 475–492). Armonk, NY: M. E. Sharpe.

Graeff, C. L. (1983). The situational leadership theory: A critical view. *Academy of Management Review, 8*, 285–291.

Graeff, C. L. (1997). Evolution of situational leadership theory: A critical review. *Leadership Quarterly, 8*, 153–170.

Graen, G. (1976). Role-making processes within complex organizations. In M. D. Dunnette (Ed.), *Handbook of industrial organizational psychology* (pp. 1201–1246). Chicago: Rand-McNally.

Graen, G. B. (2006). To share or not to share leadership: New LMX-MMX network leadership or charismatic leadership on creative projects. In G. B. Graen (Ed.), *Sharing network leadership* (pp. 25–36). Greenwich, CT: Information Age.

Graen, G. B., & Cashman, J. F. (1975). A role-making of leadership in formal organizations: A developmental approach. In J. G. Hunt and L. L. Larson (Eds.), *Leadership frontiers* (pp. 143–165). Kent, OH: Kent State University Press.

Graen, G. B., & Uhl-Bien, M. (1998). Relationship-based approach to leadership. Development of leader-member exchange (LMX) theory of leadership over 25 years: Applying a multi-level multi-domain perspective. In F. Dansereau & F. J. Yammarino (Eds.), *Leadership: The multiple-level approaches* (pp. 103–158). Stamford, CT: JAI Press.

Graham, G. (2004). *Eight theories of ethics*. London: Routledge.

Grant, J. A., King, P. E., & Behnke, R. E. (1994). Compliance-gaining strategies, communication satisfaction, and willingness to comply. *Communication Reports, 7*, 99–108.

Grayson, D., & Larson, K. (2000). How to make the most of the coaching relationship for the person being coached. In M. Goldsmith, L. Lyons, & A. Freas (Eds.), *Coaching for leadership: How the world's greatest coaches help leaders learn* (pp. 121–130). San Francisco: Jossey-Bass/Pfeiffer.

Green, E. (2016, October 16). As hurricane rages, Lowe's teams surge into action. *Inside Lowe's.*

Greenleaf, R. K. (1977). *Servant leadership.* New York: Paulist Press.

Griffin, E. (2009). *A first look at communication theory* (7th ed.). New York: McGraw-Hill.

Groth, A. (2013, December 30). Zappos is going holacratic: No job titles, no managers, no hierarchy. *Quartz.*

Grover, S. L. (1997). Lying in organizations: Theory, research, and future directions. In R. A. Giacalone & J. Greenberg (Eds.), *Antisocial behavior in organizations* (pp. 68–84). Thousand Oaks, CA: Sage.

Grow, B., Foust, D., Thornton, E., Farzad, R., McGregor, J., Zegle, S., & Javers, E. (2007, January 15). Out at Home Depot. *Business Week*, pp. 56–62.

Grunig, L. A., Grunig, J. E., & Dozier, D. M. (2002). *Excellent public relations and effective organizations: A study of communication management in three countries*. Mahwah, NJ: Lawrence Erlbaum.

Guadine, A., & Thorne, L. (2001). Emotion and ethical decision-making in organizations. *Journal of Business Ethics, 31*, 175–187.

Guarrero, C. A. (1998, October). The leadership challenge. *Security Management*, 27–29.

Gudykunst, W. B., & Kim, Y. Y. (2003). *Communicating with strangers: An approach to intercultural communication* (4th ed.). New York: McGraw-Hill.

Guinness, O. (Ed.). (1999). *Character counts: Leadership qualities in Washington, Wilberforce, Lincoln, and Solzhenitsyn*. Grand Rapids, MI: Baker Books.

Gumbel, P. (2007, July 5). BMW drives Germany. *Time.*

Hackman, J. R. (2002). *Leading teams: Setting the stage for great performances.* Boston, MA: Harvard Business School Press.

Hackman, J. R., & Wageman, R. (2005). A theory of team coaching. *Academy of Management Review, 30*, 269–287.

Hackman, J. R., & Wageman, R. (2005). When and how team leaders matter. *Research in Organizational Behavior, 26*, 37–74.

Hackman, M. Z. (1988). Audience reactions to the use of direct and personal disparaging humor in informative public address. *Communication Research Reports, 5*, 126–130.

Hackman, M. Z. (1988). Reactions to the use of self-disparaging humor by informative public speakers. *Southern Speech Communication Journal, 53*, 175–183.

Hackman, M. Z. (1989). The inner game of public speaking: Applying intrapersonal communication processes in the public speaking course. *Carolinas Speech Communication Annual, 5*, 41–47.

Hackman, M. Z., & Johnson, C. (1994). *A cross-cultural investigation of innovativeness, willingness to communicate and need for cognition.* Paper presented at the Speech Communication Association convention, New Orleans, LA.

Haidt, J. (2012). *The righteous mind: Why good people are divided by politics and religion.* New York: Pantheon Books.

Haidt, J., & Graham, J. (2007). When morality opposes justice: Conservatives have moral intuitions that liberals may not recognize. *Social Justice Research, 40*, 98–116.

Hall, E. (1977). *Beyond culture.* Garden City, NY: Anchor.

Hampden-Turner, C. M., & Trompenaars, F. (2000). *Building cross-cultural competence: How to create wealth from conflicting values.* New Haven, CT: Yale University Press.

Hample, D. (2003). Arguing skill. In J. O. Greene & B. R. Burleson (Eds.), *Handbook of communication and social interaction skills* (pp. 439–477). Mahwah, NJ: Lawrence Erlbaum.

Handbook for new employees. (2012). Retrieved from http://www.valvesoftware.com/company/Valve_Handbook_LowRes.pdf

Hannah, S. T., & Avolio, B. J. (2010). Ready or not: How do we accelerate the developmental readiness of leaders? *Journal of Organizational Behavior, 31*, 1181–1187.

Hanna, S. T., Avolio, B. J., Luthans, F., & Harms, P. D. (2008). Leadership efficacy: Review and future directions. *Leadership Quarterly, 19*, 669–692.

Hannah, S. T., Jennings, P. L., Bluhm, D., Chunyan Peng, A., & Schaubroeck, J. M. (2014). Duty orientation: Theoretical development and preliminary construct. *Organizational Behavior and Human Decision Processes, 123*, 220–238.

Hannah, S. T., & Parry, K. W. (2014). Leadership in extreme contexts. In D. V. Day (Ed.), *The Oxford handbook of leadership and organizations* (pp. 613–637). New York: Oxford University Press.

Hannah, S. T., Uhl-Bien, M., Avolio, B. J., & Cavarreta, F. L. (2009). A framework for examining leadership in extreme contexts. *Leadership Quarterly, 20*, 897–919.

Hart, D. K. (1994). Administration and the ethics of virtue. In T. L. Cooper (Ed.), *The handbook of administrative ethics* (pp. 107–123). New York: Marcel Dekker.

Harvard Business School. (2004). *Coaching and mentoring: How to develop top talent and achieve stronger performance.* Boston: Harvard Business School Press.

Harvey, J. (1974, Summer). The Abilene Paradox: The mismanagement of agreement. *Organizational Dynamics*, 63–80.

Harvey, J. (1988). *The Abilene Paradox and other meditations on management.* New York: Simon & Schuster.

Harvey, M. (2006). Leadership and the human condition. In G. R. Goethals & G. L. J. Sorenson (Eds.), *The quest for a general theory of leadership* (pp. 39–45). Northampton, MA: Edward Elgar.

Harvey, P., Martinko, M. J., & Gardner, W. L. (2006). Promoting authentic behavior in organizations: An attributional perspective. *Journal of Leadership and Organizational Studies, 12*, 1–11.

Haslam, S. A., & Platow, M. J. (2001). The link between leadership and followership: How affirming social identity translates vision into action. *PSPB, 27*, 1469–1479.

Hauerwas, S. (1981). *A community of character.* Notre Dame, IN: University of Notre Dame Press.

Hawkins, P. (2014). *Leadership team coaching: Developing collective transformational leadership.* London: Kogan-Page.

Hawkins, P. (Ed.). (2014). *Leadership team coaching in practice: Developing high-performing teams.* London: Kogan-Page.

Hays-Thomas, R. (2004). Why now? The contemporary focus on managing diversity. In M. S. Stockdale & F. J. Crosby (Eds.), *The psychology and management of workplace diversity* (pp. 3–30). Malden, MA: Blackwell.

Hays-Thomas, R., Kossek, E. E., Lobel, S. A., & Brown, J. (2006). Human resource strategies to manage workplace diversity: Examining "the business case." In A. M. Konrad, P. Prasad, & J. K. Pringle (Eds.), *Handbook of workplace diversity* (pp. 53–74). London: Sage.

Heagney, J. (2012). *Fundamentals of project management* (4th ed.). New York: AMACOM.

Heath, R. L. (1997). *Strategic issues management: Organizations and public policy challenges.* Thousand Oaks, CA: Sage.

Heath, R. L. (2002). Issues management: Its past, present and future. *Journal of Public Affairs, 2*, 209–214.

Hecht, T. D., Allen, N. J., Klammer, J. D., & Kelly, E. C. (2002). Group beliefs, ability, and performance: The potency of group potency. *Group Dynamics: Theory, Research, and Practice, 6*, 143–152.

Heilman, M. E., & Eagly, A. H. (2008). Gender stereotypes are alive, well, and busy producing workplace discrimination. *Industrial and Organizational Psychology, 1*, 393–398.

Hemphill, J. K. (1949). The leader and his group. *Journal of Educational Research, 28*, 225–229.

Hendricks, J. W., & Payne, S. C. (2007). Beyond the Big Five: Leader goal orientation as a predictor of leadership effectiveness. *Human Performance, 20*, 317–343.

Hersey, P. (1984). *The situational leader.* Escondido, CA: Center for Leadership Studies.

Hersey, P., Blanchard, K. H., & Johnson, D. (2008). *Management of organizational behavior: Leading human resources* (9th ed.). Upper Saddle River, NJ: Prentice-Hall.

Heskett, J. L., Sasser, W. E., Jr., & Hart, C. W. L. (1990). *Service breakthroughs.* New York: Free Press.

Hespe, G., & Wall, T. (1976). The demand for participation among employees. *Human Relations, 29*, 411–428.

Hicks, N. (2016, June 9). Lawsuits: Uber, Lyft violated labor law in Austin shutdown. *American-Statesman.*

Hiebert, M., & Klatt, B. (2001). *The encyclopedia of leadership: A practical guide to popular leadership theories and techniques.* New York: McGraw-Hill.

Higgs, M. (2009). The good, the bad and the ugly: Leadership and narcissism. *Journal of Change Management, 9*(2), 165–178.

Hill, N. (1976, August). Self-esteem: The key to effective leadership. *Administrative Management, 51*, 24–25.

Hill, T. A. (1976). An experimental study of the relationship between opinionated leadership and small group consensus. *Speech Monographs, 43*, 246–257.

Hinken, T. R., & Schriesheim, C. A. (1989). Development and application of new scales to measure the French and Raven (1959) bases of social power. *Journal of Applied Psychology, 74*, 561–567.

Hirokawa, R., & Pace, R. (1983). A descriptive investigation of the possible communication-based reasons for effective and ineffective group decision making. *Communication Monographs, 50*, 363–379.

Hirokawa, R. Y., & Scheerhorn, D. R. (1986). Communication in faulty group decision-making. In R. Y. Hirokawa & M. S. Poole (Eds.), *Communication and group decision-making* (pp. 63–80). Beverly Hills, CA: Sage.

Hise, R. T. (1968, Fall). The effect of close supervision on productivity of simulated managerial decision-making groups. *Business Studies, North Texas University*, pp. 96–104.

Hock-Pen, S., Nahrgang, J. D., & Morgeson, F. P. (2009). Understanding why they don't see eye to eye: An examination of leader-member exchange (LMX) agreement. *Journal of Applied Psychology, 94*, 1048–1057.

Hodis, G. M., Bardhan, N. R., & Hodis, F. A. (2010). Patterns of change in willingness to communicate in public speaking contexts: A latent growth modeling analysis. *Journal of Applied Communication Research, 38*(5), 248–267.

Hoffman, B. J., Woehr, D. J., Maldagen-Youngjohn, R., & Lyons, B. D. (2011). Great man or great myth? A quantitative review of the relationship between individual differences and leader effectiveness. *Journal of Occupational and Organizational Psychology 84*, 347–381.

Hoffman, J. (2014, May 8). Secrets of the Ritz-Carlton's "legendary" customer service. *PSA Perspective.*

Hofling, C. K., Brotzman, E., Dalrymple, S., Graves, N., & Pierce, C. M. (1966). An experimental study of nurse-physician relationships. *Journal of Nervous and Mental Disease, 143*, 171–180.

Hofstede, G. (1991). *Cultures and organizations: Software of the mind.* London: McGraw-Hill.

Hofstede, G. (1993). Cultural constraints in management theories. *Academy of Management Executive, 7*, 81–94.

Hofstede, G. (2001). *Culture's consequences: Comparing values, behaviors, institutions, and organizations across nations* (2nd ed.). Thousand Oaks, CA: Sage.

Hofstede, G., & Bond, M. H. (1988). The Confucius connection: From cultural roots to economic growth. *Organizational Dynamics, 14*, 483–503.

Hogg, M. A. (2001). A social identity theory of leadership. *Personality and Social Psychology Review, 5*, 184–200.

Hogg, M. A., van Knippenberg, D., & Rast, D. E. (2012). Intergroup leadership in organizations: Leading across group and organizational boundaries. *The Academy of Management Review, 37*(2), 232–255.

Hollander, E. P. (1978). *Leadership dynamics: A practical guide to effective relationships.* New York: The Free Press.

Hollander, E. P. (1992, April). The essential interdependence of leadership and followership. *Current Directions in Psychological Science,* 71–75.

Hon, L. C., & Grunig, J. E. (1999). *Guidelines for measuring relationships in public relations.* Tallahassee, FL: Institute for Public Relations.

hooks, b. (2013, October 28). Dig deep: Beyond lean in. *The Feminist Wire.*

Hopkins, S. A. (1997). Case #1: Downsizing at Simtek. In W. E. Hopkins (Ed.), *Ethical dimensions of diversity* (pp. 119–121). Thousand Oaks, CA: Sage.

Hornstein, H. A. (1996). *Brutal bosses and their prey.* New York: Riverhead Books.

Horowitz, J. (2014, July 29). Home Depot's disaster preparedness initiatives set to boost retail sales. *TheStreet.*

Hosman, L. A., Huebner, T. M., & Siltanen, S. A. (2002). The impact of speech style, argument strength, and need for cognition on impression formation, cognitive responses, and persuasion. *Journal of Language and Social Psychology, 21*(4), 361–379.

Hough, J., & Neuland, E. W. (2000). *Global business.* Oxford: Oxford University Press.

House, R. J. (1971). A path-goal theory of leadership effectiveness. *Administrative Science Quarterly, 16*, 321–338.

House, R. J. (1977). A 1976 theory of charismatic leadership. In J. G. Hunt & L. L. Larson (Eds.), *Leadership: The cutting edge* (pp. 189–207). Carbondale: Southern Illinois University Press.

House, R. J., (1996). Path-goal theory of leadership: Lessons, legacy, and a reformulated theory. *Leadership Quarterly, 7*, 323–352.

House, R. J., Dorfman, P. W., Javidan, M., Hanges, P. J., & Sully de Luque, M. F. (2014). *Strategic leadership across cultures: The GLOBE study of CEO leadership behavior and effectiveness in 24 countries.* Thousand Oaks, CA: Sage.

House, R. J., Hanges, P. J., Javidan, M., Dorfman, P. W., & Gupta, V. (2004). *Culture, leadership, and organizations: The GLOBE study of 62 societies.* Thousand Oaks, CA: Sage.

House, R. J., & Mitchell, T. R. (1974). Path-goal theory of leadership. *Journal of Contemporary Business, 3*, 81–97.

Hovland, C. I., Janis, I., & Kelley, H. H. (1953). *Communication and persuasion.* New Haven, CT: Yale University Press.

Hovland, C. I., & Weiss, W. (1951). The influence of source credibility on communication effectiveness. *Public Opinion Quarterly, 15*, 635–650.

Howard, P. S., & Howard, J. M. (2001). *The owner's manual for personality at work.* Atlanta, GA: Bard Press.

Howell, G. V. J., & Miller, R. (2010). Organizational response to crisis: A case study of Maple Leaf Foods. *Northwest Journal of Communication, 39*, 91–108.

Howell, J. M. (1988). Two faces of charisma: Socialized and personalized leadership in organizations. In J. A. Conger & R. N. Kanungo (Eds.), *Charismatic leadership: The elusive factor in organizational effectiveness* (pp. 213–236). San Francisco: Jossey-Bass.

Howell, J. M., & Avolio, B. J. (1992). The ethics of charismatic leadership: Submission or liberation. *Academy of Management Executive, 6*, 43–54.

Hoyt, C. L., Murphy, S. E., Halverson, S. K., & Watson, C. B. (2003). Group leadership: Efficacy and effectiveness. *Group Dynamics: Theory, Research, and Practice, 7*, 259–274.

Hsieh, T. (2010). *Delivering happiness: A path to profits, passion and purpose.* New York: Business Plus.

Huggins, N. (1987). Martin Luther King, Jr.: Charisma and leadership. *Journal of American History, 74,* 477–481.

Hughes, R. L., Beatty, K. M., & Dinwoodie, D. (2005). *Becoming a strategic leader: Your role in your organization's enduring success.* San Francisco: Wiley.

Hughes, R. L., Ginnett, R. C., & Curphy, G. J. (2009). *Leadership: Enhancing the lessons of experience* (6th ed.). Boston: McGraw-Hill Irwin.

Hult, G. T. M. (2003). An integration of thoughts on knowledge management. *Decision Sciences, 34,* 189–195.

Hunt, D. M., & Michael, C. (1983). Mentorship: A career training and development tool. *Academy of Management Review, 8,* 475–485.

Hunt, J. M., & Weintraub, J. R. (2011). *The coaching manager* (2nd ed.). Thousand Oaks, CA: Sage.

Hunter, J. E., & Boster, F. J. (1987). A model of compliance-gaining message selection. *Communication Monographs, 54,* 63–84.

Hunter, S. T., Bedell-Avers, K. E., & Mumford, M. D. (2009). Impact of situational framing and complexity on charismatic, ideological and pragmatic leaders: Investigation using a computer simulation. *Leadership Quarterly, 20,* 383–404.

Hunter, S. T., Cushenbery, L., Thoroughgood, C., Johnson, J. E., & Ligon, G. S. (2011). First and ten leadership: A historiometric investigation of the CIP leadership model. *Leadership Quarterly, 22,* 70–91.

Hunter, S. T., Tate, B. W., Dzieweczynski, J. L., & Cushenbery, L. (2010). Understanding the antecedents of unintentional leader errors: A multilevel perspective. In B. Schyns & T. Hansbrough (Eds.), *When leadership goes wrong: Destructive leadership mistakes and ethical failures* (pp. 405–443). Charlotte, NC: Information Age.

IGDA satisfaction survey. (2015). International Game Developers Association. Retrieved from http://www.igda.org

Ilies, R., Morgeson, F. P., & Nahrgang, J. D. (2005). Authentic leadership and eudaemonic well-being: Understanding leader-follower outcomes. *Leadership Quarterly, 16,* 373–394.

Ilies, R., Nahrgang, J. D., & Morgeson, F. P. (2007). Leader-member exchange and citizenship behaviors: A meta-analysis. *Journal of Applied Psychology, 92*(1), 269–277.

Inch, E. S., & Warnick, B. (2002). *Critical thinking and communication: The use of reason in argument* (4th ed.). Boston: Allyn & Bacon.

Infante, D. (1988). *Arguing constructively.* Long Grove, IL: Waveland Press.

Infante, D. A. (1995). Teaching students to understand and control verbal aggression. *Communication Education, 44,* 51–63.

Infante, D. A., & Gorden, W. I. (1985). Superiors' argumentativeness and aggressiveness as predictors of subordinates' satisfaction. *Human Communication Research, 12,* 117–125.

Infante, D. A., & Gorden, W. I. (1989). Argumentativeness and affirming communicator style as predictors of satisfaction/dissatisfaction with subordinates. *Communication Quarterly, 31,* 81–90.

Infante, D. A., & Gorden, W. I. (1991). How employees see the boss: Test of an argumentative and affirming model of supervisors' communicative behavior. *Western Journal of Speech Communication, 55,* 294–304.

Infante, D. A., & Rancer, A. S. (1982). A conceptualization and measure of argumentativeness. *Journal of Personality Assessment, 46,* 72–80.

Infante, D. A., & Rancer, A. S. (1996). Argumentativeness and verbal aggressiveness: A review of recent theory and research. In B. Burleson (Ed.), *Communication Yearbook 19* (pp. 319–351). Thousand Oaks, CA: Sage.

Isenhart, M. W., & Spangle, M. (2000). *Collaborative approaches to resolving conflict.* Thousand Oaks, CA: Sage.

Ives, W., Torry, B., & Gordon, C. (2000). Knowledge sharing is human behavior. In D. Morey, M. Maybury, & B. Thuraisingham (Eds.), *Knowledge management: Classic and contemporary works* (pp. 99–129). Cambridge, MA: MIT Press.

Jacobi, M. (1991). Mentoring and undergraduate academic success: A literature review. *Review of Educational Research, 61*(4), 505–532.

Jacobs, T. O. (1970). *Leadership and exchange in formal organizations.* Alexandria, VA: Human Resources Research Organization.

Jaffe, C. (2007). *Public speaking: Concepts and skills for a diverse society* (5th ed.). Belmont, CA: Wadsworth/Thomson.

James, E. H., Crane, B., & Perry Wooten, L. (2013). Managing the crisis life cycle in the information age. In A. J. Dubrin (Ed.), *Handbook of research on crisis leadership in organizations* (pp. 177–192). Cheltenham, UK: Edward Elgar.

Jamieson, K. H. (1995). *Beyond the double bind: Women and leadership.* New York: Oxford University Press.

Janis, I. (1982). *Groupthink* (2nd ed.). Boston: Houghton Mifflin.

Janis, I. (1989). *Crucial decisions: Leadership in policymaking and crisis management.* New York: The Free Press.

Janis, I., & Mann, L. (1977). *Decision making.* New York: The Free Press.

Jarvenpaa, S. L., & Leidner, D. E. (1999). Communication and trust in global virtual teams. *Organization Science, 10,* 791–815.

Javidan, M., Dorfman, P. W., Sully de Luque, M., & House, R. J. (2006, February). In the eye of the beholder: Cross cultural lessons in leadership from Project GLOBE. *Academy of Management Perspectives,* 67–90.

Jenner, H. (1990). The Pygmalion Effect: The importance of expectancies. *Alcoholism Treatment Quarterly, 7,* 127–133.

Jennings, L. (2015, December 10). Experts unimpressed with Chipotle's crisis management. *Nation's Restaurant News.*

Jennings, L. (2016, February 15). Chipotle's road to recovery. *Nation's Restaurant News.*

Jennings, M. M. (2006). *The seven signs of ethical collapse: How to spot moral meltdowns in companies . . . before it's too late.* New York: St. Martin's Press.

Jensen, A. D., & Chilberg, J. G. (1991). *Small group communication.* Belmont, CA: Wadsworth.

Johannesen, R. L. (1991). Virtue ethics, character, and political communication. In R. E. Denton (Ed.), *Ethical dimensions of political communication* (pp. 69–90). New York: Praeger.

Johannesen, R. L., Valde, K. S., & Whedbee, K. E. (2008). *Ethics in human communication* (6th ed). Long Grove, IL: Waveland Press.

Johnson, C. E. (1997, Spring). A leadership journey to the East. *Journal of Leadership Studies, 4,* 82–88.

Johnson, C. E. (2002). Evaluating the impact of emotional intelligence on leadership performance: Resonance or dissonance? Selected Proceedings of the 2002 International Leadership Association convention.

Johnson, C. E. (2007). Best practices in ethical leadership. In J. A. Conger & R. E. Riggio (Eds.), *The practice of leadership: Developing the next generation of leaders* (pp. 150–171). San Francisco: Jossey-Bass.

Johnson, C. E. (2016). *Organizational ethics: A practical approach* (3rd ed.). Thousand Oaks, CA: Sage.

Johnson, C. E. (2018). *Meeting the ethical challenges of leadership: Casting light or shadow* (6th ed.). Thousand Oaks, CA: Sage.

Johnson, C. E., Dixon, B., Hackman, M. Z., & Vinson, L. (1995). Willingness to communicate, the need for cognition and innovativeness: New Zealand students and professionals. In J. E. Aitken & L. J. Shedletsky (Eds.), *Intrapersonal communication processes* (pp. 376–381). Plymouth, MI: Midnight Oil and the Speech Communication Association.

Johnson, C. E., & Hackman, M. (1993). The status of leadership coursework in communication. *The Michigan Association of Speech Communication Journal, 28,* 1–13.

Johnson, C. E., & Hackman, M. (1995). *Creative communication: Principles and applications.* Long Grove, IL: Waveland Press.

Johnson, C. E., & Hackman, M. Z. (1998). *Public relations, collaborative leadership and community: A new vision for a new century.* Paper presented at the National Communication Association convention, New York City.

Johnson, C. E., & Vinson, L. (1987). Damned if you do, damned if you don't?: Status, powerful speech and evaluations of female witnesses. *Women's Studies in Communication, 10,* 37–44.

Johnson, C. E., Vinson, L., Hackman, M., & Hardin, T. (1989). The effects of an instructor's use of hesitation forms on student ratings of quality, recommendations to hire, and lecture listening. *Journal of the International Listening Association, 3,* 32–43.

Johnson, J. R. (1984). The role of inner speech in human communication. *Communication Education, 33,* 211–222.

Jones, D. (2007, May 30). Do foreign executives balk at sports jargon? *USA Today,* pp. B1, B2.

Jones, J. (2013). Factors influencing mentees' and mentors' learning throughout formal mentoring relationships. *Human Resource Development International, 16,* 390–408.

Jones, L. B. (1996). *The path: Creating your mission statement for work and life.* New York: Hyperion.

Jones, T. M. (1991). Ethical decision making by individuals in organizations: An issue-contingent approach. *Academy of Management Review, 16,* 366–395.

Joyce, L. (2005, March 1). It's Google mania! *R and D.*

Judge, T. A., Bono, J. E., Ilies, R., & Gerhardt, M. W. (2002). Personality and leadership: A qualitative and quantitative review. *Journal of Applied Psychology, 87,* 765–780.

Judge, T. A., & Piccolo, R. F. (2004). Transformational and transactional leadership: A meta-analytic test of their relative validity. *Journal of Applied Psychology, 89,* 755–768.

Julien, M., Wright, B., & Zinni, D. M. (2010). Stories from the circle: Leadership lessons learned from aboriginal leaders. *Leadership Quarterly, 21,* 114–126.

Jussim, L., Madon, S., & Chatman, C. (1994). Teacher expectations and student achievement: Self-fulfilling prophecies, biases, and accuracy. In L. Heath et al. (Eds.), *Applications of heuristics and biases to social issues* (pp. 303–334). New York: Plenum Press.

Kahane, A. (2010, March 14). Learning from experience: The Mont Fleur scenario exercise. *Reos Partners.*

Kahn, R. L. (1956). The prediction of productivity. *Journal of Social Issues, 12,* 41–49.

Kahnweiller, J. (2009). *The introverted leader: Building on your quiet strength.* San Francisco: Berrett-Koehler.

Kaiman, J. (2014, September 19). Jack Ma profile—Alibaba's powerful but humble billionaire. *The Guardian.*

Kant, I. (1964). *Groundwork for the metaphysics of morals* (H. J. Ryan, Trans.). New York: Harper & Row.

Kanter, R. M. (1977). *Men and women of the corporation.* New York: Basic Books.

Kanter, R. M. (1977). Some effects of proportions on group life: Skewed sex ratios and responses to token women. *American Journal of Sociology, 82,* 969–990.

Kanter, R. M. (1979, July–August). Power failure in management circuits. *Harvard Business Review, 57,* 65.

Kanter, R. M. (2001). An Abilene defense: Commentary one. *Organizational Dynamics, 17,* 37–39.

Kanter, R. M. (2010, July/August). Powerlessness corrupts. *Harvard Business Review,* 36.

Kantor, J., & Streitfeld, D. (2015, August 15). Inside Amazon: Wrestling big ideas in a bruising workplace. *The New York Times.*

Kanungo, R. N., & Conger, J. A. (1990). The quest for altruism in organizations. In S. Srivastva and D. L. Cooperrider and Associates (Eds.), *Appreciative management and leadership: The power of positive thought and action in organizations* (pp. 228–256). San Francisco: Jossey-Bass.

Kanungo, R. N., & Mendonica, M. (1996). *Ethical dimensions of leadership.* Thousand Oaks, CA: Sage.

Karanika-Murray, M., Bartholomew, K. J., Williams, G. A., & Cox, T. (2015). Leader-member exchange across two hierarchical levels of leadership: Concurrent influences on work characteristics and employee psychological health. *Work & Stress, 29,* 57–74.

Kassing, J. W. (2002). Speaking up: Identifying employees' upward dissent strategies. *Management Communication Quarterly, 16*, 187–209.

Kassing, J. W. (2005). Speaking up competently: A comparison of perceived competence in upward dissent strategies. *Communication Research Reports, 22*, 227–234.

Kassing, J. W. (2011). *Dissent in organizations*. Cambridge, UK: Polity Press.

Kassing, J. W., & Kava, W. (2013). Assessing disagreement expressed to management: Development of the Upward Dissent Scale. *Communication Research Reports, 50*, 46–56.

Katz, D., Maccoby, N., Gurin, G., & Floor, L. (1951). *Productivity, supervision, and morale among railroad workers*. Ann Arbor: University of Michigan, Institute for Social Research.

Katz, D., Maccoby, N., & Morse, N. (1950). *Productivity, supervision, and morale in an office situation*. Ann Arbor: University of Michigan, Institute for Social Research.

Katz, R. L. (1955). Skills of an effective administrator. *Harvard Business Review, 33*, 33–42.

Katzenbach, J. R. (2003). *Why pride matters more than money: The power of the world's greatest motivational force*. New York: Crown Business.

Katzenbach, J. R., & Smith, D. K. (1993). *The wisdom of teams*. Boston: Harvard Business School Press.

Katzenbach, J. R., & Smith, D. K. (1993, March–April). The discipline of teams. *Harvard Business Review*, 111–120.

Kayworth, T. R., & Leidner, D. E. (2001–2002). Leadership effectiveness in global virtual teams. *Journal of Management Information Systems, 18*, 7–40.

Kearney, P., Plax, T. G., Sorenson, G., & Smith, V. R. (1988). Experienced and prospective teachers' selections of compliance-gaining messages for "common" student misbehaviors. *Communication Education, 37*, 150–164.

Keil, M., & Montealegre, R. (2000, Spring). Cutting your losses: Extracting your organization when a big project goes awry. *Sloan Management Review, 41*, 55–68.

Kelion, L. (2013, September 23). Valve: How going boss-free empowered the games-maker. *BBC*.

Kellerman, B. (2004). *Bad leadership*. Boston: Harvard University Press.

Kellerman, B. (2008). *Followership: How followers are creating change and changing leaders*. Boston: Harvard Business School Press.

Kelley, H. (2016, August 11). Uber's never-ending stream of lawsuits. *CNNMoney*.

Kelley, R. (1988, November–December). In praise of followers. *Harvard Business Review, 66*, 142–148.

Kelley, R. E. (1992). *The power of followership: How to create leaders that people want to follow and followers who lead themselves*. New York: Doubleday/Currency.

Kelley R. E. (1998). Followership in a leadership world. In L. C. Spears (Ed.), *Insights on leadership: Service, stewardship, spirit, and servant-leadership* (pp. 170–184). New York: Wiley.

Kelman, H. C., & Hovland, C. I. (1953). "Reinstatement" of the communicator in delayed measurement of opinion change. *Journal of Abnormal and Social Psychology, 48*, 327–335.

Keltner, D., Langner, C. A., & Allison, M. L. (2006). Power and moral leadership. In D. L. Rhode (Ed.), *Moral leadership: The theory and practice of power, judgment and policy* (pp. 177–194). San Francisco: Jossey-Bass.

Kemp, K. F., & Smith, W. P. (1994). Information exchange, toughness, and integrative bargaining: The roles of explicit cues and perspective-take. *The International Journal of Conflict Management, 5*, 5–12.

Kenny, D. A., & Zaccaro, S. J. (1983). An estimate of variance due to traits in leadership. *Journal of Applied Psychology, 68*, 678–685.

Kernis, M. H. (2003). Toward a conceptualization of optimal self-esteem. *Psychological Inquiry, 14*, 1–26.

Ki, E-J., & Hon L. C. (2007). Testing the linkages among the organization-public relationship and attitude and behavioral intentions. *Journal of Public Relations Research 19*, 1–23.

Kim, L. (1998). Crisis construction and organizational learning: Capability building in catching-up at Hyundai Motor. *Organization Science, 9*, 506–521.

Kim, Y. (2001). Searching for the organizational-public relationship: A valid and reliable instrument. *Journalism & Mass Communication Quarterly, 78,* 799–815.

Kirkman, B. L., Rosen, B., Gibson, C. B., Tesluk, P. E., & McPherson, S. O. (2002). Five challenges to virtual team success: Lessons from Sabre, Inc. *Academy of Management Executive, 16,* 67–79.

Kirkpatrick, S. A., & Locke, E. A. (1991). Leadership: Do traits matter? *The Executive, 5,* 48–60.

Kline, T. (1999). *Remaking teams: The revolutionary research-based guide that puts theory into practice.* San Francisco: Jossey-Bass.

Knittel, R. E. (1974). Essential and nonessential ritual programs of planned change. *Human Organization, 33,* 394–396.

Koch, J. (2001, March). Thinking outside the box at The Container Store. *Workforce,* pp. 34–38.

Kogler Hill, S. E., Bahniuk, M. H., & Dobbs, J. (1989). The impact of mentoring and collegial support on faculty success: An analysis of support behavior information adequacy, and communication apprehension. *Communication Education, 38,* 15–33.

Kolditz, T. A. (2005, Fall Supplement). The in extremis leader. *Leader to Leader,* pp. 6–18.

Kolditz, T. A. (2007). *In extremis leadership: Leading as if your life depended on it.* San Francisco: Jossey-Bass.

Kolditz, T. A., & Brazil, D. M. (2005). Authentic leadership in extremis settings: A concept for extraordinary leaders in exceptional situations. In W. L. Gardner, B. J. Avolio, & F. O. Walumbwa (Eds.), *Authentic leadership theory and practice: Origins, effects and development* (pp. 345–356). Amsterdam: Elsevier.

Koleva, S. P., Graham, J., Iyer, R., Ditto, P. H., & Haidt, J. (2012). Tracing the threads: How the five moral concerns (especially purity) help explain culture war attitudes. *Journal of Research in Personality, 46*(2), 184–194.

Konrad, A. M. (2006). Leveraging workplace diversity in organizations. *Organization Management Journal, 3,* 164–189.

Kotler, S. (2016, February 23). The eight principles that made Google the most innovative company on earth. *Observer.*

Kotter, J. P. (1990). *A force for change: How leadership differs from management.* New York: The Free Press.

Kotter, J. P. (1999). *On what leaders really do.* Boston: Harvard Business School Press.

Kouzes, J. M., & Posner, B. Z. (1987). *The leadership challenge: How to get extraordinary things done in organizations.* San Francisco: Jossey-Bass.

Kouzes, J. M., & Posner, B. Z. (2002). *The leadership challenge: How to get extraordinary things done in organizations* (3rd ed.). San Francisco: Jossey-Bass.

Kouzes, J. M., & Posner, B. Z. (2007). *The leadership challenge: How to get extraordinary things done in organizations* (4th ed.). San Francisco: Jossey-Bass.

Kouzes, J. M., & Posner, B. Z. (2011). *Credibility: How leaders gain and lose, why people demand it* (Rev. ed.). San Francisco: Jossey-Bass.

Kouzes, J. M., & Posner, B. Z. (2012). *The leadership challenge: How to get extraordinary things done in organizations* (5th ed.). San Francisco: Jossey-Bass.

Kram, K. E. (1985). *Mentoring at work: Developmental relationships in organizational life.* Glenview, IL: Scott, Foresman and Company.

Kram, K. E., & Bragar, M. C. (1992). Development through mentoring: A strategic approach. In D. H. Montross & C. J. Shinkman (Eds.), *Career development: Theory and practice* (pp. 221–254). Springfield, IL: Charles C. Thomas.

Kram, K. E., & Isabella, L. A. (1985). Mentoring alternatives: The role of peer relationships in career development. *Academy of Management Review, 28,* 110–132.

Kramer, R. M. (1999). Trust and distrust in organizations: Emerging perspectives, enduring questions. *Annual Review of Psychology, 50,* 569–598.

Kramer, R. M., & Tyler, T. R. (1996). *Trust in organizations: Frontiers of theory and research.* Thousand Oaks, CA: Sage.

Krantz, M., & Hansen, B. (2011, April 4). CEO pay soars while workers' pay stalls. *USA Today*.

Krech, D., & Crutchfield, R. (1948). *Theory and problems of social psychology*. New York: McGraw-Hill.

Kriegel, R., & Brandt, D. (1996). *Sacred cows make the best burgers: Paradigm-busting strategies for developing change-ready people and organizations*. New York: Warner Books.

Kriegel, R. J., & Patler, L. (1991). *If it ain't broke . . . break it!* New York: Warner Books.

Kriger, M., & Zhovtobryukh, Y. (2016). *Strategic leadership for turbulent times*. New York: Springer, p. 139.

Kurchner-Hawkins, R., & Miller, R. (2006). Organizational politics: Building positive political strategies in turbulent times. In E. Vigoda-Gadot & A. Drory (Eds.), *Handbook of organizational politics* (pp. 328–351). Cheltenham, UK: Edward Elgar.

Kumar, R., & Sethi, K. (2006). *Doing business in India: A guide for Western managers*. New York: Palgrave Macmillan.

Kumkale, G. T., & Albarracin, D. (2004). The sleeper effect in persuasion: A meta-analytic review. *Psychological Bulletin, 130*, 143–172.

Ladkin, D. (2008). Leading beautifully: How mastery, congruence and purpose create the aesthetic of embodied leadership practice. *Leadership Quarterly, 19*, 31–41.

LaFasto, F., & Larson, C. (2001). *When teams work best*. Thousand Oaks, CA: Sage.

Lake, N. (2006). *The strategic planning handbook* (2nd ed.). London: Kogan Page.

Landauer, T. J. (1962). Rate of implicit speech. *Perceptual and Motor Skills, 15*, 646.

Langer, E. J. (1989). *Mindfulness*. Reading MA: Addison-Wesley.

Lao-Tzu. (1993). *Tao te ching* (Trans. S. Addiss & S. Lombardo, Ch. 8). Indianapolis, IN: Hackett.

Larrabee, W. (1972). Paralinguistics, kinesics, and cultural anthropology. In L. Samovar & R. Porter (Eds.), *Intercultural communication: A reader* (pp. 172–180). Belmont, CA: Wadsworth.

Larson, C. E. (1969). Forms of analysis and small group problem-solving. *Speech Monographs, 36*, 452–455.

Larson, C. E., & LaFasto, F. M. J. (1989). *Teamwork: What must go right/What can go wrong*. Newbury Park, CA: Sage.

Lashinsky, A. (2016, March 4). Why Amazon tolerates Zappos' extreme management experiment. *Fortune.com*.

Lawrence, P. R., & Lorsch, J. W. (1967). *Organization and environment*. Cambridge, MA: Harvard University Press.

Learman, L. A., Avorn, J., Everitt, D. E., & Rosenthal, R. (1990). Pygmalion in the nursing home: The effects of caregiver expectations on patient outcomes. *Journal of the American Geriatrics Society, 38*, 797–803.

Learn the lingo: 10 sports terms that became business terms. (2013, December 3). *Gal's Got Game*.

Leathers, D. G., & Eaves, M. H. (2008). *Successful nonverbal communication: Principles and applications* (4th ed.). New York: Macmillan.

Lee, Y-T., Chen, W., & Chan, S. X (2013). Daoism and altruism: China-USA perspective. In D. A. Vakoch (Ed.), *Altruism in cross-cultural perspective* (pp. 85–99). New York: Springer.

Lee, Y-T., Haught, H., Chen, K., & Chan, S. (2013). Examining Daoist Big-Five leadership in cross-cultural and gender perspectives. *Asian American Journal of Psychology, 4*, 267–276.

Lee, Y-T., Yang, H., & Ming, M. (2009). Daoist harmony as a Chinese philosophy and psychology. *Peace and Conflict Studies, 16*, Article 5.

Lengnick-Hall, C. A., Beck, T. E., & Lengnick-Hall, M. L. (2011). Developing a capacity for organizational resilience through strategic human resource management. *Human Resource Management Review, 21*, 243–255.

Leslie, J. B., & Van Velsor, E. (1996). *A look at derailment today: North America and Europe*. Greensboro, NC: Center for Creative Leadership.

Lester, P. B., Hannah, S. T., Harms, P. D., Vogelgesang, G. R., & Avolio, B. (2011). Mentoring impact on leader efficacy development: A field experiment. *Academy of Management Learning & Education, 10*, 409–429.

Levere, J. L. (2016, August 15). Airbnb for business travelers: More wi-fi, fewer hosts in towels. *The New York Times.*

Lewin, K., Lippitt, R., & White, R. K. (1939). Patterns of aggressive behavior in experimentally created "social climates." *Journal of Social Psychology, 10,* 271–299.

Ley, R. (1966). Labor turnover as a function of worker differences, work environment, and authoritarianism of foremen. *Journal of Applied Psychology, 50,* 497–500.

Lichtenwainer, B. (2011, March 1). *Fortune's* best companies to work for with servant leadership. *Modern Servant Leader.*

Lien, T. (2016, May 2). Uber sued again over drivers' employment status. *Los Angeles Times.*

Lim, Y-S., & Van Der Heide, B. (2015). Evaluating the wisdom of strangers: The perceived credibility of online consumer reviews on Yelp. *Journal of Computer-Mediated Communication, 20,* 67–82.

Lipman-Blumen, J. (2005). *The allure of toxic leaders.* New York: Oxford University Press.

Litzinger, W., & Schaefer, T. (1982, September–October). Leadership through followership. *Business Horizons,* 78–81.

Livingston, J. S. (1969). Pygmalion in management. *Harvard Business Review, 47,* 81–89.

Locke, E. A. (1991). *The essence of leadership: Four keys to leading successfully.* Lanham, MD: Lexington Books.

Locke, E. A., & Latham, G. P. (1990). *A theory of goal setting & task performance.* Englewood Cliffs, NJ: Prentice-Hall.

Lombardo, M. M., & McCauley, C. D. (1988). *The dynamics of management derailment.* Technical Report No. 34. Greensboro, NC: Center for Creative Leadership.

Lord, R. G., & Brown, D. J. (2004). *Leadership processes and follower self-identity.* Mahwah, NJ: Lawrence Erlbaum.

Lord, R. G., De Vader, C. L., & Alliger, G. M. (1986). A meta-analysis of the relation between personality traits and leadership perceptions: An application of validity generalization procedures. *Journal of Applied Psychology, 71,* 402–410.

Lord, R. G., & Maher, K. J. (1991). *Leadership and information processing: Linking perceptions and performance.* Boston: Unwin Hyman.

Louw, D. J. (2001). *Ubuntu and the challenges of multiculturalism in post-apartheid South Africa.* Available from http://www.phys.uu.nl/~unitwin/ubuntu.html

Lovegrove, I. (2013). Leaders in Antarctica: Characteristics of an Antarctic station manager. In C. M. Giannantonio & A. E. Hurley-Hanson (Eds.), *Extreme leadership: Leaders, teams and situations outside the norm* (pp. 47–61). Cheltenham, UK: Edward Elgar.

Lowe, K. B., & Kroek, K. G. (1996). Effectiveness correlates of transformational and transactional leadership: A meta-analytic review. *Leadership Quarterly, 7,* 385–425.

Lowery, W., Leoning, C. D., & Berman, M. (2014, August 13). Even before Michael Brown's slaying in Ferguson, racial questions hung over police. *The Washington Post.*

Lubit, R. (2002). The long-term organizational impact of destructively narcissistic managers. *Academy of Management Executive, 16(1),* 127–138.

Lublin, J. S. (2006, October 12). Executive pay soars despite attempted restraints. *Associated Press Financial Wire.*

Lucas, S. E. (2003). *The art of public speaking* (7th ed.). Boston: McGraw-Hill.

Luke, J. S. (1994). Character and conduct in the public service. In T. L. Cooper (Ed.), *The handbook of administrative ethics* (pp. 391–412). New York: Marcel Dekker.

Luke, J. S. (1998). *Catalytic leadership: Strategies for an interconnected world.* San Francisco: Jossey-Bass.

Lumsen, G., Lumsen, D., & Wiethoff, C. (2010). *Communicating in groups and teams: Sharing leadership.* Boston: Wadsworth.

Lundin, S. C., Paul, H., & Christensen, J. (2000). *Fish! A proven way to boost morale and improve results.* New York: Hyperion.

Luria, A. R. (1982). *Language and cognition.* J. V. Wertsch (Ed.). New York: Wiley.

Luria, G., & Berson, Y. (2013). How do leadership motives affect informal and formal leadership emergence? *Journal of Organizational Behavior, 34,* 995–1015.

Lustig, M. W., & Koester, J. (2006). *Intercultural competence: Interpersonal competence across cultures* (5th ed.). Boston: Allyn & Bacon.

Lutz, A. (2014, October 13). Nordstrom's employee handbook has only one rule. *Business Insider.*

Lutz, W. (1989). *Doublespeak.* New York: Harper & Row.

Lynam, D. R., & Milich, R. (1999). Project DARE: No effect at 10-year follow-up. *Journal of Consulting & Clinical Psychology, 67,* 590–594.

Maas, A., & Clark, R. D. (1984). Hidden impact of minorities: Fifteen years of minority influence research. *Psychological Bulletin, 95,* 428–450.

MacLeod, C. (2014, September 19). Alibaba's Jack Ma: From "crazy" to China's richest man. *USA Today.*

MacIntyre, A. (1984). *After virtue: A study in moral theory* (2nd ed.). Notre Dame, IN: University of Notre Dame Press.

Mackinnon, J. B. (2015, May 21). Patagonia's anti-growth strategy. *The New Yorker.*

Magaziner, I. C., & Patinkin, M. (1989). *The silent war: Inside the global business battles shaping America's future.* New York: Random House.

Mahortra, A., Majchrzak, A., & Roson, B. (2007). Leading virtual teams. *Academy of Management Perspectives, 21,* 60–70.

Manning, G., & Curtis, K. (2015). *The art of leadership* (5th ed.) Boston: McGraw-Hill.

Manz, C. C., & Neck, C. P. (1995). Teamthink: Beyond the groupthink syndrome in self-managing work teams. *Journal of Managerial Psychology, 10,* 7–15.

Manz, C. C., & Sims, H. P. (1989). *SuperLeadership: Leading others to lead themselves.* New York: Prentice-Hall.

Marquand, R. (2010, July 28). Robert Dudley, a Yank, takes BP helm. *The Christian Science Monitor.*

Marquardt, M. (2005). *Leading with questions.* San Francisco: Jossey-Bass.

Marquardt, M. J., & Berger, N. O. (2000). *Global leaders for the 21st century.* Albany: State University of New York Press.

Martin, F. (2002, April). So you failed . . . so what? *Unlimited,* p. 48.

Martin, H. (2012, May 25). Clothier's products all come in green. *Los Angeles Times,* p. B1.

Martin, J. (1992). *Cultures in organizations.* New York: Oxford University Press.

Martin, J. (2002). *Organizational culture: Mapping the terrain.* Thousand Oaks, CA: Sage.

Martin, J., & Powers, M. E. (1983). Truth or corporate propaganda: The value of a good story. In L. R. Pondy, P. J. Frost, G. Morgan, & T. C. Dandridge (Eds.), *Organizational symbolism* (pp. 93–107). Greenwich, CT: JAI Press.

Martin, P., & Tate, K. (2001). *Getting started in project management.* New York: Wiley.

Maslow, A. H. (1970). *Motivation and personality.* New York: Harper & Row.

Masnick, M. (2016, November 21). Theranos's insane campaign to punish whistleblower, who happened to be famous board member's grandson. *Techdirt.*

Masters, C. (2007, August 30). How Boeing got going. *Time.*

Matta, F. K., Scott, B. A., Koopman, J., & Conlon, D. E. (2015). Does seeing "eye to eye" affect work engagement and organizational citizenship behavior? A role theory perspective on LMX agreement. *Academy of Management Journal, 58,* 1686–1708.

Mattera, P. (n.d.). Deutsche Bank: Corporate rap sheet. *Corporate Research Project.*

Maxwell, J. (2000). *Failing forward: Turning mistakes into stepping-stones for success.* Nashville, TN: Thomas Nelson Publishers.

Mayer, D. M., Bardes, M., & Piccolo, R. F. (2008). Do servant-leaders help satisfy follower needs? An organizational justice perspective. *European Journal of Work and Organizational Psychology, 17*(2), 180–197.

Mayer, R. C., & Gavin, M. B. (2005). Trust in management and performance: Who minds the shop while the employees watch the boss? *Academy of Management Journal, 48,* 874–888.

Mayer, J. D. (2001). A field guide to emotional intelligence. In J. Ciarrochi, J. P. Forgas, & J. D. Mayer (Eds.), *Emotional intelligence in everyday life: A scientific inquiry* (pp. 3–24). Philadelphia: Psychology Press.

McCall, M. W. (2010). Recasting leadership development. *Industrial and Organizational Psychology, 3*, 3–19.

McCauley, C. D. (2001). Leader training and development. In S. J. Zaccaro & R. J. Klimoski (Eds.), *The nature of organizational leadership: Understanding the performance imperatives confronting today's leaders* (pp. 347–383). San Francisco: Jossey-Bass.

McClelland, D. C. (1975). *Power: The inner experience.* New York: Wiley.

McClelland, D. C. (1982). Leadership motive pattern and long-term success in management. *Journal of Applied Psychology, 67*, 737–743.

McCrae, R. R., & Costa, P. T. (1987). Validation of the five-factor model of personality across instruments and observers. *Journal of Personality and Social Psychology, 52*, 81–90.

McCroskey, J. C., & Richmond, V. P. (1990). Willingness to communicate: Differing cultural perspectives. *Southern Communication Journal, 56*, 72–77.

McCroskey, J. C., & Richmond, V. P. (1996). *Fundamentals of human communication: An interpersonal perspective.* Long Grove, IL: Waveland Press.

McCroskey, J. C., & Richmond, V. P. (1998). Willingness to communicate. In J. C. McCroskey, J. A. Daly, M. M. Martin, & M. J. Beatty (Eds.), *Communication and personality: Trait perspectives* (pp. 119–131). Cresswell, NJ: Hampton Press.

McCroskey, J. C., & Young, T. J. (1981). Ethos and credibility: The construct and its measurement after three decades. *Central States Speech Journal, 32*, 24–34.

McCuddy, M. K., & Cavin, M. C. (2008). Fundamental moral orientations, servant leadership, and leadership effectiveness: An empirical test. *Review of Business Research, 8*(4), 107–117.

McGee-Cooper, A., & Trammell, D. (2002). From hero-as-leader to servant-as-leader. In L. C. Spears & M. Lawrence (Eds.), *Focus on leadership: Servant-leadership for the 21st century* (pp. 145–146). New York: Wiley.

McGregor, D. (1960). *The human side of enterprise.* New York: McGraw-Hill.

McGuire, W. J. (1989). Theoretical foundations of campaigns. In R. E. Rice & C. K. Atkin (Eds.), *Public communication campaigns* (2nd ed., pp. 43–65). Newbury Park, CA: Sage.

McKay, J. (2014, September 12). Chief resilience officers: Coming to your city? *Emergency Management.*

McMahan, E. M. (1976). Nonverbal communication as a function of attribution in impression formation. *Communication Monographs, 43*, 287–294.

McNatt, D. B. (2000). Ancient Pygmalion joins contemporary management: A meta-analysis of the result. *Journal of Applied Psychology, 85*, 314–322.

McPhate, M. (2016, June 28). Ikea recalls 29 million chests and dressers after 6 children die. *The New York Times.*

Mednick, S. A. (1962). The associative basis of the creative process. *Psychological Review, 69*, 221.

Meilander, G. (1986). Virtue in contemporary religious thought. In R. J. Nehaus (Ed.), *Virtue: Public and private* (pp. 7–30). Grand Rapids, MI: Eerdmans.

Meinert, D. (2014, July 22). Leadership development spending is up. Society for Human Resource Management 2015 training industry report (n.d.). *Training.*

Mellor, W., Chen, L. Y., & Wu, Z. (2014, November 9). Ma says Alibaba shareholders should feel love, not no. 3. *Bloomberg.com.*

Meltzer, L. (1956). Scientific productivity in organizational settings. *Journal of Social Issues, 12*, 32–40.

Michelli, J. A. (2012). *The Zappos experience: 5 principles to inspire, engage, and WOW.* New York: McGraw-Hill.

Miczo, N. (2004). Humor ability, unwillingness to communicate, loneliness, and perceived stress: Testing a security theory. *Communication Studies, 55*(2), 209–226.

Miethe, T. D. (1999). *Whistleblowing at work: Tough choices in exposing fraud, waste, and abuse on the job.* Boulder, CO: Westview Press, p. 209.

Miller, A. N. (2002). An exploration of Kenyan public speaking patterns with implications for the American introductory public speaking course. *Communication Education, 51,* 168–182.

Miller, B. K., Rutherford, M. A., & Kolodinsky, R. W. (2008). Perceptions of organizational politics: A meta-analysis. *Journal of Business Psychology, 22,* 209–222.

Miller, D., Kets De Vries, M. F. R., & Toulouse, J-M. (1982). Top executive locus of control and its relationship to strategy-making, structure, and environment. *Academy of Management Journal, 25,* 237–253.

Miller, G. R. (1969). Contributions of communication research to the study of speech. In A. H. Monroe & D. Ehninger (Eds.), *Principles and types of speech communication* (6th brief ed., pp. 334–357). Glenview, IL: Scott Foresman.

Milner, J., Ostmeier, E., & Franke, R. (2013). Critical incidents in cross-cultural coaching: The view from German coaches. *International Journal of Evidence Based Coaching and Mentoring, 11,* 19–31.

Mirvis, P. (1996, March). Can you teach your people to think smarter? *Across the Board,* 26–27.

Mishra, A. K. (1996). Organizational responses to crisis: The centrality of trust. In R. M. Kramer & T. R. Tyler (Eds.), *Trust in organizations: Frontiers of theory and research* (pp. 261–287). Thousand Oaks, CA: Sage.

Mishra, R. (2003, August 27). Probe hits NASA in crash of shuttle. *The Boston Globe,* p. A1.

Misumi, J., & Peterson, M. F. (1985). The Performance-Maintenance theory of leadership: Review of a Japanese research program. *Administrative Science Quarterly, 30,* 198–223.

Mitroff, I. I. (2005). *Why some companies emerge stronger and better from a crisis.* New York: AMACOM.

Mitroff, I. I., & Alpasian, M. C. (2003, April). Preparing for evil. *Harvard Business Review,* 109–115.

Mitroff, I. I., & Anagnos, G. (2001). *Managing crises before they happen.* New York: American Management Association.

Mitroff, I., & Denton, E. A. (1999). *A spiritual audit of corporate America: A hard look at spirituality, religion, and values in the workplace.* San Francisco: Jossey-Bass.

Mitroff, I., & Denton, E. A. (1999, Summer). A study of spirituality in the workplace. *Sloan Management Review, 40,* 83–92.

Mitroff, I. I., & Pearson, C. M. (1993). *Crisis management: A diagnostic guide for improving your organization's crisis-preparedness.* San Francisco: Jossey-Bass.

Mitroff, I. I., Pearson, C. M., & Harrington, L. K. (1996). *The essential guide to managing corporate crises: A step-by-step handbook for surviving major catastrophes.* New York: Oxford University Press.

Mohr, L. B. (1971). Organizational technology and organizational structure. *Administrative Science Quarterly, 16,* 444–459.

Moorhead, G., Neck, C. P., & West, M. S. (1998). The tendency toward defective decision making within self-managing teams: The relevance of groupthink for the 21st century. *Organizational Behavior and Human Decision Processes, 73,* 327–351.

Mor Barak, M. E. (2011). *Managing diversity: Toward a globally inclusive workplace* (2nd ed.). Thousand Oaks, CA: Sage.

Morreale, S. P. (2007). *Assessing motivation to communicate: Willingness to communicate and personal report of communication apprehension* (2nd ed.). Washington, DC: National Communication Association.

Morrison, A. M., White, R. P., & Van Velsor, E. (1987, August). Executive women: Substance plus style. *Psychology Today,* 18–26.

Morse, R. S. (2008). Developing public leaders in an age of collaborative governance. In R. S. Morse & T. F. Buss (Eds.), *Innovations in public leadership development* (pp. 79–100). Armonk, NY: M. E. Sharpe.

Morse, R. S. (2010). Integrative public leadership: Catalyzing collaboration to create public value. *Leadership Quarterly, 21,* 231–245.

Mortensen, C. D. (1966). Should the discussion group have an assigned leader? *The Speech Teacher, 15,* 34–41.

Moscovici, S., Mugny, G., & Van Avermaet, E. (Eds.). (1985). *Perspectives on minority influence.* Cambridge: Cambridge University Press.

Moss, G. (2010). Introduction. In G. Moss (Ed.), *Profiting from diversity: The business advantage and the obstacles to achieving diversity* (pp. 3–18). Houndmills, UK: Palgrave Macmillan.

Moxley, R. S., & Pulley, M. L. (2004). Hardships. In C. D. McCauley, R. S. Moxley, & E. Van Velsor (Eds.), *The Center for Creative Leadership handbook of leadership development* (2nd ed., pp. 183–203). San Francisco: Jossey-Bass.

Mullen, E. J. (1998). Vocational and psychosocial mentoring functions: Identifying mentors who serve both. *Human Resource Development Quarterly, 9,* 319–331.

Mulvey, P. W., & Padilla, A. (2010). The environment of destructive leadership. In B. Schyns & T. Hansbrough (Eds.), *When leadership goes wrong: Destructive leadership mistakes and ethical failures* (pp. 49–71). Charlotte, NC: Information Age.

Mumford, M. D. (2006). *Pathways to outstanding leadership: A comparative analysis of charismatic, ideological, and pragmatic leaders.* Mahwah, NJ: Lawrence Erlbaum.

Mumford, M. D., Antes, A. L., Caughron, J. J., & Friedrich, T. L. (2008). Charismatic, ideological, and pragmatic leadership: Multi-level influences on emergence and performance. *Leadership Quarterly, 19,* 144–160.

Mumford, M. D., Marks, M. A., Connelly, M. S., Zaccaro, S. J., & Reiter-Palmon, R. (2000). Development of leadership skills: Experience and timing. *Leadership Quarterly, 11,* 87–114.

Mumford, M. D., & Van Doorn, J. R. (2001). The leadership of pragmatism: Reconsidering Franklin in the age of charisma. *Leadership Quarterly, 12,* 274–309.

Mumford, M. D., Zacarro, S. J., Connelly, M S., & Marks, M. A. (2000). Leadership skills: Conclusions and future directions. *Leadership Quarterly, 11,* 155–170.

Mumford, M. D., Zaccaro, S. J., Harding, F. D., Jacobs, J. O., & Fleishman, E. A. (2000). Leadership skills for a changing world: Solving complex social problems. *Leadership Quarterly, 11,* 11–35.

Munyaka, M. & Motlhabi, M. (2009). Ubuntu and its socio-moral significance. In M. F. Munyaradzi (Ed.), *African ethics: An anthology of comparative and applied ethics* (pp. 63–84). Scottsville, South Africa: University of KwaZulu-Natal Press.

Muringham, J. K., & Leung, T. K. (1976). The effects of leadership involvement and the importance of the task on subordinates' performance. *Organizational Behavior and Human Performance, 17,* 299–310.

Murray, M. (1991). *Beyond the myths and magic of mentoring.* San Francisco: Jossey-Bass.

Muscovici, S., Mugny, G., & Van Avermaet, E. (Eds.). (1985). *Perspectives on minority influence.* Cambridge, MA: Cambridge University Press.

Nahavandi, A. (2006). *The art and science of leadership* (4th ed.). Upper Saddle River, NJ: Pearson Prentice-Hall.

Nanus, B. (1992). *Visionary leadership.* San Francisco: Jossey-Bass.

Neale, M. A., & Bazerman, M. H. (1983). The role of perspective-taking ability in negotiating under different forms of arbitration. *Industrial and Labor Relations, 36,* 378–388.

Neck, C. P., & Houghton, J. D. (2006). Two decades of self-leadership theory and research: Past developments, present trends, and future possibilities. *Journal of Managerial Psychology, 21,* 270–295.

Neck, C. P., Manz, C. C. & Houghton, J. D. (2017). *Self-leadership: The definitive guide to personal excellence.* Los Angeles: Sage.

Neff, T. J., & Citrin, J. M. (1999). *Lessons from the top.* New York: Doubleday.

New college students and risky alcohol behaviors. (2016). *National Social Norms Center.*

Newsom, D., Van Slyke Turk, J., & Kruckeberg, D. (2004). *This is PR: The realities of public relations* (8th ed.). Stanford, CA: Wadsworth/Thompson Learning.

Nichols, R. G. (1961). Do we know how to listen? Practical helps in a modern age. *The Speech Teacher, 10,* 120–124.

Nielsen, R. P. (1998). Quaker foundations for Greenleaf's servant-leadership and "friendly disentangling" method. In L. Spears (Ed.), *Insights of leadership* (pp. 126–144). New York: Wiley.

Nordstrom, Inc. (2016). *Great place to work reviews*. Retrieved from http://reviews.greatplacetowork.com/

Northouse, P. (2010). *Leadership: Theory and practice* (5th ed.). Thousand Oaks, CA: Sage.

Northouse, P. (2013). *Leadership: Theory and practice* (6th ed.). Thousand Oaks, CA: Sage.

Novicevic, M., Harvey, M. G., Buckley, H. R., Brown, J. A., & Evans, R. (2006). Authentic leadership: A historical perspective. *Journal of Leadership and Organizational Studies, 23,* 64–76.

Nowack, K. M., & Mashihi, S. (2012). Evidence-based answers to 15 questions about leveraging 360-degree feedback. *Consulting Psychology Journal: Practice and Research, 64,* 157–182.

Nye, J. S. (2008). *The powers to lead*. Oxford, UK: Oxford University Press.

Oakley, G. (2000). Gender-based barriers to senior management positions: Understanding the scarcity of female CEOS. *Journal of Business Ethics, 27,* 321–334.

O'Barr, W. (1984). Asking the right questions about language and power. In C. Kramarae, M. Schulz, & W. O'Barr (Eds.), *Language and power* (pp. 260–280). Beverly Hills, CA: Sage.

Offermann, L. R., & Hellmann, P. S. (1997). Culture's consequences for leadership behavior: National values in action. *Journal of Cross-Cultural Psychology, 28,* 342–351.

Ohlott, P. J. (2004). Job assignments. In C. D. McCauley, R. S. Moxley, & E. Van Velsor (Eds.), *The Center for Creative Leadership handbook of leadership development* (2nd ed., pp. 151–182). San Francisco: Jossey-Bass.

O'Keefe, D. J. (1987). The persuasive effects of delaying identification of high and low-credibility communicators: A meta-analytic review. *Central States Speech Journal, 38,* 63–72.

Olaniran, B. A., & Williams, D. E. (2001). Anticipatory model of crisis management: A vigilant response to technological crises. In R. L. Heath (Ed.), *Handbook of public relations* (pp. 487–500). Thousand Oaks, CA: Sage.

Olen, H. (2016, October 13). Why the Wells Fargo scandal is different. *Slate.*

Olson, A. K., & Simerson, B. K. (2015). *Leading with strategic thinking: Four ways effective leaders gain insight*. Hoboken, NJ: Wiley.

Olson, D. A., & Jackson, D. (2009). Expanding leadership diversity through formal mentoring programs. *Journal of Leadership Studies, 3,* 47–60.

Onishi, N. (2014, August 20). Clashes erupt as Liberia sets an Ebola quarantine. *The New York Times.*

Opotow, S. (1990). Moral exclusion and injustice: An introduction. *Journal of Social Issues, 46,* 1–20.

Orsag Madigan, C., & Elwood, A. (1983). *Brainstorms and thunderbolts*. New York: Macmillan.

Ortega, A., Van den Bossche, P., Sanchez-Manzanares, M., Rice, R., & Gil, F. (2014). The influence of change-oriented leadership and psychological safety on team learning in healthcare teams. *Journal of Business Psychology, 29,* 311–321.

Osborn, K. (2015, September 15). General Electric is moving 500 U. S. jobs overseas. *Time.*

Otto, M. L. (1994). Mentoring: An adult developmental perspective. In M. A. Wunsch (Ed.), *Mentoring revisited: Making an impact on individuals and institutions*. San Francisco: Jossey-Bass.

Paek, H-J., & Hove, T. (2012). Determinants of underage college student drinking: Implications for four major alcohol reduction strategies. *Journal of Health Communication, 17,* 659–676.

Palmer, P. (1998). Leading from within. In L. C. Spears (Ed.), *Insights on leadership: Service, stewardship, spirit, and servant-leadership* (pp. 197–208). New York: John Wiley.

Park, H., & Reber, B. H. (2011). The organization-public relationship and crisis communication: The effect of the organization-public relationship on publics' perceptions of crisis and attitudes toward the organization. *International Journal of Strategic Communication, 5,* 240–260.

Park, H. S., Smith, S. W., Klein, K. A., & Martell, D. (2011). College students' estimation and accuracy of other student's drinking and believability of advertisements featured in a social norms campaign. *Journal of Health Communication, 16,* 504–518.

Parnes, S. J. (1975). "Aha!" In I. A. Taylor & J. W. Getzels (Eds.), *Perspectives on creativity* (pp. 224–248). Chicago: Aldine.

Pasternack, B. A., & O'Toole, J. (2002, Second Quarter). Yellow light leadership: How the world's best companies manage uncertainty. *Strategy + Business,* 74–83.

Patton, B. P., & Downs, T. M. (2003). *Decision-making group interaction: Achieving quality* (4th ed.). New York: Allyn & Bacon.

Pauchant, T. C., & Mitroff, I. I. (1992). *Transforming the crisis-prone organization: Preventing individual, organizational, and environmental tragedies.* San Francisco: Jossey-Bass.

Paulus, D. L., & Williams, K. M. (2002). The dark triad of personality: Narcissism, Machiavellianism, and psychopathy. *Journal of Research in Personality, 36,* 556–563.

Pearce, C. L. (2004). The future of leadership: Combining vertical and shared leadership to transform knowledge work. *Academy of Management Review, 18,* 47–57.

Pearce, C. L., & Conger, J. A. (2003). All those years ago: The historical underpinnings of shared leadership. In C. L. Pearce & J. A. Conger (Eds.), *Shared leadership: Reframing the hows and whys of leadership* (pp. 1–16). Thousand Oaks, CA: Sage.

Pearce, T. (2013). *Leading out loud: A guide for engaging others in creating the future* (3rd ed.). Hoboken, NJ: Wiley.

Pearce, W. B. (1989). *Communication and the human condition.* Carbondale: Southern Illinois University Press.

Pellegrini, E. K., & Scandura, T. A. (2008). Paternalistic leadership: A review and agenda for future research. *Journal of Management, 34*(3), 566–593.

Pellegrini, E. K., Scandura, T. A., & Jayaraman, V. (2010). Cross-cultural generalizability of paternalistic leadership: An expansion of Leader-Member Exchange theory. *Group & Organization Management, 35*(4), 391–420.

Perloff, R. M. (2009). *The dynamics of persuasion: Communication and attitudes in the 21st century.* Hoboken, NJ: Routledge.

Perrow, C. (1999). *Normal accidents: Living with high-risk technologies.* Princeton, NJ: Princeton University Press.

Peters, T. (1992). *Liberation management.* New York: Ballantine.

Peters, T., & Austin, N. (1985). *A passion for excellence: The leadership difference.* New York: Random House.

Peters, T. J., & Waterman, R. H., Jr. (1982). *In search of excellence.* New York: Harper & Row.

Peterson, C., & Seligman, M. E. P. (2004). *Character strengths and virtues: A handbook and classification.* Washington DC: American Psychological Association/Oxford University Press.

Peterson, D. B. (2007). Executive coaching in a cross-cultural context. *Consulting Psychology Journal: Practice and Research, 59,* 261–271.

Pettigrew, T., & Tropp, L. (2006). A meta-analytic test of intergroup contact theory. *Journal of Personality and Social Psychology, 90,* 751–783.

Petty, R. E., & Cacioppo, J. T. (1986). *Communication and persuasion: Central and peripheral routes to attitude change.* New York: Springer-Verlag.

Petty, R.E., & Wegener, D. (1999). The Elaboration Likelihood Model: Current status and controversies. In S. Chaiken & Y. Trope (Eds.), *Dual process theories in social psychology* (pp. 41–72). New York: Guilford.

Peus, C., Wesche, J. S., Streicher, B., Braun, S., & Frey, D. (2012). Authentic leadership: An empirical test of its antecedents, consequences, and mediating mechanisms. *Journal of Business Ethics, 107,* 331–348.

Pfeffer, J. (1992, Winter). Understanding power in organizations. *California Management Review,* 29–50.

Pfeffer, J. (2015). *Leadership bs: Fixing workplaces and careers one truth at a time.* New York: HarperBusiness.

Pierce, J. L., & Newstrom, J. W. (2011). *Leaders & the leadership process: Readings, self-assessments & applications* (6th ed.). New York: McGraw-Hill Irwin.

Piliavin, J. A., & Charng, H. W. (1990). Altruism: A review of recent theory and research. *Annual Review of Sociology, 16,* 27–65.

Pina e Cunha, M., Rego, A., Clegg, S., & Neves, P. (2013). The case for transcendent followership. *Leadership, 9,* 87–196.

Pittinsky, T. L. (2010). A two-dimensional model of intergroup leadership. *American Psychologist, 65,* 194–200.

Pittinsky, T. L., & Simon, S. (2007). Intergroup leadership. *Leadership Quarterly, 18*(6), 586–605.

Pittman, E. (2011, November 11). What big-box retailers can teach government about disaster recovery. *Government Technology.*

Policing Baltimore's police. (2015, May 4). *Baltimore Sun.*

Polonec, L. D., Major, A. M., & Atwood, L. E. (2006). Evaluating the believability and effectiveness of the social norms message "most students drink 0 to 4 drinks when they party." *Health Communication, 20,* 23–34.

Poole, M. S. (1983). Decision development in small groups II: A study of multiple sequences in decision making. *Communication Monographs, 50,* 206–232.

Poole, M. S. (1983). Decision development in small groups III: A multiple sequence model of group decision development. *Communication Monographs, 50,* 321–341.

Porter, M. E. (1979, March). How competitive forces shape strategy. *Harvard Business Review.*

Porter, M. E. (1985). *Competitive advantage: Creating and sustaining superior performance.* New York: The Free Press.

Post, S. G. (2002). The tradition of agape. In S. G. Post, L. G. Underwood, J. P. Schloss, & W. B. Hurlbut (Eds.), *Altruism & altruistic love: Science, philosophy, & religion in dialogue* (pp. 51–64). Oxford: Oxford University Press.

Podsakoff, P. M., MacKenzie, S. B., Moorman, R. H. & Fetter, R. (1990). Transformational leader behaviors and their effects on followers' trust in leader, satisfaction, and organizational citizenship behavior. *Leadership Quarterly, 1*(2), 107–142.

Power, M. (2008, November). K2: The killing peak. *Men's Journal.*

Priddle, A., & Bomey, N. (2014, April 2). GM restructures engineering team to better respond to safety problems. *Detroit Free Press.*

Pruitt, D. G., & Carnevale, P. J. (1993). *Negotiation in social conflict.* Pacific Grove, CA: Brooks/Cole.

Pushkala, P., Pringle, J. K., & Konrad, A. M. (2006). Examining the contours of workplace diversity: Concepts, contexts and challenges. In A. M. Konrad, P. Prasad, & J. K. Pringle (Eds.), *Handbook of workplace diversity* (pp. 1–22). London: Sage.

Quesenberry, K. A. (2016). *Social media strategy: Marketing and advertising in the consumer revolution.* Lanham, MA: Rowman & Littlefield.

Quick Take: Women in the workforce. (2016, August 11). *Catalyst.*

Rafaeli, A., & Worline, M. (2000). Symbols in organizational culture. In N. M. Ashkanasy, C. P. M. Wilderom, & M. F. Peterson (Eds.), *Handbook of organizational culture and climate* (pp. 71–84). Thousand Oaks, CA: Sage.

Ragins, B. R., & Kram. K. E. (2008). *The handbook of mentoring at work: Theory, research, and practice.* Los Angeles: Sage.

Rai, H., & Singh, M. (2013). A study of mediating variables of the relationship between 360 degree feedback and employee performance. *Human Resource Development International, 16,* 56–73.

Rajah, R., & Arvey, R. D. (2013). Helping group members develop resilience. In A. J. Dubrin (Ed.), *Handbook of research on crisis leadership in organizations* (pp. 149–173). Cheltenham, UK: Edward Elgar.

Ramesh, R. (2008, August 5). K2 tragedy. *The Guardian* (London), p. 2.

Ramperstad, A. (1997). *Jackie Robinson.* New York: Knopf.

Rancer, A. S., & Avtgis, T. A. (2006). *Argumentative and aggressive communication: Theory, research, and application.* Thousand Oaks, CA: Sage.

Raven, B. H. (2010). The bases of power: Origins and recent developments. *Journal of Social Issues, 49,* 227–251.

Rawls, J. (1971). *A theory of justice.* Cambridge, MA: Belknap Press.

Rawls, J. (1993). Distributive justice. In T. Donaldson & P. H. Werhane (Eds.), *Ethical issues in business: A philosophical approach* (4th ed., pp. 274–285). Englewood Cliffs, NJ: Prentice-Hall.

Rawls, J. (1993). *Political liberalism.* New York: Columbia University Press.

Rawls, J. (2001). *Justice as fairness: A restatement* (E. Kelly, Ed.). Cambridge, MA: Belknap Press.

Ray, S. J. (1999). *Strategic communication in crisis management: Lessons from the airline industry.* Westport, CT: Quorum Books.

Reardon, K. K. (1995). *They just don't get it, do they?* New York: Little, Brown.

Reave, L. (2005). Spiritual values and practices related to leadership effectiveness. *Leadership Quarterly, 16*, 655–687.

Reed, L. L., Vidaver-Cohen, D., & Colwell, S. R. (2011). A new scale to measure executive servant leadership: Development, analysis, and implications for research. *Journal of Business Ethics, 101*, 415–434.

Reingold, J. (2016, March 15). How a radical shift left Zappos reeling. *Fortune.com.*

Rest, J. R. (1986). *Moral development: Advances in research and theory.* New York: Praeger.

Rest, J. R. (1993). Research on moral judgment in college students. In A. Garrod (Ed.), *Approaches to moral development* (pp. 201–211). New York: Teachers College Press.

Rest, J. R. (1994). Background: Theory and research. In J. R. Rest & D. Narvaez (Eds.), *Moral development in the professions: Psychology and applied ethics* (pp. 1–25). Hillsdale, NJ: Lawrence Erlbaum.

Reston, L. (2015, July 17). Tony Hsieh's workplace dream: Is holacracy a big failure? *Forbes.*

Reuters. (2016, November 24). "It's final!": Colombian president signs revised peace deal. *New York Post.*

Rhoads, K. V. L., & Cialdini, R. B. (2002). The business of influence: Principles that lead to success in commercial settings. In J. P. Dillard & M. Pfau (Eds.), *The persuasion handbook: Developments in theory and practice.* Thousand Oaks, CA: Sage.

Rice, R. E. (2001). Smokey Bear. In R. E. Rice & C. K. Atkins (Eds.), *Public communication campaigns* (3rd ed., pp. 276–279). Thousand Oaks, CA: Sage.

Richardson, R. J., & Thayer, S. K. (1993). *The charisma factor.* Englewood Cliffs, NJ: Prentice-Hall.

Richter, A. W., West, M. A., Van Dick, R., & Dawson, J. F. (2006). Boundary spanners identification, intergroup contact, and effective intergroup relations. *Academy of Management Journal, 49*, 1252–1269.

Riecken, H. (1975). The effect of talkativeness on ability to influence group solutions of problems. In P. V. Crosbie (Ed.), *Interaction in small groups* (pp. 238–249). New York: Macmillan.

Riggio, R. E., Ciulla, J. B., & Sorenson, G. J. (2003). Leadership education at the undergraduate level: A liberal arts approach to leadership development. In S. E. Murphy & R. E. Riggio (Eds.), *The future of leadership development* (pp. 201–236). Mahwah, NJ: Lawrence Erlbaum.

Riggio, R. E., Riggio, H. R., Salinas, C., & Cole, E. J. (2003). The role of social and emotional communication skills in leader emergence and effectiveness. *Group Dynamics: Theory, Research, and Practice, 7*, 83–103

Ringland, G. (2016). *Scenario planning: Managing for the future* (2nd ed.). Chichester, UK: Wiley.

Rivera Vargas, M. I. (2011). Organizational learning model for sustainable innovation: Elements for a new innovation approach in developing countries. *Projectics/Proyectica/ Projectique, 1*, 37–47.

Robinson Hickman, G., & Sorenson, G. J. (2014). *The power of invisible leadership: How a compelling common purpose inspires exceptional leadership.* Los Angeles, CA: Sage.

Rockstuhl, T., Seiler, S., Ang, S., Van Dyne, L., & Annen, H. (2011). Beyond general intelligence (IQ) and emotional intelligence (EQ): The role of cultural intelligence (CQ) on cross-border leadership effectiveness in a globalized world. *Journal of Social Issues, 67*, 825–840.

Rodin, J. (2014). *The resilience dividend: Being strong in a world where things go wrong.* New York: PublicAffairs.

Rogers, E. M. (2003). *Diffusion of innovations* (5th ed.). New York: The Free Press.

Rogers, E. M., & Steinfatt, T. M. (1999). *Intercultural communication.* Long Grove, IL: Waveland Press.

Rohman, J. (n.d.). With an "employee-first" mentality, everyone wins. *Great Places to Work.*

Rokeach, M. (1973). *The nature of human values.* New York: Free Press.

Roloff, M. E., & Barnicott, E. F. (1978). The situational use of pro- and antisocial compliance-gaining strategies by high and low Machiavellians. In B. Ruben (Ed.), *Communication Yearbook 2* (pp. 193–208). New Brunswick, NJ: Transaction Books.

Roloff, M. E., & Paulson, G. D. (2001). Confronting organizational transgressions. In J. M. Darley, D. M. Messick, & T. R. Tyler (Eds.), *Social influences on ethical behavior in organizations* (pp. 53–68). Mahwah, NJ: Lawrence Erlbaum.

Roloff, M. E., Putnam, L. L., & Anastascou, L. (2003). Negotiation skills. In J. O. Greene & B. R. Burleson (Eds.), *Handbook of communication and social interaction skills* (pp. 801–833). Mahwah, NJ: Lawrence Erlbaum.

Rosener, J. B. (1990, November–December). Ways women lead. *Harvard Business Review*, 119–125.

Rosenfeld, P., Giacalone, R. A., & Riordan, C. A. (1995). *Impression management in organizations: Theory, measurement, practice.* New York: Routledge.

Rosenthal, R. (1993). Interpersonal expectations: Some antecedents and some consequences. In P. D. Blanck (Ed.), *Interpersonal expectations: Theory, research and applications* (pp. 3–24). Cambridge: Cambridge University Press.

Rosenthal, R., & Jacobson, L. (1968). *Pygmalion in the classroom.* New York: Holt, Rinehart and Winston.

Ross, J., & Staw, B. M. (1993). Organizational escalation and exit: Lessons from the Shoreham nuclear power plant. *Academy of Management Journal, 36*, 701–732.

Rost, J. C. (1993). *Leadership for the twenty-first century.* New York: Praeger.

Rost, J. C. (1993). Leadership in the new millennium. *The Journal of Leadership Studies, 1*, 92–110.

Rotter, J. B. (1966). Generalized expectancies for internal versus external control of reinforcement. *Psychological Monographs, 80*, 1–28.

Rothwell, J. D. (2013). *In mixed company: Small group communication* (8th ed.). Fort Worth, TX: Harcourt Brace.

Rothwell, W. J. (2016). *Executive succession planning* (5th ed.). New York: AMACOM.

Rubin, J. Z., & Brown, B. R. (1975). *The social psychology of bargaining and negotiation.* New York: Academic Press.

Rudin, S. A. (1964). Leadership as psychophysiological activation of group members: A case experimental study. *Psychological Reports, 15*, 577–578.

Russell, C. A., Clapp, J. D., & DeJong, W. (2005). Done 4: Analysis of a failed social norms marketing campaign. *Health Communication 17*, 57–65.

Ruya, C. L., & Bryant, J. B. (2004). The impact of age, speech style, and question form on perceptions of witness credibility and trial outcome. *Journal of Applied Social Psychology, 34*, 1919–1944.

Ryan, L. (2014, October 1). What business jargon says about us. *Forbes.*

Ryan, M. K., & Haslam, S. A. (2005). The glass cliff: Evidence that women are over-represented in precarious leadership positions. *British Journal of Management, 16*, 81–90.

Ryan, M. K., Haslam. S. A., Hersby, M. D., & Bongiorno, R. (2011). Think crisis-think female: The glass cliff and contextual variation in the think manager-think male stereotype. *Journal of Applied Psychology, 96*, 470–484.

Ryan, M. K., Haslam, S. A., & Kulich, C. (2010). Politics and the glass cliff: Evidence that women are preferentially selected to contest hard-to-win seats. *Psychology of Women Quarterly, 34*, 56–64.

Sack, K., Fink, S., Belluck, P., & Nosssiter, A. (2014, December 29). How Ebola roared back. *The New York Times.*

Sadler, P. (2001). Leadership and organizational learning. In M. Dierkes, A. Berthoin Antal, J. Child, & I. Nonaka (Eds.), *Handbook of organizational learning and knowledge* (pp. 415–427). Oxford: Oxford University Press.

Sagarin, B. J., & Cialdini, R. B. (2004). Creating critical consumers: Motivating receptivity by teaching resistance. In E. S. Knowles & J. A Linn (Eds.), *Resistance and persuasion* (pp. 259–282). Mahwah, NJ: Erlbaum.

Salovey, P., Bedwell, B. T., Detweiler, J. B., & Mayer, J. D. (2000). Current directions in emotional intelligence research. In M. Lewis & J. M. Haviland-Lewis (Eds.), *Handbook of emotions* (2nd ed., pp. 504–520). New York: Guilford Press.

Sandberg, S. (2013). *Lean in: Women, work, and the will to lead*. New York: Alfred Knopf.

Sanghera, P. (2008). *Fundamentals of effective program management: A process approach based on the global standard*. Ft. Lauderdale, FL: J. Ross.

Sattler, W. M. (1947). Conceptions of ethos in ancient rhetoric. *Speech Monographs, 14*, 55–65.

Schawbel, D. (2014, October 7). Kip Tindell: How he created an employee-first culture at The Container Store. *Forbes*.

Schein, E. H. (1983). The role of the founder in creating organizational culture. *Organizational Dynamics, 12*, 13–26.

Schein, E. H. (1992). *Organizational culture and leadership* (2nd ed.). San Francisco: Jossey-Bass.

Schermerhorn, R., & Bond, M. H. (1997). Cross-cultural leadership dynamics in collectivism and high power distance settings. *Leadership & Organization Development Journal, 18*, 187–193.

Schmidt, E., Rosenberg, J., & Eagle, A. (2014). *Google: How Google works*. New York: Grand Central Publishing.

Schoenberg, A. (2005, Spring). Do crisis plans matter? A new perspective on leading during a crisis. *Public Relations Quarterly, 50*, 2–6.

Schriesheim, C. A., Castro, S. L., & Cogliser, C. C. (1999). Leader-member exchange (LMX) research: A comprehensive review of theory, measurement, and data-analytic practices. *Leadership Quarterly, 10*, 63–113.

Schrodt, P., Cawyer, C. S., & Sanders, R. (2003). An examination of academic mentoring behaviors and new faculty members' satisfaction with socialization and tenure and promotion processes. *Communication Education, 52*, 17–29.

Schultz, B. G. (1979). Predicting emergent leaders: An exploratory study of the salience of communicative functions. *Small Group Behavior, 9*, 109–114.

Schultz, B. G. (1980). Communicative correlates of perceived leaders. *Small Group Behavior, 11*, 175–191.

Schultz, B. G. (1982). Argumentativeness: Its effect in group decision making and its role in leadership perception. *Communication Quarterly, 30*, 368–375.

Schultz, B. G. (1996). *Communicating in the small group: Theory and practice* (2nd ed.). New York: HarperCollins.

Schwartz, T. (2015, August 21). Why Jeff Bezos should care more for Amazon's employees. *The New York Times*.

Schyns, B., & Hansbrough, T. (Eds.). (2010). *When leadership goes wrong: Destructive leadership, mistakes, and ethical failures*. Charlotte, NC: Information Age.

Sebeok, T. A., & Rosenthal, R. (Eds.). (1981). *The clever Hans phenomenon: Communication with horses, whales, apes, and people*. Annals of the New York Academy of Sciences, Vol. 364. New York: New York Academy of Sciences.

Sebeok, T. A., & Umiker-Sebeok, J. (1979). *Speaking of apes: A critical anthology of two-way communication with man*. New York: Plenum.

Seeger, M. W., Sellnow, T. L., & Ulmer, R. R. (1998). Communication, organization, and crisis. In M. E. Roloff (Ed.), *Communication Yearbook 21* (pp. 231–275). Thousand Oaks, CA: Sage.

Seeger, M. W., Sellnow, T. L., & Ulmer, R. R. (2003). *Communication and organizational crisis*. Westport, CT: Praeger.

Segal, D. (2015, August 9). Petrobras oil scandal leaves Brazilians lamenting a lost dream. *The New York Times*, p. BU1.

Sellnow, T. L., & Seeger M. (2013). *Theorizing crisis communication*. Hoboken, NJ: Wiley.

Senge, P. M. (1990). *The fifth discipline: The art and practice of the learning organization*. New York: Doubleday/Currency.

Shaw, M. E. (1955). A comparison of two types of leadership in various communication nets. *Journal of Abnormal and Social Psychology, 50*, 127–134.

Shear, M. D., & Joachim, D. S. (2014, May 31). Shineski apologizes for misconduct at V. A. hospitals. *The New York Times*.

Sheldon, K. (1999). Learning the lessons of Tit-for-Tat: Even competitors can get the message. *Journal of Personality & Social Psychology, 77*, 1245–1253.

Shen, L. (2016, October 13). Here's how much Wells Fargo CEO John Stumpf is getting to leave the bank. *Fortune.*

Shih, C. (2011). *The Facebook era: Tapping online social networks to market, sell, and innovate.* Upper Saddle River, NJ: Prentice-Hall.

Shockley-Zalabak, P., Ellis, K., & Winograd, G. (2000). Organizational trust: What it means, why it matters. *Organization Development Journal, 18,* 35–47.

Shockley-Zalabak, P., Morreale, S., & Hackman, M. Z. (2010). *Building the high-trust organization: Strategies for supporting the five key dimensions of trust.* San Francisco: Jossey-Bass.

Shoemaker, P. H. H., Krupp, S., & Howland, S. (2013, January–February). Strategic leadership: The essential skills. *Harvard Business Review,* 2–5.

Simmons A. (2016, June 7). Clinton is set to make history, but female leaders are nothing new in other parts of the world. *Los Angeles Times.*

Simons, H. W., & Jones, J. G. (2011). *Persuasion in society* (2nd ed.). New York: Routledge.

Simons, T. (2002, September). The high cost of lost trust. *Harvard Business Review,* 18–19.

Sims, H. P., & Manz, C. C. (1996). *Company of heroes: Unleashing the power of self-leadership.* New York: John Wiley.

Singelis, T. M., Triandis, H. C., Bhawuk, D. S., & Gelfand, M. (1995). Horizontal and vertical dimensions of individualism and collectivism: A theoretical and measurement refinement. *Cross-Cultural Research, 29,* 240–275.

Singhal, A., & Rogers, E. (1999). *Entertainment-education: A communication strategy for social change.* Mahwah, NJ: Lawrence Erlbaum.

Singhal, A., & Rogers, E. M. (2003). *Combating AIDS: Communication strategies in action.* New Delhi: Sage.

Skogstad, A., Einarsen, S., Torsheim, T., Shanke Aasland, M., & Hetland, H. (2007). The destructiveness of laissez-faire leadership behavior. *Journal of Occupational Health Psychology, 12,* 80–92.

Skyrme, D. J. (2000). Developing a knowledge strategy: From management to leadership. In D. Morey, M. Maybury, & B. Thuraisingham (Eds.), *Knowledge management: Classic and contemporary works* (pp. 61–83). Cambridge, MA: MIT Press.

Slaughter, A-M. (2013, March 7). Yes, you can. *The New York Times.*

Smart, C., & Vertinsky, I. (2006). Designs for crisis decision units. In D. Smith & D. Elliott (Eds.), *Key readings in crisis management: Systems and structures for prevention and recovery* (pp. 321–342). London: Routledge.

Smith, A. E. (2015, Fall). On the edge of a glass cliff: Women in leadership in public organizations. *Public Administration Quarterly, 39,* 484–517.

Smith, A. E., Jussim, L., & Eccles, J. (1999). Do self-fulfilling prophecies accumulate, dissipate, or remain stable over time? *Journal of Personality and Social Psychology, 77,* 548–565.

Smith, P. B., Misumi, J., Tayeb, M., Peterson, M., & Bond, M. (1989). On the generality of leadership style measures across cultures. *Journal of Occupational Psychology, 62,* 97–109.

Smith, T. W. (1990). *Ethnic images.* National Opinion Research Center, GSS Topical Report No. 19. Chicago: University of Chicago.

Smithson, J., & Venette, S. (2013, September–October). Stonewalling as an image-defense strategy: A critical examination of BP's response to the Deepwater Horizon explosion. *Communication Studies, 64,* 395–410.

Snyder, L., & LaCroix, J. M. (2013). How effective are mediated health campaigns? A synthesis of meta-analyses. In R. Rice & C. Atkin (Eds.), *Public communication campaigns* (4th ed., pp. 181–190). Thousand Oaks, CA: Sage.

Snyder, N. H., & Graves, M. (1994). Leadership and vision. *Business Horizons, 37,* 1–7.

Soki, A. (2015, May 25). How an English teacher conquered China: Wisdom of Jack Ma condensed into 33 quotes. Retrieved from alok@yourstory.com.

Solomon, M. (2013, September 18). A Ritz-Carlton caliber experience requires employee empowerment and customer service standards. *Forbes.*

Solomon, M. (2014, March 15). Take these two steps to rival Nordstrom's customer service experience. *Forbes*.

Solomon, R. (1988). Internal objections to virtue ethics. *Midwest Studies in Philosophy, 8,* 428–441.

Sorensen, R., & Pickett, T. (1986). A test of two teaching strategies designed to improve interview effectiveness: Rating behavior and videotaped feedback. *Communication Monographs, 35,* 13–22.

Sosik, J. J., Avolio, B. J., & Kahai, S. S. (1997). Effects of leadership style and anonymity on group potency and effectiveness in a group decision support system environment. *Journal of Applied Psychology, 82,* 89–103.

Spears, L. (1998). Tracing the growing impact of servant-leadership. In L. Spears (Ed.), *Insights on leadership: Service, stewardship, spirit and servant-leadership* (pp. 1–15). New York: Wiley & Sons.

Spector, R. (2001). *Lessons from the Nordstrom way.* New York: Wiley & Sons.

Spector, R., & McCarthy, P. (2012). *The Nordstrom way to customer service excellence: The handbook.* Hoboken, NJ: Wiley.

Spreitzer, G. M. (1995). Psychological empowerment in the workplace: Dimensions, measurement, and validation. *Academy of Management Journal, 38,* 1422–1465.

Spreitzer, G. M. (1996). Social structural characteristics of psychological empowerment. *Academy of Management Journal, 39,* 483–504.

Staw, B. M. (2001). The escalation of commitment to a course of action. *Academy of Management Review, 6,* 577–587.

Stech, E. L. (1983). *Leadership communication.* Chicago: Nelson-Hall.

Stegner, W. (1954). *Beyond the hundredth meridian: John Wesley Powell and the second opening of the West.* New York: Penguin Books.

Stehl, S. K., Felfe, J., Elprana, G., & Gatzka, M. B. (2015). The role of motivation to lead for leadership training effectiveness. *International Journal of Training and Development, 19,* 81–97.

Stengel, R. (2011, December 26). 2011 person of the year: The protester. *Time,* pp. 53ff.

Steward, C. (2010, June 21). BP chief under fire for yacht trip. *The Herald (Glasgow) News,* p. 2.

Stewart, C. J., Smith, C. A., & Denton, R. E. (2012). *Persuasion and social movements* (6th ed.). Long Grove, IL: Waveland Press.

Stogdill, R. M. (1948). Personal factors associated with leadership: A survey of the literature. *Journal of Psychology, 25,* 35–71.

Stogdill, R. M. (1950). Leadership, membership and organization. *Psychological Bulletin, 47,* 1–14.

Stogdill, R. M. (1965). *Managers, employees, organizations.* Columbus: Ohio State University, Bureau of Business Research.

Stogdill, R. M. (1974). *Handbook of leadership.* New York: Free Press.

Stogdill, R. M., & Coons, A. E. (1957). *Leader behavior: Its description and measurement.* Columbus: Ohio State University, Bureau of Business Research.

Stone, B. (2013). *The everything store: Jeff Bezos and the age of Amazon.* New York: Little, Brown.

Stoneking, D. (n.d.). News of the day—what do Waffle Houses have to do with risk management? *FEMA.gov.*

Strauss, G. (2012, January 24). More CEOs rake in $50M and up; Firms "tone deaf" to spirit of times. *USA Today,* p. 1A.

Stretcher Sigmar, L., Hynes, G. E., & Hill, K. L. (2012). Strategies for teaching social and emotional intelligence in business communication. *Business Communication Quarterly, 75*(3), 301–317.

Strom, S. (2016, December 13). Chipotle, still struggling after food safety issues, will lose one of its C.E.O.s. *The New York Times,* p. B3.

Strong, S. R., & Dixon, D. N. (1971). Expertness, attractiveness, and influence in counseling. *Journal of Counseling Psychology, 18,* 562–570.

Strong, S. R., & Schmidt, L. D. (1970). Expertness and influence in counseling. *Journal of Counseling Psychology, 17,* 81–87.

Stross, R. (2008). *Planet Google: One company's audacious plan to organize everything we know.* New York: The Free Press.

Sturges, D. L. (1994). Communicating through crisis: A strategy for organizational survival. *Management Communication Quarterly, 7,* 297–316.

Stutman, J. (2015, January 27). IBM could lay off every American employee (and then some). *Wealth Daily.*

Suddath, C. (2012, April 27). Why there are no bosses at Valve. *Bloomberg.*

Sutcliffe, K. M., & Vogus, T. J. (2003). Organizing for resilience. In K. S. Cameron, J. E. Dutton, & R. E. Quinn (Eds.), *Positive organizational scholarship: Foundations for a new discipline* (pp. 94–110). San Francisco: Berrett-Koehler.

Sy, T. (2010). What do you think of followers? Examining the content, structure, and consequences of implicit followership theories. *Organizational Behavior and Human Decision Processes, 113,* 73–84.

Tannenbaum, R., & Schmidt, W. H. (1958). How to choose a leadership pattern. *Harvard Business Review, 36,* 95–101.

Tannenbaum, S. I., & Cerasoli, C. P. (2013). Do team and individual debriefs enhance performance? A meta-analysis. *Human Factors, 55,* 231–245.

Taras, V., Kirkman, B. L., & Steel, P. (2010). Examining the impact of *Culture's consequences*: A three-decade, multilevel, meta-analytic review of Hofstede's cultural value dimensions. *Journal of Applied Psychology, 95,* 405–439.

Taylor, J. (2008, August 5). What makes K2 the most perilous challenge a mountaineer can face? *The Independent* (London), Comment, p. 30.

Teather, D. (2005, June 9). Fatboy Ronald McDonald downsizes to head off critics. *The Guardian,* p. 19.

TED staff. (2012, November 13). TED reaches its billionth video view! *Ted Blog.*

Tee, E. Y. J. (2015). The emotional link: Leadership and the role of implicit and explicit emotional contagion processes across multiple organizational levels. *Leadership Quarterly, 23,* 654–670.

Tee, E. Y. J., Paulsen, N., & Ashkanasy, N. M. (2013). Revisiting followership through a social identity perspective: The role of collective follower emotion and action. *Leadership Quarterly, 24,* 902–918.

Tenney, G. (2012, May 2). When disaster strikes, FEMA turns to . . . Waffle House. *Fox News.*

Terrace, H. S., Pettito, L. A., Sanders, R. J., & Bever, T. G. (1979). Can an ape create a sentence? *Science, 206,* 891–902.

Teven, J. J., McCroskey, J. C., & Richmond, V. P. (2006). Communication correlates of perceived Machiavellianism of supervisors: Communication orientations and outcomes. *Communication Quarterly, 54*(2), 127–142.

Teven, J. J., Richmond, V. P., McCroskey, J. C., & McCroskey, L. L. (2010). Updating relationships between communication traits and communication competence. *Communication Research Reports, 27*(3), 263–270.

The corporate woman: A special report. (1986, March 24). *Wall Street Journal,* supplement.

The most popular talks of all time. (n.d.). *TED.com.*

Theobald, T. (2013). *Creating success: Develop your presentation skills.* London, UK: Koran Page.

The 10 greatest all time speeches by 10 inspired women. (n.d.). *Marieclaire.co.uk.*

Thibault, J. W., & Kelley, H. H. (1978). *Interpersonal relations: A theory of interdependence.* New York: John Wiley.

Thomas, D. A., & Ely, R. J. (1996, September–October). Making differences matter: A new paradigm for managing diversity. *Harvard Business Review,* 79–90.

Thomas, D. C., & Inkson, K. (2004). *Cultural intelligence: People skills for global business.* San Francisco: Berrett-Koehler.

Thomas, K. W., & Velthouse, B. A. (1990). Cognitive elements of empowerment: An "interpretive" model of intrinsic task motivation. *Academy of Management Review, 15,* 666–681.

Thoroughgood, C. N, Padilla, A., Hunter, S. T., & Tate, B. W. (2012). The susceptible circle: A taxonomy of followers associated with destructive leadership. *Leadership Quarterly, 23,* 897–917.

Three directors say VW hid deceit from the board. (2015, October 24). *The New York Times*, p. A1.

Tichy, N. M. (1997). *The leadership engine.* New York: HarperBusiness.

Tindell, K. (2014). *Uncontainable: How passion, commitment and conscious capitalism build a business where everyone thrives.* New York: Grand Central.

Ting, D. (2016, November 29). This is why Airbnb is doing what it's doing with trips and more. *Skift.*

Ting, S., & Hart, E. W. (2004). Formal coaching. In C. D. McCauley & E. Van Velsor (Eds.), *The Center for Creative Leadership handbook of leadership development* (2nd ed., pp. 116–150). San Francisco: Jossey-Bass.

Ting, S., & Scisco, P. (2006). *The CCL handbook of coaching: A guide for the leader coach.* San Francisco: Jossey-Bass.

Tompkins, P. K. (1982). *Communication as action: An introduction to rhetoric and communication.* Belmont, CA: Wadsworth.

Toppo, G. (2013, June 11). At-risk cities ramp up disaster-response planning. *USA Today.*

Top 10 greatest speeches. (2016). *Time.com.*

Torricelli, R., & Carroll, A. (Eds.). (1999). *In our own words: Extraordinary speeches of the American century.* New York: Kodansha International.

Tourish, D. (2008). Challenging the transformational agenda: Leadership theory in transition? *Management Communication Quarterly, 21,* 522–528.

Tourish, D., & Pinnington, A. (2002). Transformational leadership, corporate cultism and the spirituality paradigm: An unholy trinity in the workplace? *Human Relations, 55*(2), 147–172.

Transcript: Read the speech Pope Francis gave to Congress. (2015, September 24). *Time.com.*

Trevino, L. K., & Weaver, G. R. (2003). *Managing ethics in business organizations: Social scientific perspectives.* Stanford, CA: Stanford University Press.

Triandis, H. C. (1993). The contingency model in cross-cultural perspective. In M. M. Chemers & R. Ayman (Eds.), *Leadership theory and research: Perspectives and directions* (pp. 167–188). San Diego: Academic Press.

Trice, H. M., & Beyer, J. M. (1984). Studying organizational cultures through rites and ceremonials. *Academy of Management Review, 9,* 653–669.

Trice, H. M., & Beyer, J. M. (1985). Using six organizational rites to change culture. In R. H. Killmann, M. J. Saxton, & R. Serpa (Eds.), *Gaining control of the corporate culture* (pp. 370–399). San Francisco: Jossey-Bass.

Trice, H. M., & Beyer, J. M. (1993). *The cultures of work organizations.* Englewood Cliffs, NJ: Prentice-Hall.

Trist, E. L., & Bamforth, K. W. (1951). Some social and psychological consequences of the long-wall method of coal-getting. *Human Relations, 4,* 3–38.

Trompenaars, F. (1994). *Riding the waves of culture: Understanding diversity in global business.* Burr Ridge, IL: Irwin.

Trompenaars, F., & Woolliams, P. (2009). Getting the measure of intercultural leadership. In M. A. Moodian (Ed.), *Contemporary leadership and intercultural competence: Exploring the cross-cultural dynamics with organizations* (pp. 161–174). Los Angeles: Sage.

Tropman, J. (2003). *Making meetings work: Achieving high quality group decisions* (2nd ed.). Thousand Oaks, CA: Sage.

Tropman, J. (2014). *Effective meetings: Improving group decision making* (3rd ed.). Los Angeles: Sage.

Tuckman, B. W. (1965). Developmental sequence in small groups. *Psychological Bulletin, 63,* 384–399.

Tuckman, B. W., & Jensen, M. A. (1977). Stages of small-group development revisited. *Group & Organization Studies, 2,* 419–427.

200 highest-paid CEOs 2016. (2016, May 27). *Equilar/The New York Times.*

Two surprisingly good corporate apologies. (2015, May 19). *SorryWatch.*

Uhl-Bien, M. (2003). Relationship development as a key ingredient for leadership development. In S. E. Murphy & R. E. Riggo (Eds.), *The future of leadership development* (pp. 129–147). Mahwah, NJ: Erlbaum.

Ulmer, R. R., Seeger, M. W., & Sellnow, T. L. (2007). Post-crisis communication and renewal: Expanding the parameters of post-crisis discourse. *Public Relations Review, 33*, 130–134.

Ulmer, R. R., Sellnow, T. L., & Seeger, M. (2008). Post-crisis communication and renewal: Understanding the potential for positive outcomes in crisis communication. In R. L. Heath & H. D. O'Hair (Eds.), *Handbook of risk and crisis communication* (pp. 302–322). Hoboken, NJ: Routledge.

Upper 1 percent of Americans are rolling in the dough. (December 12, 2012). *The Oregonian*, p. A2.

Useem, M. (1998). *The leadership moment.* New York: Times Books.

Valle, M. (2006, May/June). The power of politics: Why leaders need to learn the art of influence. *Leadership in Action*, 8–12.

Van Breukelen, W., Schyns, B., & Le Blanc, P. (2006). Leader-member exchange theory and research: Accomplishments and future challenges. *Leadership, 2*, 295–316.

van Knippenberg, D., van Knippenberg, B., De Cremer, D., & Hogg, M. A. (2004). Leadership, self, and identity: A review and research agenda. *Leadership Quarterly, 15*, 825–856.

Van Velsor, E., & McCauley, C. D. (2010). Introduction: Our view of leadership development. In *The Center for Creative Leadership handbook of leadership development* (3rd ed., pp. 1–22). San Francisco: Jossey-Bass.

Veechio, R. P., Justin, J. E., & Pearce, C. L. (2008). The utility of transactional and transformational leadership for predicting performance and satisfaction within a part-goal theory framework. *Journal of Occupational and Organizational Psychology, 81*, 71–82.

Viesturs, E., & Roberts, D. (2009). *K2: Life and death on the world's most dangerous mountain.* New York: Broadway Books.

Vigoda, E. (2003). *Developments in organizational politics: How political dynamics affect employee performance in modern work sites.* Cheltenham, UK: Edward Elgar.

Vigoda-Gadot, E., & Drory, A. (2006). Organizational politics, leadership and performance in modern public worksites: A theoretical framework. In E. Vigoda-Gadot & A. Drory (Eds.), *Handbook of organizational politics* (pp. 3–15). Cheltenham, UK: Edward Elgar.

Vinson, L. (1988, November). *An emotion-based model of compliance-gaining message selection.* Paper presented at the Speech Communication Association convention, New Orleans, LA.

Vinson, L., & Johnson, C. E. (1990). The relationship between the use of hesitations and/or hedges and listening: The role of perceived importance as a mediating variable. *Journal of the International Listening Association, 4*, 116–127.

Vise, D. A., & Malsee, M. (2005). *Google story.* Westminster, MD: Dell.

von Drehle, D., & Baker, A. (2014, December 10). The Ebola fighters: The ones who answered the call. *Time.*

von Oech, R. (1986). *A kick in the seat of the pants.* New York: Harper & Row.

Vroom, V. H., & Mann, F. C. (1960). Leader authorization and employee attitudes. *Personnel Psychology, 13*, 125–140.

Vygotsky, L. (1986). *Thought and language* (Trans. A. Kozulin). Cambridge, MA: MIT Press.

Wack, P. (1985, September). Scenarios: Uncharted waters ahead. *Harvard Business Review.*

Wack, P. (1985, November). Scenarios: Shooting the rapids. *Harvard Business Review.*

Wahba, P. (2016, May 19). Why Container Store's founder is quitting CEO job. *Fortune.*

Walker, S. (1983). *Animal thought.* London: Routledge & Kegan Paul.

Wallas, G. (1926). *The art of thought.* New York: Harcourt.

Walsh, B. (2012, February 12). The upside of being an introvert (and why extroverts are overrated). *Time*, pp. 40–45.

Walumbwa, F. O., Avolio, B. J., Gardner, W. L., Wernsing, T. S., & Peterson, S. J. (2008). Authentic leadership: Development and validation of a theory-based measure. *Journal of Management, 34*, 89–126, 94.

Walumbwa, F. O., Cropanzano, R., & Goldman, B. M. (2011). How leader-member exchange influences effective work behaviors: Social exchange and internal-external efficacy perspectives. *Personnel Psychology, 64*, 739–770.

Walumbwa, F. O., Hartnell, C. A., & Oke, A. (2010). Servant leadership, procedural justice climate, service climate, and organizational citizenship behavior: A cross-level investigation. *Journal of Applied Psychology, 95*, 517–529.

Wang, H., Sui, Y., Luthans, F., Wang, D., & Wu, Y. (2014). Impact of authentic leadership on performance: Role of followers' positive psychological capital and relational processes. *Journal of Organizational Behavior, 35*, 5–12.

Warner, J. (2014, March 7). Fact sheet: The women's leadership gap. *Center for American Progress.*

Warr, P. (2013, July 9). Former Valve employee: "It felt a lot like high school." *Wired.*

Warren, I. D. (1969). The effects of credibility in sources of testimony and audience attitudes toward speaker and topic. *Speech Monographs, 36*, 456–458.

Wasden, M., & Guzley, R. (2004, November). *Guided freedom leadership: Competent and capable individuals in the 21st century.* Paper presented at the International Leadership Association Conference, Washington, DC.

Watson, D. (2003). *Death sentences: How cliches, weasel words, and management-speak are strangling public language.* New York: Gotham Books.

Watson, T., & Noble, P. (2014). *PR in practice: Evaluating public relations.* London, UK: Kogan Page.

Watts, J. (2014, January 13). Eleven U.S. cities to receive funds to increase resiliency. *Bond Buyer.*

Weber, M. (1947). *The theory of social and economic organization.* (A. M. Henderson & T. Parsons, Trans.) Glencoe, IL: The Free Press.

Weick, K. E. (1995). *Sensemaking in organizations.* Thousand Oaks, CA: Sage.

Weick, K. E. (2001). Leadership as the legitimation of doubt. In W. Bennis, G. M. Spreitzer, & T. G. Cummings (Eds.), *The future of leadership: Today's top leadership thinkers speak to tomorrow's leaders* (pp. 91–102). San Francisco: Jossey-Bass.

Weick, K. E., & Sutcliffe, K. M. (2001). *Managing the unexpected: Assuring high performance in an age of complexity.* San Francisco: Jossey-Bass.

Weir, D., & Ortenblad, A. (2013). Obstacles to the learning organization. In A. Ortenblad (Ed.), *Handbook of research on the learning organization* (pp. 68–85). Cheltenham, UK: Edward Elgar.

Weise, E. (2016, October 19). Airbnb and New York City go head to head. *USA Today.*

Weise, E. (2016, November 14). In shift, Airbnb agrees to San Francisco regs. *USA Today.*

Weissman, R. (2011, May 25). Deregulation and the financial crisis. *The Huffington Post.*

Wells, N. (2016, October 13). The "gig" economy is growing—and now we know by how much. *CNBC.*

Weschler, I. R., Kahane, M., & Tannenbaum, R. (1952). Job satisfaction, productivity, and morale: A case study. *Occupational Psychology, 26*, 1–14.

West, E. (2015, October 16). 5 car quality myths, busted. *JD Powers.com.*

Westland, J. (2007). *Project management life cycle: A compete step-by-step methodology for initiating, planning, executing, and closing a project successfully.* London: Kogan.

What we stand for. (n.d.). *The Container Store.*

Wheelan, S. A. (2010). *Creating effective teams: A guide for members and leaders.* Thousand Oaks, CA: Sage.

White, L. A. (1949). *The science of culture.* New York: Farrar, Strauss and Cudahy.

White, R., & Lippitt, R. (1968). Leader behavior and member reaction in three "social climates." In D. Cartwright & A. Zander (Eds.), *Group dynamics* (pp. 318–335). New York: Harper & Row.

White, S. S., & Lock, E. A. (2000). Problems with the Pygmalion effect and some proposed solutions. *Leadership Quarterly, 11*, 389–416.

Whitely, P., Sy, T., & Johnson, S. K. (2012). Leaders' conceptions of followers: Implications for naturally occurring Pygmalion effects. *The Leadership Quarterly, 23*, 822–834.

Whitener, E. M. (1997). The impact of human resource activities on employee trust. *Human Resource Management Review, 7*, 380–405.

Whitman, R. F., & Foster, T. J. (1994). *Speaking in public.* New York: Macmillan.

Wigmore, I. (2016, May). What is gig economy? *WhatIs.com.*

Wilcox, D. L., Cameron, G. T., Ault, P. H., & Agee, W. K. (2003). *Public relations: Strategies and tactics* (7th ed.). New York: Longman.

Williams, G. R. (1993). Style and effectiveness in negotiation. In L. Hall (Ed.), *Negotiation: Strategies for mutual gain* (pp. 151–174). Newbury Park, CA: Sage.

Winsten, J. A., & DeJong, W. (2001). The designated driver campaign. In R. R. Rice & C. K. Atkin (Eds.), *Public communication campaigns* (3rd ed., pp. 290–294). Thousand Oaks, CA: Sage.

Witherspoon, R. (2000). Coaching smart: Clarifying coaching goals and roles. In M. Goldsmith, L. Lyons, & A. Freas (Eds.), *Coaching for leadership* (pp. 165–188). San Francisco: Jossey-Bass.

Witt, J. L., & Morgan, J. (2002). *Stronger in the broken places: Nine lessons for turning crisis into triumph.* New York: Times Books/Henry Holt.

Wolf Mann, E. (2015, August 21). Remember the ice bucket challenge? Here is what happened to the money. *Money.*

Wood, E. D., & St. Peters, H. Y. Z. (2014). Short-term cross-cultural study tours: Impact on cultural intelligence. *International Journal of Human Resource Management,* 558–570.

Woodward, G. C., & Denton, R. E. (2014). *Persuasion & influence in American life* (7th ed.). Long Grove, IL: Waveland Press.

Wooten, L. P., & Hayes James, E. (2008). Linking crisis management and leadership competencies: The role of human resource development. *Advances in Developing Human Resources, 10,* 352–379.

Workplace profile. (n.d.). *Ford Sustainability Report* 2015/16.

Wright, M. (2011, November 7). Success means telling people to buy less. *Guardian Unlimited.*

Wysocky, R. K. (2009). *Effective project management: Traditional, agile, extreme.* Hoboken, NJ: Wiley.

Yanovitzky, I., Stewart, L. P., & Lederman, L. C. (2006). Social distance, perceived drinking by peers, and alcohol use by college students. *Health Communication, 19,* 1–10.

Yen, H. (2013, June 13). White majority in U.S. gone by 2043. *Associated Press.*

"You've got to find what you love," Jobs says. (2005, June 14). *Stanford News.*

Yukl, G. (1999). An evaluation of conceptual weaknesses in transformational and charismatic leadership theories. *Leadership Quarterly, 10,* 285–305.

Yukl, G. (2013). *Leadership in organizations* (8th ed.). Upper Saddle River, NJ: Pearson Prentice-Hall.

Yukl, G. A., & Becker, W. S. (2006). Effective empowerment in organizations. *Organization Management Journal, 3,* 210–231.

Yukl, G., & Falbe, C. M. (1991). Importance of different power sources in downward and lateral relations. *Journal of Applied Psychology, 76,* 416–423.

Yukl, G., Falbe, C. M., & Youn, J. (1993). Patterns of influence behaviors for managers. *Group & Organization Management, 18,* 5–28.

Yukl, G., Gordon, A., & Taber, T. (2002). A hierarchical taxonomy of leadership behavior: Integrating a half century of behavior research. *Journal of Leadership & Organizational Studies, 9,* 15–32.

Yukl, G., Guinan, P. J., & Sottolano, D. (1995). Influence tactics used for different objectives with subordinates, peers, and superiors. *Group & Organization Management, 20,* 272–296.

Zaccaro, S. J. (2007). Trait-based perspectives of leadership. *American Psychologist, 62,* 6–16.

Zaccaro, S. J., Ardison, S. D., & Orvis, K. L. (2004). Leadership in virtual teams. In D. V. Day, S. J. Zaccaro, & S. M. Halpin (Eds.), *Leadership development for transforming organizations: Growing leaders for tomorrow* (pp. 267–292). Mahwah, NJ: Lawrence Erlbaum.

Zaccaro, S. J., Kemp, C., & Bader, P. (2004). Leader traits and attributes. In J. Antonakis, A. T. Cianciolo, & R. J. Sternberg (Eds.), *The nature of leadership* (pp. 101–124). Thousand Oaks, CA: Sage.

Zachary, L. J. (2000). *The mentor's guide.* San Francisco: Jossey-Bass.

Zhang, S., Schmader, T., & Forbes, C. (2009). The effects of gender stereotypes on women's career choice: Opening the glass door. In M. Barreto, M. K. Ryan, & M. T. Schmitt (Eds.), *The glass ceiling in the 21st century: Understanding barriers to gender equality* (pp. 125–150). Washington, DC: American Psychological Association.

Zhu, W., May, D. R., & Avolio, B. J. (2004). The impact of ethical leadership behavior on employee outcomes: The roles of psychological empowerment and authenticity. *Journal of Leadership and Organizational Studies, 11,* 16–26.

Ziller, R. C. (1954). Four techniques of group decision making under uncertainty. *American Psychologist, 9,* 498.

Zorn, T. E. (1991). Construct system development, transformational leadership and leadership messages. *Southern Communication Journal, 56,* 178–193.

Zuckerman, P., & Padoan, A. (2012). *Buried in the sky: The extraordinary story of the Sherpa climbers on K2's deadliest day.* New York: Norton.

Zula, K., Yarrish, K., & Christensen, S. D. (2010). Initial assessment and validation of an instrument to measure student perceptions of leadership skills. *Journal of Leadership Studies, 4,* 48–54.

Zuwerink Jacks, J., & Cameron, K. (2003). Strategies for resisting persuasion. *Basic and Applied Social Psychology, 25,* 145–161.

Zuwerink Jacks, J., & Devne, P. G. (2000). Attitude importance, forewarning of message content, and resistance to persuasion. *Basic & Applied Social Psychology, 22,* 19–29.

Index